I0983510

HOMOSEXUAL DESIRE IN REVOLUTIONARY RUSSIA

DAN HEALEY

Homosexual Desire in Revolutionary Russia

THE REGULATION OF SEXUAL AND GENDER DISSENT

The University of Chicago Press
Chicago and London

HQ
76.3
.S653
H42
2001

BIB ID: 281017

DAN HEALEY is lecturer in history at the University of Wales Swansea.

The University of Chicago Press, Chicago 60637
The University of Chicago Press, Ltd., London
© 2001 by The University of Chicago
All rights reserved. Published 2001
Printed in the United States of America
10 09 08 07 06 05 04 03 02 01   1 2 3 4 5

ISBN: 0-226-32233-5 (cloth)
ISBN: 0-226-32234-3 (paper)

Library of Congress Cataloging-in-Publication Data

Healey, Dan.
   Homosexual desire in Revolutionary Russia : the regulation of sexual
and gender dissent / by Dan Healey.
      p. cm.
Includes bibliographical references and index.
   ISBN 0-226-32233-5 (cloth : alk. paper) — ISBN 0-226-32234-3 (paper :
alk. paper)
      1. Gays—Soviet Union—Social conditions. 2. Gays—Legal status,
laws, etc.—Soviet Union—History. 3. Homosexuality—Soviet
Union—History. 4. Social values—Soviet Union—History. I. Title.
   HQ76.3.S653 H42 2001
   305.9′0664′0947—dc21

                                                                00-012078

To
TOM SUDDON (1957–1992)
and
DAVID SANDERS (1953–1993)

CONTENTS

F I G U R E S

Plates

Following page 180

Tables

ACKNOWLEDGMENTS

The world has changed considerably since the days when community activists and private scholars labored outside the academy to lay the foundations of a lesbian and gay historiography. Yet I was constantly reminded while working on this project how many fine historians of sexualities still toil without institutional support. My debt to them is great, especially when I have stood on their shoulders the better to see my own field of study.

I was fortunate to begin my project at the end of the cold war, when coincidentally lesbian and gay studies were acquiring greater recognition. These factors made both the possibility of doing research on the history of same-sex love in Russia, and the prospect of academic funding for such a topic, realities. I gratefully acknowledge support for my doctorate from the Province of Ontario (an Ontario Graduate Scholarship and a Queen Elizabeth II Scholarship) and from the Social Sciences and Humanities Research Council of Canada (a Doctoral Fellowship). A Wellcome Trust postdoctoral fellowship (grant no. 488142) enabled me to convert my thesis into this book. The Stalin Era Research and Archives Project (SERAP) also provided financial assistance with travel expenses and a research assistantship. SERAP's institutional base, the Centre for Russian and East European Studies of the University of Toronto, and the university's history department offered congenial homes for this unconventional project. I received much encouragement from the department's Lesbian and Gay History Discussion Group. In the final stages of writing, the lively scholarly communities at the University of Dundee and the University of Glasgow welcomed me, and I salute my Scottish friends who endlessly demonstrated that Brian Souter and Cardinal Winning know nothing about the soul of Scotland.

The obscurity of my subject dictates that I owe much to those who led me to sources and shared their understanding with me. I pay tribute in particular to the Russians of all sexual orientations who generously led a foreigner to rare articles, books, archival documents, and informal publications on the outrageously unscholarly topic of "homosexualism." Among these I want to mention Elena Chernykh, Masha Gessen, Mikhail Anikeev, Natal'ia Ismailova, Sergei Ivashkin, Oleg Khlevniuk, Aleksei Kilin, Igor Kon, Dmitrii Kuznetsov, Vladimir Shakhidzhanian, Irina Sirotkina, Vitalii Startsev, Elena Tiurina, and Ol'ga Zhuk. Viktor Gulshinskii and Elena Gusiatinskaia, each in their characteristic ways, nurtured me intellectually in 1995—1996 as I gathered the material for this study. I profited from their thoughtful and well-informed comments on individual documents and on the "theme" in Russia, past and present. Leonid Veintraub offered invaluable comments on my Moscow materials. In St. Petersburg, I had illuminating discussions with Daniil' Aleksandrov on the history of Soviet science and with Natal'ia Lebina on prostitution and crime in the northern capital. Among non-Russian scholars who also passed me material or supplied me with valuable contacts, I am especially indebted to Frances Bernstein, Jonathan Bone, Jeffrey Burds, Richard Davies, Gaby Donicht, Laurie Essig, Julie Hessler, David Hoffman, Paul Legendre, Amy Randall, Joshua Sanborn, David Shearer, Stephen Smith, Peter Solomon, Jr., Christie Story, and Ellen Wimberg.

The guidance of numerous scholars of Russia has enlightened my work on this project. Linda Edmondson invited me repeatedly to the Gender Seminar at the University of Birmingham's Centre for Russian and East European Studies, where some of this book's ideas were first presented and critiqued. Don Filtzer, Jane Grayson, and William Butler at London's School of Slavonic and East European Studies gave me encouragement at the earliest stages, as did the International Study Group on the Russian Revolution. Among those who took time to comment on aspects of my work, I mention with gratitude Diana Lewis Burgin, Simon Dixon, Laura Engelstein, Sheila Fitzpatrick, David Hoffman, Moshe Lewin, Kevin Moss, Barbara Norton, and Doug Weiner. My supervisor, Lynne Viola, taught me much about pedagogy by example. Susan Gross Solomon with equal doses of patience and enthusiasm educated me in the history of medicine. Lynne and Susan, along with Robert Johnson and David Higgs at Toronto, joined by

Mark Von Hagen at Columbia, energetically combed through the thesis upon which this book is based. The book manuscript was closely read and criticized by Stephen Smith and Eric Naiman, whose comments I found unfailingly stimulating. The book is a stronger work thanks to the sensitive guidance of all these people; I, however, am responsible for its perversities and deviations.

In 1980, Professor Simon Karlinsky answered my callow undergraduate query about gay Russians by sending back an envelope stuffed with articles. That generous act sowed the seeds of this book, and if their germination has been slow, I hope that the harvest is worth the wait. Whatever differences with Professor Karlinsky I have expressed in this book, I honor him unreservedly as a pioneer whose work made mine possible. Ralf Dose, Jonathan Ned Katz, Michael Sibalis, James Steakley, George Chauncey, and Jeffrey Weeks, and friends at the Toronto Centre for Lesbian and Gay Studies, the Canadian Lesbian and Gay Archives, Homodok in Amsterdam, the Magnus Hirschfeld Gesellschaft and the Schwulesmuseum in Berlin, and Moscow's GenderDok happily answered queries and shared materials. Sadly, Alan Suddon died before seeing this book (dedicated in part to his son Tom) in print. Alan brought several émigré memoirs to my attention, sharing with me their piquancy with characteristic Suddon delight. I benefited from Brian Pronger's profound knowledge of postmodern theories of the body. Chandak Sengoopta generously provided me with an early draft of his marvelous article on "glandular politics." Audiences in Russia and elsewhere who heard talks derived from my research gave me invaluable, often tough, commentary that launched me in new directions.

Since my first visit to Moscow and Leningrad in 1974, I have learned about Russia from many friends, both expatriates and Russians, who were Intourist guides, fellow travelers, sympathetic ears, linguistic advisers, *bania* buddies, archive rats, or fully paid-up members of the Homintern. Among them, I thank Debbie King and David Geer, Bill Bowring, Eduard Liushin, Tim Ross, Alan Winterman, Kate Griffith, Dick Hoagland, Kevin Gardner, Rebecca Friedman, Roman Kalinin, David Tuller, Peter Falatyn, Robert Pleass, Julie Gilmour, Colleen Craig, Richard Schimpf, Oleg Kuz'min, Michelle Patterson, Marjorie Farquharson, Gerry Oxford, and Antony Louis and my friends at *The Moscow Tribune*. Rachel Giese gave me the chance to play with ideas in the pages of *Xtra*. I finished thanks to Adrian Mills. In Moscow, Tracy McDonald saved me from a mouse, falling plaster, and all too often, myself. Brian Pronger and Jim Bartley assisted in a thousand practical ways. My fine eccentric parents, Rita Grave and Ed Healey, indulged me extravagantly. And I cannot express the debt I owe to my chosen one, Mark Cornwall, for everything he has taught me.

Finally, it saddens me deeply that Tom and David are not here to see this book; their gifts to me flicker too faintly through these pages.

Swansea, Wales
June 2000

APRF	Arkhiv Prezidenta Rossiiskoi Federatsii (Archive of the President of the Russian Federation)
Cheka	Chrezvychainaia komissiia po bor'be s kontrrevoliutsiei i sabotazhem (Extraordinary Commission for the Struggle against Counterrevolution and Sabotage; the security police, 1918–22)
GARF	Gosudarstvennyi arkhiv Rossiiskoi Federatsii (State Archive of the Russian Federation)
GPU	Gosudarstvennoe politicheskoe upravlenie (State Political Administration, security police, 1922–23)
KGB	Komitet gosudarstvennoi bezopasnosti (Committee of State Security, security police in post-1953 Soviet Union)
MVD	Ministerstvo vnutrennykh del (Ministry of Internal Affairs)
NKVD	Narodnyi komisariat vnutrenykh del (People's Commissariat of Internal Affairs, incorporated security police, 1934–46)
OGPU	Ob'edinennoe gosudarstvennoe politicheskoe upravlenie (Unified State Political Administration, security police, 1923–34)
RGALI	Rossiiskii gosudarstvennyi arkhiv literatury i iskusstva (Russian State Archive of Literature and Art)
RGASPI	Rossiiskii gosudarstvennyi arkhiv sotsial'no-politicheskoi istorii (Russian State Archive of Sociopolitical History)
RGIA	Rossiiskii gosudarstvennyi istoricheskii arkhiv (Russian State Historical Archive)
RSFSR	Russian Soviet Federative Socialist Republic

TsGAKD SPb   Tsentral'nyi gosudarstvennyi arkhiv kinofotofonodoku-
              mentov Sankt-Peterburga (Central State Archive of Film,
              Photographic, and Sound Documents of St. Petersburg)

TsGAMO   Tsentral'nyi gosudarstvennyi arkhiv moskovskoi oblasti
              (Central State Archive of Moscow Province)

TsGIAgM   Tsentral'nyi gosudarstvennyi istoricheskii arkhiv goroda
              Moskvy (Central State Historical Archive of the City of
              Moscow)

TsMAM   Tsentral'nyi munitsipal'nyi arkhiv Moskvy (Central Mu-
              nicipal Archive of Moscow)

ZAGS   Zapis' aktov grazhdanskogo sostoianiia (Registry of Acts
              of Civil Status; civil registry offices in the Soviet era)

If Russian history is famously littered with "blank spots," then the
story of the understanding and treatment of homosexuality in this society must surely be one of the most obscure. Serious scholars of the
region have accorded little attention to sexuality in general. The intimate aspects of personal life have long been regarded as trivial and
un-illuminating when contrasted with the epoch-making events that
shook Russia in the last century. Both Russian and foreign historians
have generally trained their gaze on the singular triumph or tragedy—
depending on their perspective—of the Russian nation in war, revolution, and modernization. In doing so they have followed traditions of
historical narrative in the field that, until recently, sought to confine
most questions of dissenting sexuality to polemics, journalism, or medicalized discourses.[1] Silence on the problem of sexual and gender dissent
in Russian history has been a productive taboo in domestic and Western
historical writing, reinforcing myths of a natural, elemental, and un-
changing heterosexuality and underpinning a modern system of gender
relations, one dependent on a dominant masculinity and subordinate
femininity.[2]

   This book joins the many recent histories of same-sex love that have
challenged the presumptions behind the modern sex and gender system.[3] Most of these studies have been written about industrialized societies of the West, but important work is emerging about other nations
and cultures, suggesting that the migration of ideas about sexuality and
gender from Europe and the United States has had important consequences for the construction of power relations in the societies that
absorbed them.[4] The story of sexual and gender dissent in Russia is
not a detour from some imagined mainstream historical narrative to-

ward an account of the rise of a "sexual minority." It is rather a pressing historical theme, for it exposes how all sexuality is marshaled into the single groove of a heterosexuality made to appear natural.[5] Without homosexuality in our gaze we cannot see power as it was manifest in the twentieth century in Russia. By this I mean that we will not understand gender as a form of power, in a developing nation in which gender would be a key arena for contesting power relations, if we fail to appreciate same-sex relations as significant constituents of gender and sexual identity.

For different reasons, Soviet and Western accounts of Russia's history of gender and sexuality have all but ignored dissenting genders and desires. When they have touched the issue of homosexuality, they have usually underestimated its significance. An examination of the treatment of these themes in the historical literature can illuminate the problems this poses for a better understanding of Russia's sex and gender heritage.

Thinking about Same-Sex Desire in Russian Contexts

Discussions about the late-Soviet approach to sex usually begin with a nod to the glasnost era's famous cliché, a Leningrad woman's exclamation during a U.S.-Soviet telebridge broadcast that in the USSR "we have no sex."[6] The Communist regime had confined discussions of sex to a professional literature that was closely, often absurdly, policed.[7] Ideological conventions forged during the Stalinist era dictated that there was no need to discuss "normal" sexual relations between men and women. Socialism had constructed "hygienic" conditions (economic stability, rational marriage legislation, maternity and childcare support) in which an unproblematic natural heterosexuality could take its course. Sexual perversions (*polovye izvrashcheniia*) had apparently ceased to exist, for socialism had eliminated the wellsprings of satiety, excess, and exploitation of women said to produce such distortions in capitalist societies. Male homosexuality was discreetly and harshly condemned as a crime, while the tiny number of other perversions that came to light could easily be dealt with by "sexual pathologists" (*seksopatologi*) in the nation's network of psychiatric centers.[8]

In accordance with this late-Soviet paradigm, sex was an ageless, natural phenomenon without a history. The history of the "women's question" (*zhenskii vopros*), said to have been resolved in the construction projects and social engineering of the first Five Year Plan, furnished one arena in which modest discussion of the debates on socialism and sex, before and after the Bolshevik Revolution of 1917, could be aired.[9] Historians nevertheless were bound in this literature to vindicate the norms established by "mature socialism," and to do so with the probity displayed by Lenin himself. Soviet historians were trained to regard any interest in sexuality in literary or cultural biography as excessively "sexological," more appropriate to medicine than the historical profession.[10] In addition, Soviet hostility toward and incomprehension of male homosexuality grossly distorted much biographical scholarship when Russian chauvinism felt itself threatened by evidence of same-sex desire.[11] Soviet ideological prudery extended to the sequestering of biographical documentation that could have undermined the myth of universal heterosexuality and patriotic sexual restraint.[12]

Little in Western historical writing existed to challenge the compulsory heterosexuality of Soviet myth making. Few sustained, systematic discussions of same-sex relations were attempted, and fewer still made a serious impact on the political and social historiography. The earliest treatments of homosexuality in twentieth-century Russia were limited to ethnographic descriptions or to polemics over the ideologies of sex reform.[13] Scholarly attention to this history began with the groundbreaking literary and cultural studies of Simon Karlinsky.[14] In his most recent survey articles, Karlinsky consolidated his material within a totalitarian interpretation of the Soviet 1920s and 1930s. This analysis has been well received in post-Communist Russia, where various versions of his work have appeared in both gay and mainstream publications.[15] Karlinsky's Russian publications have furnished much-needed antihomophobic historical perspectives for lesbian and gay activists and for wider audiences in the former Soviet Union. Western authors, even those diametrically opposed to Karlinsky's intellectual position, remain dependent on his texts.[16]

Karlinsky's discussions of Soviet homosexuality are, however, not without problems for historians of tsarist and Soviet society. His account of the removal of sodomy as a prohibited act in the RSFSR criminal codes of 1922 and 1926 and his explanations for political and medical attitudes toward same-sex love in the interval of Soviet Russian sodomy decriminalization (1922–33) have necessarily been founded on a limited base of published sources. They have also been shaped by his totalitarian schema, thereby obscuring the diversity of Russia's radical traditions and revolutionary utopian dreams.[17] Karlinsky asserts that Bolshevik leaders had no intention of legalizing homosexuality when they abrogated tsarist criminal statutes in 1917. He implies that sodomy decriminalization in 1922 was the result of neglect or oversight.[18] Such a view satisfies a desire to discredit Russian social democracy (as lawless, arbitrary, and anachronistically, homophobic), but it evades a compelling truth: Bolsheviks conspicuously removed sodomy from the books. Karlinsky's account passes over or presents incompletely the medical, legal, and social contexts within which Bolsheviks deliberately chose to legalize sodomy between consenting adults.[19]

Karlinsky represents Soviet medical views of same-sex love as uniformly "morbidizing" and thus inherently hostile to "gays." His most influential text offers a very limited picture of medical opinion and conveys distorted impressions of its intent and influence.[20] Beginning with Michel Foucault, historians have produced accounts of the rise of medical views of same-sex love allowing for more nuanced understandings. Scientific discourses furnished "homosexuals" with a language and an identity, often manipulated by "patients" in opposition to the intentions of medical experts. Numerous turn-of-the-century homosexual emancipationists—some of them scientists themselves—exploited medical theories of homosexuality to advance their claims.[21] Morbidizing views of same-sex love were not the exclusive province of a scientific establishment under the thumb of tsar or commissar, but circulated more widely and had complex effects both in tsarist and revolutionary Russia. Recent research on prerevolutionary medicine provides a framework for understanding the roots of Soviet doctors' views on sexual "perversions."[22] In the rich literature of forensic medicine and psychiatry in tsarist Russia and in the unexplored criminal case files, the tsarist antecedents of the various Soviet visions of "homosexuality" can be traced. Recent works on the history of Soviet medicine provide the necessary backdrop, highlighting specifics of the Russian setting, the institutional environment, and the influence of foreign colleagues and ideas.[23] The Soviet regime permitted a multiplicity of views on the issue to coexist and develop until Stalin's recriminalization of male sodomy in 1933. Until that rupture, jurists, doctors, and Marxist commentators expressed tolerance of some forms of "homosexuality" and apprehension about others. Bolsheviks singled out certain social groups (for example, Russian Orthodox clerics and central Asian men) for the backwardness of their customs or daily life (*byt*), which produced undesirable same-sex relations. Meanwhile, certain Russian medical experts and some "homosexuals" interpreted the rhetoric of the sexual revolution in an emancipationist fashion.[24] Revolutionary attitudes toward same-sex love were neither as monolithic nor as homophobic as Karlinsky claims. Moreover, a closer examination of these attitudes is necessary not merely to decide whether the Russian Revolution was good for "gays," but to unravel the Bolsheviks' often unspoken assumptions about gender and sexuality. These assumptions were instruments in their armory for the construction of a socialist society.

Karlinsky's status as a leading literary scholar and his preference for a totalitarian school reading of the Soviet past licensed his pioneering articles on homosexual Russians despite the Cold War sex phobia of Russian and Soviet studies. While his articles were appearing in the 1970s and 1980s, social historians were nevertheless beginning to challenge the totalitarian picture of Soviet life and politics. They argued that Russian society under Communist rule had a history that could answer many questions about the regime that the totalitarian model dismissed or ignored in its focus on the state. The turn in Russian studies to social history was nourished in part by New Left critiques of Stalinism and Western Cold War conservatism, by feminism, and to a lesser extent, by the "sexual revolution" in industrialized nations in the 1960s–70s. New historical narratives addressed the social roots of the Stalinist turn of the 1930s, the role of women in tsarist and Soviet history, and family, marriage, and heterosexuality in this region.

Social historians' approaches to Russian sexual and gender dissent have been marked by either a reluctance to engage with the problem or by an assumption that homosexuality in Russia was no different from gay experience in Western societies. The first approach was not always a result of homophobia but reflected a sensible concern about the apparent lack of sources to discuss sexual dissent in a serious fashion. While Karlinsky had demonstrated that prerevolutionary literary and cultural discourse bore rich seams of material on same-sex love, androgyny, and gender fluidity, before 1991 it was acknowledged that sources then available to Western scholars for the Soviet period were far less likely to address these issues. The central party and state press familiar to researchers scarcely mentioned such questions; in classic ideological terms, the problem did not seem to exist. Revisionist historians writing about the "sexual revolution" of the Soviet 1920s under the constraints imposed by Soviet information controls[25] were confined largely to a published record that had virtually erased same-sex love and gender ambiguity.[26] Historians' views of the sexual dimension of the Russian Revolution have thus reproduced the antihomosexual silence characteristic of much Soviet discourse, whether of the revolutionary, Stalinist, or post-Stalinist eras. Much recent historical research about early-Soviet sexuality has demonstrated that the "sex question" (*polovoi vopros*) was dogged with confusion and dissatisfaction and that during NEP it served as a lightning rod for political discontent.[27] Our histories of the sex question have thus far neglected to investigate whether in this era of sexology and the dissemination of sex-hormone and psychoanalytic theories across Europe, same-sex relations in revolutionary Russia would be subject to heightened attention as an integral aspect of the construction of heterosexuality.

If revisionists did mention homosexuality, it was usually in the context of the "Great Retreat" from revolutionary values, which was said to have accompanied the rise of Stalinism in the 1930s.[28] The moment of retreat was the 1933–34 recriminalization of sodomy between males, although sources regarding this episode were thin, limited to terse legislative statements and a handful of attacks on homosexuals in Soviet publications. In these histories, the prohibition on male homosexuality was associated with measures in 1936 that banned abortion, promoted maternity, and made divorce less accessible. Historians of women and the family plausibly argued that the retreat from early revolutionary utopian and antipatriarchal ideals about sexual and romantic love entailed the construction during the 1930s of a conservative and family-centered heterosexuality.[29] These authors viewed the 1933–34 prohibition of male homosexuality as a herald of the turn to traditional familialism and gender relations. They said very little about the place of same-sex love in revolutionary values or in Soviet everyday life prior to the sodomy ban, leaving the impression that homosexuality in early-Soviet Russia was a constituent feature of the Bolshevik sexual revolution, like radical marriage legislation and abortion regulation. Yet the Bolsheviks' own silence about the issue appeared to contradict this thesis; further scholarship on Soviet abortion regulation and sexual reform has introduced additional qualifications to the revisionists' early emphasis on the emancipatory thrust of these measures.[30] Abortion was implemented with medical priorities in view, despite women's interpretation and use of the procedure to control fertility and enhance personal freedom.[31] Bolshevik social policy rapidly disappointed those who expected it to free women from traditional unpaid labor. Radical divorce, marriage, and alimony legislation left women vulnerable to abandonment and single motherhood in a period of high female unemployment.[32] Barbara Clements and Elizabeth Wood have recently emphasized the degree to which the Bolsheviks actively rebuffed feminist aspirations. Soviet women found their paths toward advancement in politics and industry blocked by a male-dominated party and managerial elite. These authors point out that, despite the lip service paid to women's emancipation, Bolshevik men failed to examine their gender prejudices in any systematic way.[33] These unexamined assumptions about gender would also dog the often contradictory approaches displayed toward same-sex love and gender dissent.

Most historians of Russia have until quite recently assumed that masculinity was unproblematic, natural, essentially thrusting and "active," certainly heterosexual, and not constructed by political, disciplinary, or cultural manipulation. These assumptions prevail despite the evidence for constructed gender roles that has accumulated as the academic research about Russia's women has developed. As yet we have little understanding of the history of gender formation among Russian men, although recently some historians have indicated how the renovation of military formations before and after the revolutionary watershed depended not merely on technological or ideological innovation, but on medical constructions of a masculine identity as well.[34] Histories of masculinity in Western societies have emphasized the role of political and disciplinary practices in shaping respectable or hegemonic male identities and have pointed to the intensification of state interest in defining and suppressing same-sex love between men as part of this process.[35] By examining same-sex love between men in revolutionary Russia, we can test the relationship that these histories posit between the modernization of masculinity and the "invention" of the homosexual.

If historians of Russia proved reluctant to approach the question of same-sex love in their region, the issue has often been broached by Western gay and lesbian scholarship outside and inside the academy. Many if not most gay liberationist, gay journalistic, and recent queer accounts of Soviet policies on homosexuality continue to work from a New Left template depicting a positive revolutionary (or Leninist) socialism, which gave "gays" their freedom, and a "degenerate" or "bureaucratized" Stalinism, which revoked it.[36] Many of these writers have invoked this history to criticize the communist or socialist movements of their own countries, while troubling little to analyze the roots of these policies in Russian culture and society.[37] Their information depends on the Freudian and Marxist sex reformer Wilhelm Reich, whose "The Struggle for a 'New Life' in the Soviet Union" (1936) presented an account, presumably composed of reports reaching Reich through intermediaries, of the Soviet 1933–34 crackdown on male homosexuals.[38] In the 1960s, New Left interest in Reich's ideas revived awareness of this text, and gay theorists on the left relied upon it to bolster their critiques of homophobia in Stalinist and European Communist parties.[39] In addition to the Reich account, a handful of official pronouncements, and the articles on homosexuality in three successive editions of the *Great Soviet Encyclopedia* (Bol'shaia sovetskaia entsiklo-pediia), have been repeatedly cited when literary scholars, historians, and queer theorists have sought to explain Stalinist maneuvers against homosexuals in the 1930s.[40]

Beyond the history of European sex reform politics and gay activist attacks on the hidebound gender politics of the traditional Left in the West, gay and lesbian historians (with the exception of Karlinsky) have had little to say about sexualities in Russia. The peculiar position of Russia as neither European nor Asian, but both, has tended to mean that students of sexualities for both continents have ignored it.[41] Survey histories of same-sex love have relied on a handful of authorities when treating Russia or the Soviet Union; less satisfactory has been the decision by one recent popular author to ignore this vast, variegated region completely.[42] The outcome has been a historical literature that grossly reduces the experience of a major nation (and many lesser ones under its domination) to a few notorious individuals and episodes. The absence of any awareness of the contradictory ways of understanding gender and sexual dissent in the tsarist Russian Empire and later in the USSR amounts to a serious gap in queer studies.

Same-sex love was not uniformly viewed as a medical condition throughout the entire region. Russia provides an excellent (and heretofore neglected) example of a European society's discordant, incoherent views of same-sex eros across national and ethnic boundaries.[43] "Homosexuality" among non-Christian peoples on the periphery of empire was read differently, and inconsistently, from the ways it was interpreted among Great Russians at the center. Gender-transgressive shamans in Far Eastern indigenous societies could be deemed to suffer from "perversion of the sexual instinct" by turn-of-the-century anthropologists, following the medical model; yet Muslim males who exploited boy prostitutes were judged by Russian doctors to be depraved, not diseased.[44] The history of the Western idea of homosexuality in Russia must be understood not only in relation to the autocratic or Soviet structures of power in which the model was deployed but in relation to the ways the model was reworked or rejected to account for sex and gender dissidence among "uncivilized" peoples beyond this empire's European heartland.[45] There was a differentiated "geography of perversion" in operation in nineteenth- and twentieth-century Russia, and this book, while primarily confined to the study of European Russia, attempts to set out some of the contours of that geography as it was mapped in the Russian imagination.

In summary then, the existing literature on the history of Russian and Soviet society, by ignoring or misinterpreting sexual and gender dissent, suffers from more than the regrettable failure to record the experience of a "sexual minority." It has overlooked a crucial element in the exercise of power by assisting in the reproduction and dissemination of the myth of a universal, natural, and timeless Russian or Soviet heterosexuality. By virtually ignoring same-sex relations between women, it has overlooked a feature historians of other nations have judged to be constituent of modern feminine roles. Having left Russian and Soviet masculinity all but unexamined, it has overlooked a key building block in the ordering of relations of power in society. Meanwhile, lesbian and gay historians and queer theoreticians have misunderstood or ignored the social and cultural basis that underpinned the turbulent history of the regulation of same-sex desire in the Russian Revolution. Historians of homosexuality have not adequately explored the links and discontinuities between the revolutionary ambitions of the Bolsheviks and the practices they used to modernize the empire they inherited.

Finding Sexual and Gender Dissent in Russian Contexts

Two key questions animate this study. The first is simply, what is knowable about the experience of same-sex desire in the Russian past? By examining various forms of evidence, which are described later in this section, it should be possible to establish the social, cultural, and gendered contexts within which love between persons of the same sex occurred in important parts of tsarist and Soviet Russia. From this springboard, it then should be possible to address the second key question. How was the regulation of sexual and gender dissent modernized in revolutionary Russia, and how did this modernization compare with that taking place in the West? The evidence used to discuss this question comes primarily from government administration, from legal and medical practitioners and researchers, statistical records, and from various types of social commentary.

The modernization of sex in the industrialized West is inextricably linked to medicine and its development of a discourse of sexuality to describe, diagnose, treat, and discipline sex. Foucault invited a generation to examine the microenvironments of the clinic, the schoolroom, and the boudoir to uncover the construction of sexuality in the negotiations between doctor and patient, adult and child, husband and wife. By deploying discourses of sexuality, societies crossing the "threshold of modernity" achieved greater control over the individual's body and over the health and growth of the population of which it formed a part.[46] The discourse of sexuality has widely been interpreted by historians of European and American homosexuality as an attribute of modernity, and homosexuality itself has been proposed as a modern invention, a product of dialogues between psychiatrists and patients, sodomites (and later "perverts"), and police.[47]

Laura Engelstein's studies of the ideologies of sex and gender in tsarist society have suggested how the modern discourse of sexuality was received, absorbed, rejected, and reshaped in Russia.[48] Engelstein has argued persuasively that disciplinary power in liberal democracies—what Foucault called "power/knowledge," or regimes of knowledge and methods of scientific practice as deployed on specific populations—never had the chance to flourish in Russian conditions. Tsarism "was as unwilling to allow alternative sources of custodial influence as it was jealous of the intrinsic power of the law."[49] Tsarist absolutism was replaced by a Bolshevik *Polizeistaat* rejecting rule of law liberalism; Bolshevism "harnessed professional disciplines to its own repressive ends."[50] The historical progression inherent in Foucault's analysis of modernity, from absolutism to enlightened despotism to liberalism, did not apply in Russia. Engelstein revised Trotskii's concept of "combined development" (calling it instead "combined underdevelopment") to describe the "superimposition" of these successive forms of power simultaneously in the Leninist-Stalinist polity. "The regime of 'power/knowledge' never came into its own in the Russian context" since there was no legal basis, no rule of law state, to frame its authority.[51]

Yet, as Engelstein admits in her consideration of Foucault's ideas for the Russian case, elites there did absorb Western ideas, and men of science took up the "new disciplinary mechanisms," albeit within a shifting political context that placed limits on them. The willingness of psychiatrists, biologists, and sexologists to advance claims for custody of the "homosexual" despite the authoritarian contexts they inhabit has been observed in a range of non-European industrializing societies.[52] One of the central questions of this study is how these disciplinary mechanisms were adapted to authoritarian power, or more precisely, how homosexuality as a diagnosis was deployed by scientists in tsarist and Communist Russia. I argue that the specific local uses of these disciplinary mechanisms within the vast space of Russia were at least as significant as the rise of a monolithic approach to homosexuality characteristic of existing historical accounts. New evidence urges us to weigh the differences espoused by practitioners in various disciplines and the political implications they carry. Equally, the geographic and national limits of homosexuality as a disciplinary category and the ways Bolsheviks and experts perceived same-sex love and gender nonconformity beyond the European heartland will define the boundaries of modernity in their eyes.

I have endeavored to avoid the most egregious anachronisms by working from the following linguistic conventions. I have sought to distinguish between "homosexuality," a specific psychosexual condition defined by Western medicine beginning in the last third of the nineteenth century, and "same-sex love" (or eros, or relations, or sexual acts), observed in most societies in history. I have employed variations on the latter terms when requiring a temporally or culturally neutral designation for relations between members of the same sex.

In this study I have attempted to listen carefully to the sources and to adhere as nearly as possible to the medical, legal, and popular terminologies their authors employed. By doing so, I have sought to allow non-Russian speaking readers to obtain the flavor of the language used by tsarist and Soviet psychiatrists, physicians, jurists, and the men and women who engaged in same-sex eros. At times this threatens to produce confusion, which I have tried to minimize and explicate, but that conceptual confusion is part of the story. The appropriation and circulation of European concepts of homosexuality took many trajectories inside the Russian and Soviet Empires. Russians did not speak with a single voice about this issue, and their linguistic and conceptual differences illuminate more profound divisions in their worlds.

When not directly citing the terms used by legal and medical practitioners, I have tended to refer to historical individuals as "homosexuals" only when it seemed plausible that they operated within and identified with a subcultural context. A male homosexual subculture began to emerge in Russia's cities in the 1870s–80s. "Female homosexuals" (as Russian psychiatrists tended to call certain women who had sex with women) appeared in more scattered locations, often off the public stage, in the 1890s. Ordinary educated Russians apparently did not begin to use the word "homosexual," which had only entered the language in 1895, until after 1905.[53] Many persons having same-sex relations after this date were not "homosexual," and I use neutral designations ("person who experienced same-sex desire" or "person who had sex with members of their own sex") where the sources suggest no identification with a homosexual role. I have included in this category those whose same-sex relations took place in coercive or extraordinary contexts (for example, in prison or as participants in certain subcultures of prostitution).

In late-nineteenth- and early-twentieth-century Russia, the terms "lesbian love" and "lesbian" (as nouns) were confined to an intellectual elite, and carried literary connotations which meant their use was avoided by psychiatrists, who preferred terms such as "female homosexuality" and "female homosexual."[54] Diana Lewis Burgin has carefully and convincingly questioned whether more than an inchoate sense of the lesbian roles existed for late-Imperial and early-Soviet women loving women, while Ol'ga Zhuk has unproblematically embraced popular and elite examples of female same-sex eros as "lesbian."[55] For clarity, I have used this word only when it appears in source materials; more neutral phrases are otherwise employed.

The history of modern ideas of homosexuality is tied to a plethora of forms of what Russians currently call (without irony) "nontraditional sex." Queer theorists have celebrated the diversity of gender and sexual deviations from Western culture's pervasive and historically contingent constructions of sexual dimorphism (the concept that only two discrete sexes exist) and heterosexuality.[56] Identities are now claiming their own histories from a past that in the 1970s and 1980s was cataloged "lesbian and gay." Bisexuals, intersex (hermaphroditic) individuals, and transgendered and/or transsexual persons are now demanding narratives of their own; meanwhile, anthropologists and queer theorists point to parallels and differences with non-Western cultures.[57] A reductionist understanding of the homosexual as standing in for these other actors is unsustainable in the face of these historiographical currents. This book can only signal points of departure for nuanced histories of other transgressors of gender and sexuality in Russian and Soviet experience. To acknowledge the distinctiveness of this experience, I use the formula "gender and sexual dissent" when referring to categories of existence associated with homosexuality in the language and thinking of early-twentieth-century Russians. With this formula I want to remind readers that some agents fashioned their disobedience not around their choice of sexual partner but around their interpretations of gender.[58] By deliberately adapting the concept of dissent to this sphere, I propose to foreground the agency of those who chose to transgress the dominant sex/gender system.[59] People who wore clothing appropriate to the opposite sex, people who presented themselves in public (by cross-dressing, using specific manners, or forging identity documents) as a member of the opposite sex, those who wished to change their sex, people whose public gender performance veered toward the margins of respectability (effeminate men and mannish women), and hermaphrodites are the chief examples of sex and gender dissidents who were often identified in this language with homosexuals.[60] Since this is a book about homosexuality and the medico-legal conceptions of it, these dissidents often appear in the story, but their histories must not be presumed to be identical to that of Russian same-sex love.

Significant limitations to this study exist, some self-imposed, others dictated by the sources available (or inaccessible) for use. The first caveat is that the questions and sources animating this book reflect a historiography of sexualities that has concentrated attention on the regulation of public sex between males and on the construction of masculinity.[61] Attention to women in these regulatory schemes has usually been limited, although more research on jurisdictions where "unnatural acts" between women were criminalized, for example, the Austro-Hungarian Empire, and some of its successor states, could challenge Anglo-American assumptions about lesbian impunity. My task in attempting to integrate Russian histories of male and female same-sex love is to find the connections between male and female homosexuality made by the structures that sought to regulate, control, and cure them. To ignore one sex or the other would, in the Russian case, severely truncate and distort aspects of the larger picture. Moreover, without pleading for the illusory "cultural unity" sought by the essentialist historian Rictor Norton, there is an urgent need for integrated narratives to nourish post-Soviet queer activism.[62] Western scholarship on Russia's social and cultural past, which has ignored these histories, also needs them. Undoubtedly, because the focus here is on regulatory and disciplinary issues, some readers may feel this book does not adequately explore women's same-sex love as a theme in its own right and on its own terms. I can only agree in advance with this criticism and encourage scholars to consider the ways that such studies might be possible in the Russian context.

The chronological limits imposed on this story were also selected with this historiographical focus in mind. The transition to modernity brought with it new ways of thinking about the body, gender, and sex, many of them mediated by science and notions of rationality. This book begins with the first appearance of the medical model of same-sex love in late-tsarist Russia from about 1870. The peculiar and illiberal resolution of the dilemmas this model suggested—the Stalinist imposition of a compulsory heterosexuality in the late 1930s—constitutes its point of conclusion. In an epilogue I sketch out just some of the effects of this resolution on Russian society from the 1940s through to the 1990s and suggest areas in need of more research.

A further caveat involves the accessibility of sources and the limits on research in post-Soviet Russia. Almost a decade after the collapse of the Soviet regime, Western audiences have become accustomed to a stream of unprecedented revelations from the archives of the Russian Federation. This book makes use of tsarist and Soviet court cases, medical and legal documents, and personal papers, all sources that have only been possible to examine as a result of the new openness of the archives. There remain, however, certain significant types of sources that I was unable to locate and topics I was unwilling to pursue. During the course of my research I concluded that the most detailed materials on the enactment and enforcement of the 1933–34 antisodomy statute were probably held in the archives of Russia's Ministry of Internal Affairs (MVD, the ordinary police), of the Federal Security Service (FSB, the successor of the OGPU/NKVD/KGB, the political police), or of the President of the Russian Federation (APRF). All of these collections retain highly restrictive access policies, and specialists will appreciate the difficulties inherent in approaching them on this topic.[63]

The holdings of these archives could answer some of the questions of high politics for which I offer hypotheses in this book. The reasons for the state's sudden interest in male homosexuals in 1933, discussed here in chapter 7, remain shadowy. It is not known to what extent police or Communist Party leaders discussed and considered female same-sex relations as a problem during this episode. The total number of men arrested and imprisoned for homosexual acts from 1933 to at least 1959 is still unknown. We do not know if post-Stalin party or government reviews of the antisodomy legislation took place or what decisions were taken about its enforcement over time. The question of whether authorities in the late 1950s worried about returnees from the Gulag carrying its sexual practices (including same-sex relations) back to wider society remains unexplored. We have only a fragmentary picture of the treatment of homosexuality in the Soviet military. Research on these issues must still be done, but the decision to release materials that would enable us to address these questions depends on a continued commitment to democratic reform in the Russian Federation. Even with that commitment, inquiry on sexual topics remains comparatively taboo in post-Soviet academic life, and this taboo affects the research agendas and proposals of those who would ask questions about the regulation of homosexuality in Soviet history. There are few rewards, and many disincentives, for even the most senior researchers who might seek access to the key documents in these special archives.

I therefore elected to confine my investigations to the records of humbler institutions, but I was rewarded by the richness of the information these contained. The key materials I have drawn upon are the published Imperial Russian and Soviet medical and legal literature on sexual deviance and unpublished court records of sex crime cases (sodomy, various forms of sexual abuse of minors, and same-sex rape). Archival materials from the RSFSR People's Commissariats of Health and Justice, from the USSR Procuracy, and from the Communist Party of the Soviet Union contextualize these cases. Diaries and memoirs present perspectives not accessible in these official documents.

The medical literature can be divided into a few chief disciplines, beginning in the nineteenth century with forensic medicine (*sudebnaia meditsina*) and continuing from the 1880s with psychiatry and forensic psychiatry (*sudebnaia psikhiatriia*). Endocrinology, and to a much lesser extent social hygiene, also took up the issue of homosexuality, from very different standpoints, during the 1920s. A popular-scientific literature of morality and sexual enlightenment was instrumental in spreading prescriptive discourses of sexuality beyond a specialist audience in the years between 1905 and 1930.[64] Soviet professional discussions of homosexuality were drastically curtailed by the mid-1930s, and only brief references in forensic medical and psychiatric literature persisted into the 1940s–1950s. In all, the medical case histories of individuals engaged in same-sex relations derived from this literature describe over one hundred persons, with the earliest cases dating from the 1860s and the latest discussed here dating from the 1960s.[65]

The court cases I use date from 1862 to 1959. The majority of these are from Moscow city courts and were obtained from the Central State Historical Archive of Moscow (TsGIAgM) and the Central Municipal Archive of Moscow (TsMAM). A small number of criminal cases from other cities and regions were obtained from prerevolutionary forensic literature. Another source of tsarist criminal cases was the personal archive of St. Petersburg jurist A. F. Koni located in the State Archive of the Russian Federation (GARF), which contains copies of investigation and trial documents he assembled, including seven cases of same-sex rape, abuse, or consensual sex. An informative civil war file, the prosecution in Moscow of a Bishop Palladii for "unnatural acts" with his fourteen-year-old novice, is found in GARF holdings for the RSFSR Commissariat of Justice on the separation of church and state. Militant atheist publications provide a further source for early Soviet convictions for clerical same-sex offenses. I was not permitted to scrutinize Moscow province (*oblast'*) criminal court inventories at the Central State Archive of Moscow Province (TsGAMO), where Moscow's crime records are held for the years 1917 to 1930.[66] I therefore treat the 1920s (a

period in which sodomy was nominally legal) using sources from forensic literature. Few persons in Russia (excepting perhaps religious adherents) would have been formally prosecuted for sodomy between consenting adults during this period, although published reports make it
clear that men and women did come under legal scrutiny for displaying
their same-sex desire in public or toward children and young people.
These cases are examined in chapter 6.[67]

TsMAM, which holds the city of Moscow's post-1930 court records,
yielded a total of sixteen case records of sodomy or same-sex abuse of
minors, for the years between 1935 and 1959. (It must be remembered
that these represent cases that proceeded through the ordinary courts,
during a time when the political police arrested and convicted Soviet
citizens in unknown numbers for similar "crimes," often on false or
coerced evidence.) Among these ordinary criminal cases from TsMAM,
eight involving adult males are concentrated in the years 1935 to 1941,
naming and describing a total of thirty-six individual defendants
charged chiefly with consensual sodomy. Of these trials, seven survive
in the form of sentencing documents and appeal records, which sum-
marize the cases in considerable valuable detail, including the circumstances of the crimes and the age, occupation, education, and civil and
party status of most defendants.[68] A single case heard in 1940 records,
through the sentencing and appeal documents, a sexual relationship
between a woman in her thirties and a girl who was between sixteen
and eighteen years old at the time of their affair. One sodomy case file
(dated 1941) contains a complete dossier of the criminal investigation
documents, interrogation transcripts, and trial documentation and supplies a vivid record of homosexual practice in the late 1930s, as well
as an example of police and courtroom procedure deployed against homosexuals.[69] No same-sex offenses were observed in these holdings for
the war years (1941–45).

Eight full case files from the late 1940s and the 1950s were viewed
at TsMAM. Two cases (1950 and 1955) are extremely interesting prosecutions of pairs of adult men on the charge of consensual sodomy. The
remainder involved forced same-sex acts by adults on minors ranging
in age from six to sixteen. TsMAM conservation protocols provided for
the destruction of all but 2 percent of the "most representative" of
these post-war (generally 1945 to 1960) city court case files, and there
are no other records of the other 98 percent found in inventories.[70]
As a result, from the Moscow city court records between 1861 to 1960
(excluding 1917–30), a series of twenty-three prosecution records of

same-sex crimes were identified, indicting a total of fifty-six defendants, with the most important cluster of defendants coinciding with the Stalinist recriminalization of sodomy and the Great Terror.[71]

If records from Russia's most secretive police and policy-making institutions have of necessity been excluded, those of humbler governing institutions are fruitfully employed in this study, including documents from the archives of the RSFSR Justice and Health Commissariats. Early drafts (1918, 1920) of Russia's first revolutionary criminal code survive, although the accompanying commentaries and records of discussions relating to crimes against the person are brief. Holdings for the RSFSR Commissariat of Health include a discussion in the Expert Medical Council (*Uchenyi meditsinskii sovet*, the commissariat's top body for reviewing scientific and regulatory medical issues) in 1929 on the question of "transvestites" and the "intermediate sex." Also of use are the commissariat's revisions to instructions for detecting the signs of sexual crime (including same-sex offenses) on the bodies of victims and material on the role of forensic psychiatry in the judicial system of the 1930s. These documents provide an important perspective on the development of medical views of the homosexual in Soviet conditions and offer oblique suggestions about the political environment in which they were shaped.

The chapters devoted to the experience of men and women who expressed their same-sex desire are derived from the court records and psychiatric literature already mentioned. As in the psychiatric literature on homosexuality and other "sexual perversions" in Europe and America, Russian medical literature often included long autobiographical accounts of the subjects' lives. These sources are primarily external to the subjects in question and, therefore, must be interpreted cautiously. Nevertheless, in their diversity and geographic spread, they cannot be dismissed as mere medical ventriloquism. To overcome the unfavorable filtering imposed by medical editing, these sources have been supplemented with reference to biographical literature on a few notable individuals. In this regard, I have also relied upon the diaries of Mikhail Kuzmin, symbolist poet and the author of the world's first coming-out novel, *Kryl'ia* (*Wings* [St. Petersburg, 1906]); the diaries are held at the Russian State Archive of Literature and Art (RGALI). Kuzmin's diary describes everyday life in a self-consciously homosexual Leningrad household. The confiscation of his journals by the secret police in the 1930s was apparently intended to facilitate the roundup of Leningrad homosexuals during the Great Terror.[72] The excellent biographical accounts of poet Sofiia Parnok by Sofiia Poliakova and Diana Lewis Burgin serve in part as an analogous "control" source for same-sex relations between educated women.[73]

With these considerations in mind, this book is divided into three parts. Part 1 explores the evolving social basis of the lives of sex and gender dissidents in urban Russia under late tsarism and the early Bolsheviks (from approximately 1870 to 1927). Chapter 1 sketches the traditional ethos of sex between men and its evolution in the Russian city into a male homosexual subculture. Chapter 2 traces the contours of mutual female sexual relations as they formed increasingly noteworthy networks in the same period.

Part 2 turns to examine the regulation of homosexual desire across the revolutionary divide of 1917. Chapter 3 sets out how the tsarist policing of sodomy and tribadism operated in an atmosphere of hypocrisy and indulgence accompanied by a weak and overstretched medical profession. Chapter 4 presents the evolution of critiques of this situation and the appearance of successive proposals to decriminalize sodomy (from the draft penal code of 1903 through to the Bolsheviks' enacted codes—for the Russian Republic—of 1922 and 1926). Early Soviet medical interest in the homosexual and perspectives on homosexual emancipation are the subject of chapter 5. Chapter 6 examines countervailing tendencies in the new Soviet regime toward increasingly hostile views of gender and sexual dissent. Chapter 7 concludes part 2 with the story of the recriminalization of male sodomy in 1933–34 and the resocialization of the "masculinized" Soviet woman.

Part 3 begins a project that merits far more attention than is possible in a work of this length: the exploration of the fate of homosexuals as the system of Stalinist socialism evolved from the recriminalization of sodomy in 1934 to the collapse of the Communist regime in 1991. In chapter 8, the treatment of homosexuals in the ordinary municipal courts of Moscow during the era of terror and social consolidation (using trial records from 1935 to 1941) is analyzed. An epilogue suggests some themes for further inquiry and proposes hypotheses based on the conclusions of this book. It describes the character of same-sex relations in prison and the Gulag camp and looks at how medicine and police worked after 1953 to enforce a gendered solution to the problem of homosexuality in late-Soviet society.

PART I

Same-Sex Eros in Modernizing Russia

1

Depravity's Artel'

TRADITIONAL SEX BETWEEN MEN AND THE
EMERGENCE OF A HOMOSEXUAL SUBCULTURE

The place of sex between males in traditional Russian culture has generally been neglected by historians. Igor' Kon characterizes Russia's sexual culture, even in the nineteenth century, as having been divided between "high" and "low" culture more deeply than were Western European sexual cultures. The popular, everyday (*bytovoe*) sexual patterns and practices of the mass of Russians were marked by pagan survivals (orgies, nonreproductive sex acts), which Russian Orthodoxy, with its comparatively weak institutions and priesthood, had been incapable of eradicating. Ecclesiastical authorities "turned a blind eye" to popular sexual culture with resigned indulgence, while publicly the Church "compensated with a strengthened spirituality and unworldly asceticism in its religious doctrine" on sexuality and marriage. Sexual folklore as expressed in erotic tales, verse (*chastushki*), and profanity (*mat*) reflected values utterly at odds with Christianity.[1] Kon does not speculate on how this chasm between sacred and profane affected Russian understandings of sex between men. Yet it seems plausible that the apparent ease with and (from a Western European perspective) tolerance of male same-sex eros grew from the popular repertoire of earthy narratives of "sexual mischief" and from the relative weakness of early modern Orthodox regulation of sexual matters generally.[2] Foreign observers of pre-Petrine Muscovy reported the widespread practice and talk of "sodomy," apparently unfettered by any religious sensibilities or sense of civic dignity.[3] Russian Orthodoxy's formal penalties for "sodomy" (*muzhelozhstvo*) had been indulgent in comparison with Western European canon and secular law, prescribing penances equal to those for adulterous male-female relations. Mutual male relations not involving anal penetration were regarded as little worse than masturbation in this ecclesiastical tradition. Nevertheless, Eve Levin rightly emphasizes that in this same tradition, all sexuality was regarded with suspicion as a source of impurity and sin, even intimacy within marriage.[4]

The state in Russia only turned its attention to the regulation of sodomy later than Western polities and did so as part of efforts to introduce new forms of social control. The military prohibition of sodomy introduced by Peter the Great in 1716 imposed on soldiers and sailors new forms of discipline patterned after the lessons of the European "military revolution."[5] Extending this regulation to the civilian male population in 1835, Nicholas I sought to instill those religious sensibilities and civic virtues that Russian males apparently still lacked.[6]

Efforts to instill these sensibilities imply that a masculine tradition indulgent of mutual eros continued to exist into the nineteenth century. Medical, legal, and diaristic sources from the years after 1861 demonstrate that such a tradition flourished. Men who experienced same-sex desire expressed it according to the social roles they played. Workshops, bathhouses, and large households were sites for same-sex relations within this tradition, and significantly, both provinces and capitals provided such sites. Masters and servants, coachmen and their passengers, bathhouse patrons and attendants, craftsmen and apprentices, and clergy and their novices exploited the opportunities of their positions to obtain or offer sexual favors. These men and youths should not be mistaken for homosexuals in a modern, European sense; their culture of masculinity *included* indulgence in same-sex eros, and it did not enforce the necessarily severe penalties associated in a later era with the stigmatized, medicalized condition of homosexuality.[7]

Depravity's Artel'

Russia in the mid-nineteenth century remained a society relatively untouched by the forces of industrialization and urbanization transforming Western Europe. The vast majority of the population were peasants, and some twenty million remained serfs until the Emancipation Edict of 1861. Relations between gentry landlords and their servants and peasants were patriarchal, with landlords frequently intervening in the sexual and intimate lives of their charges. Similarly, patron-client hierarchies dominated the worlds of work and worship in Russia's towns and church establishments. Same-sex eros between males occurred in these environments and reflected their characteristic patterns of domination and subordination.

The sexually available subordinate male was found in numerous settings. Men of means, often exploiting the license that money and vodka conferred, made use of such youths or men. A Moscow merchant (himself of the peasant estate) provides a rich example of these relations. In 1861, Pavel Vasil'evich Medvedev kept a diary recording his emotional and sexual experiences.[8] Unhappily married, Medvedev sought consolation alternately in church and at the tavern. When drunk, he indulged in "lustfulness" with both males and females—and recorded these encounters in his diary. The document speaks chiefly of a traditional masculine culture indulgent of sex between men. Yet the cash exchanges accompanying some of Medvedev's encounters and their location outside the household point to the seeds of a transition to a modern homosexual subculture.

Medvedev and his companions repeatedly turned to subordinate males for sex when lust was unleashed by vodka. An account of an evening of theater, dining, and drinking "to excess" ended with Medvedev's reflections on how to satisfy one's arousal during the journey homeward:

> For some time now my lust leads me to pick a younger cabdriver, who I make fun of along the way—with a little nonsense you can enjoy mutual masturbation. You can almost always succeed with a fifty-kopek coin, or thirty kopeks, but there are also those who agree to it for pleasure. That's five times this month.[9]

Cabdrivers who supplemented their income (or simply took pleasure) in this fashion are not unusual characters in Russian legal and psychiatric literature of the era.[10] One particularly colorful example of this sexual exchange comes from the provincial town of Uman'. There a pair of brothers, injudiciously hired as coachmen by one Prince Obolenskii in 1882, exploited his sexual interest in them ruthlessly. The prince, married with children, became infatuated with Petr and Fedor Filonovskii. They left their old employer and joined Obolenskii's staff as drivers. Before long, police observed that the Filonovskii brothers were living in a newly rented flat, were driving new phaetons and horses, and "went boozing in public houses . . . their hands decorated with diamond rings." Leaving his wife and children at home in the country, Obolenskii would visit Petr and Fedor at the rooms in town, which he had paid for and furnished luxuriously; the prince came bearing parcels containing expensive wines and foodstuffs. The brothers engaged in anal intercourse with their employer, and for a time, were handsomely rewarded. Eventually they became greedy, passing false promissory notes in Uman'. The police learned of their relations with their employer through a third coachman, who, it emerged, had also had sex for cash with Obolenskii. (Police referred to all three as gigolos [al'fonsy].) Letters found in the infamous flat exposed Obolenskii as their patron and lover, and he along with the Filonovskiis came to trial in March 1883. The outcome of this criminal case was not revealed in an article for jurists and forensic doctors that presented the Prince's sophisticated medical defense in great detail.[11]

Coachmen were not alone among male servants willing to service male employers sexually. Medical reports described how youths and young men profited in this fashion as waiters, household staff, and as simple soldiers or officers' servants.[12] It is not always possible to gauge whether subordinates were motivated solely by incentives of money and advancement. The apparent willingness of Russia's serving classes to tolerate even unpaid "gentlemen's mischief" (barskie shalosti), as St. Petersburg venereologist V. M. Tarnovskii said they called it, might imply a relative indulgence of mutual male relations. (Tarnovskii's perceptions of prostitution clashed with those of most of his colleagues and must be viewed cautiously.) There is also little hint in the various medical accounts that these subordinates experienced anxiety about their own masculinity.[13]

Another example of traditional mutual male sexuality in the provinces highlights the apparent patriarchal confidence accompanying such encounters. It also suggests that peasants evaluated same-sex relations with employers from varying moral perspectives. A petition for legal separation from her spouse, initiated by Anna Nikolaevna Kazakova in 1891, alleged that her husband of ten years, Konstantin Nikolaevich Kazakov, lured peasant servants and their children's tutors into sexual liaisons. The dossier of Kazakova's plea, read and granted by Tsar Nicholas II in 1893, contains depositions from household servants describing their encounters with the master (barin) in salty language. "The master commits sin with muzhiki [peasant adult males], using them in the buttocks [v zadu]," insisted one informant, reporting rumors in her village. Another peasant woman said, "Konstantin Nikolaevich uses muzhiki in the buttocks instead of women." Bykovskii, a male peasant serving in the household, told how the master plied him with vodka and instructed him to visit at night; after his first vodka-soaked sexual encounter with the master, he woke up to find a three-ruble note in his pocket. Bykovskii disregarded the warnings he received from other household employees (of both sexes) about the master's "sinful" acts. A peasant hired as the household driver, Mikhail Ushakov, admitted he had been sexually involved with both husband and wife. In 1887 he had been repeatedly propositioned by Konstantin Kazakov, and though the driver refused to allow the master to penetrate him anally, they did have intercourse once with the master taking Ushakov's member ("khui," the coarsest term for this body part) and placing it between his own buttocks. Both husband and wife gave their driver tips of three to five rubles for sex. Ushakov was fired when it was discovered that Anna had been made pregnant by him.[14] Unhappy families were indeed unique in their misery. These depositions reveal that peasants circulated warnings about this gentry landlord's "sin" with males, indicating that at least some regarded such transgressions negatively. Others operated within a different moral economy. For Bykovskii and Ushakov, drunkenness could excuse "sin," and perhaps even launder the money they received for it.

In urban workshops, men in positions of authority subjected youths to sexual advances or assaults. Medvedev wrote that he repeatedly masturbated with a member of his household, a "boy" of eighteen, an apprentice or servant, who "satisfied me according to my desire with manual onanism, and I did the same for him."[15] Medvedev consoled his religious anxieties by writing that the young man enjoyed their encounters, arguing that he was old enough to know what he wanted. Court records of male rapes demonstrate a similar if more sinister pattern. In one Moscow workshop, a twenty-six-year-old craftsman, Reshetnikov, was notorious for his sexual advances toward apprentice boys, and his unmasking in 1892 initially provoked laughter rather than opprobrium.[16] The same year saw the trial of a baker, Chelnokov, whose sexual involvement with his apprentices aroused the ire of a Moscow charity.[17] Pedagogic arrangements, informal and unsupervised, were similar sites for abuse. One victim of sexual interference from his fifty-five-year-old teacher explained in court in 1881, "I came not long ago to Petersburg from the village, and not knowing the customs here did not complain, because I thought that's the way things were with every master."[18]

In a similar fashion, clerical training and mentorship could be accompanied by same-sex erotic activity, sometimes of an enduring nature. The 1919 trial in Moscow of a Bishop Palladii for "corruption of a boy and for unnatural vice (pederasty)," revealed not merely the hidden sexual side of this cleric's relations with his fourteen-year-old novice, but a history of such partnerships.[19] Monastic tradition demonstrated the temptation to mutual sexual activity that patron-client relationships of this type could generate. Young male novices had long been viewed, in penitential texts and monastic practice, as a stimulant to the lustful impulses of older monks.[20] Custom and regulation formed a network of surveillance, closely scrutinizing the material and spatial aspects of seminary and monastic life thought to encourage sensuality. Convention dictated that religious community members kept a close watch on who shared cells with whom, whether doors were locked when two brothers were alone together, and whether younger brothers assisted older ones in dressing or bathing.[21] Palladii had begun his ecclesiastical career as a seminary inspector in Moscow and later Saratov, charged with overseeing the daily lives and morality of teenage religious scholars. Inspectors monitored the older boys and young men, who lived in private accommodation outside the seminary, where the temptations of alcohol, tobacco, and illicit sex were harder to control.[22] Investigations into the bishop's past identified a number of youths, and two adult monks, whose ecclesiastical careers had been launched during the late tsarist era with Palladii's assistance.[23] These patron-client transactions fit within the wider pattern of traditional mutual male eros.[24]

From as early as the seventeenth century, the Russian bathhouse (*bania*), was perhaps another site for this traditional sexual indulgence between men. Here again, the power held by older, wealthier males over young subordinates inflected relations. By the late nineteenth century, medical discourse had identified baths as a significant locus of male prostitution in Russian cities.[25] The first commercial baths appeared in Moscow in the mid-1600s, and the state mandated that the sexes should be scrupulously segregated.[26] Authorities differ on how rigorously segregation was actually observed and on whether the baths represented a desexualized space in Russian culture.[27] Certainly, separate steam rooms for men and women created a homosocial environment, which contributed to the evolution of bathhouse male prostitution in a later era. A seventeenth-century miniature illustrating a visit by bearded, mature males to the baths shows four beardless, youthful males serving them (fig. 1). One youth, in trousers, removes an older man's boots; another trousered lad draws water from a well. A naked young man pours water on the stove to produce steam, as another, also unclothed, beats a bearded older visitor, lying nude on a bench, with a leafy switch. While there is no intimation of sexual acts in the illustration, the serving boys' subordinate social position is emphasized by their youthful beardlessness. The fifteenth-century Metropolitan Daniil and archpriest Avvakum in the seventeenth century condemned men who shaved their beards as inciting immorality, because smooth faces made them resemble women and thus were an invitation to sodomy.[28] With the growth of commercial relations in the eighteenth century, youths may have sought out careers in bathhouses. A group of sixteen-year-old peasant males apprehended entering Moscow in 1745 claimed they came to seek work in commercial baths.[29] By the late tsarist era, Moscow's bathhouse staff reportedly came from generations of male (and some female) migrants all bound by ties to the same handful of rural districts (affiliation by *zemliachestvo*).[30] Urban spas, staffed by beardless youths, may have been sites of mutual male sexual relations long before the recorded instances of the nineteenth century.

Male bathhouse attendants appear in a range of sources of the 1860s to 1880s as sexually serving a male clientele. Pavel Medvedev wrote of a visit with a friend to an unnamed Moscow bathhouse in 1861, where they found "onanism and *kulizm* (anal intercourse)" awaiting them.[31] Few references to a bathhouse male sex trade in Moscow appear in forensic texts or the city court records, but there are enough discussions of the phenomenon in St. Petersburg to suggest that what Medvedev described here persisted in Moscow until the 1917 revolution. The link between baths with private rooms and the exploitation of young males was evident from the 1919 trial of Bishop Palladii. Twice he testified that while he and his novice Volkov had indeed been to "public" (*obshchie*) baths or baths for the upper clergy (*arkhiereiskie bani*) in Moscow, they had never visited baths with private rooms (*bani s nomerami*). He claimed "it was the custom that two boys went with me, to allay the suspicions of bystanders."[32] The notoriety of private rooms in Moscow's spas was sufficiently widespread to move Palladii to repeated denials on this point. There is little reason to doubt that the city's baths harbored casual male prostitution earlier in the Imperial era.

Evidence from St. Petersburg on this trade is more detailed, suggesting that it was organized according to peasant traditions until perhaps the 1890s. The migrants' practice of mutual assistance and solidarity in the city with fellow-villagers or countrymen (based on *zemliachestvo*), and the peasant pattern of working in a team (the *artel'*) for an equally apportioned share of earnings, was observed among bathhouse sex workers from the 1860s to the 1880s. These customs were a feature of recruitment, apprenticeship, and labor relations in the self-contained bathhouse world. Such peasant strategies were evident in the 1866 case of a St. Petersburg "depraved work team" (*artel' razvratnikov*). Vasilii Ivanov, a twenty-year-old bath attendant, testified in court that he had come to work in the bathhouse where another attendant from his native village worked. Once there, his colleagues recruited him into the practice of sexually servicing clients. Customers who, Ivanov observed, "did not need to be washed," would ask for other attentions: "[the client] lies with me like with a woman, or orders me to do with him as with a woman, only in the anus, or else leaning forward and lying on his chest, and I [get] on top of him, all of which I did." Ivanov reported that he and his colleagues earned about one ruble for each session of "sodomy" they provided. They operated as an *artel'*, pooling the proceeds from sexual services, after the baths' manager, acting as the team's *starosta* or leader, took his cut. "All the money we got for that [sodomy] we put together and then divided it up on Sundays," he testified, also declaring that "all the attendants in all the baths in Petersburg" were engaged in sodomy.[33]

The temporal threshold between the formation of this "depraved work team" and the arrival of more commercial prostitution, with a brothel-keeper managing atomized male sex-trade workers, remains indistinct from existing sources. In the 1880s, Tarnovskii noted the continued existence of youths he called "commercial catamites" (*prodazh-nye kinedy*) servicing bathhouse clients.[34] They still worked within the *artel'*, which the venereologist admired and romanticized. In discussing bathhouse prostitution, he celebrated the shrewdness of the so-called "Russian simple folk" (*russkii prostoliudin*) and their exploitation of the baths as a site for profit. "Among us, especially in Petersburg, thanks to the numerous baths with private rooms and bathhouse attendants, there exist a plethora of pederast prostitutes living, as it were, on the *artel'* principle."[35] Attendants were reportedly happy to indulge "congenital and aged catamites" who sought release at the baths; Tarnovskii estimated that perhaps three-quarters of male attendants were willing to engage in "active" anal intercourse with this category of pederast for cash, while "the passives are only few among them [i.e., the attendants]."[36] Although the venereologist did not fully approve of bathhouse prostitution, his comments were consistent with his controversial praise for the tsarist system of licensed (heterosexual) brothels.[37] There was also a national smugness in Tarnovskii's assertion that in Russia there was less blackmail of pederasts than in European capitals because of the traditional *artel'*. Tarnovskii saw in the *artel'* a source of public order:

> Here in Petersburg, remuneration of catamites is practically the same as paying a prostitute; in these circumstances blackmail [*shantazh*] on the part of bathhouse attendants living by the *artel'* and equally sharing the profits is unthinkable; there is no surveillance [by police of blackmailers, as in Europe].[38]

In Russia's bathhouses, according to Tarnovskii, immoral relations were concealed from the public, and persons of substance who could afford to rent a private room in better spas indulged themselves without exposing their reputations to unseemly accusations. The mutual responsibility (*krugovaia poruka*) and surveillance characteristic of *artel'* relations supposedly kept commercial catamites honest and compliant.[39] Upper-class male desire, satisfied by male prostitutes organized according to traditional peasant patterns, could be socially harmless or neutral so long as the sexual transaction took place within the commodified privacy offered by better-quality urban bathhouses.

The late nineteenth and early twentieth centuries in Russia were a period of rapid social transformation, and same-sex relations were marked by these changes. The emancipation of the serfs in 1861 and industrialization in the 1880s and 1890s brought large numbers of people (principally but not exclusively males) to cities in search of work. A significant proportion of these newcomers stayed only temporarily or seasonally; many left wives and families behind in the village. Others settled and became the basis of an urban proletariat in St. Petersburg, Moscow, and a handful of other centers. Urban workers' housing was crowded. A huge proportion lived in barracks, flophouses, or shared rooms and even shared beds; a significant percentage lived in employers' households and workshops.[40] The rapid expansion of Russia's industrial base was accomplished by large numbers of male workers living in cities where there was neither space nor money for the replication of peasant marriage and family patterns. In tsarist Moscow, working men in the sexually active younger age groups outnumbered women, and they were crowded together in accommodations precluding any possibility of starting families or of bringing a wife and children from the village to join them.[41] While traditional forms of patriarchal solidarity and mutual supervision such as the *artel'* and *zemliachestvo* functioned in the town, they could not always serve to enforce the compulsory heterosexuality of village life. Men found opportunities for sexual expression with each other in Russia's industrializing centers. As they exploited these new possibilities, they transformed Russian masculinity's traditional patterns of mutual male eros. An urban, homosexual, subculture took shape.

The "Little Homosexual World" Emerges

A homosexual subculture began to appear as Russia's two capitals grew in size and complexity at the end of the nineteenth century. It developed its own geographies of sexualized streetscapes, its rituals of contact and socialization, its signals and gestures, and its own fraternal language. In these rituals, gestures, and language, the subculture elaborated roles for participants, often based on the principles of the market in male sex. The subculture also flourished in private spaces and created domestic environments. Off the streets, in flats and bathhouses, some male homosexuals sought to intensify and further commodify mutual male sexuality and male prostitution. Others used domestic and other indoor spaces to forge emotional partnerships, to develop a poetics and a historiography of homosexuality, and to celebrate a culture of gender and sexual dissent. Continuities and contrasts between tsarist and Soviet homosexual practices can be established through an examination of the geographies of homosexual Petersburg-Petrograd-Leningrad and Moscow, the semiotics of the subculture, and the subculture's use of domestic and commodified interiors across the political divide of 1917.

From the 1870s, mechanisms of mutual recognition and contact beyond the confines of the traditional patron-client relations associated with older forms of mutual male eros began to develop. Denizens of the "little homosexual world" (*gomoseksual'nyi mirok*, as an acid-tongued satirist would dub it in 1908)[42] began to use specific streets, parks, public toilets, and other city amenities to meet and exchange information, to display themselves, and to find sexual and emotional partners. These sexualized territories also served as the meeting ground between males who sold sex (who were not always identified with the homosexual subculture) and their clients. Sources for these patterns are again more modest for Moscow than for St. Petersburg and suggest a slower evolution toward a homosexual subculture in the older capital. Medvedev's 1861 diary made no mention of cruising or male prostitution in Moscow's streets. Respectable upper-class individuals like composer Peter Tchaikovsky found willing sexual contacts in Moscow among servants or through louche friends, rather than risk scandal by public cruising.[43] One surviving Moscow sodomy trial of 1888 indicates that lower-class males could find "devotees" of same-sex relations on the city's Boulevard Ring, later an arena of homosexual liaisons well into the 1920s and 1930s. On Prechistenskii Boulevard, townsman Petr Mamaev was arrested after a drunken dispute with a younger man named Agapov. Mamaev told police, "For the past eight years I have been committing sodomy with different, unknown persons. I go out to the boulevard at night, strike up a conversation, and if I find a devotee [*liubitel'*], then I do it with him. I cannot identify who I did it with . . . I attempted to do just the same with Agapov, without money, without any exchange of money in mind, just to obtain pleasure for myself and for him."[44]

This testimony suggests that by 1888 even Moscow's police expected an "exchange of money" to be associated with "sodomy," yet as Mamaev claimed and as Medvedev had also admitted in his diary, Moscow harbored many males willing to engage in sex "just to obtain pleasure." Nevertheless, sources for an early geography of Moscow's homosexual subculture remain scarce.

It is instructive to compare this obscurity with the richness of material available on St. Petersburg for the late nineteenth and early twentieth centuries. The St. Petersburg streetscape had acquired a specifically homosexual geography by the 1870s. The new capital's main thoroughfare, Nevskii Prospekt, had reportedly been a place for "pederastic depravity" as early as the 1830s, although this was evidently within the context of traditional mutual male eros.[45] Especially notorious was the *Passazh* (Passage), a covered gallery completed in 1848 connecting the busy Nevskii with another contact point, Mikhailovskaia (now Iskusstvo) Square. This central, public arcade of shops proved ideally suited, especially in the winter, for the discreet pursuit of same-sex liaisons. By the 1860s, the Passage was already attracting blackmailers who preyed on the men picking up available youths in its upper reaches.[46] The Mikhailov gang, a group of accomplished extortionists caught in 1875, was well known to the operators of nearby Dominic's Restaurant and of the billiard hall located inside the Passage itself.[47] In the late 1880s or early 1890s, a nameless individual penned an elaborate denunciation of St. Petersburg's *tetki* (literally "aunties," a term describing men whose sexual inclinations were primarily oriented toward men; *tetki* were frequently the clients of men selling sex).[48] He noted that "On Sundays in the winter *tetki* stroll in the Passage on the top gallery, where cadets and schoolboys come in the morning; at around six in the evening, soldiers and apprentice boys appear."[49]

By the late 1880s, the pavements of Nevskii from Znamenskaia Square to the Anichkov Bridge (both locations where public toilets were reportedly used for making contacts) and on toward the Public Library and the Passage formed a promenade visible to initiates. This was apparently the city's most enduring homosexual cruising ground, with participants reporting encounters into the 1910s and 1920s. Seasonal favorites were the exhibitions and fairs held in the Mikhailovskii Manège (now the Winter Stadium). Prerevolutionary Shrovetide fairgrounds, with their *balagany* (amusement booths and crude temporary theaters) erected in the nearby Field of Mars (*Marsovoe pole*), were reportedly stalked by some *tetki* looking for young spectators to corrupt. Wednesdays saw a gathering of upper-class *tetki* at the ballet performances of the Mariinskii Theater. A similar class patronized restaurants, with their private dining rooms, discreetly (if sporadically) serving as meetings places for "pederasts." [50] The Palkin Restaurant, located at 47 Nevskii Prospekt, which was the same building that housed the notoriously homosexual Prince Meshcherskii's reactionary *Grazhdanin* newspaper, was a busy gathering spot in the late 1880s.[51]

Saturdays were reserved by some who sought "apprentice boys" or youths from the "lower orders" at the more plebian amusements of the Cinizelli Circus.[52] The embankment of the Fontanka Canal and the gardens adjoining the circus remained hubs of male prostitution into the 1920s.[53] By 1908, one jaundiced critic was able to map the daily routine for "an entire band of suspicious young people," the male prostitutes he judged to be part of the "little homosexual world." In the mornings they gathered in the garden adjoining the circus that served as a dog run, then moved on to Nevskii Prospekt and the Café de Paris in the Passage during the afternoon, and returned to the Fontanka Embankment or the Tauride Gardens to attract clients in the evening.[54] The critic's observations about the availability of male lovers (some for hire) in the Tauride Gardens are confirmed in Mikhail Kuzmin's diary and his correspondence with Val'ter Nuvel'.[55]

If most of these cruising paths centered on or around Nevskii Prospekt, with the infamous Passage and the Cinizelli Circus as their hubs, other places were important for civilian males seeking sex with military men. According to the anonymous citizen who denounced the capital's *tetki* in the late 1880s or early 1890s, a busy fair-weather spot served this trade near the Peter and Paul Fortress:

> In the summer the *tetki* gather almost daily in the Zoological Garden, but their assemblies are especially populous on Saturdays and Sundays, when soldiers come from their quarters and when Junker cadets, regimental choirboys [*polkovye pevchie*], cadets, gymnasium pupils, and apprentice boys have the day off. The soldiers of the L[ife]-Gu[ard] Mounted Regiment, cavalry guards, and both Urals and Ataman Cossacks come to the Zoological Garden solely for the purpose of earning a few twenty-kopek pieces without any labor on their part. They know all the *tetki* to see them, and so—a soldier, passing one of them, glances significantly at him and goes off in the direction of the water-closet, checking to see if the *tetka* is following him. If he does, then he [the soldier] pretends to see to his bodily functions, and tries to show off his member [*chlen*]. The *tetka* stands next to him and if the member is really big, he feels it with his hand and pays the soldier twenty kopeks.

In the course of an evening the *tetka* conducts several such probings and, having chosen a member to his taste [*vybrav sebe chlen po vkusu*], he sets off with the soldier to the nearest bathhouse, where he uses him in the anus, or conversely, the soldier uses the *tetka* that way, for which he would receive three to five rubles from him.[56]

Tetki were also to be found strolling along Konnogvardeiskii (Horse Guards, now Profsoiuznyi) Boulevard, usually earlier in the day. This street, with its barracks and riding school for the eponymous regiment, was conveniently located for escorting young recruits to the nearby Voroninskie and other bathhouses.[57] Soldiers who enjoyed sex with men continued to meet each other on Nevskii Prospekt during the world war and the 1917 revolution, and one male prostitute reported that in the 1920s, Aleksandr Gardens was a good place to meet "old soldiers" in the summertime.[58] The local subculture celebrated the availability and beauty of the cultivated young male body in uniform. Meanwhile, the perennial reality of low military pay meant that some soldiers and sailors in the northern capital continued to offer sex in exchange for cash or other considerations well into the 1930s.[59]

The most singular institutions of St. Petersburg's prerevolutionary homosexual subculture were those bathhouses that became places of resort for the *tetki* and their male friends. In the bathhouse, the traditional masculine indulgence of same-sex eros confronted and mixed with an emerging homosexual subculture. The proliferation of voices describing bathhouse homosexual relations reflects this confrontation. In 1906, the poet and diarist Mikhail Kuzmin signaled the place of the bathhouse in Russia's urban homosexual subculture in *Kryl'ia* (Wings), his notorious novel celebrating a young man's coming out. Simultaneously, foreign apologists for homosexuality in the modern, Western sense, sang the praises of the Russian bath as a place of particular opportunity.[60] Meanwhile, outsiders decried the influence of an identifiable minority of males abusing the traditions of bathhouse sociability.[61] Critics also voiced concern about male prostitution in the baths. In the wave of sex-themed journalism following the 1905 revolution, lurid descriptions appeared of bathhouses as virtual male brothels. St. Petersburg's Znamenskie Baths near the square of the same name (today's Vosstanie Square) supposedly catered to the "little homosexual world":

Hardly do you penetrate this "cloister" but the massive figure of bath attendant Gavrilo, famous in the homosexual sect, approaches with a ducklike waddle. Gavrilo is an obese man of forty to forty-five with an ugly, repulsive face and an obsequious look that bores into your soul. This "gentleman" doesn't shrink from offering you his "services" on the spot or those of somebody else . . . Gavrilo will bring you an album of photographic pictures where all these homosexual "Frinas" and "Aspazias" are depicted, dandyfied and decorated, some even in women's finery . . . You just point to one of these "miniatures" in the album, and in about five minutes the "original" is at your disposal. And incidentally, you are immediately informed of the price.[62]

This 1908 satire of the "little homosexual world" likened the baths to the familiar tsarist institution of the licensed (heterosexual) brothel.[63] The representation of the male "Frinas" and "Aspazias" (aliases employed by female prostitutes) in a photographic catalog, and their presentation as feminine, may have been exaggerations for the amusement of readers rather than actual marketing devices to attract clients. Yet Mikhail Kuzmin's diary recorded a strikingly similar scene in December 1905. He wrote,

> In the evening I thought I would go to the bathhouse just for style, for pleasure, for purity [*chistota*] . . . The man who met me at the door, on hearing that I required an attendant, a sheet, and soap, slowly turned and asked, "Perhaps you want a good-looking attendant?"—"No, no."—"Well alright then." I do not know what came over me, for I was not even aroused.—"No, just send an attendant."—"Then I'll send you a good-looking attendant," he said, with a persistent look.—"Yes, please, a good-looking one," I said distractedly, sliding farther downhill. Lowering his voice, he then asked, "Maybe you would like one a little younger?" Thinking a bit, I replied, "I'm not sure."—"Right away, sir."[64]

Aleksandr, the young man sent to Kuzmin, "began to wash me unambiguously," and as he did so "he stood too close to me and generally behaved without the slightest shame." The attendant told the poet that he could enjoy himself now and pay his debt later; he hinted that a tip at Kuzmin's discretion would be welcome.

> After some mutual groping and banter, we began to talk to each other like thieves . . . Aleksandr is twenty-two years old, has been in the bathhouse for eight years, obviously they sent me a professional [*professional*]. He claimed that the manager only told him to "wash" me, that he was not supposed to be my attendant but the others were all sleeping; that they don't go into the private rooms that often, that you can tell

from the eyes and manner. And kissing me good-bye, he was surprised when I shook his hand. For the first time he blushed, said, "Thank-you very much," and accompanied me out. With Aleksandr leading me past the ranks of other attendants, already getting up, I did not feel entirely comfortable, as though they all knew what we had done, but despite that I gazed at them more easily and attentively.

The perpetually impecunious poet returned in January 1906 to pay off his debt. Kuzmin somehow found the cash to visit Aleksandr repeatedly in spring 1906.[65] At about the same time, a cousin of Tsar Nicholas II, Grand Duke Konstantin Romanov, agonized in his diary about sexual encounters with Petersburg bath attendants who were clearly available on demand.[66]

These vignettes indicate that male sex work was becoming more commercialized. The absence of references to the *artel'* of male attendants, pooling their earnings from "sodomy," suggests that figures like Gavrilo and the persistent manager encountered by Kuzmin now operated more like Russia's licensed brothel-keepers, who engaged female prostitutes with financial contracts.[67] Youths selling sex, and pimps who organized them, were commodifying the sideline in "sodomy" described by bath attendants a half-century earlier. The frequent mention of baths with private rooms for hire make it clear that commodified privacy in the late tsarist era facilitated both sexual encounters "for pleasure" and those for payment.

The fate of bathhouse mutual male sexuality after 1917 is difficult to establish. The tsarist homosexual subculture had depended in part on the commodification of private spaces, such as bathhouses and restaurants.[68] Soviet rule brought new constraints on access to this kind of space. Even during the limited capitalism of the New Economic Policy (NEP, 1921–28), when restaurants and baths were available for lease or hire to entrepreneurs, allocation was controlled by functionaries aware of the sexual disorder associated with such establishments.[69] Hotel rooms were, at least nominally, reserved for visitors from out of town (*priezzhie*) and even heterosexual couples encountered difficulty resorting to them for sex.[70] Reports of organized male prostitution in the bathhouse cease after 1917,[71] but individuals continued to strike up acquaintances and have both voluntary and paid sex either on the premises or after meeting there. In 1927, a sixteen-year-old thief who engaged exclusively in sex with boys told a psychiatrist that he preferred partners from among his fellow *besprizornye* (homeless youths). He took them to the bathhouse to "wash them first," and they had sex there in private rooms.[72] The male prostitute P. informed his doctor that he found mutual male backscrubbing in the bathhouses often led to more tender attentions, and the psychiatrist himself noted that P. had been arrested for theft in 1926 after a liaison begun in the baths had soured.[73]

The near-disappearance of commodified space had predictable consequences. Public toilets, which had been a durable arena for the rituals of acquaintance in the male homosexual world, apparently increased in significance for that world. Dr. Belousov said that his patient P. told him that "after the revolution . . . meetings in toilets have become the most predominant [means of contact]." The male prostitute's description of the toilet in the cinema Maiak in Khar'kov in the 1920s as "particularly convenient" betrays an awareness of the perverse applications of architectural accidents that might afford privacy. He identified only two "meeting places" in 1920s Leningrad, both of which were sites with public toilets (although Belousov declined to mention this fact, referring to them with the abstract *mestnost'*, a term recalling *otkhozhee mesto*, a euphemism for a privy). The two sites were "the vicinity of the Cinizelli Circus with its little benches, and the area on Nevskii Prospekt near the Anichkin [*sic*] Palace."[74] It seems likely that male prostitutes continued to haunt public toilets "on squares and railway stations" as they had prior to 1917.[75] The revolution, by virtually eliminating commodified indoor space available for private rental and enjoyment, relegated male homosexuals to what one recent observer has dubbed a "culture of the toilet."[76]

In Moscow, sources suggest that sexualized territories used by a homosexual subculture appeared in the last years of the tsarist regime, signifying a later development of this subculture compared with its more Westernized northern rival. The testimony of the male prostitute P., described by Dr. Belousov in 1927, is very informative. Before and after 1917, according to P., the Boulevard Ring (*Bul'varnoe kol'tso*) remained the city's most notorious male homosexual territory. This ring of connected boulevards (each with its own name) surrounded the heart of Moscow in a semicircular band of greenery dotted with benches, refreshment kiosks, public pissoirs, and toilets. The boulevards provided pleasant places to sit, smoke, and converse; there was a constant circulation of pedestrians; links with public transport made them accessible. From them it was an easy walk to Moscow's greater and lesser theaters, to the Conservatory, and to shops and department stores. P. accurately noted, "You can find and meet men on any boulevard."[77] His own urban sexual career had begun on Prechistenskii Boulevard, where in

1912 at seventeen years of age he had first encountered "*svoi liudi*" (my own kind) and became a male prostitute. The Boulevard Ring's reputation as an arena for male prostitution continued into the 1920s and 1930s. Nikitskii Boulevard led to Moscow's "most important 'den,'" (according to P.), the square named Nikitskie Gates. A Yugoslav Communist also named this square as the site of a "secret market" of homosexual men in the late 1920s.[78] P. identified Sretenskii and Chistoprudnyi Boulevards as places where "an especially important public" among Moscow's homosexuals made assignations. Defendants in criminal trials for sodomy held between 1935 and 1941 (discussed in chapter 8) frequented these same boulevards; a number admitted to having sex in the public toilets and darkened corners of these streetscapes during the 1930s.

Codes of mutual recognition in gesture and speech imbued these locations with significance for the homosexual subculture. Men who wished to have sex with youths or other men identified themselves to each other in diverse ways. Some gestures were clearly devices used by prostitutes to attract potential clients. Others sought to elicit or exploit a wealthier man's tender concern. A narrative of poverty ran through many stories told by poorer young men seeking contact with more affluent males. Conspicuous clothing, the use of rouge and powder, and the adoption of effeminate mannerisms were mechanisms some youths and men in this subculture used to draw attention and to signal their intentions.

The single most important gesture was the significant glance, the most widely acknowledged form of discreet self-proclamation. It was something even outsiders knew about, judging from the comments of the anonymous denouncer of St. Petersburg's sodomites: "The *tetki*, as they call themselves, recognize each other with one glance, by signs unnoticeable to passersby, yet by these experts can even define the category of *tetka* we are dealing with."[79] An exchange of sustained eye contact, especially in a location with a notorious reputation, established participation in the subculture. Soldiers and *tetki* performed this ritual in the vicinity of the public toilets of the Zoological Gardens, as did rent boys and their clients outside a facility next to the Cinizelli Circus, as observed in 1908.[80] The rituals of requesting, offering, and lighting cigarettes were also employed, although some "hooligan" male prostitutes dispensed with such niceties and simply approached potential clients with a bluff "Hi!" (*Dras'te*) and an outstretched hand. Their clients, commented a prerevolutionary social critic, could be recognized by their "nonchalantly thrown glance" and the "particular, specific mask of desire" on their faces.[81] This set of signals did not change after 1917. A knowledgeable sailor arrested in 1921 at a "pederastic party" in Petrograd admitted that he was aware of the sexual intentions of those present: "I saw it in their glances, conversations, and smiles."[82] The prostitute P. claimed that between 1925 and 1927 he had "seen in person, met somewhere, [or] recognized as one of his kind" no less than five thousand homosexual men in Moscow.

Once contact was made, conversation developed. St. Petersburg jurist A. F. Koni reported some of the tales told by the Mikhailov gang of extortionists in the 1870s. The gang relied on narratives of impoverished but deserving youth to entice prosperous men into compromising situations. These tales were probably not only used by blackmailers but by male prostitutes as well. A justice of the peace on his way to his Mikhailovskaia Square club via "the fateful Passage" was accosted by a gang member, who asked him for money to save his dying mother. When in the street the naive judge gave him three rubles, the youth raised the alarm, claiming he deserved fifty rubles for "that *filth* you suggest." Other gang members told tales of having been excluded from school for nonpayment of fees. Another favorite pretext they (and doubtless, other youths) exploited was to loiter by the entrance to the Cinizelli Circus, asking wealthy gentlemen to buy them tickets to the performance.[83]

The class division evident in these encounters could also reflect the chasm between city and countryside. Mikhail Kuzmin recorded how he met a "professional," apparently new to city life, on Nevskii Prospekt in 1924. Despite the postrevolutionary date of this encounter, both actors—prostitute and potential client—read from a familiar script that had changed little from the tsarist era:

On Nevskii I glanced at a sweet-looking lad. He turned and came back to me. Began a conversation, "How to get to Ligovka [Street]." Then the usual story. From the country, some place, doesn't want to perish . . . et cetera. Why did he speak to me? I see you are a good man. And why was I looking at you? I don't know, it pleased me to. Yes? so I please you just a little? Practically on the spot—[he] dreams of a life together, of going for walks, of learning, culture, et cetera, of the train to the countryside. Naive, false, lying, simple-minded. He wrote down his address, I gave him mine. Just like all country folk, he plays the hypocrite. But it's been so long since I've seen a Russian lad who is good-looking. If he's a professional, so much the better. Am I married, do I live with someone? . . . We walked along Nadezhdinskaia [Street, now Maiakovskaia], but it was too well lit everywhere.[84]

The following day, the "professional" turned up at Kuzmin's flat, and the diarist took him out for a drink:

> Of course, he has a heart, and dreams, even if they're the most stupid and confused ones. A "backward" [*temnyi*] person, as he says. We went to a beer hall. It was incredibly boring and awkward; what was I to do with him? Yes, it's no longer 1907 when I could get into such adventures. The main thing is I can't stand it when people build something up on me. I ran off like one liberated . . .[85]

The script of client-prostitute transactions, however tattered in Kuzmin's hands, was nevertheless fresh enough for his interlocutor, a country youth, who was sufficiently familiar with its lines to rehearse them until he bored his hapless "client" to distraction. Through this script ran several oppositional relationships: town versus country, education versus ignorance, supposed wealth versus probable indigence, experience versus youth. Little in the patter employed by the city's male prostitutes had changed as a result of revolution.

In tsarist Petersburg, effeminate gesture and dress or simply conspicuous clothing were sometimes trademarks of "commercial catamites" and of the *tetki* who resorted to them. The degree to which these semiotics were deliberately adopted by each group (and not just attributed by outsiders) is difficult to establish. Perhaps more effeminacy was ascribed to participants, and they displayed more effeminacy, as an urban homosexual subculture developed. Mid-nineteenth-century medical sources describing more traditional male sexual barter (for example, of the bathhouse or serving-class varieties) made no mention of effeminacy among youths and men selling sex. But some male prostitutes in Petersburg streets appear to have used effeminate signals to identify themselves to customers. A Dane who picked up a young man for paid sex in the Passage in 1869 said he recognized that he was "prepared to offer himself for sodomy; it was understood in his manner of addressing me, which had the appearance of feminine courtesy (*zhenskaia liubeznost'*)."[86] Members of the Mikhailov extortion gang reportedly wore "strange outfits"—velveteen trousers and red boots, or in one case, a "much too long" velvet tie.[87]

The anonymous denouncer of the capital's *tetki* appended to his diatribe a lengthy list of suspects, characterizing many of them by their feminine traits. Several were said to be flamboyantly effeminate in public, and a few had feminine nicknames such as "Dina" and "Aspaziia." The author labeled many of his subjects "ladies" (*damy*), apparently because they enjoyed the receptive role in anal intercourse.[88] Post-1905 sensationalized portrayals of similar individuals were laden with images of distorted femininity and exaggerated class pretensions. Aliases as baronesses, duchesses, and *baby* (peasant women) proliferated among the male prostitutes based near the Cinizelli Circus. This yellow journalism also asserted that color codes distinguished "homosexual" men. Coquettish homosexuals sported "their bright red cravats, a kind of homosexual uniform, and some have a bright red handkerchief blazing from the pocket." Male prostitutes, both seasoned professionals and newcomers, sometimes wore makeup in the street. A German hairdresser wandered the town after he closed his shop "to catch a pederast" by wearing rouge, "so that they'll see I'm a girl."[89] Some signals are confirmed in the contemporary antics of Kuzmin and his friends. Appearing in public in makeup or sporting beauty marks and vibrantly colored waistcoats blended dandyism, decadent taste, and hints of the underworld of male prostitution. The best-known portrait of Kuzmin, painted following the success of *Wings* in 1909 by homosexual artist Konstantin Somov, depicted him wearing a prominent bright red necktie.[90] These eye-catching signals teased the boundaries of conventional masculinity.

Soviet sources of the 1920s continue to mention the use of female nicknames and occasional indulgence in cross-dressing, although these practices were evidently reserved for private events and spaces. Discussions of male effeminacy in psychiatric literature dwindled toward the late 1920s. Among the sailors arrested in Petrograd at a "pederastic party" in 1921 were men known to their friends as "Zoia" and "Vial'-tseva." The latter sailor, by appropriating her name and imitating her famous fashion sense, evidently paid homage to "the incomparable" Anastasiia Vial'tseva, a cabaret singer whose flashy stardom helped to transform commercial celebrity in Russia and inspired fanatical devotion. Other men arrested that evening and later interviewed were like one Red Army soldier who "loves to dress in women's clothing, and despite his poverty, possesses women's outfits."[91] The male prostitute P. supposedly boasted that he had attended prerevolutionary parties in Moscow dressed as a Ukrainian peasant woman, but he said little about effeminacy or cross-dressing in postrevolutionary homosexual life. Poverty and fear of the political dangers of public flamboyance undoubtedly curbed extravagant effeminacy by male homosexuals during the early Soviet era.

By the late nineteenth century, Russia's homosexual subculture deployed at least a handful of code words to refer to its denizens. Some were euphemisms that gave very little away to noninitiates; expressions such as "our circle" (*nash krug*), reportedly used in 1898 by a Petersburg gentry woman who loved women, implied affiliation without betraying its source.[92] Referring to men, the label "*tetka*," literally "auntie," circulated among participants in the subculture and their observers. The word had both foreign and domestic resonance. In France, the equivalent *tante* was in use in the mid-nineteenth century to denote a male prostitute, and by the end of the century, it had appeared in print referring to all homosexuals in general.[93] It was in the first sense that Petersburg doctor Vladislav Merzheevskii had used its Russian variant in his 1878 manual on forensic gynecology.[94] Ten years later, Peter Tchaikovsky was perhaps already using the more generalized secondary meaning of *tetka*, with its nuances of preening lubriciousness (close to that heard in today's Anglo-American term "queen"), in his diary.[95]

The anonymous denouncer of Petersburg's *tetki* of the late 1880s and early 1890s extended this meaning to refer to the clients of male prostitutes.[96] The denouncer distinguished between the *tetka's* "vice" as an essential characteristic possibly derived from "sexual satiety" and disgust with women on the one hand, and the opportunistic "pederasty" of the "impoverished, young . . . victims serving to satisfy" them on the other.[97] In this view, the *tetka* was predominantly an affluent character, tempting victims into sex acts—which they otherwise found repugnant—with the lure of easy money and luxury. It is unlikely that all partners of the *tetka* were so repulsed by same-sex acts; undoubtedly, as in the case of Medvedev's coachmen, "some agree[d] to it for pleasure" alone and did not seek payment. The actual class profile of these identities also remains sketchy, although most sources present the objects of the *tetka's* "exploitation" as young men newly arrived from the countryside, working as apprentices in workshops or commerce, living rough on the street, studying, or engaged as soldiers or sailors. As they circulated through the homosexual subculture, these men and youths confronted the prospect of a gradual life transition from desirable "commercial catamite" to aging *tetka*, perhaps an unpalatable career sweetened by hopes of material advancement. A loyal patron might offer the young "pederast for money" the opportunity to leave the sexual marketplace and form a partnership of sorts. Meanwhile, those with steady occupations (like military recruits) engaging in more casual forms of male prostitution abandoned this trade when age reduced their appeal or when military service took them from the city.[98] Unlike the very visible persona of the *tetka*, the boys and men who sold sexual favors did not acquire a stable subcultural label in Russian. This eloquent silence perhaps testifies to the transitory nature of this role. It also highlights the discomfort the masculine sex trade provoked and the concealment that participants felt was necessary. Outsiders might refer to these sexually available men as "pederast-prostitutes," "commercial catamites," and later on, as "homosexuals," but their apparent refusal to name themselves underlines their tenuous claim to masculine respectability that rested on keeping their sexual activity hidden.

The masculine style displayed by some of these men and youths had erotic appeal when viewed through the eyes of sexual dissidents. In contrast to the vivid figure of the effeminate *tetka*, the soldiers, sailors, and schoolboys prowling the territories of St. Petersburg's homosexual underworld were dressed in distinctive official uniforms, redolent of an exemplary masculinity. Outwardly forced to conform to public standards of self-control and sobriety imposed by their clothing, military men and students nevertheless found it a convenient and flattering camouflage for their participation in the subculture. Linked to the idealized manly images projected with the help of such clothing was another subcultural label in circulation in both capitals, that of the "woman-hater" (*zhenonenavistnik*). "Balls of women-haters" (*baly zhenonenavistnikov*) with some men attending in drag, were reportedly staged in Moscow before 1914, while a Petrograd sailor, interviewed after his arrest at the 1921 "pederasts' party," said he enjoyed sex with men, "especially when a woman-hater came his way, someone of a masculine appearance who did not make himself up to be a woman."[99] The term apparently invoked a masculinist solidarity to banish the effeminacy and, perhaps, the ruralizing nuances audible in the label *tetka*.[100]

The interaction between these characters—the *tetka*, the "pederast for money," and the "woman-hater"—remains obscure from these fragmented sources. Emerging from the traditional hierarchical world of eros between men, they were the public faces of a modern homosexual subculture.[101] The subculture was not confined to public territory, however. Some men, with the resources to rent or purchase flats or homes, organized domestic partnerships with members of the same sex. Others used private space to host gatherings and create opportunities for socializing and sexual contact. Hostile observers noted that such parties could offer their hosts the chance to earn money from either pimping or sales of alcohol. Yet these gatherings, some lavish and exuberant, cemented emotional and romantic bonds that strengthened a common identity around sexual preference.

The crowded and impoverished conditions of worker housing dictate that surviving traces of domestic partnerships between lower-class men are rare. In a 1909 textbook on sexual psychology, a psychiatrist described one Petersburg working-class male couple's domestic arrangements:

> They concluded a formal agreement between themselves, in which each swore faithfulness to the other to the grave, and they adopted the mutual appellations of man and wife. They occupied a single room and at night slept in one bed. As a ruse there were two beds in the room, and they each went to bed separately for several minutes, and then the one who had to play the role of "husband" in this revolting union [*otvratitel'nyi soiuz*] came to his "wife" and they would spend the night together.[102]

Middle-class and aristocratic homosexuals were able to construct more elaborate settings behind closed doors for their identities and partnerships. In 1908, a sarcastic critic of "homosexual Petersburg" described a hotel suite supposedly occupied by a "conscious and convinced partisan of same-sex love." On the "partisan's" desk lay a collection of pornographic cards illustrating "all the forms and positions of same-sex love," while on the wall hung a photographic portrait of a naked coachman. Bookshelves were laden with works by "authors of the Kuzmin type." "Porcelain statuettes and other knickknacks on étagères scream about it too—in other words, the room of an enlightened society homosexual reminds one of a little homosexual museum [*malen'kii gomoseksual'nyi muzei*]."[103]

In the denunciation of Petersburg's *tetki* of the late 1880s or early 1890s, the self-righteous author describes (with the detail of an eyewitness) a "ball" that turned into a "dreadful, disgraceful orgy" in the home of a rich *tetka.* Beginning as a housewarming in the wealthy host's "luxuriously furnished flat practically in the center of town," the guests danced and drank until four in the morning, when a sumptuous supper was served. The host and several guests wore "ladies' outfits." After dining, several *tetki* took off their clothes and continued dancing, while drunken groups of men engaged in sexual activity in a room equipped with "fine Turkish furnishings." "They are not at all shy in front of the servants at these parties," the observer noted, "because these are chosen from among their own (*iz svoikh*)." The same document records that a relatively less affluent resident of the capital operated as a "procurer" (*svodnia*) of "boys, soldiers, and domestic servants" for prosperous *tetki.* This enterprising man used his flat as a discreet clearing-house for young men who sought introductions to upper-class *tetki;* the youths paid the procurer a fee for his services.[104]

Despite homosexuals' increasing difficulty under Soviet rule in controlling private spaces, they occasionally managed to use domestic or other semiprivate venues (halls, cabarets) to gather. Parties, masquerades, and artistic performances brought scores of men together to socialize and be socialized, and to make sexual contacts. The relative openness of homosexual entertainments tapered off rapidly after the civil war, but a few sources hint at their more discreet continuation. Many of the best records of gatherings come from the Petrograd-Leningrad subculture, where a tradition of popular private homosexual assemblies was well established.

The best description of organized, possibly commercially run, Soviet-era private gatherings of homosexual men comes from psychiatrist V. M. Bekhterev's articles on sexual deviance mentioning the Petrograd raid on a "pederasts' club" of 15 January 1921.[105] On that evening ninety-five men were arrested in a flat belonging to a military policeman's father (*otets militsionera svodno-boevogo otriada*); the policeman himself was said to have invited guests "promising an interesting evening with ladies."[106] This gathering was one of a series that had first been observed and later even organized by a policeman. The agent, known only as "Sh.," alleged that several "such evenings" (for "pederasts") in a variety of private flats had taken place around Petrograd.[107] Who began organizing these parties was not clear from Bekhterev's reporting of Sh.'s deposition, but the doctor wrote that "the police agent *himself* had later run several evenings, 'in order to find out their [the participants'] opinions.' "[108] One seaman in custody told Bekhterev that "the parties were organized about twice a month"; he had been to many of them and recognized many guests from previous parties. The presence of so many sailors and soldiers at these gatherings seems to have been the most likely reason for police interest.

"B.," a Red Army soldier arrested in the raid, described how he came to be at the event and what he saw there.

I heard there would be a party at M.'s and that they were inviting people to come: there were a lot of people at the party I knew. I heard it would be an original party in the form of a wedding. When I arrived with X., we found the following: from a room off the corridor the young ones [*molodye*] came out into the large room—S. was dressed as the bride, Sh. [presumably not the police agent] was the groom, behind them walked many whose names I didn't know, dressed in women's gowns. Where they solemnized the marriage [*blagoslovliali ikh khlebom*], I didn't see, but we congratulated them in the big room. Some of the participants kissed. Then afterward there was dancing, and lots of people kissed.

The costumes were not confined to wedding garments, nor were the dances apparently raucous or orgiastic. Another guest reported the following:

We arrived at the flat at around 11 P.M.; the party was already in full swing. When we got there, we found some kind of masquerade: there was a bride, several Spanish costumes, and two individuals in white wigs. I invited one of them to dance a waltz and then a minuet.

Nevertheless, this party was not merely a masquerade but was explicitly set up to bring together men searching for sex with men.[109] A "flying post" (*letuchaia pochta*) enabled men to send messages to others they fancied; one lucky sailor received notes inscribed with the words, "I fancy you" and "I'd like to get to know you." Another seaman, Andrei K., serving on a torpedo boat, made it clear he understood the sexually specific nature of these parties he frequented:

it wasn't my first time at these parties, I knew lots of people, I know the persons dressed in women's garments. I personally don't engage in pederasty, but I knew that many of the guests at these parties did engage in pederasty, because I saw it in their glances, conversations, and smiles.

Same-sex affection that evening was not confined to flying missives, smiles, and looks. Bekhterev interviewed the arresting officers, who told him that in police cells, "two of the arrested men stroked each other on the back and hands, and kissed each other . . . these were a *sailor* from the transport Kama and citizen A. P. P." When questioned by Bekhterev, citizen P. admitted that "the sailor Ch. really did kiss me on the cheek. I don't know why, but I think he likes me."[110]

Bekhterev's interviews with arrested men from this party indicate that while few claimed they had been invited "by chance," several acknowledged that they knew they were attending a "pederasts' party" (*vecherinka pederastov*), and others insisted "it was not possible to be a chance visitor" at these affairs. Several acknowledged that they knew many of the other guests from previous gatherings. The soldier B. and his "partner" regularly attended these parties and asserted that the guests were "in one way or another were all acquainted with each other."[111] In the diary of Mikhail Kuzmin, a characteristically laconic but suggestive entry records that this particular evening and its unhappy end made an impression among his circle of homosexual friends. Kuzmin's partner, Iurii Iurkun, came home late that evening reporting "impressions of masquerades," and visitors to his flat the next day continued conversations about "masquerades."[112] With their cross-dressing, flirtations and dances, parodies of "normal" weddings, and idolization of military men, these parties were a vivid expression, carried over from Petersburg's tsarist era, of the city's rich male homosexual subculture.

Few parties, masquerades, or similar amusements appear in the sources for the later 1920s, which are dominated by generally unsympathetic forensic psychiatric texts. Dr. Belousov's "male prostitute" P. did not describe any large parties occurring after the revolution, although he asserted that he believed that from 1925 to 1927 he had seen, met, or recognized thousands of homosexuals in Moscow.[113] In addition, P. reported traveling around the Soviet Union with "letters of introduction" to like-minded men in distant cities, who "received him like a friend and let him stay the night" (usually expecting sexual favors in return). In each town he contrived through his first contact to meet "a wide local acquaintance" from which one or another "old fellow of about fifty" would take him in for a month.[114] A Leningrad homosexual, Sergei E., told a doctor how in 1923 he met a like-minded man "by chance": "He brought me into a circle of 'that kind' of person. From that moment a new era in my life began." After a year of fleeting "erotic joys and temptations," he settled down with a lover and began to live with him.[115] One 1935 sodomy trial referred to a private flat in which "a citizen named Petr and nicknamed "the Baroness" (*Baronessa*), who had an entire den of homosexuals," offered his visitors alcohol and conviviality.[116] Private parties arranged by and for homosexuals, as well as suggestions of a lively if discreet sociability, also figured in trials as late as 1941.[117] These men apparently had some secure access to private domestic space and in controlled circumstances were willing to share it.

The rental of cabarets or halls for cultural events organized by members of the homosexual subculture was increasingly difficult, but not entirely impossible, during NEP. *Antinoi* (Antinous), a private arts circle devoted to the appreciation of "male beauty" in prose, verse, drama, and music, functioned in Moscow during the early 1920s, staging readings of consciously homosexual poetry, recitals of music by "our own" composers, and even an all-male ballet. The group made plans to publish an anthology of homosexual verse from ancient to modern times, an attempt to construct an ennobling past.[118] The collection went unpublished, and the record of this group's activity begins and ends with correspondence relating to Mikhail Kuzmin's May 1924 reading to the Antinoi group in the Blue Bird Café, just steps from Tverskoi Boulevard. The group apparently disbanded, as it became more difficult to rent meeting space or publicize its activities even by word of mouth.[119]

Kuzmin's last public reading, in Leningrad in 1928, encapsulated the problems posed by Soviet power for those who would promote homosexual culture. Organizers of the reading (from the Institute of the History of Art) included it in a series of literary evenings but had to seek special permission from the institute's director to invite Kuzmin. They realized that "undesirable persons" (homosexuals) would be keen to hear the author of *Wings*. No advertisement of the evening was permitted, and admission was limited to invitation only. Despite these precautions, on the appointed evening, the auditorium was filled to capacity, with people standing in the aisles and seated on the floor. Many in the audience were male homosexuals, "exactly those most feared by the director":

> Most were middle-aged or mature. They began elbowing their way toward the stage; many had bouquets of flowers in their hands. When Kuzmin finished reading, they dashed up to the stage and began throwing these bouquets upon it. As Orlov [a student among the organizers] put it, this was "the last demonstration of the Petersburg pederasts." The performance turned into a genuine, happy triumph for Kuzmin, but for the organizers of the evening it all nearly ended badly: they only just managed to convince the director that they had been incapable of handling the crowd.[120]

Tsarist St. Petersburg's male homosexual subculture still existed as a network of affiliations, with its own means of disseminating information and a powerful cultural memory. To these "middle-aged or mature" men who recalled their youth as a time of carefree amusements and sexual "adventures" (persistent themes in Kuzmin's diary), the outspoken poet "dressed in prerevolutionary fashion . . . and reading with the assistance of old-fashioned spectacles, occasionally using them as a monocle" was a talisman from that time, and perhaps a rebuke to the world they now lived in.[121]

Conclusion

During the late Imperial era a Russian, urban, male homosexual subculture developed from indigenous patterns of a traditional mutual masculine sexuality. The male homosexual world was not alien to the national body, but was a vigorous and resourceful part of society. It is heterosexist and nationalist chauvinism to claim that in tsarist Russia or in the USSR, this homosexual subculture was imported from abroad or created by Communist misrule.[122]

Intimate relations within the traditional male social hierarchies of late tsarist Russia, such as those between masters and servants, belonged to this society's older masculine sexual culture. Here there was little identification with a specific group of "one's own people," with an effeminate self-image, or with an exclusive sexual orientation. Individuals in positions of authority indulged in same-sex erotic acts for pleasure, while their subordinates apparently often acquiesced with a view to material if not personal profit. Yet many also tolerated or welcomed "gentlemen's mischief" and did not always expect to be compensated. This was a sexual culture that grew from a popular and elite indulgence of masculine sexual release and perhaps from a perception that "normal" outlets for male "lustfulness" (especially female prostitutes) could be expensive or contaminated by venereal disease.[123] The impression of relative indulgence (in comparison to Western views of eros between men) must not be exaggerated. As diaries and other sources reveal, Russian men irrespective of class often appeared to view these acts as "sinful" even if they repeatedly committed them.[124]

Parallel with this traditional sexual pattern, a modern homosexual subculture took form against the backdrop of rapid urbanization and the accelerated introduction of market relationships and the more impersonal bond between employer and employee. In the subculture, forms of speech and mutual recognition identified participants across the barriers of class, age, and education. A proportion of the denizens of the homosexual world used boldly effeminate manners, gestures, and forms of dress. Others perhaps adopted a more discreet symbol, such as the red cravats or handkerchiefs said to have constituted a "homosexual uniform" in 1908. A sense of self-consciousness appeared, as some men having erotic relations with their own sex now referred to themselves and their friends as *tetki* or "our own kind." Others (like the "women-haters" or some "pederasts for money") resisted such marginalized identities, exploiting instead their public projection of a normative masculinity for hidden and transgressive purposes. Commercialization catered to this specialized market. By the late tsarist era, bathhouse "mischief" conducted by the peasant *artel'* had developed into efficiently organized, discreet but notorious male prostitution in the bathhouse, now more closely resembling the licensed female sex trade. "Balls of women-haters" and bars run by *tetki* could apparently survive on the proceeds generated by "our own kind" alone.

After 1917, revolutionary legislation perhaps indicated to some that homosexuality might be tolerated. Yet the male homosexual world's uses of space would prove to be out of step with the Communist goal of reconstructing everyday life. Gradually losing control over commodified public interiors, such as hotel rooms, bathhouse cabinets, restaurant chambers, halls for poetry readings or cabarets for entertainments, some homosexuals retreated into a narrowing private realm. But it would be misleading to claim that Soviet policies alone "drove people into the toilets." Marginal public spaces were well established sexualized territories, geographic expressions of a lively urban male homosexual subculture. After 1917, male homosexuals and their male sexual partners continued resorting to public lavatories and other civic amenities like parks and boulevards because they were spaces where participants could recognize and meet each other according to familiar rituals. Even Mikhail Kuzmin, the bourgeois founder of Russia's literary homosexual tradition, who after all had more or less a room of his own, found the pursuit of a "sweet-looking" young "professional" on the streets of Leningrad one autumn evening in 1924 a stimulating "adventure," reminiscent of his prerevolutionary escapades. Sex in public was an affirmation of self.

"Our Circle"

SEX BETWEEN WOMEN IN
MODERNIZING RUSSIA

For my part, my love for an individual of my own sex is just as great, pure and sacred, as the love of a normal woman for the opposite sex; I am capable of self-
sacrifice, I would be ready to die for that beloved person who would understand me.
How sad that we are considered depraved and diseased.
—From "transvestite" and "homosexual" Evgeniia Fedorovna M., "History of
my illness (the brief confession of a person of the intermediate sex, a male
psycho-hermaphrodite)"[1]

nlike their male counterparts, Russian women who had erotic
relations with members of their own sex had less access to the
public sphere and so were less able to construct for themselves
a coherent subculture with the attributes of the male homosexual
world. This is not to suggest that no female homosexual subculture
existed in revolutionary Russia. Traces in the historical record of the
nature and extent of the semiotics of a subculture are slight. Scraps of
evidence suggest that among certain urban women, dress, mannerisms
and deportment served as signals to other women that same-sex erotic
approaches were welcome. Psychiatrists, both before the revolution and
in their burst of interest in female homosexuality during the 1920s,
failed to display any concern about the social connections between individual "patients," treating them instead in their discourse as isolated
"misfits" without linkages to similar women. There was little or no
policing of female mutual sexual relations during these decades, so data
on the customs and geography of a subculture such as that available
from prosecutions of homosexual men, do not exist. Yet this does not
necessarily mean that women did not form circles or networks in the
private sphere that facilitated mutual recognition by individuals who
felt same-sex desire. The record is episodic, briefly illuminating the
varied sites of women's mutual relations and leaving the historian to
speculate on continuities in the evolution of these hidden worlds.

Despite the fragmented sources, it is possible to propose at least some social locations for female homosexuality in late tsarist and early Soviet Russia. Psychiatric, criminological, and biographical records can be examined for indicators of these social contexts. The medical sources, which offer some of the earliest biographical accounts of male and female same-sex desire produced by Russians, only begin in the 1880s to describe women who loved other women in any detail. Erotic relations between women of earlier eras cannot be ruled out, but the character of these affinities is seldom intelligible in nonmedical genres.[2]

Class position seems to have been a significant determinant of the range of opportunities available for the expression of same-sex desire between women. In late-tsarist and early-Soviet sources, lower-class women having mutual relations were normally featured in this literature when they were prostitutes or in prisons.[3] In the epilogue, studies by criminologists of prison life and Gulag memoir literature, are examined as sources on same-sex love between women. This chapter considers the single-sex environment of the tsarist licensed brothel, which created a rather different culture of self-preservation in conditions of relative autonomy. The medical literature also reveals that more fortunate women could find avenues within and beyond the conventional family to express same-sex desire. Economic independence, whether gained through education or entrepreneurship, greatly enabled these women to achieve a measure of self-determination, including the expression of same-sex love. The widely observed phenomenon of the "passing woman" in Russian society offers a further perspective on love between women and the gender dissent that frequently accompanied it.

Women Apart: The Culture of Brothels and Prostitution

Prior to 1905, Russian medicine had seldom linked "lesbianism" to female prostitution, in contrast to Western forensic medicine and criminal anthropology where the association was well established as a moralistic trope in medico-legal literature. After the 1905 revolution, experts in Russia began to discard their view of the prostitute as the innocent, often peasant, victim of urban male depravity, and gradually adopted the bourgeois discourse of the marginalized and masculinized sexually deviant woman.[4] Fragmentary evidence from medical case histories and records of criminal trials before and after the 1905 watershed suggest that whatever the ideological transformations of the category "prostitute-as-lesbian," at the level of actual experience some women exploited the homosocial space provided by licensed brothels of the ancien régime to foster same-sex relations.[5]

Wealthy women could even constitute clients of female prostitutes. In the early 1880s one affluent gentry woman, Iuliia Ostrovleva (referred to as "Miss N." by her psychiatrist) was introduced to "unnatural sexual directions" with other women after meeting a prostitute on the streets of St. Petersburg. Ostrovleva claimed that in the hidden space of the public brothel a world of women who loved women flourished. Her psychiatrist V. F. Chizh recorded:

> Among her many acquaintances with perverted sexual feeling, she lived the most varied life of love and sexual feeling; here there was platonic love, and courtship, and jealousy, and satiety, betrayals, a connection [*sviaz'*] with two women simultaneously; the joys of victory and the bitterness of failure, in a word, the whole life of Miss N. was absorbed by this perverted love. She loved to get dressed in men's clothing and drive out in a troika with the objects of her love; dressing in men's suits she went to public houses and spent a great deal of money on women. According to her assurances, there are by far more women with perversion of the sexual feeling than we usually think, and in fact they occupy the most varied social positions.[6]

This case history, Russia's first psychiatric study of "contrary sexual feeling" in either sex, thus explicitly indicated that a nascent culture of women who recognized their sexual affiliation across the barriers of class already existed in the Petersburg of the early 1880s. The brothel was one institution that could discreetly provide a meeting point for these women.

A criminal case caught the attention of experts in the capital about ten years after the study of Ostrovleva or "Miss N." was published. A Petersburg tobacconist who had married a prostitute, Krasavina, was charged with her murder. In 1893 he had discovered his wife in bed with a prostitute, one of her former colleagues; he stabbed his wife to death on the spot. The story of Pelageia Krasavina's relationship with her female lover was heard in court and later recounted by gynecologist I. M. Tarnovskii in 1895.[7] Krasavina's life as a "tribade-prostitute," like that of Ostrovleva and her circle, had been sheltered in the official brothel and tolerated by her colleagues if not by the owner of the various houses she worked in. Anna Ivanova, a twenty-four-year-old sex worker from one of these establishments, testified in court that Krasavina and her lover had been inseparable, that they had had sexual relations together, and that "in a word, they became what we call in public houses *koshki* [female cats]"——an argot term for female prostitutes who shared sexual favors.[8] Female same-sex relationships were apparently common enough in the brothels of St. Petersburg to have a specific label in the vocabulary of sex workers. Love letters between the two women were heard as evidence in court. In one note, Krasavina's girlfriend had written "you are my Polly, my sweet and dear and my own [*rodnaia*], I love you." Similar expressions of romantic endearment were exchanged by prostitutes in venereal wards, where "touchingly affectionate pairs" of public women were observed conducting relationships of a passionate character.[9]

The tsarist public house provided a potential material basis for the "*ménages de tribades*" observed in similar licensed establishments in turn-of-the-century France, where some owners deliberately favored same-sex relations between their sex workers as a stabilizing influence as well as a commercial attraction.[10] The degree to which Russia's brothel operators consciously mirrored this policy remains obscure. The owner of the various brothels on Vasil'evskii Island and Chubarov Alley where Pelageia Krasavina worked apparently put up with the disruption caused by her attempts to establish intimate relations with fellow prostitutes, as long as she was generating income. She was eventually dismissed for evading relations with paying customers.[11] Claims of "lesbianism" (*lesbiianstvo*) in Russian brothels come from St. Petersburg physician Boris Bentovin, who wrote that managers regarded mutual "adoration" (*obozhanie*) between sex workers with approval, as a guarantee against strong ties to male clients. Likewise, Bentovin pointed to the existence of mentoring relationships between "very young prostitutes only starting out in their profession" and "more solid and experienced girlfriends (*podrugi*)."[12] Older prostitutes offered advice and support during "critical moments" to younger girlfriends and taught them necessary skills. Bentovin made no mention in his 1909 study of prostitution of the lesbian tableaux vivants, popular attractions in Paris *maisons de tolérance* at this time, but he noted that female couples bonded by mentorship appeared together in Petersburg's brothel drawing rooms. In this peculiar space blending the sexual market with trappings of domestic respectability, the younger partner served as a "attracting magnet" drawing in the wealthiest clients. Meanwhile, her older mentor "who could hardly count on success on her own," was able to attract "a less demanding suitor" in the wake of her younger girlfriend. "That is how the adoring and the adored live, complementing each other, as it were, and bringing each other a degree of profit . . ."[13] Bentovin's indulgent depiction of mentoring same-sex relations inside the brothel must be balanced against the harsh realities faced by most licensed prostitutes. Conditions in Russia's brothels were usually squalid, with deleterious psychological and physical effects on prostitutes. Medical surveillance was brutal and invasive, threatening public women with physical harm and financial ruin. While brothels constituted a social sphere that undoubtedly sheltered some same-sex relationships, this harsh environment offered sex workers rather limited prospects for agency and self-expression.[14]

The Soviet abolition of the medico-legal regulation of brothels and the subsequent rise in the informal and covert sex trade made prostitution a less predictable social sphere for women who turned to this profession. The housing shortage and the decline in private control over sheltered urban spaces appeared to drive illicit heterosexual sex into the streets, railway stations and carriages, restaurants, bathhouses, and taxicabs. The revolutionary regime repeatedly declared that women who sold their bodies were victims of economic exploitation, not to be criminalized, and campaigns to discourage them from taking up sex work were launched. The abolition of licensed brothels turned prostitution into a very unstable and dangerous livelihood for female sex workers.[15] Russian historians have argued that more urban women and more declassed women from the former elite supposedly turned to casual or occasional heterosexual prostitution in the 1920s as urban unemployment hit them hardest.[16] Whether in fact these practices can be measured by historians using existing sources may be disputed, but the end of regulation and the regime's eagerness to rescue the female prostitute undoubtedly changed the environment for same-sex relations within the sex trade.[17]

A 1926 case history of "Sh.," a so-called "female homosexual" (*gomoseksualistka*) who murdered her partner, "L.", a prostitute, illustrated these social conditions. It also suggested that Soviet doctors would pursue the link made in the Western medical imagination between prostitution and female homosexuality.[18] Before meeting L. in a Moscow cafeteria where they both worked, Sh. had been married twice, once apparently for love before the world war, and a second time for "material reasons" during the civil war. By 1919, however, Sh. had been widowed, and she drifted to Moscow in search of a living. Sh. and L. shared a flat, and later a room, while L. alternated between earning a living at a succession of unstable menial jobs and bringing home men for paid sex. Sh. also found employment in short-term and unreliable jobs as a maid and in a canteen. Later she took in mending and laundry and cooked meals for L. Sh. reported to Moscow penal psychiatrists Krasnushkin and Kholzakova that L. had made sexual advances to her and that eventually she had been provoked to murder L. with an axe. The psychiatrists doubted Sh.'s evasive and vague claims that the sexual relationship with L. had been brief and episodic, and they suggested that the "bisexual" Sh. not only had regular physical relations with L. but had also engaged in prostitution periodically.[19]

The actual role of commercial heterosexual sex in the partnership of L. and Sh. was not explained by the psychiatrists. Unlike Bentovin, they hesitated to draw a direct connection between "lesbian" relations and initiation into prostitution through mentorship, preferring instead to see in Sh.'s "masculinized" body a biological explanation for her deviance. Other observers of the heterosexual prostitution market in early Soviet Russia had remarked upon the financial partnership of younger women (to sell sex) and older women (with rooms to rent), but no suggestion that same-sex relations lay behind this symbiosis was mooted.[20] Between L. and Sh., a same-sex relationship appeared to supply the glue that cemented the household formed by these two women. Whatever the elements of domestic and economic cooperation here might have been (and psychiatrists had little to say about the nongenital aspects of this couple's relationship), experts viewed their engagement in the sex trade and their "female homosexuality" as masculinizing and degenerate.

Three years later, the psychiatrist Krasnushkin published a series of lectures on "criminal psychopathy" featuring the case of a "poetess" whose verse "sang the praises of lesbian love [*lesbosskaia liubov'*]" and whose forays into heterosexual prostitution brought her in contact with the police and psychiatry.[21] Krasnushkin's colorful description painted this "patient" in the stereotypes of the "prostitute-as-lesbian." The "poetess" had been arrested for "keeping a den [of vice]":

> She recruited some kind of actress from a labor registry, luring her into a homosexual [*gomoseksual'naia*] liaison, and finally committed a homosexual act in the presence of two men, who had treated them [the two women] to food and drink and paid ten rubles for this sexual spectacle.[22]

Krasnushkin supplied no details of the nature of his "patient's" liaison with the out-of-work actress. Yet he took pains to present her poetic efforts "dedicated to lesbos [*sic*]" in a comparatively positive light, suggesting that her "indisputable giftedness" mitigated her "adventurist history." In his lecture he included one of her love-poems, judging it "socially degraded" as a result of her addictions to alcohol and cocaine, but nonetheless attesting to her talent:

> Sanctified love I have not known,
> Nor have I known maiden's tears,
> I have not sought offspring through marriage,
> And I have never woven wreathes of roses . . .
>
> From afar, encounters have always lured me,
> Brilliant sin beckoned wickedly,
> The passion of girlfriends, the tears
> And their heavy, hidden laughter . . .
>
> To their circle I was devoted,
> Drank their caresses—with caresses, their bodies,
> Brunettes captivated me more than once,
> And often my sin with blondes was bold.
>
> I loved them day and night,
> And in the weaving of our bodies,
> I loved their eyes filled with languor
> And on their breasts I loved sleep.
>
> But all is past, all irretrievable,
> I now know, it's all deceit
> I cannot go back by this same path,
> For life is but an intoxicant![23]

Krasnushkin, a vigorous and successful figure in Soviet psychiatry, evidently felt there was pedagogic value in the "sexual spectacle" furnished by this "patient-poetess" and her verses. Here was a memorable example of the "gifted psychopath," an exceptional case with which to instruct psychiatry students at Moscow State University. Yet the passion of the woman behind these verses and the circumstances of her case history were also perhaps evidence of the survival of same-sex relations and of mentorship among female prostitutes.

Domesticity, the Salon Lesbian, and Masculinization

If female same-sex eros between prostitutes sometimes bore the stamp of a brutalized lower-class culture, there were also women whose privileged economic position allowed them to express their desires, if more discreetly. Tsarist psychiatric literature yields a handful of biographies of gentry or bourgeois women like Dr. Chizh's Iuliia Ostrovleva, whose strong will and access to education and resources permitted them to explore same-sex self-expression.[24] The lives chronicled in this medical sources paralleled in their material aspects those of literary "lesbians" of late-tsarist salons.[25] In the early Soviet era, women with cultural capital were also sometimes able to invest this resource to construct a domestic environment sheltering same-sex desire. The political and economic stability requisite for a culture of the literary salon declined during the 1920s, eventually becoming submerged in the social transformations of the first Five Year Plans. The historical roots of Russia's "lesbian subculture," always fragile and tentative in the first three decades of this century, were greatly undermined by these changes, which are discussed in part 2.

One source of domestic shelter for same-sex relations was the heterosexual family. The conventional Russian family was not totally inimical to the gender nonconformity and same-sex relations in its midst. Families strove to contain, control, or accommodate these phenomena, often employing considerable adaptivity. Tsarist and early-Soviet psychiatric case histories suggest that parents reacted with equanimity when female children displayed interest in boy's clothing and games. Tomboyishness and even failure to learn housekeeping skills was tolerated in childhood, but the same girl was expected to adapt at sixteen or so and agree to marriage.[26] Some families went to unusual lengths to accommodate gender and sexual dissent. Ostrovleva's mother claimed she had "lost control" of her daughter as early as age twelve; yet this widowed matriarch and her family expressed only respect for her daughter's "love of work" and "energy" in her extraordinary chosen profession as manager of a horse-drawn cab service. Ostrovleva, who supposedly had an annual allowance of "three to four thousand [rubles]," kept her business finances separate from her mother's household accounts. Theirs was not a relationship of economic dependency. When the psychiatrist Chizh considered this young woman's development, he concluded that "with more discipline in her upbringing and life, the matter would not have gone as far as it had."[27] Perhaps Chizh implied that the lack of a firm paternal presence in the family had allowed Ostrovleva's "many peculiarities" to arise.

Families adapted to the personal characteristics of gender dissidents in their midst, and despite Chizh's implied faith in paternal gravitas, fathers too could be indulgent when it came to daughters' refusals to be socialized into feminine roles.[28] In the first decade of the twentieth century, Evgeniia Fedorovna M. (a "passing woman" in adult life) was expelled from school for refusing to wear a skirt; her rebellion was

accommodated by her father, who educated her at home and later arranged for her to write external gymnasium examinations.[29] In 1919,
a teacher, Ol'ga Shch., lived in a household in Ozery, near Moscow that
included her brother Boris and an adult sister. That year Ol'ga invited
sixteen-year-old Valentina P., with whom she had been having a sexual
relationship for over a year, into her home after the teenager was orphaned. They shared a bed and continued a love affair until 1922, when
quarrels over Valentina's membership in the Komsomol destabilized
the liaison. During this time Ol'ga's siblings adapted to the lesbian
relationship under the family roof, referring ironically to Valentina as
"your [Ol'ga's] husband" and noting that they kissed "not the way
women kiss, but another way." Yet the teenager's growing dishonesty
and violence led Boris to cut short the family's experiment in adaptation. He forbade further contact between Ol'ga and her lover, even
summoning his sister home from a posting in a factory as a teacher in
Saratov (where Valentina had followed), and he apparently persuaded
Ol'ga to consider offers of marriage from local men.[30] Standing in for
the absent patriarch, Boris reasserted masculine authority in his family
and attempted to reimpose heterosexual norms of behavior on his sister.

A little later, another family accommodated a gender and sexual
dissident in its midst for financial reasons, since the "female homosexual" it harbored was a capable market trader. When in 1925 after being
arrested and eventually given a course of hypnotherapy to "cure" her,
authorities returned her to a different, better-off branch of her family
for surveillance. The police apparently did not trust her closest relatives
to restrain her from donning a Nepman's garb and returning to the
marketplace; these siblings had grown dependent on her earnings.[31]
This use by authorities of the heterosexual family as a site for the
rehabilitation of a social "misfit" was unusual in Soviet psychiatric
literature about the homosexual. What was more common in this discourse was the degree of adaptability families displayed. Families did
not simply expel so-called "homosexuals" from their midst, but often
exerted some effort to accommodate or adapt to the sexual or gender
dissident member.

Beyond the ties of the biological family, Russian women who experienced same-sex desire and who possessed sufficient resources established their own households and, in urban centers, even circles of
like-minded friends. These circles formed the beginnings of a lesbian
subculture among women of the tsarist intelligentsia. As Diana Lewis
Burgin has established, the word "lesbian" was little used, and these
women only sporadically expressed a sense of selfhood defined by a

specific sexuality. Nevertheless, the case of Ostrovleva from the Petersburg of the early 1880s indicates that there were prosperous women-loving women who crossed class boundaries to express their desire with prostitutes open to the same sexual tastes. Another Petersburg psychiatric case (of 1898) described the less affluent, but equally adventurous, "Z., a virgin, twenty years old, from an extremely degenerated family" of provincial gentry origins. She had begun an erotic affair at the age of eighteen with another woman, who was apparently kept as a gentleman's mistress. Z.'s interviews with her doctor emphasized the cohesion of what she referred to as "our circle" (*nash krug*), a group of women who had mutual sexual relations:

> The patient affirms that women such as her, that is, who love women, are found not at all infrequently; they among themselves form a kind of particular world. Such women recognize each other by manners, expressions of the eyes, mimicry, and so on. She herself learned to discern such women virtually from her very first experience. "We," the patient says, "in no way become jealous when the object of our love belongs to a man: we know that that woman (only of course if she belongs to our circle) cannot love her husband and only fulfils her role passively. But it is a different matter if a beloved woman gives herself or pays attention to another woman: then we feel a strong jealousy and we are prepared to set off a great scandal or dispute."[32]

In this case, Z.'s family had compelled her to refer to the psychiatrist for advice about her sexual difference. It appeared that her financially straitened parents had counted on her to accept one of the many proposals of marriage she had rejected. Yet Z. was keener to remain in the company of her "circle" of female friends. Other contemporary medical case histories of same-sex relations between Russian women of upper-class families evaded any mention of a social world formed by these women themselves.[33] Medical discourse was not alone in depriving love between women of contextualization. In Russia's literary salons of the late Imperial era, the discourse of lesbianism in all its French "vocabulary and stereotypes" remained an exotic spectacle for the male gaze, and "lesbians" were a decadent species confined to an indoor, artificial world and isolated from any social roots. This construction was supported both by those who explored this aesthetic and by those who condemned it. Virtually all "lesbian" authors of this era, according to Burgin, consciously suppressed information about their sexuality in their public writing and utterances. G. S. Novopolin, scourge of the "pornographic element in Russian literature," dismissed the proposition that "lesbian love," now making an appearance on the literary stage, was also enjoying a parallel prevalence in Russia's comparatively "primitive" society.[34] Once the possibility of lesbian love had been acknowledged in imitation of the French aesthetic canon with the publication of Lidiia Zinov'eva-Annibal's *Tridtsat' tri uroda* (*Thirty-three Monsters* [St. Petersburg, 1907]), salon culture embraced sexual ambiguity within the confines of this aesthetic discourse, and certain salons became stages where these ambiguities might be paraded.[35]

Conditions for the survival of tsarist bourgeois salon culture, which might have harbored continuing explorations of sexual dissidence, "eroded and finally collapsed" in the two decades following the 1917 revolution, in the words of Beth Holmgren.[36] Significant figures who had contributed to the elaboration of aestheticized sexual ambiguity (Zinaida Gippius, Marina Tsvetaeva) emigrated during the revolution, and those who remained, especially Sofiia Parnok (1885–1933), endured an increasingly unstable material and political situation. An unabashed celebrant of mutual female relations in her verse, Parnok led a bohemian existence, migrating from one set of lodgings to the next and never establishing a permanent home, supporting herself on the margins of intellectual work with a succession of poorly paid publishing and translation commissions in the 1920s and early 1930s.

Translator and photographer Lev Gornung was an intimate friend of Parnok and of one of her partners, the mathematician Ol'ga Tsuberbiller. Gornung's description of their dress and intellectual circle fleetingly opens a window on what Burgin has described as "the totally closeted lesbian subculture, which was well-represented in the theatrical, artistic, and university communities" of Russia.[37] Of Parnok and Tsuberbiller, Gornung observed,

> [t]hey dressed very simply, and almost alike, always wearing severe, almost masculine attire consisting of jackets and skirts with hems below the knees. Both of them wore shirts and ties. Their shoes were invariably the same style of brown, low-heeled oxford.

Parnok's biographer Burgin posits that such "almost masculine" dress was a signal of their sexual preference, an urban code that could be read by other women who loved women. Photographs of the poet and the mathematician from the mid-1920s suggest that they consciously manipulated this code, wearing shirts and ties only in the city, and donning skirts and dresses to avoid "unwanted attention" when visiting the countryside.[38] Another fragment (again, the product of a man's ob-

servation) from Parnok's biography recorded an awareness of this nascent subculture and perhaps linked it with gentle teasing to the street-
walkers of Moscow's Tverskaia-Iamskaia Street. In a friendly parody on
one of Parnok's most overtly homosexual verses (included in the cycle,
"Wise Venus," in *Roses of Piéria*), a member of her literary circle wrote:

> "Some intractable girls find a girlfriend more dear than a boy-
> friend."
> Not for masculine hearts have my arrows been sharpened by Love.
> So she sang in Piéria (on the Fourth, on Tverskaia Iamskaia)
> The sister of Sappho, a daughter of Lesbos true-blue.
> Well, one can't argue tastes. Blest she who embodies the feat
> Of the girlfriend of girlfriends here on Tverskaia Iamskaia
> Streets.[39]

If there was any sign of a lesbian subculture moving into the public
realm of urban streetscapes, the workplace, or halls of study, it was in
the "almost masculine" styles cultivated by some women entering public life. Medical and lay sources confirm that, at least in towns, the
woman regarded as "masculine" was a fixture of early-Soviet society,
adopting styles of dress and behavior that at least metaphorically facilitated the occupation of masculine social terrain.[40] To a great degree,
perceptions of masculinization in women, especially women performing
public roles, must have been fueled by the anxieties about appropriate
dress and comportment that consumed so much energy in debates about
everyday life (*byt*).[41] Nevertheless, female Bolsheviks assiduously cultivated hardness (*tverdost'*) as a key feature of their political personalities,
and the image of the ruthless, efficient, emotionally controlled, and
coldly rational Communist woman was supported by thousands of ex-
emplars.[42] The image evidently deteriorated into a stereotype. People's
Commissar of Health Nikolai Semashko admitted and regretted that
"masculinized" women were a "type . . . frequently encountered: tou-
sled (often dirty) hair, *papiroska* [a crude Russian cigarette] clenched
in the teeth (like a man), deliberately awkward manners (like a man's);
a deliberately coarse voice (like a man's)." The "masculinized" woman
had "completely lost feminine traits and had turned into a man—
for the moment, still in a skirt (or more accurately, in half-trousers)."
Semashko deplored the trend as "vulgar 'equality of the sexes,'" but
he stopped short of questioning the political credentials of women who
embodied it.[43] This was a discussion about appropriate values among
friends of the regime; Semashko did not suggest that such women be
removed from the offices they held. Enough women had served loyally

in uniform during the civil war and continued to receive praise (if no encouragement to enlist) for their contributions in military and police work to produce the impression that "masculinized" women were somehow politically conscious and valued citizens.[44] The mannish Bolshevik female also became the subject of considerable foreign scrutiny in the early Soviet era.[45] Of course, women who donned collars and ties, trimmed their hair like a man's, and walked with a businesslike gait, were neither always drawn to their own sex, nor unique to Soviet Russia in the 1920s and 1930s. But the outward symbols of masculinity, which were associated (probably more from long-standing perceptions of fashion and politics than from Bolshevik intentions) with women's emancipation, were replete with positive value. Masculine styles conferred revolutionary credibility while disguising other motives. Some women who loved women used these styles as a semaphore code to like-minded women. They adopted a masculine style not merely because they wished to resemble men, but because they wished to attract other women.[46]

Until Stalinist initiatives to reconstruct femininity of the mid-1930s, women choosing to occupy masculine social roles who happened to be "happy, well-adjusted Lesbians"[47] were tolerated as part of the revolutionary social landscape. Their image as energetic and enterprising participants in the new society's political, economic, and military life earned the so-called "active" (that is, imitative of "masculine" traits) female homosexual admiration from some sexological authorities.[48] Some women evidently exploited this stereotype to realize their own sexual desires and personal objectives. Women-loving women who manipulated the symbols of masculinity in this era successfully, attracted little attention from the authorities for this very reason. We consequently have only occasional references to them such as the passage from Gornung's diary cited by Burgin. These successful individuals were probably able, as the widow and intellectual Tsuberbiller was, to disguise their same-sex desire behind a series of claims to respectability: an education, perhaps a previous marriage, a "quiet" way of life. Soviet Russia's apparitional "lesbian subculture" literally spoke "half-voiced," evaporating as soon as it might be broached.[49]

"I want to be a man": Transformations of Bodies, Clothing, and Society

A twenty-three-year-old female respondent to Izrail Gel'man's 1923 sex survey of students at Moscow's Sverdlov University ended a "confes-

sion" of her career as a "homosexual" with the words, "I want to be
a man, I impatiently await scientific discoveries of castration and grafting of male organs (glands)."[50] Her faith that one day science would
be able to give her the biological attributes of masculinity (and that a
surgical intervention would be sufficient to confer "manhood" upon
her) was not exceptional, nor was her desire to "change sex" unusual
among so-called "homosexuals" of the 1920s. The medical techniques
of gender reassignment in Soviet Russia in the 1920s were as rudimen-
tary and broadly unsuccessful as those then available in the West. Despite such limits, clinical psychiatrists and biologists engaged in the
emergent study of the mechanisms of sex differentiation were sought
out by "homosexuals," who believed these experts could transform
them into beings of the opposite sex.[51] As noted, within Russia's embryonic urban lesbian subculture, a limited masculinization of the individual left her still recognizably female (recall Health Commissar Semashko's reference to these mannish women dressed "for the moment,
still in a skirt"). Expressions of literary lesbianism sometimes employed
masculine grammatical gender or ambiguously gendered devices, but
readers and audiences knew that they confronted a female voice, albeit
in a decadent or exotic key. In this milieu it was a woman-centered
sexuality, rather than gender, that formed the basis of identity. By contrast, a demand for a surgical change of sex like that put to Gel'man
in 1923 may be interpreted as evidence of transgenderism. It was argu-
ably a precocious expression of a transgendered individual's desire that
science make physical sex correspond to a gender identity viewed as
paramount by the respondent.[52] Other women diagnosed as "female
homosexuals" may have "wanted to be a man" without necessarily
expecting medicine to intervene. Outside of Russia's great cities, some
"female homosexuals" turned to more traditional methods of appropriating the privileges of masculinity, effecting self-transformations with
clothing and gesture that allowed them to "pass" as men. Some used
their acquired masculinity as a pathway to sexual relations with other
women. These total transformations typified the survival of the "passing woman" in Russian culture.

The existence of women who successfully lived as men has been
well documented for traditional European and non-European societies.[53] (Men, too, have been observed performing the female gender.)[54]
Late-twentieth-century sexological interpretations of these performances may be anachronistic lenses through which to consider these
durable and varied patterns of identity appropriation as they functioned
in different times and cultures. Homosexuality, transvestism, and trans-

sexuality are recent U.S. and European constructs imposed on the infinite varieties of human sexual and gender diversity. In certain cultures, the performance of a gender transformation has been more significant to both actors and observers than any accompanying same-sex erotic activity. Our sexology-focused perception of these phenomena can blind us to important social, economic, and symbolic motivations for the activity. In seventeenth- and eighteenth-century Netherlands, for example, many "passing women" were motivated by poverty or by a desire for adventure in military service, and many women who adopted male identities in this context found it easy to do so because of their marginal or foreign status in a relatively fluid society.[55] Moreover, the disguise of a polar gender as intelligibly masculine or feminine was (and frequently, remains) a socially necessary performance for intersexual persons (hermaphrodites).[56] In examining case histories of women who passed as men, accepting medical labels of "homosexuality" at face value can thus obscure aspects of gender and identity in unfamiliar contexts.

Gender ambiguity in itself was not a modern or imported phenomenon in Russia. Masculine women (and feminine men) were already sufficiently common in the everyday experience of nineteenth-century Russians of far-flung regions that a number of words had been coined, apparently by peasants, to name and describe them. The lexicographer Vladimir Dal' who gathered his material between the 1830s and 1850s in central Russia found that the manly woman was known as *muzhlanka, muzhlatka, borodulia, suparen', and razmuzhich'e*. Dal' reported that his informants defined these women as "resembling a man in their appearance, movements, voice, et cetera," or "by structure, by body formation"; they might even approach the condition of a "hermaphrodite-woman" (*germafrodit-zhena*).[57] The lexicographer found an analogous vocabulary describing the feminine male.[58] In addition, Dal' reported that the verb *devulit'sia* was used of men who "luxuriate, take women's habits, manners."[59] None of the words describing mannish women was reportedly used as a deliberate insult, but some terms for an effeminate man (*babatia, babulia*) could "in this sense sometimes be abusive, like '*baba.*'"[60] The elaboration of a verb to describe male effeminacy suggests that peasants exercised more judgmental scrutiny of this behavior than of analogous activities on the part of masculine women (for whom no verbs were coined). The closest Dal' came to recording a critical estimate of the mannish woman was found in the entry for "borodulia." From Novgorod province he recorded the phrase "Borodulia ne muzhik" [A bearded lady is no man].[61] The saying reminded its audience that such a woman remained subordinate to the men around her, but it was not as bluntly abusive as some of the words used against effeminate males. In a patriarchal society, women who exploited their manly traits might acquire respect and status, whereas males who forsook their manhood caused more damage to their reputations.[62] Peasants confronting hermaphroditic offspring may have preferred, where plausible, to have them christened as boys, evidently for the social and economic advantages that would ensue.[63] Rural and lower-class Russians possessed an array of terms to describe individuals who appeared or behaved like members of the opposite sex. They associated this gender marginality with hermaphroditism observed in domesticated animals, linking social qualities with the familiar phenomenon of physical sexual indeterminacy.[64]

The case of the peasants Mariia Pavlovna Shashnina and Ekaterina Ivanovna Demicheva, accused of poisoning Demicheva's husband apparently so that the two might live together as lovers, suggests how Russian peasants might interpret same-sex relations between women within a framework of hermaphroditism. In 1886 the two women were arrested after Demicheva admitted poisoning her husband's kvass at the urging of Shashnina. They came to trial in the Nizhnii Novgorod circuit court; nine years later, St. Petersburg physician I. M. Tarnovskii examined the trial documents and wrote about the case in his study of "female sexual perversion."[65] Investigators discovered that Demicheva had had a sexual relationship with Shashnina before the marriage and that Shashnina had previously had similar relations with three other peasant women. According to Tarnovskii, Demicheva and other peasants said Shashnina, as well as possessing female genitalia, "also had something resembling a male member": "Several of her women lovers said they had felt a sexual organ entering their vagina and had touched and even seen this member emerging from Shashnina's genital cleft." The women reported that with her they experienced the same sexual satisfaction they got from men. The peasants of this village said they knew Shashnina to be "double-sexed" (dvukhpolaia) or "double harnessed" (dvukhsbruinaia).[66] In addition to her reputed physical difference, she smoked tobacco, did not wear her hair in the customary kerchief, and dominated her mother and brother in household matters. Nevertheless, various medical experts examined Shashnina four times between June 1886 and June 1887, and all agreed no signs of hermaphroditism and no enlargement of the clitoris were present. Evidently, peasants interpreted Shashnina's sexual approach to other women as the result of having attributes of both sexes and expected that this included possession of a phallus or something like one.[67] Shashnina's reputation as "double-harnessed" had paradoxically fixed her gender role as female, making it less likely that she might attempt to "pass" as a man, at least within her own community. Russian examples of the "passing woman" demonstrate that greater female mobility facilitated this phenomenon.

Soviet psychiatry of the 1920s took an interest in women who convincingly occupied a male gender identity and in accordance with the evolving sexological categories of European science, labeled them "female homosexuals" or occasionally, "transvestites." The reasons why some women decided to acquire manhood by changing their identity documents, assuming male variants of their names, and altering their dress, manners, and hairstyle, are hard to reconstruct. In the cases discussed in Soviet psychiatric literature of this era, same-sex desire appeared to be a prime motive. Some of these women were undoubtedly not aware of the existence of any lesbian subculture in the capitals. They would have had less access to the possibilities open to masculinized women who courted respectability while wearing selected pieces of male clothing (such as the collars and ties sported by Parnok's circle). "Passing" as a man could, for these isolated women, serve as a means of gaining sexual access to other women. Yet others who adopted a man's identity were clearly attracted by the full range of male participation in the revolutionary struggle, including the military life. Sexuality may have been less urgent for them. The assumption of a male identity could satisfy numerous sexual, social, and personal ambitions for women engaged in these performances of gender.

One common feature in the life histories of women who lived as men in revolutionary Russia was the fact that many apparently lived far from the capitals, the sites of the embryonic lesbian subculture, where this alternative to full gender transformation was evolving fitfully. The displacements of the era also produced opportunities for self-transformation. The story of Aleksandr Pavlovich, a "female homosexual" Nepman, illustrates these factors. This biological woman, described in 1925 by psychiatrist A. P. Shtess of the Saratov Bureau of Criminal Anthropology, had been trained and raised "like a son" by her father. The "patient's" childhood more resembled a boy's than a girl's, according to Shtess. When the family patriarch died in 1919, the patient's older sister, concerned that the wider household not lose the market income she generated, compelled the young trader to marry a "weak-willed groom." The marriage ended after just three weeks, as the patient, disgusted with conjugal relations, began to don masculine apparel and then ran away to Astrakhan', formally assuming the name "Aleksandr Pavlovich."[68]

For a period in Astrakhan' Aleksandr Pavlovich "continued to engage in trade"; presenting herself as a man in the marketplace, "she enjoyed a great success among the female traders." In 1920 she returned to Saratov as "Aleksandr," resumed trade in small silver goods, and compelled her extended family to address her as her masculine persona. She began a series of romantic and sexual liaisons with women, including one relationship lasting two years during which the partners "considered the question of marriage."[69] Aleksandr's assumption of a masculine social role was so complete that "he" even gave vent to "his" jealousy by giving this partner beatings, once hospitalizing her for two weeks.

This "Nepman's" prosperity was sufficiently persuasive to quell disputes in the extended family over her assumption of a masculine identity. "Aleksandr" lived for approximately four years in Saratov assisting her sisters' households financially with the proceeds of her market activities, which eventually included a large volume of gaming at cards ("orlianka" and "konfetka") as well as trade in silver. Her success at these forbidden activities led to administrative fines, brawls with rivals and clients, and conflict with the authorities until she was arrested in 1924 and later transferred to the Bureau of Criminal Anthropology for examination and compulsory therapy.[70]

Using a combination of Freudian psychoanalysis, seventeen sessions of hypnotherapy, and "persuasion" (*ubezhdenie*), Shtess claimed he was able to "cure" this patient completely of her "homosexuality." Her willingness to relinquish her masculine identity (a point of resistance early in their encounter) was the ultimate proof of the doctor's successful intervention. The patient gave up smoking after her last hypnosis session,

> her manners and behavior are more feminine and reserved; to the question of having a child, she thinks for a bit and then expresses the wish to have a baby at some point; her mood is cheerful. On 13 October the patient signed out of the clinic, dressed in women's clothing.[71]

Shtess published photographs of this woman "before therapy" in her masculine garb, then naked ("Habitus") to reveal her body as typically female, not hermaphroditic, and finally, "after therapy," docilely posed in a skirt (figs. 10–12). She was dispatched to a branch of the family that would not be tempted by her earning capacity as a "man" to allow her to return to her old way of life. This patient's attempt to occupy a masculine gender role was the exterior manifestation of her "homosexuality," which the doctor said produced "internal conflicts with the [social] environment." Shtess regarded as pathological the fact that for four years, this "homosexual" had successfully negotiated those supposed conflicts—as a man.

Aleksandr Pavlovich was not an isolated, exceptional example of the "female homosexual" who deployed a masculine social persona over a sustained time period. Her interest in the turbulent world of the NEP market was mirrored by an apparently widespread attraction on the part of women living as men, to the even more dramatic arena of soldiery.[72] The most widely discussed case of the female soldier as "homosexual" (and "transvestite") was described by psychiatrist A. O. Edel'shtein in 1927.[73] Evgeniia Fedorovna M. had represented herself as a man since being orphaned in 1915 at seventeen. During the revolution, she found work in the Cheka as a political instructor (*politruk*), in "investigatory-penal organs," and took part in "requisitions and searches of monasteries," later traveling to the Southern front where "she took part in operations against banditry." During this time she altered her identity documents to the masculine Evgenii Fedorovich; she also began to have sexual relations with a series of women.

In 1922, while posted by the GPU in a provincial town, Evgeniia met and courted "S.," a woman postal employee, and they concluded an officially registered marriage with Evgeniia presenting her altered (male) identity documents. Edel'shtein, who appears to have been able to interview S., reported that at first this woman did not suspect that her "husband" was not male. Evgeniia's ability or willingness to sustain her performance as a man faltered not long after the marriage. Rumors reached S. that Evgeniia was a woman, and Evgeniia finally admitted as much to her. This did not end the partnership, however.[74]

Evgeniia's indiscretion "brought attention to herself and doubt about her sex," apparently inspiring local authorities to charge her with a "crime against nature." The poorly constructed case against Evgeniia failed, and the Commissariat of Justice was compelled to recognize the two women's marriage as "legal, because concluded by mutual consent." The pair remained together for another two or three years. After S. had an affair with a male coworker, she had a child, which Evgeniia legally adopted, and the two women and the infant formed a family until Evgeniia's GPU regiment was transferred to Moscow. Evgeniia appears to have abandoned her wife and child to follow her soldiering career, only to be fired in 1925 soon after arrival in the capital.[75]

The loss of her life in a man's uniform devastated Evgeniia, and she was unable to make a successful transition to civilian life. She began to drink, causing disturbances, and leading a promiscuous sex life with women, eventually acquiring a second (unofficial) "wife." In 1926 complaints began to accumulate that she was impersonating bureaucrats and party members for profit, and her drinking led to disorderly conduct. She found herself repeatedly before police and courts for hooliganism and extortion, until Dr. Edel'shtein examined her at the Moscow Health Department's Bureau for the Study of the Personality of the Criminal and Criminality. Throughout this decline and during the psychiatric observation, Evgeniia maintained her self-presentation as a man. The doctor did not report any attempt to cure his patient, remarking cryptically that "the social future of such a subject is very difficult."[76]

Evgeniia's performance of a male gender role lasted for more than ten years. Others, like Dr. Shtess's Aleksandr Pavlovich, sustained similar performances for considerable lengths of time.[77] Given more favorable circumstances, these women might never have been detected in their assumption of a masculine social position. These performances were not solely staged for the pursuit of material gain or for the opportunities of living as a man in a man's world. Same-sex desire was integrally connected to these women's desire to redefine themselves. They chose not only to become military "men" or (in Aleksandr Pavlovich's case) a gaudy Nepman, but to "chase after ladies" (*ukhazhivat' za baryshniami*), to engage in "many affairs with women."[78] They found the masculine gender role well suited to satisfying this desire, and they eagerly exploited its potential.

Nevertheless, while exploring their same-sex desire these women wanted to remain physically female. Their "failed copies" of masculinity (in Judith Butler's phrase) reveal to us an otherwise hidden transcript of gender.[79] In an atmosphere in which the transformation of the biological sex of animals was sensationally publicized and the role of hormones in the definition of biological sex was entering popular awareness,[80] these women did not seek out medical interventions to change their sex. Evgeniia and Dr. Skliar's "P. A.," both scientifically knowledgeable, were almost certainly aware of recent advances in hormonal theories.[81] Other individuals (as noted above) were already presenting themselves by the late 1920s to Soviet medical professionals requesting surgical sex changes; Evgeniia, P. A., and Dr. Shtess's Aleksandr Pavlovich were not among this cohort of precocious transsexuals.[82] In her "History of my illness" published by her psychiatrist,

Evgeniia Fedorovna M. did assert that women of her type "consider their sex a misunderstanding and wish to transform themselves into persons of the opposite sex," but she did not argue for surgery to transform her body. Instead, she pleaded for acceptance of "same-sex love . . . as a particular variation" in humanity. She argued that once members of the "intermediate sex" were "no longer oppressed and smothered by their own lack of consciousness and by petty-bourgeois disrespect," their lives would become socially worthwhile.[83]

Evgeniia pleaded, in effect, for the social and political rights of the "intermediate sex" using arguments consciously borrowed from the essentializing, scientific justifications of homosexual emancipationism. Her assumption of a male gender persona, one traditional way for the sexually ambiguous to order their position in the world, was thus transitional, for she envisioned a world in which gender and sexual ambiguity would be understood by medicine and respected in a knowledgeable society. The revolutionary faith in science to end archaic moral strictures and to bring rationality to human sexual relations, was a powerful tool not only in the hands of Bolshevik legislators and medical practitioners, but in the hands of ordinary individuals who manipulated it to justify their own desires. Evgeniia Fedorovna M. wrote "History of my illness" for her psychiatrist, explaining her personality in scientific terms, and elite psychiatrists acknowledged that her reading of recent international scientific literature was impressive.[84] How much reading Evgeniia had in fact done is difficult to establish from existing sources. She dealt primarily with theories of "pseudohermaphrodites" and "psycho-hermaphrodites," terms that by the 1920s had been propagated by Krafft-Ebing and Havelock Ellis for persons who experienced varying degrees of desire for persons of either sex (anticipating modern "bisexuals").[85] Evgeniia spoke of "pseudohermaphrodites" as purely interested in same-sex relationships, echoing the concepts of apologists for same-sex love who used the term "intermediate sex" (*srednii pol*).

"Pseudohermaphrodites, both male and female, have a particular predisposition to same-sex sexuality," she argued, and "the attraction to a woman of a woman of the intermediate sex is just the same in nature as the normal man's attraction to a woman." The fact of a congenital predisposition was proved by erotic dreams about the same sex.

In sleep a person does not govern themselves, and if during involuntary erotic ecstasy the image of a woman and not a man appears to a woman, it means that such is her nature, which she is incapable of overcoming. These women are unable to reverse this attraction in themselves, which from their point of view is natural, even if they wanted to. Once we come to accept that along with the usual love there exists same-sex love as well, as a particular variation, then we must make the logical conclusion and permit persons of the intermediate sex access to their form of sexual satisfaction.

Evgeniia argued that society must learn to distinguish between the signifiers of sex (external sex organs) and the determinants of sexual desire, which were "mental particularities . . . established by nature itself in the gonads." She borrowed verbatim from a tsarist apologist for the "intermediate sex" the assertion that science was well aware of the distinction:

> Prof. [Sigmund] Freud justly points out that people who are in a sexual sense perverted ought not to be considered degenerates. . . . No one can consider people of the intermediate sex physically or mentally ill. . . . One may count among the number of men with an abnormal deviation of sexual desire leading writers (Oscar Wilde, Whitman, Verlaine), artists (Michelangelo), and musicians (Tchaikovsky), and this clearly proves that it is impossible to dismiss people of the intermediate sex to the category of the mentally and psychically disturbed.[86]

Evgeniia returned to her own words to argue that the scientific evidence about sexual intermediacy obliged society to deal humanely and rationally with people like herself: "It would be preferable when judging homosexual persons [gomoseksual'nye liudi] if their personality and mental capabilities were taken into account before all else, and not their actions, which are a private matter [chastnoe delo] just as for normal people." In "History of my illness," Evgeniia combined traditional ways of thinking about sexual ambiguity (as a form of hermaphroditism), with more recent scientific understandings (as a manifestation of anomalous function of the sex glands). The expression of the wish for self-transformation into a person of the opposite sex—so that her desire for women might make sense in a world overwhelmingly ordered according to a heterosexual norm—blended with the vocalization of a new identity, that of an "intermediate sex," of "homosexual persons." If the world could not reconfigure Evgeniia's "misunderstood" body with male sex organs or recognize her adopted masculine gender (her persona as Evgenii), then it ought to accept her sexual desire, her sexuality directed toward women, as the misunderstood element of her being. In this fashion Evgeniia appropriated scientific and emancipationist language to explain and to vindicate both her same-sex desire and her gender dissent.

Conclusion

Same-sex relations between women in tsarist and early Soviet Russia reflected the general transformation of women's roles and opportunities. For increasing numbers of women, the ties of the patriarchal village were loosening and breaking, and as with migrant men in the city, links to family, *zemliachestvo*, or *artel'* were not always sufficient to maintain traditional forms of surveillance, including the monitoring of sexual behavior.[87] If opportunities for an independent existence were hampered in the town by gendered legal disadvantages and the threat of medico-legal supervision (under the tsarist regime of licensed prostitution), there were still occasional avenues for the expression of same-sex love. Adequate sources about this love between lower-class women have yet to emerge, and its character must be judged through the distortions of a single ubiquitous occupation, prostitution. In this realm, same-sex relations could be sheltered and even tolerated, particularly in licensed brothels, and the freedom (or opportunity) to express same-sex love in this environment was evidently sought by some women as prostitutes and as clients. As with men, however, the loss of control over this form of commodified private space in the early Soviet era broke up an arena for women's mutual sexuality. Women who sold sex during NEP did so in more precarious public spaces; perhaps some found a symbiosis in combining mutual protection in a dangerous enterprise with mutual emotional and sexual relations.

"Lesbian love" between women of the educated middle social strata was even more indistinct, for these women successfully (and dutifully, if they were Bolsheviks)[88] concealed their personal lives. It would be unreasonable to look for a lesbian subculture where women were not in a position to establish one. Moscow of the 1920s was not Paris or Berlin, capitals in which same-sex relations between women found expression in an elite salon culture, in a commercial sector of sometimes louche bars and cafés, as well as in the disreputable world of the sex trade. The sites of a potential Russian lesbian subculture were constrained by material scarcity and, after 1917, by a political mistrust of affluence and pleasure. The semipublic environment of the salon (making a public stage from domestic space) became constricted during the 1920s and died off in the fearful middle years of the 1930s. Networks and circles of like-minded women nevertheless exploited the regime's disregard for the home, and for them as homemakers, to preserve their affinities.

A code of "masculinized" dress and manners enabled urban women who sought mutual erotic relations to recognize each other. There were pockets of tolerance for the mannish woman in military formations and in academic or cultural institutions, which permitted some self-conscious "female homosexuals" to earn a living and apply their talents. These women apparently exploited the valorization of social and economic activity in the public sphere promoted for women by the revolution. Education and paid labor provided claims to socialist respectability that might deflect criticism for the failure to marry or produce children. It appears that few women in this embryonic lesbian subculture came from the peasantry; nor did urban women who loved women flaunt their sartorial "masculinization" while in the country-side, reverting instead to a conformist femininity. Lesbian love supposedly required the oxygen of sophisticated city life, and early revolutionary Russia offered only a handful of cities with this degree of modernity.

Russian women, in contrast to men, did not take control of public space to express same-sex desire through the definition of sexualized territories. A few, nevertheless, found a site upon which to inscribe their desire: their own bodies. Through the performance of a "masculinized" womanhood, or, more traditionally, in the assumption of a completely male identity, some women made their desire for their own sex intelligible within the confines of a culture which imagined the sex drive as universally heterosexual. If desire flowed only through "active" and "passive" channels, then a woman's passionate desire for another woman might be constructed as "active" and therefore "masculine." By combing and reworking known gender possibilities, such as the familiar phenomenon of hermaphroditism, or the utopian prospect of sex transformation promised by experimental biology, they inhabited one gender without abandoning another biological sex. If female masculinity was an affirmation of self, and even a badge of emancipation and political consciousness (in its "hardness," *tverdost'*), it was also potentially alarming for those who would insist upon women's maternal essence.

PART II

Regulating
Homosexual
Desire in
Revolutionary
Russia

Euphemism and Discretion

POLICING SODOMITES AND TRIBADES

ussia's patterns of mutual male and mutual female relations existed within a comparatively indifferent legal and medical regime. In contrast to the increased policing of sex between men observable in France, England, and Germany during the nineteenth century, the tsarist justice system did not engage in systematic and sustained surveillance of "pederasts" or "sodomites." Despite the existence of a statute forbidding "sodomy" after 1835, authorities in Russia called upon doctors, and later, psychiatrists to produce expertise about so-called pederastic bodies and practices less frequently than their Western European counterparts. Forensic doctors and psychiatrists in Russia became aware of French and German forms of medical expertise for demonstrating anal intercourse and of European psychiatric models of homosexuality as mental illness. They were, however, unenthusiastic about applying these discourses in Russian conditions. Medical professionals were in a subordinate relationship with the tsarist regime and police, and doctors regarded their unpaid forensic duties as burdensome. At the same time, as a discipline, psychiatry received little respect from the tsarist government, which preferred to leave the control of socially disruptive elements in the hands of police and jailers.

Meanwhile, tsarist law had nothing explicit to say about sex between women, who were regarded in this patriarchal and archaic legal system as less than complete sexual and civil subjects. Legal medicine imagined mutual female sexuality as a problem only when force was used or when a woman imposed her sexual attentions on younger women and girls in her care. While some legal physicians observed and recorded single-sex relationships between licensed female prostitutes, these liaisons did not constitute an especially heightened focus of concern (as was the case in France, for example). In this climate, Russian psychiatrists were also relatively indifferent to the phenomenon of lesbian love as a form of sexual psychopathology.

Underlying the disinclination to medicalize "homosexuality" in Imperial Russia was a comparatively indulgent view of same-sex practices by both rulers and police. Male same-sex relations were outlawed, yet enforcement and prosecution of the law was episodic. An examination of evidence from criminal cases and from statistical records reveals the extent to which the policing of the "sodomite" under the old regime was a business more of euphemistic administrative discretion than one of formal justice. Changes in policing patterns apparent after the 1905 revolution further demonstrate the degree to which arbitrary enforcement continued to prevail, now accompanied by new concerns about homosexuality as a problem in crucial spheres of Imperial life.

Moral Legislation and the Reluctance to Pathologize

The legislative basis for the prosecution of sodomy in tsarist Russia was the product of forces quite different from those leading to similar prohibitions in old regime France, the German states, and England. While Western and Eastern Europeans shared the Christian tradition's prohibition of the "sodomitical sin" (*sodomskii grekh*), Russian Orthodoxy did not express the harsh and persistently punitive view advanced by Roman Catholicism since the twelfth century.[1] Orthodoxy was less able to enforce those sexual norms it did espouse, having only begun the task of Christianization of Rus' in the tenth century, in a territory that was vast and underpopulated in comparison with Western sees. The Russian Orthodox Church regarded all sex as dangerous and sinful, even sex within matrimony. Pre-1700 Orthodox Church sources (ecclesiastical court records, commentaries on church law, catechisms for lower clergy) demonstrate that male same-sex contacts were viewed within this framework as sinful but also that this framework ordered some acts as less dangerous than others.[2] Anal intercourse between men attracted penances as severe as those for (heterosexual) adultery, while other nonpenetrative forms of mutual male contact were excused with the lighter penalties associated with masturbation. Eve Levin has suggested that this differentiated scale of penalties was based on Russian Orthodoxy's inheritance, through Byzantine canon law, of classical Athenian evaluations of anal intercourse. Orthodoxy sought to preserve the integrity of the male gender role, which was thought to be endangered if one man were willing to be penetrated anally by another.

Meanwhile, nonpenetrative forms of erotic contact were viewed less severely. This role-based distinction between forms of male same-sex activity lingered in later Russian legal definitions of sodomy.

The significance of phallic penetration to Orthodox assessments of same-sex offenses was highlighted too by the penalties that female same-sex acts attracted. Penances for mutual masturbation between women were somewhat higher than those imposed on men for the same offense, but not as harsh as penalties for male anal intercourse. Sexuality between women attracted less attention from church hierarchs. Russian Orthodoxy had, for example, devised a large body of penitential codes to deal with the problem of mutual male erotic acts in monasteries while no comparable set of texts on women's relations in convents was elaborated.[3] The degree to which ecclesiastical authorities enforced prohibitions of same-sex relations remains unexplored, and accounts of punishment in later legal commentaries are rare. In one report, individuals of both sexes were executed by fire for "sodomy" (*sodomskoe delo*) in seventeenth-century Muscovy.[4] Systematic church attention to the issue was likely confined to the closed worlds of monasteries and convents, where the ascetic rejection of the flesh, supposedly made easier by single-sex environments, could be enforced most readily.

Secular incursions into the regulation of same-sex sexual acts came later in Russia than in Western Europe. In France, England, and the Holy Roman Empire, states consolidating their control over local church courts or hierarchies between the fourteenth and sixteenth centuries enacted their own laws against sodomy.[5] Often this legislation continued to assert religious reasoning for the prohibition. Moreover, Western legal understandings of sodomy during this era included not only anal intercourse (whether between two men, or a man and woman), but other nonprocreative sexual acts as well. It was only towards the end of the seventeenth century that sodomy came to denote a specific sexual act, as moral campaigners in northwestern Europe concentrated their attention on emerging urban subcultures of mutual male sexuality.[6] Moralists acting from religious motives condemned male prostitution and public sex as wickedness, and there were episodic waves of sodomy prosecutions in the Netherlands and England. It was in this era that Peter the Great visited these nations during his tour of Europe, the so-called Grand Embassy of 1697–98, unprecedented for a Russian ruler.

Peter was rumored to have experienced sodomy firsthand, as testimony in a contemporary buggery trial of an English captain in London revealed.[7] Rather later in the course of his reign, on the advice of German advisers, Peter enacted Russia's first secular statute against same-sex relations. If the Orthodox church had concentrated its surveillance efforts on the same-sex environment of men's monasteries, the tsar turned a similar regulatory zeal on the army and navy, another homosocial sphere. Russia's armed forces were at this time the objects of major reforms in recruitment, training, and equipment. In Peter's Military Articles of 1716, as Laura Engelstein has explained, sodomy (named in an explicit and specific fashion as *muzhelozhstvo*, derived from the roots for "man" and "to lie") was punished not as a private moral failing but because it threatened the stability of military hierarchies.[8] The innovation was not "hypocritically" motivated,[9] but reflected the mature tsar's abiding concern that Russia replicate the results of what historians call the "military revolution," which had made the armies of Europe vastly superior to Muscovy's unruly and ill-equipped forces.[10]

Increased contact with Western Europe during the eighteenth century and the gradual penetration of Western mores among Russia's ruling elite were reflected in the adaptation of Western sexual values. In a draft criminal code for civilians, proposed during the reign of Elizabeth I in 1754, an article "on the sodomitical sin" employed Biblical labeling to identify the crime in much less specific language than that used in the military legislation. The article otherwise made the same distinction as Peter's Military Articles between consensual acts and those accompanied by force.[11] The proposal was apparently an attempt to extend the military concern for hierarchies to society at large and to frame it in a recognizably religious context as a moral norm. A proposed penal code of 1813 included an even more euphemistic formulation prohibiting "unnatural shamelessness" (*protivoestestvennoe stydodeianie*).[12] The language of this draft law expressed a moralistic fear of naming the crime in more explicit terms (following the widespread presumption of rulers that describing "sodomy" would only serve to spread the vice). This proposal also preserved and intensified the religious basis for punishment first seen in the 1754 draft. The early-nineteenth-century proposal indicated that in addition to penalties (differentiated by social estate), offenders would be required to make "a public church confession" (*publichnoe tserkovnoe pokaianie*). The enlistment of the Church in the moral redemption of sexual outlaws coincided with the extension of Russian Orthodoxy's responsibilities for regulating personal and family matters in the post-Napoleonic reaction.[13] When in 1835 a new criminal code was finally enacted (replacing a code that had been in force for 186 years), sodomy was prohibited

for civilians. In this and the 1845 code that supplanted it, the requirement that Russian Orthodox subjects seek penance for sodomy cemented the religious and moral link that had been mooted in preceding
proposals. Consensual sodomy was punished with exile to Siberia (under what was later article 995 of the penal code); aggravated sodomy,
that is, with minors or with the use of force or the abuse of a position
of authority, netted exile with hard labor (article 996). The legislation,
which remained in effect until 1917, extended the secular regulation
of male same-sex relations from a point of military discipline to the
moral and social control of civilians.[14]

The state's increased concern for an orderly society was also reflected
in the introduction of regulated female (heterosexual) prostitution in
1843. This measure, evolving in the following decades, subordinated
medical expertise to policing functions. Prostitutes with licenses, "yellow tickets," to practice their trade were screened at regular intervals by
physicians recruited by urban "medical-police committees."[15] Focusing
solely on public women, municipal medical-police committees under
the direction of the Ministry of Internal Affairs conducted the most
systematic surveillance of deviant sexuality in the Russian state until
the 1917 revolution. The medical approach to same-sex erotic relations
in Russian science originated in the extension of medical-police functions beyond the regulation of prostitution.

Early-nineteenth-century forensic medicine in Russia had comparatively little to say about the detection of sexual crime or the examination of living persons.[16] The development of this branch of legal medicine was only stimulated by radical changes in judicial practice
accompanying the Great Reforms of the 1860s. The new system of
justice relied on "rational" standards of evidence, presented orally and
subject to questioning in cross-examination, in contrast to the prereform
practices of written testimony and adjudication. The reforms also introduced jury trials in criminal cases, an important departure from other
continental legal systems, where adjudication was based on scholarly
knowledge rather than popular notions of justice. Doctors were now
expected to answer in court for their opinions and to defend them from
challenges by procurators, witnesses, and the accused.[17] In criminal
cases against same-sex erotic practices, whether consensual sodomy,
sodomitical rape, or (at least potentially if not in practice) adult female
sexual abuse of girls in their care, medical opinions about the signs of
forbidden activity could be pivotal.

During the 1850s and 1860s, forensic doctors in Western Europe
had systematized knowledge of the physical signs of anal intercourse

between males and, to a lesser extent, other traces of same-sex erotic contact, including contact between women. Particularly influential were the studies of forensic doctors Ambroise Tardieu of Paris and Johann Ludwig Casper of Berlin. Tardieu's 1857 book on the forensic medical indications of sexual crime, including chapters on anal intercourse based on over two hundred pederasts identified for the Parisian police, enjoyed great influence well into the twentieth century.[18] Russian medical professionals who developed an expertise in this field were aware of Tardieu's catalog of cases yet were quick to criticize his claims with reference to counterevidence from local examples.[19] Casper's studies of Berlin pederasts (published in the 1850s) were perhaps more influential than Tardieu's among Russian forensic doctors, who expressed a preference for the German's apparent caution and objectivity, even as they blended citations from both authorities and produced a hybrid of the German and French points of view on the indications of sodomy in males.[20] The Russian forensic medical approach to sodomy detection was much less systematic than apparent reliance on any single Western authority might imply.[21]

The institutions supplying expertise in cases of sexual crime had only modest support from tsarist resources. Legislation (the Medical Statutes of 1857 and 1892) prescribed "onerous forensic duties" for private practitioners where state physicians could not serve police and courts; any doctor might be required to make legal depositions or commit the insane.[22] Expertise varied widely in quality, with "humble provincial employees"—district, municipal, and police doctors—providing laconic and relatively unenlightened opinions (zakliucheniia), while professors from medical faculties in university towns delivered courtroom lectures "developing the scientific breadth and depth of their thought."[23] Doctors received little or nothing for providing these services to police and courts. In 1890, the Ministry of Justice ruled that forensic medical examinations had to be provided without remuneration, and at least one doctor found his demand for payment refused after providing expertise in a sodomy trial.[24] In the last years of the tsarist regime, forensic medicine was on the curriculum in some medical schools and had its own faculty at Moscow University, although it remained a marginal discipline. Few dedicated forensic medical facilities existed in the empire. Police customarily referred to the nearest doctor, pharmacy, laboratory, or clinic, and operatives at this level "had no contact with faculties of forensic medicine."[25]

Following the judicial reforms, and in these circumstances, the methods for identifying the stigmata of sodomy were absorbed by the medical profession fifteen to twenty years after their articulation in France and Germany. They were applied to a preexisting—but in some ways quite different—urban culture of mutual male sexual relations. Legal medicine's tendency in Europe to elide the practice of "pederasty" with the identity of the habitual "pederast," to construct an identity out of behavior, was also apparent in Russian texts on sodomy detection. Yet Russia's low incidence of sodomy prosecutions moderated any nominative effect, which constant police attention directed toward the stigmatized group had produced in Germany and France. As a result, Russian forensic medicine's interest in sodomy detection was modest. An even weaker interest was displayed in female mutual sexual relations, although forensic gynecology was not without a role in uncovering evidence of victimization.

The first Russian attempt to domesticate foreign knowledge about indications of same-sex couplings appeared in *Forensic Gynecology* (Sudebnaia ginekologiia) by Vladislav Merzheevskii, published in 1878 in St. Petersburg. The author, a member of the Interior Ministry's Medical Council, devoted most of his manual to indications of female victimization by male sexual criminals. Nevertheless, a fifty-seven-page chapter on "pederasty" and brief sections on "lesbian love" and bestiality were included. These chapters on "unnatural intercourse" directly followed one about heterosexual rape, the most prevalent sexual crime. This ordering, and the placement of same-sex acts within a context of forensic gynecology, suggested that sodomy was merely an expression of unbridled male lust, which might choose as its object a woman, a boy, another man, or an animal. Yet within the chapter on sodomy a shift toward the "pederast" as a personality is discernible.

Merzheevskii began by discussing the history of legislation against "the unnatural satisfaction of sexual lust," then reviewed the European literature on sodomy detection. He briefly noted that Casper proposed the "vice" was usually "congenital" (although he qualified this statement with a bracketed question mark), defining it as "mental hermaphroditism" (*umstvennyi germafroditizm*). Also acknowledged without further comment was Karl Westphal's recent assertion that "abnormal sexual attraction" was very often a psychopathic or neuropathic disorder.[26] Merzheevskii then turned to the social milieux in which the "vice is hidden from 'the uninitiated,'" and produced forty-two sodomitical case histories culled from Casper, Tardieu, and the St. Petersburg circuit court.[27] Here the Russian cases turned chiefly on identification of the "passive pederast" through examination of the anal region and comparison with a catalog of deformities. Following Casper, Merzheevskii attacked Tardieu's claim that the "active pederast" displayed signs of his vice on the penis. Nevertheless, he included a case from the French physician, labeled "Habitual active and passive pederasty. Characteristic conformity of the penis," without commenting on these descriptions.[28]

A similar eclecticism pervaded the venereologist V. M. Tarnovskii's discussion of forensic medical technique in relation to the pederast, in his "forensic-psychiatric study" of the "perversion of sexual feeling," published seven years after Merzheevskii's manual.[29] This landmark text straddles the paradigm shift from forensic medicine to psychiatry on same-sex perversion. Drawing on Westphal and Richard von Krafft-Ebing, Tarnovskii sought to downplay the reliability of forensic medical examinations as an evidentiary tool for the courts and to emphasize the possibilities for psychiatry as a way of explaining perversions. Yet despite this primary argument, the author devoted some twenty pages (out of 105) to a technical description of anatomical examinations. Tarnovskii wanted his professional readers to acquire precise, reliable techniques for detecting "passive pederasty":

> For the examination I have the boy stand across a wide bed, on his knees; his chest lies on a pillow, with his head somewhat lower than the buttocks which he projects; the legs should be parted so that his knees and heels do not touch each other. In this position, I repeat, if the subject does not know the purpose of the examination and has no wish to conceal or dissimulate, the indications of habitual sodomy [*privychnaia sodomiia*] stand out in bold relief.[30]

Tarnovskii noted that catamites (*kinedy*) who were aware of the doctor's intent frequently clenched their buttocks, obscuring the indications of their sexual practices. He recommended compelling these youths to assume the posture described for protracted periods, to exhaust their resistance. This was more effective than Tardieu's suggested frequent changes of position.[31]

The indications of passive sodomy in Tarnovskii's assessment varied little from Merzheevskii's catalog but were presented in more precise anatomical detail. Tarnovskii had examined twenty-three "notorious catamite boys" and found that the surest sign of the practice of passive sodomy was a weakening of the sphincter muscle. This could be detected by any doctor "without specialist training." Tarnovskii dismissed Tardieu's list of deformities of the active pederast's penis as evidence of degeneration rather than a specific sexual practice.[32]

While Tarnovskii cooperated with the police to identify pederasts for the courts, as a doctor he believed he was often seeing the effects of congenital illness rather than acquired vice, verifiable with the techniques of psychiatry, not forensic medicine. The central question he proposed—"What are we dealing with, a congenital deformity, an illness, or a debauched habit (*porochnaia privychka*)?"—was not to be answered by a search for the stigmata of sodomy alone.[33] The indicators of sodomy were only one pathway toward a forensic conclusion, because not all pederasts were alike. It was necessary first to establish "with what kind of pederast we are dealing." Here Tarnovskii supplied his professional readership with a detailed checklist to enable physicians to distinguish between culpable and innocent varieties of pederasts. These criteria highlighted the transitional tension in Tarnovskii's approach from anatomical principles to psychiatric ones.

The first step was to detect the indications of sodomy in the anus. If these were discovered and the patient was a youth, the doctor was then to seek physical signs of degeneration or mental deviations, indicators of a "psychopathic subject." Such youths were "congenital pederasts" and should not be prosecuted. They were inclined to passive anal relations and found intercourse with women impossible, Tarnovskii claimed. "Healthy" youths lacking clues to degeneration or mental illness were to be judged "acquired pederasts," which could be corroborated if they took both anal active and passive roles and were able "to have normal intercourse with women." Rare cases of the "congenital active pederast" might be distinguished by markers of degeneration (mental deviations, "abnormally developed genitals") and an aggressive loathing of women (as opposed to the mere indifference of the passive counterpart).[34]

In youths one had to rely chiefly on somatic indicators, while with adults, Tarnovskii counseled a psychiatrist's approach: "You must know the man closely" to distinguish between past and present personality characteristics. A full biography was crucial:

> The careful collection of data regarding heredity, the most detailed anamnesis, following the patient's life step by step, especially the period of sexual maturation, along with an all-encompassing investigation of the physical and mental status of the patient will help to decide whether we are dealing with a congenital or acquired perversion of the sexual drive.[35]

The circumstances of the crime needed to be examined to eliminate the possibility of "the most dangerous and least culpable" variant, "periodic pederasty," where violent bouts of sexual disorder caused by organic maladies punctuated an otherwise peaceful existence. Evidence in the patient history of degenerate heredity, epilepsy, progressive paralysis, and in the aged, senility, might exculpate the adult pederast. "Only the elimination of all above-mentioned pathological states . . . will permit one reliably to confirm the debauchery, moral corruption, and completely punishable, conscious, voluntary depravity of the examined subject."[36]

Tarnovskii argued strongly that Russian legal practice regarding acts of sodomy failed to distinguish between congenital (innocent) and acquired (culpable) perpetrators and that anatomical techniques inherited from Casper and Tardieu were inadequate to the psychiatric task of determining who ought to be prosecuted. Perhaps recognizing that legislative change was unlikely, he observed that "only the mutual labor of the doctor and the jurist—the investigator and the philosopher" could set a new boundary between "physiology and pathology," between "the correction of the healthy, the rehabilitation of those with pathological predispositions, and the curing of the sick."[37] A handful of cases in the medical literature demonstrated that an eclectic blend of forensic medical and psychiatric understandings of "pederasty," similar to Tarnovskii's, circulated in late-nineteenth-century Russia.[38] In these texts, the weight of authority was already shifting from forensic medicine to psychiatry, but the claim to uncover sexual practice from the physical signs of "pederasty" reserved a potential labeling role for forensic physicians.

Another signal of the shift from physical indicators of "pederasty" as an act to indicators of same-sex perversion as an identity was the attention forensic authorities paid to the subculture of Russia's urban "pederasts." If, as Merzheevskii claimed, Petersburg lacked "the completely organized society of pederasts as in Paris," he still furnished readers with details of the capital's pederastic demimonde, considering it a less elaborate version of that found in Western Europe.[39] Merzheevskii's descriptions of Parisian male prostitution dominated by effeminized youths, some in female costume, were set next to local cases presented without references to unmasculine behavior; he implied that Petersburg "pederasts" were untroubled by anxieties about their masculinity.[40]

European psychiatric models of men's same-sex perversion first began to express a closer link between male effeminacy and physiological concepts of hysteria and degeneration during the 1870s and 1880s with the influential work of Karl Westphal and Richard von Krafft-Ebing.[41]

These fusions of behavioral phenomena (unmanly acts) with supposed biological conditions (frequently reduced to "degeneration," the cumulative effect of venereal disease, addiction, or hysteria on successive generations) allowed psychiatrists to posit a congenital origin for sexually deviant personalities.[42] Following these authorities, Tarnovskii emphasized effeminate characteristics in his subjects more than Merzheevskii had, while linking these to a social sphere in which pederasts flourished, giving it a distinctly caste-like character:

> The pederast always seeks the society of those similar to himself, because only in their presence can he give satisfaction to his abnormal instinct without punishment, and find sympathy for his pathological condition or encouragement for vice. What is more, the active pederast, by the walk, manner of comportment, gesture, speech, looking in the eye, et cetera, will recognize a passive pederast more easily than would a normal man. From his point of view the catamite, by the tone of the conversation, quickly guesses what is going on. Thus, pederasts in general rapidly become acquainted with each other and live to a great extent among circles in which all types of the sexual deviant activities described are met.[43]

The intimations in Merzheevskii of a personal identity characterized by pederasty were fully realized only a few years later in Tarnovskii's assessment of the pederastic subculture of St. Petersburg he observed.

If there was a uniquely Russian aspect to forensic medical lore on "pederasty," it was concentrated on the bathhouse as a locus for male prostitution. Authorities associated male commercial sex offered by bathhouse attendants with national peasant customs. Merzheevskii sought to warn forensic medical practitioners of the potential exploitation of bathhouses by pederasts by presenting the 1866 Petersburg case of the "depraved work team." Tarnovskii, perhaps under the influence of patriotic affection for the baths and their associations with hygiene, viewed them instead as a guarantor of public order because they purportedly kept male prostitution off the streets, ordered it according to peasant custom, and curbed extortion rackets. Discursively he distinguished extortionists' solidarity from that displayed by bathhouse attendants as the collusion of urban "gangs," despite the fact that their "rewards were divided equally between the participants," just like those of the bathhouse *artel'*. In his reluctance to condemn the "Russian simple folk" for organizing themselves to exploit these opportunities, there was a hesitation to pathologize all aspects of same-sex erotic practice.

A presumption that the lower orders, in their economic and cultural subordination in Russia's urban life, were sexually innocent prevented Tarnovskii from medicalizing all mutual male sexual activity.[44]

Forensic specialists also regarded women as comparatively "innocent" of same-sex depravities. Since such relations between women were not a crime in tsarist (nor subsequently, in Soviet) law, legal medicine paid far less attention to the anatomical indications of what was usually referred to as "lesbian love" (*lesbiiskaia liubov'*) or "tribadism" (*tribadiia*) in forensic studies. An early Russian article on medicolegal expertise in same-sex crimes published in 1870 by one Dr. Zuk of the Ministry of Internal Affairs stated, "If a woman uses another woman for the satisfaction of her sexual excitement, then this crime [*prestuplenie*] is called lesbian love [*lesbiiskaia liubov'*]." Despite the use of this language, Zuk then asserted that such love could only be a crime if a woman abused a position of power over a ward or pupil. If there was no such relationship between two females apprehended in mutual sexual relations, then "it was not our affair" to judge and punish them, and in any case, "lesbian love leaves extremely rare traces."[45] Very few cases of sexual assaults between women, or of women's seduction of female minors, appear to have reached the courts.[46]

Merzheevskii's manual of forensic gynecology similarly abdicated any role for the doctor when "lesbian love" was suspected. Even in court cases in which minors or the mentally deficient were seduced by women, doctors were obliged "to declare themselves not competent" to give testimony, unless it could be shown that the victim's hymen had been ruptured. The use of dildoes (*kauchukovye muzh'ia*, literally, "rubber husbands") and mutual masturbation between adult women might leave minor traces (enlarged clitoris, enlargement or pigmentation of the labia minora) but nothing reliable as evidence, for these could be observed on "innocent individuals." In his brief discussion of the issue, Merzheevskii made no references to European authorities, citing only the ancient poets and one modern author, Adolphe Belot, whose novel, *Mademoiselle Giraud ma femme* (Paris, 1870), was said to be typical of a Western popular literature cloaked in morality while stimulating "passionate natures" to vice.[47] Without a legal sanction against female same-sex love, forensic medicine saw little need to develop expertise in its detection. There were few further passages mentioning lesbian love in forensic medical texts published before 1917.[48]

European forensic gynecological lore about "pederasty" or "lesbian love" had little impact in Russian medical practice because the enforcement of laws against same-sex erotic acts (discussed below) was comparatively modest. Medical practitioners were seldom compelled to furnish evidence in cases of this type and did not accumulate experience or circulate observations about the detection of vice with the energy of their continental European counterparts. Medical understandings of the problem did not acquire the authority they enjoyed in France and Germany. With the European paradigm shift in explanations for same-sex love from forensic medicine to psychiatry, the potential development of the medical model of "homosexuality" became even less likely in Imperial Russian conditions. Michel Foucault has proposed that psychiatry in Europe was a "bourgeois" science, deploying a medical understanding of sexuality first on the middle class itself before turning its attention to other social groups.[49] The professional position of the discipline of psychiatry in late tsarist Russia, a society with a notoriously small middle class, was confined by this bourgeois orientation. Psychiatrists formed a tiny corporation (of only three hundred fifty practitioners in 1916) concentrated in the largest cities and earning a substantial portion of income from private clinical practice.[50] Like the urban middle class as a whole, psychiatry in autocratic Russia lacked political leverage, even after the quasi-constitutional settlement following the 1905 revolution. If forensic gynecologists and physicians had a problematic relationship with the regime and its police, tensions between psychiatry and authority were even worse. Conflict over the forced incarceration of criminal and political prisoners (confined in chains and accompanied by jailers) in mental asylums undermined psychiatrists' claims to manage these institutions as centers for therapy. Indeed, the discipline's therapeutic claims were the subject of great pessimism, with asylums chronically underfunded and mistrusted. Forensic psychiatrists commanded little respect in courtroom battles over the defense of nonresponsibility by reason of derangement.[51] Defensive and deprived of respect and resources, Russian psychiatry was scarcely positioned to advance claims for expertise and financial support beyond the familiar problems of insanity and neuropathy.

When Russia's psychiatrists in this era did discuss same-sex love as a medical question, their thinking was as much determined by the particular environment they inhabited as by the groundwork laid by Europe's pioneers of sexual psychopathology. Veniamin Tarnovskii's 1885 forensic-psychiatric treatise on "pederasty" in its varied congenital and acquired forms did not stimulate a flood of case histories confirming his findings from Russian psychiatrists, and neither did the appearance of a Russian translation of Krafft-Ebing's *Psychopathia sexualis*, the landmark psychiatric taxonomy of perversions, in 1887.[52] Tarnovskii's work, with its medical-police origins, did not elicit enthusiasm from colleagues. His resolute defense of tsarist prostitution regulation and his close identification with state authority discounted in their eyes his pathologizing views of the prostitute and perhaps of the pederast as well.[53] Another Tarnovskii, Ippolit Mikhailovich, a St. Petersburg obstetrician-gynecologist, produced a study of "perversion of the sexual feeling" in women, explicitly adopting a view of female same-sex relations as normal and natural.[54] Despite his awareness of Western theories of congenitally perverted sexuality, and somewhat inconsistent reasoning (itself a product of the inherent contradictions of the medical model of sexualities), Ippolit Tarnovskii's sympathies lay with the women of all social classes he described. His view was tempered by the widespread feminism and the sense of disempowerment shared by male members of the intelligentsia engaged in the medical profession under tsarist constraints.[55]

The single most influential Russian proponent of the medical model of same-sex relations, Vladimir M. Bekhterev (1857–1927), confined his application of the psychiatric paradigm almost entirely to ethnic Russian upper-class males drawn from clinical, not forensic, practice.[56] His focus on a narrow range of male deviance among the respectable elements of the dominant gender and ethnicity of the empire mirrored Western psychiatry's interest in applying the paradigm of perverted sexuality in the first instance to bourgeois males. Bekhterev's celebrated opposition to the abuse of forensic medicine by the regime[57] and his interest in the clinical rather than forensic aspects of sexual perversion made his promotion of the medical model of "homosexuality" more palatable to his discipline. Finally, his emphasis on a nurturist etiology for sexual perversions appealed to a profession searching for a role in public life. By explaining the mechanisms of sexual development (and derailment) psychiatrists could claim expertise in the prophylaxis of perversions.

Bekhterev's interest in same-sex love originated in his experiments with hypnosis as a form of psychotherapy. His earliest article on what he termed "perverse sexual drives" (*prevratnye polovye vlecheniia*), appearing in 1898, described two case histories of male patients suffering from attraction to their own sex, and the doctor's efforts to cure them using hypnotic suggestion. In this article Bekhterev did not examine the etiology of sexual perversion. He did refer allusively to perversions as a syndrome similar to degeneration, and he noted the terminology used by Krafft-Ebing to describe same-sex love.[58] Where the article broke new ground for Russians was in his assertion that hypnosis was "a completely effective means" of therapy for sexual deviance. There was no longer a need for doctors to "limit themselves in such cases to a virtually passive role" when confronted with these disorders, Bekhterev declared.[59] The French psychiatrists Jean-Martin Charcot and Valentin Magnan had proposed a similar therapy for sexual inversion in 1882, but Veniamin Tarnovskii had scarcely addressed therapies in his monographs on perversion, and Bekhterev, Russia's chief advocate of suggestion therapy, was the logical promoter of its application to sexual perversion.[60]

Bekhterev's principle contribution to Russian psychology and psychiatry was his theory of reflexology, and his later writing about sexuality concentrated on the interpretation of case histories using this theory. Applying a model of stimulus and instinctual reaction to human behavior, Bekhterev emphasized the environment as the source of mental pathologies including sexual perversions.[61] Perverse sexual drives, he wrote in 1913, were the result of childhood sexual traumatization, careless upbringing, and later experiences. Inappropriate sexual stimuli formed "combined reflexes" (*sochetatel'nye refleksy*), which developed in puberty to produce habitual perversion. His conclusions were based not only on clinical observation and comparison of patient histories, but on laboratory examinations of the human brain. He rejected various hypotheses for a congenital origin to homosexuality, including Magnan and Gley's theory of the woman's brain in man's body, noting that brains of "homosexuals" he examined revealed no discernible differences from normal brains. Bekhterev reserved a small, and secondary, role to degeneration as a biological factor that might in some cases be contributory. The appearance of a strong sexual appetite in early childhood was a degenerate characteristic that could "awaken the sex drive at an early age in unusual circumstances, with which it would closely compose itself and then soon solidify as a result of its production over time in analogous external circumstances . . ."[62] The implications of this etiology were clear: monitoring childhood sexual experience was crucial to the development of "normal sexual attraction."[63]

The medical model of homosexuality in late tsarist Russia owed its relative weakness to a combination of chronological and developmental circumstances. The delay, in comparison with its Western rivals, of the Russian Empire's efforts to adopt liberalizing reforms, slowed the arrival and evolution of this very specific form of forensic and medical expertise. Even after forensic medical lore about detecting "pederasty" and "lesbian love" had been domesticated, for the most part it failed to circulate and develop in significant local ways. Legal medical practitioners generally lacked institutional platforms and served the state unenthusiastically. Despite the existence of legislation that might have called for a vigilant and frequent surveillance of the "sodomite" (if not the "tribade"), tsarist policing of the prohibition would be sporadic or indifferent, and expertise in detection remained a peculiar sideline of forensic medical knowledge.

The paradigm shift from forensic medicine to psychiatry in theories about the medical significance of same-sex love contributed to the reluctance of medicine in Russia to pathologize the "homosexual." The psychiatrist in tsarist Russia was embroiled in institutional battles that threatened the existence of the profession. There was little energy for the extension of the discipline beyond the primary concerns of the care of the insane, the funding and operation of asylums, and (for an urban elite) the cultivation of a private practice. Russian psychiatric attention, when it was focused on the problem of homosexuality, rejected the full range of stigmatization when applying the discourse to women or members of the lower classes, out of sympathy with their subordination. Psychiatrists themselves suffered from the same subordination in the autocratic state. A regime jealous of power and suspicious of technical expertise was unreceptive to disciplinary discourses developed in bourgeois and generally liberal societies.

Euphemism in the Policing of Sodomy

Late tsarist Russia had inherited unambiguous legislation against male same-sex relations. Criminal sanctions for sodomy between consenting adults were relatively harsh until 1900, and were still severe after revisions to punishments following this date.[64] Tsarist discourse gave no quarter to male practitioners of same-sex love, even as it virtually ignored female same-sex eros as a possibility. Yet a swarm of contradictions in the administration of the antisodomy statute lay beneath "the smooth surface of euphemized power."[65] Until 1905, prosecutions appeared to be dwindling, with criminal proceedings affecting less privileged members of society disproportionately. Convictions for consensual sodomy in particular appeared to have become increasingly rare. In the aftermath of the 1905 revolution, specific groups and Imperial districts bore the brunt of heavier enforcement, further highlighting the inequitable policing and juridical practice surrounding this legislation. The concealed but notorious indulgence by the last two tsars of men who had sex with other men, both within the royal family and among the government's servitors, completed the circle of contradictions that surrounded the issue of "homosexuality" and the law.

In the decades before 1914, unlike other European powers penalizing male same-sex relations, Russia did not produce its own Oscar Wilde, Philipp Prince zu Eulenberg or Colonel Alfred Redl, figures whose public downfall dramatized male homosexuality as a political problem, an expression of anxieties about masculinity and military preparedness.[66] There were plenty of potential Russian candidates available to fill the role, yet society was habituated to the observance of discretion and concealment in such matters.[67] When that discretion was breached, the miscreant used his connections to suppress scandals before they came to procurators' attention. The autocratic state itself was inclined to apply administrative punishments that would obviate any courtroom session.[68] In practice, the demands on elite men having sex with men of maintaining minimal discretion and of husbanding connections dictated that the autocracy needed only very small investments in administrative coercion to maintain the euphemism that "sodomites" did not exist in elite society and government. Informal public pressures need not even involve the regime. Composer Peter Tchaikovsky learned the value of such discretion after being linked in journalistic accounts during his student days to a group of "pederasts" said to frequent St. Petersburg's Chaumont Restaurant.[69] The ultraconservative editor of the newspaper *Grazhdanin,* Prince Vladimir Meshcherskii, taxed his connections to Tsars Alexander III and Nicholas II to the limit, obtaining not only subsidies for his publication, but advancement for a host of young military men he fancied and sponsored. Because of his "peccadilloes," Meshcherskii was not received at court, but the tsars met and corresponded with him privately and were aware that the prince "discreetly advertised" this relationship to obtain favors for his friends and journal.[70] Alexander III ordered the suppression of proceedings against the prince in an 1887 scandal involving a youth in the Imperial Guard, despite the disapproval of Meshcherskii's family and the active pursuit launched by chief procurator of the Holy Synod Konstantin Pobedonostsev. A further sexual scandal, implicating some two hundred men including Meshcherskii and members of the Imperial family, was similarly quashed.[71] "There were at least seven gay grand dukes at the time (uncles, nephews, or cousins of the last two tsars)," according to Simon Karlinsky; of these, the brother of Alexander II, Grand Duke Sergei Aleksandrovich stood "at the top of the 'homosexual pyramid'" of Russia's social life.[72]

Accompanying these contradictions of the formal prohibition of sodomy at the highest level was a system of unequal and (until 1905) declining enforcement. Critics agreed that "one of the worst evils" of the statute was "the actual *disuse* of the law, the random and unjust character of repression, ruinous to some but sparing others, those strong in position, influence, connections."[73] Euphemism—the concealment of the elite's dirty linen—operated most tellingly in the courts, where only a tiny percentage of cases involved privileged persons, or so it appeared. A statistical study of the 440 convictions for sodomy from 1874 through 1904 in Imperial Russia contradicted this perception, claiming 5 percent of "pederasts" were from the upper classes, yet these same classes were only responsible for 2.8 percent of criminal convictions for all offenses in these years.[74] When examined by occupation, the same sample showed, however, that a disproportionately small number of state servitors were convicted for sodomy. Members of the "free professions" (artists, physicians, men of letters, teachers, the clergy) and servants and craftsmen were among those most likely to be convicted.[75] A similarly large proportion of convictions for sodomy, compared with their shares of convictions for all crime, were borne by non-Russians and, in particular, by "Eastern peoples characterized by the most passionate temperaments," although in strictly numerical terms, 72 percent of sodomy convictions fell to European Slavs (Russians, Ukrainians, and Belorussians).[76]

Other forms of inequity were alleged by critics of the sodomy law. The justice system prosecuted these cases much less successfully than the average crime, with only about 41 percent of sodomy indictments leading to conviction (compared with a conviction rate of 66 percent for all other crimes).[77] Juries were increasingly inclined to acquit persons accused of the offense in the late Imperial era, and those they did pronounce guilty frequently received moderated or reduced penalties.[78] The actual number of cases prosecuted per year was very modest, and in the thirty-one years up to 1904 a gradual falling trend in the proportion of sodomy to all criminal indictments was observed.[79] Procurators in St. Petersburg and Moscow appear to have read a political message in the suppression of the scandals of the late 1880s involving Prince Meshcherskii and the grand dukes and abandoned prosecutions for consensual sodomy altogether.[80]

Policing practices regarding consensual and aggravated sodomy, to judge from available sources of the era, relied on complaints from members of the public or from the parents of victims. Not surprisingly, if "pederasts" engaged in public sex (especially if drunk and disorderly while doing so), they ran a greater risk of detection. In archival records of sodomy trials, and in the forensic medical and psychiatric literature, the police rarely figure as initiators of arrests. Rather, they acted when a denunciation was received or when other circumstances drew their attention to a particular "pederast." In 1871, two drunken men were apprehended when police happened to discover them engaged in anal intercourse near a railway embankment in St. Petersburg.[81] A porter spied through the keyhole of a Vitebsk hotel room as nobleman Pavel Petrovich Pizani "copulated with [a young Jewish gymnasium student] via the anus" in 1887, leading to a denunciation of Pizani's "strange way of life" and police questioning of his youthful partners.[82] Petr Mamaev, arrested in 1888 on a Moscow boulevard and eventually charged with "passive pederasty," had been drunk and brawling with another man at the time of his arrest.[83] In contrast to the surveillance routines typical from the mid-nineteenth century in Paris and Berlin, Russian police devoted little energy to the pursuit of this crime. Given that "the intimate character of homosexual actions makes these relations practically undetectable," only a handful of cases came to court.[84] Cases under article 996, in which a younger or weaker male was raped or abused, were more vigorously prosecuted with the help of forensic medical evidence and probably constituted the vast majority of sodomy convictions. Article 995 against voluntary sodomy was virtually a dead letter in the largest of Russia's cities by the end of the Imperial era.

Cases of the rape (*iznasilovanie*) of men and boys constitute the most frequently recorded same-sex sexual crime pursued by the tsarist courts. It was estimated that for each conviction under article 995, there were four for article 996 (using force, or abusing the dependency of the victim, or with a minor) during the years from 1874 to 1904.[85] Both Merzheevskii and Tarnovskii doubted that male rape could actually be committed, where both parties were at least youths if not fully grown. Delicately, they implied that the barrier of the sphincter muscle could only be breached voluntarily; because of anatomy and predisposition the receptive male in a same-sex "rape" was incapable of being victimized.[86] The realities of rape between males in tsarist Russia were considerably more brutal and complex, and forensic medical practice did not discard the notion of the penetrated boy or youth as victim, despite the theoretical musings of these authorities. Perhaps the violence of these cases moved most doctors to produce detailed evidence to assist police in securing convictions. The principal signs of anal rape were traumatic bruising and abrasions or cuts to the victim's anus or body or blood blistering observed on the penis of the perpetrator. Forensic doctors reported on these indications using formulas of words that occasionally appear to lead investigators to conclusions that would swiftly resolve these cases. The more defenseless the victim (by virtue of age), the more doctors openly employed conjecture and suggestion in their testimony.[87]

In the last peacetime decade of the tsarist regime, a surge of convictions for "sodomy" was registered.[88] This increase surpassed the general 35 percent rise in criminal convictions (reflecting the unrest following the 1905 revolution), documented for the first decade of the twentieth century by Ministry of Justice statisticians.[89] There was a virtual trebling of the number of sodomy offenses recorded, with the substantial weight of new convictions after 1910.[90] The government's published statistics did not distinguish between consensual and aggravated sodomy, but following Piatnitskii's assumption that men who were convicted of the crime without accomplices were probably guilty of aggravated sodomy, it appears that about 78 percent of the 504 individuals convicted from 1905 to 1913 acted on their own. These were most likely convictions under article 996, and their proportion did not vary from previous decades.[91]

These statistics did, however, point to a shift of enforcement of the sodomy statutes away from St. Petersburg and Moscow toward the towns and rural districts of southern Russia and the Caucasus.[92] In the last two years during which statistics were gathered, almost half the total sodomy indictments for the Russian Empire originated in the Tiflis district (including the towns of Tiflis [Tbilisi], Baku, Ekaterinoslav, Erevan, and other settlements in the region). Convictions of ethnic Slavic groups declined sharply, accompanied by an equally acute rise in the proportion of convictions of individuals from nationalities of the Caucasus.[93] The unspoken reasons for the shift of sodomy policing away from Russia's largest and most "European" centers to the south and east and to the peoples who inhabited those regions, appear to be the result of two complementary factors. On the one hand, within "European" or "civilized" Russia, indulgence of nonviolent male same-sex relations prevailed and was supplemented by arguments, however weak in this context, that a biological or psychological anomaly predisposed the (civilized, European, male) individual to "homosexuality." In medical terms, a carving up of turf could be discerned, whereby forensic gynecologists and physicians continued to supply expertise in cases of coercive or abusive same-sex relations, while psychiatrists, albeit reluctantly and with nothing like the enthusiasm of their Western colleagues, began to explore the homosexual personality. Whether doctors,

jurists, and cultural critics (discussed in chapter 4) viewed the "homosexual" in their own society as morally corrupt, as benign but anomalous, physiologically deformed, or psychopathic, he was now rapidly
becoming a public personality imbued with a specific sexual desire.

On the other hand, no such personality was accorded to men who
engaged in "pederasty" by medico-legal experts looking at the problem
in the south and east of the empire. They argued that the phenomenon
was primarily a result of local cultures, regardless of the incidence of
"sexual psychopathy" among the populations of the region. Here Russian men of science had little doubt that the medical model was inappropriate, for (they said) the customs and habits of the "natives" of
Georgia and Armenia, of the regions around Baku, and the towns of
Tashkent and Samarkand, bred same-sex relations, often of a coercive
variety. The "savage morals of the native population" (*dikie nravy tu-
zemnogo naseleniia*) were responsible for the supposedly widespread
Caucasian practice of abduction of male youths and boys for sexual
purposes.[94] In Tashkent and surrounding regions, the seclusion of
women, masculine "parasitism" in the *chaikhana* (teahouse) and local
traditions of boy prostitution (*bachebastvo*, the keeping of itinerant
troupes of *bachi*, boy dancers who also engaged in paid sex), contributed
to the prevalence of "pederasty" in Central Asia.[95] More bewildering
for Russian observers was the cultural crossroads of the Caucasus, where
"civilized" (*kul'turnye*) peoples lived side by side with "primitive" ones,
and "sexual psychopathy" and "degeneration" interacted with the socially produced indulgence of male same-sex relations supposedly prevalent among "primitive" nationalities. "[T]he larger the city and
the greater the number of Moslems" it held, the more "pederasty"
flourished.[96] The vice, while chiefly blamed on Islamic traditions of
female seclusion, was in this region also supposedly urban, the result
of male mobility and the opportunities created by commodified private spaces. Baku and Tiflis inns, "Persian bazaars," and bathhouses
were known as places where males, reportedly usually "Persians or
Tatars . . . offer their passive services to active pederasts." Male migrants from Nagorno-Karabakh to the oil industries of Baku returned
having grown accustomed to "passive pederasty" to earn "a piece of
bread."[97] The urban lifestyle of the Armenians, with the "corruptions
of city restaurant life" (*izbalovannosti gorodskoi restorannoi zhizni*),
nurtured pederastic relations, especially since men of this commercially successful nationality often traveled throughout the region.
Meanwhile, the wealth of Baku's Islamic entrepreneurs—Persians and
Tatars—allowed them to indulge in "all the Eastern delights," in-

cluding "active pederasty" with "passive" prostitute-males. As one Russian psychiatrist-anthropologist wrote, "for a prosperous, infamous and corrupt Persian or Tatar, a boy is the highest requirement of a refined taste, like the tainted egg for a Chinese mandarin of the highest rank, or Roquefort cheese or the high carcass of a hazel hen for a gourmand of the Petersburg aristocracy."[98] In Russia's Orient, the exotic Other included the sexually "savage" male, often a non-Christian or tainted by his location on the periphery of Christendom.[99] Such men were scarcely worthy of medical attention, with the exception of the provision of forensic evidence in criminal investigations. Russian doctors argued rather that customs and habits needed to be studied and (by implication) radically changed; only "schooling and the accessible printed word" could combat and reduce the harm done by socially sanctioned pederasty.[100] While the Ministry of Justice's statistical gazettes failed to explain the conspicuous local increase in sodomy convictions, Russian forensic and psychiatric practitioners in these regions expressed attitudes that doubtless lay behind the police activity of the late tsarist era in these districts.

Conclusion

Euphemistic practices characterized the regulation of same-sex love in the Russian Empire. Despite the enactment of legislation designed to impose a conservative European moral norm, the law enjoyed little force. Enforcement was naturally difficult to implement without adopting the policing methods (entrapment, routine surveillance) favored by the authorities in Berlin and Paris. Russia's police, while duly concerned with maintaining order and public decency, lacked the resources to devote to the active detection of sodomy. The Great Reforms stimulated medical-police interest in forensic techniques of supplying evidence to prove "sodomy" or "lesbian love" in open courtroom trials, modeled on continental forms of jurisprudence. This arcane knowledge fit within the existing framework of forensic gynecology as practiced by medical-police committees established to supervise licensed heterosexual prostitution. Yet in spite of the reforms, the production of evidence in "sodomy" cases (for cases of "lesbian love" were ignored) was generally constrained by policing priorities. By World War I, only the forensic medical task of identifying the "pederast" who committed rapes on males had been routinely established in police and court procedure. Merzheevskii and V. M. Tarnovskii remained the domestic authorities on this subject, as the demand for such expertise was modest.

By the first years of the twentieth century Russian psychiatry was reluctantly but occasionally challenging forensic medicine as the principal interpreter of same-sex love in Russian medical discourse. The key texts on the criminological meaning of "homosexuality" (as it was increasingly called) in late tsarist Russia abandoned descriptions of the body of the sodomite or tribade and turned to psychiatric medicine, both domestic and Western European, for the newest explanations of the phenomenon.[101] Forensic medicine retained an ongoing role as purveyor to the courts of expertise in cases of violent sexual assaults between males.

Policing of the antisodomy statute did little to extend the medicalization of same-sex love in the Russian Empire. Authorities were principally concerned with the detection and the punishment of acts of sexual violence. Yet their enforcement of the law betrayed attitudes toward male same-sex relations that were notably inequitable, especially in the years of violence and instability following 1905. Indulgence at the highest levels shielded friends of the Imperial court, and few cases, even of male rape, were tried in St. Petersburg and Moscow. No exemplary trial of a Russian Wilde or Eulenberg, staged to mark the homosexual as dangerous outsider, took place. Meanwhile, an increasingly vigorous stance against mutual male sexual relations characterized police methods in the southern and eastern fringes of empire. Here even doctors who within the Russian heartland might concede a role for "psychopathy" in explaining the sexual dissident refused to apply the medical model to the phenomenon of "native" pederasty. A moralistic law, its unequal enforcement, and the contradictory theories circulating about the problem it was meant to regulate: these factors generated a robust debate in late tsarist Russia and determined the shape of legal reform that came in the wake of its collapse.

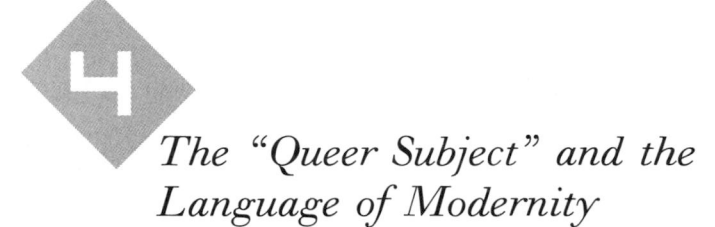

The "Queer Subject" and the Language of Modernity

REFORMING THE LAW ON SAME-SEX LOVE
BEFORE AND AFTER 1917

I n St. Petersburg in 1908, a pseudonymous apologist for the "intermediate sex" defended his decision to speak in print about this "new
question, which it had been forbidden to raise before":

> A queer subject [*strannyi sub'ekt*], feeling revulsion toward women and
> sexual attraction to men, may turn up in any family. How should this
> kind of young man be viewed? How is he to be raised? Should he be
> considered a freak [*urod*] or a debauched individual? To parents, all
> these questions are extremely important.[1]

The pain of the young "queer subject" and the confusion of his parents
were a function of the silence that surrounded this "new question."
The author proposed to illuminate it in a "popular and accessible"
manner, with a bricolage of texts drawn from a range of scientific and
respectable European sources. The voice of this Russian "queer subject," combining the language of medicine with individual rights, spoke
behind a veil of anonymity, a ventriloquist of Western and modern
homosexual emancipation. In the final years of the tsarist era, a handful
of obscure translators and publishers reproduced the latest European
texts, sexological and apologetic, on "homosexuality," for a domestic
Russian market. Doctors and jurists were often the ostensible audience
for these works; but most significantly, authors, translators, and publishers of these texts sought to reach an educated lay public. The claims
of the "intermediate sex" were now heard not only in discreet offstage
negotiations between "pederasts" and authority, but in the emerging
public domain created by the relaxation of print censorship after the
1905 revolution.

The brief interlude of quasi-constitutional rule and Duma (parliamentary) politics (1905–17) was marked by fresh discussions conducted by liberals and socialists on the problems of regulating sexuality. When the Bolsheviks came to power in 1917, this subject was apparently not a concern of the first order. Yet very soon revolutionary intentions regarding the relationships between the state, science, and church on the one hand, and the equality of men and women envisioned in the socialist program on the other, forced the problem of sexuality further up the regime's list of priorities. Same-sex relations figured in these priorities. In addressing them, Russian revolutionaries would draw from numerous sources to fashion a new discourse for the coming sexual order, including ambivalent socialist traditions and a legacy of local patterns of regulation.

The "Queer Subject" and Tsarist-Era Politics of Sexual Dissent

Late tsarist Russia had a comparatively rich and vigorous range of voices speaking about same-sex love. Works of literature and criticism, satires and counterblasts, and translations of foreign tracts and apologetics brought the question within the reading public's reach, disseminating new concepts and languages to describe mutual male and mutual female eros. Meanwhile, jurists sought to explain how both past and present societies regulated this love, as they put before their peers and their public audience suggestions for sexual legislation in the Russian Empire that was more just. Marxists stood on the margins of this discursive flood: yet their few declarations on the coming sexual revolution were not without relevance to the issue of homosexuality.

It was in literary form that Russian authors excelled in defending same-sex love. In no other European great power before 1914 was there as optimistic and confident an expression of the homosexual self as that portrayed by Mikhail Alekseevich Kuzmin in his notorious and best-selling novel, _Wings._[2] It was the first modern coming-out story with a happy ending in any language. This autobiographical fiction described a middle-class Petersburg youth, Vania, who grows aware of his difference and struggles to make sense of it. The narrative welded local elements of the homosexual subculture and of the philosophy of the fundamentalist Old Believer sect to a framework of classicism and cosmopolitanism in order to convey the particularity of Vania's—and Kuzmin's—emotional and intellectual journey to self-acceptance. For participants in the homosexual subculture of St. Petersburg and Moscow, the familiar landmarks of Russian life in the novel rooted it in a shared experience and gave it a power exceeding its literary value. *Wings*, Simon Karlinsky observes, became the "catechism" for what poet Nikolai Gumilev described in 1912 as "a whole array of people, united by a common culture, who have quite justly risen to the crest of life's wave."[3] Gumilev recognized the novel's political appeal and Kuzmin's status as a "spokesman" rooted in a "common culture" of same-sex love. *Wings* enjoyed a *succès de scandale*, its moral viewpoint distinguishing it from contemporary Western European analogs and serving, unlike those texts, to propose an uncompromisingly positive evaluation of same-sex love in the Russian cultural landscape.[4]

A less successful novel, but one frequently paired with *Wings* as the equivalent for celebrants of "lesbian love," was *Thirty-three Monsters*, published in 1907 by Lidiia Zinov'eva-Annibal.[5] The fiction, a series of melodramatic diary entries written by an unnamed narrator, depicted a lesbian relationship between the diarist, a woman of extraordinary beauty, and her lover Vera, a famous actress. Their love is portrayed as hysterical, tearful, and passionate, yet the affair ends when Vera deliberately sacrifices the object of her happiness to the appropriating gaze of thirty-three male artists. Their thirty-three portraits of the diarist capture her beauty (freezing it like Dorian Gray's), but in the process also transforming her into a multiple "mistress" and "prostitute." Vera's "magnanimity" exacts a terrible price, and she commits suicide rather than endure the loss of her bisexual lover to the men. Diana Lewis Burgin comments that Zinov'eva-Annibal's novel is as much about aesthetics as lesbian love, yet because of its scandalous content (coming so soon after the publication of *Wings*), it acquired lasting notoriety as Russia's first novel of lesbianism.[6] In contrast to Kuzmin's novel of male love, *Monsters* imported a foreign (specifically a French) language of lesbianism and confined it to a cushioned and carpeted interior setting with little that was recognizably Russian. Its pessimism and the suffocating masculine gaze it deployed to destroy the two women's love conformed to the formulas of cosmopolitan literary decadence. *Monsters* was nobody's "catechism," and as the poet Zinaida Gippius remarked; it did not reflect the truth about women.[7]

Somewhat later, in 1915, an authentically lesbian poetic voice did emerge in the work of Sofiia Parnok, but critics who lacked a language for evaluating her most explicitly female-loving verses greeted them with "silence" and "consternation."[8] Parnok's work rejected the St. Petersburg-centered salon conventions of literary homosexuality, which heavily aestheticized works like Zinov'eva-Annibal's had helped to inaugurate. Experimenters with idiosyncratic sexualities and genders dotted the landscape of the tsarist capital's literary salons, imbuing the theme of same-sex love and the blending of gender with exotic and mystic colors. Decadence, the aesthetic fashion across Europe, made its mark on Russian literary culture, and sexual and gender dissent were integral if highly controversial features of the trend.[9]

Literary scholars and historians have mapped the terrain of Russian decadence and its interest in sex and gender transgression; but little has been said about texts that defended transgressive sexualities in genres of nonfiction. In part this is because only a modest number of such works appeared in Russia and because they remain bibliographic rarities that until recently were sequestered in the "special collections" of Soviet libraries, inaccessible to researchers. Other books of this type were simply translations of foreign texts. Nevertheless, a literate public that was fascinated by sex and not always concerned about hierarchies of genre apparently consumed these tracts and translations about same-sex relations. Such publications supplied readers who might not be committed devotees of the modernist avant-garde with access to the new languages for describing and understanding same-sex love.

One significant nonliterary introduction to the issue, written and produced in Russia, appeared in 1908 under the title *People of the Intermediate Sex* (*Liudi srednego pola*). Composed by the pseudonymous P. V. Ushakovskii, its 226 pages summarized for jurists and doctors, for worried parents of the "queer subject," and for "any educated person," all that was necessary to acquire "a proper and completely scientific view of same-sex (*odnopolaia*) love" according to the latest European theories.[10] This popular manual opened with an introduction to the medical explanations for "homosexuality" (*gomoseksual'nost'*), ranging from the "female soul in a male body" of Karl Ulrichs to the psychopathological model of Krafft-Ebing and the psychoanalytic proposals of Freud. It provided important extracts from autobiographical accounts of the "psychology of the perverted individual," including letters to Emile Zola from an Italian "invert,"[11] and an account of a visit to Berlin's "uranian" (male homosexual) restaurants and gathering spots, as well as a description of a meeting of Hirschfeld's Scientific-Humanitarian Committee, founded in 1897 to promote the emancipation of homosexuals.[12] Medico-legal descriptions of male prostitution in European capitals were culled from P. Brouardel and A. von Schrenck-Notzing.[13] British expertise was represented with biographies of the "invert" first published by Havelock Ellis, followed by a long excerpt from André Raffalovich's account of the trial of Oscar

Wilde.[14] After a substantial chapter devoted to quotations from Moll, Ferré, and Bloch on "bisexual perversion" (*dvupoloe izvrashchenie*), Ushakovskii concluded his bricolage with an assessment of the "general view of persons of the intermediate sex," quoting again from Krafft-Ebing, Carpenter, Hirschfeld, and Bloch.

At first glance, this precocious manual was of limited originality; yet it provided ordinary literate Russians with translations of a surprising array of key contemporary works about homosexuality, many of them emancipationist in tone. The book's conclusion imported that sentiment in a domestically written plea for tolerance. Ushakovskii departed from bricolage to argue not merely for the decriminalization of same-sex relations in Russia but for their acceptance as a natural part of the human sexual order. Legislation against same-sex love was illogical and impossible to enforce. "The law should protect children and the insane and forbid all manner of assaults. But that which two adult persons, in their own room (*u sebia v komnate*), do with their bodies by mutual consent and causing no harm does not concern the state."[15] Driving persons of the intermediate sex to hide their true selves from society only generated evil. Those intermediate types who sought to hide within heterosexual marriage created tragedies for their spouses and possibly produced offspring with a damaged heredity. The recognition that healthy and moral individuals suffered from this "flaw" (*nedostatok*) would overturn society's assumption that all manifestations of same-sex love were depraved and antisocial. By discussing his aspirations in abstract terms and avoiding any mention of the local variations on public order offenses associated with the sodomy ban (such as male prostitution in bathhouses), Ushakovskii elevated his argument to a case made on principles of liberalism.[16]

Translations of European studies of the homosexual, conducted by homosexuals themselves, formed a substantial volume of the pertinent literature available to a Russian readership in the late tsarist era. Hirschfeld's celebrated ethnographic description of "Berlin's third sex" was published in a Russian edition just four years after the German original.[17] An undated translation of Havelock Ellis's study of "sexual inversion" (banned in Britain but issued in the U.S.), appeared after 1909.[18] The English socialist Edward Carpenter's various essays on the "intermediate sex" appeared in a handsome edition approved by the military censor in 1916.[19] Studies of same-sex love and manuals on the sex question containing chapters on the issue by respected European medical experts appeared in translation as well.[20] In addition to these respected works at the loftier end of the genre, there was no shortage of less elevated, frankly commercial depictions of the "perverted world," usually produced by marginal men of medicine. One of many piquant volumes on sexual perversion by French physician Jean Fauconney was issued in a Russian version produced by a Moscow entrepreneur.[21] Fauconney's "sapphists" and "pederasts" formed "an international union of vice" (vsemirnyi soiuz poroka), the women recognizing each other on the Bois de Boulogne "with quasi-masonic signals, the rapid movement of the tongue and lips," while the men found each other "[e]verywhere: in Palermo, at the Louvre, in the highlands of Scotland, in Petersburg, in Barcelona."[22] Cosmopolitan vice might attract readers, but in 1908, Moscow's Committee of Press Affairs prosecuted Evdokiia Konovalova and her translator for publishing six thousand copies of this small book, "with the clearly expressed aim of popularization" not the presentation of psychiatric research.[23] Russian Fauconneys, some rather more prestigious (and therefore better able to clothe their texts in the trappings of dispassionate science and thereby evade the courts) churned out similar volumes that evidently reached an eager audience.[24]

As in other parts of Europe, individuals in Russia who experienced same-sex desire turned to these texts and sifted them for clues to their own differences. The answers they received were not always encouraging, yet evidence suggests this literature influenced a popular readership. One army officer recalled how his first physical relationship with another male, when both he (as a gymnasium student) and his roommate (a seminarian) shared a bed each evening, came to an end as a result of fears aroused by books like these. "One fine day he came home . . . and showed me a book (I forget which), where the kind of relations we had were called criminal and unnatural. . . . We quarreled."[25] A man who had been a prostitute on the boulevards of Moscow between 1912 and 1914 reported that the only two books he had read were August Forel's Polovoi vopros (The Sex Question) and "the book by Moll on homosexuality." He comfortably accepted that he was "a stepson of nature" (pasynok prirody).[26] Another Soviet psychiatric patient, a "female homosexual," was evidently well versed in Hirschfeld's arguments for tolerance of sexual anomaly and understood herself by them.[27] A Red Army soldier, interviewed after the 15 January 1921 raid on a Petrograd "pederasts' party," admitted "he had read many books, attempting to find an explanation for his condition, and had become convinced that 'he had been born into this world with this unfortunate feeling [homosexuality].' "[28]

Commentators on both left and right for the most part greeted claims for a medical or aesthetic basis for same-sex love, and for a politics of tolerance flowing from these models, with derision. Many critics poured scorn on Kuzmin's *Wings* and on its decidedly unmedical view of male love as an exalted experience, superior to the love of men for women, mediated by classical learning and mentorship. One journalist on the left accused Kuzmin of "petty-bourgeois individualism" and of celebrating the "common Russian bath" with its corrupting relations between respectable gentlemen and their sexual victims, peasant youths. Critics "of a socialist cast" read the novel's exalted promise of "new people" whose appreciation of beauty would open ordinary people's eyes as evidence of the degeneracy of the upper classes.[29] Kuzmin's *Wings* inspired little sympathy from the left because its vision appeared to perpetuate existing forms of exploitation, supposedly embodied inside the bathhouse microcosm by cross-class male prostitution.

One of the most vitriolic reactions to both *Wings* and *Thirty-three Monsters* came from a social democrat, in G. S. Novopolin's critique of the "pornographic element" in contemporary Russian literature.[30] This critic deplored the temerity of authors "openly propagandizing for this unnatural vice" and was particularly appalled that a woman writer (*zhenshchina-pisatel'nitsa*) who had feminine traditions of virtue and martyrdom to uphold chose instead to publish "an apologia for refined depravity." The physicality of *Monsters* he found intolerable. Zinov'eva-Annibal added "many piquant details" to the annals of Krafft-Ebing with repeated "queer [*strannaia*] speech about legs, arms, the lines of the stomach, breasts . . ." She wrote about "a purely clinical phenomenon" with far too much "relish" for Novopolin's taste, and her chief protagonist reveled in "male-phobia" (*muzhefobstvo*).[31] Both Kuzmin and Zinov'eva-Annibal wreathed perversion in "a cult, an aura of beauty," and their obsession with a "narrow sphere of sexual desires" was no basis for an aesthetic, or by implication, a politics.[32] Novopolin insisted that what these writers depicted was alien to Russian social reality, in contrast to Western Europe, where neurasthenia and its companions, the sexual perversions, flourished in the lap of affluence. The sources of vice in innocent Russia, he argued, were either Eastern or Western. Pederasty "is widely practiced, they say, in the Caucasus and in aristocratic circles of both our capitals [i.e., Moscow and St. Petersburg]"; it was, in other words, the vice either of Russia's internal Orient or that of its most European elite. Meanwhile, the sins of Russia's "bourgeoisie" (by which Novopolin presumably meant, its urban merchants) were said to be "coarse and simpleminded."[33] In the pure Russian heartland, homosexuality did not exist, although he conceded that "[l]ast year, it is true, a book about Petersburg homosexuals [*peterburg-skie gomoseksualisty*] did appear. But we think if everything in that book is true, then it is an affair for St. Petersburg, not for all of Russia."[34]

The volume to which Novopolin alluded was a spicy tract by V. P. Ruadze, a minor poet, journalist, and satirist. Ruadze's indictment of homosexuality in the capital bore the attention-grabbing title *On Trial! . . . Homosexual Petersburg,* yet the book was in reality a quasi-fictional Baedecker to the homosexual subculture. The author strove to embellish not the sexual or moral depravities of his subjects, but their vanities and obsessions, and the result was scarcely a documentary catalog of crimes to be punished, but a peep show of private vice intended to titillate and amuse.[35] Thirty-five brief sketches dissected the social dimensions of homosexual Petersburg, from the "society" mansions of titled aristocrat and the more modest hotel lodgings of the "bourgeois" *tetka,* to "the street [which] is the mirror of public mores." The book concluded with a section devoted to "orgies and parties," where all classes and estates mingled shamelessly. Ruadze's attempt to stimulate police and public interest in "the little homosexual world" was taken up by at least one social democratic critic in much the same tone.[36]

On the far right, the most peculiarly Russian discussion of same-sex love appeared in 1911, in an unconventional philosophical work by the anti-Semitic and antirationalist Vasilii Rozanov. Entitled *People of the Lunar Light,* Rozanov's book celebrated the gender and sexual deviations (*ukloneniia*) of people (metaphorically "of the moonlight") as natural intermediaries on the spectrum between potent, polar (and "sunlit") masculinity and femininity.[37] A feature of Rozanov's analysis of these "sodomites" (*sodomity*) was his sustained polemic against psychiatry and its theories of sexual psychopathy, anticipating quite recent readings of patient-doctor interaction. Krafft-Ebing's subjects did not write to him with complaints or pathos, yet, Rozanov charged, the Austrian psychiatrist labeled their conditions sexual "suffering." "Fatuous medics" and a trusting public buried truth about sex under "revolting medical terms and fantastic, utterly stupid conceptions," labeling all sexually transgressive individuals " 'perverted,' 'depraved,' 'diseased,' 'deformed.' " ("The prattlers—if they were to meet Socrates, they would only write: 'Weighs 4 *puda* 10 *funtov.*' ")[38] Fascinated by case histories of gender nonconformity and autobiographies of people obsessed with non-procreative sex, Rozanov argued that they proved that sex was more dynamic (*tekushchii*) than medical men understood it to be. For Rozanov, the "third sex," in its rejection of procreation and of

the joys of family and home, was capable of deeper spirituality. In
this "sodomites" resembled monastic religious, who truly lived by the
teachings of the New Testament (which represented, for Rozanov, the
apex of a European civilization he deplored for its lack of fecundity).
Castigating the "seedlessness" (*bessemennost'*) of Christianity, he insisted that a monastic community of 1,001 "depraved" monks realized
New Testament precepts more fully than "1,001 happy fathers, even
if they were as virtuous as Abraham," who in their paternity got no
further than the Old Testament.[39] Rozanov's difficult and often convo-
luted work still proposed in characteristically contradictory fashion tolerance for "sodomites," both male and female. If his influence was
limited by stylistic and political considerations, he nevertheless spoke
for a patriarchal vision of sex and commanded the attention of a range
of philosophers and avant-garde intellectuals.[40]

Many of the positions reflected in this post-1905 intellectual ferment
had been anticipated in the more specialized debate among jurists over
the value of the existing, but little-used, sodomy statute. Discussions
about revisions to tsarist criminal law unfolded over two decades from
the 1880s until a new code was partially adopted in 1903. This Draft
Code of 1903 was widely regarded as a model of current European
jurisprudence.[41] The decision to retain a ban on consensual sodomy in
this code was based on what Laura Engelstein terms "the refusal of
the private," a conservative resistance to the notion of personal sexual
autonomy exercised in private space. Jurists approached their justifications for retention from different aspects of this refusal. Arkhangel'
procurator Richard Kraus expressed most clearly the belief that sexual
perversions were characteristic of the town, and of educated society; he
denied the right to control one's body when it led to the violation of
"laws of nature" or "the basic principles of human existence and community." Commenting on the sodomy ban, jurist Leonid Vladimirov
argued that it had an educative value, offering guidance and discipline
for the morally weak. St. Petersburg procurator A. F. Koni, who disap-
proved of European efforts to strike down antisodomy statutes, argued
that homosexuals, like the *skoptsy* (a sect of dissenting Orthodox, who
practiced self-castration), threatened the social order by promoting nonprocreative sexuality. The sodomy ban must therefore remain, just as
the castrates' sect was outlawed.[42]

The most articulate defender of decriminalization was Vladimir D.
Nabokov, whose liberal defense of privacy in this matter brought him
very close to the positions promoted by homosexual emancipationists
led by Germany's Dr. Magnus Hirschfeld.[43] Legislation should not be

used to impose morality or even a medical "norm," nor was it consistent or necessary for the educative effect of law to be brought to bear on this single example of supposed immorality. Nabokov acknowledged, if he did not completely accept, the medical arguments circulating in Germany and elsewhere in Europe that some proportion of homosexuals were congenital, so that the contention expressed in Russia's criminal statute that sodomy was a vice (and, therefore, a willful act) was mistaken in many cases. A "secular law, based on abstract and universal principles" should not punish sodomy committed in private between consenting adults.[44] The liberal view of the issue was endorsed by the St. Petersburg Juridical Society and by members of the Samara circuit court; nine out of twenty-three members of the Moscow Juridical Society also supported decriminalization during deliberations over the 1903 draft statute.[45] Well after the 1903 code had been partially enacted, jurists continued to question the wisdom of keeping the sodomy ban, arguing still from liberal legal principles and attacking tsarism's inequitable policing of the law, while acknowledging the persuasive claims of medicine to interpret same-sex love.[46]

Liberal lawyers, arguing from principles of secularization, the right to privacy, and personal autonomy, were among the most articulate defenders of homosexual emancipation in Imperial Russia, and yet they did so not from the subject position of homosexuals themselves, but from that of jurists striving to create a liberal, rule-of-law regime. The absence of a unified, self-conscious movement of homosexuals calling for a lifting of the ban in Russia should not be regarded as unusual, since only Germany could boast such a unique enterprise.[47] As in France and elsewhere in Europe, the most influential Russian apologies for homosexuality were found in literary works and cultural criticism, the products of individual rather than collective effort. In tsarist Russia, voices calling for the end of criminal sanctions for same-sex love used liberal arguments defending the individual's right to privacy and autonomy.

Radicals on the left would have had little time for arguments about sexuality proceeding solely from unfettered individualism or rule-of-law liberalism. Bolsheviks made no specific contributions to the question of homosexual emancipation, and historians of revolutionary approaches to sex and gender have excluded the issue from their analyses.[48] Nevertheless, the traditions of the Russian left on sexuality can be examined for indications of the directions social democratic thought probably took on the issue, when it considered it at all. The left's views on sexuality divided into two potentially contradictory camps, between forces for the deconstruction of the old order and those intent on defining the new. Utopian libertarians sought to eliminate the influence of church and state over the private sexual lives of citizens; while rationalizers looked to modern disciplines (medicine, pedagogy) to enhance "biopower," the health, reproductive, and productive capacity of the new socialist society.[49]

The thirst for freedom from arbitrary regulation of "the sex question" (usually defined as pertaining to different-sex sexuality, marriage and divorce, licensed prostitution, and birth control), was a byword in late-tsarist intellectual life. The libertarian socialist tradition, along with many other radical and liberal viewpoints, argued that neither church nor state should interfere in the sexual lives of adults. Authentic relationships, "based on the unfamiliar ideas of complete freedom, equality and genuine friendship,"[50] would flourish after private property had been destroyed, and with it, the hypocritical morality of the bourgeoisie. To libertarians in sexual matters, it was self-evident that the archaic mechanisms of bourgeois morality, whether ecclesiastical or state regulation of the sex lives of citizens, would be discarded on the morning after the revolution. The radical redefinition (or indeed, elimination) of marriage and the easing of divorce was an eagerly anticipated outcome.[51] Following in this tradition, the discarding of religious and disproportionate sanctions against incest, bestiality, and sodomy as sexual practices offensive to God or to "bourgeois morality," was logical. If Russian Marxists did not discuss these issues, they were nevertheless associated with the German Social Democratic Party's support for the decriminalization of male same-sex acts, based on these principles. The link was clearest in the Russians' enthusiastic embrace of August Bebel's theories on sexual politics in his extremely popular *Women and Socialism* (1879).[52] Early editions of Bebel's book presented negative opinions on same-sex relations as the consequence of upper-class or urban excesses.[53] He nonetheless was later an early signatory to Magnus Hirschfeld's petition to repeal paragraph 175 of the German criminal code against male same-sex acts. As leader of the German Social Democrats in 1898, he was the first politician to speak in any legislature in favor of homosexual emancipation, in an address to the Reichstag supporting the Hirschfeld campaign.[54] Bebel's conversion on this matter represented the logical extension of the principle of personal choice in private sexual matters, from heterosexual relations to homosexual ones. In later editions of *Women and Socialism* he acknowledged Hirschfeld's persuasive biologistic arguments that homosexuality could be an inborn condition and that for the "third sex," same-sex love was as natural and aesthetically noble as "normal" relations.[55]

This foregrounding of private choice in sexual matters as a political principle was "a powerful libertarian motif in nineteenth-century socialist ideology," more of a motive force than has usually been recognized.[56] Popular expressions of homosexual emancipation from post-1917 Soviet sources (such as Evgeniia Fedorovna M.'s "History of my illness") suggest that self-identified homosexuals in Russia believed the revolution had ended the state's "refusal of the private" for same-sex relations, licensing their right to love. Early-Soviet legal and medical experts frequently reflected these libertarian expectations in their interpretations, discussed in chapter 5, of same-sex relations. Aleksandra Kollontai, the best-known Bolshevik thinker on sexuality, promoted a libertarian view of the future of eros freed from the constraints of private property, sex inequality, and hypocritical moral convention. Kollontai acknowledged the value of experimentation in (heterosexual) love relationships, a rare admission among senior figures of the personally ascetic Bolshevik movement. Kollontai's association in the 1920s with the World League for Sexual Reform (based in Berlin and inaugurated by Magnus Hirschfeld) would link her to campaigns in Western Europe for homosexual emancipation.[57] Yet her published works never directly addressed "homosexuality," concentrating on love "between the sexes" and on the problems of women workers coping with maternity.[58]

Europe's parties of the left brought much more than sexual libertarianism to bear on thinking about personal life. Highly significant was the fact that Marxists claimed an "objective," "scientific" viewpoint and expected science to contribute to the rationalization of society once socialism was proclaimed. Marxists (like liberals and others) were influenced by Darwinism and theories of individual and racial degeneration and eugenics, all of which put sexuality at the heart of strategies for social engineering. Sex, understood as part of untamed nature, was to be channeled toward "natural," procreative heterosexuality through self-discipline and the inculcation of social responsibility in personal relations.[59] Medical disciplines, rather than religious dogma or outdated legal codes, would define what was "healthy" or "unhealthy" in sexual relations. The congenital model of homosexuality promoted by Hirschfeld was not universally or always wholeheartedly accepted. Many— and not only socialists—worried that greater liberty would lead to an increase in the number of cases of "acquired" (environmentally in-duced) perversion. Even those on the left who expressed tolerance of private same-sex relations among adults felt that public displays or culturally transmitted forms of such intimacies would lead to an undesirable spread of nonprocreative practices.[60]

Vladimir Lenin's thinking on sexuality fell, as Richard Stites and Wendy Goldman have demonstrated, into the rationalizing and not the libertarian camp.[61] The few sources on Lenin's views on sex say nothing about same-sex relations, although certain passages offer indications of the Bolshevik leader's likely attitude toward the homosexual emancipation movement of Western Europe and its arguments. In 1915, in correspondence with the French social democrat Inessa Armand, Lenin with blunt clarity listed in order of value his understandings of "freedom of love" (*svoboda liubvi*).[62] The relief of "love matters" from material considerations he listed foremost as most significant for the proletariat, "and thereafter," he indicated that love was to be freed from the constraints of religious prejudice, patriarchal and social strictures, the law, police, and courts. The thrust of this correspondence with Armand was that opponents of socialism would seize upon notions of "free love" to accuse the left of promoting freedom "from the serious in love . . . from childbirth . . . [and] freedom for adultery." The implication of his remarks for a politics of homosexual emancipation under socialism was that this particular "freedom of love" should wait (as would all sexuality) until a proletarian revolution reconstructed the material order.[63] Of secondary importance to the proletariat would be the tearing down of the old order's "prejudices" and "prohibitions," and here one could include by implication the religious and legal ban on consensual sodomy. Also implied in Lenin's remarks on the critique that he foresaw from the right was a rationalizing direction for the new society: toward "the serious" in love, toward childbirth, away from adultery or promiscuity. His revulsion for light-hearted or casual and temporary relations might be compatible with homosexual apologists' insistence on the nobility of same-sex relationships. Lenin's anticipation that some devotees of "free love" intended to flee from the responsibilities of parenthood was nevertheless potentially problematic for the "homosexual" who failed to procreate.

In a conversation between Lenin and German Communist Clara Zetkin, reportedly conducted in 1920 and later widely circulated as evidence of the leader's probity in sexual politics, Lenin developed these themes.[64] Lenin's comments suggested that a political critique devoted narrowly to questions of sexual dissent would find little favor in his proletarian revolutionary movement. On German Communist plans to organize Hamburg's female prostitutes, "—how shall I put it?—to be a special revolutionary militant section" with its own newspaper and campaigning, Lenin was scathing. He argued that "other working women in Germany" better deserved the attention of agitators. Socialist sympathy for prostitutes had been at one time "healthy," a laudable "rebellion against the virtuous hypocrisy of the respectable bourgeois."[65] But to devote energy on such projects while bourgeoisie and proletariat struggled over power was now "corrupted and degenerate." If Lenin believed that a "special revolutionary militant section" for prostitutes was diversionary, he doubtless would have regarded a "militant section" for homosexual emancipation in the same light. Marxist thinkers, especially Engels and Bebel, he contended, had written everything that needed to be known by the conscious worker on this subject, and they had seen little need for such particularistic campaigning. New theories about sexuality merely tinkered with superstructural phenomena and pandered to bourgeois anxieties. Impatient with Freudianism as mere "modern fashion," as "ignorant [and] bungling" for privileging sexuality over more pressing material matters, Lenin launched into a diatribe against sexual particularism:

> It seems to me that these flourishing sexual theories, which are mainly hypothetical, and often quite arbitrary hypotheses, arise from the personal need to justify *personal abnormality or hypertrophy in sexual life* before bourgeois morality, and to entreat its patience. This masked respect for bourgeois morality seems to me just as repulsive as poking about in sexual matters. However wild and revolutionary the behavior may be, it is still really quite bourgeois. It is, mainly, a hobby of the intellectuals and of the sections nearest to them. There is no place for it in the party, in the class conscious, fighting proletariat.[66]

Lenin seemed to be saying that those who suffered from a "personal abnormality . . . in sexual life" ought to do so in silence, while working for the revolution. Indulging in transgressive sexual behavior was "really quite bourgeois," while seeking the sympathy of middle-class morality was capitulation to the enemy.[67] For the young "queer subject" imagined by Ushakovskii in 1908, the Lenin of 1920, refracted through the even more conservative mood of 1924, proposed an existence of sacrifice of the "personal" to the revolutionary movement.[68]

Yet this was hardly different than Lenin's prescription for heterosexuals. He firmly opposed the idea that the pleasures of sex could be a purely private affair, even if they were "normal" or "healthy." Sex was not reducible to a physiological act. The "glass of water theory" that promised the satisfaction of sexual desire under communism as easily and as simply as taking a drink of water, was "completely un-Marxist, and moreover, antisocial":

> Of course, thirst must be satisfied. But will the normal man in normal circumstances lie down in the gutter and drink out of a puddle, or out of a glass with a rim greasy from many lips? But the social aspect is most important of all. Drinking water is, of course, an individual affair. But in love two lives are concerned, *and a third, a new life, arises.* It is that which gives it its social interest, which gives rise to a duty toward the community.[69]

Sex, in its potential for procreation, was thus a social act, and the new society would regulate and supervise it. Lenin mistrusted public interest in the sex question (he mentioned women and young people as particularly preoccupied with the issue). While insisting that he was not moralizing in a Western, middle-class fashion, he argued that there was an inherent unhealthiness in the contemplation of these issues by ordinary members of society. Lenin's fears proceeded too from a decidedly generational viewpoint ("This [revolutionary interest in sex] does not impress us old people.") Sex concerns would divert youthful energies from revolutionary work; discussions of sex, especially outside the bounds of scientific inquiry (in, for example, the Komsomol club or Party cell) would merely lead to self-indulgence.[70] His protests articulated a prudery determined to confine this troublesome question to the custody of science and the judicious counsel of experienced (and therefore, mostly male) Communists.

Yet these precepts of Lenin's come to us heavily mediated, published five years after they were said to have been uttered, and later so often reproduced because they suited the sexual politics of Stalinism. In contrast, when the Bolsheviks came to power in October 1917, they inherited a variety of liberal and leftist attitudes toward the comparatively unanticipated issue of homosexuality. Not surprisingly, their responses to same-sex relations as a legal and administrative problem reflected these multiple perspectives. Obviously influential would be the dominant, ascetic strain in Russian Marxist thinking about sex and its rationalistic view of human energy as available to be channeled toward social objectives. Yet libertarian aspirations also colored revolutionary ideals and may well have motivated some with an interest in resolving this particular issue. Those who dealt with the question were undoubtedly aware too of the broad range of publicity that same-sex love had received in the prerevolutionary era and of the scientific, cultural, and social claims made by contending parties in debates about homosexuality.

"History knows no miracles": Codifying Bolshevik Sexual Ethics

War and then revolution moved these ideas from the realm of abstraction, but the reform of the sodomy statute was always a subsidiary of the larger questions of governance. In 1915, the tsarist regime briefly considered the full implementation of the 1903 draft criminal code, under which sodomy would have remained an offense. There were no further revisions, and the project was abandoned as the war worsened. Following the February 1917 revolution, the Provisional Government established "a commission to review and implement the [1903] Criminal Code," and as it had Nabokov among its members, the liberal position on sodomy decriminalization would have been influentially represented. Neither Nabokov nor Nikolai S. Timashev refer to any substantive work completed by the commission, which existed during the last four months of the increasingly unstable Provisional Government.[71]

The trail of evidence leading from the potentialities of 1917 to the first Soviet Russian criminal code of 1922, which decriminalized sodomy, is rather unclear. There are no records of substantive debate among the framers of the criminal code over the section on crimes against the person, which is where sexual crime was located in the new code.[72] (Chapter five of the 1922 redaction was entitled "Crimes against the Life, Health, Freedom and Dignity of the Individual.") Historians have sought to explain the abolition of the sodomy penalty with reference to contextual factors. Simon Karlinsky regards decriminalization as at best a benign oversight, the result of the elimination of all tsarist law during the Bolshevik revolution. In his surveys he has discounted whatever deliberate reforming intention lay behind the legalization as a "misreading of the Bolshevik leaders' position on gay liberation" said to be common to observers in England and Germany in the 1920s, and on the left in the West generally since the 1970s.[73]

Attempts to recover the origins of a "principled decision" (in Laura Engelstein's words) to remove sodomy from the code have sought to place the decision within a " "modernist consensus" in scientific, juridical, and cultural circles"[74] or within the evolution of modern criminal sanctions in Russia, beginning with the draft code of 1903.[75] These mutually compatible replies to Karlinsky were based on published sources available in the West. They can be reinforced with reference to evidence from the archives of the RSFSR People's Commissariat of Justice. While these documents do not discuss the sodomy statute in detail, they do demonstrate a principled intent to decriminalize the act between consenting adults, expressed from the earliest efforts to write a socialist criminal code in 1918 to the eventual adoption of legislation in 1922. This intention coincided with prosecutions for "unnatural vice [pederasty]" and "crime[s] against nature" conducted by the Bolsheviks at considerable cost in the heat of the civil war, or soon thereafter. The outcome of the prosecution of such crimes was to modernize the language of criminal sexual deviance, but also, as with all law in the Bolshevik state, to leave opportunities for arbitrary application of legal norms available to procurators and policymakers.

Within weeks of the October 1917 revolution, the Commissariat of Justice, headed by Left Socialist Revolutionary (LSR) Isaak Shteinberg, drafted a criminal statute as part of an ambitious Code of Laws of the Russian Revolution.[76] The LSRs made no secret of their admiration for the 1903 draft criminal code, and the deputy commissar of justice and editor of the commissariat's "codification department" A. Shreider noted in his commentary that the LSRs' 1918 version relied on that draft, "reworked and revised in depth from the point of view of the new revolutionary legal consciousness."[77] The table of contents to Shreider's code further emphasized the reliance on the 1903 draft, presenting a concordance of 1903 and 1918 articles.[78]

In the debates over the 1903 draft code the prohibition against consensual sodomy had been criticized by liberals, yet they had not been successful in abolishing the offense. Shreider's 1918 variant, however, stripped away the clause against consensual acts while retaining the elaborate language describing acts imposed against the weak or with the use of force. The relevant article was entitled "sodomy" (*muzhelozhstvo*), and as in 1903 fell within a chapter specifically devoted to sexual offenses headed "On indecent conduct" (*O nepotrebstve*).[79] The resulting sodomy law was a balance between principles of consent, capacity to understand "the character and significance" of the act, and protection for the weak as argued by Nabokov some sixteen years earlier.[80] Not only would simple sodomy between adults, defined as persons sixteen and over, be legalized, but by doing so and by keeping the remaining language of the 1903 draft legislation, knowledgeable consent from fourteen- and fifteen-year-old boys would have exonerated sodomy with certain youths as well. In this respect the first occupants of the Justice Commissariat were heeding Nabokov's argument that the law could not treat young "catamites" who operated as prostitutes in urban Russia in the same way as "innocent" youths.[81]

Nowhere in the commentary that accompanies the 1918 version does Shreider offer more than declarative reasoning as a clue to this modification to the 1903 draft. This code had represented "a powerful step forward from the archaic, unwieldy and contradictory" 1845 statute in effect until Soviet rule. Referring to the evolution of "democratic" legal systems out of the tyrannies of the "ancient satrap" and Louis XIV's "l'état, c'est moi," Shreider argued that a state must resort to coercion to curb "anarchy," but that this was an "unfortunate necessity." A criminal code was needed to regulate the norms of a state's legal resort to force. The statute he was proposing would compel the state to serve the law, and not vice versa. Norms evolved with the legal consciousness of a society; what was required was "not the minimum of individual rights that the collective should not infringe [upon], but rather the maximum of demands put to the collective by the individual." The criteria upon which his revisions to the 1903 code were based were "the welfare of the genuine human individual and the interests of international labor solidarity."[82] Shreider's insistence on maximizing individual rights within a state constrained by something approaching the rule of law would seem to be consistent with the elimination of the antisodomy statute.

The March 1918 resignation of the LSRs from their coalition with the Bolsheviks over the Treaty of Brest-Litovsk entailed a Bolshevik take-over at the Justice Commissariat, with P. I. Stuchka then appointed people's commissar, who was supplanted in 1919 by D. I. Kurskii. Shreider was dismissed as deputy commissar and Bolshevik M. Iu. Kozlovskii was assigned to review criminal legislation. The LSR draft code was criticized by Stuchka for defending bourgeois interests and for insufficient revolutionary consciousness.[83] In the subsequent two years, the Justice Commissariat made little substantive progress toward a Bolshevik criminal code, as a result of the intense pressure on personnel during the civil war and the relatively low priority accorded by the Soviet government to the commissariat in its allocation of resources.[84] Nevertheless, top jurists monitored the experience of Soviet courts without explicitly codified criminal law, and proposals for a code did periodically surface for discussion in the Justice Commissariat's collegium. "Guiding principles of criminal law of the RSFSR" were drafted by Kurskii in the course of 1919 and published in December of that year, serving as the basis for the general part of the 1922 criminal code. By 1920, the collegium was convinced that explicit, centralized norms that reflected Moscow's view of revolutionary consciousness would be more reliable than the inconsistencies and anachronisms of local legal officials, and it turned to the drafting of the special part of the code.[85]

Prior to this renewed exercise in codification, during the interlude without written criminal law, a centrally directed trial for "pederasty" suggested how officials in the Justice Commissariat viewed issues raised by homosexual offenses. In late 1919, the Justice Commissariat's Eighth Department, charged with implementing the separation of the Orthodox church from the state, devoted considerable resources to the prosecution of a Bishop Palladii of Zvenigorod for "corruption of a boy and for unnatural vice (pederasty)."[86] Palladii was a trusted friend of Patriarch Tikhon, who had sent the bishop to defend the New Jerusalem Monastery from nationalization in early 1919. When Bolsheviks finally seized the monastery, they uncovered allegations about Palladii's relationship with Ivan Volkov, a fourteen-year-old "lay brother" (keleinik). Militant atheist jurists in the Eighth Department launched a wide-ranging investigation into the bishop's sexual career; Palladii was tried in Moscow in October 1919, sentenced to five years' imprisonment and later released under a general amnesty in January 1920.

For Bolshevik jurists, the political significance of Palladii's case resided in both the bishop's damaging connection to the patriarch and in the timing of its revelations. As Palladii came under investigation, Patriarch Tikhon was seeking to establish a modus vivendi with the hostile Soviet regime. Tikhon's 1918 pronouncement of anathema on the Bolsheviks had generated disastrous results for the Church; he now made a series of declarations enunciating a new policy of ecclesiastical neutrality in politics.[87] The Justice Commissariat's atheist jurists intended to tarnish Tikhon's retreat from worldly matters to a moral high ground by exploiting this episode of clerical depravity.[88] Their activity was supervised by People's Commissar of Justice Kurskii and the commissariat's collegium, including Eighth Department chief P. A. Krasikov and collegium member N. A. Cherlunchakevich. These same men would eventually be responsible for the drafting of the first Bolshevik criminal legislation.[89]

The Palladii trial demonstrated some of the assumptions underlying early Bolshevik juridical thinking about same-sex offenses. Most significant was the willingness to prosecute an adult for "unnatural vice (pederasty)," where political factors warranted. Wartime propaganda needs outweighed any consideration that clergy were entitled to the sexual autonomy promised by the revolution. The sexual revolution would have a class basis, and the enemies of the victorious class would not be entitled to the autonomy accorded to full citizens. Later clerical sex trials would demonstrate an equally flexible, instrumental approach to the application of laws on sexual crime.[90]

Of equal importance for the codification to come was the decision to present Volkov as an innocent "victim" of clerical depravity. At fourteen years old, Volkov was on the threshold of "knowledgeable" sexual self-determination as defined in the 1903 and 1918 draft codes, with their allowance that certain youths (urban "commercial catamites") could give informed consent to sodomy. Volkov's complex relationship to the bishop included the receipt of benefits (education, lodging, payment, and a career) in apparent exchange for domestic and sexual services.[91] Yet Bolshevik jurists elected to extend previous definitions of sexual childhood or minority to encompass this knowledgeable fourteen-year-old. Eventually, in the 1922 criminal code, Bolsheviks would arrive at a medicalized benchmark for sexual autonomy defined not by age but by "sexual maturity," to be determined by physicians in cases of sexual activity with, or assaults against, young persons.

Bolshevik intentions to medicalize sexual deviance are further evident in the Palladii case from the jurists' turn to psychiatrists for forensic expertise and for assurances that the bishop would not commit new crimes after his amnesty. Volkov was sent to the newly established Institute of the Defective Child for observation during the investigation; the Eighth Department hoped to call upon psychiatrists at Palladii's trial to testify to the harm done to the boy.[92] In early 1920, when Palladii was granted amnesty, he spent three months in a psychiatric hospital "for isolation and therapy in a special medical establishment." Krasikov and his team apparently expected medical science to explain and interpret the signs of sexual disorder and believed that "therapy" for "unnatural vice" could be had from psychiatric hospitalization.

In 1920, the Justice Commissariat collegium took up the task of codifying criminal law with renewed interest, delegating to M. Iu. Kozlovskii (formerly a legal "nihilist," now an advocate of standardized penal norms) the task of working up a "scheme" of chapter headings for a code.[93] The jurist produced a draft code and commentary by June of that year, and the evolution of the provisions he made regarding sexual crime may be traced from archival documents.[94] These documents represent the earliest surviving Bolshevik proposals for such legislation. Kozlovskii's original primitive conception of sex offenses acquired refinement with reference to the 1903 draft criminal code, and possibly to the Palladii case and French revolutionary legislation as well.

In a first handwritten scheme, under the chapter heading "Crimes against personal rights," Kozlovskii listed only a single offense with sexual content: "Insult to feminine honor."[95] Apparently only female victims of sex crimes were imaginable to this jurist and only in the archaic framework of reputation and honor; his second version restated the offense in this manner. Yet here another hand had crossed out the typescript of this phrase and replaced it with "Crimes against morality [*nravstvennosti*] (infringements of female honor, sodomy [*muzhelozhstvo*], etc.)." The sphere of potential offenses was widened, and the reference to "insult" was dropped; as well, the offenses fell under a more elaborate chapter heading, "Crimes against the life, health and property [*dostoianie*] of the individual." (The reference to "property" was swiftly corrected to read "dignity.")[96]

In Kozlovskii's clean copy of his June 1920 draft of this chapter, sexual crimes had been considerably developed from these early schemes, and the influence of the 1903 and 1918 drafts was evident. The names of four of the five sex offenses were borrowed from the 1903 code, although the overall language of each article was simplified. Sodomy was to be one of these five crimes, but only when imposed on children or with the use of force. Simple sodomy between consenting persons of fourteen or over was not to be a crime.[97] This was a clear reduction in the age of consent over the 1903 draft. The threshold ages of fourteen and fifteen years in that version and Shreider's 1918 redaction, had been subject to a test of the younger person's character (sodomy "with his consent, but through abuse of his innocence" would be punished); now, in this draft, the age of consent for all sexual acts was fourteen. There is no evidence linking Kozlovskii to the Palladii episode, but the clarification of the age of consent in sodomy cases, evident in the draft he proposed, could reflect the collegium's experience with this awkward case.

Kozlovskii understood that his criminal code, like early French revolutionary penal law, was "transitional," and that only when the gains of revolution were consolidated would new norms acquire stability. His commentary indicated his familiarity with the course of French codification after 1789, the history of which he viewed as the prime teacher for the commissariat's legal draftsmen.[98] The degree to which this understanding influenced his view of the sodomy statute cannot be determined from his explicit statements. French revolutionary secularization

and rationalization of statutes had (perhaps unintentionally at the outset) included the decriminalization of sodomy in 1791, later deliberately
confirmed by Napoleonic fiat in 1805 and in the penal code of 1810.[99]
It is arguable that Kozlovskii knew of this aspect of the French codes
he cited in this commentary, although his comments did not dwell on
specific offenses. Kozlovskii did think that many crimes prohibited under the old regime would remain illegal, but he singled out "religious
crimes" as a specific category of offenses that would "drop away" under
the revolutionary order.[100] Secularization was the fundamental principle
of his penal renovation. But crimes against the person (including what
he archaically called "crimes against . . . female honor") he believed
would undergo less change than any other section of the criminal code:

> Human nature with its good and evil passions is more stubborn and
> conservative than political institutions and social slogans. The latter may
> and do have a great influence on the direction of the statistical curve
> of criminality, but of themselves they are powerless to recreate human
> nature rapidly. History knows no miracles or sudden leaps.[101]

For this reason he counseled the creative adaptation of the 1903 draft
statute, "with the elimination and alteration of those specific offenses
on which traces of the capitalist relations of the previous era remain."
In the absence of a direct statement endorsing the legalization of sodomy, what Kozlovskii's drafts and comments demonstrate is a clear intention to remove the act from Bolshevik criminal law. This intention
followed from a principled commitment to the secularization and modernization of legal norms and from a prevailing conviction that a medical interpretation of sexual disorder accorded with Bolshevik visions.

Unfortunately, the path from these proposals to the final language
of the 1922 RSFSR criminal code on crimes against the individual
(adopted by the Justice Commissariat's collegium on 21 December
1921),[102] remains obscure. Collegium protocols suggest that in the
eighteen-month interval between Kozlovskii's draft and the approval of
the eventual wording, "a special commission of experts of the General
Consultation Department of the Justice Commissariat" led by P. A.
Krasikov and L. A. Savrasov was chiefly responsible for the considerable
revisions in language that resulted.[103] Consultation between the collegium and the Institute of Soviet Law late in 1921 resulted in the institute putting forward its own draft code, which was rejected by the
commissariat for its "bourgeois" orientation.[104] At the December 1921
collegium session approving the final wording of the chapter on crimes

against the individual, among those present were Krasikov and Cherlunchakevich, who had presided over the Palladii case. Also present
was N. V. Krylenko, who as people's commissar of justice would one
day publicly justify the 1934 reversal of the revolutionary decision to
decriminalize sodomy.[105] The entire criminal code was assembled in its
final form by January 1922, when the Justice Commissariat published
it for circulation to justice officials, the Council of People's Commissars
(Sovnarkom), and the Central Executive Committee of the All-Russian
Congress of Soviets (VTsIK). After discussion in Sovnarkom (February
1922) and in a committee and plenary sessions at VTsIK in May, the
criminal code became law on 1 June.[106]

The Language of Modernity

In its final form, the 1922 Russian criminal code radically modernized
the archaic language of Kozlovskii's 1920 proposals. Its minimalist formulas enshrined the general conception of sexual crime as a violation
of the individual's right to "life, health, freedom, and dignity."[107] The
Kozlovskii draft had employed tsarist legal terms for various forms of
sexual misconduct; all of these were discarded.[108] Sodomy and incest
were not named at all in the new code. Archaic labels for sexual misconduct were reformulated with terminology drawn from forensic medical
and even police-blotter language.[109] Thresholds for consent (the age
at which sexual autonomy was granted by the state) were especially
medicalized as explicit age limits were abandoned, and the concept of
"sexual maturity" (*polovaia zrelost'*), to be determined by medical opinion in each case, was introduced instead. A person having achieved
sexual maturity could consent to sexual intercourse, to defloration, or
to "perverted forms" of sexual behavior.[110] The effect of this new language was to deprive sexual crime statutes of any pretense of safeguarding religious or transcendent morality and to thrust such offenses
squarely into the remit of the guardians of public health and order.
When in 1926 a revised RSFSR criminal code was issued, the same
language and principles were reaffirmed, including the absence of a
ban on consensual same-sex relations.[111]

In their exegesis of the 1922 and 1926 Russian criminal codes, jurists
noted instances for which certain homosexual acts could be prosecuted.
The innovative principle of gender-neutrality in the formulation of
most sex offense articles suggested that victims and perpetrators might
be of either sex.[112] A new tendency to consider the possibility of female
same-sex offenses appeared in juridical commentaries as a result. The

articles that gave rise to jurists' speculation regarding homosexual acts were numbers 167 and 168 in the 1922 code (articles 151 and 152 in 1926). The first prohibited (in addition to defloration) the "satisfaction of sexual lust in perverted forms" with sexually immature persons.[113] It was generally agreed that "perverted forms" included "unnatural sexual intercourse whether between men, that is, sodomy or pederasty, or between women, that is, lesbian love or tribadism, and also anal copulation . . . regardless of the sex of the victim or accused person."[114] The second article (number 168/152) punished "depraved acts" with children or minors (defined for purposes of punishment in the 1922 code as under fourteen in the case of children [*maloletnie*], and fourteen to eighteen years as minors [*nesovershennoletnie*]). Definitions of "depravity" evoked less certainty in jurists; one included homosexual anal intercourse and "lesbian love," effectively introducing a redundancy since he had already comprehended such acts under the preceding article.[115] Others adopted heterocentric and phallocentric views. Liublinskii asserted that "depraved acts" could include "those forms of same-sex contacts that cannot be compared with [hetero-] sexual intercourse."[116] "Lesbian love," not explained in anatomical terms except to note that genital contact "without the aim of copulation" was intended, could be understood as a depraved act when nonadults were the object.[117] The article was apparently an inarticulate attempt to criminalize nonpenetrative and nonprocreative sex acts that were believed to contribute to the "corruption of children and minors." Among these acts, male *and* female same-sex contacts were included, doubtless because of the socialist belief that "acquired" as opposed to "congenital" homosexuality could and should be prevented in an ideal society.

Curiously, anal intercourse inflicted violently on an adult was not enumerated as specific offense in the code. Some commentators believed that the gender-neutral article 169/153 on rape included this offense, whether homosexual or heterosexual; others disagreed, arguing incorrectly that tradition reserved the terms "rape" and "sexual intercourse" to heterosexual acts.[118] From a purely legalistic viewpoint, rape between men could readily have been prosecuted under either the gender-blind rape statute alone or by application of the principle of analogy.[119] In 1928, in reply to an inquiry about the treatment of homosexuals in Russia from Magnus Hirschfeld's Scientific-Humanitarian Committee, the People's Commissariat of Justice wrote from Moscow that the first section of article 153 did indeed prohibit "homosexual acts accompanied by physical or mental violence."[120] Central legal and forensic medical publications of the interval of sodomy decriminalization (1922–33) are devoid of references to contemporary prosecutions of male rape, which may indicate that the crime went unpunished, or if it was, then unpublicized. Legislators, determined to modernize the language of criminal law on sexual crime, may have opted to eradicate a specific reference to "sodomy . . . by means of force," reasoning that a gender-blind definition of rape would serve the same purpose, while upholding principles of sex equality. The law's drafters could thereby rid the code of the word "sodomy," a term with religious and moralistic associations. They could also sidestep the dilemma of how to name homosexual rape, posed by having chosen to define all other sex crimes in forensic medical or criminological terminology. An associated benefit of this textual strategy would have been the code's total silence on same-sex offenses, a silence that some rulers have believed deprived homosexuality of publicity and imitation by example.[121]

Conclusion

In the final years of tsarist rule, when the quasi-constitutional settlement following the 1905 revolution relaxed censorship, self-consciously homosexual voices (and parodies of them) emerged in avant-garde literature and in journalistic, satirical, and popular scientific texts. The "queer subject" appeared in the public domain, and with a boldness and ease not always evident elsewhere in Europe, was heard calling for toleration and respect for the "third sex." These appeals were greeted by some with derision and vulgar parody. Entrepreneurs exploited the new press freedom to publish speculative tracts, dressed up in the dispassionate language of medicine, but actually offering voyeuristic tours of the homosexual subcultures of Russian and European capitals. Increasingly, popular scientific texts, both domestic and foreign, spoke about "sexual psychopathologies" or the "third sex" to a nonprofessional reading public.

Fresh awareness of the ferment in European ideas about the "homosexual" was accompanied by liberal attacks on the antiquated and arbitrary antisodomy statute. In Russia, it was liberal jurists and not homosexuals themselves who voiced the most cogent arguments against this law. Liberals proposed to eliminate that law's moralizing focus on a single repugnant act, which they believed like other forms of immorality might best be confined to the private sphere and eliminated by education. They voiced a principled stand for a right to privacy in adult, consensual sexual matters, within a framework of law based on abstract and universal principles. The vehicles for a rule of law state, whether the Duma monarchy or the republic of February 1917, were however not politically viable, and liberal spokesmen for homosexual emancipation were swept aside in the October 1917 revolution.

Russia's victorious social democrats were the bearers of conflicting traditions, counseling on the one hand libertarianism in sexual relations between adults, while also anticipating a social claim on sex in the new society, to be mediated by a rationalist political ideology and modern medicine. It was a tension that would characterize revolutionary approaches to same-sex love for much of the subsequent decade. Despite this conflict of values, there was agreement over the form of regulation most appropriate in a socialist society. While briefly holding the Justice Commissariat, Left Socialist Revolutionary jurists deliberately eliminated the ban on consensual sodomy in their proposed criminal code. Two years later, when Bolshevik legal experts returned to the issue of codification, they too made the same explicit decision. The legislation that they finally approved secularized and modernized the language of violations to the sexual autonomy and inviolability of the person. Religious terminology for physical acts was replaced by forensic medical and criminological discourse, and the range of offenses was simplified. The status of homosexual love in this new dispensation was apparently clarified by the absence of a penalty for sodomy between consenting adults. The repeal of this ban was a real political advance, and Soviet Russia was the most significant power since revolutionary France to decriminalize men's same-sex love, while sentences for similar "crimes" ranged from five years (for "unnatural vice") in Germany to life imprisonment (for "buggery") in England.[122] The medicalization of sexual offenses that accompanied the ambitious new legislative regime nevertheless offered police, jurists, and medical officials opportunities for the continued regulation of sexual and gender dissent.

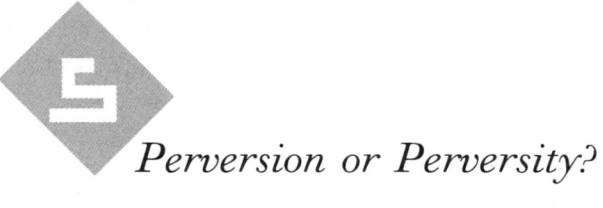

Perversion or Perversity?

MEDICINE, POLITICS, AND THE REGULATION
OF SEX AND GENDER DISSENT AFTER SODOMY
DECRIMINALIZATION

How would Soviet power understand and regulate same-sex love? One ambitious junior psychiatrist in 1922 had no doubt that the latest scientific knowledge dictated a medical view of the issue:

> Doctors look upon homosexuals as unfortunate stepchildren of fate. They are like cripples, similar to the blind, deaf-mutes, et cetera, who owe their defect only to a physiological deformation; but they can in no way be considered ill-intentioned, debauched people offending public morality and therefore, the term *perversion* [*izvrashchenie*] (inversio), and not *perversity* [*izrashchennost'*] or even less so, *debauchery* [*razvrashchennost'*], is used to designate this pathological condition.[1]

V. P. Protopopov of Petrograd argued for a potentially progressive approach. By banishing the old regime's religious, moralistic understanding in favor of a view already widely supported in Western medical circles, Soviet jurisprudence and medicine would rationalize the treatment of this sexual anomaly. As "homosexuals" were thought to be victims of a biological deformity and not responsible for their sexual drives, a modern society relieved of bourgeois philistinism would no longer condemn them to prison but invite them instead into the clinic. Writing as Russia's new criminal code was still under discussion in the People's Commissariat of Justice, Protopopov expressed what some held to be the rationale for the eventual decriminalization of sodomy.

The Communist Party's preoccupation with the fundamental questions of rule dominated its politics in the 1920s. A succession struggle followed Lenin's incapacitating strokes beginning in 1922 and his death in January 1924; the associated debate over industrialization between

Stalin and his opponents occupied the first peacetime years of Soviet rule. Bolshevik ambiguities about same-sex relations should be considered in this context. Communists generally believed that sexual questions, despite their evident importance for the revolution, were superstructural matters that would resolve themselves once collectivist economic and social foundations were laid. Moreover, medical science would be enlisted by the state (which had, under the old regime, mistrusted technocratic expertise) to define the "healthy" and the "pathological" citizen on a basis assumed to be materialist. When these expectations were combined with the deliberate deletion of "sodomy" from the first revolutionary criminal code, a discursive vacuum opened and permitted various agents to express a plurality of approaches to sex and gender dissent. There was no single or official position on homosexuality during the period of sodomy decriminalization (1922–33), but instead a diversity of views among a range of experts and administrators.

Few experts sought to stake their careers on the issue of homosexuality in the way Protopopov did. If disputes seldom erupted in public between those who espoused diverging views, nevertheless the implications of these arguments may be distilled from the percolating discussions of the period. Certain jurists and police remained suspicious of the homosexual, despite the new penal code. Meanwhile, a few psychiatrists and endocrine experts seized upon apparent discoveries about the determination of sexual orientation to claim the homosexual as theirs. To these authorities, same-sex erotic attraction was supposedly the result of hormonal anomaly; some regarded it as a natural human variant, with its own legitimate historical and cultural precedents. Others asserted a biosocial view, claiming the origins of sexuality resided not principally in the glands but in society or in the individual's developmental history. By looking at these psychiatrists' studies and their approaches to methodological and gender issues, the range of alternatives in circulation in the new society can be reassessed and the potential for a politics of sex and gender diversity in revolutionary Russia can be evaluated.

Sexual Revolution, Medicine, and Sexual Anomalies

The discursive vacuum left by the Bolsheviks around issues of sexual and gender dissent created opportunities for Soviet legal and medical experts of the 1920s. Seeking to make their disciplines "Soviet," they used the possibilities for interpretation and research afforded by encounters with "homosexuals" and members of the "intermediate sex" to promote views that would differentiate them from their tsarist predecessors. Jurists, most trained under the old regime, struggled to reconcile the experience of revolution and civil war, an era without positive law, with the new requirements of a return to a formal legal framework under the New Economic Policy. Where same-sex relations were concerned, the new criminal norms said little, and jurists filled the discursive vacuum with speculation about the medical or emancipatory implications. Meanwhile medical experts and, in particular psychiatrists, examined "homosexuality" and "transvestism" with vigor not seen before 1917. As Susan Gross Solomon has argued in the case of social hygiene, novelty was not necessarily required to confer positive political credentials on a line of research. Under the patronage of the astute and charismatic People's Commissar of Health Nikolai Semashko, sponsorship could come if the ideas were new to Russia.[2] Despite the considerable resource limitations on the new Health Commissariat, which in budgetary priorities ranked low in the Soviet state,[3] an impressive volume of research and discussion on problems of sex and gender anomaly took place during the 1920s.

Experts in law and medicine wasted little time in claiming their turf. Three months after the enactment of the 1922 RSFSR criminal code, in the weekly journal of the Commissariat of Justice, an obscure jurist published "Trials of Homosexuals," an article describing two cases and arguing that homosexual behavior, in the absence of a sodomy statute, could still be illegal under the new code.[4] The item dealt with one trial, apparently completed, against a large number of men arrested in a Petrograd "pederasts' club" in a private flat, where several males were apprehended in women's clothing. This party had been one of a series of gatherings organized in and around Petrograd as masquerades, with dancing, matchmaking rituals, and mock wedding ceremonies. The other case, said to be under investigation, was that of a woman, Evgeniia, who had impersonated a man to marry her female friend in a civil registry office (ZAGS, an agency of the Commissariat of Justice). The two women had successfully argued against local prosecutors seeking to invalidate the marriage. Psychiatrists too discussed these cases, both in print and behind closed doors, and their accounts diverged substantially from that offered by the Justice Commissariat.[5]

The article's author, identified only as G. R., offered broad interpretations of criminal code articles against "hooliganism" and brothel-keeping to secure convictions against "homosexuals." Charges of hooliganism would presumably have proved successful in the women's case, while the brothel-keeping charge covered "dens" like the "pederasts' club." This jurist argued that forensic psychiatric expertise provided a medical justification for the prosecution of homosexuals. He cited testimony, warning of the influence of perversion on "normal" persons, that he claimed Russia's leading psychiatrist, academician V. M. Bekhterev, had given during the trial of the Petrograd men.[6] Medicine and law in the young Soviet republic were apparently united in their determination to repress "homosexuals" as harmful elements, despite the decriminalization of sodomy.[7]

Yet jurists who approached the question did not display unanimity on the proposed treatment of "homosexuals." It is doubtful that "Trials of Homosexuals" necessarily reflected the attitude of all jurists or that provincial officials closely read and obeyed the commissariat's journal.[8] The author of this article noted himself that the higher judiciary had not been moved to produce guiding determinations "on this subject." His conclusions were couched in the cautious language of a jurist offering an opinion rather than the confident tones of a bureaucrat relaying a fiat from the desk of the people's commissar.[9] Legal commentaries on Soviet Russia's new criminal code ignored these suggestions at least as often as they agreed with them, but significantly, none ever referred to this article.[10] Many Soviet jurists commenting on the new code understood the absence of a ban on sodomy as a progressive measure. Sodomy had been decriminalized, one jurist wrote, because

> science, and much legislation following from it . . . had taken the view that the commission of the act of sodomy with adults infringed no rights whatsoever, and that [adults] were free to express their sexual feeling in any form, and that the intrusion of the law into this field is a holdover of church teachings and of the ideology of sinfulness.[11]

Adults who committed consensual same-sex acts could thus be regarded as beneficiaries of the sexual revolution, emancipated from religious prejudice by science. Other legal experts explicitly invoked the authority of medicine to justify decriminalization, citing the range of theories of the origins of same-sex desire from psychopathological disturbance to the latest biological hypotheses of Iwan Bloch, Magnus Hirschfeld, and Eugen Steinach.[12] Scholars also cited a history of retreating criminal sanctions against homosexual acts; they noted that a "more humanitarian point of view" was responsible for the gradual easing of penalties in European legislation.[13]

Psychiatrists—including Bekhterev—also contradicted G. R.'s analysis. Evidence that this lawyer's proposals represented only an isolated expert's opinion is found in articles by psychiatrists describing the same cases dealt with in "Trials of Homosexuals." In a 1927 case history of "transvestism" and "homosexuality," Moscow psychiatrist A. O. Edel'shtein presented a woman, Evgeniia Fedorovna M., whose actions closely resembled those of "Evgeniia" in the 1922 Justice Commissariat item.[14] The psychiatrist dryly noted as fact the information that the Commissariat of Justice had conceded the legality of his patient's 1922 marriage to another woman on the grounds of "mutual consent."[15] The two texts may well describe the same Evgeniia/Evgenii. Yet even if they do not, Edel'shtein's article indicates that justice officials did recognize *his* subject's same-sex marriage in 1922. The legal strategies promoted in "Trials of Homosexuals" were certainly not heeded by those jurists investigating the woman who eventually became Edel'shtein's patient.[16]

Medical articles relating to the case of the "pederasts' club" contradicted the 1922 Justice Commissariat's account of the psychiatric expert testimony provided. Psychiatrists also challenged the timing of this trial as reported in this item.[17] As with the women's case, available evidence precludes an indisputable connection between the Petrograd raid on a private party at which sailors and other men staged a masquerade wedding, as described in the commissariat's weekly journal, and the similar incident described separately by Petrograd psychiatrists Bekhterev and his student, V. P. Protopopov.[18] But the circumstances of the cases are so similar and extraordinary to suggest that they were the same. Even if they were not, the credibility of "Trials of Homosexuals" as conclusive evidence of a supposed prevailing Soviet approach toward same-sex relations is undermined when these two accounts are compared.

The Justice Commissariat's jurist implied that the raid on the "pederasts' club"—or at least the subsequent trial—had taken place after the 1 June 1922 enactment of the new criminal code.[19] The author presented the timing of the case in this way to strengthen his argument that homosexuality should now be criminalized as disorderly conduct, since sodomy was no longer a prohibited act. Yet Bekhterev's accounts of his activities during the investigation following a Petrograd raid on a "pederasts' club" undermined this timing and suggested that his professional opinions had been distorted in the Commissariat of Justice's version. In 1922, the psychiatrist published an account of the arrest of "an entire club of homosexuals, about ninety-eight individuals altogether, during their festive wedding party."[20] This article was addressed to a professional audience of psychiatrists and physicians. Bekhterev said police telephoned on the night of the raid to invite him to examine the men for research (*nauchnye*), not forensic, purposes, and a footnote indicates his examinations must have taken place before 28 February 1921 (fifteen months before the new criminal code was adopted).[21] He reported nothing here about being required to furnish forensic psychiatric opinions or to attend a trial.

Bekhterev again described the police raid and his interviews with the men who were arrested in a chapter dated December 1924 addressed to an audience of professional educators and included in a twice-published, respected volume on sexual education.[22] In this version, the psychiatrist aggressively strove to correct the Justice Commissariat's account without directly mentioning it. Bekhterev claimed to have studied the police investigation files, and he gave the date of the raid as 15 January 1921. He noted that police surveillance of similar gatherings in a succession of private flats had begun in late 1920.[23] Bekhterev made no comment about this surveillance, but his terse observation about his own official role in the aftermath of the raid is a distinct contradiction of the Commissariat of Justice official's representation of the academician in court. "I was required to give an opinion on the case, and naturally, it was for the quashing of the case, for neither seduction nor propaganda for homosexuality were possible to establish in this instance."[24]

At issue in the discussion between psychiatrists, jurists, and the shadowy author of "Trials of Homosexuals" was the question of the status of "homosexuals." Were they still to be regarded as criminals (as the police and some jurists apparently viewed them), or would they now be patients awaiting psychotherapy (as Bekhterev, an advocate of hypnosis, recommended) or maybe even a hormonal adjustment (as Protopopov's study implied)? Perhaps homosexuals were now "free to express their sexual feeling" like other adult citizens, as some legal commentaries argued. Fragmentary evidence suggests that emancipatory and medical views were preferred (when no public disturbance, or politically disloyal act took place) over likely police preferences for a tougher line.

A similar dispute over the correct approach to women as (heterosexual) prostitutes raged at this time between police, jurists, medical experts, and social activists, offering instructive indicators of official attitudes toward sexuality in public.[25] A chaotic range of views about prostitution had been expressed during the civil war years by authorities, resulting in a patchwork of rehabilitative and repressive measures. Social workers and Zhenotdel (the Women's Department of the early Communist Party) activists promoted communal housing experiments and sex education programs, while police in some jurisdictions simply rounded up prostitutes and confined them in labor camps. An early effort at coordination, an interdepartmental commission set up in 1919 under the auspices of the Commissariat of Welfare, tried to promote policies of education and social assistance. In December 1922, after legislators had rejected any suggestion that prostitutes themselves should be criminalized in the new RSFSR criminal code, another, much broader, interdepartmental commission for the struggle against prostitution led by Health Commissar Semashko was established. This commission rejected police methods on ideological grounds, arguing instead that social assistance and education for the woman who sold sex (regarded as a victim of economic circumstance and masculine disrespect) would win her for "useful labor." In the course of debate, police proposals for a special unit (a "moral militia") to target brothel-keepers and male clients were attacked by Clara Zetkin and venereologists for threatening to revive the tsarist regulationist system while driving prostitution underground, leaving disease to flourish unchecked.[26] Where female prostitution was concerned, Soviet medicine would coordinate policy, which would be predicated not on punitive practices like those of the tsarist regime, but on therapeutic and redemptive strategies intended to combat disease and restore women's dignity.

Less clarity surrounded policy on same-sex love. No one of Zetkin's stature commented publicly, inside the USSR, on the legal and medical discussion about "homosexuals." Nor was the question dramatized with the formation of a committee of experts. But one month after the interdepartmental commission on prostitution had been established, Health Commissar Semashko, during a visit to Berlin, indicated to German allies in the international movement for sex reform that the Soviet legalization of male same-sex relations was a deliberately emancipatory measure, part of the sexual revolution. The research and sex-reform activities of Dr. Magnus Hirschfeld's Institute for Sex Research, founded in Berlin in 1919, were followed with interest by Soviet social hygienists, and apparently by their patron, Semashko.[27] In January 1923, Semashko paid a visit to the institute with a delegation of Soviet doctors. They particularly requested a screening of the film, *Anders als die Andern*, a cinematic documentary about same-sex love made in 1919 with Hirschfeld's participation. The institute's journal on sexual intermediate types reported that the Soviet viewers expressed amazement that the film had been regarded as scandalous and had been banned. The journal then observed that Semashko

> stated how pleased he was that in the new Russia, the former penalty against homosexuals has been completely abolished. He also explained

that no unhappy consequences of any kind whatsoever have resulted from the elimination of the offending paragraph, nor has the wish that the penalty in question be reintroduced been raised in any quarter.[28]

This careful and allusive statement (not published in the USSR) was the most positive expression of homosexual emancipationist sentiment by a senior figure in the Soviet regime. It suggested that the emancipation of homosexuals was a logical outcome of the revolution. The health commissar ignored the call, expressed in "Trials of Homosexuals" (and reminiscent of police proposals for a moral militia), for a return to the regulation of homosexuality by other means. Semashko appeared optimistic about the consequences of the new legal dispensation.

Semashko's link with social democrat and sex reformer Magnus Hirschfeld was one of many associations with German medicine which the people's commissar cultivated as evidence of Soviet Russia's radical break with tsarist public health policy.[29] Two years after Semashko's visit to Hirschfeld's institute, social hygienist Grigorii Batkis, a "young hothead Bolshevik doing his graduate studies at Moscow University,"[30] published a German-language pamphlet, *The Sexual Revolution in Russia*, in Berlin. Here Batkis said that in the USSR homosexuality was a private matter, to be treated like "so-called 'natural' intercourse."[31] Later Batkis and other Soviet representatives spoke at conferences of the World League for Sexual Reform (WLSR), the international face of Hirschfeld's Institute for Sex Research. In the late 1920s, the WLSR became an arena in which Soviet social hygienists enjoyed the spotlight thanks to radical Bolshevik legislation on sexual matters. At the earliest league conferences, Soviet decriminalization of male homosexuality was routinely hailed. The presence of Aleksandra Kollontai, the Bolshevik Party's foremost spokesperson on sexual issues, along with Batkis and a Ukrainian professor on the organization's "international committee" of directors gave it the appearance of official Soviet support.[32] Yet Kollontai's oppositional agitation within the Party and her poorly understood and easily distorted sex radicalism gave opponents pretexts to mount attacks on her in the Soviet press for promoting "free love" and "bourgeois feminism" during 1923.[33] Kollontai had less influence on these issues in Soviet politics after that year in her new role as ambassador to Norway.[34] The impression that Soviet approval extended to the full roster of the WLSR's goals (which specifically included homosexual emancipation) must be seen in the context of an increasingly bifurcated policy on sexual politics in Communist discourse, especially in the second half of the 1920s. Internationally, it was popular and profitable

where Communists were out of power to support the sex reform movement, while inside Soviet Russia where the gains of the sexual revolution were institutionalized, rationalizing and not libertarian forces were
gathering political momentum, often with substantial popular support.[35]

Interest in and sympathy for the homosexual in early-Soviet medicine came not only as a byproduct of participation in the international
sex reform movement. Health Commissar Semashko, as a patron of
research in the emerging field of endocrinology, indirectly prompted
psychiatrists to examine the links thought to exist between hormonal
functions and mental disorders. Again, the commissar was backing ideas
that aroused intense interest among scientists in central and eastern
Europe and which had the potential to make medicine "Soviet" if important breakthroughs could establish a contrast with tsarist medical
research.

The apparent discovery in 1918 that sex gland functions determined
sexual orientation was part of a wider body of endocrinological study
by Austrian biologist Eugen Steinach. His prewar and postwar research
on animals had contributed to a revolution in the understanding of
the sex glands; with publicity and encouragement from Hirschfeld,
Steinach turned to the question of altering human sexual behavior by
controlling glandular secretions. In 1918, Steinach and the surgeon
Robert Lichtenstern completed a successful partial transplant of a "normal" (heterosexual) human testicle to a male homosexual, who reportedly then lost his effeminate mannerisms, enjoyed sexual relations with
a female prostitute, and later married.[36] Hirschfeld seized upon these
results as the most compelling basis for his "biomedical construction
of a new homosexual identity" and publicized them widely in the early
1920s.[37] Russians were aware of Steinach's experiments, especially because of his related work on animal and human rejuvenation therapy
(omolozhenie). The supposedly rejuvenating surgical procedure, fashionable in Europe and the USSR during the 1920s, received wide publicity in the Soviet press. To Bolshevik visionaries, rejuvenation seemed
to promise mastery over the mysterious processes of life itself, and many
hundreds of such operations were carried out on animals and (mostly
male) humans in NEP Russia.[38]

Against this backdrop of sex reform politics, interdisciplinary approaches to female prostitution, and endocrinological advance, a comparatively significant body of psychiatric studies on the question of homosexuality appeared during the 1920s in the Soviet Union. Psychiatric
studies of homosexuals had the potential to differentiate the Soviet

psychiatric discipline radically from its tsarist antecedent, which had been so reluctant to medicalize the homosexual. In clinical and forensic psychiatric studies of modest numbers of "homosexuals," psychiatrists gathered data and speculated, sometimes with great polemical force, about the etiology of same-sex desire. Most agreed that social and biological factors combined to produce the anomaly, but there were sharp disagreements about the appropriate emphasis to be placed on biological causes. A temporal coincidence had conferred revolutionary élan on endocrinological discoveries, endowing glandular research with a residual political glamor. If the question of the etiology of homosexuality could lead psychiatrists and biologists to new discoveries about hormonal functions, it would contribute prestige as well as new knowledge to Soviet medicine.

The first and most confident statement of the endocrinological hypothesis for the origin of homosexuality was made by the laboratory assistant who accompanied academician Bekhterev to examine the men arrested in the January 1921 Petrograd "pederasts' club" raid. V. P. Protopopov disagreed publicly with his teacher and used the issue of homosexuality to stake out his own scientific territory, not without success. At the police station that evening Bekhterev had dictated notes of interviews with at least seven men to a Doctor Mishutskii, who "for some reason" subsequently refused to hand them over.[39] Protopopov meanwhile conducted extensive interviews with forty men detained by police. He not only wrote up ten of the most interesting case histories from his sample but also used the material as a springboard to survey the current state of medical thinking on homosexuality. Protopopov concluded that his material supported Steinach's endocrinological hypothesis as proposed in 1918; the gland-centered etiology was diametrically opposed to Bekhterev's nurturist viewpoint.[40] Protopopov was made director of the Faculty of Psychiatry at Khar'kov State University in 1923, and five years later he supervised an experiment based on the Steinach hypothesis, an attempt at sex-gland implants conducted by psychiatrist Ia. I. Kirov.[41] The procedure, adapting techniques of rejuvenation therapy as applied to women, was undertaken to reverse the sex drive of a determined "female homosexual" (*gomoseksualistka*). Sheep and pig ovary sections were implanted under the right breast of twenty-eight-year-old patient "Efrosiniia B.," who was said to have consented to the operation.[42] It proved a dismal failure, and neither Protopopov nor his student Kirov revisited homosexuality as a research topic.

Early supporters of the hormonal theory for the origins of same-sex desire were also found among the first cohort of Soviet-era psychiatrists trained during the civil war by P. B. Gannushkin, the profession's leader in Moscow.[43] After qualifying, Mark Ia. Sereiskii specialized in mental disturbances produced by endocrinological processes, publishing a monograph on the subject in 1925 and later a general psychiatric textbook with another Gannushkin associate, M. O. Gurevich.[44] Unsurprisingly, given his research interests, Sereiskii was the most committed of Soviet psychiatrists to the theory that homosexuality constituted a hormonal anomaly. During the cultural revolution (in circumstances discussed in chapter 6), his assertion of the theory would attract wide attention.

Evgenii K. Krasnushkin had also been encouraged by Gannushkin to examine endocrinological factors in mental illness. During the civil war he assumed forensic and penal psychiatric responsibilities, and in the 1920s he specialized in the assessment and rehabilitation of criminals with mental disorders at the V. P. Serbskii Forensic Psychiatric Institute, the Moscow Bureau for Study of the Personality of the Criminal and Criminality, and the city's labor reformatory for minors, Mostruddom.[45] It was in a forensic capacity that Krasnushkin studied sexual and gender dissent. In his 1926 joint article with N. G. Kholzakova on "female murderer-homosexuals," the two psychiatrists had proposed a constitutional etiology for homosexual desire originating in the sex glands, with secondary significance attached to environmental factors.[46] They relied on an interpretation of Hirschfeld's complex modeling of "intersexuality," a modeling that predated the Steinach testicular transplant breakthrough. The two Russian doctors appear to have been heavily influenced by Hirschfeld's Die Transvestiten. In this groundbreaking 1910 work on cross-dressing, the German sexologist had elaborated a theory of sexual "intermediaries" to classify all forms of gender and sexual nonconformity between the extremes of an innate and heterosexual masculinity and femininity. Krasnushkin and Kholzakova confusingly designated all "intermediaries" as "transvestites" and referred to "homosexuals" and "bisexuals" as subcategories.[47] Their reading ignored Hirschfeld's clear distinction between crossdressing and same-sex eros. It also paved the way for later disputes in Soviet medicine about the "transvestite" as citizen and patient.

Krasnushkin and Kholzakova's two subjects had murdered their female partners, in one case from jealousy when the lover had announced her intention to marry a man, and in the other instance from apparent sexual provocation. The criminality of the "female homosexuals" under review did not prevent the two psychiatrists from introducing the topic in terms that reflected the influence of emancipationist arguments for tolerance of the harmless or gifted homosexual. Unenlightened "popular" (*khodiachee*) opinion of sexual intermediary types as "unnatural" (*protivoestestvennye*) ignored a growing body of scientific evidence that found these types to be widespread. Anthropologists demonstrated the existence of same-sex desire and gender intermediacy across boundaries of "civilization," class, and culture. Hirschfeld, the foremost authority on intermediaries, was hailed as "the most prominent expert of modern sexology." Finally, Krasnushkin and Kholzakova argued that homosexuals were not always linked to crime or illness. "Both male and female homosexuality are frequently combined with high aesthetic giftedness," they observed. "A classical example of this combination is the Greek poetess (*poetessa*) Sappho; the name of the island of 'Lesbos,' where she so successfully cultivated love between women, to this day gives the name "lesbian" to this love."[48] Elsewhere Krasnushkin asserted that persons "suffering from sexual perversions" were few in number and had little harmful effect on society: "as long as they do not harm the rights and physical well-being of others, their perversions in and of themselves" should not be punished. The "genuine sexual revolution" included Soviet understanding on this point, in contrast to Western European law, which treated perversions harshly.[49] These arguments for a medical and historicizing approach to same-sex love resembled those used by some tsarist-era apologists, and by Hirschfeld's Scientific-Humanitarian Committee, the German campaigning organization for homosexual emancipation.

A similar biological emphasis, drawing on Hirschfeld, was evident in the work of forensic expert N. P. Brukhanskii of Moscow's Institute of Neuropsychiatric Prophylaxis. In a 1927 monograph on "sexual psychopathology," he described a number of cases of female and male "homosexuality" that arose in the capital's provincial court. In these cases of murder or attempted murder motivated by jealousy, Brukhanskii had served as an expert witness, authenticating for the court the psychology of same-sex desire expressed in defendants' and victims' letters. Not infrequently, the cases ended in the hospitalization of defendants rather than imprisonment (in the international context, a progressive outcome). He supported the decriminalization of sodomy, while professing doubts about all scientific theories for homosexuality given the current state of knowledge.[50] In his forensic psychiatric textbook published in 1928, he gave more explicit indications of the theories he favored, suggesting that "authentic homosexuality" was the result of constitutional factors (citing Hirschfeld), while acknowledging that culture could force individuals into same-sex relations against "their nature."[51]

In Leningrad, where clinicians explored blood testing as a means of identifying "sexual anomalies," similar sentiments were evident. While one pair of researchers claimed that "homosexuality must be viewed as a particular biological imperfection," they rejected any quick presumption that homosexuals were thus psychologically impaired. Presenting the "confession" of twenty-three-year-old "Sergei E." neuropathologist N. F. Orlov asserted that the "moral level" of this subject "was no lower than that of the majority of healthy, normal heterosexual men."[52] Yet these assertions were clouded with ambiguity, for Sergei E. had in his own words sought psychiatric help to "be reborn, to become different, to become like everybody else." He wanted "to start a family" and believed same-sex love was too unstable a basis upon which "to build a life." Orlov posited that the roots of homosexuality were the likely result of "profound biochemical phenomena" and not merely hormonal anomaly; in his view, "the activity of all the cells of the organism" was implicated. His sympathetic presentation of four cases of male homosexuality (explored in a clinical, not penal, setting)[53] suggests that, as in Hirschfeld's work, Soviet medical practice could wed a humane approach to the individual who experienced same-sex desire with a biomedical understanding of homosexuality.

In June 1926, in his capacity as a sexologist, Hirschfeld visited the Soviet Union sponsored by Semashko's Health Commissariat. Hirschfeld returned from the USSR apparently disappointed with Bolshevik prudery, remarking that scientific interest in homosexuality was in decline and that homosexual behavior was regarded as "unproletarian" in the new socialist state. The German activist-physician realized that no open, organized group of homosexuals existed in the new Russia and that Soviet journalism and literature were silent about the question. Hirschfeld was uncharacteristically laconic about this journey and only published a brief newspaper article describing it.[54] It is not known if he encountered any of the Soviet psychiatrists mentioned here for his influence on their work.[55] (He made a poor impression on Mikhail Kuzmin, who along with Nikolai Kliuev attended a "deadly dull" meeting with the sexologist on 8 June 1926.)[56] Yet Hirschfeld's influence on Soviet views of the sex and gender dissident, however modest, had nevertheless been powerful, and it was far from exhausted in 1926.

Biosocial Perspectives on Homosexuality

While hormonal etiologies for sexual anomaly attracted attention for their novelty and promise, many Soviet psychiatrists promoted explanations that acknowledged a role for biology, but emphasized the social environment in which sexualities developed. Biosocial understandings of social anomalies (such as criminality, suicide, prostitution, and drug addiction) were the dominant paradigm shared by experts in many Soviet disciplines in the 1920s. Like-minded psychiatrists tended to invoke the flexible and dynamic concept of psychopathy when discussing the sex or gender dissident. The psychopathic model for this type of patient gained ground in the late 1920s, and is discussed in chapter 6. Earlier in the decade, groups of psychiatrists put forward alternative biosocial explanations for sexual anomalies, and these challenged the highly biological Steinach-Hirschfeld hormonal model. In their privileging of the influence of environment (or nurture), Bekhterev's reflexology and psychoanalysis as interpreted in Russia also had a potential political appeal to Marxist sponsors.

The theory that sexual attraction was a complex reflex had been expounded by Bekhterev well before 1917, and his sober promotion of "sexual health" and of scientific sex education apparently accorded with the rationalizing sexual politics of the Communist Party leadership. His success after October 1917 was based, however, on the vigorous range of his psychiatric activities and on his political credentials. He embraced the Bolshevik regime and energetically participated in institution building while remaining outside the Party. Bekhterev's principal tsarist base for research and therapy, the Petrograd Psychoneurological Institute, became in the 1920s the nucleus for a Psychoneurological Academy, grouping fifteen research facilities under his presidency, including the Institute for the Study of the Brain and Mental Activity (established in 1918).[57]

Little in Bekhterev's etiology for homosexuality and other "sexual deviations and perversions" changed after 1917, but in 1922 he published an extensive survey of the clinical material he had collected over more than two decades.[58] (This article would be the longest single work on sexual anomalies to be published in Soviet Russia until 1974.[59]) In his survey, Bekhterev interpreted recent claims about glandular influences on sexuality to underpin his environmental theory of perversion. Noting that the sex drive "was facilitated by development of the sex glands and their hormones," Bekhterev argued that the hormonal system in humans was subordinate to the mediation of "socio-cultural conditions" (such as modesty taboos, literature, and courtship practices), which ordered sexuality. "Inversion" (same-sex attraction) resulted from the habit of mutual masturbation between boys or girls, "when the inclination to normal sexual intercourse is weakened or absent" or from the influence of deliberate sexual stimuli, especially during puberty.[60] Taking pains to explain Sigmund Freud's theories of the emergence of sexual anomalies, Bekhterev nevertheless argued robustly against the Viennese psychoanalyst's eroticization of "parts of the body not intended for sexual attraction" and the imprecision of psychoanalytic categories of sexual pathology and health. Bekhterev confidently stated that nature "intends" sex to end in procreation, and he evaluated patients experiencing same-sex attraction according to whether they could easily ignore this urge and engage in "natural" (procreative) sex. The "inversion" of desire felt by those who could still have natural relations he set aside as a sexual "deviation" (*uklonenie*), admittedly an "unnatural" one. Those, however, whose inverted desire "had taken root" (*vkorenilos'*), were "pathological" (*patologicheskie*). The Petrograd psychiatrist in effect divided homosexual patients into those who might be persuaded from their deviation by psychotherapy, and those whose pathology suggested a pessimistic prognosis.[61]

Until Bekhterev's death in 1927, his authority in the Soviet Union on the scientific basis of sexual development was considerable, but with the breakup of his institutional networks after his death, the reflexological viewpoint lost its most vocal advocate.[62] A perspective on sexuality that attracted more modest attention from psychiatrists in the Soviet Union was offered by psychoanalysis. While enthusiasm for Sigmund Freud's theories among a new generation of psychiatrists marked the last years of tsarist rule, little about homosexuality found its way into the Russian psychoanalytic movement's journal, *Psikhoterapiia* (*Psychotherapy*).[63] Freudian explanations of · homosexuality were infrequently rehearsed in Soviet Russian psychiatric literature, notwithstanding the widespread receptivity to Freud's psychotherapeutic practices in the early 1920s. In the later 1920s, officially sponsored attacks on "Freudianism" (*freidizm*) as a worldview as well as a psychotherapeutic technique mounted. Psychoanalysis fell under proscription until the 1970s.[64]

Freud's work was translated into Russian and published in NEP Russia, and his theories circulated widely among the reading public. His influence on early-Soviet pedagogy and cultural criticism was significant.[65] Yet psychiatric writing on "homosexuality" in this period does not reflect the appeal of psychoanalysis. One reason why few psychoanalytic interpretations of same-sex perversion appeared in Russia is that while Freud's work was well known, few institutionally powerful psychiatrists actively sought to work with and develop his concepts. There were structural and ideological reasons for this. To the tsarist psychiatric profession struggling for recognition and resources, minor psychiatry (*malaia psikhiatriia*, the treatment of neuroses and everyday life problems)[66] had been a significantly lower priority than in affluent Germany or France. Both Bekhterev and Gannushkin opposed the Freudian view, the former from his biological and reflexological approach, while the latter, from his training under Emil Kraepelin, an opponent of psychoanalysis.[67] Two students of Gannushkin, Krasnushkin and Lev Rozenshtein, exhibited interest in Freud before the revolution. Yet there is no trace of this influence on Krasnushkin's later work about sexuality. Rozenstein's activities as director of the Institute of Neuropsychiatric Prophylaxis in Moscow were said by Wilhelm Reich in 1929 to be influenced by Freud, but the Soviet doctor said little about sex or psychoanalysis in print.[68] Rozenshtein's views are difficult to recon struct. He undoubtedly continued in the 1920s to be interested in sexuality and its place in mental hygiene. He devoted precious time during a research trip to Berlin in the mid-1920s to visiting Hirschfeld and the psychiatrist Arthur Kronfeld at the Institute for Sex Research. Yet he came home disappointed that Kronfeld held a position no more important than psychotherapeutic counselor in the institute, "an institution of the commercial type with a fine-sounding (*gromkoe*) name."[69] The Institute of Neuropsychiatric Prophylaxis apparently continued to conduct counseling and sex education work during the late 1920s.[70] Rozenshtein's sanguine view of female sex and gender dissent, reported in 1933 by a U.S. observer, was frankly emancipationist but lacked any hint of the psychoanalytic approach. As a clinical psychiatrist, he apparently believed it was appropriate to assist patients in accepting same-sex desire and finding suitable and productive social roles. He invited "Lesbians, militiawomen and Red Armyists" in uniform to come and give their life histories to his students, while claiming that "women [in Soviet Russia] may legally take men's names and live as men."[71] (Whether in fact such bureaucratic procedures existed is examined in chapter 6.) Perhaps Rozenshtein was speaking in the discourse of the sexual revolution as cultivated for the foreign left. Yet by the time of this conversation, in 1932 or 1933, events were shaping a new and far harsher discourse around the "individual misfit." Psychiatrists would be left without guidance once the new discourse criminalized the male homosexual and made the position of "women [who] take men's names and live as men" untenable.

Isolated case histories of same-sex relations from practitioners in Russia's regions displayed enthusiastic applications of psychoanalytic concepts and are indicative of the remarkable penetration of Freudian theories beyond Moscow.[72] The most explicitly Freudian analysis of a "homosexual" emerged from the Bureau of Criminal Anthropology in Saratov. Bureau psychiatrist A. P. Shtess's 1925 case history is a psychoanalytic profile of a "female homosexual," unparalleled in Soviet psychiatric literature, with its creative application of the Oedipal complex, penis envy, and castration fear to interpretations of the patient's psyche. Suggestion therapy, Freud's technique of free association, and seventeen hypnosis sessions gradually secured the patient's cooperation and her supposed rehabilitation. Shtess, like U.S. psychoanalysts in a later era, used the techniques of Freudian analysis to "cure" homosexuality, which he believed "serves as a barrier to the development of a [healthy] outlook, and lowers the social worth of the human personality." He also combined psychoanalysis with hypnosis, a blending much explored in Russia but condemned by Freud, who also rejected the dogmatic and hostile pathologization of homosexuality.[73]

Gender and the Soviet Homosexual

Studies of same-sex desire in early Soviet Russia seldom voiced concern about the "social worth" of the individual homosexual as explicitly as did Dr. Shtess in Saratov. Psychiatrists in this period frequently presented homosexual "patients" with little comment on their life prospects, effectively inviting a professional audience to supply its own readings of extraordinary anamneses. Yet in the selection of cases for consideration, doctors were already signaling the types of deviations they found socially troubling and perhaps those they felt would interest their institutional sponsors. Frequently, in the study of sexual anomaly, gender was a key factor they pursued. Implicitly, in studies focusing on the gender-transgressive "homosexual," psychiatrists sought to erect boundaries between anomalous and "normal" gender identities. Their studies, and the silences in them, suggested much about their readings of appropriate femininity and masculinity in the new socialist state and about their aspirations for the problem of "homosexuality" in their discipline.

If tsarist psychiatry had been reluctant to explore female homosexuality, early-Soviet psychiatrists were relatively eager to study this virtually uncharted phenomenon. Almost all of their texts discussing "female homosexuality" were the result of encounters with women who violated conventional gender norms.[74] Soviet psychiatrists of the 1920s recorded with considerable consistency the "mannish" (*muzhepodobnyi*) character of their principal subjects. Such gender nonconformity was found to have begun early in childhood. Women's case histories of homosexuality paid at least as much attention to girlhood gender transgression as to early sexuality, in contrast to case histories of male homosexuals that privileged the *sexual* development of boys and downplayed their effeminacy. V. P. Osipov described how a female soldier, who sought his assistance with her sexual deviance, had "loved the company of the boys she grew up among in childhood, and often wore their clothing."[75] Another woman who had served in the civil war as a commander told N. I. Skliar in 1924 that she had played with boys as a child and loved "climbing trees, playing Cossacks, war games." She did not begin wearing men's clothing until her military service, when she "began to go by a masculine name" and refer to herself using masculine grammatical forms.[76] Forensic psychiatrists likewise found elements of masculinization in the histories of childhood they obtained from their patients. Valentina P., who murdered her lover Ol'ga Shch., said that she "began to wear men's clothing in childhood . . . I loved men's clothing." Valentina had applied to join the Red Army while a young teenager but her older, more feminine lover had prevented it. Ol'ga's brother said that Valentina "had trouble in school because she was always chasing after girls, writing them notes"; at home she would refuse to wear her skirt and put on trousers instead.[77] Similar accounts appeared in the work of Krasnushkin and Kholzakova who also reported on Valentina P. and another "female homosexual-murderer" in 1926 and in Edel'shtein's 1927 study of Evgeniia Fedorovna M.[78]

Psychiatrists were fascinated by individuals like Evgeniia who publicly transformed their gender identities, taking male names, changing their passports, adopting masculine occupations, gestures, and habits. Cases of women's gender identity transformation aroused the interest of (overwhelmingly male) psychiatrists whether they promoted hormonal or biosocial etiologies for sexual anomaly.[79] Their curiosity about the phenomenon, for which science had no conclusive explanations, implicitly reflected the anxiety about appropriate gender roles for women, which was widespread in NEP society.

Much ambivalence accompanied descriptions of "masculinized female homosexuals." On the one hand, these individuals enacted public roles that accorded with generally accepted notions of revolutionary equality. Three of the passing women in this psychiatric literature had served in military formations as commanders or soldiers during and after the civil war, conducting political education work, and in one case, later managing a clinic.[80] These were women with education and talent whose service to the revolutionary state was impossible to gainsay.

Likewise, two anonymous "female homosexuals" described as masculine in their appearance and temperament by sexologist I. G. Gel'man in his 1923 survey of the sex lives of Moscow's Sverdlov University students were from worker and peasant backgrounds; in their potential they embodied Soviet goals for women's education and promotion in the public sphere.[81] Even "female homosexuals" whose criminality brought them into view displayed a perverse competence in a masculine world, apparently appropriating the gender equality promised by the revolution, while subverting its economic values.[82]

In the 1920s, some forensic doctors viewed the rise in Russian women's suicide after the revolution as an unfortunate index of progress, a measure of the rise in women's assumption of public duties and burdens.[83] While psychiatrists did not express similar notions explicitly, their interest in the "masculinized female homosexual" perhaps suggested that they saw in her another potential index of the stresses of emancipation. As People's Commissar of Health Semashko had indicated in 1924, vulgarized "equality of the sexes" led some women in urban life to crop their hair, drink, smoke and swear, and stride about in "half-trousers."[84] Along the way, these "masculinized" women had ignored the "feminine constitution, designed for the functions of childbirth," which he said they possessed. Women who rejected a "natural" femininity, the destiny Semashko argued had been ordained by their biology, had in his scheme exceeded the limits of emancipated Soviet womanhood. The pathology of the "masculinized" woman evidently lay in the hint that she might reject maternity. Psychiatrists studying the "female homosexual" seldom made this connection an explicit justification for their research, yet it implicitly underpinned their interest in the gender-transgressive woman.

While masculinization and its problematic relation to revolutionary values appeared to fuel psychiatric interest in the female homosexual, early-Soviet doctors who encountered men who had sex together said rather little by comparison about male effeminacy (*zhenopodobnost'*). Of the prerevolutionary psychiatric authorities on sexual perversion, only Veniamin Tarnovskii expressed thinly disguised contempt for boys and men of Russia's elite who failed to internalize the values of courage, controlled emotions, and devotion to duty. According to his classification of "pederasts," the most effeminate were deemed to have a congenital disorder. Effeminacy was observed in some pederasts from early in childhood and was a symptom of degeneration.[85] Tsarist psychiatrists after Tarnovskii avoided descriptions of unmanly behavior and expressed far less interest in gender role patterns in their perverse subjects. This lack of attention to effeminacy was a symptom of psychiatrists' reluctance to pathologize same-sex relations wholeheartedly.[86] Bekhterev's prerevolutionary, upper-class men were described with sparing reference to their gestures or forms of dress.[87] It was actually in popular-scientific, literary, and journalistic depictions of male same-sex relations published after 1905 that images of the decadent, effeminate homosexual began to appear with any frequency in Russian discourse.

Revolution briefly revived psychiatric interest in the male effeminacy—homosexuality link. Osipov recycled Tarnovskii's accounts of the soft pederast, now rechristened the "homosexual," for a new generation of psychiatrists in his 1923 textbook on mental illness.[88] Bekhterev's and Protopopov's articles about the 1921 raid on the Petrograd "pederasts' club" described transvestite parties and male parodies of heterosexual relations, a world of transgressive behavior in gesture and language depicted with an ethnographer's eye. This world of the "women-haters' ball" was also reflected in Moscow forensic psychiatrist V. A. Belousov's 1927 case of the "male prostitute" known as "P."[89] The momentary revival of interest in the gender-transgressive male homosexual stemmed from concerns about public order. Most of the relevant case histories emerged from police initiatives to control private gatherings (the "pederasts' club") or economic crime (the "male prostitute"). Psychiatric expertise was apparently sought by authorities in these cases to confirm the dangers of "mental infection" if suggestible individuals associated with homosexuals.[90] Occasionally, forensic psychiatric expertise exculpated the homosexual by desexualizing him or by claiming to have cured him, and in such texts effeminacy was minimized or ignored.[91]

Far more consistent were the rigid roles with which Russians viewed sexual activity between men, assigning holistic identities according to positions supposedly adopted in anal intercourse ("passive" and "active pederasts"). The passive/active binarism could be expressed in explicitly gendered terms from the earliest moments of Russian reception of medical discourses of homosexuality.[92] Case histories of males, when describing sexual postures, employed phrases such as "D. offered himself as a woman,"[93] and "he generally prefers to be in the woman's position."[94] The Russian language possesses a vivid means of shaping this gendered perception in the verbs "to use" (*upotrebliat'*, *ispol'zovat'*), to describe the insertive, "man's" role in sex acts.[95] The division of pederasts into active and passive types, reinforced in the reception of Casper and Tardieu, resonated in Russia with the deep cultural divide

between men and women and the mechanistic understanding of lust
as a masculine drive to which women submitted passively.[96] Where
other forms of sexual relations were described, they could be recast
within this binarism.[97] The official language of criminal dossiers and
the recorded speech of sodomy-trial defendants in the 1930s–1940s reflected the enduring presence of this vision of gender and sexual relations in Russian society.[98]

Psychiatric attempts to link male passivity with congenital homosexuality, and an active sexual posture, to acquired forms, appeared frequently. Doctors sought to distinguish cases caused by neuropathy, hormonal imbalance, or degenerate constitution, from supposedly less
authentic, acquired forms of homosexuality.[99] The link was tightest in
writing on the 1921 "pederasts' club," in which Bekhterev to a limited
extent, and Protopopov more radically, insisted that "pederasts" who
also had relations with women were exclusively "active" users of the
male anus "as *ultimum refugium*." Protopopov went further, adding
that such men were not true or "congenital homosexuals" at all. Both
psychiatrists disassociated the medically interesting "homosexual" (as
opposed to the morally corrupt "pederast") from the practice of anal
intercourse, seeking to exculpate the homosexual by distancing him
from the most reviled of sexual acts.[100]

Men and women who conformed to gender role expectations
("manly" men, "feminine" women) but engaged in same-sex practices, were seldom regarded by psychiatrists as genuinely "sick." Doctors often asserted that removal from the influence of the gender-
transgressive "homosexual" partner or a course of suggestion therapy
or hypnosis was all that was needed to restore this "normal" individual
to health. In their medical histories of homosexuality, psychiatrists discussed gender-conforming women differently from men. Their attitudes toward these potentially recoverable individuals anticipated later
differences between the approaches to same-sex love taken by authorities in law and medicine.

In psychiatric case histories of the 1920s, partners of the "mannish"
female homosexual were often represented as "normal" (heterosexual),
and their femininity was taken as read. Feminine partners appeared
fleetingly in the cases, often indulging the masculinized principals, then
rejecting them for marriage to males.[101] Feminine partners in this literature also conformed to gender expectations by exposing themselves
to psychological and physical abuse from their masculinized partners.[102]
Ol'ga Ivanovna Shch., a librarian and teacher, murdered by Valentina
P., was described by Krasnushkin and Kholzakova (who did not meet

her alive) as "a woman with a soft, kind, generous character, a feminine (*zhenstvennaia*), subtle, refined figure, of slight height, with a sweet face." [103] The fascination with the mannish female homosexual was accompanied by the implicit denial of the possibility of a feminine "genuine" homosexual as partner. Psychiatrists suggested that the womanly partners of masculinized female homosexuals were actually normal women who had only temporarily come under the influence of a scheming and forceful homosexual personality. The resolution of the feminine woman's problem was implicit in her "passive" role in these case histories and scarcely needed to be spelled out. Sexual relations with a man, and preferably marriage, would close this unfortunate chapter in her life.

The manly, uneffeminate man who engaged in same-sex love was also felt to be less pathological, but his rehabilitation could seldom be left to a "natural" resumption of heterosexuality. Often enough, these subjects had once been or still were married. Tarnovskii had invented the category of the congenital "periodic pederast" to describe how such men might live peacefully in the family bosom between sex romps with bathhouse youths or male street prostitutes.[104] In his landmark 1922 article on sexual perversions, Bekhterev's portraits of homosexuals included many masculine males. Men and boys in single-sex environments were at risk of acquiring homosexual tastes, he argued, illustrating the point by relating how one individual could corrupt an entire *artel'* of lumberjacks or how a man still capable of relations with women could, through mutual masturbation, develop a taste for rough lower-class men.[105] Both before and after 1917, Bekhterev's prescription for rehabilitation was confidently interventionist: courses of hypnosis and sessions of talk therapy were often undertaken, with doubts about effectiveness only expressed in the case of effeminate males.[106] In 1927, Belorussian psychiatrist A. K. Lents described how he had cured or lessened homosexual desire with hypnosis. Two patients had been inclined to the insertive role and were not effeminate, but another homosexual spoke in a "effeminate" tone, and Lents judged him less susceptible to hypnotherapy.[107]

The masculine male who had sex with other males was in the eyes of Russian psychiatry less authentically pathological because of his "active" sexual role and the positive prognosis this suggested. Yet these men, unlike their female counterparts, could not be trusted to resume heterosexual relations without therapeutic intervention. "Normal" masculinity was more fragile and socially determined than the "feminine constitution, designed for the functions of childbirth" imagined by Semashko. Therefore, normal masculinity had to be reconstructed through hypnosis or persuasion. Effeminate homosexual men, however, posed a more profound psychiatric dilemma: how to redirect sexual desire from a passive to an active posture, and how to resocialize the unmanly male who preferred such acts? Psychiatrists appear to have avoided discussing these questions after the interest displayed in the early 1920s, and reports of effeminacy in males dropped dramatically by the end of the decade.[108]

Conclusion

Some early-Soviet psychiatrists, following developments in European sexology and endocrinology, examined the question of homosexuality, apparently hoping that important discoveries might enhance their discipline's links to key revolutionary values. The silence in the penal code on same-sex relations offered new opportunities for medicine in an area formerly dominated by police approaches. A vanguard role in the international sex reform movement, and friendly ties with Hirschfeld, its leading sexologist, were cultivated by the Health Commissariat. By conducting research in sexual anomalies, psychiatrists could potentially attract patronage for work that would distinguish them from tsarist predecessors and raise their prestige within and outside the Soviet Union in the quintessentially modern discipline of sexology. Hirschfeld's promotion of a hormonal etiology for sexual intermediaries also afforded a potential avenue for psychiatrists to contribute to revolutionary ambitions to master nature. By incorporating and attempting to replicate the Steinach breakthroughs in identifying the source of sexual anomalies, psychiatrists could enhance their association with the pioneering work of endocrinologists.

Despite the promise of these initiatives, their contradictory political potential rendered problematic the question of a biological basis for homosexuality. Methodological limitations highlighted this dilemma. For psychiatrists reliant on anamnesis, finding sufficient material to make a case for problematizing same-sex relations was a formidable hurdle.[109] It was not that there were no "homosexuals" to study—one Leningrad psychiatrist, extrapolating from Hirschfeld's attempt at demographic analysis, said that two to three million probably lived in Soviet Russia.[110] A more significant obstacle was the epistemological threshold, the point at which dozens of scattered case histories constituted a critical mass pointing to a recognized social entity. No psychiatrists of the 1920s managed to assemble studies of large numbers of "homosexuals." After the articles produced by Protopopov and Bekhterev in the aftermath of the 1921 "pederasts' club" raid, only a handful of psychiatrists published *comparative* multiple case histories of homosexuality, and these were not quantitative studies of large samples but anecdotal reviews of a few patients.[111] There was no Russian version of Hirschfeld's Institute for Sex Research, which studied sexual variety and educated the public, nor of the U.S. Committee for the Study of Sex Variants, formed to conduct a systematic mass study.[112] Soviet social hygienists in their sexological research confined themselves to surveys of relations *between* the sexes; the only deviance they added to this agenda was female prostitution. Studies of homosexuals that did appear in Soviet medical literature were usually based on modest clinical samples or on individuals processed through a penal psychiatric facility. Psychiatrists in revolutionary Russia tended to encounter the homosexual fortuitously rather than actively seeking him or her out.

As a result of this reactive posture, these psychiatrists eschewed the methodologies of quantification that other disciplines embraced in the 1920s to make "Soviet" their studies of the socially anomalous. Questionnaires, structured surveys, and gathering of statistics were among the ways in which social hygienists and forensic doctors studied forms of social anomaly such as female prostitution and suicide.[113] These tools connected the individual case to the social body and dramatized the problem for researchers asserting claims for their disciplines inside the Health Commissariat, as well as for Party activists and political agitators who took interest in the political issues flowing from these claims. Demonstrating the significance of the object of research depended, in part, on being able to count its prevalence in society and to situate it (by markers of class, gender, education, and so on) within the social body. As the individual case history became part of a larger whole, the research topic acquired a firmer claim to political relevance, and doctors could present themselves as "physician-sociologists" (*vrachi-sotsiologi*), diagnosticians of society.[114]

Material difficulties also arose for psychiatrists who asserted a primarily hormonal origin for same-sex desire and gender nonconformity. A constant problem in Soviet biological experimentation was the short supply of healthy tissues, both animal and human, for research work of every kind. An attempt to replicate the Steinach transplant and cure a male "homosexual" in 1923, conducted by leading biologist M. M. Zavadovskii of Second Moscow State University, proved unsuccessful.

While skeptical of the procedure, Zavadovskii nevertheless noted that failure could also be ascribed to the lack of appropriate tissues for transplant.[115] In 1928, Kirov in Khar'kov similarly complained that "we were unable to obtain a necessary high-quality ovary satisfying all the present requirements" in his implant experiment on Efrosiniia B.[116] As in Western European nations, the directions taken by researchers of the sex hormones in the Soviet Union were often determined by the materials most readily available to gather and manipulate.[117] Human testicular and ovarian tissue supplies were difficult enough to obtain in peacetime, and the Soviet Union's geographic position and economic limitations constricted access to gorilla or monkey glands.

Ultimately, unlike rejuvenation therapy, which appeared to work at least temporarily, the Steinach-Lichtenstern gland transplants to alter sexual orientation produced no material results. Numerous attempts to replicate the Austrians' breakthrough were made in the early 1920s in Central and Eastern Europe. By the mid-1920s, biologists in the region were generally convinced that the techniques were ineffective, and the few reversals of sexual appetite observed were solely the products of doctors' influence on suggestible patients. Hirschfeld, a physician not a biologist, continued to hope for an endocrinological etiology of sexual intermediaries, because a congenital basis for same-sex love had underpinned the logic of his brand of emancipationism.[118] In the late 1920s, some Soviet psychiatrists would also continue to anticipate the day when biologists would reveal the hidden mechanisms of sexual orientation in the sex-gland system. Yet in NEP Russia, material obstacles to sex-gland transplantation and the failures of transplants undertaken made it clear that the existing procedure was a fruitless drain on scarce resources.

Embedded in the transfer of the question of sex and gender dissent from the law to medicine were a number of dilemmas that made doctors cautious. Without explicit political signals, how were doctors to know what medical involvement was intended to achieve? Were doctors meant, through the techniques of "minor psychiatry," to assist the individual who embodied sexual anomaly to accept her- or himself as fully capable citizens of the new society? Were doctors supposed to be curing "individual misfits"? Or were they supposed to be unlocking the secrets of sexual anomaly in order to create "a life that will not produce misfits"? Unlike other social anomalies, homosexuality's political significance was far from clear. Suicides were unambiguously regarded as losses to the new society, and while female prostitution evoked contradictory responses from police, social workers, and medical practitioners, they nonetheless could agree that the phenomenon was undesirable. In the 1920s, as Bolsheviks surveyed the social landscape and considered ways of transforming it according to Marxist aspirations, sex and gender dissent evoked a variety of responses that were dependent on their context. Doctors assessed their position astutely when they remained cautious about medicalizing all forms of sexual anomaly.

6

"An Infinite Quantity of Intermediate Sexes"

THE TRANSVESTITE AND THE CULTURAL REVOLUTION

In NEP Russia, doctors were the chief creators of a new discourse around homosexuality and other forms of sex and gender dissent, but they were not alone in their encounters with these individuals. While it appears that police reluctantly ceded jurisdiction over homosexuals to psychiatrists after the 1922 RSFSR criminal code was published, significant departures from this division of labor existed simultaneously. These exceptions to the presumption that it was the job of medicine to speak about the "homosexual" or the "transvestite" demonstrated the limits set by Soviet authority on medical models of sexual and gender anomaly.

Bolshevik campaigners engaged in battles with certain "backward" (*otstalye*) elements of the Soviet Union's population had no doubts that this emerging medical model was irrelevant to the forms of same-sex relations they encountered. An examination of their confrontations with Christian clergy and with the sexual customs of "primitive" peoples of the south and east of the Soviet Union reveals the consistent application of a view of sexual deviance supposedly created by social conditions. As they pried open the secret world of the monastery or sought to "modernize" the cultural practices of Islamic and Caucasian peoples, campaigning Bolsheviks developed a politics of sexual difference that was strikingly at odds with "advanced" European psychiatric and endocrinological hypotheses. Bolshevik enthusiasts in the antireligious movement and Russian Bolsheviks devising legislation for the new peripheral republics of the Soviet Union approached the regulation of same-sex offenses as remnants of the old ways of life (*staryi byt*) that they were determined to eradicate. In doing so they produced a counter-discourse to the medicalizing and libertarian voices heard from certain psychiatrists and jurists in the RSFSR.

The cultural revolution, which accompanied the first Five Year Plan (1928–32), did not leave the problem of gender and sexual dissent untouched. It generated a debate, traceable in various episodes, about the viability of the "transvestite" (a category that stood for all varieties of the "intermediate sex") in the new society. This debate reflected both the influence of Bolshevik campaigners' experience in combating remnants of old ways of life and the passions of medical men considering the scientific problem of sexual anomaly. As in other technical fields, the medical approach to the question displayed a utopian phase (during 1929 and 1930), when psychiatrists restated their optimism about the promises of both sexual emancipation and endocrinological discoveries. This medical claim to custody of a particular socially anomalous identity came into conflict with tougher strategies for dealing with "deviant" behaviors and ways of life. The discursive space within which anomalies like the "homosexual" or "transvestite" could exist unmolested in the Soviet Union of the first Five Year Plan began to shrink.

The Refusal of the Medical

The decriminalization of sodomy in the 1922 RSFSR criminal code had suggested to the Health Commissariat and some scientists and jurists that homosexuality would be a medical and not a police matter. There were, nevertheless, forms of (usually male) same-sex relations that particular groups of Bolshevik activists refused to regard as medical problems. They rejected claims of congenital origins for same-sex love and denied that historical evidence of same-sex love in other cultures demonstrated its universality. Activists argued that certain "depraved" remnants of the old regime (among Russian Orthodox clergy) or "primitive" nationalities within the Soviet Union (southern and eastern ethnic groups) were prone to display socially produced forms of "sexual perversion." With a consistency not always apparent elsewhere in the handling of gender and sexual dissent, Bolsheviks pursued campaigns and policies to eliminate class elements or social patterns that they perceived as formative of "perversions." These initiatives put clear limitations on the biomedical claim to knowledge about sex and gender dissent, depriving technocratic expertise of an unfettered, leading role. They also produced political discourses about anomalous sexualities that ran counter to the Health Commissariat's excursions into the international politics of sex reform and implied limits to libertarian readings of revolutionary legislation on sexual crime.

In the early Soviet era, militant atheist campaigners, based during the civil war in the Commissariat of Justice and later in the Party's Agitation and Propaganda Department, were engaged in a struggle to discredit the moral and political authority of the Russian Orthodox Church.[1] Sexual misdemeanors committed by clergy and monks became a powerful if minor theme in antireligious activities and publicity. Building on the experience of the 1919 Bishop Palladii case, atheist journalists and prosecutors pursued exposés of ecclesiastical life, replete with excesses of appetites for food and sexual gratification.[2] Procedural standards in trials of Orthodox churchmen on sex charges (as in Palladii's case) took second place to the production of public demonstrations to impress "a population not liberated from religious prejudices."[3] Trials of clerics for sexual improprieties usually dealt with heterosexual relations, and if between consenting adults, could expose a tension between the regime's declarations of sexual autonomy between citizens, and the same regime's determination to undermine the moral authority of the Church. Some element of coercion or abuse of minors normally had to be unveiled to give such cases a legal basis, but moral "hypocrisy" and counterrevolution were the underlying crimes prosecutors believed they were pursuing.[4] Since clergy, monks, and nuns were members of social groups formally deprived of electoral rights and full citizenship in Soviet law (until the Stalin Constitution of 1936) the legal bases for these prosecutions could be elastic.[5]

The Bolshevik atheists' analysis of the culture of "monastic depravity" rejected suggestions that sexual deviance had a biological etiology or that "homosexual monks" could be victims of a mental illness. In Vologda, during the 1922 trial of one Father Vasilii for sex with male novices, his superior Archbishop Aleksandr organized a sophisticated defense. A local doctor was found to give the court an expert opinion,

> that the guilty monk was a sick man with a perverted sexual psyche, that this illness was widespread not only in ancient Greece and Rome, but also in modern foreign states, and that since the boy-victims were not subjected to any bodily harm, these acts were not particularly blameworthy.[6]

The court ignored these opinions based on medical and historical appeals, sentencing Vasilii to the maximum five years' imprisonment, while Aleksandr and another cleric each received one year in prison for concealing the crime. The Justice Commissariat report of this case, and the prosecutor in court, insisted on the inadmissibility of medical "mercy and sympathy for the monks in the docks." The author of the account of the trial rejected the defense doctor's opinion that homosexuality was an illness of sexuality, and that "sodomy was one of the most prevalent illnesses in human history." "And the prosecutor was correct," the reporter wrote,

> when . . . having described the conditions and circumstances of monastic life, he proved that this life, which is supposed by outsiders to be an example of zeal, asceticism, morality, and cleanliness, in reality is one of wholesale deceit and hypocrisy . . . and that the cause of sexual feeling in perverted forms originates in the conditions of this life, in the evasion of censure for, or accusations of, the violation of monastic vows.[7]

Later reports in the atheist press suppressed any mention of the details of clerical defense strategies that appealed to medical models of sexual deviance.[8] Indeed, in contrast to the failure of the Justice Commissariat's attempt to convict Palladii on the basis of medical evidence from the Institute of the Defective Child, atheist campaigners later in the 1920s were successful in obtaining medical expertise to support their environmentalist arguments. Criminologist L. G. Orshanskii gave such testimony in a 1927 Leningrad show trial of child-abusing clerics.[9] To have accepted a medical basis for homosexuality, "pederasty," or other forms of sexual disorder (as evidence of "sexual psychopathy," or hormone malfunction), would have been to undermine the militant antireligious credo that class and environment spawned such phenomena.

Bolshevik atheist campaigners, in the pages of their publications, projected confidence about their ability to conduct successful anticlerical sex scandal trials, which attracted great popular interest. Accounts of legal proceedings in this discourse claimed that "open" (*otkrytye*) or "show" (*pokazatel'nye*) trials were eagerly attended by large audiences, said to be composed of religious "believers."[10] Spectators supposedly listened with "loathing" or "incomprehension" to descriptions of male same-sex acts. Popular disgust with these revelations was said to lead the "believing masses . . . [to] recoil from the church" and make a clean break with religion.[11] Atheists constructed a discourse of popular loathing for the abuse of boys by adult males, linking it to the moral purity of the audiences who heard these trials. The innocence of courtroom audiences was clearly ascribed to their class origins, with healthy proletarians knowing nothing of these outrages. At Father Vasilii's 1922 trial in Vologda, the represented innocence of peasant and worker spectators was violated by the defense's medical and historical justifications of homosexuality:

> There's no point talking about foreigners or the prevalence of this illness among certain layers of society. You had to see the incomprehension written on the faces of the witnesses [i.e., Vasilii's accusers] when they were told of this phenomenon. You had to grasp the effort with which the witnesses attempted to comprehend, digest, and believe in the possibility of those acts, in order to say that among the mass of peasants and workers this illness has not only not become widespread, but is totally alien and incomprehensible.[12]

In a report on the 1927 show trial in Leningrad's Okhta House of Enlightenment of the deacon Khranovskii and two subdeacons for sex acts with children, the worker-audience's "natural" decency threatened the accused with a taste of mob justice, which had to be restrained by rational authority. During the reading of the indictment, giving the ages of the boys and one girl cited as victims,

> the gleam in the eyes of the workers gathered in the House of Enlightenment for the trial of the *batiushki* [fathers], and the muffled whispers of "scoundrels," "bastards" [*negodiai, merzavtsy*], and the fact that the accused were under increased police protection all became clear.[13]

The young age of Khranovskii's victims and the "gleam" of purity in his accusers assured that he got the maximum five-year sentence, to be followed by an exceptional two years' banishment from both Leningrad and Moscow.[14]

Atheist journalists invoked a similar discourse of popular revulsion and class-based innocence or evil to divide the faithful from clerical leaders when adult same-sex relations were on trial. The formal legality of these relations in Soviet Russia was ignored. In the 1927 trial of deacon Tkachenko in Vladikavkaz, two days were spent dwelling on the colorful facts of his career as a "passive pederast" with fellow clerics, despite the formal charge he faced, of having negligently spread venereal disease. Tkachenko was "already corrupted to the marrow in monasteries" and now "wallowed in a swamp of depravity, allowing himself to sink to the very bottom of this stinking mire" by engaging in sodomy. His class origins determined both his "pederasty" and his diseased state: he had been infected with syphilis during a liaison with a White Army officer while fighting the Reds in the civil war. Tkachenko's partners in "pederasty" were also benighted by religious conviction. They included a member of his parish council and an adherent to the flagellant *khlysty* sect. "The believing masses present at the trial listened with a feeling of loathing to the testimony about what their 'spiritual shepherds' had committed."[15]

Whether Bolsheviks mined existing seams of popular hatred for adult "pederasts" (as opposed to abusers of children) is difficult to gauge from these brief newspaper accounts. Yet clues to sentiment inside the Party can be gleaned from a brief dispute in 1923 over the Sodom episode in the Bible and its political significance for militant atheists.[16] In an essay entitled "Sodom's Sinners and Sodom's Righteous Men," the editor of *Bezbozhnik* Emelian M. Iaroslavskii proposed (while acknowledging the evils of clerical "depravity in the form of sodomy") that the Church's traditional reading of the Sodom tale imposed "the morality of remote Biblical times" on today's "workers."[17] The interest of the inhabitants of Sodom in "pederasty" was explicable in historical, ethnographic, and sociological terms. The first Sodomites had "the mores that we encounter among many peoples of the East; pederasty, that is, copulation with a man, was widespread in Greece, Rome, everywhere in Christian monasteries where monks swore vows of chastity" in regard to women, "yet they cohabited with monks and novices." Not shrinking from accusing Russian Orthodox clergy of the "seduction of boys" and of widespread official indulgence of such practices, Iaroslavskii nevertheless implied that the religious prohibition of sodomy was misguided and obsolete. He emphasized that the part of the Sodom story that "priests always ignore" in their moralizing was the conclusion, in which, following Sodom's destruction, Lot's daughters conspire to make their father drunk and then conceive sons by him in order to repopulate "their tribe." Iaroslavskii's attempt to draw attention to the Church's condoning of this case of incest, which he likened to "snokhachestvo" (in Russian peasant families, the sexual abuse of young wives by their fathers-in-law), evoked a visceral reaction. One P. Masliankovskii, a Moscow party activist, attacked Iaroslavskii in a private letter for his supposedly mistaken reading of the crucial passage about the Sodomites' demands "to know" (*poznat'*) the two angels Lot harbored in his house. "Not to know the meaning of *poznat'* and the crimes and sins of the Sodomites" who "insisted on raping only men" was deplorable.[18] Iaroslavskii replied in the pages of the atheist movement's journal:

It turns out that Biblical sinners are pederasts and righteous men commit incest. P. Masliankovskii is indignant with pederasts but is not bothered by incest. This he calls impartiality, objectivity. Amazing! Surely in certain eras in certain classes cohabitation with men was quite legal, open, and recognized? Especially in monasteries it was, and is practiced even today.[19]

Iaroslavskii had no intention of defending "pederasts," but he had attempted to situate "Sodom's righteous men" in their historical context, to expose the irrational moral universe of what he called "the Jewish Bible" and its irrelevance to proletarians in the contemporary era. Yet just the sort of activist he had hoped to enlighten balked at Iaroslavskii's historicizing view of "pederasty." This party member was not alone. In a populist atheist newspaper edited by one of Iaroslavskii's rivals, a mocking retelling of the Sodom story published at this time dwelt on the "disgusting lust for buggery" (*gnusnoe muzhelozhnoe vozhdelenie*) displayed by Lot's neighbors, ignoring the refinements of ethnocultural contextualization.[20] In the antireligious movement of the 1920s, there was apparently more political ground to be gained from crude exploitation of popular revulsion for sexual difference than from careful discussion of the historical and social roots of same-sex desire.

In the rare but potent treatments of this topic during NEP in the atheist press and in the trials of clerics themselves, a language of purity and depravity was elaborated. Discourse on clerical same-sex relations united fears of corruption of minors, of sexual disease and moral defectiveness, all determined by the swamplike, stinking environment of religious communities. The discourse contrasted these deceitful swamps with the moral and political purity of ordinary spectators, workers and peasants whose faith in religion was invariably said to have been corroded by courtroom exposure of clerical depravities. Bolshevik atheist campaigners blocked Orthodox clergy from exploiting medical interpretations of homosexuality in their own defense and laid the foundations for a Soviet discourse of sexual anomaly as alien to the "normal" worker and peasant.

Certain nationalities in the Caucasus region and Central Asia were also believed to be unsuited to biomedical models of anomalous sexualities. Bolshevik activists engaged in state-building in the new Soviet republics of these regions continued, like tsarist governors, to assume that male same-sex relations were widespread there. Like Russian medical men practicing in these regions before the revolution, Bolsheviks too considered that these supposedly harmful and undesirable relations were socially generated and, therefore, susceptible to policy interventions. There was some difference between perceived sexual practices in the Caucasus and Central Asia, and these were reflected in early Bolshevik sex crime legislation that was enunciated in the individual criminal codes of the region's union republics. The regulation of sexuality in these republics was broadly based on the RSFSR penal code of 1922, but important legislative differences indicated that legal drafters perceived some societies to be less prepared for sexual modernity than others. An examination of the asymmetries of antisodomy regulation introduced in these republics suggests how Bolsheviks' perceptions of local social conditions informed their policy on the question outside the European heartland.

The Transcaucasian republics of Azerbaidzhan and Georgia (but not Armenia) had antisodomy articles in their first Soviet penal codes during the 1920s. These articles apparently prohibited consensual and aggravated forms of sodomy between adults.[21] As in the revolutionary penal codes of RSFSR, Belorussia, and Ukraine, sexual crimes in the codes of the Transcaucasian republics were enumerated in a small cluster of articles, in language that did not differ greatly from the Russian example.[22] These societies received relatively modern revolutionary regulation on sex crime, a measure of Bolshevik perceptions of the level of their economic and social development in the Soviet Union. Despite this modernity, comparatively simple prohibitions (using the word "sodomy," *muzhelozhstvo*) formed a bridge of linguistic continuity with old regime legislation. In this region, the Bolsheviks believed a sufficiently high degree of mutual male sexual activity prevailed to justify the retention of the prerevolutionary sodomy law, regardless of the modernity of the rest of their sex crime legislation. Here their perception was perhaps influenced by tsarist-era levels of enforcement of the old antisodomy statute in the region, which were disproportionately high compared with conviction rates in European Russia.

In Central Asia in the late 1920s, after longer battles to establish Soviet rule, Bolshevik legislators drafting criminal codes departed significantly from the language of modernity in their work. Activists here confronted traditions of entertainment and commercial sexuality that differed significantly from Russian amusements and from patterns of same-sex relations observed in the Caucasus. Uzbek and Turkmen young male prostitutes, *bachi*, were organized into brothels or dancing troupes by procurers who recruited boys with the collusion of parents and guardians.[23] Bolshevik legislators were determined to eradicate this form of male prostitution as one of the region's "crimes constituting survivals of primitive custom," along with bride price and polygamy.[24] Their views welded the socialist mission to rescue the (normally female) prostitute with Marxist dogma establishing historical hierarchies of civilized versus primitive societies. Just as revolutionary jurists had rejected the criminalization of female prostitutes in Russian republic, in Uzbek and Turkmen law the male prostitute himself was not banned, but virtually every other aspect of the masculine sex trade was prohibited. As with legislation against other "survivals of primitive custom," the articles in the Uzbek and Turkmen criminal codes prohibiting male prostitution eschewed the legal minimalism and medicalized language characteristic of the laws governing sex crime in "modern" parts of the Soviet Union. Instead, the codes described the social practices they sought to eradicate in almost ethnographic detail. The *bachi* and their patrons were not to be included among the various categories of "congenital" sexual deviants supposedly found in "civilized" societies. These measures were the result of a concerted effort between 1925 and 1928 on the part of jurists, Party activists, and scholarly experts on the region's nationalities to study local customs in order to design legislation to eliminate "backwardness" in family, gender, and intimate relations.[25]

The Uzbek SSR criminal code, first adopted in 1926, contained the most elaborate prohibitions against male same-sex relations of any Soviet republican code, providing eight articles against various practices (articles 276–283). These offenses were grouped with others constituting "survivals of primitive custom," in contrast to sex crimes which were located as a separate subsection among offenses against the person. Consensual and aggravated adult sodomy (named both in Russian, *muzhelozhstvo*, and Russified Uzbek, *besakalbazstvo*) were prohibited in the first two articles; a further article prohibited the act with a child or minor. Unique in Soviet legislation was this code's article 278, prohibiting the sexual harassment of men. Its language inverted the gendering of the RSFSR's pathbreaking statute against the sexual harassment of women, first adopted in the Russian republic in 1923.[26] The enactment of this extraordinary prohibition against the harassment of adult males eloquently voiced Bolshevik anxieties that Uzbek men might be recruited into prostitution. Like women in the Russian republic, Uzbek men were to be protected from advances and pressures that, it was felt, could force them into informal sexual barter or indeed prostitution. The harassment law also highlighted the application of an environmental understanding of same-sex relations in this context: suggestible but "normal" males could be influenced by "primitive" elements and forced to commit sodomy against their supposed authentic natures.

Traditional positions of authority, this time over young males, were the focus of articles 280, 281, and 282, which concentrated specifically on offenses related to *bachi.* The "maintenance of persons of the male sex (*bachi*) for sodomy, and also the preparation and education of them for this" (article 280), attracted maximum sentences of five years when the victims were adult males, and eight when they were minors. Agreements or contracts between those who maintained *bachi* and the parents or guardians who sold their sons into service as prostitutes were forbidden in article 282. The maximum sentence for parents under this offense was three years, while the individuals who maintained *bachi* ("soderzhateli," brothel owners) could receive five years' imprisonment. "Procuring and also recruitment of men for sodomy" was a separate offense, again reversing the usual gendering of this prohibition against recruitment (explicitly of women) into prostitution found elsewhere in Soviet criminal law.[27] Another provision in this body of law, which was unique among Soviet penal codes, was the prohibition of "the organization of public amusements (*bazmy*) with the participation of *bachi*" (article 281), which attracted a maximum penalty of three years. The men who kept youthful male prostitutes were regarded by Bolshevik legal drafters as class aliens, capitalists making deals with families to maintain male children and youths, "educating" their charges, and exploiting them sexually while providing public entertainment. In their first Soviet criminal code of 1927, Bolshevik jurists in the Turkmen SSR adopted similar but less elaborate language, primarily directed against those who committed offenses involving *bachi* who were minors.[28]

Some legal commentaries produced by jurists in Soviet Russia and Ukraine reflected the distinction between the biomedical approach to homosexuality in their republics and the environmental model applied elsewhere in the Soviet Union. From Moscow, P. I. Liublinskii argued that in "the East," where traditions enabled "more affluent and powerful elements to exploit the dependency of weaker" persons, homosexuality is rightly judged a "crime of daily life" (*bytovoe prestuplenie*).[29] Odessa jurist E. P. Frenkel' viewed the prohibition of sodomy in Azerbaidzhan as a means of protecting the innocent "in view of its [sodomy's] extreme prevalence." A "new culture" would replace the old ways of life as sport and education brought health to sexual relations, and assaults on young persons would become rarities ascribed to pathologies of character.[30]

The socialist determination to stop culturally produced forms of same-sex eros in non-Slavic republics underlined the fragmentation of approaches in effect: a medicalized condition of a minority in the European, "civilized" heartland became an endemic form of depravity on the non-Christian, "primitive" periphery. It was of no significance that some individuals in the peripheral republics might be "congenital homosexuals" and therefore less culpable for their sexuality. This contradiction between the Soviet Union's declared sexual vanguardism and its policies in outlying regions seemed unproblematic to jurists and Justice Commissariat bureaucrats who referred to the matter in any detail. They passed over the reasons for these distinctions with the briefest of explanations or none at all.[31] According to a 1928 letter from the RSFSR People's Commissariat of Justice replying to inquiries about the status of Soviet homosexuals made by Hirschfeld's Scientific-Humanitarian Committee, "[i]n particular republics where pederasty is especially common" it was punished.[32] The commissariat felt no need to explain its belief that the practice was common or the decision to prosecute "pederasty" outside the European republics of the Soviet Union. Such laconic treatment of the subject was apparently due at least in part to the contradictions inherent in Bolshevik views of same-sex love. Nevertheless, the language of the legislation itself, especially in the discursive gender inversions practiced by drafters of the Uzbek articles on sexual harassment and procuring, threw light on inversions of masculinity in "primitive" republics that were evidently embarrassing to the Soviet regime. It seemed preferable to wage the struggle against these aspects of the "survivals of primitive custom" without drawing excessive attention to them, since these "backward" practices contradicted the modernity of regulation in the European Soviet republics.

Utopian Medicine Imagines the "Transvestite"

Few aspects of Soviet society remained untouched by the first Five Year Plan. The transformation of the Soviet Union into a socialist economy in a single country was a Promethean venture, an attempt to achieve in a decade what Western Europe had accomplished in a century of industrial revolution. Peasant smallholdings would be consolidated into collective farms, and economies of scale in the countryside would allow mechanization and huge productivity gains. State-directed investment in industry (coal, oil, electricity, iron, and steel) would permit the expansion of a modern (in Marxist terms, industrial and urban) society, and secure the revolution with a military-industrial complex to rival those of the capitalist powers. None of these ambitious projects would be undertaken without enormous social costs, and in the case of agriculture, without a virtual civil war in the countryside. Communists set about to change Russia not solely in economic terms, but in human terms as well. A cultural revolution would transform the way individuals worked and played, thought and acted; indeed, it would seek to transform their desires.

In the earliest phase of the first Five Year Plan, utopian dreams proliferated in a political atmosphere of optimistic enthusiasm. As Sheila Fitzpatrick explains, enthusiasm was not confined to the Communist Party or to its youth wing (the Komsomol), but spilled over into the sciences and academic disciplines, where both Marxists and non-Marxists floated ideas that were "distinctly eccentric."[33] The cultural revolution "unleashed" visionaries who even put forward "previously ridiculed" schemes for the transformation of economic and social life. Government departments, under the simultaneous pressure of an antibureaucracy campaign, answered the call to abandon their usual caution and supported visionaries in architecture, engineering, and culture.[34] Public health was not immune from this moment of mobilization against established hierarchies.

A debate about the nature and value of the "transvestite" and other members of the "intermediate sex," which had been percolating in clinical and forensic psychiatric literature during the later 1920s, would advance to a new stage during the cultural revolution in discussions held within the People's Commissariat of Health. During the NEP era, psychiatric analysis of the transvestite began with the cases of "female homosexuals" examined by Moscow forensic psychiatrists E. K. Krasnushkin and N. G. Kholzakova in 1926, and their problematic interpretation of Magnus Hirschfeld's taxonomy of sexual intermediaries.[35] This study appeared in the first annual collection of articles produced by psychiatrists and other medical researchers associated with the Moscow Bureau for the Study of the Criminal Personality and Criminality. In the next edition of the bureau's yearbook, Krasnushkin and Kholzakova's reading of Hirschfeld's category of the "transvestite" was challenged in a pair of articles. While colleagues criticized their clumsy handling of "transvestism," Krasnushkin and Kholzakova's comparatively benign view of the sexually anomalous individual as victim of biology was also implicitly dismissed. These articles insisted instead that "transvestites" and "homosexuals" were environmentally produced psychopaths.

Publishing separate studies of a female "transvestite" (Evgeniia Fedorovna M.) and a "male prostitute" ("P.") in the 1927 edition of the bureau's review, A. O. Edel'shtein and V. A. Belousov undermined the sexological theories proposed by Krasnushkin and Kholzakova.[36]

Edel'shtein, citing Hirschfeld and European case histories, restated in detail the German sexologist's detachment of the impulse to cross-dress from homosexual desire. Transvestism was a discrete sexological category, which could exist independently of homosexuality. Moreover, both the transvestism and homosexuality observed in Evgeniia's case unquestionably "originated from purely mental (*psikhicheskie*) factors." Her hysteria, "pseudologicality," and sexual "perversions" were psychopathic, determined not by hormones or constitutional factors but by "the absence of correct upbringing" or, indeed, "in this case a clearly wrong upbringing, a harmful education." Belousov's assessment of the "male prostitute" P. offered the same general diagnosis of psychopathy, based on "infantilism": "hysterical traits and mechanisms, psychopathological instability, childish traits and behavior."[37] Both Edel'shtein and Belousov offered pessimistic prognoses for their patients. "Undoubtedly the social future of such an individual is very difficult," Edel'shtein observed of Evgeniia, about whose fate after his examination he said nothing.[38] Belousov was yet more pessimistic in the face of "the typical aspects of homosexual life (*gomoseksual'nyi byt*)" as led by the male prostitute:

> [P.'s] lack of any interests at all, and his association with the backward [*otstalye*] layers of society, the total submergence in the interests of his profession [prostitution] and the absence of a genuine desire for labor force us to pronounce an *unfavorable prognosis* for the future of the patient: he will remain faithful to his profession and it follows that his future "friends" will protect him like a thief.[39]

Belousov's assessment echoed both the views expressed by the Russian Health Commissariat's interdepartmental commission for the struggle against [female] prostitution, and the fears voiced in legislation against the Uzbek *bachi*. Like those charged with the fight to end prostitution among women, the psychiatrist describing P.'s "homosexual life" viewed the male prostitute as a labor deserter. At the same time, Belousov understood the social location of P.'s way of life in terms similar but not identical to those used by jurists in Central Asia. The male prostitute was an element from "backward layers of society," in this case, a minority within Russia itself, rather than in a Soviet Uzbekistan now defined as historically "backward," where "survivals of primitive custom" were universally practiced.

There was no suggestion in these correctives to Krasnushkin and Kholzakova that therapeutic intervention was undertaken to "save" such patients. Krasnushkin quickly moved toward a psychopathy-based etiology for same-sex "perversion," apparently in response to failures of the therapeutic claims for the hormonal theory. In 1927, he wrote that he had witnessed attempts to transplant animal-to-human "sex glands" in a male homosexual and also in an older male for rejuvenation purposes. The failure of these procedures had left him skeptical about the Steinach claims. A biological predisposition for homosexuality perhaps existed, but remained unproved, and there were instances in single-sex institutions (such as prisons, where Krasnushkin had devoted his practice) in which "compensatory homosexuality" arose that was not congenital. Despite these reservations, Krasnushkin continued his robust support for the noncriminalization of harmless sexual deviations. By 1929, in a published collection of his lectures on psychopathy in criminals, he had virtually abandoned any role for constitutional factors in forming the homosexual personality, adopting a nurturist position instead. He remained, however, convinced that there were "socially useful and valuable psychopaths," including among these homosexuals.[40]

Krasnushkin's volte-face on the biological causes of sexual anomaly, combined with his continued defense of the homosexual as "socially useful," was not an isolated position within the psychiatric profession. Opinions blending a range of theories and evaluations of gender and sexual dissent were heard that year in the Commissariat of Health Expert Medical Council's deliberations about "transvestites." These discussions, undertaken during the utopian phase of the cultural revolution, featured highly positive evaluations of the individual "transvestite" (including the suggestion that same-sex marriages could, "in exceptional circumstances," be recognized), as well as concerns that the "intermediate sex" could also generate problems beyond the reach of medicine. Medical experts found the question of regulating sexual and gender dissent in its totality a contradictory challenge, but nonetheless one that they were unwilling to abandon to police and courts.

Defining the problem initially provoked disagreements between a forensic gynecologist and clinical psychiatrists. In January and February 1929, subcommittees of the Expert Medical Council were called upon by Commissar of Health Semashko to assist the Justice Commissariat in formulating a response to a request from a citizen Kamenev of the Tatar ASSR for a change of sex (*peremena pola*).[41] Semashko evidently passed the brief to the commissariat's Chief Forensic Medical Expert, Ia. Leibovich, a specialist in forensic gynecology. In correspondence with the Expert Medical Council, Leibovich referred to the problem as one of "homosexuals" (*gomoseksualisty*), some of whom were "psychic hermaphrodites" (*psikhicheskie germafrodity*). For this reason, he argued they should be handled under regulations (laid down by the Commissariat of Internal Affairs in 1926) pertaining to the civil registration of hermaphrodites.[42] The presidium of the council, reviewing this recommendation, rejected Leibovich's references to hermaphroditism and defined the question as one of "the changing of sex, name, and conducting operations [to change sex]." The Expert Medical Council presidium referred to the persons in question as "transvestites."[43] The confusion of categories (sex changer, hermaphrodite, homosexual, transvestite) and the eventual choice of the term "transvestite" were consistent with existing sexological taxonomy in Europe. When confronted with persons requesting changes of biological sex in the decades before doctors devised programs of hormone and surgical treatment for "transsexuals," sexologists frequently labeled such individuals "transvestites."[44] When the full Expert Medical Council met, even more definitional slippage took place, and more forms of gender and sexual dissent were considered.

Psychiatrist L. Ia. Brusilovskii opened the 8 February 1929 council discussion of citizen Kamenev's petition with a report "about transvestites." Citing Magnus Hirschfeld's research and political activism, Brusilovskii claimed the "question of transvestites . . . in the conditions of the USSR is not particularly frequent," while in Germany the phenomenon was "extraordinarily widespread." He pointed out that Moscow psychiatrist Edel'shtein had recently published "an interesting case" from local experience—the 1927 article about "transvestism" describing Evgeniia Fedorovna M.[45] Brusilovskii then read from Evgeniia's "History of my illness," implicitly endorsing her self-definition by referring to the "confession" as Evgeniia's defense of "her intermediate sex" (*svoi srednii pol*). In his summary he called her a "*transvestistka*" (female transvestite).[46]

Biologist N. K. Kol'tsov joined the discussion, declaring, "Of course, there is no intermediate sex, but rather an infinite quantity of intermediate sexes." The phenomenon was demonstrable in the animal world, but "in humans it occurs very frequently, perhaps more often than among animals; it is acquired or intensified by imitation (*podrazhenie*) on the basis of a mental infection (*psikhicheskaia zaraza*)." He related his experience with a male patient (also from Kazan') who had pleaded for a sex change and whom he had supposedly cured with injections of a "sperm-based liquid" (*spermin-zhidkost'*).[47] Having recently visited Central Asia, Kol'tsov disagreed with Brusilovskii's suggestion that "this question" was of less significance for the Soviet Union. The biologist said concern was due "not in the RSFSR, but in such republics as Kazakhstan," where the *bachi* suffered "extraordinary economic exploitation." Here was a domestic group whose gender and sexual deviation was socially produced, not congenital, and whose supposed miserable position could be worsened if concessions were made "on a general basis" to "transvestites."[48] Kol'tsov's argument illuminated the national fault lines underlying the medical model of sexual perversion in the Soviet Union. As a biologist, Kol'tsov made generous claims for the congenital and especially hormonal model of the "intermediate sex," where an urban, apparently European patient presented himself. Yet sexual deviance seen as the result of backward social practices was to be excluded from the realm of medicine, as a problem instead for the law.

Further discussion raised the theme of the "intermediate sex" in military formations, and a clear divide in the evaluation of male and female recruits appeared.[49] Brusilovskii took up Kol'tsov's fear of contagion among males to warn that "subjects of this type, declaring that they are homosexuals, lead to the creation, due to a great mental infection [*pri bol'shoi psikhicheskoi zaraze*], of a contingent refusing military service. Numerous criminal cases of this type take place."[50] Only one psychiatrist present was aware of a routine procedure for dealing with recruits claiming unfitness on grounds of homosexuality. "If someone now were to refuse military service on this pretext," A. V. Rakhmanov pointed out, "he [*on*, that is, a male person] would first be sent to a psychiatric institution for a examination. So the question would be resolved in this direction."[51] Rakhmanov did not explicitly state that the army would automatically reject a male "homosexual," although his comments when taken with those about "mental infection" from Brusilovskii strongly suggest this policy. Rakhmanov insisted that psychiatrists should conduct lengthy evaluations of such recruits, "and without fail, in a psychiatric establishment, where there are forces sufficiently competent to decide the issue." The comparatively rare contemporary psychiatric texts about mental infirmities in the military mentioned sexual perversion only in the most oblique terms, but the metaphor of "mental infection" was influentially employed in dealing with suicide and other problems doctors and political educators encountered among soldiers and officers.[52] The Expert Medical Council was quick to agree that "mental infection" *among males* led to undesirable consequences for military recruitment.

In contrast to the anxiety expressed about male cohorts "infected" with homosexuality, Rakhmanov quickly turned to defend the presence of "masculine" women in the army, whether married to men or being unlikely to marry because of their "masculinization." These were women "who did not make claims to anything except [military] service." Rakhmanov described them as "women one encounters in military service, especially among commanders, dressed up [*pereodetye*] in men's clothing." He had personally observed two cases:

> They are women of a masculine appearance, they wear military uniforms, but one of them was at the time the wife of a man and had children, thus while being a commander of the Red Army and occupying a rather high command post, she had a family. The other woman did not have a family and was of a more masculinized type [*maskulizirovannyi tip*]. Here, obviously there was no need to apply special measures. So I think the decree we are presenting, to require expertise in every individual case, it will resolve the issue.

No one in the room ventured to disagree with Rakhmanov's views on women whose gender nonconformity rendered useful services to the state. The cross-dressing female (whatever the unvoiced implications about the sexuality of the "masculinized type" might be) supposedly occupied positions of authority within the Red Army and was therefore a figure worthy of "individual" and not standardized consideration.

A similar call for "careful" and individualized consideration greeted the information that a same-sex marriage had been approved by Soviet officials in the past and the suggestion that the council consider whether the right to such marriages be formally granted to "transvestites." Again, this indulgent view was extended solely to individuals understood to be biological women. On hearing of Evgeniia's successful fight to have her marriage to a woman recognized by the Commissariat of Justice, Kol'tsov worried that

> the wife, that is, the woman who married the other woman [meaning Evgeniia's partner, "S."], certainly suffered as a result. That woman was done serious harm, for she could hardly remain as normal [*normal'naia*] as she would have if she had been married to a man. I suggest that in such circumstances we must be extremely careful. Only in exceptional circumstances and with the concurrent testimony of experienced experts should this be permitted.[53]

The biologist was in fact proposing that same-sex marriages could take place, under specialist medical supervision. No one in the room challenged the proposition. Later in the discussion, Kol'tsov did argue that a specific law should forbid a woman dressed as a man from marrying another woman, but the minutes record no support from colleagues, and his suggestion did not figure in the final resolution prepared for Semashko. Psychiatrist Brusilovskii did point to the danger of disruption in women's bathhouses if the right to be a transvestite with some form of state sanction were recognized.[54] Yet the overwhelming balance of anxiety tipped toward male representatives of the "intermediate sex" and the "mental infection" that threatened their effectiveness as fighting men. The gathering of Russia's top neuropsychiatric specialists was virtually silent about "feminized" males, men "dressed up" as women, or same-sex marriages between male "transvestites." Femininity in men was a marker of backwardness, imagined not in the Russian homosexual but in the "unfortunate *bachi* of Turkestan," boys of "an utterly clearly defined masculine sex" who "were dressed in feminine clothes and spoiled forever" by sexual and economic exploitation.[55] Male femininity could only be imagined as foreign, backward, and tragic, while masculinization in women endowed them with competence, authority, and crucially, loyalty to the modernizing (and implicitly Russian) values of the revolution.

One last issue examined in this discussion gave voice to the utopian aspirations of the moment, which was Kamenev's request that he be transformed into a woman both surgically and bureaucratically. Leading clinical psychiatrist P. B. Gannushkin contended that he "constantly encountered" requests for changes of sex; it was an issue relevant to Russia, apparently not to be dismissed as a German problem. Currently under observation in his Moscow clinic he had a woman who wished to be transformed into a man, and he worried about the legal position of doctors attempting sex change surgery. The prospect of changing sex, like transvestism, thrust the problem of the citizen's registered sex to the fore, and Gannushkin and others present repeatedly expressed concern that doctors could not work independently on such patients. Cooperation with legal officials to enable changes to the individual's officially recorded sex (through ZAGS, an agency of the Justice Commissariat) would be required.[56] Equally worrying was the question of doctors' criminal liability in such cases. Gannushkin recounted a 1928 case he reviewed in Moscow's city health department (Moszdrav) of a medical practitioner who "changed sex and made women of men and vice versa, using rather primitive surgical operations. We found ourselves reviewing a huge quantity of case histories with one and the same patients featuring as 'Konstantin,' 'Ekaterina,' et cetera." The case never reached the courts, because Moszdrav was able to bury it: "We got out of difficulty thus: we wrote that it was a rare incidence when psychopathic patients fell into the hands of a doctor-psychopath. Whether it was the right thing to do or not, it eased the matter."[57] Gannushkin probably doubted that this resolution had in fact been "the right thing to do"; this was as near as any council member would come to a plea for ethical guidance. Yet Gannushkin's extraordinary revelations also suggested to his colleagues that changes of sex for humans were feasible or imminent, a prospect made plausible by recent developments as well as the utopianism of the cultural revolution.[58]

The question of the "intermediate sex" looked destined to acquire a definite shape as a result of these discussions. Soviet Russia's leading neuropsychiatric experts advised that "an expert opinion be established in each individual case" of "transvestism." They directed that "this entire question in all its breadth, with all possible deviations," should be reviewed by an interdepartmental commission drawn from the Commissariats of Health and Justice.[59] Like the interdepartmental commission established in 1922 under the Health Commissariat to coordinate the struggle against female prostitution, the mixed commission "on transvestites" was intended to dramatize the interdisciplinary problem of sexual anomaly. The diverse, contradictory, and complex issues raised by sex and gender dissent would be handled under the aegis of medicine and biological (and in particular, hormonal) science, in consultation with those who administered justice and the regime of identity registration. By calling for an interdepartmental commission, the Health Commissariat's Expert Medical Council signaled that medicine would consolidate its custody of the issue. Indeed, health officials looked forward to the clarification of "the right (*pravo*) of transvestites to enter into marriage with persons of the same sex and . . . the right [of doctors] to produce operations to change the sex of transvestites."[60]

This "distinctly eccentric" episode in the cultural revolution helps to explain others. By coincidence, the specific volumes in two key Soviet encyclopedias that would contain articles on "homosexuality" (*gomoseksualizm*) appeared in 1929 and 1930.[61] The articles conveyed a heady optimism about the imminence of discoveries about the biological mechanisms of sexual anomaly as well as a libertarian enthusiasm for the acceptance of the individual homosexual. The editor of the first edition of the *Great Medical Encyclopedia*, Health Commissar Semashko, commissioned psychiatrist Mark Ia. Sereiskii to write the article on homosexuality; it was an endorsement of the young psychiatrist's authority in the field of endocrinological anomalies. In this piece Sereiskii argued tenaciously for a biological and constitutional etiology of same-sex attraction, based primarily on the Steinach findings, but relying also on Hirschfeld's sexological research and support for the endocrinological hypothesis. He also poured scorn on psychopathological theories of same-sex attraction and on legislation prohibiting homosexual acts, as outdated. In 1930, Sereiskii's *Great Soviet Encyclopedia* article on the same topic linked the endocrinological hypothesis to a robust endorsement of Hirschfeld's campaign for homosexual emancipationism and for the integration of the alienated homosexual "into the new collective."[62] The limits of this medical and political argument were fixed by the editors, who appended an "ethnographic sketch" from classicist P. Preobrazhenskii on the subject of "homosexual love" among "s[o] c[alled] uncivilized peoples."[63] In the cultures of the small peoples of the Far North (among the Chuchki, Koriaki, and Kamchadal) or in Soviet "Asiatic" cultures (by which he meant Islamic cultures), the origins of homosexuality "to a significant extent bear a social character," not a biological one. The vast territory of the Soviet Union harbored examples of the two European interpretations of gender and sexual dissent, one medical and suited for "civilized" societies (where homosexuals constituted a minority), the other anthropological and appropriate to "primitive" cultures (where homosexuality was endemic).

Sereiskii's articles were the tip of an iceberg. The isolation and eccentricity of his endorsements of the hormonal hypothesis and emancipationist politics were illusions created by the policy turn to come. In the utopian enthusiasm for the transformation of society and the implementation of visionary schemes, the ideas Sereiskii proposed were far from alien to scientific leaders within the People's Commissariat of Health. Utopian visionaries there ignored the negative prognoses advanced by promoters of the psychopathological model of sexual perversion and entertained the prospect of a social blueprint, however limited by considerations of gender and culture, for the viable Soviet "transvestite."

Utopia without "Social Anomalies"

Like many a blueprint from this era, the vision of the socially viable transvestite was buried as the political atmosphere of the first Five Year Plan shifted from unbridled optimism to ruthless pragmatism. Achieving the fantastic targets announced in the plan would require a marshaling of resources into a narrow range of endeavors. Science, sponsored by the state, would be expected to contribute to these efforts, and those doing the science would come under greater political scrutiny as Marxists attacked nonparty experts across a range of disciplines. The consequences of this turn toward an increasingly coercive pragmatism for the "transvestite" or "homosexual" are often only implicit in the available evidence. Yet the campaign against "biologizing" (from the verb frequently employed in the era, *biologizirovat'*) in psychiatry and criminology and the fate of the so-called "social anomalies" during the course of the first Five Year Plans provide contexts for understanding the events of 1933–34.

The pragmatic turn in public health was signaled by a change of leadership and a shakeup in the provision of medical care. A reorganization of the Commissariat of Health was ordered by a decree of the Central Committee of the Communist Party on 13 December 1929, directing the commissariat to place more emphasis on the needs of industrial workers and collectivized farmers. The charismatic old Bolshevik Semashko, Health Commissar since 1918, was replaced for still undisclosed reasons in 1930 by Mikhail F. Vladimirskii. The new man was also an old Bolshevik and physician, but was probably regarded as a safe pair of hands for his brief: during the 1920s he had served in the RSFSR Commissariat of Internal Affairs and as a Party leader in Ukraine.[64] Audits and institutional restructuring followed, and psychiatrists did not escape change. A decree from the Workers' and Peasants' Inspectorate of 26 October 1931 noted several deficiencies in psychiatric provision, including the limited network and low quality of hospitals and staff; the inadequate use of "labor therapy"; and the inordinate number of hospitalized patients who could be supervised as outpatients. There were further directives to the commissariat to intensify the industrial applications of psychiatric medicine and the labor content of therapies, with more resources to be directed to "workers in the leading branches of industry," and the expansion of labor colonies and workshops in psychiatric institutions.[65] The emphasis on labor as therapy predated the first Five Year Plan. The degree to which research and therapies were channeled to specific "productive" sectors of the population was novel, reflecting the plan's stringent filtering of all spending priorities through the prism of class. For the modest resources invested in mental health, the best possible return (measured by labor productivity) was sought. The commissariat's Expert Medical Council disbanded subcommittees that did not reflect these priorities. No evidence exists that the interdepartmental commission on "transvestites" ever met, but a 1933 memorandum indicates the neuropsychiatric subcommittee of the council (where the plan for an interdepartmental commission originated) had by then been eliminated.[66]

Research agendas saw corresponding adjustments. Psychiatrists devoted more energy to the problems of major psychiatry (schizophrenia and disorders with known biological causes) and trained the resources devoted to minor psychiatry (neuroses and problems of life adjustment) on the urban worker in an effort to enhance output. Studies of the anomalous personality were no longer to be the result of random selection in the reception rooms of clinics but were to originate in planned agendas focusing on the needs of workers and collective farmers.[67] In Soviet psychiatric literature of the 1930s, sexual anomaly virtually disappeared as a problem worthy of attention in its own right, emerging usually as a symptom within the contexts of major mental illness, physical deformity, or the restoration of labor capacity (*trudosposobnost'*).[68] A similar decline during the first Five Year Plan in Soviet studies relating to sexuality, in some cases more precipitous, took place in social hygiene, sexual enlightenment, and eugenics.[69]

Loud attacks on "biologizing" scientists, accused of looking for the roots of social ills in individual biology, helped to hasten the abandonment of sexological studies during this period. The complaint from Bolsheviks that some scientists paid too much attention to nature and not enough to nurture in their assessments of human pathologies had a long pedigree. During the cultural revolution, however, these complaints became dogma as the campaign to open academic disciplines to scholars with Party credentials, and a simultaneous campaign attacking the political loyalty of "bourgeois specialists" (inherited from the old regime), imposed an unprecedented degree of ideological conformity on intellectual work.[70]

In this atmosphere various strands of endocrinological research were vulnerable, and one enthusiast for rejuvenation therapy now admitted it was ideologically flawed because it contradicted the laws of history.[71] The hormonal hypothesis for the origins of homosexuality was also potentially under fire, yet criticism of the high-profile Sereiskii encyclopedia articles failed to materialize. Editors perhaps believed that a critique would necessitate too much discussion of an embarrassing and increasingly taboo theme.[72] Only a single article, in a journal of experimental biology, appeared to contradict Sereiskii. In 1931, biologist M. M. Zavadovskii published the results of a bid to cure a male homosexual soldier of the Red Army. The experiment had taken place in

1924, when the soldier had come to the biologist, an expert on sex transformation in animals, seeking assistance on his homosexual feelings. Zavadovskii wrote:

> We pointed out to our patient that our modern knowledge of the mechanism of the origins of homosexual individuals was extremely insufficient, that many of our postulates were based only on conjectures, and so he could hardly seriously count on real help from medical intervention.[73]

The suicidal patient was offered first "suggestion therapy" with an unnamed psychiatrist, and when this failed, the opportunity to undergo a "biological experiment," the removal of one-eighth of a testicle and the grafting of a similar portion of testicular tissue from a rhesus monkey. The experiment produced no effect in the patient, but it enabled the biologist to study the soldier's tissues. Here the chief "deviation from the norm" was reduced sperm production combined with structural peculiarities, and Zavadovskii intuited a possible link between these phenomena and the anomalies of the patient's "instinct."[74] Despite this conjecture, he clearly felt his results disproved any simplistic endocrinological model of homosexuality. These results, similar to outcomes in central European experimental biology published in the mid-1920s, lacked much claim to currency in Zavadovskii's own discipline, and his intention in releasing them was evidently to debunk Sereiskii's highly public claims for the endocrinological hypothesis.[75]

Psychiatrists who had previously expressed skeptical but friendly interest in the hormonal model, such as Osipov and Gannushkin, were now wary of the "biologizer" accusations, and clarified their rejection of the Steinach experiments and Hirschfeld's claims for them in stronger terms.[76] They reiterated their support for the psychopathy model, underscoring psychogenous and social factors in their etiologies for sexual perversion. Leningrad's Osipov included significant new passages in his 1931 psychiatry textbook (a revision of a 1923 manual), expressing a much more negative prognosis for the "homosexual" in line with those given by Edel'shtein and Belousov. Osipov drew overt conclusions about therapy that these two Moscow psychiatrists had left implicit: physical labor, sport, and hypnosis could reclaim "ambivalent" cases, "but most homosexuals consider their perverted desire to be normal," so therapy was useless for them. He also sharpened his estimate of the low social value of the homosexual. In class terms, they were tiny number of aliens who shied away from heavy labor, preferring decoration and dress design. Paranoia drove them to "gather conspiratorially," while some even "demand[ed] support for pederasty from the state." While Soviet legislation did not punish sexual perversions as long as they did not present a social danger, "this element is far from excluded"; Osipov implied that any impression created by the legislation of a soft line on "pederasty" was mistaken.[77]

It is ironic that those who now conclusively abandoned hormonal explanations of sexual anomaly would find that the diagnosis of psychopathy was being hulled of any significance outside the clinic by the same campaign against "biologizing." At issue was the use of the psychopathic label when doctors made expert determinations on the legal responsibility (vmeniaemost') of mentally unstable persons accused of crimes. During the 1920s, psychiatrists had classed a large number of these defendants as "psychopaths," and substantial numbers of "psychopaths" were judged not legally responsible (nevmeniaemyi). These patient-defendants did not stand trial but were subject to "compulsory therapy" in psychiatric institutions.[78] Psychiatrists, using the diagnosis in specialist institutes for the study of the criminal personality and at the leading V. P. Serbskii Forensic Psychiatric Institute in Moscow, were accused of reviving the biological determinism of criminal anthropologist Cesare Lombroso. Others who had once invoked the authority of psychoanalysis were accused of "Menshevizing idealism," a reference to doctors' supposed deviation from materialist foundations (like the Bolsheviks' revolutionary rivals, the gradualist Mensheviks) toward the propositions of Freudianism.[79] By 1930, forensic psychiatrists Krasnushkin and Brukhanskii, practitioners associated with the Serbskii Institute since its establishment, had been removed to other posts following press attacks for their "biologizing" approach.[80] New personnel at the institute established their credentials by repeating these accusations well into the 1930s and by insistently protesting their tough new line on the psychopath as liable to answer for his crimes and as fit for rehabilitation through the corrective labor camp system.[81] Any juridical meaning for the diagnosis of psychopathy had been surrendered, and thus the "social future" of the "homosexual" or "transvestite," if classed as a psychopathic personality, looked even more difficult than Edel'shtein had suggested when he considered Evgeniia Fedorovna M.'s prognosis in 1927.

Another campaign of the first Five Year Plan focused on identities previously often grouped with the psychopath (the female prostitute, the homeless, the "professional" beggar, and the alcoholic) and further contributed to the narrowing of discursive space in Soviet life for the sexual or gender dissident. The targets of this campaign were those who, for the most part, formed distinct subcultures of the urban street as they eked out a living from illicit market activities. These deviant personalities were, like the criminal psychopath, to be removed from medical custody (and any suggestion that biology caused their deviance), and handed over to agencies of social intervention. The first plan explicitly enumerated "social anomalies" (*sotsanomaliki*) to be the object of rehabilitative measures, administered by the People's Commissariat of Welfare.[82] A significant proportion of the *sotsanomaliki* were female prostitutes, and among other measures the plan called for the creation of three thousand places in labor "prophylactoria." These urban institutions provided "former" prostitutes with industrial training and treatment for sexually transmitted diseases; upon release, they were placed in factory employment and expected not to revert to prostitution. For all categories of the socially anomalous, nine thousand places in labor (agricultural and workshop) dormitories were projected. In addition, there were to be ten special camps for "inveterate" (*zlostnye*) prostitutes, not mentioned in the planning documentation.[83]

The plan's approach was criticized in January 1929 by the Central Council on the Struggle against Prostitution (as the interdepartmental commission of the early NEP years was now named). The principle of compelling women prostitutes to enter institutions would drive the prostitute underground and render their reclamation, and the control of venereal diseases, much more difficult. A public conflict between these sentiments of "charity" expressed primarily within the Health Commissariat and an authoritarian use of "barracks" espoused by the Welfare Commissariat was quickly settled by government decrees, which clarified institutional roles for fulfilling the plan on the socially anomalous. Health officials lost most of their influence. The Commissariat of Welfare received overall control of the prostitute (and the Central Council devoted to her) and would operate virtually all of the projected prophylactoria and the rural labor colonies and special camps for the socially anomalous.[84] Individuals similar to the sexual and gender dissident, who had previously been subject to medical supervision, were now to be reclaimed through an authoritarian system of compulsory labor.

According to Lebina and Shkarovskii, historians of female prostitution in Leningrad, welfare officials there did not wholly abandon less coercive strategies, but during the first Five Year Plan and at the outset of the second, impatience with the continued existence of prostitutes and other "anomalies" grew. Offices of "social patronage" opened in districts of the city between 1930 and 1931, identifying (among the "anomalous") homeless women at risk of prostitution. "Patronage" meant finding these persons jobs or temporary shelter, giving legal or housing advice, and increasingly, giving them train tickets "home" (presumably to the villages, now torn apart by the brutal collectivization drive, from which they had escaped). The Commissariat of Welfare in 1931 declared its intention to use patronage centers as distribution points, from which the "socially anomalous" would be sorted into those who would cooperate with voluntary placement (in factories now desperate for labor, or in "open" workshops), and those requiring more persuasion (in the form of semiclosed workshops and "rural special regime colonies," agricultural camps meant to be self-financing). Recidivists would be handed over to the Commissariat of Internal Affairs and sent to its growing network of work sites and camps (the Gulag system). By 1931, the cities of Moscow and Leningrad each had a big "special regime" colony nearby, where professional beggars and prostitutes were sent for labor and rehabilitation, operated by the Welfare Commissariat. Boredom, illness, and squalor reigned at the Svirsk colony north of Leningrad, and the colony's male director was sacked in 1932 for drunkenness and sexual relations with his charges. Inmates were not informed of the criteria by which review panels declared individuals "rehabilitated," and many of those who were released (via Leningrad's social patronage offices) into factory employment reportedly continued to sell their bodies. Faith in patronage measures declined, and in Leningrad, the city's welfare department decided at the beginning of the second Five Year Plan to spend less on preventative aid to women at risk of prostitution and to send more women directly to the Svirsk colony. In early 1933, at a Leningrad conference on the struggle with *sotsanomaliki*, a professor studying the question declared that the colony could hardly be regarded as "cruel," since unemployment, the supposed cause of prostitution, had been eliminated. There was no longer any justification for young women to engage in antisocial behavior. In September of that year, the journal of the Welfare Commissariat sharpened the rhetoric of impatience, warning that the "old bourgeois principle of 'philanthropy and alms' hovers over these questions . . . Where is the struggle with social anomalies? Where is the political analysis of this work? Where is the class vigilance?"[85]

The struggle with social anomalies fused with a wider process of urban social cleansing conducted by both regular militia and secret police, which accelerated in late 1932 with the introduction of internal passports and accompanying city residence permits. These bureaucratic measures not only served to fix who the rightful residents of the socialist city would be, but legitimated the deportation of "former persons" (*byvshie liudi*), politically disenfranchised members of the tsarist nobility, bourgeoisie, clergy, and other "class aliens." Their status was now inscribed in their identity documents, and they could easily be denied permission to reside in the capitals or turned upon as "class enemies" when campaigns needed scapegoats.[86] The process of identifying the "socially anomalous" was greatly facilitated by "passportization," and David Shearer argues that "socially dangerous elements" identified in this way were increasingly being purged from important cities without ever seeing a court or being formally charged with a crime.[87] In Leningrad in this period, some male homosexual intellectuals associated with these stigmatized groups, were already under greater scrutiny from the secret police. [88] Those men who participated in the subculture of public sex also became more vulnerable as urban social cleansing gathered strength.

Conclusion

After the departure of the members of the village soviet [council], a second gathering of women was summoned by the [church] bell, where a protocol was decreed about the dismantling of the collective farm. At that same meeting, the women elected their own chairman and secretary of the village soviet, namely, Chairman Starodubtseva Varvara Moiseevna, a middling peasant, . . . and as secretary Starodubtseva Natal'ia Vasil'evna, the daughter of a kulak (deprived of electoral rights for conducting private trade), who, after the election got dressed up [*pereodelas'*] in men's clothes and named herself Antonenko Vasilii Vasil'evich.
—From an OGPU summary of disturbances against collectivization, led by women near the village of Butovsk, 14 March 1930[89]

Medicine's domination of the question of homosexuality in revolutionary Russia was never total. "Homosexuality" was not a single idea or phenomenon in the Bolshevik imagination as it turned to consider the regulation of same-sex relations and gender dissent during the 1920s. The issue had many readings, dependent not on a single, ideologically invariable interpretation of the "homosexual" or "transvestite," but on a range of values in the developing political canon. Class and loyalty to the revolution were paramount, and nationality within the Soviet Union could play a crucial role. The reach of medical understandings of sex and gender dissent and of the emancipatory ethos closely tied to certain medical views in revolutionary Russia was confined to urbanized, modern regions and to citizens whose loyalty was not in doubt. Beyond this context, the regime viewed anomalous sexuality and gender through political, not medical, prisms. Natal'ia Starodubtseva's extraordinary gesture of triumph over her adversaries imposing the collective farm on her village, relayed in a secret police report, illustrates these limits. Natal'ia turned the world upside down and became Vasilii. Her gendered protest (whatever its motives) could not and would not be interpreted as the "transvestism" of a woman of the "masculinized type." Natal'ia/Vasilii was a class enemy, the daughter of a rich peasant engaged in trade, and these essentialized attributes determined the policeman's lexicon for defining her rebellion. To this informer, and his intended audience, the discourse of hormonal anomaly or sexual psychopathy would have sounded utterly alien.[90]

By 1930 counter-discourses about the "homosexual" or "pederast" among particular enemies of the Bolshevik project had been elaborated, with Orthodox leaders and "backward" elements on the periphery of the Soviet Union as their primary targets. If there was a common theme in these discourses, it was the role of *byt*, everyday life or lifestyle, in shaping the relations that Communists regarded as harmful and dangerous. "Remnants of the old ways of life" in the "modern," European heartland, or "survivals of primitive custom" on its fringes in "backward" societies, equally threatened the development of socialism. The monastic "pederast" and the Uzbek procurer of *bachi* both diverted youthful male energy into undesirable grooves, leading youths from "normal" relations to perverse ones by seduction, religious instruction, or worse still in the *bacha*'s case, contractual agreement. Biologizing theories of hormonal imbalance, reflex formation, or psychopathic personality development were irrelevant in cases in which disloyalty to the revolution (from religious or economic motives) and the perverse upbringing of boys were the immediate defects of *byt* as identified by the Bolsheviks in these peculiar situations.

The gendering of this counter-discourse influenced utopian visions of the transvestite discussed in the Health Commissariat's Expert Medical Council in early 1929. Implicitly, the psychiatrists (and biologist Kol'tsov) expressed more interest in promoting the "rights" of the transvestite with medical and biological justifications, as long as she was a woman underneath her army uniform. Her prognosis could be imagined positively, since her loyalty to the state was evident in her leadership ability and since her gender nonconformity, her masculinity, brought her increased respect.[91] By contrast, they imagined the insufficiently masculine male as a victim of "mental infection" (the recruit shirking military service after contact with homosexuals) or economic exploitation fused with backwardness (the "unfortunate *bachi*" of Turkestan"). Implicitly they revealed their own dread of feminization, a word they were incapable of uttering, even as they spoke dispassion-ately of "masculinization" in the women they discussed. Underlying the council's deliberations was a sense that the male member of the "intermediate sex" was the product of nurture, of conditions of *byt* gone wrong. These were deviations that were evidently preventable (except perhaps in a small number of congenital cases). Their sense of the female "transvestite" was more deeply "biologized" and intracta-ble: no hormonal injections could apparently restore her femininity, and indeed, to doctors it appeared that society might have to adjust to the female "transvestite" by conceding same-sex marriage. This was a gendered utopianism, libertarian in the extreme toward the woman seeking to become like a man, but pathologizing men who willfully evaded or tragically lost their masculinity. At its extreme, it reached for control over the very mechanisms of gender through operations to change sex in humans, which hardly seemed far-fetched in the atmo-sphere of cultural revolution. Agents of psychiatry and biology imag-ined that they would retain primary custody of the "transvestite" who requested a change of sex, with a consultative administrative role for state officials. In this expectation, medical men displayed even greater utopianism than the dream of turning Konstantin into Ekaterina.

The Five Year Plan and the accompanying campaigns, against "biol-ogizing" in the human sciences, and for class-consciousness and party-mindedness in intellectual work took custody of various social problems away from the realm of medicine. Where the "homosexual" or "trans-vestite" would fit in this restructuring of responsibilities was not imme-diately evident, for the question had never been quantified by NEP-era "doctor-sociologists" who had measured and counted suicide, women's prostitution, or homelessness. Psychiatrists and Health Commissariat leaders in some cases did not think that there was a "pathology" of the "intermediate sex" to be counted. As a result, there was no statisti-cal discourse to reify the problem of gender and sexual dissent, no table of figures to display in the planners' calculations of the "social anoma-lies." The discursive space occupied by anecdotal patient histories of the "individual misfit" narrowed, especially as various diagnoses (hor-monal, psychopathic) lost political force. In a society with no need for sexology, still less a sexual psychopathology, there was little room for the "homosexual" or "transvestite." Osipov's 1931 description of the "homosexuals" who "gathered conspiratorially," and who, in their paranoia, erroneously sought "support for pederasty from the state," proved disastrously prescient.

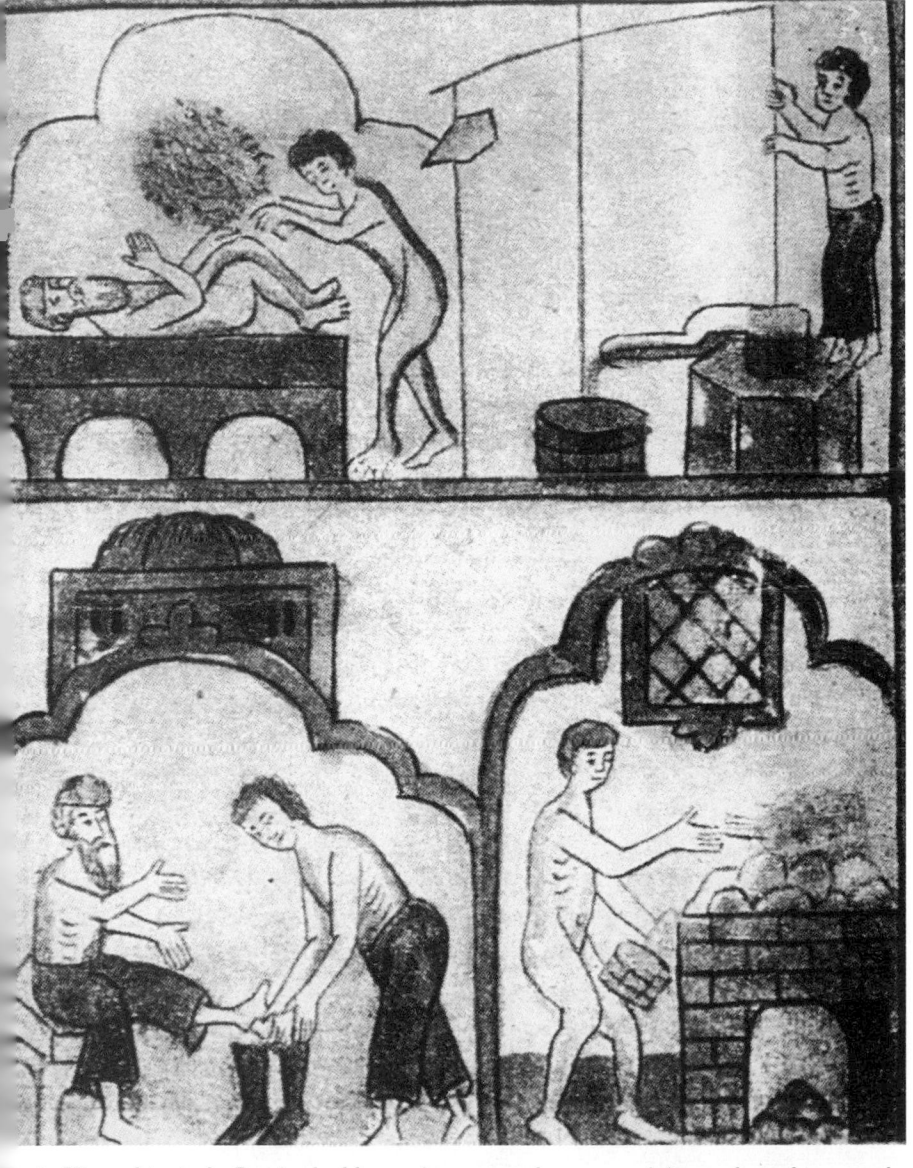

. 1. Hierarchies in the Russian bathhouse. A seventeenth-century miniature shows four smooth-ed younger men serving two mature, bearded visitors to a Moscow *bania*. Two clothed youths rform services outside the steam chamber (helping a visitor to undress [*bottom left*] and drawing ter [*top right*]) while within one youth pours water on the stove to make steam (*bottom right*) another beats an older visitor with the *venik*, a leafy switch used to raise the blood circulation *left*). Youthful attendants were a fixture of Muscovy's commercial bathhouses starting in this ., but the first evidence of sexual exchange between male customers and attendants dates from mid-nineteenth century. Gosudarstvennyi Istoricheskii Muzei, Moscow.

Fig. 2. Egorov Bathhouse, Kazachii Lane, St. Petersburg, ca. 1910. In this posed scene taken [by] the capital's most famous studio photographer, Karl K. Bulla, something of the masculine sociabil[ity] of the late Imperial *bania* can be glimpsed. In a *myl'nia* or chamber for washing, nude sen[ior] attendants soap up, scrub, and rinse off customers, while more junior attendants in traditio[nal] Russian shirts await their orders in the background. TsGAKD SPb, ed. khr. D2150.

Fig. 3. Egorov Bathhouse, Kazachii Lane, St. Petersburg, ca. 1910. Another scene staged by B[ulla,] this time with suds and energetic scrubbing in a heated antechamber leading to shower stalls. [The] walls here were decorated with an Arabic motif. TsGADK SPb, ed. khr. D133.

g. 4. Egorov Bathhouse, Kazachii Lane, St. Petersburg, ca. 1910. Interior of a cabinet for private
laxation. The luxurious appointments were intended for an exclusive and affluent clientele, who
aid five rubles in the late Imperial era for access to the establishment's hydrotherapy treatments,
airdressers, salons, and restaurants, as well as the bathing facilities including a large indoor plunge
ol. For sixty kopeks, poorer clients gained admission to an "Eastern" steam room on the same
emises. This bathhouse first opened in 1804 and was reconstructed in the 1870s and 1880s.
GAKD SPb, ed. khr. D2145.

. 5. Nevskii Prospekt, St. Petersburg, ca. 1910. The commercial heart of the Imperial Russian
ital was also the site of a clandestine sexual marketplace, where men seeking sex with each
er met for both paying and free sexual exchange. *Far right*, the infamous Passazh (Passage), a
lery of shops where the *tetki* and the men who offered them sex cruised, winter and summer.
lection of the author.

Fig. 6. The Passazh, Nev[s] Prospekt, St. Petersburg, 20[] This covered shopping gall[e] opened in 1848, became a c[on]venient spot especially in [] colder months for men seek[ing] same-sex contacts. "On S[un]days in the winter *tetki* strol[] the Passage on the top gall[e] where cadets and schoolb[oys] come in the morning; at arou[nd] six in the evening, soldiers [] apprentice boys appear." P[ho]tograph by the author.

Fig. 7. Cinizelli Circus, St. Petersburg, ca. 1914. Another place for youths seeking sexual patron[s.] Apprentice boys and "hooligans" struck up conversations with prosperous-looking men, asking[] tickets to the performances. Nearby, a public toilet was used by rent boys as a place to dis[play] themselves, and a yard for exercising dogs reportedly served as a gathering spot for "an e[xtra] band of suspicious young men." Collection of the author.

8. Prince Feliks Iusupov and his family, 1901. Feliks Iusupov senior (*right,* standing), governor-
eral of Moscow (1914–15), was one of Russia's wealthiest aristocrats. Iusupov, who also held
title of Count Sumarkov-Elston, was probably the "Count S.-E.," described as a sexual patron
he "male prostitute, P.," whose case history was published by psychiatrist V. A. Belousov in
7. Iusupov's son, also named Feliks, here fourteen years old (*far left,* seated), had a penchant
opulent cross-dressing and flirting with officers. He was one of the conspirators who murdered
gorii Rasputin in 1916. Of his father he wrote, "As he grew older, he showed signs of eccentricity
His nature was so different from my mother's that he never really understood her . . . The
on I saw so many queer and eccentric people is that they amused my father. I often admired
kindness and patience of my mother, whose house was invaded by these strange characters,
she received them all with the same good grace." F. Youssupoff, *Lost Splendours* (London:
than Cape, 1953).

Fig. 9. The First Petrograd Women's Battalion, organized by the Provisional Government, 191
A postcard depicting the military formation that was later mocked for its ineffective defense
the Provisional Government headed by Aleksandr Kerenskii during the October events that brougl
the Bolsheviks to power. Soldiering attracted a significant minority of women who sought to stret
the boundaries of femininity, including some women who sought sexual fulfillment with the
own sex. Wallwork Collection, MS 1172, Brotherton Library, Leeds University, U.K.

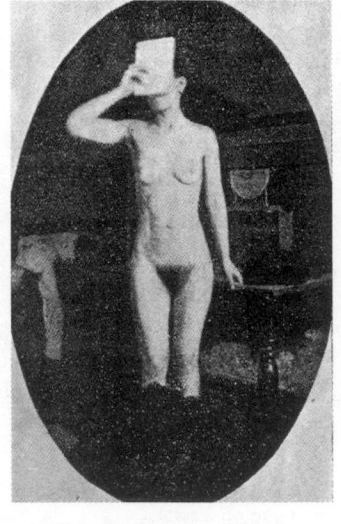

Figs. 10, 11, 12. "Female homosexual" A. P., Saratov, 1925. Arrested for economic infractions
Saratov's marketplaces, this women living as a man using the name Aleksandr Pavlovich v
diverted from prison to forensic psychiatric treatment. After a course of Freudian analysis a
seventeen hypnosis sessions (like the one "before treatment"; *far left*), Aleksandr Pavlovich ab
doned her masculine dress, stopped smoking, donned women's clothing, and expressed a desire
have a baby. The middle photograph was published to demonstrate that in this case, the pati
was not a hermaphrodite. Released to the care of relatives ("after treatment"; *far right*), "A.
now wore a skirt, a fashionable navy blouse, and more feminine footwear. From A. P. Sht
"Sluchai zhenskogo gomoseksualizma pri nalichii situs viscerum inversus, ego psikhanaliz i gipr
erapiia," *Saratovskii vestnik zdravookhraneniia* 3–4 (1925): 1–19.

Fig. 13. Advertisement for "Spermokrin," late 1920s. The European-wide fascination with endocrinology was felt in Soviet Russia, where rejuvenation therapies (including testicular grafts, ovary implants) and hormone-based preparations were explored as avenues to the transformation of humanity. This ad from the Health Commissariat's Institute of Experimental Endocrinology proclaimed that "Spermokrin is medically prescribed for neurasthenia, arteriosclerosis, feebleness in old age, thinning blood, sexual impotence." To Soviet scientists, endocrinology beckoned with its apparent potential for quick breakthroughs in research. The hypothesis that homosexuality was linked to sex hormone anomalies, first propounded in Austria by Eugen Steinach and publicized by German homosexual emancipationist and socialist Dr. Magnus Hirshchfeld, found adherents in the USSR. Attempts to manipulate sexual orientation with sex hormones, using the same grafting and implant techniques employed in hundreds of Soviet rejuvenation procedures, were undertaken in the early 1920s. As in Central Europe, these experiments failed, but the allure of the sex hormones was a formative experience for the first generation of Soviet doctors. GARF, f. A-406, op. 12, d. 2223, l. 215.

Figs. 14, 15. Examples of the *bachi* of Uzbekistan. Samarkand, 1913. Photographed by Edmun James Pearse, British representative of the Gramophone Company (resident in St. Petersburg from 1909 to 1917), during a tour of southeastern territories of the Russian Empire. On these tours Pears visited his network of distributors of gramophones and records; he also made sound recordings an took snapshots of musicians. The *bachi* (literally, "boys") were itinerant entertainers, maintaine by school masters who taught them poetry, dance and song, as well as pimping for them in the role as male prostitutes. Costumed in outfits that combined elements of feminine and masculin attire, the *bachi* performed at festive gatherings and attracted the dismayed attention of Russia officialdom. Socialists seeking to establish their authority after 1917 found the institution intoler ble for its commercial as well as sexual features, and associated it with social elements alien the revolution. Soviet Uzbekistan's successive criminal codes sought to eradicate all trace of th "survival of primitive custom." E. J. Pearse Collection, MS 1231, Brotherton Library, Leeds Unive sity, U.K.

Figs. 16, 17. *Bachi* in Samarkand, 1913. The same British commercial traveler witnessed this performance by *bachi* dancers (*above*), with an assembled crowd of Uzbek adults and a Russian official in the foreground. Below, the same two dancers at rest posed for his camera. Their very long hair and multicolored costumes are clearly visible. E. J. Pearse Collection, MS 1231, Brotherton Library, Leeds University, U.K.

Fig. 18. Soviet Moscow's cruising grounds: Nikitskie Gates Square, 1930. Until the opening of th
Moscow Metro altered male homosexual cruising patterns, the Boulevard Ring, with its gree
spaces, benches, kiosks, and public toilets, was the chief meeting place for men seeking sex wit
men in the Soviet capital. Nikitskie Gates Square was one of the most frequented hubs of th
Boulevard Ring in the subculture. Even before World War I, a bar "with an electric organ, ru
by an old *tetka*" offered dancing and conviviality in the immediate neighborhood. After the Revolu
tion, men continued to gather here for paid and unpaid sexual transactions. They congregated i
the underground toilet, located to the left behind the monument to botanist K. A. Timiriaze
according to sodomy trial records from 1930s. Some met partners there and sought privacy in th
courtyards, basements, and entry halls of tenement blocks nearby, while others had sex on th
spot. Collection of the author.

Москва. Площадь им. Свердлова   фото М. Радина ф-3533

ɟs. 19, 20. Soviet Moscow's cruising grounds—Okhotnyi Riad Metro Station, 1925 (*above*) and
erdlov Square, 1938 (*below*). The circulation of pedestrians in central Moscow was transformed
the major building projects of the first Five Year Plans, including the Moscow Metro, which
ened its first line in 1935. A key station on this line was Okhotnyi Riad, which deposited passen-
rs just steps away from Red Square and the model socialist city's newest attractions. Mezzanines
d passageways offered shelter from winter weather and opportunities for making contact. Passen-
rs from Okhotnyi Riad station emerged at surface level on Sverdlov Square, with its little trees
d benches offering a pleasant place to wait for trams and buses, to pass the time, and to meet
e-minded men. This square stood opposite the opulent Metropole Hotel (which opened in 1905;
ow) and just in front of the Bol'shoi Theater (*to the left, out of frame*). First mentioned in sodomy
ls of the late 1930s as a place where soldiers, sailors, and civilians open to sexual propositions
m other men could be found, the square became a chief hub of male homosexual street cruising
1950s and 1960s Moscow. Collection of the author.

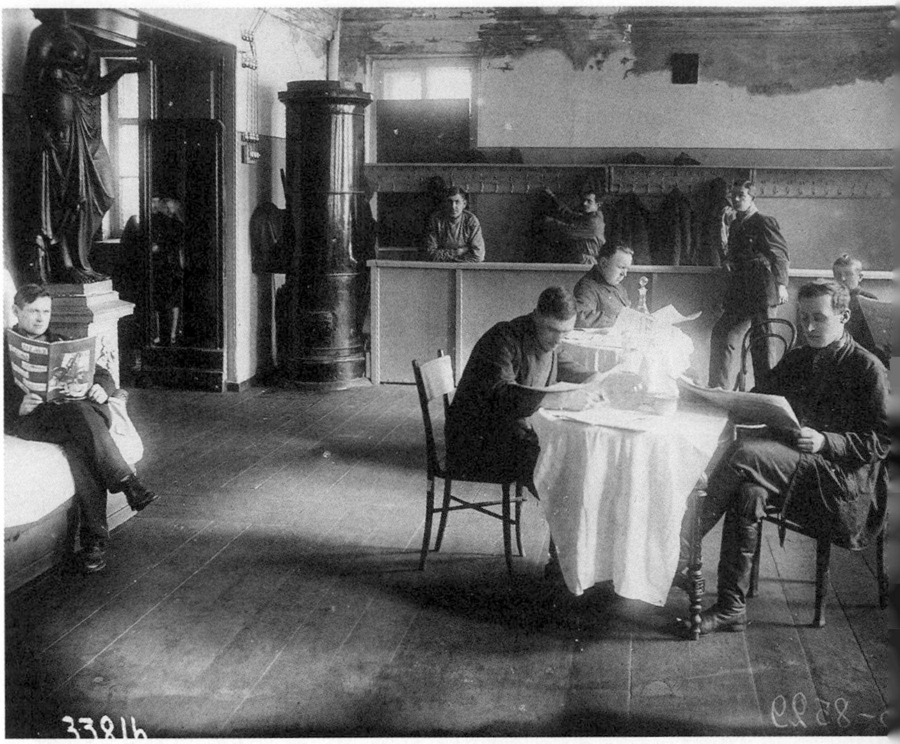

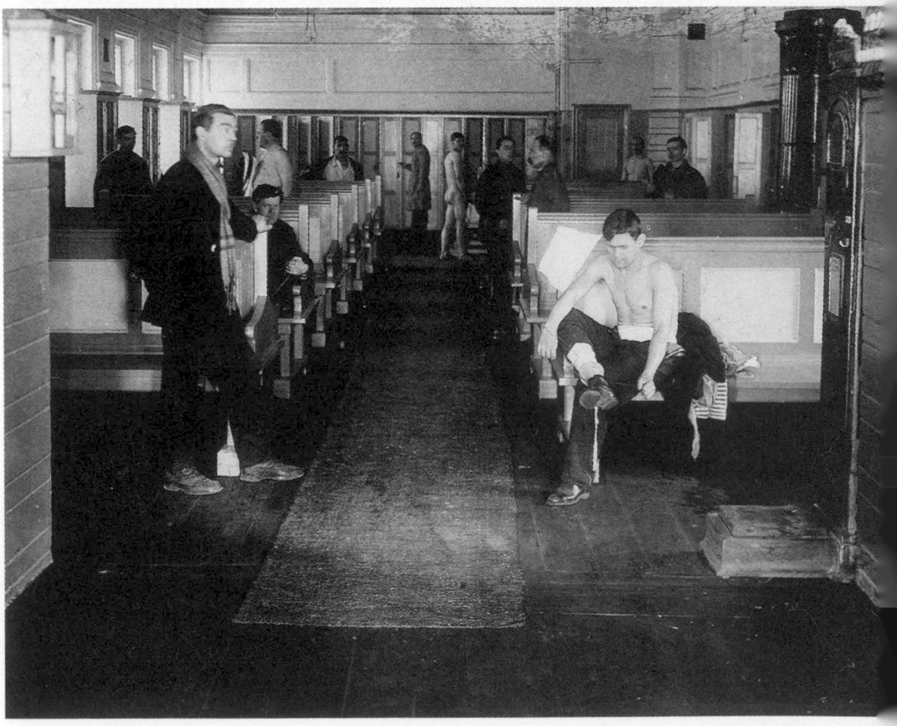

igs. 21, 22, 23. Inside the Soviet bathhouse—hygiene above suspicion. In photographs of the *ania* equally as posed as the prerevolutionary compositions of Karl Bulla, Soviet photographers ›ught to emphasize the earnest pursuit of self-improvement and hygiene in places formerly de-›ted to the elemental celebration of all bodies. In the cloakroom of a Leningrad bath (1932; *left ›p*), visitors make a show of reading newspapers and magazines, ignoring the crumbling tsarist ›cor and each other. The men's disrobing chamber of another Leningrad bathhouse (1939; *left ›ttom*) appeared to be an equally sullen and uncomradely environment. This photo too may have ›en taken in an establishment built before 1917. A Spartan chamber for washing (1932; *above*) ›mpletes the impression of businesslike solitude while surrounded by fellow bathers. These pic-ires were produced for Leningrad's Bathing and Laundry Trust. Despite the somber mood depicted ›re, men open to same-sex relations continued to meet in the baths, but the surveillance of private ›oms and the larger, communal spaces of newer bathhouse buildings made consummation far less asible, and systematic prostitution, impossible. TsGAKD SPb, ed. khr. Dr. 8528, Dr. 8526.

Fig. 24. Pathologized sexualities—the Soviet transvestite, 1957. From a textbook of forensic gyn cology, a composite photograph of "K.," first diagnosed a transvestite in Kazan' (apparently 1937). There a people's court accorded him permission "to wear women's clothing, [his] passpc was changed with the adoption of a woman's name, and he was removed from the military recru ment rolls." Moscow's forensic medical clinic confirmed these facts after a referral from city poli M. G. Serdiukov, *Sudebnaia ginekologiia i sudebnoi akusherstvo* (Moscow: Meditsina, 1957), 47—4

̄ʒs. 25, 26. Pathologized sexualities—a female homosexual and transvestite, ca. 1965. The cap-
̄n below states, "O. A., an active female homosexual. A man according to her passport (Andrei
̄ɪnovich), in which a registered marriage to a woman is recorded." Together with her wife and
̄ɪ̄e's children from a heterosexual involvement, O. A. lived as the head of what the psychiatrist
̄zaveta Derevinskaia described as her "homosexual family." The children even called her "papa."
̄ese images from Derevinskaia's doctoral thesis formed part of her study of "female homosexuals"
̄ɪducted in Karaganda, Soviet Kazakhstan, between 1955 and 1965. O. A. was one of nine "free"
̄men encountered in the local university psychiatric clinic; the remaining eighty-seven were
̄soners from a nearby women's corrective labor camp. E. M. Derevinskaia, "Materialy k klinike,
̄ogenezu, terapii zhenskogo gomoseksualizma," Kandidatskaia dissertatsiia meditsinskikh nauk,
̄̄aganda State Medical Institute, 1965. With permission of GTsNMB, Moscow.

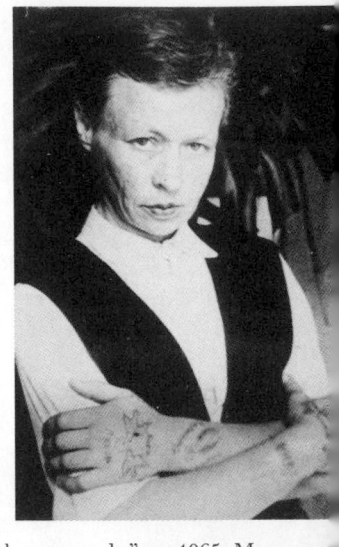

Figs. 27, 28, 29, 30, 31. Pathologized sexualities—"female homosexuals," ca. 1965. More wom
from Derevinskaia's Karaganda University study of lesbians. The trainee psychiatrist divided
subjects in "active" and "passive" homosexuals, along rigid stereotypical lines that reflected
gender expectations of consumer socialism. "Passive" female homosexuals (*top middle, bottom rig*
cooked and cleaned, enjoyed sewing outfits for themselves, wore jewelry, and if they worked, t
"feminine" jobs. Their "active" counterparts (*above right, above left*) kept their hair short, w
"masculine" clothing or sometimes passed as men, smoked, controlled the family finances,
took "men's" jobs. Derevinskaia presented pictures too of "female homosexual couples" alw
composed of one "active" and one "passive" partner. In the bottom left photograph, for exam
the "passive" woman avoids the gaze of the camera while her "active" partner smokes as she lo
directly into the lens.

7

"Can a Homosexual Be a Member of the Communist Party?"

THE MAKING OF A SOVIET COMPULSORY HETEROSEXUALITY

Despite the advances claimed for the forced-pace industrialization program of the first Five Year Plan, crises marked the years 1932 and 1933 that threatened to undo all that (from the leadership's point of view) had been accomplished. If, in material terms, the plan had laid the foundations for a huge expansion of the heavy industrial base of the nation, in social terms the results were appalling. The most disastrous effect of the drive for wholesale collectivization had been a virtual civil war in the countryside with deportations of better-off peasant families (the "liquidation of the kulaks as a class"), accompanied by the confiscation of grain for urban consumption and export. Meanwhile, party activists backed with police and legal officials forced poorer peasants, their tools and livestock into the new collective farms. The expropriation of seed grain and peasant demoralization contributed to mass famine in 1932–33 in Ukraine and southern Russia, killing three to five million people.[1] Many millions fled the village and sought refuge and employment in the rapidly expanding factories of the new industrial complexes and towns invoked by the plan. There they found that despite the new enterprises' hunger for labor, little had been done to provide for workers' needs on a scale commensurate with planned growth: housing in particular was improvised, cramped, distant from work, and unhygienic. Thousands who arrived to work in the steel mills of a plan centerpiece, the new town of Magnitogorsk, lived summer and winter in the early years of the decade in tents and mud huts. In Moscow the number of inhabitants per room rose from 2.71 in 1926 to 3.91 in 1940.[2] The flow of new arrivals in the cities "ruralized" them, bringing thousands of new residents who knew little of urban and industrial ways. Workers dissatisfied with poor housing and living standards took advantage of the labor shortage to change jobs with increasing frequency, and the result was a huge turnover of employees, and consequently of urban residents, what Moshe Lewin has dubbed a "quicksand society."[3] In social terms, the first Five Year Plan had produced rural famine, serious labor shortages, urban chaos, and decline in the health and welfare of the proletariat, in whose name the Communist Party ruled. While seeking to stabilize the food situation (with the worst of the famine peaking in winter and spring 1933–34), the leadership acted to conceal the scale of village suffering from the urban population and to weed out and repress critics. A purge (*chistka*) of the Communist Party, which during the previous four years had accepted large numbers of new worker and peasant members, was ordered in December 1932 and continued through 1933.[4] The purge, with its review of biographies and its intense scrutiny of Communists' political and intimate actions, contributed to a mentality of suspicion and a search for scapegoats. In this atmosphere, the impatience with the continued existence of urban "social anomalies," and the impulse to social cleansing in the cities increased.

In 1933, urban male homosexuals would fall within the larger net of these trends. In the case of this group, international developments also significantly contributed to justifications for the decision to recriminalize sodomy. The legal measure, first proposed in September 1933 by the deputy chief of the secret police (OGPU), G. G. Iagoda, was preceded by the rupture in German-Soviet relations occasioned by Hitler's coming to power and the intensification of a virulent propaganda war in Europe between Fascism and Communism. Accusations of homosexuality (hurled as an insult to the masculine honor of the opposition) had already become a significant new feature of this political discourse. This international homophobic rhetoric significantly elevated a modern antihomosexual discourse to the diplomatic arena for the first time in the 1930s.[5] Its crucible had been Weimar Germany. There, politicians inheriting the legacy of the Eulenberg scandal in the Wilhelmine era confronted the visibility of a national homosexual emancipation movement, an interest group that successfully established the voices of "homosexuals" as citizens in Weimar political culture.[6] Until Hitler's accession, the German Communist Party (KPD) generally supported Magnus Hirschfeld's campaign for the abolition of paragraph 175 in the German criminal code that prohibited male homosexual relations.[7] Weimar Communists had argued, with perhaps more faith in historical progress than comprehension of sexual dissent, that decriminalization would be the logical consequence of removing all "reactionary" legislation on sex. The Social Democratic Party (SPD) also supported these goals but had failed to do so with the consistency of the KPD. In 1931 and1932, lurid reports in the social democratic press about the homosexuality of the Nazi *Sturmabteilung* (SA) leader Ernst Röhm generated a morals scandal. The KPD's Richard Linsert criticized SPD disclosures about Röhm's personal life as "sexual denunciation"; yet in April 1932 the KPD joined in the irresistible attacks on the SA chief, while continuing to support the abolition of paragraph 175.[8] The ideological purity displayed by Linsert was less sustainable once the stakes became more desperate, and the left was erased from the German political landscape in 1933.

When ex-Communist Marinus van der Lubbe was arrested after the Berlin Reichstag fire on the night of 29 February 1933, Nazis seized on his political ties to blame international Communism for the attack. In response, the Communist International exploited the fact of van der Lubbe's homosexuality in a resonant campaign to disassociate him from the left. A widely distributed book by a collective of exiled German Communists accused van der Lubbe of being in the pay of the Nazi Party and under the sexual and moral influence of SA leader Röhm.[9] Homosexuals were branded as violent, unreliable, and morally degenerate in this tract and in the war of words within the left, and between left and right, that it generated.[10] The central European nationalist and later Fascist institution of *Männerbund* (associations for young men's physical and moral education) came under increasingly scaring attacks from the left as fountainheads of homosexuality and other moral impurities.[11] Meanwhile, the Nazis linked Magnus Hirschfeld's leftist politics and his Jewish faith to his long campaign to abolish the German statute prohibiting male same-sex relations. The closure of Germany's homosexual publications, organizations, and bars in February and March 1933 and the ritualized destruction of Hirschfeld's Institute for Sex Research (6 May 1933) gave expression to Nazi moral outrage. A "battle for the birthrate" with military objectives firmly in view would determine the new regime's outlook on sexuality.[12]

By contrast to Hitler's loud and crude antihomosexual campaigning of the 1920s and early 1930s, the proscription of male homosexuality throughout the USSR in 1933–34 was imposed without public discussion. The orchestrated press campaigns which accompanied other new measures (on juvenile crime in 1935, or on abortion in 1936) were not an aspect of the adoption of the sodomy law. As with decriminalization in the first RSFSR criminal codes, historians have been forced to speculate on the reasons for the change, and a small number of texts and clues have been sifted repeatedly for what they can yield. In addition, little has been said in this historiography about the decision not to prohibit lesbian relations. With fresh evidence on the legislative process and on the administrative and medical consequences of the adoption of the antisodomy law, new light can be shed on the reasons for the change and on the way experts and citizens greeted it. Significant gaps in our knowledge still exist. Without further access to archival materials, particularly ordinary and secret police archives and the Presidential archives,[13] the political motives for the recriminalization of sodomy remain speculative. Nevertheless, it is possible from the new sources to construct a clearer picture of the development and reception of this legislation and of the silence on women who loved women that accompanied it.

"Destroy the homosexuals—Fascism will disappear"

According to documents from the Archive of the President of the Russian Federation (APRF) published in 1993, after the decriminalization of sodomy by Boris Yeltsin in April of that year, the immediate initiative for the enactment of the antisodomy law in 1933 came from the political police.[14] OGPU deputy chief G. G. Iagoda wrote to Iosif Stalin on 15 September 1933 to argue for the need for legislation against "pederasty" as a matter of state security. Iagoda reported that raids had recently been conducted on Moscow and Leningrad "organizations of pederasts" and that 130 persons had been arrested. Iagoda wrote that they were guilty of

> establishing networks of salons, centers, dens, groups, and other organized formations of pederasts, with the eventual transformation of these organizations into outright espionage cells . . . Pederast activists, using the castelike exclusivity of pederastic circles for plainly counterrevolutionary aims, had politically demoralized various social layers of young men, including young workers, and even attempted to penetrate the army and navy.

Stalin forwarded Iagoda's letter to Politburo colleague L. Kaganovich, noting that "these scoundrels must receive exemplary punishment, and a corresponding guiding decree must be introduced in our legislation."[15]

Iagoda sent Stalin the text of a draft law on 13 December 1933, with a covering letter outlining the OGPU's arguments in favor of the measure.[16] Iagoda did not mention spying by the homosexuals who had been arrested earlier that year; instead, he noted that the OGPU had established that organized groups of "pederasts" had operated "salons" for "orgies," engaging in the "recruitment and corruption of totally healthy young people, Red Army soldiers, sailors, and individual students." The OGPU's attention, at least in this letter, appeared after three months to have shifted to the potential security danger that closed groups presented and the threat to "healthy young people" drawn into them. Iagoda's interest was concentrated on male rather than female sociability (which he did not mention). At no point in the subsequent development of this legislation was the question of female homosexuality explicitly raised. This does not mean that women's same-sex love continued to be held in the positive regard characteristic of some circles in the 1920s. The factors that would impinge on women are examined later in this chapter.

The draft decree for the Presidium of the USSR Central Executive Committee (TsIK) attached to Iagoda's December letter consisted of a proposed wording of the new law, a clause ordering the inclusion of the statute in each union republic criminal code, and a final paragraph confirming the continued validity of laws dealing with rape and prostitution. This draft was approved by the Politburo on 16 December 1933.[17] The following day the USSR All-Union Central Executive Committee adopted virtually the same decree, distributing it to the analogous RSFSR body for the development of corresponding draft decrees.[18]

There were significant variations between the original statute proposed by Iagoda and the version finally adopted by the highest organs of the USSR (7 March 1934)[19] and RSFSR (1 April 1934) governments.[20] Perhaps the most eloquent expression of the distance in mentalities between the Party leadership and the legal theorists who administered Soviet justice was apparent in the language they used to discuss the issue. Intraparty correspondence and even the Politburo's 16 December 1933 decree employed the crude expression *pederastiia* (pederasty) to refer to the offense in question. The traditional legal term *muzhelozhstvo* (sodomy) was used in all Russian government documents and the draft law itself. The Iagoda draft proposed maximum, but no minimum, sentences for simple and aggravated forms of sodomy. Moreover, the forms of aggravated sodomy that the OGPU deputy chief proposed to make crimes specifically included such acts "for payment (*za platu*), as a profession or in public."[21] These qualifications were only dropped from the decrees at a very late stage, and *minimum* sentences were also added (three years for simple and aggravated sodomy) the week before the USSR decree's publication on 7 March 1934.[22] The insertion of sentencing minimums suggests legislators intended to underline the seriousness with which the new offense was to be viewed and set this sex offense apart from others in the code.[23] The late deletion of Iagoda's formulas mentioning male prostitution and public displays is unexplained in the available sources; some possible reasons are examined below.

Despite the apparent uniformity imposed by the all-union decree of 7 March 1934, the timing and language of adoption of the sodomy law unaccountably varied in some republics. Ukraine was by far the first union republic to incorporate the statute in its penal code, on 11 January 1934; it used the language of Iagoda's original proposal as found in the 16 December 1933 Politburo decree. Male prostitution and public homosexuality were thus explicitly named as crimes in the Soviet Union's second largest republic. In addition, no minimum sentences were spelled out for sodomy in Ukraine's penal code.[24] The effect of these anomalies on enforcement and sentencing practices was potentially great, with local policing patterns influenced by the concern expressed in the code about public and prostitution-related manifestations of male homosexuality. Ukrainian judges may have had little option but to impose the union-level decree's minimum sentences, although undoubtedly they found the same means to evade these minimums as those employed later in the 1930s by their Russian counterparts.

The same textual variant was for some reason adopted in the Tadzhik SSR penal code.[25] Elsewhere, local justice drafters generally followed the RSFSR wording patterned on the USSR decree of 7 March, adopting their versions in April 1934. The location of the new statute within penal codes reflected a rough division in Stalinist perceptions of modernity and backwardness in matters of sexuality, with some codes incorporating it into existing sections on sexual crime (reflecting a modernized sexual ethic), and others placing it among crimes constituting survivals of primitive custom. In the Belorussian SSR and Ukraine, the new article was situated with articles on sexual offenses. The Transcaucasian republics of Armenia and Georgia followed this comparatively modern categorization.[26] In the Tadzhik and Uzbek codes, the prohibition figured among local customary offenses instead of sex crimes.[27] Turkmen and Azerbaidzhan penal codification had no distinction between sexual and customary crime, and the existing antisodomy statute among these articles was simply revised to reflect the all-union decree.[28]

The Stalinist leadership was silent about these legislative changes, leaving little in the available documentary record to indicate why it responded in this enthusiastic and draconian fashion to Iagoda's initiative. The OGPU's initial extralegal arrests in late summer 1933 of male homosexuals in Moscow and Leningrad demonstrated that no law need hamper the work of the secret police, if "castelike" groups were suspected of conspiracy. More than enough legislative latitude existed to combat espionage and counterrevolution, and indeed in the Five Year Plan atmosphere of campaign justice, the OGPU had a comparatively free hand to deal with these crimes.[29] Iagoda's proposal for new legislation after these raids and the changes to the legislation as it developed suggest that while suspicions of espionage were present, other concerns were paramount. As the process of urban social cleansing accelerated in late 1932 with the introduction of internal passports and city residence permits, "social anomalies" and "class aliens" were increasingly becoming the targets of security police action. "Recidivist" female prostitutes, "professional" beggars, the homeless, and unrepentant "criminal elements" formed visible subcultures of the street that the new identity document regime was supposed to weed out of the socialist city.[30] Male homosexuals in their most public subcultural guise, meeting on the sexualized territories of Moscow's Boulevard Ring and Leningrad's Nevskii Prospekt, apparently drew police attention to a further anomalous subculture of the urban landscape.[31] While Iagoda seized Stalin's attention with his first letter's warnings about espionage among homosexuals, the legislation he proposed and most of his arguments for it targeted a subculture. Private circles of homosexual men could constitute potentially treasonous "salons" and "dens," but it was the public aspects of homosexual sociability and its "demoralizing" effect that attracted sustained concern. Iagoda's anxiety about the "recruitment and corruption of totally healthy young people," actually young men, in the military and higher education, was reminiscent of the concerns voiced by psychiatrists discussing "mental infection" among cohorts of "normal" army conscripts. What homosexual sociability threatened was a crisis of mental or sexual hygiene, imagined by police and Politburo in the crude language of the street as the seduction of innocent young men by "pederasts." Moreover, Iagoda's first draft of the legislation singled out sodomy "for payment, as a profession or in public" as particular features he sought to eliminate with stiffer penalties. These were (in the context) striking descriptions of social behavior, resembling the quasi-ethnographic language of laws against "crimes constituting survivals of primitive custom," explicitly enumerated in peripheral republican codes. Evidently, this language proved too vivid, for it was excised in the week before publication, perhaps on the advice of the RSFSR Commissariat of Justice or jurists of the USSR and RSFSR Supreme Courts. One may speculate that jurists argued for a less explicit, more euphemistic law that would not inspire the "mental infection" created by publicity of forbidden practices. They probably suggested as well that public sexual acts, male prostitution, and "professional" sodomy could all be prosecuted under existing legislation.[32] It also seems likely that jurists pointed out the inconsistency of formally outlawing the male prostitute, while female prostitutes had never been made official criminals.

Soon after the relatively low-key official adoption of the new antisodomy statute, Stalin was made aware of the kind of reaction it would receive among the Western European left. In a letter received in May 1934, British Communist and Moscow resident Harry Whyte, an editorial employee at the *Moscow Daily News,* asked Stalin to justify the new law.[33] (He also chronicled his efforts to learn the whereabouts of his lover, a Russian man arrested in secret police raids on Moscow homosexuals between December 1933 and March 1934.) In its thorough exposition of contemporary Marxist views on homosexuality, the letter made evident the problems of presentation that the new law would attract and probably influenced the direction of the subsequent Stalinist public pronouncements on the sodomy law.

Whyte's long missive opened with a question for Stalin: "Can a homosexual be considered a person fit to become a member of the Communist Party?" The journalist laid out Marxist arguments against the blanket prohibition of sodomy, which, he claimed, introduced unwarranted contradictions in Soviet social life by imposing "sexual leveling" on a harmless minority and by ignoring science on the issue. The new law jettisoned the achievement of the previous Soviet legislation protecting sexual liberty and inviolability, legislation that represented Soviet power's resolution of capitalist contradictions on the question. Whyte likened the social position of homosexuals to that of other groups in society suffering arbitrary discrimination, naming women, "colored races," and national minorities. He drew a fine distinction between a Communist's personal life (to which private sphere his sexual proclivity ought to be consigned), and cases in which homosexuality became a public, political issue in bourgeois societies. The letter cataloged Marx and Engels on political aspects of homosexuality, noted with approval the Comintern line on van der Lubbe's alleged contacts with homosexual Nazis, and pointed to the hypocrisy of fascist policy inherent in the destruction of Hirschfeld's sexological institute. Whyte reminded Stalin of his criticism at the Seventeenth Party Congress in 1934 of "leveling" (*uravnilovka*) in wages, living standards, and "tastes and personal *byt*" as a form of "primitive asceticism" unworthy of

Marxism. These comments against leveling "have a direct connection to the question" of homosexuality, the journalist argued, since the new law forced a biologically distinct minority to comply with "sexual leveling."[34]

Stalin directed that the letter be archived, recording his opinion of its author: "An idiot and a degenerate."[35] The document was retained in a file with others relating to the introduction of the new legislation, suggesting that its arguments were not viewed as an idiot's prattle, but served as a useful guide to an unfamiliar discourse. To counter it, Stalin apparently turned to a mouthpiece for whom the European terms of this rhetoric were familiar. Cultural spokesman Maksim Gor'kii's article, "Proletarian Humanism," appearing in *Pravda* and *Izvestiia* on 23 May 1934, was the regime's first public explanation of the recriminalization of male homosexuality, and it placed the question squarely within the terms of the propaganda war between Fascism and Communism.[36]

The themes of this war were the moral degradation and outright seduction of a nation's youth and, particularly, of young men as the nation's productive and fighting force, by the evils of the opposing political system. Underlying this ideological anxiety about corrupted youth was an appeal to more venerable stereotypes. Gor'kii deployed the myth of elemental Russia's purity to set up a familiar contrast with an over-civilized West, declaring that proletarian humanism was transforming the huge reserves of "barbaric" Russia's "physical energy" into productive, "intellectual energy." Meanwhile, capitalism now hired Fascism to mobilize the physically and morally depleted scions of the bourgeoisie, the sons of alcoholics, hysterics, and syphilitics. "In the thousands of gray, desiccated faces, it is especially rare to see healthy, full-blooded individuals, because there are few of them." Among the "hundreds of facts speaking of the destructive, demoralizing influence of Fascism," homosexuality was but one of the most "revolting" features. At stake was not only the purity and health of a population but of its culture. Where the proletariat ruled, homosexuality was regarded as a force for corrupting youth and was punished, while "in the land of the great philosophers, scientists and musicians [Germany], it is practiced freely and with impunity." Fascism's "poison" of nationalism and anti-Semitism was schooling youth in "social cynicism, a sadistic passion for murder." Yet Gor'kii dismissed any claim that homosexuals might constitute a social minority (like Jews or "the unarmed Hindus, Chinese, and Negroes") worthy of safeguarding by the workers' state, with his notorious slogan, "Destroy the homosexuals—Fascism will disappear."[37] One could infer from the content of this article, much cited as the reflection of the intentions behind recriminalization of sodomy in 1934, that an obedient Gor'kii was briefed about Whyte's letter to Stalin and the arguments against the new legislation he was required to demolish.[38]

The unanticipated sodomy ban threw functionaries, including literary officials and medical experts, into confusion. Not all were inclined to accept the consequences for their fields of competence. The best documented example of this disarray concerns the purchase, by the State Literary Museum director V. D. Bonch-Bruevich, of the well-known diary and papers of Leningrad poet Mikhail Kuzmin. In November 1933 Kuzmin received 25,000 rubles for these papers, comprising a daily record of his life from August 1905 to December 1931. They contained frank references to his and others' homosexuality.[39]

On 1 February 1934 (that is, between the December Politburo and March Soviet government decrees enacting the sodomy ban) an OGPU official demanded and received from Bonch-Bruevich the complete archive. In April, a special commission of the Cultural Enlightenment Department of the Party Central Committee began an investigation of the museum director. The purchase of the Kuzmin papers, for the large sum, was the focus of the inquiry. Bonch-Bruevich defended the worth of the archive and its homosexual themes, which he noted were essential to an understanding of "bourgeois left symbolism," in letters to Iagoda and Commissar of Enlightenment A. S. Bubnov in May 1934.[40] Three days after these letters were written, Gor'kii's article "Proletarian Humanism" appeared in *Pravda* and *Izvestiia*, but Bonch-Bruevich did not immediately abandon the defense of the purchase.[41] On 20 June, the Party commission reprimanded Bonch-Bruevich for paying "dearly" for "material of an uncommonly trashy (*makulatornyi*) character," ordered a purge of museum staff, and directed that future purchases be vetted by Bubnov's commissariat. Kuzmin himself escaped arrest, dying of natural causes in 1936, while most of the diary and papers he had sold to Bonch-Bruevich were returned to the museum in 1940.[42] Iurii Iurkun, Kuzmin's partner during the Soviet era, was arrested in 1938 during the Great Terror by the NKVD (on charges of counterrevolution, not homosexuality) in a sweep against Leningrad's literary figures. He was executed after seven months of interrogations in September 1938.[43]

Other homosexuals and their literary works met similar fates during the 1933–34 crackdown.[44] Nikolai Kliuev, poet of the Russian village and of homosexual love, drew the ire of Ivan Gronskii, chief editor of

Izvestiia VTsIK and the thick literary journal *Novyi mir* in the 1930s. Gronskii had (he would claim in 1959) allotted the indigent bard a generous academician's ration in 1932. Kliuev moved to the country with his male lover (the artist A. Iar-Kravchenko; they first met in 1928), wrote poems, and eventually sent Gronskii some verses for publication. The editor was outraged by their homosexual content and endeavored to persuade the poet to "write normal verses." When Kliuev flatly refused, Gronskii did not hesitate to telephone Iagoda (later confirming the decision with Stalin), demanding the poet be deported from Moscow.[45] The call apparently took place immediately before Kliuev's arrest on 2 February 1934. The poet was interrogated in Moscow's Lubianka and charged under criminal code article 58(10)—counterrevolutionary agitation—not homosexual offenses, probably because of the inflammatory invective of his poems denouncing collectivization. On 5 March he was exiled to Narym territory in Siberia. Kliuev was re-arrested while in exile and shot as a counterrevolutionary in October 1937.[46] Gronskii's response to Kliuev's refusal to heterosexualize his verses was to "cleanse" Moscow of the poet and his homosexuality. With more self-interest than Bonch-Bruevich, this literary functionary comprehended what political costs a subsidy to an outlawed (and anti-Soviet) homosexual artist could incur. The OGPU's decision to apply counterrevolutionary articles of the criminal code in Kliuev's case does not diminish the impression that the poet fell into the hands of the security police for his unrepentant homosexuality, but more enlightened investigation of his secret police file would be required to substantiate this.[47]

Doctors and even Commissariat of Justice officials were less aware of the new legislation and of the "homosexual conspiracy" upon which it was founded. One psychiatrist, approached by Harry Whyte, checked with the Justice Commissariat (Whyte does not say when) before twice assuring the *Moscow Daily News* staffer that the Commissariat had no objection to the treatment of patients "if they were honest citizens or good Communists," and that these homosexuals could organize their personal lives as they wished. Whyte consulted another psychiatrist, who refused to believe in the existence of the antisodomy law until the journalist produced a copy of the legislation. Whyte contacted the Commissariat of Justice himself (between the December 1933 and March 1934 decrees) and was told that the law was being enacted because "homosexuality is a form of bourgeois degeneracy." Seeking information about his arrested lover, Whyte also contacted the security police directly, and obtained differing responses to his questions before and after the legislation was published in its final form, suggesting a shift in the way it was being implemented. During the interval between decrees, when speaking to OGPU officials, Whyte was told that the arrests being carried out had a "political character" (and not a public morality basis). The journalist understood this to mean that a distinction would be drawn between politically loyal homosexuals, who would not be targeted, and those deemed counterrevolutionary, who would be arrested. After the publication of the law of 7 March 1934, however, an OGPU employee told Whyte that "the law would be strictly applied in every observed case of homosexuality."[48] It appears that with the published law came fresh instructions widening the scope of its enforcement, but evidence of these directives remains scant.

In contrast to other criminal legislation enacted during the 1930s, the antisodomy decree left no trail of circulars informing procuracy and judiciary of the intent behind the measure or how the law ought to be enforced. Normally, such directives assisted court investigators and judges in carrying out their duties in the regular criminal justice system.[49] Instructions on the antisodomy law could have been transmitted orally or via closed circulars, which were returned after being read.[50] In this study's sample of eight Moscow sodomy trials dating from 1935 to 1941, only one case (the first, dating from March 1935) offers any evidence that courts were informed of the meaning of the law of 7 March 1934. In its sentence, the municipal court justified its qualification of defendants' acts under this law by noting

> that the law of 7 March 1934 is directed against sodomy not in the narrow meaning of the term, but against sodomy as an antisocial system [*pravlenie*] of sexual liaisons between men in whatever form they may take and especially when they occur among groups of persons organized on that basis.[51]

The court used this reasoning to acquit one defendant and give another a greatly reduced sentence. The RSFSR Supreme Court confirmed this reasoning in its review of the case and even acquitted a further defendant on the basis that no proof of sodomy after 7 March 1934 had been presented.[52] None of the remaining seven cases up to 1941, nor any of the six cases found in the same archive dating from 1949 to 1956, offer any similar statement suggesting courts had been given directives on the interpretation of this law.

Clinical psychiatrists received no direct guidance regarding the new law, and they were left to learn about it fortuitously. Forensic psychia-

trists evidently knew about the shift and quickly altered their definitions of psychopathy to fit.[53] In 1935, psychiatrist E. A. Popov radically
deconstructed "homosexuality" as a category of mental illness. Without
mentioning the recriminalization of sodomy, he sought to purge psychiatry of the homosexual. Classifications of sexual perversion based on
symptoms rather than etiologies were a "remnant" that betrayed the
discipline's diagnostic and therapeutic weakness. A variety of primarily
exogenous causes could account for homosexuality: normal sex life was
"perverted" by "a lack of success, difficulties, disappointments, chance
factors which cause revulsion toward women." Men of this type still
have a "normal sexual basis [*ustanovka*)" that continued to influence
their choice of sex object (preferring effeminized youths] and sex act
["striving to imitate normal coitus by means of the pederastic act"].
Applying the full force of the nurturist psychopathic model, he spoke of
the "nonuniformity of that group of phenomena figuring in psychiatric
systems under the name of homosexuality."[54] In Popov's prescient
scheme, eros between men would only be the object of medical attention as an aspect of a mental disorder or psychopathy, not as an entity
in itself.

The state abruptly shifted the nexus of medico-legal supervision of
same-sex love to practitioners of forensic medicine and gynecology, disciplines undergoing significant restructuring as a result of the Five Year
Plans.[55] In late 1933, the newly founded Central Institute of Forensic
Medicine drafted Soviet Russia's first comprehensive guidelines for
doctors acting as expert examiners in cases of sexual crime. These
rules for "forensic medical obstetric-gynecological examination" were
adopted by the Health Commissariat in consultation with the Procurators of the RSFSR and USSR, and a representative of the main administration of the regular police three months after the sodomy law, in
June 1934.[56] The rules were under discussion just as the new antisodomy statute was being drafted, but evidence of a link between the two
initiatives has not emerged. Yet the guidance for legal doctors contained specific instructions for detecting the signs of "pederasty":

13. In examinations regarding depraved acts, accompanied by rape or
not, and as well regarding sexual perversions (with or without the use
of force), the expert, . . . examines (in the case of pederasty [*pederastiia*])
the anal orifice and should note its form (crater- or funnel-shaped),
whether it gapes or not, the flabbiness or slackness of the mucous mem-
brane of the rectum, the presence or absence of ray-shaped folds of skin
around the anal orifice, of fissures and wounds, the status of the sphinc-

ter, levator, the dilation of the ampulla, prolapsus of layers of the rectum; particular attention is to be paid to the presence of rectal gonorrhea, especially in victims who are men (or boys) . . .[57]

The location of this passage on the anatomical indications of "pederasty" directly following a discussion of heterosexual rape, in a code of rules governing gynecological examinations, echoed Vladislav Merzheevskii's treatment of the issue in his manual fifty-six years previously. Yet this was not simply a return to pederasty-as-vice according to the old regime's formula, but part of a larger process by which the state attempted to standardize forensic medical practice in matters of sexual crime.[58] A more systematic procedure for the detection of pederasty conformed with authorities' determination to impose routine and standard values on the haphazard production of medical expertise in criminal investigations of rape, defloration, and sexual abuse.

In a manual of forensic gynecology, published in 1935 by doctors who contributed to the formulation of these rules, male homosexuality was, nonetheless, treated with a degree of inconsistency that betrayed the authors' political and scientific bewilderment. Gynecologists N. V. Popov and E. E. Rozenblium, at the end of a chapter entitled "Rape," discussed "rape with sexual perversions," and devoted two pages to etiologies of "homosexuality" and "lesbian love." The authors presented a neutral review of endocrinological and reflexological theories, listing foreign and domestic authorities by name, and even stating, unusually for the period, that hormonal theories "deserve . . . full attention."[59] Popov and Rozenblium then turned abruptly from scientific discourse and wrote:

> Finally, the role of specific class conditions must be emphasized: homosexuality has obtained a special prevalence in such countries as Germany, among the aristocratic military bosses and generally among the "big shots" of the Fascist movement.[60]

Noting that homosexuality was now punished in all union republic criminal codes, the authors argued that because it was an offense between men, there was no need to deal with it in their volume.[61] Forensic gynecologists, responsible for gathering evidence from victims and perpetrators of sexual crimes, appeared reluctant to take on the duty of detection of voluntary sodomy in males. By minimizing the crime's prevalence, suggesting that the problem was better understood by psychiatrists and even endocrinologists, and finally, by putting a class-enemy gloss on the offense, Popov and Rozenblium apparently rejected any involvement for their discipline. Yet immediately after these passages, they presented the case of a wife whose husband demanded "perverse" sex (anal and oral), referring to her as a "passive pederast" (*passivnyi pederast*). The authors then rehearsed all the classic stigmata of receptive anal intercourse, in language reminiscent of Merzheevskii and Tarnovskii, and concluded with remarks on the differences in signs of anal gonorrhoea between women and men.[62] Perhaps the authors, by presenting a case of "passive pederasty" gendered as female, were emboldened to transmit a heritage of medical lore on male sodomy.[63]

In an apparent attempt to dispel confusion surrounding the antisodomy statute, RSFSR People's Commissar of Justice N. V. Krylenko spoke at some length about it in a March 1936 speech before legislators in the Central Executive Committee (VTsIK).[64] The commissar extended the regime's homophobic rhetoric by explicitly adding homosexuals to the list of class enemies, declassed elements, and criminal elements that had been the subject of urban social cleansing campaigns. Since the end of the first Five Year Plan, various types of crimes of "daily life" (including group rapes), said to be committed by members of these social layers, had become the target of higher penal sanctions and concealed but ongoing scrutiny.[65] By linking homosexuals with the preexisting categories of social deviance, Krylenko closed a gap that had left officials and experts perplexed about how to understand "ordinary" homosexuals without any apparent connection to centers of espionage or Nazi ruling circles.

Krylenko referred in his address to a number of legal changes designed to eliminate "the remnants of enemies . . . who do not wish to admit that they are doomed by history to finally concede their place to us." The changes were to be transformational for all Soviet society; they were enacted "to rework ourselves, to foster in ourselves the new man . . . and new attitudes toward *byt* (daily life)." The law against sodomy, he noted, had been the subject of comment in the Western press, adding that until recently, Soviet thinking on the problem of "this type of crime" was dominated by the "Western bourgeois school," which taught that "this type of action is always a phenomenon of illness." Krylenko argued that homosexuality and alcoholism were analogous conditions: just as alcoholics were responsible in law for their criminal acts, except in a tiny number of cases where "a genuine illness is present," so homosexuals were in the overwhelming majority of cases criminally responsible for their behavior.[66]

It is clear in the published text, from the gradually intensifying reaction in the hall, that this extravagantly masculine people's commissar manipulated his (primarily male) audience's emotions associated with love between men, as he reached the climax of his argument:

> In our environment, in the environment of the workers taking the point of view of normal relations between the sexes, who are building their society on healthy principles, we don't need little gentlemen [*gospodchiki*] of this type. Who then for the most part are our customers in these affairs? Workers? No! Declassed rabble. (*Mirthful animation in the hall, laughter*) Declassed rabble, either from the dregs of society or from the remnants of the exploiting classes. (*Applause*) They don't know which way to turn. (*Laughter*) So they turn to . . . pederasty. (*Laughter*)[67]

Krylenko appealed to the political and (at least unconsciously) to the masculine anxieties of his audience, cloaking a disturbing topic with humorous political banter, to establish a distance of class and loyalty between the panicking sexual social refuse and the healthy toiling Soviet man (and woman). He then rapidly shifted to an earnest tone, pointing out that pederasts "in secret filthy hiding places and dens" were frequently engaged in counterrevolutionary activity. The law against sodomy was justified in bantering language that located male homosexuals within familiar class and social categories, and distanced Soviet medical views of them from "bourgeois" theories. Krylenko thus reduced the ambiguity in the regime's construction of the "ordinary" homosexual to a minimum.

Compulsory Motherhood, Compulsory Families, Compulsory Heterosexuality

If the male "pederast" was reconfigured in the Stalinist imagination to fit the discourse of the declassed, the woman who loved women did not appear in this dehumanizing polemical realm at all. The reasons for this gendered dichotomy in the Stalinist treatment of homosexuality have not been revealed in archival discoveries. We know, by contrast, that in Nazi Germany discussions among police, doctors, and Nazi officials did take place about whether women having sex together should be classed as criminals, but nothing comparable has emerged to illuminate the attitudes of Soviet leaders on this issue.[68] The "female homosexual" or "masculinized" woman did not excite interest during the laconic discussions of what to do with the male homosexual. It is, however possible to reconstruct an official perspective on these apparitional figures from the well-known measures adopted in the area of family policy and from evidence in medical and legal practice of the 1930s.

The conservative turn in social and family policy under Stalinism has long been familiar to students of the Russian Revolution as a "betrayal" of revolutionary principles or as a "great retreat."[69] Historians more recently have pointed out the syncretic nature of policy on marriage, divorce, and family during the period of the first Five Year Plans. Stalinism did not simply turn back the clock to 1917, but mixed elements of the revolutionary drive for women's emancipation with expectations (never seriously examined by Russian Marxists) that biology ordained a feminine social role.[70] The accumulation of the state's measures in the middle and late 1930s blended appeals for women to join the expanding industrial labor force with an increasingly insistent promotion of maternity and family. Women's employment increased massively, especially during the second Five Year Plan (1932–37), when 82 percent of all new workers joining industry were women; by 1940, 39 percent of industry's work force was female.[71] Yet the threat of war, which underlay the planning priorities of the new command economy, also prompted the Stalinist leadership to worry about the Soviet Union's falling birthrate. A 1934 study of fertility rates in Soviet society by economist S. G. Strumilin evidently had an important impact on the leadership's thinking, undermining the consensus around health arguments that had supported the 1920 abortion legislation.[72] In this climate, new penalties and incentives were intended to revise attitudes toward procreation, childrearing, and family obligations and to compel women to combine motherhood and waged work. Abortion, a common form of birth control among employed urban women who enjoyed priority of access through insurance schemes, was banned, and divorce was made less accessible in a comprehensive decree on family policy in June 1936. The same decree announced new welfare entitlements for women with seven or more children and promised greater funding for new maternity homes and day care facilities. It also laid out more stringent norms for alimony payments from breadwinner salaries (almost always men's) in divorce cases. Access to birth control devices was simultaneously and secretly curbed in an order to the Commissariat of Health, further limiting women's reproductive autonomy.[73]

Preceding and accompanying these open and secret measures intended to make women carry more pregnancies to term, press campaigns were orchestrated to inculcate sexual probity and to emphasize that maternity was a social duty. Family life became the subject of prescriptive scrutiny, where before Bolshevik leaders had said little about the internal dynamics and psychology of the husband-wife relationship. *Pravda* condemned "so-called 'free love' and all disorderly sex life" as unquestionably bourgeois and against Soviet morality and pointed out the dominant pattern of family relations among the "elite of our country [who] are as a rule also excellent family men who dearly love their children." The same article condemned "the man who does not take marriage seriously"; somewhat later, extracts from the correspondence of Lenin to Inessa Armand were published to underline his concern for "the serious in love."[74] Underlying the nostrums against male promiscuity was the implicit assumption that it was naturally and correctly always women who assumed the nurturing role after childbirth. The alimony provisions in the 1936 decree evoked genuine approval from women who feared or had experienced abandonment, and some of this emotion was evident in accounts of reaction to the new law. From the pages of the press, a cult of motherhood was celebrated, reaching proportions critical observers found grotesque, as the lives of mothers of seven, eight, or ten children were vaunted as examples of patriotism, and women were depicted rhapsodizing over "the first cry, the first smile of a child."[75] The cumulative effect of these measures was to impose a state-sponsored compulsory heterosexuality on all women of childbearing age. Women who had sex with men and who chose to limit their fertility in order to advance in education or work were now driven to abstinence, backstreet abortions and their dire consequences, or the abandonment or curtailment of a hard-won career.

An integral part of the recasting of socialist heterosexuality was the selective revival of femininity as a promoted public identity for key groups of Soviet women. The most prominent heroines of the first Five Year Plans included female aviators, tractor drivers, and exemplary factory and collective farm workers who overfulfilled production targets. Women like Valentina Grizodubova, Polina Osipenko, and Marina Raskova, who completed the first nonstop flight from Moscow to the Soviet Far East in 1938, were celebrated for their embodiment of the ideals of emancipation and technical accomplishment. Productivity gains, the mastering of technology, and the military applications of women's participation in industry and warfare were the significant themes emphasized in the promotion of these exceptional women to national notoriety. The externals of their femininity were not as significant as their technical achievements. Yet simultaneously, the movement of "wife-activists" (*obshchestvennitsy*), launched in 1936 with the sponsorship of Sergo Orzhonikidze, the Commissar for Heavy Industry, extolled a public role for wives of industrial executives, engineers, and army officers.[76] The femininity of these women, and its association with prosperity, was a striking and deliberate feature of their public personae. Cast as mothers, housewives, and "mistresses of the great Soviet home," these wives without paid employment were recruited by the wife-activist movement to supervise factory amenities and to organize cultural, educational, and leisure activities for workers. They were also exhorted to care for their husbands and children in a fashion that combined the wider theme of maternity as national duty, with new notes of consumerism and (where appropriate) of deference to husbands. In the propaganda of the movement, such women were told to provide a hygienic, cosy, and soothing domestic environment, to watch over the "moral condition" of their husbands, and to talk to them about their work in a constructive and frankly productivity-enhancing manner. Likewise, they were to accept criticism and tutoring from their husbands; but this was not to stand in the way of their participation in social activism, nor blind them to antistate acts or words from family members. The usually nonparty wife-activist, in the words of Rebecca Neary, "with her permanent wave, fur-collared coat, and stylish cloche," presented a blunt contrast with the "plainly dressed, severely countenanced" woman Communist, who had no time for fashionable clothing or hair treatments. To the stereotype of the "plain and stern" or "principled and selfless" Bolshevik woman was now added a maternal, gentle and more feminine alternative, "as would befit the denizens of a land in which life had become 'better' and 'more joyous.' "[77] For select groups of Soviet women, a new ideal, "[f]eminized without being overtly sexualized," completed the construction of a Stalinist version of socialist heterosexuality.

It would seem that Stalinist leaders did not perceive a need to prohibit or pathologize explicitly the "masculinized" woman or "female homosexual" despite these exertions to construct a new heterosexuality. There were several possible explanations for this apparent lack of concern. The first was the virtual absence, already noted, of a female subculture of same-sex relations exploiting public space. Women who loved women were less able (and perhaps inclined) than their male counterparts to create and exploit special urban territories for socializing and sexual contact. Had such an open subculture existed, it would have suffered the same fate as the street cultures of female prostitutes and of male homosexuals. Another probable reason for the lack was the perception, evident in Soviet medical encounters with female homosexuals in the 1920s, that "genuine" or "congenital" female homosexuals were extremely rare in Soviet society and, moreover, that their partners consisted of "normal" women who had been diverted from heterosexual relations, perhaps after unsatisfactory affairs with men.

The abortion and contraception bans theoretically meant that such women would no longer have the option of rejecting motherhood if they engaged in heterosexual relations. As in Nazi Germany, leaders considering the possibility of mutual female relations may well have assumed that intercourse with a man was sufficient to "cure" the lesbian.[78] Finally, the image of the old-style female Bolshevik with her selflessness and political consciousness (embodied, for example, in the person of Lenin's widow, Nadezhda Krupskaia) and the acquired rather than inborn traits of "masculinization" (such as technological skill and courage) could not be written off lightly. Political literacy, technical prowess, and strength under pressure were assets to be cultivated among the vast numbers of new women workers entering industry. By contrast, the "feminization" of the image of the wife-activist was a badge of special status, linking her to membership in the managerial elite raised to positions of responsibility by Stalinist promotion policies.[79] The syncretic nature of Stalinist policies on the family produced numerous tensions and contradictions between new and old ways of thinking about appropriate gender roles for women.

An echo of this unstable combination of expectations was present in the work of forensic gynecologists in the middle 1930s. When in 1933–34 the forensic medical discipline in conjunction with jurists and police drafted rules for "forensic medical obstetric-gynecological examination," they avoided explicit mention of female same-sex offenses comparable to those on "pederasty." One passage on gathering evidence of sexual crime indicated that assaults by women on girls, of the type understood in the RSFSR Criminal Code's gender-neutral article 152, were anticipated. When conducting examinations on individuals (who could be either alleged assailants or victims),

> establishing VIRGINITY or RAPE with DEFLORATION, or DE-
> PRAVED ACTIONS, or SEXUAL MATURITY the expert should
> verify:
> a) GENERAL STATUS OF THE EXAMINED PERSON: body structure
> corresponding in external appearance to her [*eiu*] stated age, infantilism,
> virilism (masculinization [*omuzhestvlenie*]), abnormalities of hair cover,
> defects of general development, etc.[80]

Guidelines then directed doctors to check whether the person being examined displayed "masculine" or "feminine" patterns of hair growth. They were also instructed, depending on the aims of the examination, to collect information about the "sexual life" of the person in question, and the terse directive spelled out only two key questions: "from what age did [sexual life] commence (perversions)." In the formulation of these instructions, forensic experts and jurists, led by the gender-neutral language of the law, anticipated that assaults on sexually immature females could be inflicted by adult women. Yet the criminal code had always been silent about the assailant's or victim's body structure or "virilism": these were medical concepts reflecting a constitutional view of the "masculinized" female, and their inclusion in the medico-legal guidelines pointed to a shared expectation that at least one female in a same-sex act would belong to this category. The representatives of the police and judiciary who presided over the adoption of these rules in 1934 allowed these discursive shadows of the "masculinized" woman to remain, regardless of the antibiologizing campaigns of the cultural revolution. A year later, the guidelines were published in the forensic gynecological manual that handled the question of "pederasty" so awkwardly. N. V. Popov and E. E. Rozenblium only briefly addressed the issue of female same-sex assaults in a commentary on "rape with sexual perversions." They completely avoided any discussion of masculinization in women sex offenders or victims of female same-sex assaults, which the guidelines in the same textbook indicated were an important factor in these kinds of crimes.

Instead, Popov and Rozenblium, not wishing to highlight the proscribed NEP-era "biologization" of the female homosexual implied in the guidelines, said that lesbians were seldom encountered, mostly foreign to Russia, and not really relevant to forensic gynecology. "Lesbian love" figured among the rare, but not specifically criminalized, sexual perversions of which the medical examiner ought to be aware. "Tribadism" left "no changes in the genital region," although "rare cases observed in Paris" of clitoral wounds caused by teeth were known. "Active partners" could have an enlarged clitoris, and their victims often displayed hysteria or more complex mental disorders.[81] If Popov and Rozenblium revived the archaism of treating pederasty under the rubric of forensic gynecology, then by ignoring domestic authorities on female homosexuality, they also returned to the trope of innocent Russia and sexually depraved Western Europe. The only source they cited on this issue was Louis Martineau's 1883 *Leçons sur les déformations vulvaires et anales*, a text that by its temporal and cultural remoteness rendered "lesbian love" that much more exotic.[82] It could be dismissed by the casual reader as a symptom of bourgeois degeneracy, whether Imperial Russian or, more probably, Parisian. Simultaneously, by pointing to the potential for mental disorders among "tribades," Popov and

Rozenblium also hinted that they preferred to leave the problem with psychiatrists. In its evasions and denials, their commentary on "lesbian love" reflected the contradictory gender currents of the middle 1930s: the dilemma about "masculine" qualities in women and the anxiety about the woman who avoided maternity.

Conclusion

The syncretism that marked the construction of the Stalinist system of gender and family relations had an effect on Soviet constructions of same-sex love developed during the 1930s. Elements of the variegated tsarist and NEP-era approaches to sexual and gender dissent were combined with the slogans and exigencies of the Five Year Plan era. Stalinism revived and strengthened the primary divide in prerevolutionary views, that between male and female forms of homosexuality. The gender-neutral language of sex crime in the first Bolshevik criminal codes that were applied to the "modern" Soviet republics was repudiated in the new sodomy law of 1933–34: this was a stunning reversal of a key principle of the sexual revolution. Nevertheless, it was a retreat that had precedents in NEP legislation beyond the "modern" heartland, in the "backward" republics where "survivals of primitive custom" encouraged the cataloging of clearly gendered offenses. Within Soviet Russia, prosecutions of clerical same-sex offenses presented another Bolshevik precedent where "survivals" of the past were mapped on society as defects created by class rather than the historical backwardness of "primitive" societies. The ambition that a secular, medicalized, and gender-blind modernity would inform the way revolutionary justice dealt with sexual crimes was already reserved for a vanguard population (workers and peasants) within a vanguard "nation" (Russia and its "civilized" partners in socialism).

The attention paid exclusively to male homosexuality reflected the vanguard role in which men were habitually cast by Russian Marxist thinking. While both male and female proletarians were nominally equal, Party activists from the revolution's inception to the consolidation of the Stalinist system feared the politically unconscious female and revolutionary iconography represented the Bolshevik movement as resolutely masculine.[83] The demoralization of the "healthy young people, Red Army soldiers, sailors, and . . . students" seduced by "pederasts" deflected the cream of this male vanguard from its historical mission, just as the "double dealers" and "turncoats" inside the Party supposedly tried to derail it during the economic and social crisis of 1933.

Both elements had to be eliminated from the leading institutions of the regime so that "mental infection" could be reduced and new cases of pederasty or political disloyalty averted. The same intentions underpinned the social cleansing of the leading cities of the Soviet homeland. Ultimately, the vanguard class, gender, and cities would rework themselves, sloughing off the "bourgeois degenerates" who haunted them in secret dens and salons, as life itself was transformed and remnants of the former classes disappeared.

Women's role in this drama was a supporting one, but in its class dimensions it acquired complexity and contradiction. As peasants in "backward" regions, as collective farmers, and as proletarians, women were called upon in greater and greater numbers during the 1930s to enter public life and wage labor. Women in these spheres were compelled and encouraged to emancipate themselves from patriarchal fathers and husbands, who were not to stand in the way of their progress toward careers beyond the home. They were becoming more like men, even in some cases becoming what some could regard as "masculinized." Meanwhile, the wife-activist movement promoted a feminine and materialistic ideal for a new elite entitled to the fruits of socialism. The two conflicting norms coexisted in an uneasy moral equilibrium, the heroism of self-transformation and productivity gains on the one hand, and the dutiful concern for bringing culture to the existence of those around her, on the other. Compulsory motherhood bridged the gap between the two roles. The cult of motherhood could be called upon to redeem an excess of "masculinization" acquired by working-class women on the shop floor or at the aerodrome. The experience of maternity gave the wife-activist in her potentially delicate role as do-gooder a common reference point with women at the factory bench.[84]

The "grotesque hybrid"[85] of Stalinist family policy produced a crude form of compulsory heterosexuality, which depended heavily on pronatalist coercion. It was a heterosexuality composed of many fears and impulses, a nervous amalgam worthy of the arriviste "culture" the new Soviet elite sought to acquire.[86] Male homosexual subcultures threatened the purity of the healthy Soviet young man and perhaps harbored opportunities for sedition. Degenerate remnants of a defeated bourgeoisie, aristocracy, and clergy—survivals of Russia's own backwardness—lurked in these salons and dens, encouraging male prostitution and the practice of "sodomy . . . as a profession." Mental infection perhaps threatened to contribute to an already falling birthrate, just as war loomed. Men whose sexuality was too unstable would require a spell of corrective labor to teach them "normal" ways. Women did not run the same risk, since there was no visible network of female homosexuals. The supposedly rare, anomalous "masculinized" female who preyed on "normal" young women could be recognized by doctors and isolated if necessary, without the need for legislative revision. The "normal" young woman, meanwhile, was to be reminded (in the words of Lenin) that her freedom to love was not freedom "from the serious in love . . . from childbirth." Her biology naturally assured her status as "normal," and the motherhood cult would remind her of the purpose of her sexuality.

PART III

Homosexual Existence and Existing Socialism

"Caught Red-Handed"

MAKING HOMOSEXUALITY ANTISOCIAL
IN STALIN'S COURTS

F rom the moment that OGPU deputy chief G. G. Iagoda's attention turned to the 130 men arrested in raids on Moscow
and Leningrad "pederasts" in late summer 1933, a new rivulet
of the socially anomalous joined the torrent of victims seized and processed by the system of extralegal punishment. The number of individuals who entered this stream as convicted "pederasts" remains unknown, because of the inaccessibility of the records.[1] It is possible,
however, with new archival material to examine the process by which
a second stream of men designated as "pederasts" and "homosexuals"
were treated in the conventional criminal court system. The nature and
meaning of the trials of these men in Stalin-era courts can be gleaned
from the fragmentary sources at our disposal, mostly sentencing and
appeal records. These cases, while modest in number, can suggest how
Soviet justice helped to construct a Stalinist heterosexuality.

The cold war view of the Soviet Union inclined some historians to
dismiss the notion of "Stalinist justice" as oxymoronic. A regime supported by extralegal terror and repression could hardly be serious about
maintaining a functioning system of criminal justice.[2] Yet what the
historian observes for the 1930s and afterward are episodes of surging
illegal repression and violence coinciding with the ongoing administration of ordinary justice. There were moments when the terror system
threatened to extinguish conventional jurisprudence. During the collectivization drives of 1932–1933, the use of legal machinery in the dispos-
session and deportation of the "kulaks" embroiled jurists, judges and
procurators in the virtual civil war raging in the countryside. At the
height of the Great Terror in 1937–38, as Peter Solomon points out,
the procuracy participated in the dynamic of accusation and repression,

with lethal results.[3] Yet after 1938, a compartmentalization emerged in the apparent functions of secret, extralegal repression (which reinvented itself as a more selective system), and the public administration of justice (which eventually strove to improve with legal education for new cadres under late Stalinism). Solomon argues that conventional justice was allowed to continue to operate essentially for reasons of international window-dressing. It was expedient to appear to be a "normal state" with European legal machinery and the appearance of legality in the propaganda war with Fascism, and later, too, during the cold war. Conformity to expectations of fairness, order, and (in its most extreme version) "perfection" in the administration of justice was an aspect of the image the Soviet leadership strove to project after the adoption of the 1936 "Stalin" Constitution. The realization of this plan for Soviet legality would for the most part have to wait until after 1945, when more legal officials received specialist education.[4]

While Solomon acknowledges that the decision to put resources into the Soviet legal system also enabled the state to extend its reach, an emphasis on the international public relations function of Soviet law turns our attention away from the microenvironment of the courtroom and the dramas that were played out there. Without a focus on the courtroom itself, it becomes impossible to gauge the significance of sexual crime in Soviet jurisprudence, for whether from prudery or out of a fear of stimulating base tastes, most trials in cases of sexual crimes took place behind closed doors. Scarcely visible to outside observers, these trials nonetheless had an immediate meaning for their participants. An examination of the formal progress of sodomy cases from arrest to conviction can reveal this significance. The cases also suggest how the male homosexual subculture in Moscow responded to the escalation of force used against it. A 1940 trial of two women offers further evidence of the gendering of same-sex offenses and the medico-legal concerns lesbianism raised. Finally, the stories of these trials begin the process of restoring the individuality and humanity of homosexuals to our narratives of Stalinist repression.

"He showed me the places where pederasts meet"

By comparison with the rhetorical forms used to explain them, the actual extent of arrests and trials of homosexuals conducted during and after the enactment of the 1933–34 decree remains difficult to establish. The Iagoda-Stalin correspondence of late 1933 and the Whyte-Stalin letter of May 1934 add substance to statements from a cluster of memoir and journalistic sources that arrests of Soviet homosexuals began from sometime in 1933 and continued into 1934. While the details vary somewhat, read together they suggest that raids occurred in major Russian and Ukrainian centers and that observers believed espionage, probably for Germany, motivated OGPU action.[5] One Russian witness to these events said that in 1933 numerous homosexuals were arrested for participating in gatherings that were "made . . . to appear as counterrevolutionary, Trotskyite, or even Hitlerite." He reported that in the absence of an explicit law against homosexuality, these men were forced to sign false confessions of counterrevolutionary crimes. Others were netted under an elastic reading of the RSFSR Criminal Code's article 155 (compelling someone to prostitution and the maintenance of vice dens).[6]

Iagoda's September 1933 letter to Stalin suggests that during the earliest phase of this assault the OGPU conducted these arrests of "pederasts," and one may infer that existing laws were used when it was "discovered" that no antisodomy statute was available to give the arrests a legal basis.[7] Harry Whyte had discussed these actions of late 1933 ("when arrests of homosexuals had only begun") with his superior at the *Moscow Daily News*, its editor-in-chief, M. M. Borodin, who regarded Whyte as a "top shock-worker" and had even recently promoted him. Borodin knew about Whyte's sexuality but believed that only politically unreliable homosexuals were being targeted.[8] The British Communist carried his inquiries further for personal motives. Whyte spoke twice to operatives of the OGPU because between the decrees of 17 December 1933 and 7 March 1934 the security police had arrested a Russian with whom he was involved in "homosexual relations" (as he wrote to Stalin). He indicated that sweeps of homosexual circles by security police continued into this period, at least in Moscow. Yet neither his letter to Stalin nor the published Iagoda-Stalin correspondence said anything of substance to indicate the scale of the OGPU's raids on homosexual circles. It is likely that some information on this question available in the Presidential Archive was deliberately left out of the 1993 *Istochnik* article, for example, on Ukrainian arrests.[9] It is also probable that some OGPU (or, from July 1934, NKVD) arrests and prosecutions of men who came under surveillance for "pederasty" were then charged with counterrevolutionary crimes (the fate of Nikolai Kliuev and Iurii Iurkun, discussed in chapter 7). Such victims will be extremely difficult to disaggregate from the larger mass, even if access to the relevant files were permitted.

The earliest record of a case under the antisodomy legislation reach-

ing the conventional legal system of Moscow (as opposed to OGPU/
NKVD tribunals) dates from arrests conducted in November 1934.[10]
From the Moscow city court sample of eight sodomy trials with thirty-
six named defendants held between 1935 and 1941, two probable means
of initiating investigations emerge. (In seven of the cases for which
only the sentencing and appeal documents survive, the origins of the
cases must be inferred.) Denunciation, either by men who had been
the objects of sexual advances or by those who observed homosexual
behavior and chose to report it, was evidently a significant factor initiating most cases. Persistent importuning drove some to complain to the
authorities. On 20 February 1941, a student of the Glazunov Musical
Theater College (a Komsomol member), denounced twenty-three-year-
old fellow student Andreevskii, who had on three separate occasions
invited him to take the "passive" role in intercourse. He also said, "Rumors about Andreevskii being a pederast are rife among the students
of the college." The denunciation led to the trial of three men associated with the college later that year.[11] In one 1937 case, which combined charges of counterrevolutionary agitation with sodomy, the sex
crime was probably an aggravating charge added by court investigators
or the procuracy to the first arrested man's file; eventually his confession
brought two other men accused of sodomy and treasonous agitation
into the same trial brief.[12] Police actions account for the initiation of
other cases. The 1938 case against Tereshkov and nine others began
with the arrest of Tereshkov and another man on 3 December 1937,
"caught red-handed during mutual masturbation" in a raid on the public toilet at Nikitskie Gates.[13] This was the sole police sweep on a "meeting place for homosexuals" (*mesto vstrech gomoseksualistov*) mentioned
in the court records, but it is apparent from the documents that the
courts were made aware that such places existed, and police doubtless
kept them under surveillance.[14]

Whether by denunciation or on police initiative, once a "homosexual" had been identified, investigators moved quickly to gather as much
information as possible about his sexual and social contacts. The sentencing records, which indicate the dates of arrest for each person convicted, suggest that police understood they had a narrow window of
opportunity to unravel the dense web of ties between these men, before
lovers and friends might manage to hide themselves or destroy evidence. The twelve men figuring in the 1935 Bezborodov case were
arrested individually or in pairs between 22 November and 12 December 1934. The man whose arrest sparked that of the eleven other defendants, the forty-nine-year-old cook Bezborodov, evidently divulged the
names of at least three men he had had sexual relations with in the

previous years. Within five days of the cook's detention, these men plus two friends who had facilitated their acquaintance had also been arrested. The cook's most recent liaison, an affair with a Communist Party member and white-collar employee, Venediktov, which had lasted from June to September 1934, evidently led police to another cluster of men not known to Bezborodov. In this way, two more white-collar employees and two former priests were soon detained. The police collected considerable documentary evidence to accompany the confessions they obtained, including a "seized notebook . . . containing numerous addresses of men, who Gribov for some reason no longer knows."[15] Postcards and intimate correspondence belonging to others were also taken during arrests and were used in the investigations; incriminating passages were read out in court. In raids leading to other such trials, photographs and diaries were taken by investigators. The search of the room belonging to Glazunov Musical Theater College student Andreevskii, conducted on 28 February 1941, yielded "ten photographs, a notepad with phone numbers, three notebooks with addresses and phone numbers, a trade-union card, a passport, a Komsomol membership card, a military service card, a student identity card, and various correspondence addressed to [the student]." Another search of a second defendant's room produced an intimate letter from a former lover and "four photographic cards of his comrades."[16]

The police gathered statements to be used as evidence primarily from the arrested men, but they also relied on witnesses to supply information about the defendants' behavior. It is difficult to ascertain how reliant police were on neighbors and colleagues to testify against "homosexuals," but one group of special witnesses does emerge in these documents: young objects of homosexual advances. Police and procurators appear to have exchanged immunity from prosecution for witness testimony from these individuals, contradicting the original antisodomy decree. They may have reasoned that the position of these young males was analogous to that of the teenage female prostitute, who in the otherwise severe 1935 decree on juvenile crime was not criminalized; instead, their adult procurers faced new penalties.[17] In most cases these were boys and youths like the teenager ("*podrostok*") Kirill, who met Svechnikov, a physician in his forties, in July 1937 at the Moscow Zoo and accepted an invitation to the older man's home. Kirill received alcoholic drinks and an offer to stay the night. "Later Svechnikov, using the fact that the youth was quarreling with his parents, systematically invited him to his flat, gave him alcohol and money, touched his sex organs, kissed Kirill, was jealous of his girlfriends (*revnoval ego k devushkam*) and repeatedly suggested that the teenager Kirill have a sexual affair with him." The court viewed Kirill's testimony as plausible, for it confirmed details from the confession of Tereshkov, this case's ringleader figure, who had had "intimate relations" with Svechnikov between 1932 and 1934. Kirill may not have been charged in return for testimony that incriminated this former lover probably named in Tereshkov's personal address book.[18] In the 1939 case of Leont'ev and Baikin, the physical education instructor Leont'ev was shown to have "corrupted and inveigled a [named] minor to commit sodomy" and to have "systematically committed depraved acts in relation to children and minors" whose names appeared with those of other witnesses in the court's documentation. The teenager with whom Leont'ev engaged in sodomy was not prosecuted, as investigators and judges viewed him as a victim rather than a fellow criminal. The practice of indulging the young victim of the scheming "pederast" could be highly elastic when procurators wished to shield "normal" young men, even those well into "sexual maturity," from prosecution as homosexuals in their own right. The trial in November 1937 of Ivan Siniakov, a thirty-nine-year-old film executive, for aggravated sodomy ("with the use of force or with the use of the dependent situation of the victim") deftly exculpated the twenty soldiers and sailors and seven civilian men, who had consented to relations with him.[19] At least five of these men gave evidence against Siniakov, and the sentencing document indicates that they ranged in age from sixteen to twenty-nine years of age; most were in their early- to mid-twenties.[20]

Criminal investigators only gathered forensic medical and psychiatric evidence in a modest proportion of these cases. Medical examinations of the bodies of accused were apparently reserved for those instances when confessions or witness testimony required confirmation of an unusual factor or a connection with other persons. Connections were established according to a gendered "active/passive" conception of mutual male relations in anal intercourse. Only two men were examined for anatomical evidence of "passive" intercourse. The first was scrutinized in 1935 to verify his claim that he had been "wounded in the sex organ during the Civil War" and was thus only capable of "passive" intercourse (he received an unusually light one-year sentence).[21] The second individual was examined for reasons that are difficult to reconstruct from the surviving sentencing document alone. In 1937, Sergeev was arrested while masturbating with Tereshkov during the police raid already mentioned on the toilet at Nikitskie Gates—in that year hardly a scenario requiring more evidence of homosexual inclinations for a court to convict—yet forensic medical evidence that

Sergeev frequently played "the role of a passive pederast" was obtained. It may be that police sought to use this evidence to link Sergeev to "active pederasts" they were later unable to arrest.[22] Sergeev did *not* launch an appeal, probably because of this expertise held against him, and unlike most defendants in the Tereshkov case, his sentence was not later suspended or reduced.

The absence of references to forensic medical examinations of the other thirty-four defendants in this sample is consistent with the sentencing documents' formulations that confessions and eyewitness testimony were the usual forms of evidence used against them. Especially in the atmosphere of the Great Terror, there was no need for scientific confirmation of that which could be "proven" by self-incrimination and denunciation. Evidence from the late 1940s and 1950s suggests that forensic medical (and psychiatric) expertise may have become more prevalent in investigations of sodomy cases as court and police investigators acquired better training.[23]

Expert psychiatric evaluations were also sparingly used, and when they were, they demonstrated that the legal impotence of the psychopathic diagnosis now applied to the criminalized homosexual. Psychiatric evaluations appear in the sample of cases where individuals were perceived as unbalanced or when they preyed on minors. They were initiated when investigators required them, never when requested by defendants or their defense advocates.[24] Film executive Ivan Siniakov underwent a psychiatric review on 22 September 1937 at the V. P. Serbskii Forensic Psychiatric Institute, where he was judged to be "a psychopathic personality with aspects of neurasthenic development and inclination to sexual perversions," yet he was pronounced liable to answer for his crimes.[25] It was a diagnosis that enabled doctors to say they had recognized an illness, while they surrendered any custodial claim over the homosexual. The diagnosis also evidently assisted procurators, who built a case against Siniakov as having "a conceited and self-lauding" personality, and displaying "demoralization in personal life" (*bytovoe razlozhenie*), the official reason given for his being stripped of the Communist Party membership he held until his arrest.[26] A member of the nobility before the revolution, Siniakov was certainly vulnerable to ideological reinterpretation as a "double-dealer", a class alien who had somehow crept into the Party. There was however surprisingly little of this rhetoric in the sentencing and appeal documents describing his trial. Instead, by presenting him as a morally degraded and mentally unbalanced personality, certified by psychiatrists, procurators could free the young (and not so young) soldiers, sailors, and civilians he had seduced from political and sexual taint by association. In this case, the function of forensic psychiatry was not merely to supply the appearance of normal judicial procedure, but to give scientific gloss to a procuratorial strategy of selective exculpation.

With a case assembled, the trial took place. None of the trials in this sample were "show trials" (*pokazatel'nye protsessy*), the dramatized processes that mobilized the press and judiciary to construct flawless spectacles of proletarian justice, sometimes in theatrical settings.[27] From the sample of eight Moscow city court trials for sodomy between 1935 and 1941, very little evidence of "campaign justice" or any determination to publicize these crimes can be discerned. Six out of eight trials on sodomy charges, involving thirty-two out of thirty-six defendants, were held behind closed doors.[28] This appears to be a higher rate of closed trials than for heterosexual sex crimes (discussed below), but the sample is admittedly small. Ben De Jong's conclusion that trials for sodomy took place behind closed doors as "a matter of course" in the 1960s and 1970s may not necessarily apply to earlier decades.[29] Nonetheless, when taken in conjunction with the veil of silence drawn over internal explanations of the crime even for jurists, it seems that judges saw little educative value, and possibly greater social harm, in opening sodomy trials to public view.

While these records (primarily of sentences and appeals) offer little sense of the conduct of the trials themselves, they often contain descriptions of the male homosexual subculture that the new statute sought to eradicate. Paradoxically, it is the survival of the subculture and not its demise that is documented in these brief summaries. The earliest trials noted the continuing existence of sociability, street cruising, and public sex, especially in the vicinity of Moscow's Boulevard Ring. In November 1934, Bezborodov and Gribov (a "ringleader" whose address book fell into police hands) "wishing to drink alcohol," visited the flat of one Petr "by nickname 'The Baroness,' who kept an entire den of homosexuals." The court designated this flat as one of the significant "meeting places of pederasts," although the fate of the Baroness and his "den" is unclear.[30] Another gathering place was Hermitage Park. The nearby Boulevard Ring linked this small green space to Trubnaia Square, where one of the capital's most frequented "meeting places," a public toilet, was located. This facility was reportedly constructed underground in a circular shape, with cubicles against the perimeter wall, facing inward. There were no doors on the stalls, which had simple holes in the floor.[31] All users were in a position to observe each other, and this perverse panopticism apparently enabled meetings as well as prevented them. Levin, investigated for sodomy in 1941, described his discovery of this facility:

> Once in autumn 1940 I left a restaurant on Tsvetnoi Boulevard and was walking toward my apartment on Neglinnaia Street. On the way I stopped in the toilet on Trubnaia Square and there, against my will, an act of sodomy was committed with me. A man came up to me and began to masturbate, touching my penis. I did not particularly object. A month and a half after this I once again went to the toilet on Trubnaia Square, but this time with the deliberate intention of committing an act of sodomy. In this manner I committed acts of sodomy about five or six times . . .[32]

Sometimes, Levin invited partners home to sleep overnight with him; others he had sex with on the spot. He claimed that his loneliness drove him to drink, and it was only the alcohol that was responsible for his cruising in the toilet, not his desire for company.[33]

Nikitskii Boulevard, running from Nikitskie Gates Square, where in 1937 Tereshkov and Sergeev had been "caught red-handed" in the men's toilet, figured in other confessions as well. One defendant explained to interrogators: "In 1936 in the apartment where I lived, Afanao'ev, an artist of the ballet, moved in . . . He showed me the places where pederasts meet: Nikitskii Boulevard and Trubnaia Square." Another defendant said that in the early 1930s, a friend "told me that the chief places for pederasts were Nikitskii Boulevard, Trubnaia [Square], a bar on Arbat [Street], and the Tsentral'nye Baths." By this time the bar and baths would have been publicly owned; these were rare references to formerly commercial spaces frequented by the subculture in this era.[34] Similarly, Sretenskii and Chistoprudnyi Boulevards, mentioned by the prostitute P. in 1927, continued to figure as meeting spots in the mid-1930s. In 1935, Anisimov and Brodskii "met by chance on Sretenskii and other boulevards of the city of Moscow with men-pederasts [muzhshchiny-pederasty] and entered into sexual intercourse with them in toilets, in apartments and on the boulevards . . ."[35]

The Boulevard Ring was one feature of central Moscow that was not drastically altered by the construction projects of the first Five Year Plans, and thus it remained a refuge from the disruptions prevailing elsewhere in the center. The remarkable catalog of the activities of film executive Ivan Siniakov suggests that the project of transforming Moscow into a model socialist city was paradoxically responsible for the emergence of a new pattern of sexualized territories in the heart of the capital. In 1936, Siniakov struck up acquaintances with sexually available soldiers and sailors in Sverdlov Square, located in front of the Bol'shoi Theater, and the following year, in nearby Manezh Square. These are the earliest references yet uncovered for homosexual contacts in these squares, located near the Okhotnyi Riad metro station. The opening of the Metro in 1935 and the reconfiguration of central traffic arteries leading to the massive Hotel Moskva (where Mokhovaia Street and Okhotnyi Riad became Prospekt Marksa in the 1930s) lured the curious. Servicemen on leave and civilians visiting the capital in the late 1930s flocked to the Metro and especially to the cluster of stations in this district. By the 1950s, probably thanks to these new transport links, Sverdlov Square with its patch of greenery in front of the Bol'shoi had become the focal point of new cruising patterns, surpassing the older haunts associated with the Boulevard Ring.[56]

Siniakov's case significantly revealed that under Stalin, some military men preserved the time-honored habit of sexual availability to men for modest compensation. The sentence highlighted Siniakov's forays in Sevastopol' and Leningrad, and it was clear that both sailors and their patron followed a scripted routine of meetings in notorious locations and innocent-looking invitations:

> In 1929, the accused Siniakov, having become acquainted with the sailor A, twenty-five years old on the boulevard in Sevastopol', and having as a result met him in Leningrad, inclined the former to the commission of sexual acts in perverted form; a year later, having met the sailor B, twenty-four years old, and using B.'s situation as a demobilized serviceman, invited him to stay with him in Moscow, where he began to incline B. to sexual perversions. . . . In [1931] in Moscow, meeting sailor C. in the street, with whom he was acquainted from Sevastopol' where they had met on the seaside boulevard, he invited the latter to drink alcohol in his flat, where subsequently he committed with C. sexual acts bearing the character of sodomy [sic].[57]

The seaside boulevards of Sevastopol' were but one infamous place for sailors who sought this kind of patronage. On an unnamed Leningrad street or embankment in 1936, Siniakov met four sailors aged twenty-two to twenty-six, whom he invited to his hotel room for drinks; they stayed the night there and had sex with him. Later that year at an unidentified Moscow theater he met a sailor "who committed a range of sexual acts during the performance" with him. He picked up another seaman that year in Gor'kii Park. On the street while on business in

Kursk (in 1931) and Penza (1934), the film executive met young men who agreed to move (evidently, temporarily) to Moscow to live and have sexual relations with him. He also found the eighteen-year-old from Penza a studentship. The entertainment world too afforded opportunities for this tireless Communist nobleman. In the stables of the Moscow Circus he met an eighteen-year-old performer and lured him into posing nude for photographs, and into bed, in 1934. In 1936, in an encounter not without rich ironies, at the House of Unions (*Dom soiuzov*, the former House of the Nobility and the scene that year of the show trial of Old Bolsheviks G. E. Zinoviev and L. B. Kamenev), Siniakov made the acquaintance of "Soso," a participant in a "festival of Georgian Art," and took him home to bed.[38] That same year he met a sea-cadet at Mosfilm Studios, with similar results.

Despite concentration in these prosecutions on public sexuality and forms of male prostitution, the records show, too, that the male homosexual subculture continued to harbor relations beyond the bluntly carnal. The voyeurism of earlier sentencing documents gave way to a dry discourse of physical relations between men. During the four days of hearings in February and March 1935 in the Bezborodov case, much time was devoted to an examination of the romantic relations between Pavlov, a forty-year-old bachelor and white-collar worker, and Shelgunov, an expriest of fifty-four. Wounded in the genitals during the civil war, Pavlov had been "deprived of the ability to lead a normal sex life." His partner gave him shelter from 1931 to 1934, and the pair testified to their "loving, tender relationship," confirmed in their private correspondence. Investigators interpreted the physical and emotional love between this pair according to a gendered, active/passive template. Incapable of an "active sexual role" because his penis was defective, Pavlov was said to be "the object of Shelgunov" and thus the receptive partner in sex. Yet emotionally, roles were reversed: Pavlov's "active strivings" were expressed "in his spiritual ties (*dukhovnye sviazy*) with Shelgunov, who on this level played the role of a woman." While evidence suggests police investigators continued to gather as much material as possible about the private lives of men charged with sodomy, trials later in the decade evidently spent less time scrutinizing mutual male relationships except ultimately for their sexual content.[39]

Sodomy in the Calculus of Sentencing and Appeals

Patterns of sentencing and appeals in these trials suggest that the antisodomy law was upheld with vigor for a brief time following enactment, then treated with some leniency except where additional factors weighed against specific individuals. The case of Bezborodov and eleven others (1935) and the case of Tereshkov and nine others (1938) demonstrate the point. Both cases involved a large number of mutually acquainted friends, pairs of individuals who had been involved in long relationships, and briefer sexual contacts. In each case, one or two defendants were singled out as "ringleaders," usually described in these documents as persons "who enabled a range of individuals to engage in sodomy."[40] Their "conspiratorial" activity amounted to running a gregarious social and sex life and keeping a personal notebook of phone numbers, material evidence that led police to others in their circles.

In the 1935 Bezborodov case, the court made a point of stating in its sentencing document that the purpose of the new law was to punish "sodomy as an antisocial system (*pravlenie*) of sexual liaisons between men"; this was the most politicized statement appearing in any of the available Moscow sodomy trial files. Eight out of twelve defendants in this case, including two viewed as ringleaders, received sentences of five years, the maximum penalty for simple sodomy. None of these convicts received any reduction of their sentence on appeal.[41] In contrast, on 1 August 1938, eight of the ten men accused of sodomy in the Tereshkov case were handed the minimum three-year sentences; only the supposed ringleader was given a maximum five-year term. Within weeks, only two of the eight men serving three-year penalties were still in prison. One received an immediate suspension, and five others launched appeals and had their sentences suspended. Five weeks after the trial, only three of the original ten defendants were still in custody.[42] In other cases from the sample, sentences of more than three years were exceptional and aggravating circumstances influenced judges to pronounce them.[43]

Comparison may also be made between sodomy cases and other sex crime cases heard before the Moscow city court between 1935 and 1941. Given the disaggregated nature of the records, only an impressionistic survey based on seventy-six convictions for sex offenses under articles 151, 152, and 153 of the RSFSR criminal code during this period in the Moscow city court is possible.[44] Initial sentences in this sample run from acquittals (nine in total) up to the death penalty (three men, later commuted to ten years' imprisonment); most (thirty-three) fall between three and five years' confinement. Eighteen terms of deprivation of liberty for less than three years were handed down. Against this very crude measure, sentences for simple sodomy during the same period, in the same courts, tended toward the three-year mark and so were roughly comparable to moderate sentences for rapes by individual men and the sexual abuse of minors and children. These were not sentences indicative of politicized or campaign justice.

A comparison that illuminates differences in trial and sentencing practice can be found by comparing trials of groups of sodomites versus rapists. Groups of men committing heterosexual rape in an organized fashion had been the subject of special attention from 1926 when Leningrad's Chubarov Alley case first raised fears that the "conscious proletariat" was capable of such barbarities.[45] In the mid-1930s, there were calls for harsher sentencing, with the application of state-crime level sanctions (ten years and even execution) for group rapes.[46] The use of politicized language in the special collegium (*spetskollegiia*) of Moscow's city court, in which offenses viewed as politically significant were tried, was more forceful against these gangs of rapists than the most propagandistic rhetoric used by judges in the regular criminal collegium where homosexuals were tried. A case of group rape of one factory worker by eight of her coworkers in 1935 attracted exceptional sentences that actually exceeded the eight-year maximum under article 153. Three sentences of ten years' confinement and three death sentences were handed down, using the application of article 59(3) against banditry. On appeal, the RSFSR Supreme Court agreed that the lower court had interpreted the case correctly as a political crime but ordered the death sentences be commuted to ten years each; the rest of the sentences, including the three other ten-year terms, were upheld.[47]

By contrast, the most politicized sodomy case in the 1935–41 sample (the trial of Bezborodov et al. already mentioned) was handled by the city court's ordinary criminal collegium, and while a large number of maximum sentences were handed down, they did not exceed the limits stated in the criminal code. The *spetskollegii* of intermediate-level courts were used after 1934 to handle politicized offenses, and a sharper rhetoric from them was the norm. Only one of the sodomy trials in the Moscow city court sample was tried at this level, suggesting that as cases against homosexuals were entering the conventional justice system, sodomy was already seen as less politically significant.[48]

Group rape and collective sodomy cases heard later in the 1930s appear to have lost the force of politicized justice. Both types of trials displayed a return to normal sentences (not exceeding criminal code limits) and the application of maximum sentences was restricted to "ringleader" figures, with lesser offenders netting briefer prison terms. On appeal, however, the RSFSR Supreme Court appeared less willing to reduce penalties for group rapes than for sodomy, suggesting that at this level there was a clear distinction made between the degrees of social danger involved in the crimes.[49]

Men convicted of sodomy in Moscow's city court between 1935 and 1941 who appealed their sentences to the RSFSR Supreme Court were more successful in getting reduced penalties than were rapists, but less successful than individuals charged with (usually nonviolent) sex crimes involving young persons.[50] Evidentiary factors probably influenced the higher court: violent sexual assaults against adult women were easier to document with forensic medical evidence and police testimony, while child abuse and sex with teenagers could be more difficult to demonstrate and might be successfully challenged by the defendant's advocate.

Successful appeals launched by men convicted of sodomy show little commonality of strategy but for one circumstance: they tended to be supported by advocates, not argued by the defendants themselves. As they did normally, lawyers relied heavily on the "personality, lack of previous convictions, and family situation" of their clients in arguing for mercy.[51] No appeals on psychiatric grounds were successful.[52] Lawyers or defendants who challenged the court's interpretation of the letter of the law were occasionally rewarded for their erudition. On 30 June 1941, advocate S. D. Bos'ko argued before the RSFSR Supreme Court's collegium for criminal cases that his client, Andreevskii (a "ringleader" figure in the trial of three men associated with the Glazunov Musical Theater College) could not be guilty of aggravated sodomy under article 154a-II. The Moscow city court had not demonstrated any use of force with his partners, nor was evidence produced of the claim that Andreevskii had actually "accomplished" the act of sodomy with the youths and children who testified against him. The advocate requested that his client's crime be requalified under article 154a-I (voluntary sodomy), and the six-year sentence correspondingly reduced. The Supreme Court agreed, and on 10 July 1941 Andreevskii was given a new penalty, the maximum of five years under article 154a-I.[53] Such comparative lenience shown after the beginning of the Nazi invasion of the Soviet Union also highlights the relative depoliticization by this time of sodomy as a crime of conspiracy or espionage. None of the documents in this trial's 132-page dossier mentions these themes.

Appeals when the convicted person was a "ringleader" figure or linked to the seduction of teenagers or young men were normally unsuccessful, as were those launched by three men who had been simultaneously convicted for counterrevolutionary crimes.[54] Here the circumstances of the crime outweighed the eloquence of any advocate. In one case of an unsuccessful appeal, a jurist's erudition appears to have struck the RSFSR Supreme Court as "too clever by half." The defendant Baikin, a former member of the nobility, at the time of arrest a lecturer in a legal institute, submitted in his own defense that while he "had sexual intercourse with various men including Leont'ev" (his codefendant), the acts were not in the form of sodomy and, therefore, could not be prosecuted under article 154a. The appellate court rejected this argument, citing both Baikin's and Leont'ev's testimony as conclusive evidence that "not only depraved acts, but sodomy itself as well" had occurred, without registering precisely what in its view was meant by "sodomy."[55]

Some defendants and their advocates, evidently responding to the state's increasingly shrill insistence on compulsory heterosexuality, put forward defenses that emphasized family and a healthy sexual desire for women. Evidence from Moscow city court sodomy trials suggests that jurists themselves could also be prepared to dispense with a distasteful law behind the fig leaf of marriage. Toward the end of the decade, Moscow city court judges sometimes fixed upon the marriages of otherwise harmless defendants as evidence of their innocence. The guise of marriage could also function as a ruse for judges to mitigate the harsh effects of the antisodomy statute. Of the twenty-nine defendants in the sample for whom civil status was recorded, nine were actually married or "family men" (*semeinye*), that is, apparently married with children; a further five were either divorced or widowers.[56] Of the six described as "family men," all from the first trial in the sample, two were ultimately acquitted, apparently for lack of contact with the "closely tied group" of homosexuals, but the rest were given exemplary punishment.[57] In this early case, having a family did little to soften the court's stern view of the crime. The three men described as "married" (*zhenatye*) were a pianist, a teacher, and an actor. The pianist was convicted of simple sodomy and given a three-year sentence during the strictest first phase of the new statute's implementation in 1935; his marital status, like that of most "family men" in the earlier trial, does not appear to have mitigated his sentence.[58] Both the married teacher and actor were tried for simple sodomy still later, when judges sought to soften the legislation's effect. Judges and investigators cooperated to produce the acquittals of these two men, relying on their marital status as an indicator of innocence. The teacher Efimov, brought to trial with nine others in 1938, had been accused of sodomy because of his association with this case's "ringleader," Tereshkov. They had allegedly shared a bed and had sexual relations, according to Tereshkov's original testimony. During the trial however, the "ringleader" withdrew his testimony, now saying that Efimov had not been aware of Tereshkov's presence in the bed because he had been sleeping so soundly. Tereshkov now said "it seemed to him that Efimov had a wet dream (*polliutsiia*)." The court heard from witnesses attesting that Efimov was "a good family man [*sem'ianin*], of whom nothing bad had been observed in his private life" and the charges against the teacher were dismissed.[59]

One of three actors from Moscow's Glazunov Musical Theater College charged with sodomy in 1941 walked free after a similar revision of the evidence first obtained. The married actor Markovskii twice admitted to investigators that he had committed sodomy while working in a Blagoveshchensk theater with a codefendant, Fedorov, who corroborated this admission when interrogated.[60] Nevertheless, in court Fedorov withdrew his corroboration, and Markovskii himself now said he had been "convinced to sign a statement saying I had sexual relations" with Fedorov. Between the investigators' gathering of evidence and the actual trial, a new script had apparently been composed and rehearsed (for performance behind closed doors). During the trial Markovskii was recast as a robust defender of "normal" relations, and conversations that had not figured in interrogation were aired. Fedorov now admitted "when I guided the conversation to sodomy, he [Markovskii] told me to quit thinking about it because it could end up badly."[61] Markovskii's version of the conversation emphasized the positive: "I told him [Fedorov] that we have a lot of pretty girls, that it [sodomy] is no good." It was also stressed that at the time of his arrest, Markovskii's wife (his second) was pregnant.[62] (The fact that this young woman lived in Kiev and was evidently estranged from her husband, who replied, "I don't know her address," when questioned upon arrest three weeks before, was now overlooked.)[63] The court also agreed to a petition from Markovskii that character witnesses in his favor be heard; they attested to his decency, vigilance, and normal relations with women.[64] A male friend claimed that Markovskii had been revolted by the "outrage" uncovered at the theater in Blagoveshchensk, that he had reported it to authorities, and now wanted to resign. A woman neighbor of the actor testified:

> I have known Markovskii since 1930. Markovskii was friendly with a girl (*druzhil s devushkoi*) in our house who died, then there was another girl. We always used to laugh at him because he was not so friendly with the guys (*on tak malo druzhit s rebiatami*). I knew Markovskii up

until his departure for the Far East. I cannot imagine that Markovskii could engage in pederasty.[65]

Even Markovskii's wife's pained and reluctant contribution ("In Blagoveshchensk I was with him in the same group, we spent all our time together, but I stayed in a separate hotel room") could not moderate the court's determination to acquit her husband.[66] Meanwhile, his two bachelor codefendants were convicted, although Andreevskii's advocate S. D. Bos'ko was successful in obtaining a one-year reduction in his client's sentence. In addition to the arguments about evidence Bos'ko used, which have already been mentioned, the advocate also relied on a version of the heterosexual defense. He suggested to the Supreme Court that during the trial "it had not been established precisely that Andreevskii has become a homosexual in full measure," because there were gaps of six months and one year between episodes of sodomy. The unmarried twenty-three-year-old student was "still young and he could rehabilitate himself during a shorter period of punishment," Bos'ko wrote in his appeal.[67] The advocate shifted the focus from an act (sodomy) to an identity and argued that his client was at base "normal" and, therefore, reclaimable. No one in any of the Moscow city court sodomy cases specifically used the term "heterosexuality" to describe relations between the sexes. Yet in the process of these contests over the definition of who was a "pederast" or "homosexual", advocates and defendants, perhaps with prompting by court investigators and judges, sought to claim a masculinity based on "normal" sexuality and familial ties. In closed court sessions where "homosexuals" were tried, male heterosexuality was being redefined.

"An unnatural sexual life with various women"

While the reconfiguration of male heterosexuality was to a significant degree conducted in courts where men were tried for sodomy, Stalinist ideals of "normal" women's sexuality were constructed without resort to a legal penalty for same-sex love. Mutual female love occurred in private space, not on the sexualized public terrain occupied by the male homosexual subculture, and did not attract police attention. Yet despite the lack of an explicit prohibition, gender-neutral legislation did anticipate offenses involving relations between adults and "persons not having attained sexual maturity," and women having sex with girls could be prosecuted. Two Moscow-district criminal cases of this type (in 1925 and 1940) illustrate a transformation in judicial attitudes toward female homosexuality, a shift that reflects the wider changes in Soviet sexual ethics and also reveals fragments of lesbian existence under Stalinism.

The first case arose in late 1923 from a complaint originating in Volokolamsk district by the mother of a teenage girl who had allegedly been raped by a female letter carrier. Nina, then 15-and-a-half years old, was said to have been convinced by Fedosiia P., twenty-two, that she was a man in disguise, and they began a romantic affair. At the end of summer 1923 Nina told her mother that she was no longer a virgin, saying that Fedosiia could not possibly be a woman. In response to the mother's complaint, a people's investigator ordered a gynecological examination of Fedosiia, which revealed that she was a woman with normal genitalia. Nina was examined and found to have reached sexual maturity and to have lost her virginity sometime in the past (reports described her as particularly "developed" for her age). Nina sought to quash the complaint at this point, "forgiving" Fedosiia for her "joke," and demanding their letters—in the hands of the investigator—be returned or burned.[68]

Published accounts give no reason for the continuation of the case, which was not heard in Moscow provincial court until April 1925, but one clue may be that "the people's investigator acquainted Fenia [Fedosiia P.] with cases of hermaphroditism."[69] Fedosiia responded with descriptions of her childhood and adult identification with males. The case attracted forensic medical interest and may have been the subject of conflict between gynecologists and psychiatry. When finally a trial was held, new gynecological examinations were conducted by V. A. Riasantsev, who reported no deviations from female norms in Fedosiia (including no evidence of hermaphroditism) and declared that Nina had long been sexually mature. By this time Nina too was well aware of the putative diagnosis for Fedosiia P.'s ambivalence and declared in court, "I don't believe it even now, that P. is a woman, she's not a woman but a hermaphrodite."[70] Forensic psychiatrist N. P. Brukhanskii testified that the pair's letters were clear evidence of their "homosexuality." The court was unable to reconcile Fedosiia's and Nina's accounts of their involvement and seized on Riasantsev's report to declare that "what had taken place were depraved acts by mutual consent (*po vzaimnomu soglasheniiu*) between persons having reached sexual maturity." Fedosiia was thus acquitted.[71] In 1925, it was possible for a court to apply forensic medical evidence, in this case of the maturity and normality of the bodies of "depraved" individuals, to untangle conflicting testimony and dispose of a confusing case on the grounds that "mutual consent" informed adult sexual choices. Gynecologists' opinions and the two women's correspondence eliminated any question of assault on Nina; hermaphroditism or an unnaturally "enlarged clitoris" were shown not to be responsible for Fedosiia's acts, although this did not remove suspicions that she had used "a rubber husband" (*kauchukovyi muzh*) in relations with the girl.[72] A gynecologist and a psychiatrist provided the court with medico-legal expertise demonstrating informed consent between the sexually mature, and judges exploited the language of sexual revolution to divest themselves of an irresolvable dilemma.

A similar case arising in Moscow city court in 1940 demonstrates the use of forensic gynecological and psychiatric evidence to convict a woman accused of "depraved acts" against a sexually immature teenager. A mother's complaint apparently also brought this affair to the authorities' attention, and in court her assertions were backed by at least three witnesses. In 1936 Irina Stepanova, Party member and researcher,[73] had met Anna, the daughter of a Leningrad associate, and during the subsequent year she befriended the sixteen-year-old. Stepanova began a sexual relationship with Anna, reportedly taking her virginity as "a test of 'honor'" (*proverka "chestnosti"*) in late 1937, then convincing Anna to leave her home in Leningrad and move to Moscow with her in January 1938, where they lived until mid-1939. Perhaps in response to a complaint by Anna's mother, police raided Stepanova's flat in the spring or early summer, a diary was seized and later used against her, and she was expelled from the Party in August. Anna was somehow convinced to testify against Irina, and the pair confronted each other as adversaries during the two-day hearing behind closed doors in April 1940.[74]

Investigators established that Stepanova "for more than ten years had engaged in an unnatural sexual life with various women (lesbian love)." Presumably, during this time Stepanova had successfully concealed her private romantic affairs from the intellectual and Party circles to which she belonged by exploiting domestic space. It is plausible to speculate that the "various women" whose connections with Stepanova were reduced to the merely physical in the court record may have constituted a network of friends or a circle of like-minded women, protecting their emotional links behind the closed doors of their flats or rooms. Stepanova's "lesbian" way of life was only uncovered when police finally searched her flat and confiscated a diary.[75] These years of careful discretion resembled the same concealment of female same-sex relations within the domestic sphere evident in the circle in Moscow around poet Sofiia Parnok and her partner Ol'ga Tsuberbiller. After Parnok's death in 1933, Tsuberbiller kept her photograph adorned with flowers in her room, and their circle continued to gather there.[76]

Stepanova, however, had courted disaster by taking a lover so young. In her trial, medical testimony was used to prove that Anna had not achieved sexual maturity before "intercourse" with Stepanova began in 1937, a distinction crucial to the qualification of the older woman's actions as a crime of sexual abuse. The examining gynecologist evidently applied the more exacting definition of "sexual maturity" set by the "forensic medical obstetric-gynecological" guidelines of 1934.[77] (Doctors had been free, before these rules, to employ whatever criteria they chose.) The court ascertained that Anna had never had relations with men, primarily to establish her virginity before relations began with Stepanova. This point was also made to emphasize the teenager's innocence and potential for a "normal" sexual life once the odious influence of her older friend, who had inculcated "a revulsion toward men," was removed.[78] For good measure, Stepanova was sent to the V. P. Serbskii Forensic Psychiatric Institute for an assessment, and there pronounced "imputable and responsible for her actions." No reported attempt to find signifiers of "masculinization" on Stepanova's body took place. The court cited Anna's testimony, the diary seized in Stepanova's Moscow flat, and forensic medical opinions as conclusive evidence against the defendant, and handed down a three-year sentence (the maximum penalty was five years).[79]

On appeal, Stepanova's advocate argued that Anna *had* reached sexual maturity before their affair (and therefore no crime under article 152 could be construed). He alleged that Anna's loss of virginity was the result of masturbation and not his client's fault; he also called for further consideration of Stepanova's "state of mental health." The RSFSR Supreme Court rejected these pleas, citing the existing forensic medical testimony. By 1940, jurists would not invoke revolutionary principles of "mutual consent" between sexually mature women, for women's duty lay within the Stalinist framework of compulsory heterosexuality. Arguments for the defense based on the medical definition of the victim's sexual maturity or on the mental health of the accused, represented a scrap of hope for Stepanova, but as in men's sodomy trials by the late 1930s, medical expertise favoring defendants was rarely if ever admitted. Nor was it acceptable to acknowledge female sexual desire unmediated by heterosexual relations: the allegations of teenage masturbation were rebuffed. In the eyes of the court, the young Anna's diversion from heterosexual relations was the social danger posed by her relationship with Stepanova, and it acted to end it. Anna had been convinced to betray her older friend and would now be reeducated into heterosexual norms in her mother's care. In a contest over definitions of sexual maturity and autonomy, Stepanova had discovered to her great cost the new boundaries of Stalinist compulsory heterosexuality.

Conclusion

Almost all of the courtroom dramas described here took place behind closed doors. Unlike the show trials of the 1920s against clergy and monks for sexual offenses, these were not edifying spectacles mounted to demonstrate Bolshevik values to a wide audience. Nor were they meant to proclaim to the capitalist world the moral purity of Stalin's socialism. No Röhm scandal ending in a Night of Long Knives erupted in the Soviet Union to sweep away any major figure inside the Party in a torrent of homophobic rhetoric.[80] These processes functioned not on the massive scale of the show trials, but primarily for the players who took part in them. Stalin's trials of homosexuals represented a micropolitical environment in which new understandings of gender, sexuality, medicine, and law were forged and inculcated. Defendants, their advocates, judges, lay assessors, and procurators enacted roles that explicated and developed the meaning of the new prescriptions about compulsory heterosexuality, whether it was the familial love and concern to be demonstrated by fathers or the instinctively maternal devotion of mothers.

Why invest so much effort in such small numbers? The answer is probably to be found by examining the occupational and class status of these individuals. Of the thirty-six named defendants in the Moscow sodomy trial sample, seven men were workers,[81] twenty-six were white-collar clerical or professional-managerial employees,[82] and three individuals were from the clergy or ex-clergy.[83] Most of these men were skilled, productive, and categorized with an acceptable class background. With few exceptions, these were not the "declassed rabble" nor the "remnants of the exploiting classes" whom Commissar of Justice Nikolai Krylenko had singled out in his 1936 address, justifying the new antisodomy law. Instead, these men (and Stepanova, too) were from those valued urban worker and intelligentsia social groups that Stalinist measures would forge into a socialist technical and managerial elite. In these trials all parties acted, in the words of Krylenko, "to rework ourselves, to foster in ourselves the new man . . . and new attitudes toward *byt* (daily life)." In these contests behind closed doors, Soviet justice helped to fashion Stalinist compulsory heterosexuality, especially in its masculine variant. The focus of concern was the male homosexual subculture of the boulevards, and the participation of these "reclaimable," sometimes even "normal," men in it. Same-sex relations were discovered by police and vigilant citizens, described by interrogators, measured by doctors, indicted by prosecutors, implicitly defended as private correspondence or diaries were made public, and excused and denied by advocates who sometimes pleaded that their clients could be reformed. It was, of course, a massively unequal contest, and the people caught in this system were shamed, made fearful, and most often, imprisoned for a sexual identity that was invoked and redefined in closed courtrooms.

With Stepanova's psychiatric assessment provided by the compliant V. P. Serbskii Forensic Psychiatric Institute and a gynecological evaluation of the harm (defloration) that she had inflicted on her young friend, Soviet justice furnished a new definition of Stepanova as lesbian in medical and legal terms. In a rare case in which same-sex relations between women came before the courts, jurists and doctors evidently drew on the institutional long-term memory of legal historians and forensic gynecologists to interpret an unfamiliar phenomenon. They also incorporated the Stalinist reworking of women's gender roles, expressing a sharp concern to channel female sexuality into heterosexual and, ultimately, maternal objectives. Their anxiety to reinforce compulsory heterosexuality was evident especially in the contest over definitions of sexual maturity. Who defined "sexual maturity" defined the age of consent, the point at which the state granted autonomy in sexual matters to its young citizens. The 1934 forensic gynecological guidelines defined sexual maturity (always gendered as female) according to a natalist focus on the ability to give birth and sustain a new life. Autonomy for women in the Stalinist sexual order was little more than the freedom to remain celibate or risk pregnancy. In 1940, jurists would not accept that young women's sexuality had legitimate purposes (such as pleasure or emotional fulfillment) other than the maternal.

These trials contributed to the "grotesque hybrid" of Stalinist gender policy by linking a previously tolerated form of sexual difference to criminality. The hostile pathologization proposed by psychiatrists who promoted the psychopathic model of sexual perversions was insufficient to the Stalinist vision. The "honest citizens or good Communists" who, according to a psychiatrist consulted by Harry Whyte in 1934, had been free to reconcile their same-sex desire with their public lives, perhaps with the aid of psychotherapy, and undoubtedly with great discretion, now faced imprisonment, particularly if they were men. Inside places of confinement, the stigma and shame of the sexual identities forged in Stalinist jurisprudence would escape the containment of discreet closed courtroom sessions.

Epilogue

THE TWIN CRUCIBLES OF THE GULAG
AND THE CLINIC

T he character and the treatment of same-sex relations in Soviet
Russia in the second half of the twentieth century would owe
much to the Gulag and the clinic, two arenas in which "pederasty" and "female homosexuality" were visible but contained. From
1934 to the mid-1950s, the NKVD and its successors operated the Gulag
system, an archipelago of camps, colonies, prisons, and "labor settlements" across some of the most inhospitable territories of the Soviet
Union. Prisoners from both the conventional justice system and the
extralegal tribunals of the secret police entered the Gulag, and those
with sentences of three years or more were sent to its "corrective-labor
camps." By the late 1930s, almost three million convicts inhabited the
places of confinement run by the Gulag, most of which functioned as
self-financing economic enterprises dependent on forced labor.[1] Subsequent waves of new convicts, and the captives of war and of the
conquest of the Baltic states, changed the social structure of the Gulag
camps. World War II also brought new groups of Soviet citizens into
the system, as persons captured by the enemy were treated as traitors
and given harsh sentences after repatriation. By the time of Stalin's
death in 1953, the population of the Gulag stood at some 2.47 million.[2]
The years after 1953 saw de-Stalinization and the proclamation of "socialist legality," as attempts were made by Stalin's successors to curb
the power of the security police. The Gulag was transferred out of secret
police hands, and ultimately the economic empire based on convict
labor was broken up. Large contingents of Soviet citizens were rehabilitated and amnestied, and returned to society during the middle to
late 1950s, with important and little-understood consequences. Men
who had been convicted on charges of sodomy were regarded as com-

mon criminals and were not amnestied. Likewise, there was apparently little effort made to withdraw or reform the antisodomy law.

This epilogue is an outline of the historical legacies of Stalinist policy against same-sex love. It is not intended to be exhaustive, but rather to suggest linkages between contemporary phenomena and the past revealed in this study. I hope that its suggestions and conjectures will stimulate more research on the history of Russian sexual and gender dissent. The kinds of evidence available on these issues for the second half of the twentieth century present exciting yet daunting methodological and logistical considerations for researchers who might wish to investigate them.[3] Here I rely on archival and published material to examine three themes. The first is a discussion of prison cultures of male and female same-sex relations and how the expansion of the Gulag system affected them. Awareness of this experience evidently weighed heavily in the elaboration of separate regulatory regimes for male and female homosexuals in post-1953 life. Thus, the second section examines de-Stalinization for its effects on sexual regulation. Finally, the epilogue sketches the significant transformations in late-Soviet society that created forces challenging post-Stalinist (and neo-Stalinist) moralizing from the police, administration, and psychiatry.

"Such is love in prison"

The sexual culture of the Gulag, which contributed enormously to late-Soviet perceptions of same-sex desire, grew from a preexisting prison culture. In the first three decades of the twentieth century, Russia's penal experts like their colleagues in Europe observed and deplored same-sex erotic practices in places of confinement. Official voices fell silent on this topic after 1930, and until memoirists took it up after 1953, the issue was suppressed, leaving a thin base of sources on the 1930s and 1940s.[4] In tsarist and early-Soviet prisons, a distinctive and harrowing role for anal rape and other sexual humiliations marked male prisoners' subculture, a brutalized version of Russia's traditional masculine culture of mutual erotic practices. Evidence of the sexual culture of men's prisons appears to reflect a degree of continuity from the late nineteenth century to the present day. It is, however, plausible to propose that the growth of the Gulag system from the late 1920s intensified the worst features of this subculture.[5] Women's prisons and later Gulag camps, reflected some critical gender differences in their hierarchies and practices. An examination of both prison cultures suggests how late-Soviet views of same-sex desire came to be constructed from widely held perceptions of criminality in confinement.

To begin with men's prisons, experts' early-twentieth-century descriptions of the place of so-called "pederasty" in prison life reflected (usually unconsciously) the general masculine traditions of mutual sexual activity. Hierarchies of age, physical strength, command of resources, and social status dictated who would become sexually accessible and who would dominate. The youthful newcomer, if raped or seduced by fellow prisoners, would rapidly be incorporated as a "pederast" into the prison's social system, at its lowest rung. Once his status was established, he might turn to prostitution as a survival mechanism, if circumstances and character allowed. Initiatory rape and prostitution were not the only routes to the status of "pederast" in prison. Some inmates were pushed outside the community of fully masculine prisoners (known as *muzhiki,* the word for peasant patriarchs) for failing to adhere to the code of prisoners' norms. These men joined the first two categories of "pederasts," often after initiatory rapes or sexual humiliations, and became part of the same caste.

As they arrived in common cells, naive teenagers were often courted with favors, tricked into compromising positions, or simply raped. On Christmas Eve in 1902 in Ekaterinburg, one youth put into a remand cell was raped by no less than six juvenile inmates. "Petia . . . did not appear more than fifteen to sixteen years old, but he looked very much like a girl."[6] This lad had the courage to complain about his attackers, and a doctor who examined him noted:

> This vice is one of the evils of prison. It is not only terrible for the individual who bears the evidence of such assaults, but because at the end of the day it creates these people who convert it into their own sort of profession, living flagrantly (*pripevaiuchi*) in prison, earning money for that profession.[7]

Once it was known that a young newcomer had been assaulted in this way, he became the object of abuse and attacks. His assailants sought to prevent him from making a complaint with a combination of violence and (if he complied), eventually with money or gifts of tea, tobacco, or food.[8] As the physician in Ekaterinburg observed, the path from initial sexual assaults frequently led to open prostitution.

In 1911, an observer vividly depicted prison inmates' view of young men, as surrogate women. The traditions of bathhouse prostitution, with youthful males assumed to be sexually available, were evident:

they go naked together [to the bath], young and old, gazing at each
other with greedy eyes, like men looking at women, at anybody a little
younger, a little paler, a bit more tender, softer to the touch. They sur-
round him on all sides, laugh and pinch, and slap him on the back. He
tears himself away, squeals and makes eyes like a woman of easy virtue.
Jokes and curses rain forth, simply bestial. Such is love in prison.[9]

The criminologist Mikhail Gernet, reproducing these words in his 1925
study of penal psychology, believed there was very little in this bathhouse vignette to distinguish it from reports of more organized homosexual vice in French prisons. Despite his contention that "sexual famine" (*polovoi golod*) was at the root of such phenomena wherever the
prison, the Russian bath was a peculiarly national institution, long associated with covert mutual male sexual activity. In this setting, youths
were viewed as sexually available, and some might exploit this circumstance "like a woman of easy virtue," as their counterparts did in the
commercial baths of St. Petersburg and Moscow. They were subjected
to a barrage of "bribes, offers of rations accompanied by seduction,
promises of protection or defense, intimidation and plain assault" by
older prisoners with sexual intentions.[10] Prisoners and expert observers
universally interpreted "pederastic" relations behind bars as gendered
into an active/passive, masculine/feminine dichotomy, with all the
assumptions about domination and subordination implied by these bi-
narisms. Younger men were assumed to be available for the "passive"
role. Social hygienist David Lass of Odessa noted in his 1927 survey
of 692 male prisoners that among the "pederasts" he surveyed, the
"passives" were most likely to be younger men, while older men were
more often "active."[11] The exchange of favors of various kinds (access
to food, housing, education) for sex was common enough between males
in Russian society from at least the mid–nineteenth century. The existence of such relations in prison was not a depravity generated by life
behind bars, as some experts believed. They ignored the fact that similar exchanges flourished beyond prison walls.[12]

The seasoned prostitute convict attracted open resentment and (less
frequently, perhaps) surreptitious expressions of kindness. In 1899, a
former convict described a male prostitute, Shuster, who wore his uniform "more decently, I would almost say, more exquisitely, than the
other prisoners," and who went by the name "Kat'ka"; he was the
object of much hatred and violence.[13] The ex-convict wrote that when
quizzed about the hostility directed at Shuster, the *starosta* (chief) of
his barracks replied:

Our fellows have their own ideas on this account. They keep to the rule: if your chance comes, take it; if not—run away. And why do they persecute him if a good half of the prison is guilty of it [sodomy]? Well, scoundrels like Kat'ka are either fed to fatten them up for the slaughter or beaten in their fat mugs.

The *starosta* implied that like a peasant's beloved cow or pig, "Kat'ka" could be stroked and fawned over, until the moment of cyclical violence (corresponding to the day of slaughter), when the prostitute must be humiliated to preserve the community's masculine honor.

In Soviet Russia's jails of the 1920s, penologist Mikhail Gernet encountered "pederasty . . . in the form of prostitution, when passive pederasts offer themselves to all comers for the going rate." Such men possessed a "psychology resembling the feminine" and used all the typical gambits of the female prostitute, "virtually up to the traditional opening of an acquaintance with a request for a cigarette."[14] Officials working with homeless youth during NEP reported that teenage boys sent to adult prisons and youths in reformatories prostituted themselves for petty gifts and protection.[15] Young men continued to be the most successful as prison prostitutes, but older men were observed "offering themselves for tea or cigarettes" during the 1950s.[16] Whole barracks of "pederasts" operating as male brothels have been reported in memoirs of prison camp life from the 1930s and 1970s.[17] Individual prostitution persists inside the "zones" to this day.[18]

Inmates who violated the common code of prisoners' norms were also relegated to the status of "pederasts" and were often forced to serve as sexual objects of the *muzhiki.* The most enduring general pretext in prison for relegation to this status was by losing at cards without being able to pay one's debts. Losers were compelled to service their victors sexually by way of compensation and afterward were regarded as "pederasts." Sources appear from the first years of the twentieth century for this particular phenomenon.[19] Symbolic humiliations such as the use of specifically feminizing insults (also noted by observers as early as the 1900s) were sufficient to consign violators of the prison moral code to this category.[20] In the memoirs of post-1953 dissidents, theft from fellow inmates or informing on them to the camp administration were by the 1960s and after also routes to the "pederast" caste.[21] Evidence from more recent research indicates that the "untouchable" status forced upon men subjected to same-sex rape and abuse has hardened into a cruel and rigidly observed pattern in late-Soviet and post-Soviet places of confinement.[22]

In 1926, E. K. Krasnushkin had permitted himself to imagine the
socialist prison,

> with physical education, with a school, with a cinema, theater, library,
> with well-organized medical care in all specializations, with a determi-
> nation to develop the prisoners' independence and inclination to social
> skills.[23]

Prison in the new society would be an arena of rehabilitation and resocialization. Life inside the prison—its *byt*—would be examined and
restructured, down to its most intimate aspects, including (as Gernet
and Lass did) even the sex lives of prisoners. Yet a major feature of
the prison environment, same-sex relations, was dealt with timidly by
these researchers. Prisoners refused to answer questions or gave evasive
replies. Penologists recoiled from probing further. They covered their
reluctance to examine this shameful aspect of prison life with optimistic
nostrums about the effect of a reformed *byt*: separate beds, better physical education, a more carefully ordered schedule of routines would obviate the problem. There was no need to inquire further into the origins
of sexual brutality between prisoners of the same sex.

Soviet places of confinement did not become centers for rehabilitation, but in the Gulag system, hypertrophied into an economic empire
for the NKVD. This expansion multiplied the sites for mutual male
sexual cruelty. (It may be true, as one Gulag survivor claims, that "those
convicted of homosexuality" in the 1930s were usually sent to the Med-
vezh'egorsk camp on the north shore of Lake Onega. Yet this presumed
concentration of victims of the sodomy law—logistically implausible
in any case—should not distract us from the more general sexual brutality of the camps.)[24] The economic exploitation of the prison camp regime squeezed resources out of prisoners, intensifying the prisoners' informal market for the barest scraps of comfort (food, clothing, tobacco,
tea, sexual release). In tsarist prisons, attitudes toward the sexually available male were shaped at least in part by lower-class views of that male
as demasculinized and therefore dehumanized. This prisoners' subculture was already brutal, especially by comparison with views evidently
held by men who had sex together in wider Russian society. Timid
examinations of the problem did nothing to alleviate the brutality in the
early revolutionary years. Under Stalinism, traditional prison hierarchies
were reinforced and even fostered by authorities who sought to intimi-
date "politicals" with violence meted out by "criminals."[25] The evidence
suggests that the "passive pederast" was at the bottom of this hierarchy

throughout the twentieth century, a gender and sexual "untouchable" whose dual role as sexual surrogate and despised scapegoat resonated with amplified masculine insecurities and vicious misogyny.[26]

As with men's places of confinement, the prison and, later, the Gulag camp were widely believed to encourage same-sex intimacies among women, to the point of generating "acquired" homosexuality, the result of a culture of "social self-regulation among prisoners."[27] Yet Russians who studied women in the penal environment in the 1920s regretted the lack of reliable data on their sexual activity. Penologist Gernet could only muster two letters illustrating "unnatural vice" in prison.[28] Lass's 1927 survey of the sex lives of 81 female and 692 male Odessa prisoners was stymied by the unwillingness of women to reveal more than a few intimate details to the expert.[29] His data based on surveys did suggest that some proportion of women engaged in same-sex relations. In his sample of women, 35.3 percent admitted they were "not abstaining" from sexual activity (which Lass interpreted as masturbation "and other sexual perversions") while in prison. Yet Lass found it either impossible to obtain, or to relay in print, further information about the nature of the "other sexual perversions" his subjects displayed, except to surmise that many subjects were reporting "pollutions" in his survey as a means of disguising events of a less solitary nature. He also noted about a third of his female subjects shared beds in prison, a practice said to encourage vice.[30]

Gernet's approach to the "psychology of prison sex life" was more anecdotal, not dependent on a questionnaire-led methodology. One of the letters he presented, from a female prisoner described "being pestered" by a masculine-looking woman, supposedly known in prison slang as one of the "'kovyrialki,' as the women-tribades taking the man's role in unnatural relations with their female cellmates are called." Gernet continued,

> According to our correspondent, these women "'have all the tricks of men, they walk, kept their hair like men, they smoke and wear Russian men's shirts (rubashki-kosovorotki) secured with a lace.' The courtship began with notes, with avowals of mad love and requests to belong to no one else. In [the correspondent's masculinized friend's] notes she wrote 'she kisses her little mouth and eyes, and wants to kiss her all over.'" The correspondent who the prison administration informed us had been seduced by her comrade, wrote to us, "I liked her, she came to me when I was alone but I was afraid to greet her: right away she was kind of mad and strong, she grasped me on the bed and began to kiss

my breasts, legs, hands so unexpectedly that I didn't have the strength to say anything."[31]

Gernet's text presents an early-Soviet portrait of the "masculinized" female homosexual in prison, accompanied with one of the earliest documented references to the prison slang term *kovyrialka.* (The word is an untranslatable derivation from the verb *kovyriat'(-sia),* a colloquialism meaning to dig in to, to tinker, to rummage in.) Sources quoting Gulag memoirs and interviews with female ex-convicts of the Brezhnev years employ the term to denote so-called "passive" sexual partners of "masculinized" prison women, rather than the "active" women themselves.[32] The female homosexual prisoner, masculinized either by her confinement or by a deeper nature, was noted by scientists in other disciplines as well.[33]

Soviet scientists fell silent on the issue of same-sex relations between women in places of confinement during the 1930s, not returning to the question until the general revival of sexology in the 1960s.[34] Literature on women's experience of the Gulag camp system offers some interesting if selective characterizations of same-sex relations in these institutions. This literature also reveals how educated Gulag victims constructed their experience in memoirs to draw crucial distinctions between themselves and persons supposedly justly imprisoned for "genuine crimes." There is a tendency in this literature to evaluate mutual female sexual relationships in an extremely hostile manner. "Lesbian love" is often ascribed selectively to women said to be criminals, that is, not incarcerated under false charges of "counterrevolution" or "anti-Soviet agitation" but for authentic crimes such as theft or murder. The Gulag lesbian is thus constructed as a dangerous character, a pitfall awaiting innocent (heterosexual) women arriving in the camp system. As one German Communist veteran of eleven years in the Gulag, Elinor Lipper, wrote,

> Most women prisoners had never even heard of the existence of sexual relations between two women. They learned about it for the first time as prisoners: for it is relatively frequent among female criminals.[35]

A Russian memoirist recalled a species of camp inmate she first saw at Kolyma in the 1930s, named simply "it" (*ono*). These individuals cut their hair in masculine fashion and took more feminine "lovers." "They went about the camp in pairs, arm in arm, defiantly displaying their love. The administration and the great majority of inmates hated the 'its.' Women in camps fretfully made way for them."[36]

Another writer, recalling Gulag existence in the early 1950s, presented a more nuanced set of reflections about the "its." The "literary-scientific word 'lesbian' " was not widely used, she reported. The camp vocabulary ran from the jocular use of "it" to refer to masculinized lesbians, to the "merciless" criminals' label "dog" (*kobel*).[37] These women tried to resemble men, wearing trousers and short hair; they were most common among criminals, but some were known to exist among German prisoners "and even among our intelligentsia." This author believed fewer Ukrainian women and peasant women fell under such "demoralization," yet she observed that there were cases of keen friendships founded on shared religiosity in which only "sublimation" drew off sexual pressures. It was among criminal inmates that same-sex relations were conducted "openly," while among "the intelligentsia, everything was of course hidden, veiled, ambivalent."[38] Influential sources on Gulag camp life of the 1940s and 1950s repeat similar observations of same-sex relations between women, with the same moral and class inflections.[39]

Ol'ga Zhuk has sketched the patterns of "butch" and "femme" behavior that mark the contemporary Russian women's prison, ascribing its roots to the Gulag system and totalitarianism.[40] The roles and terminology of *kobel* (imitating "men's" roles) and *kovyrialka* (performing "women's" functions) persist to the present day, reproducing a simulacrum of "the patriarchal and strictly regulated structure of heterosexual Soviet families." Both the masculine violence and feminine tenderness of heterosexual relations are represented in the prison role system. Lesbian prisoners "live in families" patterned after male-female relations, according to observer Vladimir Bondarenko. Like Gulag memoirists, Zhuk locates the source of these prison roles in "the criminal underworld" and notes how it persists beyond the prison "among the working class, especially among its lumpen elements."[41] A new development in post-Soviet descriptions of prison-based "butch-femme" relations is the assertion that such bonds are (in Zhuk's words) "stable" and "familiar," or in the words of Bondarenko, that "women recreate inside Russian prisons the world which they have lost." Even Soviet and post-Soviet prison psychiatrists report the formation of "homosexual families" among women prisoners with a certain degree of reluctant appreciation.[42]

De-Stalinization and the Regulation of Same-Sex Love

Stalin's death in March 1953 set in motion a process of political transformation that has generally been regarded as liberal and humane. De-

Stalinization, promoted at first cautiously by a collective leadership, then more boldly under the consolidated rule of Nikita Khrushchev (1957–64), sought to renovate the Communist Party's relationship with society by bringing the security police under strict Party control, curbing the use of terror, and dismantling the Gulag. By the late 1950s, perhaps as many as 4.5 million Gulag inmates had been released, returning to society, and in many cases, attempting to reclaim lost jobs, homes, families, and lives.[43] A key aspect of de-Stalinization was the Party's attempt to implement "socialist legality" and to liberalize Soviet criminal legislation. A third important feature of this political shift was the intellectual "thaw" that accompanied it; while censorship was not abandoned, themes and issues that had previously been taboo were licensed for controlled examination in popular and specialist media. Despite these positive developments, there was no "liberalization" regarding homosexuality, and paradoxically the result of de-Stalinization for men and women who expressed same-sex desire would be increased surveillance and incarceration.

At no point did the energetic renewal of "socialist legality" apparently lead to an examination of the value of the 1934 antisodomy statute. The period saw the drafting of new union republic criminal codes based on the adoption in 1958 of revised penal standards in the USSR Fundamental Principles of Criminal Law. As well, a legislative commission of the USSR Council of Ministers reviewed thousands of normative acts issued during the Stalin era to determine which should remain in force. Abortion was decriminalized in a decree of 1955. A new RSFSR criminal code was drafted and approved in 1960.[44] The new criminal law prescribed sentences that were generally reduced, and the antisodomy statute was marked, albeit slightly, by this policy as the prescribed minimum sentences were eliminated. There was no change in the maximum sentences provided for sodomy offenses.[45] The retention of the antisodomy law rested on a continuing consensus that at least male homosexuality was a moral failing that ought to be suppressed and eliminated from society. It was a consensus hardly unique to the Soviet Union in the postwar era.[46] Yet in the USSR, specific conditions probably combined to sustain the persecution of male homosexuals.

It seems likely, to judge from the evidence of Gulag memoir literature, that for many thoughtful inhabitants of the camps, the experience of same-sex sexuality was recalled with loathing, confusion, and denial. In men's camps in particular, mutual sexuality was embedded in a brutal system of power relations known to all. Jailers and police who ran prisons and camps were well aware of the role of "pederasty" within the culture of the establishments they operated, and in some cases, manipulated it mercilessly.[47] Both inmates and administrators— the majority of persons involved in the Gulag system[48]—observed this sexual hierarchy, collaborated with it, or at least survived alongside it. Its victims were isolated and unable to resist the ferocity with which the "passive pederast" was kept in line. Meanwhile, some might pardon the "active pederast," as certain psychiatrists had explained him earlier in the century, as a man compelled to act on his "natural" desires in "artificial" or "unnatural" circumstances. The "active pederast" could thus be interpreted in various frameworks: as a perverted outcome of the criminal element surrounding him, or as another psychological victim of Stalin's Gulag. According to these lines of reasoning, he would expect (and be expected by others) to revert to heterosexual relations once he was released. It seems doubtful that such spontaneous self-transformations were always so easily effected once the Gulag inhabitant returned to freedom. The decision, whether consciously taken or not, to retain the Stalinist prohibition against sodomy in the de-Stalinized criminal codes was perhaps born of the fear that returnees from the brutality of camp life could carry "mental infection" to society, spreading the "perversions" of Gulag existence.[49]

This logic may account for the climbing rates of convictions for sodomy observed in official statistics from 1960 to the 1970s (see appendix 1). The higher evidentiary standards introduced under the campaign for "socialist legality" also increased the number of forensic medical examinations of "passive homosexuals" and the elaboration of new techniques for identifying them. One forensic medical expert in Moscow turned the detection of sodomy into a technical specialty, and rigged up devices (in the Ministry of Health proctology laboratory) for measuring sphincter muscle tone in order to identify the receptive male partner. Other techniques included the chemical analysis of swabs taken from the suspect's penis.[50] A terse report by this expert, I. G. Bliumin of the Moscow Bureau of Forensic Medical Expertise in 1969, on the examination of 202 "passive homosexuals" for evidence of sodomy, not only attempted to bolster the scientific basis for this enterprise, but to justify the antisodomy statute as well.[51] Having conducted prostate massages on these "homosexuals" and on a control group "who did not commit the act of sodomy," Bliumin observed indications of arousal (*vozbuzhdenie*) in 156 of the "passive homosexuals." Their arousal reportedly vanished when they were examined a second time, "having ceased the commission of sodomy for a sustained period" (presumably in prison, although the physician did not indicate how he ensured this behavioral modification). In a conclusion echoing that of Dr. Shvarts, who conducted digital rectal examinations on Tashkent *bachi* at the turn of the century, Bliumin argued that the conditioned reflexes he had demonstrated, created the homosexual.[52] Logically, the legislative regime that isolated the male homosexual from society as a prophylactic measure was justified. Paradoxically it seems that anxiety about the socially harmful consequences of de-Stalinization contributed to a swelling of the numbers of men sent to prison and corrective labor camps in the late Soviet era for sodomy. An important prop of the Stalinist formula for compulsory heterosexuality survived the dictator (and indeed, the Soviet system itself), living on in a grotesque afterlife of intensified enforcement and abuse.

The renewal of the male-centered law against homosexuality also bolstered the principle of gender difference in the treatment of sexual crime that Stalin had instigated in 1934. At that time, women's deviant sexuality was left to be corrected by "life itself" in the enforcement of compulsory motherhood, an end of fertility control, and the selective promotion of femininity. De-Stalinization brought a partial return to women's control over fertility, with the legalization of abortion, although modern methods of contraception remained a low priority in the command economy. The "thaw" of the Khrushchev years fostered a very controlled revival of Soviet studies in sexology, and these were marked by the gendered criminal law on homosexuality. The organizing principle of the sexological revival was an emphasis on deviance (the discipline was known as "sexual pathology," *seksopatologiia*), since it was judged needless and prurient to study unproblematic normal sexuality.[53] In this climate, the "female homosexual," who had featured in the work of psychiatrists during the 1920s, returned to some research agendas. The consequences of this second wave of medicalization for women having sex together would be harsh.

A study of "female homosexuals" drawn primarily from the Karaganda women's corrective labor camp was perhaps the earliest, and most unlikely, of the trickle of sexological studies appearing in the post-Stalin climate.[54] Between 1954 and the early 1960s, ninety-six women were examined by a trainee psychiatrist, Elizaveta M. Derevinskaia, and her academic supervisor, psychiatrist Avram M. Sviadoshch, to build physiological and psychological profiles of each subject. Derevinskaia wrote up the results of the research in her candidate's dissertation, which she successfully defended in 1965.[55] It was not published, although Sviadoshch, who by 1973 had persuaded the Leningrad City

Health Department to establish a center for sexological consultation and research, drew liberally on his student's work in his *Female Sexual Pathology*.[56]

Derevinskaia's dissertation would be the most significant study of same-sex relations to be conducted by a scientist during the Soviet era. In the timing of the research, its unprecedented scale, and the source of its chosen subjects, the project addressed unspoken anxieties about the problems that would accompany the return of Gulag inmates to society. Foremost was the fact that this was a study of women: the reaffirmed criminalization of male same-sex love and the caution surrounding the new discipline of Soviet "sexual pathology" dictated that large-scale studies of men who loved men would be rare and subordinate to police requirements.[57] There would be no analogous study of this magnitude of "homosexual" men by psychiatrists or sexologists.

Of the ninety-six women in Derevinskaia's sample, eighty-seven came from Karaganda's corrective labor camp; the author said little about how these women came to be identified as "female homosexuals." Some had come to light during medical treatment for somatic problems. Twelve convicts remained under observation after their release. The trainee psychiatrist was extremely circumspect about the reasons for these women's incarceration; she indicated that forty-three "engaged in thefts" and had never held any employment. From the terse life histories she presented, other subjects appeared to have no association with criminality and may have belonged to the large contingent of camp inmates imprisoned in the 1940s and early 1950s on falsified political charges.[58] Nine women came to Derevinskaia's attention as "free" patients who had been treated in Karaganda's provincial psychoneurological clinic. It is possible that among this group there were former convicts who, upon release, had remained in the district because of the residence restrictions often placed on released prisoners. The group was primarily drawn from European nationalities of the Soviet Union and from the ranks of the less educated.[59]

The Karaganda study, which was remarkable for its engagement with the international medical literature on female homosexuality, argued for the classification of homosexual women as either "active" or "passive."[60] Derevinskaia hoped that by sorting her patients into these two groups, the contradictory diagnostic and therapeutic outcomes reported by earlier authorities might be avoided. Her descriptions of the "active" and "passive" female homosexual cataloged the gender desiderata of the Soviet 1950s and 1960s. The "active female homosexual plays the masculine role during sexual intimacy," undressing her partner and even carrying her off to bed, where the "active" woman "usually took the active position (on top of her partner)." The majority of these women (forty-one out of the fifty-seven "actives" in the sample) "imitate the behavior of a man as head of the family." They took all major decisions, decided how all money (including that earned by their partners) was to be allocated, held the family purse, and demanded an account of all spending. "They all refused to tolerate filth and slovenliness" and could be sharp, even rude, with their partners. "Active" women in these households scorned "work considered feminine"; "not one of them made dinner, did laundry or mending." But they did "men's work" with relish ("chopping wood, fixing a fence or roof, etc."), and twenty-one of the twenty-nine "active" women with jobs worked in "men's professions" (the author mentioned cobbling, driving, and operating a lathe as typical "men's" jobs they held). Almost half of the "active" women were described as "transvestites," wearing at least some masculine garb. One individual, a "free" patient of the psychiatric clinic, passed as a man in society, using the name "Andrei Ivanovich" in her passport (see fig. 25). With her partner she had registered their marriage officially (presumably by convincing the registry personnel that she was a man). "Together they formed a homosexual family" with her partner's children from a previous marriage, and the children knew "Andrei" as "papa." Most "active" subjects had short, boyish haircuts, and thirty-six had tattoos (evidence of lives lived in the criminal underworld of the camps). Virtually all liked their partners to wear makeup and low-cut dresses.[61]

These "passive" girlfriends conformed to feminine norms in their sexual and nonsexual lives, sometimes exaggerating "the specificities of feminine behavior." They expected and encouraged their partners to take the initiative in lovemaking; Derevinskaia quoted one woman declaring, "Undressing a woman is a man's business." Frequently they employed masculine grammatical speech when addressing their partners (*milyi, dorogoi moi*). The psychiatrist regarded their expressions of romantic love and not infrequent "masochistic tendencies" as exaggerations of the feminine principle. "Passive" women "patiently endured beatings and cynical abuse." At home they did the laundry and the cooking and made their partners comfortable. In their external appearance, "nothing distinguishes the passive female homosexual from the women around her." Many wore long hair or braids, and had a "feminine walk." Nineteen out of thirty-nine "were distinguished by coquetry." No instances of "transvestism" were recorded; on the contrary, all wore "women's clothing" and "loved to wear rings, earrings, bracelets, broaches," and makeup. Some tinted their eyebrows and hair. They were "soft" and "easily influenced" in character. Twenty-four out of thirty-nine "passives" had professions, and these were of a "feminine" type (as "seamstress, secretary-typist, cleaner").

A significant proportion of Derevinskaia's study was devoted to a review of Western literature on therapeutic approaches to the homosexual, and to her thesis that "active" female homosexuals were less susceptible to curative measures than "passive" ones. This aspect of her work had clear implications for the management of returnees from the Gulag, although Derevinskaia spoke of them only in veiled terms. She placed particular emphasis on the positive effect that the removal of influences that led "passive" women into same-sex relations would bring, suggesting that once such women were able to live among men (rather than with "active female homosexuals"), many would return to "a normal sexual life."[62] With Sviadoshch, in 1956–57 the trainee psychiatrist conducted a therapeutic program on nine women who consented, some with a high degree of skepticism, to treatment for their homosexuality. These patients received courses of a libido-deadening sedative (aminazine),[63] and they reportedly experienced significant falls in their sexual desire. When the women stopped taking the drug, homosexual desire returned and Derevinskaia concluded that the drug only acted on the sex drive without affecting its "direction." In seven cases she punctuated the drug therapy with psychotherapeutic sessions (which were not described in any detail). In this subsample, three "passive homosexuals" made the transition to "a positive result," that is, to heterosexual relations. One further "passive," and all three "active female homosexuals" experienced "no positive effect whatsoever."[64]

Almost twenty years after these extremely limited "positive" results were observed, Dereninskaia's supervisor, who by 1973 had opened his sexological clinic in Leningrad, was promoting similar techniques for curing the female homosexual. Sviadoshch had also followed Western theories of the intervening years, which concentrated attention on brain centers and their supposed function in determining sexual orientation, but he concluded that the therapeutic surgical techniques derived from these theories were too complex and dangerous. While research might one day unlock "new directions" for the control of this "sexual pathology," he implied that the drug and psychotherapy regime devised by Soviet medicine was comparatively affordable and effective.[65]

The contained evolution of "sexual pathology" as a subdiscipline of

Soviet psychiatry during the 1960s and 1970s meant that practitioners evidently devoted most of their energy to building institutions and defending their scientific projects. Whatever their personal opinions, ideologically they worked within "norms that were too narrow and dogmatic," giving expression to an authoritarian and judgmental sexual outlook that had its origins in Party supervision, Soviet intellectual isolation, and undoubtedly, the prudery of many experts as well as their masters.[66] The weakness of Soviet psychological understandings of sexuality also hindered any development of views open to sexual and gender diversity as anything but pathological. Disputes between various physiological disciplines (urology, gynecology, and endocrinology) for a share of the sexological turf had the effect of undervaluing personal experience and emotions regarding sex in favor of technical interventions designed to correct malfunctions and defects in a mechanistic fashion. Igor' Kon has indicted this attitude as "hand-in-glove with Soviet 'repressive psychiatry' which assisted the KGB in locking up dissidents in madhouses," but the problem cannot be ascribed to Party or security police pressure alone.[67] The Soviet medical profession's habits of paternalism and secrecy regarding experimentation on patients and therapeutic decision-making facilitated the practice of a sexist, uncritical, and coercive "sexual pathology."[68]

Recent investigations have reported that during the late Soviet period, women identified as lesbians by educational and medical authorities could be subjected to many of the strictures of repressive psychiatry used against political dissidents.[69] The techniques of this treatment closely resembled those pioneered by Derevinskaia and Sviadoshch. Women in same-sex relations were kept under observation for two- to three-month periods in psychiatric hospitals and given "mind-altering" medication. After release, these patients were registered as mentally ill and would be subject to periodic examinations in outpatient psychiatric clinics, sometimes with sustained drug prescriptions. Persons registered under this regime were denied access to certain forms of employment and to a driver's license. It was virtually impossible to "deregister" such individuals. By the late 1980s, registration controls appear to have been easier to evade.[70] The sexological approaches used on individual victims of this system varied regionally and by the type and degree of specialist knowledge of the administering medics.[71] Nevertheless, the heritage of the sexological view of female homosexuality as an illness, manageable through technocratic and bureaucratic mechanisms, was a result of the de-Stalinizing process that partially licensed sexologists' expertise but did not relax authoritarian systems of social control.

Decriminalization, Again

The changes within Soviet society in the 1980s leading to the search for ways to revitalize Communist rule and the command-administrative economy, and then in 1991 to the collapse of the Soviet Union, had seismic consequences for the legal and medical regulation of homosexuality in Russian life. Continued urbanization, widening education, the penetration of technocratic authority, and a cynical view of the ideological certainties that had propelled the generation of the 1930s to leading roles in public life (and kept them there), had the effect of stripping away the appeal of Communism.[72] Doubts about the historical inheritance of Stalinism and the compromises of de-Stalinization grew. Social developments contributed to skepticism. Just as growing cities fostered the appearance of sites of a male homosexual subculture before 1917, these sites proliferated and evolved as urbanization continued.[73] Despite the conviction of hundreds of men per year on sodomy charges, there appeared to be no conclusive way to rid society of men who wished to have sex together. Russia's homosexual subcultures had taken root in a society where unsupervised and informal subcultures proliferated, despite the neo-Stalinist reaction to Khrushchev's political relaxation during the late 1960s and the 1970s. Dissident movements were mostly political, in the conventional Western view; yet police and KGB regarded all nonconformity with suspicion and considered homosexuality a form of "sexual dissidence."[74]

Two significant strands of dissent contributed to Russia's second decriminalization of consensual sodomy in 1993. One strand came in the form of individual protest against the injustice of Soviet antihomosexual legislation and policing, and eventually, in the spontaneous organization of groups of gay men and lesbians in response to the AIDS/HIV crisis and the social revival of glasnost. The second strand came as experts in law and medicine pressed authorities to acknowledge the futility of Soviet policing of homosexuals and to respond to the challenge of AIDS/HIV with realistic strategies of education and treatment. The two strands, the popular and the discursive, complemented each other and also drew strength from European and U.S. examples and encouragement. Masha Gessen, Igor Kon, James Riordan, and David Tuller have chronicled the progress of this political transformation, situating it within the context of a democratizing Russia with all its uncertainties.[75] An examination of these events through an historical lens can suggest how the Stalinist heritage and the ambiguous legacy of de-Stalinization contributed to these events.

The de-Stalinizers' decision to retain Stalin's antisodomy statute and their evident fear of "infection" from "homosexuals" returning from the Gulag intensified police activity against men identified as homosexual at a moment otherwise characterized by the relaxation of police methods of social control. While the rate of sodomy convictions during the 1950s is still not known, it is clear that between 1961 and 1971, a 40 percent increase in annual convictions occurred (see appendix 1, table 2). Whatever the trend before 1961, after that date the police and courts were labeling more and more male homosexuals, with the collaboration of forensic medical specialists. In effect, this medico-legal complex created, sustained, and increased the observed incidence of "homosexuality" in Soviet society.

In the United States, increased policing and harassment of homosexuals during the 1950s and 1960s provoked first cautious and then more radical reactions from homophile organizations. Ultimately, police persecution in June 1969 enraged customers at the Stonewall Inn in New York City, resulting in the riot now credited as the moment when the gay liberation movement was born. The century's second wave of political activism conducted by those who chose same-sex love gathered strength in English-speaking nations and spread in patchwork fashion to other industrialized and industrializing countries, where local activists frequently adapted and discarded aspects of American gay liberation to suit their own cultures and politics. Leftists, often with bitter experience of the sexually conservative orthodoxies of local Communist and socialist parties, led much of this activism.[76] While there was no gay liberation movement in the Soviet Union in the 1970s, the appearance of this increasingly vocal foreign activism, with its awareness of the Stalinist role in the repression of first-wave homosexual emancipationism, changed the environment in which the Soviet policing of male homosexuals operated. For the first time since Magnus Hirschfeld's Scientific-Humanitarian Committee wrote to the Soviet Embassy in Berlin in 1928 for clarification of the psychiatric treatment of homosexuals in the USSR and since Harry Whyte asked Stalin for an ideological justification of the 1934 antisodomy statute, Soviet persecution of same-sex love was subjected to critical scrutiny by foreign homosexuals. More important, this attention was now of a more sustained nature and came within a context of wider human rights concern focused on the USSR.[77]

In particular, the pursuit by the KGB of intellectuals regarded as politically disloyal on the grounds of alleged violations of the antisodomy law attracted international attention. Georgian filmmaker Sergei Paradzhanov, given a five-year sentence in 1974 under the statute, and

Leningrad poet Gennadii Trifonov, arrested in 1976 and sentenced to four years' imprisonment for sodomy, were the most notorious examples. An Italian gay activist, Angelo Pezzana, traveled to Moscow and sought to secure leading human rights dissident Andrei Sakharov's support for a public statement against Soviet persecution of homosexuals. Undeterred by Sakharov's refusal, Pezzana staged a one-man protest on Paradzhanov's behalf in Moscow on 15 November 1977, gaining foreign press coverage and a mocking response from the intellectual broadsheet *Literaturnaia gazeta.* From prison, Trifonov rebuked this newspaper in an open letter of December 1977, castigating society's "stupidity, falsehood, cruelty, and cynicism" in its treatment of homosexuals. *Literaturnaia gazeta* did not publish the letter, but it was translated and published abroad, and in 1978 Trifonov's poem "Letter from Prison" was released simultaneously in several gay periodicals.[78] The various strands of late-Soviet political dissidence were unsympathetic to critiques of gender and sexual dogmatism and were largely influenced in these views by the intelligentsia cult of asceticism, the heritage of Stalinist ideas of the "naturally" feminine and masculine, and memoirists' accounts of labor-camp same-sex relations.[79] In the West, organizations monitoring political dissidence such as Amnesty International then regarded the oppression of homosexuals as irrelevant to their mandates. Nonetheless, by the late 1970s and early 1980s, a handful of Soviet homosexuals employed the techniques of the wider dissident movement to challenge their society's persecution of same-sex love. The short-lived "Gay Laboratory" (*Gei-laboratoriia*), a group of about thirty men and women appeared in Leningrad in 1983 under the leadership of Aleksandr Zaremba, and with contacts with Finnish lesbian and gay organizations and the International Gay Association. The Gay Laboratory sought to examine the implications for Russians of the ideals of gay liberation and to consider the new threat that AIDS posed to same-sex love in Soviet conditions. Under pressure from KGB surveillance and threats, the group disbanded in 1984 as members either emigrated or fell silent.[80]

Legal and medical experts also expressed careful or veiled calls for reform of the antisodomy statute during the 1970s and 1980s. In their views jurists and sexologists did not acknowledge the second wave of homosexual emancipationism embodied in Western gay liberation activism. In contrast to some of their counterparts in the 1920s who counted first-wave emancipationist politics as part of the sexual revolution that was supported by the Soviet Union, experts of the late Soviet years couched their arguments for the decriminalization of consensual sodomy exclusively in technical language. An example was one text-book in criminal law, published by Leningrad University in 1973, which offered a detailed critique of the statute echoing Vladimir Nabo-kov's turn-of-the-century liberal objections to the tsarist antisodomy measure. The authors in particular criticized the use of criminal law to punish failings that were merely moral in nature; they argued that the act was so well concealed it could not be consistently punished; and they pointed to the decriminalization or nonexistence of such a crime not only in capitalist countries but (by then) in socialist East Germany, Poland, and Czechoslovakia.[81] Two further initiatives to influence pol-icy on this issue remained behind closed doors. The first was a 1979 mem-orandum to the USSR Ministry of Internal Affairs written by crimin-ologist A. N. Ignatov, apparently with little effect; it was followed by historian and sexologist Igor' Kon's unsuccessful attempt, in 1982, to publish an article about sodomy legislation in the legal journal, *So-vetskoe gosudarstvo i pravo*.[82]

Jurists who argued in the 1970s and 1980s against the antisodomy statute were evidently greatly influenced by medical models of homo-sexuality, in some contrast to their predecessors early in the twentieth century. The gradual advance during these years of Soviet "sexual pa-thology" as a confident and technically sophisticated discipline in its own right was marked by significant publications from G. S. Vasil'-chenko, Kon, and others, whose works approached male as well as female homosexuality with increasing boldness.[83] Despite their often paternalistic and pathologizing character (Vasil'chenko defined homo-sexuality as one of many "violations [*narusheniia*] of psychosexual ori-entation"), this movement into the diagnosis and treatment of male homosexuality represented an important departure from Stalinist cer-tainties that love between men was a crime, not an illness. Soviet re-search followed developments in Western neuroendocrinology and ex-perimented more widely with the drug and psychotherapies for male homosexuality that colleagues had first applied to women.[84] Soviet sex-ology was once again poised to assume custody of the homosexual. In the mid-1980s, as jurists secretly drafted a new RSFSR Criminal Code, a debate between police functionaries and medicine reportedly emerged over the scrapping of the sodomy ban. By the late 1980s, the debate moved into the public realm under General Secretary Mikhail Gorba-chev's policy of glasnost, and the criminologist Ignatov openly linked his arguments for the decriminalization of male homosexuality to the "proof" offered by sexology and genetics that homosexuality was a congenital "pathology." It was thus pointless to prosecute as a crime.[85]

According to Kon, he was supported by lawyer A. M. Iakovlev and the psychoendocrinologist and pioneer of contemporary Soviet sex reassignment, A. I. Belkin, while Ministry of Internal Affairs (police) officials called for the retention of a specific ban on aggravated forms of sodomy (with force or against children).[86] This standoff between medical and police approaches to homosexuality resembled NEP-era discussions about the regulation of same-sex relations. As Masha Gessen observes, however, by the late Gorbachev era there was an emerging consensus among all parties that the law against consenting adult sodomy would be eliminated.[87]

This public debate now took place against a backdrop of invigorated organization by Russians defending the rights of so-called "sexual minorities," many adopting the tactics and strategies of Western gay liberation. In 1990, campaigning groups were established in Moscow, Leningrad, and elsewhere; gay and lesbian publications began to appear, and a sexualities studies conference was held in the Estonian SSR. Contacts with European and U.S. activists multiplied. Anti-AIDS information and campaigning often served to shelter self-organization by gay men and lesbians, too. Democratization, which mobilized many sectors of Soviet society, facilitated the rise of Russian lesbian and gay activism.[88] Campaigners, however, found constituencies identified by sexual and gender dissent were difficult to build: there would be little or no "gay community" in Russia.[89] As a result, there were significant limits to these new activists' access to the politicians and parties that assumed the direction of the Russian Federation after the collapse of the Soviet Union in 1991. Russian President Boris Yeltsin's April 1993 decree eliminating the 1933–34 law against consensual sodomy "caught gay and lesbian activists by surprise."[90] Sodomy decriminalization was implemented without input from Russian activists, as one item among the many legislative reform packages that characterized the first years of the Yeltsin administration. The presidency simultaneously released historical documents (the Iagoda-Stalin correspondence) apparently to justify its removal of a consequence of the Communist regime.[91] No enabling legislation accompanied the decree to facilitate an amnesty of the seventy-three men reported by Ministry of Internal Affairs officials as then serving time for consensual sodomy; little action to release these men was forthcoming, and most evidently served out their sentences.[92] Nevertheless, confirmation of the end of the old sodomy statute came in 1996 when legislators adopted a new criminal code for the Russian Federation, although this penal code also defined a new offense of male homosexual and lesbian sexual assault. Activists and some experts, including Ignatov and Kon, vigorously criticized drafts of the new statute for mentioning lesbianism for the first time in any Russian legislation, and for introducing new inconsistencies, based on sexual orientation, in the punishment of sexual crimes.[93]

In the interval between Yeltsin's decree in 1993 and the enactment of the new criminal code in 1996, the existing law as amended punished rapists of girls with fifteen years' imprisonment or even death, while the rape of a boy was subject to a maximum sentence of just seven years. The new code eliminated these variations, but also embedded "sodomy" (*muzhelozhstvo*) and "lesbianism" (*lesbiianstvo*) in its language as specific, but still undefined, sexual acts. This embedding reflected the triumph of the Ministry of Internal Affairs and police demand for a specific law against same-sex sexual assault and abuse. The approach advocated by the most enlightened sections of the legal and medical professions and by gay and lesbian activists that legislation should punish sexual violations of the weak and youthful without regard for the genders of the individuals involved was defeated. In the first post-Soviet code there was only a partial return to the earliest Bolshevik principles of gender neutrality in the equalization of penalties for heterosexual and same-sex assaults.[94] The elaboration of a specific article nominating "sodomy" and "lesbianism" as potential sex offenses reaffirmed the Stalinist view that the sex of perpetrators and victims in sexual assaults continued to be of significance to the state.

CONCLUSION

Though complex and often most intricate, the new geographical map of homosexual perversion both reflected and corroborated the late nineteenth- and early twentieth-century construction of race, gender and sexual identity as a single project of *civilization.*
—Rudi C. Bleys, *The Geography of Perversion: Male-to-Male Behavior outside the West and the Ethnographic Imagination, 1750–1918*

As far as homosexuals are concerned, let's keep Russia's purity (*chistota*). We have our own traditions. This form of relations between men was imported from abroad. If they think that their rights are being infringed, let them go and live in some other country!
—Valentin Rasputin, interview on British Channel Four television, early 1991[1]

Recent attempts to produce new frameworks for understanding Russia's experience of the twentieth century have focused attention on the peculiar kind of modernity this nation forged. The problem has been defined, in two important examples, as one of "Stalinism as a civilization"[2] historically rooted in European ideals, or of a "neo-traditional" society, in which the state substituted itself for the market and supplanted traditional values.[3] Stalinism, viewed by Stephen Kotkin through its determination to construct subjectivities and redefine not just economics but everyday existence, threw up a "noncapitalist" civilization with the collaboration of millions, who learned to "speak Bolshevik" and who, whatever their reservations and doubts, were largely prepared to defend "socialism." Their creation was "an integral part of the course of European history."[4] Alternatively, by examining Soviet nation-building schemes as a feature of the Communist modernization process ("national in form yet socialist in content," in the Stalinist formula), Terry Martin concludes that Soviet modernity was flawed in its construction. Measures designed to guide the USSR's non-Russian peoples past the dangerous historical stage of awakening national consciousness (dangerous because it distracted new proletarians from their class identity), instead solidified nationalisms through "affirmative action" programs and a "constant routine of ethnic labeling." Martin writes: "Modernization is the theory of Soviet intentions; neotraditionalism, the theory of their unintended consequences."[5]

For both Kotkin and Martin, the construction of new identities is a key feature of the modernizing society, an integral part of the Soviet project to industrialize, urbanize, secularize, and educate the tsarist empire the Bolsheviks inherited. What kind of homosexual identities were created by this "civilization"? Where did these identities fit in the "geography of perversion" posited by Rudy Bleys, in the epigraph that begins this chapter? As an instrument of European civilization in the late nineteenth and early twentieth centuries, how effective were Russian homosexualities? If these identities failed to coalesce, if unintended consequences prevailed, to what extent was the Russian experience of modernizing same-sex eros marked by neotraditional characteristics? Can the selective, homophobic amnesia practiced by Valentin Rasputin, in the epigraph that follows, be read as evidence of a mentality determined by neotraditionalism?

If, as Eve Sedgwick suggests, Western concepts of homosexuality are subject to "a radical and irreducible incoherence," then in the Russian Empire and later the Soviet Union, this incoherence was compounded by the fact that this huge polity straddled the boundaries between the "civilized" and the "primitive."[6] The entire atlas of Europe's "geography of perversion" might perhaps be found within this single political entity. Sedgwick's "minoritizing" understanding of same-sex love as an anomaly or pathology appeared, with lunges and lags, in Russia's European cities. Meanwhile, "universalizing" interpretations of pederasty as endemic to non-Slavs, to the peripheral and often "primitive" peoples in the empire or union, prevailed when Russians looked beyond the metropolitan center. Yet for Russians thinking at the beginning of the century about sex and modernity, this dualistic "geography of perversion" was incomplete. Their maps included a third element, distinct from both the Western European world of burgeoning industrial cities, alienation from tradition, and enervated, commercialized titillation, and from the other extreme in "primitive," colonized, societies. Russia stood largely on the brink of civilization, as yet still innocent of its artful pleasures, according to the social democrat G. S. Novopolin in 1909:

> Let's for a moment leave Western Europe where, on the one hand, neurasthenia with its inevitable and frequent companion, the sexual perversions, and on the other hand, the culture of comfort so often in tandem with the filthy artificiality of sexual variety, are making great headway. Let us return to our native soil. Naturally, the mores of a significant part of Russian society, and especially the Russian bourgeoisie, are far from a chaste purity [*tselomudrennaia chistota*]. Yet so far only coarse and simpleminded debauchery reigns. We are still a long way from the epidemic of neurasthenia and refined comfort, and thanks to this, far, too, from the [epidemic of] sexual perversions. . . . depravity on Russian soil still exhibits a primitive [*primitivnyi*] character.[7]

"Pederasty," Novopolin argued, was practiced only among urban elements of Russia's "bourgeoisie" and its "aristocratic circles," as well as "in the Caucasus." The "coarse and simpleminded" pleasures of ordinary worker and peasant Russians stood somewhere between the neurasthenic perversions of urban Europeans and the oriental depravities of the Caucasus or central Asia. The tripartite "geography of perversion" with its comparatively innocent Russia interpolated between a "civilized" Europe and a decidedly "primitive" or "backward" "East," permitted and permits Russians to imagine their nation as universally, naturally, and purely heterosexual. When Valentin Rasputin claimed, "We have our own traditions," he unwittingly appealed to a Great Russian mapping of the "geography of perversion," a mythology of national purity, imagined at the century's beginning and reinforced by subsequent events.

The ambiguity, and the silences, at the heart of Bolshevik ideas about same-sex relations and their place in the new society stemmed largely from the dissonance generated by this Russian "geography of perversion." The socialist modernization project and its civilizing mission cut across the epistemic divide between "minoritizing" and "universalizing" thinking about same-sex eros. In urban Russia, where the revolutionary project was being forged, the affirmation of modernity dictated sexual morality be secularized and that sexual questions be medicalized. In the revolutionary criminal code of the Russian republic with its language of modernity, there was no place for religious or "bourgeois" morality, and the prohibition against sodomy was erased. The erasure satisfied more than one perspective, including the myth of "chaste" Russia between two poles of sexual disorder. The erasure also left the way open to modernizers who would apply scientific understanding to sexual and gender dissent. "Morbidizing" views of same-sex love influenced both those who supported emancipatory intentions and those who attempted to pathologize homosexuality and extend psychiatry's therapeutic reach to include the homosexual. Yet even psychiatrists of the 1920s who sought custody of the homosexual often imagined Russia was comparatively innocent of such perversions. As L. Brusilovskii claimed in the Expert Medical Council in 1929, perversions were "not particularly frequent" in the USSR, in comparison to Germany. It was more comfortable to imagine these disorders not among Russian males but among a tiny minority of Russian women, whose accelerated emancipation had perhaps masculinized them too much.

Meanwhile, beyond urban Russia and the USSR's European heartland, the Bolshevik civilizing mission rejected the "morbidizing" hypotheses about same-sex eros and saw it instead as endemic, a practice characteristic of a backward social, religious, and cultural fabric. This was a twentieth-century socialist version of the European ethnographic tradition that Bleys identifies, which regarded subject "races" and peoples as universally given to "sodomy" or "pederasty." Building state structures in these regions that were "socialist in content" yet "national in form," Bolshevik legislators of the 1920s renounced the tersely modernist and revolutionary language of sexual crime that their counterparts in the RSFSR had composed. In the southern and eastern republics, they favored a language of ethnography, a catalog of "prevalent" or "widespread" local customs (including sodomy, the exploitation of male prostitutes, and the sexual harassment of men) that they hoped to eliminate. In socialist terms, such crimes were portrayed as the work of local capitalists and national leaders, groups seeking to demoralize the ordinary citizens of these regions. From the outset of the Russian revolutionary era, the socialist "civilizing mission" to eradicate "crimes constituting survivals of primitive custom" reflected a peculiarly Russian "geography of perversion." That mapping allowed the RSFSR (along with Belorussia, Ukraine, and anomalously perhaps, Armenia) an ambiguous sexual modernity where same-sex eros was concerned, in contrast to the unquestionably "primitive" vices of the Caucasus and central Asia.

The recriminalization of sodomy in the RSFSR and other "modern" Soviet republics in 1933–34 returned to neotraditionalist features of the regulation of same-sex love but also fixed important modern aspects of masculine identity. The decision to nominate and prohibit only male homosexual activity has to be seen as a neotraditionalist maneuver, especially as consolidated in language recalling moments of religious and moralistic conservatism in Russia's legal history. The important revolutionary principle of gender equality in legislative norms was violated as Stalinism borrowed a technique from the socialist "civilizing mission" on the periphery (the initially quite detailed antisodomy law) and trained it on the metropolitan center. Nevertheless, at the center there was no "primitive" society corresponding to that supposed to engage universally in sodomy in the peripheral republics. The new law did not diagnose a problem understood as "endemic" in the USSR's more "modern" nations. The thrust of the central antisodomy statute was minoritizing, and this was its paradoxically modernizing effect, for it invoked a male homosexual identity and contrasted it with the majority's supposed pure and "normal" (hetero-) sexuality. In the heart of the new civilization that socialism was constructing, "salons" of "pederasts" and "homosexuals" demoralized "normal" soldiers, sailors, and workers, diverting their imagined raw vigor (that distinguished Soviet Russia from the "depleted" West) from its "natural" channels. "Destroy the homosexuals—Fascism will disappear," Gor'kii wrote, pointing the finger at a sexual identity, not at a particular act. An urban subculture was made the subject of this legislation, confining the problem to a minority of men. Significantly, it was a subculture known by its sexualized territories, its use of urban space: as Iagoda had originally proposed, sodomy practiced "in public" would be a particular target. These territories would be cleansed of a specific social anomaly. Now the imaginary Russian nation was officially interposed in its chaste purity between neurasthenic (and in the 1930s, Fascist) Europe on the one hand, and the "primitive" depravity of the East on the other.

The pretense that only male homosexuality existed and needed to be criminalized was a neotraditional feature of Stalinist gender syncretism. "Female homosexuality" had been a somewhat novel object of "morbidization" during the early Soviet era, and even a subject for utopian visions during the cultural revolution, but medicine eventually shelved any claims to the "masculinized woman" in the 1930s. The "morbidizing" view of female homosexuality was entirely suppressed, and with it, any impulse to modernize women's sexual identities, whether through medical sympathy (including utopian notions of same-sex marriage) or with oppressive pathologization as a psychopathology. Soviet women's sexuality was now subject to demands determined wholly by masculinist and natalist regime goals. With heterosexuality made compulsory and all discourse about women's sexuality independent of men suppressed, Stalinism greatly curtailed opportunities for women's sexual agency afforded by the postrevolutionary settlement.

De-Stalinization brought Soviet Russia an illiberal form of sexual modernity in which science and police methods were combined to enforce, with more apparent efficiency than before, a compulsory heterosexual norm. (None of this varied that greatly from the oppression of same-sex love in the 1940s–60s in Britain, the U.S., or the Germanies.) Now the "female homosexual" was revived as a "morbidized" identity, and pathologized by psychiatry, perhaps under orders to control a contagion among returnees from the Gulag. The identity of "female homosexual" was now definitely assigned to a specific minority, set apart from the majority of "normal" women. Neotraditionalism persisted, however, in the continued gendered regime for suppressing same-sex love: men's mutual love remained a crime, while love between women was "merely" an illness.

The sustained denial that homosexuality existed in Russia remained a strikingly neotraditionalist feature of late-Soviet thinking about same-sex love. Soviet information controls created (for the "normal" majority) the impression that homosexuality was a vice of Western capitalism. In the press there was no reporting of closed prosecutions for male sodomy, while sexological literature about the "female homosexual" was supposed to be issued to specialists alone. The biographies of literary and cultural figures were distorted, heterosexualized, or suppressed. Late-Soviet Russians, if untouched in their personal experience by same-sex desire, could easily have concluded that their country was as sexually innocent as the tripartite "geography of perversion" imagined. The mapping of the innocent Soviet Union situated between a perverted West and the vice-ridden underdeveloped countries was especially evident in Soviet journalism about AIDS in the Gorbachev era.[8] The suppression of Russia's historical and cultural memory about same-sex love and the pretense that Russia was innocent of both Western perversion and more "primitive" depravity constituted a significant element in the gender politics of the sanitized "folkloric national identities" that communism promoted. These national identities, Terry Martin argues, were a key source of unintended neotraditionalism.[9] The assertion that same-sex relations are alien to the national culture is an increasingly frequent claim in anti-Western discourse, observed both in Communist regimes (Cuba, China) and developing market-economy countries with varying political systems (such as Zimbabwe, Iran, and

Malaysia). Such "post-colonial homophobia" from these nations is a reaction against both the imposition of the European sex/gender system, and at the same time, the institutionalization of the homo/hetero binarism, a key instrument of Western sexual politics.[10] Stalinism pioneered this homophobic discourse, but it had older roots in Russian intellectual life. Collective amnesia about sexual and gender dissent preserved and promoted the neotraditional myth of Russia's "purity" between a diseased West and a depraved East.

HOW MANY VICTIMS OF THE
ANTISODOMY LAW?

Estimates of the number of men convicted under the 1934 anti-sodomy legislation in the USSR have ranged as high as 250,000.[1] Recently, campaigners against homophobia in the Russian Federation have tended to cite a total of approximately 60,000 convictions during the fifty-nine years of the law's existence. This estimate is based on awareness from Sovietological sources that about 1,000 men were convicted each year during the late 1960s and into the 1970s; the same rate is, however, anachronistically projected backwards for earlier decades. There have also been efforts, understandable but ignoring the historical differences, to compare the figures for sodomy conviction in the Soviet Union with the total number of victims sent to concentration camps for male homosexuality in Nazi Germany.[2]

Neil McKenna was correct when he postulated that we might never know just how many men suffered as a result of this legislation. The first and most serious deficiency in any attempt to count its victims is the complete lack of data about the use of this law by the security police. To my knowledge, no foreign or Russian academic, no community organization, nor any political party or politician, has approached the KGB's successor to request access to data it may hold on the history of the arrest of homosexuals by Soviet security police and their fate in the prisons and camps it controlled. (Similarly, there have been no known initiatives to obtain fuller historical explanations from the Archive of the President of the Russian Federation or the archive of the Ministry of Internal Affairs.) The taboo on the pursuit of this topic remains strong, and the rewards for making such a request might seem modest when juxtaposed with the possible undesirable consequences. Furthermore, from the strict ration of information that was released in 1993 to justify the decriminalization of sodomy at that time, we can assume Russian officials also think there are few political rewards to be gained by more explicit disclosures.

In the present climate we are unlikely to obtain documentary confirmation of the "several thousands" reportedly imprisoned for this offense by the security police.[3] The second stream of convictions, those registered by the ordinary police and courts, has left only "snapshots," fragmentary and unsatisfactory traces in the archival holdings accessible to researchers. These are presented in the tables below. Table 1 attempts to assemble fragments of evidence for the years from 1934 to 1950. These "snapshots" from the 1930s and 1940s suggest that government officials were compiling data on sodomy convictions but that they were treated with extraordinary secrecy, especially considering that the same statisticians collected and issued data for internal use on counterrevolutionary crimes and other sexual offenses processed through the ordinary courts. In tables of convictions by criminal code article, the relevant columns were often simply left blank. Justice officials were similarly reluctant to circulate official explanations of the legislation once it was in effect. The extreme unwillingness to publish such information, even in internal secret documents, is perhaps a signal that the security police were primarily charged with enforcing the antisodomy law during the Stalin era; we do not know how many men they arrested for this crime. There is a significant gap in the accessible statistics for the years from 1951 to 1960. If it is true that security police were primarily responsible for sodomy-law enforcement, the gap may correspond to the era when this duty was transferred from security to ordinary police.

The figures in table 1 for the 1930s–40s suggest that in the ordinary justice system, the number of men convicted for both voluntary and aggravated sodomy was much lower than rates in the 1960s and later (tables 2 and 3). It would thus be hazardous simply to project figures from the late Soviet era backward in time. From the evidence presented in this study, there are good reasons to suspect that fewer persons were convicted, at least in the ordinary justice system, for sodomy during the first twenty-seven years of the law's operation. Few cases are in evidence in the limited records of the Moscow city courts, and this was an exemplary jurisdiction, the Soviet capital, where one would reasonably expect a greater number of cases to appear. We also know that noteworthy figures whose homosexual activity was known to the authorities during the 1930s (such as Nikolai Kliuev and Iurii Iurkun) were not formally convicted by the security police under the antisodomy statute but for counterrevolutionary offenses. This tendency per-

Table 1 Sodomy Convictions, 1934—50

Year	Sodomy convictions, RSFSR	Form 10: Possible sodomy convictions*	Percentage of all crimes, RSFSR
1934			
1935	15 (a)		
1936		257	0.03 (g)
1937	74 (b)	164	0.01 (b)/0.02 (g)
1938		138	0.02 (g)
1939		97	0.01 (g)
1940			
1941		109	0.01 (g)
1942			
1943			
1944	6 (c)		
1945	16 (c)/47 (d)		—/0.003 (e)
1946	39 (c)/82 (d)		0.002/0.005 (e)
1947	63 (d)		0.004 (e)
1948	34 (d)		0.003 (e)
1949			
1950	130 (f)		0.01 (e)
Total:	377/451	765	

Key to sources:

(a) Observed in Moscow city court *only*, TsMAM f. 819, op. 2 sample.

(b) All RSFSR, *first half of 1937 only*; GARF f. 9492, op. 2, d. 42, l. 155. NB: 48 were convictions for voluntary sodomy (article 154a-I), 26 for aggravated sodomy (article 154a-II)

(c) Full year, combined article 154a parts I and II, GARF, f. 9492, op. 2, d. 42, l. 140.

(d) Full year, combined article 154a parts I and II, GARF, f. 9492, op. 2s, d. 50, l. 400.

(e) Based on total convictions for all crimes shown in GARF, f. A353, op. 16, d. 20, l. 9.

(f) Full year, combined article 154a parts I and II, GARF f. A353, op. 16s, d. 121, ll. 16—24.

(g) Based on total convictions figures on Form 10.

* *Form 10:* Figures in this column are conjectural, i.e., they were not labeled as sodomy convictions in the sources used, but extracted by deduction in the following manner. (Source: RSFSR Justice Commissariat "form 10" convictions tables, GARF f. A353, op. 16s, d. 19, ll. 24—29ob. [1936]; d. 23, ll. 31—34ob. [1937]; d. 27, ll. 41—42ob. [1938]; d. 31, ll. 99—104ob. [1939]; d. 38, ll. 123—126ob [1941].) These preprinted forms listed most criminal code articles separately, but not article 154a for sodomy. Under "Crimes against the person" all but four articles were accorded separate lines. The four counted together were article 141 (incitement to suicide), articles 147—149 (kidnapping), article 154a (sodomy), article 157 (refusing medical help), all apparently aggregated into a line in this section labeled "Other crimes." On "form 10" it is possible to isolate convictions by the length of sentence they attracted. Of the four aggregated articles, only article 154a-II had a penalty minimum of five years. Article 154a-I and article 141 had five-year maximums; the others got three years or less. By extracting the number of convictions in this line netting a five-year or greater sentence, a relatively small proportion of the total, it appears possible to isolate those convictions under article 154a which attracted maximum sentences. The figure would be slightly "polluted" by the presence of a small number of convictions attracting the maximum sentence for article 141; but also "diluted" by the absence of sentences for voluntary sodomy (article 154a-I) below the five-year maximum.

Table 2 Sodomy Convictions in the USSR and RSFSR, 1961–81

Year	Sodomy convictions, USSR	Percentage of all crimes, USSR	Sodomy convictions, RSFSR	Percentage of all crimes, RSFSR
1961	705	0.09	464	N/A
1962	767	0.09	530	0.11
1963	831	0.12	592	0.14
1964	777	0.13	547	0.14
1965	627	0.11	393	0.11
1966	770	0.11	485	0.10
1967	940	0.13	617	0.13
1968	756	0.11	453	0.10
1969	993	0.12	641	0.12
1970	1,223	0.14	787	0.14
1971	1,206	0.14	854	0.15
1972	1,255	0.14	882	0.15
1973	1,319	0.16	853	0.16
1974	1,355	0.15	883	0.15
1975	1,214	0.14	803	0.14
1976	1,181	0.13	773	0.13
1977	1,320	0.16	877	0.17
1978	1,314	0.15	882	0.16
1979	1,262	0.14	822	0.14
1980	1,119	0.11	708	0.11
1981	1,229	0.12	849	0.12
Total:	22,163		14,695	

Source: GARF, f. 9492 s. ch., op. 6s, dd. 58, 69, 81, 91, 102, 112, 128, 141, 151, 161, 177, 193, 205, 221, 239, 254, 271, 285, 302, 317, 328.

haps had the effect of diminishing whatever official tallies might be compiled. It appears that in the conventional legal system, the law was used against the male homosexual subculture as a function of urban social cleansing rather than to pursue outright anti-Soviet dissent. Yet social cleansing perhaps dwindled in importance; during the late Stalin years little conventional police interest in the subculture was registered. Only six Muscovites and nine Leningraders appear among the 130 citizens of the RSFSR convicted for sodomy in 1950.[4] The conviction rate in this year is very low compared with the 464 Russians in 1961, the next year for which statistics are available.

The figures for 1961 to 1980 indicate that convictions for voluntary and aggravated sodomy increased rapidly during the late 1960s and reached a fairly constant level thereafter. This trend suggests that a modernized routine of police surveillance (raids on notorious subcultural territories, the use of entrapment, a now standard resort to generally available forensic expertise) had been adopted. The statistics say nothing about the proportion of voluntary sodomy convictions to those

Table 3 Sodomy Convictions, 1987–91

Year	Sodomy convictions, USSR
1987	831
1988	800
1989	538
1990	497
1991	482 (RSFSR only)
Total	3,148

Source: James Riordan, "Sexual Minorities: The Status of Gays and Lesbians in Russian-Soviet-Russian Society," in *Women in Russia and Ukraine*, ed. Rosalind Marsh (Cambridge: Cambridge University Press, 1996), 160–61.

for forcible or adult-minor relations, nor how it may have varied over time. We also know little about the number of citizens who had contact with the police because of suspected engagement in sodomy, but whose cases did not reach a conviction. Many men were questioned on suspicion of homosexual relations, charged but not prosecuted, or prosecuted but not convicted, as Dan Schluter correctly informs us.[5] Statistics for the early 1980s do not appear in archival sources, and to the best of my knowledge, have not been published elsewhere. The total number of convictions recorded in the sources that are accessible for the entire era of sodomy criminalization (1934–93) comes to between 25,688 and 26,076, but this must be regarded as nothing but a provisional total. We lack any numbers at all for twenty-two years out of the period, and most of the figures for the earliest two decades are fragmented and contradictory. Security police statistics are completely absent from this provisional tally. Russian citizens who wish to see democracy flourish in their country deserve a fuller account of this aspect of Stalinist oppression.

INTRODUCTION

1. The reaction of a senior historian from Russia to my 1994 graduate seminar paper, "Constructing the Soviet Pervert: Same-Sex Desire, Medicine and Law in Soviet Russia, 1917–1929," illustrates a desire to marginalize the topic: "In my opinion (and, I would suggest, not only mine), this is not the most pressing historiographical theme, but if one recalls that recently in New York 250,000 members of the so-called 'sexual minority' held a demonstration in defense of their rights, then such a peculiar interest on the part of the young scholar in a problem, which sooner belongs to the history of medicine than society, is understandable": B. G. Litvak, "Kollokvium severoamorikan oktikh istorikov-ruslstov," *Utechestvennaia istoriia* 4 (1995): 218–21, quotation, 221. Litvak's Soviet-style view of medicine as "outside" society (because of its scientific, "objective" claims) is antithetical to my position, based on social constructionist and feminist views of science as shaped by the society and culture that produce it. See, e.g., Thomas S. Kuhn, *The Structure of Scientific Revolutions* (Chicago: University of Chicago Press, 1962); Anne Fausto-Sterling, *Myths of Gender: Biological Theories of Women and Men* (New York: Basic Books, 1985); Nelly Oudshoorn, *Beyond the Natural Body: An Archaeology of Sex Hormones* (London: Routledge, 1994); Vernon A. Rosario, ed., *Science and Homosexualities* (New York: Routledge, 1997).

2. The literature on Western society's construction of heterosexuality and its reliance on contingent and politically determined gender roles is now very large. Key works include Michel Foucault, *The History of Sexuality: An Introduction. Vol. 1*, trans. Robert Hurley (London: Penguin, 1978); Jeffrey Weeks, *Sexuality and Its Discontents: Meanings, Myths, and Modern Sexualities* (London: Routledge & Kegan Paul, 1985); and Jonathan Ned Katz, *The Invention of Heterosexuality* (New York: Dutton, 1995).

3. Landmark studies in this field include Mary McIntosh, "The Homosexual Role," *Social Problems* 16 (1968): 182–92; James Steakley, *The Homosexual Emancipation Movement in Germany* (New York: Arno, 1975); Jonathan Katz, *Gay American History* (New York: Thomas Crowell, 1976); Pierre Hahn, *Nos ancêtres, les pervers: La vie des homosexuels sous le Second Empire* (Paris: Olivier Orban, 1979); Lillian Faderman, *Surpassing the Love of Men: Romantic Friendship and Love between Women from the Renaissance to the Present* (New York: Morrow, 1981); Lesbian History Group, ed., *Not a Passing Phase: Reclaiming Lesbians in History 1840–1985* (London: Women's Press, 1989); Martin B. Duberman, Martha Vicinus, and George Chauncey, Jr., eds., *Hidden From History: Reclaiming the Gay and Lesbian Past* (New York: New American Library, 1989); Allan Bérubé, *Coming Out under Fire: The History of Gay Men and*

Lesbians in World War Two (New York: Plume, 1990); Jeffrey Weeks, *Coming Out: Homosexual Politics in Britain from the Nineteenth Century to the Present* (London: Quartet Books, 1990); Lillian Faderman, *Odd Girls and Twilight Lovers: A History of Lesbian Life in Twentieth-Century America* (New York: Columbia, 1991); Emma Donoghue, *Passions between Women: British Lesbian Culture 1668–1801* (London: HarperCollins, 1993); George Chauncey, *Gay New York: Gender, Urban Culture, and the Making of the Gay Male World, 1890–1940* (New York: Basic Books, 1994); Jeffrey Merrick and Bryant T. Ragan, eds., *Homosexuality in Modern France* (New York: Oxford University Press, 1996).

4. See, e.g., Peter A. Jackson, "Thai Research on Male Homosexuality and Transgenderism and the Cultural Limits of Foucaultian Analysis," *Journal of the History of Sexuality* 1 (1997): 52–85; Gilbert Herdt, ed., *Third Sex, Third Gender: Beyond Sexual Dimorphism in Culture and History* (New York: Zone Books, 1993); James N. Green, *Beyond Carnival: Male Homosexuality in Twentieth-Century Brazil* (Chicago: University of Chicago Press, 1999); Ian Lumsden, *Machos, Maricones, and Gays: Cuba and Homosexuality* (Philadelphia: Temple University Press, 1996); Stephen O. Murray and Will Roscoe, eds., *Islamic Homosexualities: Culture, History and Literature* (New York: New York University Press, 1997).

5. Eve K. Sedgwick observes that "a radical and irreducible incoherence" prevails in Western concepts of homosexuality. A "minoritizing" view that a subgroup in the population is "really" gay coexists with a "universalizing" awareness that everyone may potentially experience same-sex desire. She suggests that "male heterosexual identity and modern masculinist culture may require for their maintenance the scapegoating crystallization of a same-sex male desire that is widespread and in the first place internal." Modernity is associated with an increasingly "minoritizing" view of same-sex sexuality, and the proscription of personal expressions of same-sex intimacy for the "majority," but Sedgwick cautions that even in modern life the incoherence of homosexuality remains; Eve K. Sedgwick, *Epistemology of the Closet* (Berkeley and Los Angeles: University of California Press, 1990), 85.

6. Described in Igor S. Kon, *Seksual'naia kul'tura v Rossii: Klubnichka na berezke* (Moscow: OGI, 1997), 1. The cliché's irony marked the moment when sex regained its voice; see, e.g., Masha Gessen, "We Have No Sex: Soviet Gays and AIDS in the Era of Glasnost," *Outlook* 3, no. 1 (1990): 42–54; Laura Engelstein, "There Is Sex in Russia—and Always Was: Some Recent Contributions to Russian Erotica," *Slavic Review* 51, no. 4 (1992): 786–90.

7. In 1995, in the academicians' reading-room in Moscow's former Lenin Library, I could not obtain a copy of the last Soviet medical encyclopedia in which the article on "sexual perversions" (E. A. Popov, "Polovye izvrashcheniia," in *Bol'shaia meditsinskaia entsiklopediia,* 2d ed. [Moscow, 1962]: 25: 942–52) had not been expertly sliced out of the volume. Sexological knowledge, revived after Iosif Stalin's death in 1953, was dispensed to professionals on a need-to-know basis: see Kon, *Seksual'naia kul'tura v Rossii,* 171–73.

8. For cogent statements of Soviet sexual norms, see, e.g., D. Gorfin, "Polovaia zhizn'," in *Bol'shaia sovetskaia entsiklopediia,* 1st ed. (Moscow: OGIZ RSFSR, 1940), 46: 163–69; "Gomoseksualizm," in *Bol'shaia sovetskaia entsiklopediia,* 2d (Moscow, 1952): 12: 35; A. Mandel'shtam, "Polovaia zhizn'," in *Bol'shaia meditsinskaia entsiklopediia,* 2d ed. (Moscow: Sovetskaia entsiklopediia, 1962), 25: 874–87.

9. E.g., P. M. Chirkov, *Reshenie zhenskogo voprosa v SSSR (1917–1937 gg.)* (Moscow: Mysl', 1978).

10. The U.S. biographer of poet Sofia Parnok encountered such attitudes among sympathetic Soviet colleagues, Diana Lewis Burgin, *Sophia Parnok: The Life and Work of Russia's Sappho* (New York: New York University Press, 1994), 6–7.

11. For example, the attributions of "pederastic" relations between Frenchman Georges d'Anthès, the murderer of poet Aleksandr Pushkin, and his adoptive father, Netherlands Ambassador to St. Petersburg Baron Heeckeren. A recent analysis of new evidence including correspondence between d'Anthès and Heeckeren indicts "Soviet prudery" for its view of same-sex relations as inherently "sordid." It demonstrates too that well before 1917 the national discussion of the tragic death of Pushkin was marked by homophobic innuendo directed against his assassin; Serena Vitale, *Pushkin's Button* (London: Fourth Estate, 1999), 335. The claim that composer Peter Tchaikovsky committed suicide to atone for his homosexuality is perhaps the most exasperating example of this genre; for an exhaustive refutation, see Alexander Poznansky, *Tchaikovsky's Last Days: A Documentary Study* (Oxford: Clarendon, 1996).

12. Material about the biographies of Tchaikovsky, film director Sergei Eisenstein, and poet and diarist Mikhail Kuzmin were kept in "special collections" and researchers were denied access; e.g., on Kuzmin, see S. V. Shumikhin, "Dnevnik Mikhaila Kuzmina: Arkhivnaia predystoriia," in *Mikhail Kuzmin i russkaia kul'tura XX veka: Tezisy i materialy konferentsii 15–17 maia 1990g.*, ed. G. A. Morev (Leningrad: Sovet po istorii mirovoi kul'tury AN SSSR, 1990); John E. Malmstad and Nikolay Bogomolov, *Mikhail Kuzmin: A Life in Art* (Cambridge, Mass.: Harvard University Press, 1999).

13. For ethnographic views, see Magnus Hirschfeld, *Die Homosexualität des Mannes und des Weibes* (Berlin: Louis Marcus, 1914), 590–92; for sex reform polemics, see Wilhelm Reich, "The Struggle for a 'New Life' in the Soviet Union," first published 1936, reprinted in *The Sexual Revolution* (New York: Pocket Books, 1969); John Lauritsen and David Thorstad, *The Early Homosexual Rights Movement (1864–1934)* (New York: Times Change, 1974).

14. Simon Karlinsky, "Russia's Gay Literature and History," *Gay Sunshine* 29/30 (1976). 1–7, "Death and Resurrection of Mikhail Kuzmin," *Slavic Review* 38, no. 1 (1979): 92–96; "Gay Life before the Soviets: Revisionism Revised," *Advocate* 339 (1 April 1982): 31–34; "Russia's Gay Literature and Culture: The Impact of the October Revolution," in Duberman et al., *Hidden From History;* introduction to *Out of the Blue: Russia's Hidden Gay Literature,* ed. Kevin Moss (San Francisco: Gay Sunshine Press, 1996).

15. See, e.g., his "Gomoseksualizm v russkoi istorii i kul'ture" *Tema* (1 1991): 4–5; idem, " 'Vvezen iz-za granitsy . . .'? Gomoseksualizm v russkoi kul'ture i literature," in *Erotika v russkoi literature. Ot Barkova do nashikh dnei. Literaturnoe obozrenie. Spetsial'nyi vypusk,* eds. I. D. Prokhorova, S. Iu. Mazur, and G. V. Zykova (Moscow: Literaturnoe obozrenie, 1992). Note Karlinsky's influence in Iaroslav Mogutin and Sonia Franeta, "Gomoseksualizm v sovetskikh tiur'makh i lageriakh," *Novoe vremia* (1993): 35: 44–47, 36: 50–54.

16. The "1917 Collective" relies rather incongruously on Karlinsky, "Russia's Gay Literature and Culture"; see "Capitalism and Homophobia: Marxism and the Struggle for Gay/Lesbian Rights," in *The Material Queer: A LesBiGay Cultural Studies Reader,* ed. Donald Morton (Boulder: Westview Press, 1996), 374–76.

17. The diversity of radical visions of the early revolutionary years is cataloged in Richard Stites, *Revolutionary Dreams: Utopian Vision and Experimental Life in the Russian Revolution* (Oxford: Oxford University Press, 1989).

18. Karlinsky, "Russia's Gay Literature and Culture," 357.

19. For an early statement of this critique, see my "The Russian Revolution and the Decriminalisation of Homosexuality," *Revolutionary Russia* 6, no. 1 (1993): 26–54. For an excellent introduction to the legal contexts, see Laura Engelstein, "Soviet Policy toward Male Homosexuality: Its Origins and Historical Roots," in *Gay Men*

and the Sexual History of the Political Left, eds. Gert Hekma, Harry Oosterhuis, and James Steakley (Binghamton, N.Y.: Harrington Park Press, 1995).

20. Karlinsky's view of Soviet medicine is based on a totalitarian-school reading of just two sources, "Russia's Gay Literature and Culture," 358. These readings are challenged in chapters 5 and 6. Observers from gay left perspectives also condemn Soviet medicalization of homosexuality. The 1917 Collective, quoting Karlinsky, perpetuates the "morbidizing" thesis, see "Capitalism and Homophobia," in Morton, *The Material Queer*, 375. Jeffrey Weeks (drawing on Lauritsen and Thorstad, *The Early Homosexual Rights Movement*, 73−74) dismisses as "biological stereotypes" the references to Magnus Hirschfeld and Sigmund Freud in the 1930 *Great Soviet Encyclopedia* article on "homosexuality": *Coming Out*, 147.

21. See, e.g., Foucault, *History of Sexuality: An Introduction. Vol. 1;* Rosario, ed., *Science and Homosexualities;* Chandak Sengoopta, "Glandular Politics: Experimental Biology, Clinical Medicine, and Homosexual Emancipation in Fin-de-Siècle Central Europe," *Isis* 89 (1998): 445−73.

22. Some pertinent texts are Nancy M. Frieden, *Russian Physicians in an Era of Reform and Revolution, 1856−1905* (Princeton: Princeton University Press, 1981); John F. Hutchinson, *Politics and Public Health in Revolutionary Russia, 1890−1918* (Baltimore & London: Johns Hopkins University Press, 1990); Laura Engelstein, *The Keys to Happiness: Sex and the Search for Modernity in Fin-de-Siècle Russia* (Ithaca: Cornell University Press, 1992); Joan Neuberger, *Hooliganism: Crime, Culture and Power in St Petersburg, 1900−1914* (Berkeley: University of California Press, 1993); Laurie Bernstein, *Sonia's Daughters: Prostitutes and Their Regulation in Imperial Russia* (Berkeley and Los Angeles: University of California Press, 1995).

23. On social hygiene and the politics of public health, see Susan Gross Solomon and John Hutchinson, eds., *Health and Society in Revolutionary Russia* (Bloomington: Indiana University Press, 1990); Susan Gross Solomon, "The Expert and the State in Russian Public Health: Continuities and Changes across the Revolutionary Divide," in *The History of Public Health and the Modern State*, ed. Dorothy Porter (Amsterdam: Editions Rodopi B. V., 1994); Frances L. Bernstein, "Envisioning Health in Revolutionary Russia: The Politics of Gender in Sexual-Enlightenment Posters of the 1920s," *Russian Review* 57 (1998): 191−217; idem, "What Everyone Should Know about Sex: Gender, Sexual Enlightenment, and the Politics of Health in Revolutionary Russia, 1918−1931" (Ph.D. diss., Columbia University, 1998). On psychology, psychiatry, and neurology, see David Joravsky, *Russian Psychology: A Critical History* (Oxford: Basil Blackwell, 1989). On psychoanalysis, Aleksandr Etkind, *Eros nevozmozhnogo: Istoriia psikhoanaliza v Rossii* (St. Petersburg: Meduza, 1993); Martin Miller, *Freud and the Bolsheviks: Psychoanalysis in Imperial Russia and the Soviet Union* (New Haven: Yale University Press, 1998). On comparative and ethical themes, Mark B. Adams, ed., *The Wellborn Science: Eugenics in Germany, France, Brazil, and Russia* (New York: Oxford University Press, 1990); Susan Gross Solomon, "The Soviet-German Syphilis Expedition to Buriat Mongolia, 1928," *Slavic Review* 52, no. 2 (1993): 204−32; Loren R. Graham, *Science in Russian and the Soviet Union* (Cambridge: Cambridge University Press, 1993).

24. Existing historiography conveys the impression that sexual dissidents were victims without historical agency. Karlinsky admits that "Soviet persecution of gay men was neither continuous nor total" under Stalin, "Russia's Gay Literature and Culture," 362. Leftist anti-Stalinist accounts imply resistance was nonexistent or futile. See Reich, *The Sexual Revolution*, 252−56; Lauritsen and Thorstad, *The Early Homosexual Rights Movement*, 62−75.

25. During the 1960s−1980s, access to Soviet archives for Western researchers was

limited by a system of controls including visa restrictions and police surveillance, vetting of topics, inaccessibility of finding aids to collections, and archival staff control of files to be released. Soviet researchers functioned under many of the same constraints. On these conditions, see introduction in *Stalinism: New Directions,* ed. Sheila Fitzpatrick (London: Routledge, 1999), 3–4.

26. For examples of reluctance to discuss what apparently was not in the sources, see, e.g., Richard Stites, *The Women's Liberation Movement in Russia: Feminism, Nihilism, and Bolshevism, 1860–1930* (Princeton: Princeton University Press, 1978), 346–91; Wendy Z. Goldman, *Women, the State, and Revolution: Soviet Family Policy and Social Life* (Cambridge: Cambridge University Press, 1993). For a careful acknowledgement of fragmentary data on "homosexuality" in sex surveys of the 1920s, see Sheila Fitzpatrick, "Sex and Revolution: An Examination of Literary and Statistical Data on the Mores of Soviet Students in the 1920s," *Journal of Modern History* 50 (1978): 252–78.

27. Eric Naiman, "The Case of Chubarov Alley: Collective Rape, Utopian Desire and the Mentality of NEP," *Russian History/Histoire Russe* 17, no. 1 (1990): 1–30; idem, *Sex in Public: The Incarnation of Early Soviet Ideology* (Princeton: Princeton University Press, 1997); Elizabeth Waters, "Victim or Villain: Prostitution in Postrevolutionary Russia," in *Women and Society in Russian and the Soviet Union,* ed. Linda Edmondson (Cambridge: Cambridge University Press, 1992); N. B. Lebina and M. B. Shkarovskii, *Prostitutsiia v Peterburge* (Moscow: Progress-Akademiia, 1994); Elizabeth A. Wood, "Prostitution Unbound: Representations of Sexual and Political Anxieties in Postrevolutionary Russia," in *Sexuality and the Body in Russian Culture,* eds. Jane T. Costlow, Stephanie Sandler, and Judith Vowles (Stanford: Stanford University Press, 1993).

28. This thesis was first proposed by sociologist and jurist Nicholas Timasheff, *The Great Retreat* (New York: E. P. Dutton, 1946).

29. Gail W. Lapidus, *Women in Soviet Society: Equality, Development, and Social Change* (Berkeley & London: University of California Press, 1978), 113; Tatyana Mamonova, *Russian Women's Studies: Essays on Sexism in Soviet Culture* (New York: Pergamon, 1985), 130; note also Chris Ward, *Stalin's Russia* (London & New York: Edward Arnold, 1993), 198–99. An important revisionist proponent of the "Great Retreat" thesis in sexual matters, Richard Stites, ignored the criminalization of sodomy entirely in his *The Women's Liberation Movement in Russia.*

30. Susan Gross Solomon, "The Demographic Argument in Soviet Debates over the Legalization of Abortion in the 1920s," *Cahiers du Monde Russe et Soviétique* 33, no. 1 (1992): 59–82; Wendy Goldman, "Women, Abortion and the State, 1917–36," in *Russia's Women: Accommodation, Resistance, Transformation,* eds. Barbara Evans Clements, Barbara Alpern Engel, and Christine D. Worobec (Berkeley and Los Angeles: University of California Press, 1991).

31. It is interesting that in deliberations over abortion in 1920, women (Inessa Armand, Nadezhda Krupskaia) appeared to emphasize a women's right to control fertility, while their male counterparts were more concerned to medicalize and control the procedure; see Elizabeth A. Wood, *The Baba and the Comrade: Gender and Politics in Revolutionary Russia* (Bloomington: Indiana University Press, 1997), 107–8.

32. Beatrice Brodsky Farnsworth, "Bolshevik Alternatives and the Soviet Family: The 1926 Marriage Law Debate," in *Women in Russia,* eds. Dorothy Atkinson, Alexander Dallin, and Gail W. Lapidus (Stanford: Stanford University Press, 1977); Barbara Evans Clements, "The Effects of the Civil War on Women and Family Relations" in *Party, State and Society in the Russian Civil War,* eds. D. P. Koenker, W. G. Rosenberg, and R. G. Suny (Bloomington: Indiana University Press, 1989).

33. Barbara Evans Clements, *Bolshevik Women* (Cambridge: Cambridge University Press, 1997); Wood, *The Baba and the Comrade.*

34. Mark von Hagen, *Soldiers in the Proletarian Dictatorship: The Red Army and the Soviet Socialist State, 1917–1930* (Ithaca: Cornell University Press, 1990); Kenneth M. Pinnow, "Making Suicide Soviet: Medicine, Moral Statistics, and the Politics of Social Science in Bolshevik Russia, 1920–1930" (Ph.D. diss., Columbia University, 1998); Joshua A. Sanborn, "Drafting the Nation: Military Conscription and the Formation of a Modern Polity in Tsarist and Soviet Russia, 1905–1925" (Ph.D. diss, University of Chicago, 1998).

35. See, e.g., J. A. Mangan and J. Walvin, eds., *Manliness and Morality: Middle-class Masculinity in Britain and America, 1800–1940* (Manchester: Manchester University Press, 1987); David D. Gilmore, *Manhood in the Making: Cultural Concepts of Masculinity* (New Haven: Yale University Press, 1990); E. Anthony Rotundo, *American Manhood: Transformations in Masculinity from the Revolution to the Modern Era* (New York: Basic Books, 1993); Robert A. Nye, *Masculinity and Male Codes of Honor in Modern France* (Berkeley: University of California Press, 1993); R. W. Connell, *Masculinities* (Cambridge, England: Polity Press, 1995).

36. See, e.g., Lauritsen and Thorstad, *The Early Homosexual Rights Movement;* Neil McKenna, "Men of the Lunar Light: A Utopian Period in Russian History," *Him* 32 (1990): 49; Jonathan Dollimore, *Sexual Dissidence: Augustine to Wilde, Freud to Foucault* (Oxford: Oxford University Press, 1991), 94; Morton, *The Material Queer,* 254–62 (for Aleksandra Kollontai's article, "Sexual Relations and the Class Struggle," evoking the "good" socialism of her heyday). A confused presentation of these politics is found in Rictor Norton, *The Myth of the Modern Homosexual: Queer History and the Search for Cultural Unity* (London: Cassell, 1997), 252.

37. See, e.g., Guy Hocquenghem, *Homosexual Desire* (1972; Durham: Duke University Press, 1996), 133–36; and, despite acknowledging the absence of a social basis for homosexual reform in the USSR, Weeks, *Coming Out,* 144–50. Karlinsky's critique of gay left understandings of this history has focused on the failure to incorporate Russian social and cultural specificities, see, e.g., "Gay Life before the Soviets."

38. By the time of the Soviet sodomy ban, Reich had been expelled from the Communist Party and was in exile in Scandinavia; see David Boadella, *Wilhelm Reich: The Evolution of His Work* (London: Vision, 1973).

39. So, e.g., Hocquenghem condemned Reich as "grossly reactionary" and his attempt to combine sex and revolution doomed to reproduce "the heterosexual norm": *Homosexual Desire,* 133–36; for Reich as hero of progressive sexual politics silenced by Stalinism, see Lauritsen and Thorstad, *The Early Homosexual Rights Movement,* 77.

40. A recent document collection presents four items of the Stalin era (from the *Great Soviet Encyclopedia, Pravda,* and other sources) that have been widely cited; despite a nuanced introduction by Laura Engelstein, these familiar sources produce the same impression of "tolerance" undermined by a Stalinist "general about-face in regulating private and sexual life" in the 1930s: Mark Blasius and Shane Phelan, eds., *We Are Everywhere: A Historical Sourcebook of Gay and Lesbian Politics* (New York: Routledge, 1997), 197–99, 214–15.

41. Thus, polyglot Rudi Bleys avoids the region entirely despite his exhaustive discussion of ethnographic literature for Asia, Africa, and the Americas, Rudi C. Bleys, *The Geography of Perversion: Male-to-Male Behaviour outside the West and the Ethnographic Imagination, 1750–1918* (New York: New York University Press, 1995); the *bachi* (boy prostitutes) of central Asian societies are confined to a single reference in Stephen O. Murray and Will Roscoe, eds., *Islamic Homosexualities: Culture, History,*

and Literature (New York: New York University Press, 1997), 208–11. More attention to sexual and gender ambiguity among Far Eastern Siberian peoples is paid in Stephen O. Murray, ed., *Oceanic Homosexualities* (New York: Garland, 1992), 314–36.

42. Modest source bases for Russia characterized the following studies, which in most respects were exhaustive: Arno Karlen, *Sexuality and Homosexuality: A New View* (New York: W. W. Norton, 1971); David Greenberg, *The Construction of Homosexuality* (Chicago: University of Chicago Press, 1988). Recent popular surveys have either relied on Karlinsky's work, in the case of Neil Miller, *Out of the Past: Gay and Lesbian History from 1869 to the Present* (New York: Vintage Books, 1994), or they have ignored Russia completely; a best-selling example being Colin Spencer, *Homosexuality: A History* (London: Fourth Estate, 1995).

43. Male-to-male sexual acts committed by Asians, Africans, and American aboriginals were perceived by nineteenth-century Europeans as endemic or "inherent to inferior races," whereas the same acts observed in Europeans tended to be interpreted as the deviance of a minority: Bleys, *The Geography of Perversion*, 270. Russia, ignored by Bleys, straddles this epistemological fault line.

44. On Siberian shamans, see excerpts from anthropological literature in Murray, *Oceanic Homosexualities*, 314, 324, 332–36; on the revival of Siberian shamanistic cultures and concomitant androgyny, see Marjorie M. Balzer, "Sacred Genders in Siberia," in *Gender Reversals and Gender Cultures: Anthropological and Historical Perspectives*, ed. Sabrina P. Ramet (London: Routledge, 1996); on Muslim males, see, e.g., V. M. Tarnovskii, *Izvrashchenie polovogo chuvstva. Sudebno-psikhiatricheskii ocherk* (St Petersburg, 1885), 50–51; and A. Shvarts, "K voprosu o priznakakh privychnoi passivnoi pederastii (Iz nabliudenii v aziatskoi chasti g. Tashkenta)," in *Vestnik obshchestvennoi gigieny, sudebnoi i prakticheskoi meditsiny*, no. 6 (1906): 816–18.

45. Scholars have begun to unravel Russians' relationships with their subject peoples, and their findings underscore the asymmetry of the ruling nation's approach to its subjects, based on hierarchies of European perceptions of development. For excellent discussions, see Yuri Slezkine, *Arctic Mirrors: Russia and the Small Peoples of the North* (Ithaca: Cornell University Press, 1994); Daniel Brower and Edward Lazzerini, eds., *Russia's Orient: Imperial Borderlands and Peoples, 1700–1917* (Bloomington: Indiana University Press, 1997).

46. Foucault, *History of Sexuality: An Introduction, Vol. 1*, 97, 143–45; Paul Robinson, *The Modernization of Sex: Havelock Ellis, Alfred Kinsey, William Masters and Virginia Johnson* (New York: Harper & Row, 1976).

47. Greenberg, *The Construction of Homosexuality*, 14; Duberman et al., introduction to *Hidden from History*, 9. For a summary of discussions, see Annamarie Jagose, *Queer Theory: An Introduction* (New York: New York University Press, 1996), 10–21.

48. Laura Engelstein, "Lesbian Vignettes: A Russian Triptych from the 1890s," *Signs* 15, no. 4 (1990): 813–31; idem, *The Keys to Happiness.*

49. Laura Engelstein, "Combined Underdevelopment: Discipline and the Law in Imperial and Soviet Russia," *American Historical Review* 98, no. 2 (1993): 338–53, quotation, 348.

50. Engelstein, "Combined Underdevelopment," 344.

51. Engelstein, "Combined Underdevelopment," 344, 351.

52. Jackson, "Thai Research on Male Homosexuality and Transgenderism"; Wim Lunsing, "Japan: Finding its Way?," in *The Global Emergence of Gay and Lesbian Politics: National Imprints of a Worldwide Movement*, eds. B. D. Adam, J. W. Duyvendak, and A. Krouwel (Philadelphia: Temple University Press, 1999), 295–96; Lumsden, *Machos, Maricones, and Gays*, 96–114; Green, *Beyond Carnival*, 107–46.

53. Late-nineteenth-century Russian medicine used the words "pederasty" (*peder-*

astiia) and "pederast" (*pederast*) to refer to males who engaged in anal intercourse, usually with other males, without imposing rigid age distinctions. In these practices, popular and educated Russian followed French usage; in the eighteenth century, Russia's elite sexual culture borrowed many French models; see Igor Kon, "Istoricheskie sud'by russkogo Erosa," in *Seks i erotika v russkoi traditsionnoi kul'ture*, ed. A. L. Toporkov (Moscow: Ladomir, 1996), 13. The first known use of the adjective "homosexual" (*gomoseksual'nyi*) in Russian was by I. M. Tarnovskii, *Izvrashchenie polovogo chuvstva u zhenshchin* (St. Petersburg, 1895); see Engelstein, "Lesbian Vignettes." After 1905, relaxation of censorship facilitated dissemination of the term beyond a scientific audience. See, e.g., P. V. Ushakovskii, *Liudi srednego pola* (St. Petersburg, 1908); V. P. Ruadze, *K sudu! Gomoseksual'nyi Peterburg* (St. Petersburg, 1908); I. B. Fuks, *Gomoseksualizm kak prestuplenie. Iruidich. i ugol.-politich. ocherk* (St. Petersburg: Obshchestvennaia Pol'za, 1914). Note also use of term "homosexual crimes with soldiers" used repeatedly by all protagonists in file on the 1909 dismissal of staff-captain A. I. Belinskii from the Imperial Army, GARF f. 117, op. 1, d. 300. I am grateful to Josh Sanborn for sharing this source.

54. Diana Lewis Burgin, "Laid Out in Lavender: Perceptions of Lesbian Love in Russian Literature and Criticism of the Silver Age, 1893–1917," in *Sexuality and the Body in Russian Culture,* eds. Jane T. Costlow, Stephanie Sandler, and Judith Vowles (Stanford: Stanford University Press, 1993); Dan Healey, "Unruly Identities: Soviet Psychiatry Confronts the 'Female Homosexual' of the 1920s," in *Gender in Russian History and Culture, 1800–1990,* ed. Linda Edmondson (London: Palgrave, 2001).

55. Burgin, *Sophia Parnok;* Ol'ga Zhuk, *Russkie amazonki: Istoriia lesbiiskoi subkul'tury v Rossii XX vek* (Moscow: Glagol, 1998).

56. For an intelligent attack on rigid sexual dimorphism, see Anne Fausto-Sterling, "The Five Sexes: Why Male and Female Are Not Enough," *Sciences* (March/April 1993): 20–24.

57. Pat Califia, *Sex Changes: The Politics of Transgenderism* (San Francisco: Cleis Press, 1997); Alice Domurat Dreger, *Hermaphrodites and the Medical Invention of Sex* (Cambridge, Mass.: Harvard University Press, 1998); Leslie Feinberg, *Stone Butch Blues* (Ithaca: Firebrand Publishers, 1993); idem, *Transgender Warriors: Making History from Joan of Arc to RuPaul* (Boston: Beacon Books, 1996); Herdt, *Third Sex, Third Gender.* For a thinly disguised history of bisexuality, see Spencer, *Homosexuality.*

58. On the "performative" aspects of gender, see Judith Butler, *Gender Trouble: Feminism and the Subversion of Identity* (New York: Routledge, 1990).

59. Some might object that these individuals were not responsible for their acts; they were simply following the dictates of their hormones, genes, or (more crudely) their sex organs. An understanding of their behavior as "dissent" is therefore unwarranted. I argue that whatever the biological baseline for same-sex desire and gender transgression, individuals who experienced them did so despite having been socialized within a hegemonic sex/gender system. They were faced with the choice of pursuing the expression of their transgressive desires or suppressing them. These choices carried life-changing consequences that made explicit a sexual politics of the normal (as will be apparent in chapter 8, when considering the fate of those who chose to have sex with their own sex in late 1930s Moscow, for example). For theoretical discussions of "identity as resistance" to a dominant sex/gender system, see Jeffrey Weeks, *Against Nature: Essays on History, Sexuality and Identity* (London: Rivers Oram Press, 1991), 74–83; Dollimore, *Sexual Dissidence.* Another objection to this application of dissent in a Russian context could come from political scientists who wish to reserve the label for the cohort of human rights activists who surfaced in late Soviet society. The objection reflects a heterosexist conceptualization of both liberty and dissent. The KGB re-

portedly considered homosexuality a form of "sexual dissidence" in the 1970s–80s, see Julie Dorf, "On the Theme: Talking with the Editor of the Soviet Union's First Lesbian and Gay Newspaper," *Outlook* 1 (1990): 55–59.

60. Hermaphrodites (persons with genitalia and anatomy blending elements of the male and female) may appear to be so biologically "damaged" that the label of "sexual and gender dissident" seems inappropriate. I argue that these individuals, who normally had to "pass" as either male or female in society, were acutely aware of the artifice of gender and their manipulation of it to shape life chances. See Fausto-Sterling, "The Five Sexes"; Dan Healey, " 'Man or Woman?': Hermaphroditism as a Medical Problem in Tsarist and Soviet Russia" (paper presented to European Social Science History Conference, Amsterdam, 13 April 2000).

61. For a critique of the masculinism of this literature, see Rosemary Auchmuty, Sheila Jeffreys, and Elaine Miller, "Lesbian History and Gay Studies: Keeping a Feminist Perspective," *Women's History Review* 1, no. 1 (1992): 89–108.

62. Alan Sinfeld's call for "more urgent and intelligent subcultural work, not less," despite skepticism about "gay" as a coherent category, could have been formulated with post Soviet Russia in mind. See Alan Sinfield, *Gay and After* (London: Serpent's Tail, 1998), 17, 79, 181.

63. One file in the Presidential Archive appears to be devoted to the implementation of the Stalinist antisodomy law: APRF, f. 3, op. 57, d. 37; see "Iz istorii Ugolovnogo kodeksa: 'Primerno NAKAZAT' etikh Merzavtsev,' " *Istochnik* 5–6 (1993): 164–65. Through a reliable intermediary, I inquired whether MVD archives held any Soviet-era studies of the Stalinist antisodomy statute (for instance, on conviction rates, the character of the crime, or enforcement patterns), but I obtained a negative response. Such studies of specific crimes (such as juvenile crime, group rapes, or "crimes directed against the emancipation of women" in central Asia) appear periodically in Justice Commissariat, RSFSR and USSR Procuracy, and USSR Supreme Court archival holdings. Documents of any kind about the sodomy law are exceedingly rare in the holdings of these agencies.

64. On the Soviet variant of this literature, see Bernstein, "What Everyone Should Know about Sex."

65. Russia has a seventy-five-year embargo on the release of archival files designated as "personal documentation." Archive directors interpret this restriction in different ways. In 1995, I was advised that patients' medical records after 1920, held by the Ministry of Health of the Russian Federation, would not be released for research purposes. (Similar restrictions are not uncommon in Europe or the U.S.) Unfortunately, this meant that I was unable to locate patient records for particularly intriguing figures, such as Evgeniia Fedorovna M., a "female homosexual" and "transvestite" described in chapter 2. (For an early look at her case, see my "Evgeniia/Evgenii: Queer Case Histories in the First Years of Soviet Power," *Gender and History* 9, no. 1 [1997]: 83–106.) Most medical case histories used in this book were gathered from published sources.

66. The seventy-five-year embargo on "personal" documents was invoked.

67. Searches of the analogous criminal records for the 1920s for the city of Ekaterinburg/Sverdlovsk in the State Archive of Sverdlovsk Province and in the city of Saratov in the State Archive of Saratov Province have failed to uncover a single sodomy prosecution in this era. I am grateful to Aleksei Kilin for conducting the review of Ekaterinburg records.

68. These seven sentencing and appeal documents, consisting of some two to ten pages each, were sifted from over eleven thousand pages of similar records for crimes (mostly counterrevolutionary agitation, theft and embezzlement, assaults, and murders)

during 1933–41 (TsMAM f. 819, op. 2, dd. 1–45 (for 1933–41): "*Moskovskii gorodskoi sud, 1933–1951.*") The documents are sorted by year but have no indexes or cataloging apparatus.

69. To preserve the anonymity of the individuals in these TsMAM trial and sentencing documents, I have assigned pseudonyms to named defendants. For ease of identification in the text, I have given each trial a short name based on the type of document it was found in (sentence or case file), followed by the leading defendant's name and the year of the case. Full citations are given in the bibliography.

70. Inventories (*opisi*) for the city courts generally open with a statement of this protocol, but nowhere are the criteria of "representativeness" revealed. This culling of court records took place in the 1970s.

71. In addition, this archive's holdings for the Moscow Holy Consistory yielded only one same-sex offense, the 1862 case of a village priest suspected of raping an eight-year-old boy: TsGIAgM, f. 203, op. 727, d. 518.

72. Shumikhin, "Dnevnik Mikhaila Kuzmina." Dr. Shumikhin generously provided me with materials and advice at RGALI. Portions of Kuzmin's diaries have been published: M. A. Kuzmin, *Dnevnik, 1905–1907*, eds. N. A. Bogomolov and S. V. Shumikhin (St. Petersburg: Iz-vo Ivana Limbakha, 2000), "Mikhail Kuzmin. Dnevnik 1921 goda," eds. N. A. Bogomolov and S. V. Shumikhin, *Minuvshee. Istoricheskii al'manakh* (1993): 12: 423–94, 13: 457–524, and *Dnevnik 1934 goda*, ed. G. A. Morev (St. Petersburg: Iz-vo Ivana Limbakha, 1998). The authoritative biography of Kuzmin is N. A. Bogomolov and John E. Malmstad, *Mikhail Kuzmin: Iskusstvo, zhizn', epokha* (Moscow: Novoe literaturnoe obozrenie, 1996), translated and revised as Malmstad and Bogomolov, *Mikhail Kuzmin: A Life in Art.* See also N. A. Bogomolov, *Mikhail Kuzmin: Stat'i i materialy* (Moscow: Novoe literaturnoe obozrenie, 1995).

73. S. Poliakova, "Poeziia Sofii Parnok," in *Sofiia Parnok: Sobranie stikhotvorenii,* ed. S Poliakova (Ann Arbor: Ardis, 1979); Burgin, *Sophia Parnok.*

CHAPTER ONE

1. I. S. Kon, "Istoricheskie sud'by russkogo Erosa," in *Seks i erotika v russkoi traditsionnoi kul'ture,* ed. A. L. Toporkov (Moscow: Ladomir, 1996), 6–8. For a rich discussion of Russia's sexual folklore, see the essays in Marcus Levitt and Andrei Toporkov, eds., *Eros and Pornography in Russian Culture / Eros i pornografiia v russkoi kul'ture* (Moscow: Landomir, 1999).

2. Kon, "Istoricheskie sud'by russkogo Erosa," 12. The range of tropes of male anal penetration expressed in *mat* is vast, and its significance to Russian systems of gender deserves further attention. See, e.g., Vladimir Kozlovskii, *Argo russkoi gomoseksual'noi subkul'tury: Materialy k izucheniiu.* (Benson, Vt.: Chalidze Publications, 1986), 96–98; F. Il'iasov et al., *Russkii mat (Antologiia)* (Moscow: Lada M, 1994).

3. Karlinsky, "Russia's Gay Literature and History," 1, discusses several reports; see also idem, "Russia's Gay Literature and Culture: The Impact of the October Revolution," in Duberman et al., *Hidden from History,* 348; and James Riordan, "Sexual Minorities: The Status of Gays and Lesbians in Russian-Soviet-Russian Society," in *Women in Russia and Ukraine,* ed. Rosalind Marsh (Cambridge: Cambridge University Press, 1996), 156–57.

4. Eve Levin, *Sex and Society in the World of the Orthodox Slavs, 900–1700* (Ithaca: Cornell University Press, 1989), 199–202; note also I. S. Kon, *Lunnyi svet na zare: Liki i maski odnopoloi liubvi* (Moscow: Olimp, 1998), 284.

5. Laura Engelstein, *The Keys to Happiness: Sex and the Search for Modernity in Fin-de-Siècle Russia* (Ithaca: Cornell University Press, 1992), 58. On the "military revolution," see Geoffrey Parker, *The Military Revolution: Military innovation and the rise*

of the West, 1500–1800 (Cambridge: Cambridge University Press, 1988); in the Russian context, see Richard Hellie, "The Petrine Army: Continuity, Change and Impact," *Canadian-American Slavic Studies* 8, no. 2 (1974): 237–53. The impact of recruitment and disciplinary practices inspired by the military revolution on the emergence of a modern homosexual identity deserves a study in itself.

6. In this sense, state regulation preceded the internalization of modern forms of morality, see Kon, "Istoricheskie sud'by russkogo Erosa," 6. The history of these regulations is discussed in chapter 3.

7. For an argument that same-sex erotic relations between early modern Europeans were part of the fabric of general masculine culture, see Michael Rocke, *Forbidden Friendships: Homosexuality and Male Culture in Renaissance Florence* (New York: Oxford University Press, 1996). The pseudonymous Konstantin K. Rotikov uses an undifferentiated and essentialized "homosexuality" to describe mutual male sexuality in St. Petersburg from its founding in 1703 to the twentieth century. In his *Drugoi Peterburg* (St. Petersburg: Liga Plius, 1998), Rotikov deploys literary gossip and legend (without source attribution) to argue that "homosexuals" have been a constant feature of St. Petersburg's private life. He conflates forms of traditional Russian mutual male eros with more recent patterns of a "homosexual" subculture.

8. Jeffrey Burds, "Diary of Moscow Merchant Pavel Vasil'evich Medvedev, 1854–1864" (Department of History, Northwestern University, Boston, photocopy). I am grateful to Jeffrey Burds for providing me with generous access to a transcript of the text of Medvedev's diary for the year 1861 which contains these vignettes. For an introduction to the diary, see A. I. Kupriianov, " 'Pagubnaia strast' moskovskogo kuptsa," in *Kazus: Individual'noe i unikal'noe v istorii*, eds. Iu. L. Bessmertnyi and M. A. Boitsov (Moscow: RGGU RAN, 1997).

9. Burds, "Diary of Moscow Merchant Pavel Vasil'evich Medvedev," 152.

10. Tarnovskii, *Izvrashchenie polovogo chuvstva*, 69–71. Tarnovskii gives the following description of one "pederast": "A third particularly exploits young coachmen, travels with them, converses with them, strikes up acquaintances with them, visits coachmen's courtyards, and never had even an unpleasant confrontation. They consented to or laughed at his propositions, but always in the most kindly fashion" (Tarnovskii, 70).

11. V. F. Golenko, "Pederastiia na sude," *Arkhiv psikhiatrii, neirologii i sudebnoi psikhopatologii* 9, no. 3 (1887): 42–56.

12. N. A. Obolonskii, "Izvrashchenie polovogo chuvstva," *Russkii arkhiv patologii, klinicheskoi meditsiny i bakteriologii* (1898): 1–20, esp. 15; V. M. Bekhterev, "O polovykh izvrashcheniiakh, kak patologicheskikh sochetatel'nykh refleksakh," *Obozrenie psikhiatrii* 7–9 (1915): 1–26, esp. 9–13; V. A. Belousov, "Sluchai gomoseksuala-muzhskoi prostitutki," *Prestupnik i prestupnost'. Sbornik* 2 (1927): 309–17.

13. Even when turning down proposals from upper-class men for sex, Tarnovskii claimed lower-class males did so without malice and without turning to the police for satisfaction, see Tarnovskii, *Izvrashchenie polovogo chuvstva*, 70. Note also the 1892 case of Moscow craftsman Reshetnikov, described below, whose sexual advances evoked mirth-making among the apprentice boys in his workshop.

14. RGIA, f. 1412, op. 221, d. 54, ll. 29–37 and passim. I am very grateful to Gaby Donicht for sharing this data with me.

15. Burds, *Dnevnik moskovskogo kuptsa*, 144.

16. TsGIAgM, f. 142, op. 2, d. 433. Note also the case of Kniazev, son of a workshop owner, convicted of raping an eleven-year old apprentice in 1874; f. 142, op. 3, d. 233.

17. TsGIAgM, f. 142, op. 1, d. 172. See also A. F. Koni dossier, GARF, f. 564, op. 1, d. 260, ll. 92–100.

18. Tarnovskii, *Izvrashchenie polovogo chuvstva*, 70.

19. GARF, f. A353, op. 3, d. 745 (*Dokumenty o kontrrevoliutsionnoi agitatsii monakhov Novoirusalimskogo monastyria i po obvineniiu episkopa Palladiia v rastlenii mal'chika, 1919 g.*), ll. 29, 70–70 ob., 72–73 ob., 81–83 ob., and passim. On this case, see Dan Healey, " 'Their Culture': Clerical Same-Sex Offenses in the Discourse of Bolshevik Militant Atheism, 1919–1930," (Department of History, University of Wales Swansea, 1998, photocopy).

20. Levin, *Sex and Society in the World of the Orthodox Slavs*, 290–92.

21. This surveillance appears in testimony from clerics who had worked with Palladii. Nuns who laundered monks' bed sheets noted the stains they contained. (GARF, f. A353, op. 3, d. 745, ll. 30, 70 ob., 72 ob., 81) One witness, denying that Palladii's relations with his novice included "sodomy," told police that "All priors, bishops etc., the high ranks in monasteries who have lay brothers—never sleep in the same room with them." (l. 30 ob.)

22. Orthodox seminaries in this period accepted boarding boys at age twelve for a six-year period. Older youths loathed seminary dormitories and often rented private rooms, while inspectors (*inspektory*) monitored their living arrangements, see T. G. Leont'eva, "Byt, nravy i povedenie seminaristov v nachale XX v." in *Revoliutsiia i chelovek: Byt, nravy, povedenie, moral'*, ed. P. V. Volobuev et al. (Moscow, 1997).

23. Cheka investigators located in Saratov two clerics, one twenty-six, the other thirty-one years of age, whose monastic careers began while they were teenagers dependent on Palladii; both denied any "disgusting acts" with the bishop. One of these men admitted having destroyed his correspondence with Palladii, and a (fruitless) police search on his quarters was conducted anyway, GARF, f. A353, op. 3, d. 745, ll. 70–70 ob., 72–73 ob., 81–83 ob., 94 ob.–95 ob., 102–102 ob.

24. For descriptions of similar relations with clerics before and after 1917, see V. A. Belousov, "Sluchai gomoseksuala-muzhskoi prostitutki," 313.

25. V. Merzheevskii, *Sudebnaia ginekologiia. Rukovodstvo dlia vrachei i iuristov* (St. Petersburg, 1878); Tarnovskii, *Izvrashchenie polovogo chuvstva*.

26. A. A. Biriukov, *Eta volshebnitsa bania* (Moscow: Sovetskii sport, 1991), 17; Anatolii Rubinov, *Sanduny: Kniga o moskovskikh baniakh* (Moscow: Moskovskii rabochii, 1990), 19.

27. Levin concludes from church sources that Russian baths constituted a desexualized space, see *Sex and Society in the World of the Orthodox Slavs*, 195–97. For a fascinating and provocative assertion that "all baths are women's baths," see Nancy Condee, "The Second Fantasy Mother, or All Baths Are Women's Baths," in *Russia—Women—Culture*, ed. Helen Goscilo and Beth Holmgren (Bloomington: Indiana University Press, 1996). Foreigners' accounts (even allowing for their Western, masculine gaze) suggest that in Russian villages and disreputable town baths, the sexes mixed freely; see Claude de Grève, *Le Voyage en Russie. Anthologie des voyageurs français aux XVIIIe et XIXe siècles* (Paris: Robert Laffont, 1990), 948–54; and N. Wraxall, *A Tour through Some of the Northern Parts of Europe* (n.p., 1776), 248, cited in Havelock Ellis, *Studies in the Psychology of Sex* (Philadelphia: F. A. Davis, 1926), 1: 31. In 1845, commercial pressures compelled Ministry of Internal Affairs officials to restate the prohibition of mixed-sex bathing; see I. A. Bogdanov, *Tri veka peterburgskoi bani* (St. Petersburg: Iskusstvo SPb, 2000), 242–43; citing RGIA, f. 1287, op. 37, d. 61, ll. 222–25.

28. Elite Russian men generally adopted shaving under Peter the Great; Muscovites who took up the practice prior to the eighteenth century were condemned for making themselves resemble women and thus departing from the image of God; Levin, *Sex and Society in the World of the Orthodox Slavs*, 202. Archpriest Avvakum refused a

request from Vasilii Sheremet'ev, governor of Kazan', to bless his son, "Matvei Brado-brits" (Mathew who shaves), citing his "shameful appearance" (*bludonosnyi obraz*): *Zhitie Protopopova Avvakuma*, ed. N. S. Tikonravov (St. Petersburg, 1861), 16. See also Kozlovskii, *Argo russkoi gomoseksual'noi subkul'tury*, 21; Kon, *Lunnyi svet na zare*, 284.

29. For discussion of this fact in the context of labor migration, see Akademiia nauk, *Istoriia Moskvy* (Moscow: AN SSSR), 2: 553.

30. In the early 1930s, one elderly peasant near Moscow reportedly told a journalist the following: "*Banshchiki* (bathhouse attendants) came from three provinces, but only from two or three districts in each, and not next door to each other, but in nests . . . From time immemorial the districts that have supplied Moscow with *banshchiki* were Zaraiskii-Riazanskii, Tul'skii-Kashirskii and Venerskii. Generation after generation of men and women went to Moscow for this reason. See, I was taken as a ten-year-old boy, just as they sent my grandfather, and father, and now our children,; in Vladimir A. Giliarovskii, "Moskva i moskvichi," in V. A. Giliarovskii, *Izbrannoe v trekh tomakh* (Moscow: Moskovskii rabochii, 1960), 3: 308.

31. Burds, *Dnevnik moskovskogo kuptsa*, 157. *Kulizm* was derived from the French *cul* (ass). See entry for "*coniste*," under which "*culiste*" is discussed in opposition, in Claude Courouve, *Vocabulaire de l'homosexualité masculine* (Paris: Payot, 1985), 84–86. Probably these words arrived in Russia during the eighteenth century as elite sexual culture adapted French models, Kon, "Istoricheskie sud'by russkogo Erosa," 13.

32. GARF, f. A353, op. 3, d. 745, ll. 39, 32 ob.

33. Merzheevskii, *Sudebnaia ginekologiia*, 239. Thirty years later, attendants in a Petersburg bathhouse were said to charge three to five rubles for similar attentions, see V. M. Bekhterev, "Lechenie vnusheniem prevratnykh polovykh vlechenii i onanizma," *Obozrenie psikhiatrii* 8 (1898): 1–11. As with female prostitution, price differentials between male prostitutes apparently indicated perceptions of value associated with the luxury or modesty of the setting, the age of the male providing sexual services, and the acts performed. See Bernstein, *Sonia's Daughters*, 86–93.

34. Tarnovskii, *Izvrashchenie polovogo chuvstva*, 89.

35. Tarnovskii, *Izvrashchenie polovogo chuvstva*, 69.

36. The medical and legal experts' obsession with "active" (insertive) and "passive" (receptive) sexual postures was a constant of Russian discourse on male (and eventually, female) same-sex love. Tarnovskii, *Izvrashchenie polovogo chuvstva*, 71.

37. In the 1880s, he called for tax exemptions for brothels, proposed that the army's soldiers should pay mandatory visits to them free of charge, and claimed public houses kept crime and immorality off the streets. His opinions shifted by the late 1890s, when he argued that without inspection of male clients, licensed brothels only spread disease; see Bernstein, *Sonia's Daughters*, 145, 176.

38. Tarnovskii, *Izvrashchenie polovogo chuvstva*, 70. In fact, blackmailers of "peder-asts" did operate in St. Petersburg and exploited bathhouse reputations and opportuni-ties to compromise clients, see Merzheevskii, *Sudebnaia ginekologiia*, 252, and A. F. Koni, *Na zhiznennom puti. Iz zapisok sudebnogo deiatelia. Zhiteiskie vstrechi* (St. Peters-burg, 1912), 1: 152–56. Similar bathhouse-centered male prostitution was observed in Turkey, see Ellis, *Studies in the Psychology of Sex*, 1: 13.

39. Bathhouse apprenticeship required boys to work their way up a hierarchy of functions, becoming fully trained attendants by age eighteen or nineteen. Giliarovskii described tsarist bathhouse attendants as a contented group, with few youngsters aban-doning their apprenticeships (in contrast to boys in bakeries and workshops): "Moskva i moskvichi," 308–12.

40. In 1882, 20 percent of Moscow's population occupied nonfamilial housing such

as factory barracks; a further 12.6 percent were clerks or workers who lived with their employers in situations like apprenticeships. In highly industrialized Lefortovskaia and Serpukhovskaia districts, the proportion in barracks and group accommodation rose to 43.7 percent. See Robert Johnson, *Peasant and Proletarian: The Working Class of Moscow in the Late Nineteenth Century* (New Brunswick: Rutgers University Press, 1979), 53–66. On worker housing, see also Victoria E. Bonnell, ed., *The Russian Worker: Life and Labor under the Tsarist Regime* (Berkeley: University of California Press, 1983), 121–30, 175–77; on urban development, Daniel R. Brower, *The Russian City between Tradition and Modernity, 1850–1900* (Berkeley: University of California Press, 1990).

41. Between 1871 and 1902, the proportion of women in Moscow's entire population rose from 40 percent to 45 percent, but the number who were dependents or women of child-bearing age remained low. In 1902, there were twice as many married men as married women in Moscow, evidence that migrant workers still left their wives in the village and lived apart for extended periods in the city, Johnson, *Peasant and Proletarian*, 55–56. Male workers thus felt justified in resorting to female prostitutes, Bernstein, *Sonia's Daughters*, 90–92. On women in the industrial workforce, see Barbara A. Engel, *Between the Fields and the City: Women, Work and Family in Russia, 1861– 1914* (Cambridge: Cambridge University Press, 1994).

42. Ruadze, *K sudu!*, 17.

43. In 1878, Tchaikovsky wrote to his homosexual brother Modest describing how a friend Nikolai Bochechkarov introduced him to a young butler. The three met on the boulevard, went to a pub, and an "infatuated" Tchaikovsky took the butler to a private room. Poznansky, *Tchaikovsky's Last Days*, 19.

44. Mamaev's wife and children lived in distant Ekaterinburg, TsGIAgM, f. 142, op. 2, d. 142, l. 148.

45. A. I. Reitblat, "Letopisets slukhov," *Novoe literaturnoe obozrenie* 4 (1993): 167– 69, cited in Konstantin Rotikov, "Epizod iz zhizni 'golubogo' Peterburga," *Nevskii arkhiv: Istoriko-kraevedcheskii sbornik* 3 (1997): 449–66, see 451.

46. On 6 January 1869, a fifty-six-year-old Dane met a young Petersburger while buying eau de cologne in this gallery. After sex with the Dane in his flat, the young man tried to blackmail him, Merzheevskii, *Sudebnaia ginekologiia*, 254.

47. Koni, *Na zhiznennom puti*, 154–55; Tarnovskii, *Izvrashchenie polovogo chuvstva*, 72.

48. The argot term *tetka* (plural, *tetki*) is discussed below. On the denunciation, see RGIA, f. 1683, op. 1, d. 199, ll. 1–13. This document was first described in Rotikov, "Epizod iz zhizni 'golubogo' Peterburga." Rotikov presented a detailed commentary of this denunciation, withholding, however, its most explicit aspects. The full document was published by RGIA researcher V. V. Bersen'ev and A. R. Markov of the Petersburg State Academy of Culture, as "Politsiia i gei: Epizod iz epokhi Aleksandra III," *Risk* 3 (1998): 105–16. Bersen'ev and Markov disagree with Rotikov's dating of 1889 for the denunciation, arguing that it was more likely composed between 1890 and 1894. All further citations of the denunciation are from Bersen'ev and Markov's publication.

49. Bersen'ev and Markov, "Politsiia i gei," 109.

50. Restaurant-based "dens" of "pederasts" were uncovered periodically, but information on these locations remains elusive. The young Tchaikovsky escaped scandal when the Chautemps Restaurant was exposed in the press, Poznansky, *Tchaikovsky's Last Days*, 10. Another scandal forced the closure of a restaurant in approximately 1893, P. V. Ushakovskii [pseud.], *Liudi srednego pola* (St. Petersburg, 1908), 6.

51. See Rotikov, "Epizod iz zhizni 'golubogo' Peterburga," 454–55; and cf. Bersen'ev and Markov, "Politsiia i gei," 112, n. 4. On Meshcherskii's career and reputation, see chapter 3.

52. Bersen'ev and Markov, "Politsiia i gei," 109.

53. Ruadze, *K sudu!,* 55–56, 102–3. For a Soviet report that the "vicinity of the Cinizelli Circus with its little benches" continued to function as a "meeting place," see Belousov, "Sluchai gomoseksuala-muzhskoi prostitutki," 314.

54. Ruadze, *K sudu!,* 102–3.

55. Malmstad and Bogomolov, *Mikhail Kuzmin: A Life in Art,* 107; for the correspondence, see Bogomolov, *Mikhail Kuzmin: Stat'i i materialy,* 229. In his diary for 24 May 1906, Kuzmin noted at the Tauride that "you can get whatever you like, a singer, a dancer, or just an ordinary young man," and that Nuvel' had recently met there Viacheslav, a regimental medic "with whom he could make love"; Kuzmin, *Dnevnik, 1905–1907,* 155.

56. Bersen'ev and Markov, "Politsiia i gei," 109. The nearby Narodnyi Dom (opened 1901, later the Velikan Cinema) became another site for same-sex military-civilian liaisons, see Ruadze, *K sudu!,* 108.

57. Rotikov, "Epizod iz 'golubogo' Peterburga," 453–54.

58. Belousov, "Sluchai gomoseksuala-muzhskoi prostitutki," 314; V. M. Bekhterev, "O polovom izvrashchenii, kak osoboi ustanovke polovykh refleksov," in *Polovoi vopros v shkole i v zhizni,* ed. I. S. Simonov (Leningrad: Brokgauz-Efron, 1927), 168–70; V. P. Protopopov, "Sovremennoe sostoianie voprosa o sushchnosti i proiskhozhdenii gomoseksualizma," *Nauchnaia meditsina* 10 (1922): 49–62.

59. Example of popular verse of 1920s about sailors, see Healey, "Evgeniia/Ev genii," 92. A 1937 sodomy trial involving military personnel from Leningrad, Moscow, and Sevastopol' is discussed in chapter 8.

60. Mikhail Kuzmin, "Kryl'ia," in *Podzemnye ruch'i. Izbrannaia proza* (St. Petersburg: Severo-Zapad, 1994), 30 (discussed in chapter 4); foreign praise, Magnus Hirschfeld, *Die Homosexualität des Mannes und des Weibes* (Berlin: Louis Marcus, 1914), 590–91; X. Mayne [E. I. Prime Stevenson] *The Intersexes. A History of Similsexualism as a Problem in Social Life* (1908; reprint New York: Arno, 1975), 431; for a condemnatory, yet lurid view, Bernhard Stern, *Geschichte der Öffentlichen Sittlichkeit in Russland* (Vienna: n.d. [1907]), 2: 570.

61. Bersen'ev and Markov, "Politsiia i gei."

62. Ruadze, *K sudu!,* 17–18.

63. A description of a "pornographic club," which offered a composite portrait of the Petersburg homosexual subculture by cataloging youthful male prostitution, strip shows with male and female dancers, lectures on unnatural love, and poetry from a figure recalling Kuzmin, is found in A. I. Matiushenskii, *Polovoi rynok i polovye otnosheniia* (St. Petersburg, 1908), 124–28, citing an article in *Stolichnoe Utro* 45 (1907).

64. Kuzmin, *Dnevnik, 1905–1907,* 85–86.

65. Kuzmin, *Dnevnik, 1905–1907,* 85–86, 102, 133.

66. "My way lay past the baths. I was sure that if I saw one of the attendants at the doors, I would not be able to resist [. . .] The doors to the bathhouse were open, but there were no attendants in sight. By some miracle I refrained and drove past [. . . a week later] I was overwhelmed by sinful thoughts during the committee meeting. I dismissed my coachman on the Morskaia before reaching the corner with the Nevskii and continued on foot. I walked up and down twice past the bathhouse doors; the third time, I went in. And so, I have once again sinned in the same way." Entries for 15 and 21 May 1904 in Andrei Maylunas and Sergei Mironenko, *A Lifelong Passion: Nicholas and Alexandra. Their Own Story* (London: Phoenix Giant, 1997), 231.

67. By the first decade of the twentieth century, bathhouse staff had ceased to

perform their conventional function in *artel'* formations; they worked as individualized employees instead. See Bogdanov, *Tri veka peterburgskoi bani*, 86.

68. In the 1920s, Leningrad's "Cafe PEPO" (i.e., *Petrogradskaia kooperatsiia*) was frequently mentioned by the poet Kuzmin in his diary as a place to meet homosexual friends; simultaneously it enjoyed a reputation as a hub for female prostitutes. Compare RGALI, f. 232, op. 1, d. 62, ll. 286, 500, with Lebina and Shkarovskii, *Prostitutsiia v Peterburge*, 79.

69. Soviet surveillance of female prostitution is examined in chapters 5 and 6, but the mechanisms of control over commercial sites for public sex in the 1920s and 1930s remain obscure. In 1925, article 171 of the RSFSR criminal code (against operating a "den of vice") was used to close down Moscow's Ermitazh Restaurant and another bar also harboring women prostitutes. In a 1924 survey, Moscow men infected with venereal disease from prostitutes were asked the locations of their trysts; the use of commodified space (hotels, "dives," and bathhouses) appeared to have declined, while public space such as railway stations and the street were resorted to; Hans Haustein, "Zur sexuellen Hygiene in Sowjet-Russland," *Abhandlungen aus dem Gebiete der Sexualforschung* 5, no. 1 (1926): 20, 28. On the partial privatization of Leningrad bathhouses during NEP, S. I. Avvakumov et al., eds., *Ocherki istorii Leningrada* (Moscow-Leningrad: Nauka, 1964), 4: 493.

70. B. R. Gurvich, "Prostitutsiia, kak sotsial'no-psikhopatologicheskoe iavlenie (Predvaritel'noe soobshchenie)," in *Sovetskaia meditsina v bor'be za zdorovye nervy: Sbornik statei i materialov*, eds. A. I. Miskinov, L. M. Rozenshtein, and L. A. Prozorov (Ul'ianovsk: Izd. Ul'ianovskogo kombinata PPP, 1926), 66.

71. One social critic found that bathhouses *outside* of Russia were "the center of homosexuality," citing these institutions in "the civilized nations of Europe and America"; L. M. Vasilevskii, *Polovye izvrashcheniia* (Moscow: Novaia Moskva, 1924), 38.

72. N. I. Ozeretskii, "Polovye pravonarusheniia nesovershennoletnikh," in *Pravonarusheniia v oblasti seksual'nykh otnoshenii*, ed. E. K. Krasnushkin (Moscow, 1927), 147. Group rapes of boys who violated *besprizornyi* norms exposed a more brutal side of sexual relations among homeless children, see, e.g., Peter H. Juviler, "Contradictions of Revolution: Juvenile Crime and Rehabilitation," in *Bolshevik Culture: Experiment and Order in the Russian Revolution*, eds. Abbott Gleason, Peter Kenez, and Richard Stites (Bloomington: Indiana University Press, 1985), 270.

73. It is unclear whether this affair began as a voluntary or commercial sexual relationship. Belousov, "Sluchai gomoseksuala—muzhskoi prostitutki," 312, 314.

74. Belousov, "Sluchai gomoseksuala—muzhskoi prostitutki." Evidently "Anichkov" Palace was intended. These had been sites of public facilities in the tsarist era.

75. A penal psychiatrist discussing young men's prostitution did not explicitly admit his subjects used toilets in this fashion, but by mentioning these busy public places— where facilities were located—the implication was clear; Ozeretskii, "Polovye pravonarusheniia nesovershennoletnikh," 150.

76. M. Anikeev [pseud.], " 'Liudi byli zagnany v tualety, i ot etogo ikh kul'tura— tualetnaia,' " *Uranus* 1 (1995): 46–47.

77. Belousov, "Sluchai gomoseksuala—muzhskoi prostitutki," 312.

78. Anton Ciliga, *The Russian Enigma* (London: Ink Links, 1979), 67.

79. Bersen'ev and Markov, "Politsiia i gei," 109. Similarly, see Tarnovskii, *Izvrashchenie polovogo chuvstva*, 62.

80. Male prostitutes lined the pavement leading to the facility and followed potential customers into it. "They became acquainted with the intimate details of their bodies, and then came to an agreement on where to go and for how much." Ruadze, *K sudu!*, 103.

81. Ruadze, *K sudu!* 105–6, 108. Kuzmin referred to the "hooligan" element among the available males haunting the Tauride Gardens: *Dnevnik, 1905–1907,* 155.

82. Bekhterev, "O polovom izvrashchenii, kak osoboi ustanovke polovykh refleksov," 170.

83. Koni, *Na zhiznennom puti,* 155–56.

84. RGALI, f. 232, op. 1, d. 62, l. 460 (28 October 1924). It appears the pair were looking for a suitable public place to have sex, but Kuzmin's diary could be coy about these "adventures."

85. RGALI, f. 232, op. 1, d. 62, l. 462 (29 October 1924).

86. Merzheevskii, *Sudebnaia ginekologiia,* 254.

87. Koni, *Na zhiznennom puti,* 154.

88. E.g., one Obrezkov, a sixty-year-old senior civil servant in the Ministry of Foreign Affairs, was described as "A lady, loves to be used by persons with large members"; Bersen'ev and Markov, "Politsiia i gei," 114.

89. Ruadze, *K sudu!,* 55–56, 90, 105, 108, 109.

90. Malmstad and Bogomolov note that Kuzmin's diary says nothing about red neckties as a symbol; see *Mikhail Kuzmin: A Life in Art,* 121–22. Reflecting on the Somov portrait in 1934, Kuzmin thought it depicted his "later, compromised, intelligentsia-inspired (*obintelligenchennyi*) period" in contrast to traditionalist elements in his earlier "look"; Kuzmin, *Dnevnik 1934 goda,* 72. We can speculate that the red tie was a symbol of that "compromised" new exterior and note that Somov did take a keen interest in Kuzmin's *Wings* and his frank diary. A contemporary Berlin sexologist did not mention the symbolism of the red necktie in a note about recognition between homosexuals: Albert Moll, "Wie erkennen und verständigen sich die Homosexuellen unter einander?" *Archiv für Kriminalanthropologie und Kriminalstatistik* 9, no. 2–3 (1902): 157–59. (My thanks to Ralf Dose for this item.) Nevertheless, von Aschenbach, the hero in Thomas Mann's *Death in Venice* (1912) encounters an ageing homosexual wearing a red tie and later dons one himself as his love for the boy Tadzio overwhelms him. (My thanks to Jonathan Ned Katz for this observation.) In urban America at this time, red neckties were widely reported as a symbol of the wearer's interest in same-sex eros; Chauncey, *Gay New York,* 3, 52, 54; and Ellis, *Studies in the Psychology of Sex,*1: 299–300. The case for the red necktie as early-twentieth-century international signal of male same-sex interest remains open. James N. Green notes that red neckties were a signal used by urban male homosexuals in Brazil from perhaps the mid–nineteenth century; he suggests that the coincidence of the red tie as visual cue among homosexuals was probably not the result of international diffusion, but a reflection of European aesthetic codes that associated the color red with "prostitution, seduction, and sensuality," Green, *Beyond Carnival,* 49–50.

91. Bekhterev, "O polovom izvrashchenii, kak osoboi ustanovke polovykh refleksov," 169–70; Protopopov, "Sovremennoe sostoianie voprosa o sushchnosti i proiskhozhdenii gomoseksualizma," 52. On Vial'tseva, see Louise McReynolds, "'The Incomparable' Anastasiia Vial'tseva and the Culture of Personality," in *Russia—Women—Culture,* eds. Helena Goscilo and Beth Holmgren (Bloomington: Indiana University Press, 1996).

92. F. E. Rybakov, "O prevratnykh polovykh oshchushcheniiakh," *Vrach* (1898): 22: 640–43, 23: 664–67; 23:8 (page numbers cited are from an offprint).

93. Courouve, *Vocabulaire de l'homosexualité masculine,* 207–9. *Tante* had similar meanings in German.

94. Merzheevskii, *Sudebnaia ginekologiia,* 205.

95. He fleetingly described a gathering of such men: "Russian *tetki* are repulsive."

See P. I. Chaikovskii, *Dnevniki, 1873–1891.* (1923; Moscow-Petrograd: Gos. iz-vo Muzy-kal'nyi sektor, reprint 1993), 203 (13 March 1888); the word retains this generalized sense today, Kozlovskii, *Argo russkoi gomoseksual'noi subkul'tury,* 69.

96. Bersen'ev and Markov, "Politsiia i gei."

97. Bersen'ev and Markov, "Politsiia i gei," 109.

98. Fragmentary evidence hints at these life transitions, suggested in the Petersburg denunciation (Bersen'ev and Markov, "Politsiia i gei," 109). Homosexual sponsorship promoted the careers of the male protégés of Prince Meshcherskii, see W. E. Mosse, "Imperial Favorite: V. P. Meshchersky and the *Grazhdanin*," *Slavonic and East European Review* 59 (1981): 529–47. In a Soviet psychiatrist's case history of a Moscow male prostitute in his thirties, the prostitute related how his engagement in the sex trade was interrupted during extended periods of sponsorship in first an aristocrat's and then an industrialist's household: V. A. Belousov, "Sluchai gomoseksuala-muzhskoi prostitutki," *Prestupnik i prestupnost'. Sbornik II* (1927): 309–17. For career structures of male prostitution in England of the same era, see Jeffrey Weeks, "Inverts, Perverts and Mary-Annes: Male Prostitution and the Regulation of Homosexuality in England in the Nineteenth and Early Twentieth Centuries," in Duberman et al., *Hidden from History.*

99. Belousov, "Sluchai gomoseksuala-muzhskoi prostitutki"; V. P. Protopopov, "So-vremennoe sostoianie voprosa o sushchnosti i proiskhozhdenii gomoseksualizma," *Nauchnaia meditsina* 10 (1922): 49–62, (see 51, case no. 5).

100. In Wilhemine Germany, these two ideals of male homosexuality found expression in the gender inversion–based theories of Magnus Hirschfeld, countered by the masculine supremacist arguments of Benedict Friedländer and his Community of the Special; see Sedgwick, *Epistemology of the Closet,* 88–89. Variations on "women-hater" as sexual identity (including "stratophiles," devotees of sex with military men) circulated in pre-1914 Europe; see Mayne, *The Intersexes,* 198, 212–23.

101. These roles appear somewhat similar to the pre-1945 system of "fairies," "punks," and "wolves" richly described by George Chauncey for men in New York City. On the "boundaries of normal manhood" implicit in the relations between "wolves" (masculine men) and "punks" (the youths they had sex with) and "fairies" (as feminized and very visibly transgressive men open to sex with other men), see Chauncey, *Gay New York,* 47–97.

102. P. I. Kovalevskii, *Psikhologiia pola. Polovoe bezsilie i drugie polovye izvra-shcheniia i ikh lechenie* (St. Petersburg, 1909), 219.

103. Ruadze, *K sudu!,* 42–43.

104. Bersen'ev and Markov, "Politsiia i gei," 110, 112. In his diary, Kuzmin referred to a "sodomitical *bal masqué*" described to him by Val'ter Nuvel' (12 April 1906): Kuzmin, *Dnevnik, 1905–1907,* 131. For a fictional depiction of a tsarist-era party in a similar vein, see Georgy Ivanov, "The Third Rome," in *Out of the Blue: Russia's Hidden Gay Literature,* ed. Kevin Moss (San Francisco: Gay Sunshine Press, 1996), 180.

105. V. M. Bekhterev, "Polovye ukloneniia i izvrashcheniia v svete refleksologii," *Voprosy izucheniia i vospitaniia lichnosti* 4–5 (1922): 644–746; idem, "O polovom iz-vrashchenii, kak osoboi ustanovke polovykh refleksov." For ten interview–life histories of men arrested at the party, Protopopov, "Sovremennoe sostoianie voprosa o sushch-nosti i proiskhozhdenii gomoseksualizma."

106. Bekhterev, "O polovom izvrashchenii, kak osoboi ustanovke polovykh reflek-sov," 168–69.

107. The 15 January 1921 party took place at 6 Simeonovskaia (now Belinskii) Street, flat 1; other parties took place at 31 Angliiskii (now Malkin) Prospekt; and 10

Ofitserskaia (in 1918, officially renamed Dekabristy) Street, "where several parties were organized." Other parties took place at the home of an ex-monk on 21 Liniia; and in another private home in Pavlovsk, near Petrograd; Bekhterev, "O polovom izvrashchenii, kak osoboi ustanovke polovykh refleksov," 169.

108. According to the protocol describing the arrests at the January party, the hosts were not running the evening for the police, but for private profit; Bekhterev, "O polovom izvrashchenii, kak osoboi ustanovke polovykh refleksov," 169.

109. Using the much less detailed description of the raid found in G. R., "Protsessy gomoseksualistov," *Ezhenedel'nik sovetskoi iustitsii* 33 (1922): 16−17, Engelstein points out that no sex acts, illegal or otherwise, had been detected, "Soviet Policy toward Male Homosexuality," 168. In Bekhterev's and Protopopov's descriptions, most of the arrested men readily admitted homosexual desire, while only some were inclined to cross-dressing.

110. Bekhterev, "O polovom izvrashchenii, kak osoboi ustanovke polovykh refleksov," 168.

111. Bekhterev, "O polovom izvrashchenii, kak osoboi ustanovke polovykh refleksov," 170 71.

112. Kuzmin, "Dnevnik 1921 goda," 438−39. These mentions of "masquerades" in Kuzmin's diary do not appear to be linked to the costume ball attended by Iurkun and Ol'ga Arbenina on 11 January 1921, at which the couple "announced their relationship"; Malmstad and Bogomolov, *Mikhail Kuzmin: A Life in Art*, 289.

113. Belousov, "Sluchai gomoseksuala—muzhskoi prostitutki," 313.

114. Belousov, "Sluchai gomoseksuala—muzhskoi prostitutki," 314.

115. A. S. Solovtsova and N. F. Orlov, "Gomoseksualizm i reaktsiia d-ra Manoilova," *Klinicheskaia meditsina* 5, no. 9 (1927): 541−47, esp. 546.

116. Sentence of Bezborodov and eleven others (1935), l. 241. Defendants in this trial were said to have visited the Baroness's flat on 7 November 1934, eight months after the publication of the antisodomy law.

117. One defendant mentioned that an older male homosexual actor from the Malyi Theater had organized a "name day" party for him, Trial of Andreevskii and two others (1941). The survival of social contacts and private gatherings is especially evident in Sentence of Krasin and Popov (1935), a pianist and an actor found guilty of "mixing with homosexuals" (l. 283); and Sentence of Tereshkov and nine others (1938), in which Tereshkov's web of "systematic" contacts among homosexuals is cited by the court (l. 47).

118. Early-Soviet homosexuals sought to construct a favorable historiography, and this projected anthology was not the sole attempt to do so. Kuzmin's diary tersely observed, "Zenger is preparing a 'work' [called] Homosexuality in Pre-Petrine Rus' " (RGALI, f. 232, op. 1, d. 65, l. 71; 16 May 1927). Zenger remains unidentified.

119. Describing obstacles to holding the reading in a letter to Kuzmin, V. V. Ruslov blamed "the generally awful mood reigning at the moment in Moscow, among Muscovites in general (the reason—mistrust and arrests) and also among 'our own,' who, as you doubtless know, are more timid than desert gazelles; as a result, frightened by the mood here, they are prostrate and at the thought of 'our' evening immediately fall into hysterics and refuse to purchase tickets." See A. G. Timofeev, "Progulka bez Gulia? (K istorii organizatsii avtorskogo vechera M. A. Kuzmina v mae 1924 g.)," in *Mikhail Kuzmin i russkaia kul'tura XX veka: Tezisy i materialy konferentsii 15−17 maia 1990 g.*, ed. G. A. Morev (Leningrad: Sovet po istorii mirovoi kul'tury AN SSSR, 1990), 187. Kuzmin, ever impecunious, was eager to appear for Antinoi, which planned to pay him a fee and travel expenses, Timofeev, "Progulka bez Gulia?" and RGALI, f. 232, op. 1, d. 62, ll. 179, 198.

120. N. A. Bogomolov and John E. Malmstad, *Mikhail Kuzmin: Iskusstvo, zhizn',* *epokha* (Moscow: Novoe literaturnoe obozrenie, 1996), 259–60. Orlov's characterization of the meeting ("posledniaia demonstratsiia peterburgskikh pederastov") is translated as the "last demonstration of Leningrad's homosexuals," in Malmstad and Bogomolov, *Mikhail Kuzmin: A Life in Art,* 349. This rendering needlessly sanitizes the language used by Orlov in his reminiscences, expressed decades after the 1933–34 restoration of the sodomy ban in conditions of late-Soviet prudery and ignorance.

121. Bogomolov and Malmstad, *Mikhail Kuzmin: Iskusstvo, zhizn',* *epokha,* 260; Kuzmin looked back to 1907–8 as a "merry" time, RGALI, f. 232, op. 1, d. 61, l. 462 and d. 66, l. 55.

122. Conservative novelist Valentin Rasputin declared on British television in early 1991 that homosexuality "was imported from abroad" and was alien to Russia's traditions; see Simon Karlinsky, " 'Vvezen iz-za granitsy . . .'? Gomoseksualizm v russkoi kul'ture i literature." More examples of this chauvinism are cited in Igor S. Kon, *The Sexual Revolution in Russia* (New York: Free Press, 1995), 222, 249; and Riordan, "Sexual Minorities."

123. On elite beliefs that regular sexual indulgence for males was tolerable and healthy, and on male workers', soldiers', and students' demand for sexual release, see Engelstein, *The Keys to Happiness,* 204–205; Bernstein, *Sonia's Daughters,* 86–93.

124. Both the peasant merchant Pavel Medvedev and the tsar's cousin Konstantin Romanov used the vocabulary of "sin" to refer to these acts in their diaries. The same language appeared in the testimony given by peasants in Konstantin Kazakov's household during the inquiries following his wife's plea for separation.

CHAPTER TWO

1. Evgeniia's case and confession are presented in A. O. Edel'shtein, "K klinike transvestitizma," *Prestupnik i prestupnost': Sbornik 2* (1927): 273–82 (quote, 277).

2. For speculation on same-sex love between Catherine the Great and Princess Dashkova, see Karlinsky, "Russia's Gay Literature and History,"; and (more cautiously), Tatyana Mamonova, *Russian Women's Studies: Essays on Sexism in Soviet Culture* (New York: Pergamon, 1985), 9–18.

3. For a fine discussion of the role of class in the experience of French women-loving women, see Francesca C. Sautman, "Invisible Women: Lesbian Working-class Culture in France, 1880–1930," in *Homosexuality in Modern France,* eds. Jeffrey Merrick and Bryant T. Ragan, Jr. (New York: Oxford University Press, 1996).

4. Engelstein, *The Keys to Happiness,* 160–64. For examples of the new discourse on lesbian-prostitutes, see A. Borisov, *Izvrashchennaia polovaia zhizn': Boleznennye izmeneniia polovoi sfery* (St. Petersburg, 1907); P. I. Kovalevskii, *Psikhologiia pola. Polovoe bezsilie i drugie polovye izvrashcheniia i ikh lechenie* (St. Petersburg, 1909); A. Koffin'on, *Izvrashchennyi mir* (Moscow, 1908), 31–40.

5. On the social environment of the tsarist licensed brothel, see Bernstein, *Sonia's Daughters;* Lebina and Shkarovskii, *Prostitutsiia v Peterburge.*

6. V. F. Chizh, *K ucheniiu ob "izvrashchenii polovogo chuvstva" (Die conträre Sexualempfindung). Soobshcheno obshchestvu Peterburgskikh morskikh vrachei v zasedanii 1-go fevralia 1882 goda* ([St. Petersburg?], 1882), 14. The same case is described using "Miss N.'s" full name and additional details, in Tarnovskii, *Izvrashchenie polovogo chuvstva u zhenshchin,* 141–54.

7. Tarnovskii, *Izvrashchenie polovogo chuvstva u zhenshchin,* 22–27; this is one of three cases presented in Engelstein, "Lesbian Vignettes," 813–31.

8. GARF, f. 564, op. 1, d. 260, ll. 28–29 ob. (A. F. Koni dossier).

9. Letters were cited in B. I. Bentovin, *Torguiushchie telom: Ocherki sovremennoi*

prostitutsii (St. Petersburg: Leonid Krumbiugel', 1909), and have been reproduced in some detail in Bernstein, *Sonia's Daughters,* 172–74. First published in 1904, Bentovin's indulgent commentaries on these letters reflected, in Engelstein's view, the prevailing reluctance among Russian doctors to pathologize the prostitute as "masculinized" or "lesbian"; *The Keys to Happiness,* 160–61.

10. Sautman, "Invisible Women," 187–89.

11. Tarnovskii, *Izvrashchenie polovogo chuvstva u zhenshchin,* 22–23.

12. Bentovin, *Torguiushchie telom,* 108–9.

13. Bentovin, *Torguiushchie telom,* 109.

14. See Bernstein, *Sonia's Daughters,* chapter 5. The classic literary portrait of Russia's official houses of prostitution, including hints of lesbian relations (between brothel-keeper Emma Eduardovna and her charges), was published in installments between 1909 and 1915 by Aleksandr Kuprin, *Iama,* reprinted in *Sobranie sochinenii v deviati tomakh,* vol. 6 (Moscow, 1964); in English, published as Alexandre Kuprin, *Yama: The Pit,* trans. Bernard G. Guerney (London, John Hamilton, 1930).

15. On conditions in the heterosexual sex trade during NEP, see, e.g., L. Eratov, "Nakazuema li prostitutsiia?" *Ezhenedel'nik sovetskoi iustitsii* 4 (1922): 4–6; Gurvich, "Prostitutsiia, kak sotsial'no-psikhopatologicheskoe iavlenie"; A. Uchevatov, "Iz byta prostitutsii nashikh dnei," *Pravo i zhizn'* 1 (1928): 50–60.

16. Lebina and Shkarovskii, *Prostitutsiia v Peterburge,* 40–60, 77–85.

17. For a survey of the evidence on class, see I. A. Golosenko and S. I. Golod, *Sotsiologicheskie issledovaniia prostitutsii v Rossii. (Istoriia i sovremennoe sostoianie voprosa)* (St. Petersburg: Petropolis, 1998), 58–88.

18. E. K. Krasnushkin and N. G. Kholzakova, "Dva sluchaia zhenshchin ubiitsgomoseksualistok," *Prestupnik i prestupnost': Sbornik 1* (1926): 105–20; case of "Sh." and "L.," 106–14.

19. Krasnushkin and Kholzakova, "Dva sluchaia," 110–12.

20. L. M. Vasilevskii and L. A. Vasilevskaia, *Prostitutsiia i novaia Rossiia* (Tver': Oktiabr', 1923), 99, 129. On the procuress in the Soviet imagination, see Julie A. Cassiday and Leyla Rouhi, "From Nevskii Prospekt to Zoia's Apartment: Trials of the Russian Procuress," *Russian Review* 58 (1999): 413–31.

21. E. K. Krasnushkin, *Prestupniki psikhopaty* (Moscow: Izd-vo pervogo Moskovskogo gos. universiteta, 1929), 10–12.

22. Krasnushkin, *Prestupniki psikhopaty,* 11.

23. Krasnushkin, *Prestupniki psikhopaty,* 12.

24. Chizh, *K ucheniiu ob "izvrashchenii polovogo chuvstva";* Rybakov, "O prevratnykh polovykh oshchushcheniiakh," also called "Misha" in Tarnovskii, *Izvrashchenie polovogo chuvstva u zhenshchin,* 28–39. Note also a probably fictionalized account: "Razskaz o sebe dokotora filosofii, Marii Vladimirovny Bezobrazovoi" in Vasilii Rozanov, *Liudi lunnogo sveta: Metafizika khristianstva,* 2d ed. (St. Petersburg, 1913), 227–60.

25. The place of the "lesbian" in Silver Age belles-lettres is discussed in Burgin, "Laid Out in Lavender." On sexual ambiguity in these salons, see Beth Holmgren, "Stepping Out/Going Under: Women in Russia's Twentieth-Century Salons," in *Russia—Women—Culture,* eds. Helena Goscilo and Beth Holmgren (Bloomington: Indiana University Press, 1996), 233.

26. In tsarist families, see Rybakov, "O prevratnykh polovykh oshchushcheniiakh"; Rozanov, *Liudi lunnogo sveta,* 228–34; in Soviet-era families, Krasnushkin and Kholzakokov, "Dva sluchaia," 107; A. P. Shtess, "Sluchai zhenskogo gomoseksualizma pri nalichii situs viscerum inversus, ego psikhoanaliz i gipnoterapiia," *Saratovskii vestnik zdravookhraneniia* 3–4 (1925): 1–19, esp. 8.

27. Chizh, *K ucheniiu ob "izvrashchenii polovogo chuvstva,"* 12, 16.

28. According to a biography in Rozanov, either concocted or highly edited, paternal indulgence facilitated deviance. Rozanov related that one Mariia Bezobrazova managed in the 1870s to convince her father, who allegedly shared the opinions of reactionary Prince Meshcherskii on the question of women's "freedom," that she could and should receive an education. Bezobrazova's father eventually employed her as a secretary (a man's occupation) in his publishing concerns. Rozanov, *Liudi lunnogo sveta*, 244–46.

29. Edel'shtein, "K klinike transvestitizma," 273–74.

30. N. P. Brukhanskii, *Materialy po seksual'noi psikhopatologii* (Moscow: M. i S. Sabashnikov, 1927), 53–54, 57; Krasnushkin and Kholzakova, "Dva sluchaia," 117. In a version of this case history edited and published posthumously by a colleague of Krasnushkin, Boris and siblings are entirely absent, Valentina's Komsomol membership is not mentioned, and Ol'ga is said to have announced her intention to marry "a worker A.," a decision implicitly taken spontaneously as a result of her decision to "experience a laboring life" firsthand in a textile factory; see E. K. Krasnushkin, *Izbrannye trudy*, ed. V. M. Banshchikov (Moscow: Medgiz, 1960), 107–9.

31. Shtess, "Sluchai zhenskogo gomoseksualizma."

32. Rybakov, "O prevratnykh polovykh oshchushcheniiakh," 8.

33. "Misha" in I. M. Tarnovskii's "triptych" of cases had had several successive girlfriends, but the gynecologist's narrative obscured any reference to a milieu of same-sex relations. *Izvrashchenie polovogo chuvstva u zhenshchin*, 34–39; see also Rozanov, *Liudi lunnogo sveta*, 234.

34. G. S. Novopolin, *Pornograficheskii element v russkoi literature* (St. Petersburg, 1909), 169.

35. Burgin, "Laid Out in Lavender," 181–94; Holmgren, "Stepping Out/Going Under," 233–34; Karlinsky, "Russia's Gay Literature and Culture," 354–56. The influence of the fin-de-siècle fashion for lesbian tableaux vivants in France's licensed brothels (Sautman, "Invisible Women," 187) on masculine bourgeois tastes cannot be discounted as a factor contributing to the rise of a more aestheticized salon discourse of "lesbianism."

36. Holmgren, "Stepping Out/Going Under," 234.

37. Burgin, *Sophia Parnok*, 261.

38. Burgin, *Sophia Parnok*. For photographs of the two women, many of them taken by Gornung who was a tireless recorder of their excursions, see Burgin, figs. 18–23. For more on Gornung, see Veronique Garros, Natalia Korenevskaya, and Thomas Lahusen, eds., *Intimacy and Terror: Soviet Diaries of the 1930s* (New York: New Press, 1995), 99–107.

39. Verse by M. Vazlinskii (1924), archive of Mariia Shkapskaia, RGALI, cited in Burgin, *Sophia Parnok*, 183–84. On the use of Tverskaia-Iamskaia and surrounding streets by high-class female prostitutes, see Gurvich, "Prostitutsiia, kak sotsial'no-psikhopatologicheskoe iavlenie."

40. Virtually all Soviet psychiatric, forensic, medical, and sexological cases describing "female homosexuals" of the 1920s featured urban women, and except for some prostitutes and one NEP-trader, most were white-collar employees, students, soldiers, or unskilled workers. Twenty-two women are identified as "female homosexuals" in the following literature; of these, the women who initially attracted psychiatric interest almost all were judged "masculine" in dress and gesture. Case histories from forensic psychiatry: Brukhanskii, *Materialy po seksual'noi psikhopatologii*, 53–61, 62–65; Krasnushkin and Kholzakova, "Dva sluchaia"; one case ("Fedosiia P.") occurring in these first two texts is also discussed in V. A. Riasentsev, "Dva sluchaia iz praktiki. 1. Gomoseksualizm?" *Sudebno-meditsinskaia ekspertiza* 2 (1925): 152–56. Other cases: Shtess, "Sluchai zhenskogo gomoseksualizma"; Edel'shtein, "K klinike transvestitizma"; Krasnushkin, *Prestupniki psikhopaty*, 11–13. From clinical psychiatry: V. P. Osipov, *Kurs*

obshchego ucheniia o dushevnykh bolezniakh (Berlin: RSFSR Gosizdat, 1923), 355–56, 365; N. I. Skliar, "O proiskhozhdenii i sushchnosti gomoseksualizma," *Vrachebnoe delo* 24–26 (1925): 1919–23; Ia. I. Kirov, "K voprosu o geterotransplantatsii pri gomoseksualizme," *Vrachebnoe delo* 20 (1928): 1587–90. Two cases, from a sexological survey: I. G. Gel'man, *Polovaia zhizn' sovremennoi molodezhi. Opyt sotsial'no-biologicheskogo obsledovaniia* (Moscow and Petrograd, 1923), 119–21.

41. On these anxieties, see Wood, *The Baba and The Comrade*, 203–8.

42. Clements, *Bolshevik Women*, 19, 59–65.

43. N. A. Semashko, "Nuzhna li 'zhenstvennost'" (v poriadke obsuzhdeniia)," *Molodaia gvardiia* 6 (1924): 205–6. The health commissar reserved his sharpest words for the "artificial surface" of the powdered, rouged, and nail-varnished would-be "lady" found in class-alien circles.

44. On women's participation in the civil war, see Clements, *Bolshevik Women*, 171–89; Fannina W. Halle, *Women in Soviet Russia* (London: Routledge, 1934), 98–105. During a discussion about "transvestites" and the "intermediate sex," held in February 1929 in the Expert Medical Council of the Commissariat of Health, psychiatrists praised "women in military service . . . dressed in men's clothing" as competent officers and citizens, GARF, f. A482, op. 25, d. 478, l. 86 ob. This discussion is examined in chapter 6.

45. Visitors from Western nations often noted the 'masculinized' female in the USSR. Their perceptions reflect their native societies' anxieties about the modernization of gender and the Soviet role in forcing the pace of change. Ernst Lubitsch's 1939 romantic satirical film *Ninotchka* allowed the sexually ambiguous Greta Garbo in the leading role to catalog the West's worries about the Soviet threat to femininity. A similar scenario, this time with Katharine Hepburn as a Soviet fighter pilot, was revived for cold war audiences in *The Iron Petticoat* (1956), an inferior film despite the casting. For impressions of female masculinization in foreigners' accounts, see John Littlepage and Demaree Bess, *In Search of Soviet Gold* (London: Harrap, 1939), 45; Ethel Mannin, *South to Samarkand* (London: Jarrolds, 1951), 92.

46. Psychiatrists occasionally published photographs of their patients in the masculine clothing they wore when they first presented themselves to doctors; Shtess "Sluchai zhenskogo gomoseksualizma"; Kirov, "K voprosu o geterotransplantatsii pri gomoseksualizme."

47. Ella Winter, *Red Virtue: Human Relationships in the New Russia* (London: V. Gollancz, 1933), 169, quoting Moscow psychiatrist Lev Rozenshtein.

48. L. G. Orshanskii, "Polovye prestupleniia. Analiz psikhologicheskii i psikhopatologicheskii," in *Polovye prestupleniia*, eds. A. A. Zhizhilenko and L. G. Orshanskii (Leningrad-Moscow: Rabochii sud, 1927), 88–89.

49. "Half-voiced" (*Vpolgolosa*) was the title of Sofiia Parnok's last published collection of verse, issued in a tiny edition in 1928, Burgin, *Sophia Parnok*, 224–25. On the apparitional nature of love between women in Western culture, see Terry Castle, *The Apparitional Lesbian: Female Homosexuality and Modern Culture* (New York: Columbia University Press, 1993).

50. Gel'man, *Polovaia zhizn' sovremennoi molodezhi*, 120.

51. In the Expert Medical Council of the Health Commissariat 1929 discussion on "transvestites" and the "intermediate sex," psychiatrist P. Gannushkin and biologist N. Kol'tsov both told of patients who sought to transform their biological sex: GARF, f. A482, op. 25, d. 478, ll. 85–87. Gannushkin described early unauthorized Soviet attempts at sex changes; see chapter 6. On European sex-change operations attempted in the 1930s, see Bernice L. Hausman, *Changing Sex: Transsexualism, Technology and the Idea of Gender* (Durham: Duke University Press, 1995), 15–19, 142.

52. "Transgenderism" refers to identities and practices that exploit or cross genders in a transgressive way; the emphasis is on gender roles, while sexual identities are secondary. Late-twentieth-century sexology defined the 'transsexual' as the chief representative of transgender identities in the West and prescribed sex-change surgery. Early sexological definitions of "sexual inversion," "transvestism," and "homosexuality" encompassed aspects of personalities later labeled "transsexual": Jay Prosser, "Transsexuals and the Transsexologists: Inversion and the Emergence of Transsexual Subjectivity," in *Sexology in Culture: Labelling Bodies and Desires,* eds. Lucy Bland and Laura Doan (Cambridge: Polity Press, 1998). Non-Western and traditional cultures display a myriad of transgender identities and social roles that undermine the universalizing sexological definitions. See, e.g., Herdt, *Third Sex, Third Gender;* Ramet, *Gender Reversals and Gender Cultures.* The argument that transgendered persons should claim a history independent of that of homosexuals or other sexuality-based categories is made in Leslie Feinberg, *Transgender Warriors: Making History from Joan of Arc to RuPaul* (Boston: Beacon Books, 1996).

53. For Russia and Europe, see Nadezhda Durova, *The Cavalry Maiden: Journals of a Russian Officer in the Napoleonic Wars,* trans. Mary Zirin (Bloomington: Indiana University Press, 1988); Julie Wheelwright, *Amazons and Military Maids: Women Who Dressed as Men in the Pursuit of Life, Liberty and Happiness* (London: Pandora, 1989). A useful systematic study based on 119 documented Dutch cases between 1550 and 1839 is Rudolf M. Dekker and Lotte C. van de Pol, *The Tradition of Female Transvestism in Early Modern Europe* (London: Macmillan, 1989; New York: St. Martin's Press, 1997).

54. Havelock Ellis, *Studies in the Psychology of Sex,* vol. 7, *Eonism and Other Supplementary Studies* (Philadelphia: Davis, 1928); Magnus Hirschfeld, *Die Transvestiten* (Leipzig, 1910).

55. Dekker and van de Pol, *The Tradition of Female Transvestism.*

56. See Michel Foucault, *Herculine Barbin: Being the Recently Discovered Memoirs of a Nineteenth-Century French Hermaphrodite* (New York: Pantheon, 1980); Alice Domurat Dreger, *Hermaphrodites and the Medical Invention of Sex* (Cambridge, Mass.: Harvard University Press, 1998). On Russian dimensions, see Healey, " 'Man or Woman?' "

57. Vladimir Dal', *Tolkovyi slovar' zhivogo velikorusskogo iazyka,* 4 vols. (St. Petersburg-Moscow, 1903–9); see relevant entries for each term; for quotations, *razmuzhich'e,* 3: 1532, *muzhlanka, muzhlatka,* 2: 934. I am indebted to Viktor Gushinskii for bringing the Dal' entries discussed here to my attention.

58. Dal', *Tolkovyi slovar'.* See entries for *devunia, devulia, babatia, babulia, razdevul'e;* if married, the effeminate male was known as *babiak, babenia.* These terms denoted the "feminine-looking, beardless" man, an "effeminate" (*zhenstvennyi*) or "softy" (*nezhenka*); for quotations, *germafrodit* and subsequent synonyms, 1: 859; *devunia,* 1: 1267.

59. Dal', *Tolkovyi slovar', devunia, devulia,* 1: 1267.

60. Dal', *Tolkovyi slovar', baba* and derivatives, 1: 86.

61. Dal', *Tolkovyi slovar',* 1: 283.

62. This aspect of status acquisition for women adopting male gender is noted for early modern Holland in Dekker and van de Pol, *The Tradition of Female Transvestism.*

63. Two cases from Iaroslavl' district were described in V. A. Raspopov, "Dva sluchaia lozhnogo muzhskogo germafrodizma (Pseudohermaphroditismus masculinis externus)," *Vrach* 50 (1884): 838–40. The first involved an intersexed infant, "taken for a boy at birth and christened 'Konstantin' "; the second, a forty-six-year-old "male" peasant who displayed many female secondary sexual characteristics, yet was married in spite of having a small penis (judged incapable of accomplishing intercourse).

64. Dal', *Tolkovyi slovar'*, entry for *germafrodit*, 1: 859. Dal' gives *mezheumok*, a person or thing lacking definite qualities, also a mediocrity, as a synonym for hermaphrodite.

65. Tarnovskii, *Izvrashchenie polovogo chuvstva u zhenshchin*, 15–21; for a partial translation of this text, see Engelstein, "Lesbian Vignettes," 818–21.

66. Another Russian term for hermaphroditism, used by forensic medical experts, was "dvusnastnoe," (double-rigged), see Eduard Gofmann, *Uchebnik sudebnoi meditsiny*, trans. I. M. Gvozdev et al. (Kazan': Tip. Imperatorskago Universiteta, 1878), 84.

67. Peasant views were so heavily mediated by judicial and medical investigators that more definite assertions about peasant belief regarding same-sex eros between women, and regarding hermaphroditism, are hazardous. A similar case of husband-poisoning, committed by two peasant women supposedly having a sexual affair, discussed by criminal anthropologist P. N. Tarnovskaia, offered only limited evidence of villagers' viewpoints on these issues. Inquiries into the way of life of the older woman, who inspired a young wife to murder her husband, revealed that she was given to alcoholic binges and "every sort of indecency" (*vsiakie nepotrebstva*). Tarnovskaia published a photograph of this woman dressed in a man's peasant shirt (*kosovorotka*) and with her hair trimmed in a very short crop; *Zhenshchiny-ubiitsy. Antropologicheskoe izsledovanie* (St. Petersburg, 1902), 377–80.

68. Shtess, "Sluchai zhenskogo gomoseksualizma," 5–8.

69. Presumably with the intention of convincing registry officials that "Aleksandr" was a man. Shtess described the clothing the "patient" particularly liked to wear: "a khaki-colored military service cap and jacket, invariably flared trousers, white shoes, a big man's ring on the little finger, and a riding crop in hand." Shtess, "Sluchai zhenskogo gomoseksualizma," 9.

70. Shtess, "Sluchai zhenskogo gomoseksualizma," 10–11.

71. Shtess, "Sluchai zhenskogo gomoseksualizma," 12.

72. The cases of women who posed as males in the army or Cheka forces include Evgeniia Fedorovna M., described in Edel'shtein, "K klinike transvestitizma"; a "case of transvestism and homosexuality" in Osipov, *Kurs obshchego ucheniia o dushevnykh bolezniakh*, 365; and "P. A." described in Skliar, "O proiskhozhdenii i sushchnosti gomoseksualizma."

73. On Evgeniia, see G. R., "Protsessy gomoseksualistov," 16–17; Edel'shtein, "K klinike transvestitizma"; GARF, f. A482, op. 25, d. 478, ll. 85–87.

74. Edel'shtein, "K klinike transvestitizma," 274.

75. Edel'shtein, "K klinike transvestitizma"; G. R., "Protsessy gomoseksualistov," 16.

76. Edel'shtein, "K klinike transvestitizma," 282. On the legal issues at stake in Evgeniia's case, see chapter 5.

77. "P. A.," a twenty-six-year-old manager of a medical clinic, spent one year in the Red Army as a commander (*voenkom*) impersonating a male, and after an unsuccessful marriage, a further three years using the same masculine persona prior to observation by a psychiatrist in 1925, Skliar, "O proiskhozhdenii i sushchnosti gomoseksualizma," 1919–20.

78. Skliar, "O proiskhozhdenii i sushchnosti gomoseksualizma," 1920; quotations from Osipov, *Kurs obshchego ucheniia*, 365.

79. Butler, *Gender Trouble*, 147.

80. On the transformation of sex in animals, see M. M. Zavadovskii, *Pol zhivotnykh i ego prevrashchenie (mekhanika razvitiia pola)* (Moscow-Petrograd: Gosizdat, 1923). Soviet journalism and cinema spread awareness of hormone research far beyond the laboratory, see M. O. Chudakova, "Posleslovie" in M. Bulgakov, *Sochineniia: Roman,*

povesti, rasskazy (Minsk: Universitetskoe, 1988), 412−14; Mikhail Zolotonosov, "Masturbanizatsiia: 'Erogennye zony' sovetskoi kul'tury, 1920−1930-kh godov," in *Erotika v russkoi literature: Ot Barkova do nashikh dnei (Literaturnoe obozrenie. Spetsial'nyi vypusk)*, eds. I. D. Prokhorova, S. Iu. Mazur, and G. V. Zykova (Moscow: Literaturnoe obozrenie, 1992), 97.

81. Evgeniia's "History of my illness" was praised by psychiatrists for its grasp of foreign literature on the topic, during the Expert Medical Council's discussion of "transvestites," GARF, f. A482, op. 25, d. 478, l. 85−85 ob. Dr. Skliar's patient P. A. had medical training and managed a clinic; Skliar reportedly had to insist that she don feminine clothing and stay in the women's ward. The vehemence of his arguments against German sexologist Magnus Hirschfeld's hypothesis that homosexuality was hormonally determined suggests he heard of this from P. A. For another well-read lesbian who argues forcefully that homosexuality was not an illness requiring medical intervention, see A. K. Sudomir, "K kazuistike i sushchnosti gomoseksual'nosti," *Sovremennaia psikhonevrologiia* 5, no. 11 (1927): 371−77.

82. Nor, apparently, was one Andrei Ivanovich, a "female homosexual" passing as a man, living in Karaganda in a registered marriage with another woman, observed in the early 1960s: E. M. Derevinskaia, "Materialy k klinike, patogenezu, terapii zhenskogo gomoseksualizma" (Kandidatskaia dissertatsiia meditsinskikh nauk, Karagandinskii gosudarstvennyi meditsinskii institut, 1965), 117. Hermaphrodites sometimes turned to doctors in the 1920s with requests for medical "clarification of sex," see Healey, " 'Man or Woman?' "

83. Edel'shtein, "K klinike transvestitizma," 279.

84. Opening the 1929 Expert Medical Council discussion on the "intermediate sex," Dr. Ia. I. Brusilovskii described Evgeniia's "diary": "This is the diary of a very rich intellect. She knew languages and had the opportunity to make use of all the decisive foreign literature on this issue and her diary is a detailed report [doklad] in defense of her intermediate sex." GARF, f. A482, op. 25, d. 478, l. 85 ob. The minutes do not say whether Brusilovskii read from an actual diary or referred to the published text of Evgeniia's "History of my illness"; Dr. Edel'shtein did not attend this discussion.

85. Alice D. Dreger, "Hermaphrodites in Love: The Truth of the Gonads," in *Science and Homosexualities*, ed. Vernon A. Rosario (London: Routledge, 1996), 59.

86. Edel'shtein, "K klinike transvestitizma," 278. This passage of Evgeniia's "History of my illness" occurs in Ushakovskii, *Liudi srednego pola*, 199−200.

87. Barbara Alpern Engel, "St. Petersburg Prostitutes in the Late Nineteenth Century: A Personal and Social Profile," *Russian Review* 48 (1989): 21−44; idem, *Between the Fields and the City: Women, Work and Family in Russia, 1861−1914* (Cambridge: Cambridge University Press, 1994).

88. Clements, *Bolshevik Women*, 86.

CHAPTER THREE

1. John Boswell, *Christianity, Social Tolerance and Homosexuality* (Chicago: University of Chicago Press, 1980), 269−302; Greenberg, *The Construction of Homosexuality*, 286−88.

2. Levin, *Sex and Society in the World of the Orthodox Slavs*, 199−203.

3. Levin, *Sex and Society in the World of the Orthodox Slavs*, 203−4, 281−83. The Stoglav, a code of religious and secular precepts propounded in 1551 by Russian Orthodox churchmen in consultation with Ivan IV ("the Terrible"), specifically condemned male ecclesiastical same-sex acts, see Ardalion Popov, *Sud nakazanii za prestupleniia protiv very i nravstvennosti po russkomu pravu* (Kazan': Imperatorskii universitet, 1904),

195–96; B. I. Piatnitskii, *Polovye izvrashcheniia i ugolovnoe pravo* (Mogilev, 1910), 6–7; James H. Billington, *The Icon and the Axe: An Interpretive History of Russian Culture* (New York: Vintage, 1966), 65.

4. Popov, *Sud nakazanii za prestupleniia protiv very i nravstvennosti,* 196; Popov cited Grigorii Kotoshikhin, *O Rossii v tsarstvovanie Aleksiia Mikhailovicha* (St. Petersburg, 1884), 130–31.

5. Greenberg, *The Construction of Homosexuality,* 302–4.

6. See, e.g., Arend H. Huussen, Jr., "Sodomy in the Dutch Republic During the Eighteenth Century," and Randolph Trumbach, "The Birth of the Queen: Sodomy and the Emergence of Gender Equality in Modern Culture, 1660–1750," in Duberman et al., *Hidden from History.*

7. A Captain Rigby was entrapped or denounced by young William Minton in London's St. James's Park in 1698 and charged with attempted buggery. A journalistic report represented Rigby's seduction thus: " 'How can that be?' says Minton. 'I'll show you,' says Rigby, 'for it is no more than was done in our forefathers' time'; and then to incite Minton thereto spake blasphemous words and further said that the French King did it and the Czar of Muscovy made Alexander, a carpenter, a prince for that purpose and affirmed he had seen the Czar of Muscovy through a hole at sea lie with Prince Alexander." Alan Bray, *Homosexuality in Renaissance England* (London: Gay Men's Press, 1982), 98.

8. Engelstein, *The Keys to Happiness,* 58–59.

9. As Greenberg charges, *The Construction of Homosexuality,* 303.

10. Thus, the same military regulations sought to banish "whores" (*bludnitsy*) from the vicinity of regiments, Bernstein, *Sonia's Daughters,* 13–14. On the "military revolution," see Parker, *The Military Revolution: Military Innovation and the Rise of the West;* in the Russian context, see Hellie, "The Petrine Army: Continuity, Change and Impact," 237–53.

11. Popov, *Sud nakazanii za prestupleniia protiv very i nravstvennosti,* 425.

12. Popov, *Sud nakazanii za prestupleniia protiv very i nravstvennosti.* Popov interpreted this term as including both sodomy (*muzhelozhstvo*) and bestiality (*skotolozhstvo*).

13. For a discussion of this trend, see G. Freeze, "Bringing Order to the Russian Family: Marriage and Divorce in Imperial Russia, 1760–1860," *Journal of Modern History* 62, no. 4 (1990): 709–46.

14. On revisions to the statute, Engelstein, *The Keys to Happiness,* 59. For penalties before 1900, "Muzhelozhstvo" in Brokgauz and Efron, *Entsiklopedicheskii slovar',* 39: 110; in 1900, exile was amended to a term of imprisonment of four to five years, V. D. Nabokoff, "Die Homosexualität in Russischen Strafgesetzbuch," *Jahrbuch für sexuelle Zwischenstufen* 3 (1903): 1161; amended text, *Svod zakonov Rossiiskoi Imperii* 15 (St. Petersburg, 1911), 15: col. 3679. An apparent rise in "pederasty" in boarding schools (*internaty*) was said to have influenced the enactment of the 1835 sodomy ban, V. M. Bekhterev, "Polovye ukloneniia i izvrashcheniia v svete refleksologii," 644–746, esp. 704–5.

15. Bernstein, *Sonia's Daughters,* 13–29.

16. On the evolution of forensic medical practice and its concerns, see V. Rozhanovskii, "Sudebno-meditsinskaia ekspertiza v dorevoliutsionnoi Rossii i v SSSR," *Sudebno-meditsinskaia ekspertiza* 6, suppl. (1927): 1–105, esp. 22–25; for early regulations on the examination of living persons, Sergei Gromov, *Kratkoe izlozhenie sudebnoi meditsiny* (St. Petersburg, 1832), 151–93; "Prilozhenie. Ukazatel' statei russkogo zakonodatel'stva otnosiashchikhsia k voprosam sudebnoi meditsiny," in Gofmann, *Uchebnik sudebnoi meditsiny.*

17. The transition to new practice in forensic evidence is recounted in A. F. Koni, *Na zhiznennom puti,* see chapter 18, "Svedushchie liudi i ekspertiza." On the Great Reforms, see Ben Eklof, John Bushnell, and Larissa Zakharova, eds., *Russia's Great Reforms, 1855–1881* (Bloomington: Indiana University Press, 1994); W. Bruce Lincoln, *The Great Reforms: Autocracy, Bureaucracy and the Politics of Change in Imperial Russia* (DeKalb, Ill.: Northern Illinois University Press, 1990). On the procedural divergence between continental and common-law legal systems, and the impact on forensic medicine, Catherine Crawford, "Legalizing Medicine," in *Legal Medicine in History,* eds. Catherine Crawford and Michael Clark (Cambridge: Cambridge University Press, 1994).

18. Ambroise Tardieu, *Étude médico-légale sur les attentats aux moeurs,* 3d ed. (Paris: J. Ballière, 1859; reprint, Jérôme Millon, 1995).

19. The key Russian texts were Vladislav Merzheevskii, *Sudebnaia ginekologiia;* V. M. Tarnovskii, *Izvrashchenie polovogo chuvstva.*

20. Johann Ludwig Casper, "Über Notzucht und Päderastie und deren Ermittelung seitens des Gerichtsarztes. Nach eigenen Beobachtungen," *Vierteljahrsschrift für gerichtliche und öffentliche Medicin* 1 (1852): 21–78; idem, *Practisches Handbuch der gerichtlichen Medizin, nach eigenen Erfahrungen,* 2 vols. (Berlin, 1857–58).

21. Engelstein suggests that Casper was preferred over Tardieu by Russian authorities on sodomy detection; yet both Merzheevskii and Tarnovskii presented so much of Tardieu's material with a minimum of comment that readers were left to draw their own conclusions; Engelstein, *The Keys to Happiness,* 132–33.

22. Frieden, *Russian Physicians,* 266–70.

23. Koni, *Na zhiznennom puti,* 352–53.

24. A Dr. Goloushev, who in 1892 gave expertise in a Moscow case of male rape of a thirteen-year-old boy, was told by a court that Ministry of Justice circular no. 10308 of 16 March 1890 required expertise be provided gratis. His appeal for an honorarium was rejected; TsGIAgM, f. 142, op. 2, d. 433, l. 96. On pay for expertise, see also Frieden, *Russian Physicians,* 266.

25. Ia. Leibovich, "Tri goda sudebnoi meditsiny," *Ezhenedel'nik sovetskoi iustitsii* 7 (1922): 7–8; Rozhanovskii, "Sudebno-meditsinskaia ekspertiza v dorevoliutsionnoi Rossii i v SSSR," 74; V. I. Prozorovskii, ed. *Sudebnaia meditsina* (Moscow: Iuridicheskaia literatura, 1968), 6–7; note also Koni on the lack of forensic medical training in legal education, *Na zhiznennom puti,* 360–61.

26. Merzheevskii, *Sudebnaia ginekologiia,* 204–5; also mentioned was H. Kaan, *Psychopathia sexualis* (Leipzig, 1844).

27. He acknowledged receiving this material from St. Petersburg procurator A. F. Koni, see Merzheevskii, *Sudebnaia ginekologiia,* 207n.

28. Merzheevskii, *Sudebnaia ginekologiia,* 217–19, 235.

29. Tarnovskii, *Izvrashchenie polovogo chuvstva.*

30. Tarnovskii, *Izvrashchenie polovogo chuvstva,* 77.

31. Tarnovskii, *Izvrashchenie polovogo chuvstva,* 78–79, 81.

32. Tarnovskii, *Izvrashchenie polovogo chuvstva,* 82, 84, 93–95.

33. Tarnovskii, *Izvrashchenie polovogo chuvstva,* 96.

34. Tarnovskii, *Izvrashchenie polovogo chuvstva,* 96–97.

35. Tarnovskii, *Izvrashchenie polovogo chuvstva,* 97.

36. Tarnovskii, *Izvrashchenie polovogo chuvstva,* 97.

37. Tarnovskii, *Izvrashchenie polovogo chuvstva,* 104–5.

38. Gofmann, *Uchebnik sudebnoi meditsiny,* 159–67; P. I. Kovalevskii, "Prof. V. M. Tarnovskii. Izvrashchenie polovogo chuvstva 1885 g.," *Arkhiv psikhiatrii neirologii i sudebnoi psikhopatologii* 5–6, no. 3 (1885): 262–64; Golenko, "Pederastiia na sude,"

42–56: N. A. Obolonskii, "Izvrashchenie polovogo chuvstva," *Russkii arkhiv patologii, klinicheskoi meditsiny i bakteriologii* (1898): 1–20.

39. Merzheevskii, *Sudebnaia ginekologiia*, 208.

40. For examples of Petersburg male prostitutes' indifference to the sex of their partners and of mutual voluntary relations between men who could not find partners in a licensed (heterosexual) brothel, see Merzheevskii, *Sudebnaia ginekologiia*, 238– 39, 241. A foreign forensic medicine textbook, translated by a University of Kazan' professor, explicitly rejected suggestions that effeminacy was psychopathic; see Gofmann, *Uchebnik sudebnoi meditsiny*, 166n.

41. Westphal, "Die conträre Sexualempfindung"; R. von Krafft-Ebing, "Über gewisse Anomalien des Geschlechtstriebs und die klinisch-forensische Verwertung derselben als eines wahrscheinlich functionellen Degenerationszeichens des centralen Nerven-Systems," *Archiv für Psychiatrie und Nervenkrankheiten* 7 (1877): 291–312; idem, *Psychopathia sexualis. Eine klinisch-forensische Studie*. 1st ed. (Stuttgart, 1886; Russian trans., 1887).

42. Vernon A. Rosario, "Pointy Penises, Fashion Crimes, and Hysterical Mollies: The Pederasts' Inversions," in *Homosexualities in Modern France*, eds. Jeffrey Merrick and Bryant Ragan Jr. (New York: Oxford University Press, 1996), 153–61; Geert Hekma, "'A Female Soul in a Male Body': Sexual Inversion as Gender Inversion in Nineteenth-Century Sexology," in *Third Sex, Third Gender: Beyond Sexual Dimorphism in Culture and History*, ed. Gilbert Herdt (New York: Zone Books, 1993), 224– 25; George Chauncey, "From Sexual Inversion to Homosexuality: Medicine and the Changing Conceptualization of Female Deviance," *Salmagundi* 58–59 (1982–83): 114– 46.

43. Tarnovskii, *Izvrashchenie polovogo chuvstva*, 62.

44. Tarnovskii, *Izvrashchenie polovogo chuvstva*, 70. Engelstein makes this point in her assessment of Russia's reception of western medical concepts of homosexuality, *The Keys to Happiness*, 132, 164. On the enduring professional presumption of Russian peasant sexual innocence into the late 1920s, see Susan Gross Solomon, "Innocence and Sexuality in Soviet Medical Discourse" in Marsh, *Women in Russia and Ukraine*.

45. Dr. Zuk, "O protivozakonnom udovletvorenii polovogo pobuzhdeniia i o sudebno-meditsinskoi zadache pri prestupleniiakh etoi kategorii," *Arkhiv sudebnoi meditsiny i obshchestvennoi gigieny* 2, sec. 5 (1870): 12–13.

46. Moscow's secular and ecclesiastic court records for the years 1865–1917 (TsGIAgM, "Moskovskii okruzhnyi sud," f. 142; "Moskovskaia dukhovnaia konsistoriia," f. 203) hold no cases of this type. Jurist A. F. Koni's criminal case files contain no lesbian convictions, although it holds details of the 1893 murder by a jealous husband of a woman, Krasikova, in a relationship with a female prostitute, GARF, f. 564, op. 1, d. 260, ll. 22–32 ob., also described in Engelstein, "Lesbian Vignettes," 813–31. Between 1874 to 1904, four women in the Russian Empire were reportedly indicted for "pederasty" in unexplained circumstances, but all were later acquitted; Piatnitskii, *Polovye izvrashcheniia i ugolovnoe pravo*, 11n.

47. Merzheevskii, *Sudebnaia ginekologiia*, 261–62. On Belot's novel and its context, see Victoria Thompson, "Creating Boundaries: Homosexuality and the Changing Social Order in France, 1830–1870," in Merrick and Ragan, *Homosexuality in Modern France*, 117–20.

48. Of the European powers before 1914, only Austria-Hungary forbade same-sex relations between women, but the degree to which this crime was enforced remains unknown. A foreign medico-legal textbook briefly mentioned "lesbian love" and the Austrian law, but doubted the worth of punishing women's "unnatural sexual abuse"; Gofmann, *Uchebnik sudebnoi meditsiny*, 159–60.

49. Foucault, *The History of Sexuality: An Introduction. Vol. 1*, 127.

50. Statistics, see Joravsky, *Russian Psychology: A Critical History*, 420.

51. On these problems, see Julie V. Brown, "The Professionalization of Russian Psychiatry, 1857–1911" (Ph.D. diss., University of Pennsylvania, 1981).

52. Krafft-Ebing's textbook of perversion circulated beyond the medical profession in Russia, as elsewhere; see Evgenii Bershtein, " 'Psychopathia sexualis' v Rossii nachala veka: politika i zhanr," in *Eros i pornografiia v russkoi kul'ture / Eros and Pornography in Russian Culture*, eds. M. Levitt and A. Toporkov (Moscow: Ladomir, 1999). This wider reception of medicalization is discussed in chapter 4.

53. It should be noted that V. P. Tarnovskii, however eminent, was a venereologist and not primarily a psychiatrist; see Engelstein, *The Keys to Happiness*, 162; Bernstein, *Sonia's Daughters*, 126–27.

54. Engelstein, *The Keys to Happiness*, 155–62. Ippolit may have been an older brother of Veniamin Tarnovskii, 155n. The study of women's same-sex love was Tarnovskii, *Izvrashchenie polovogo chuvstva u zhenshchin*, partially translated in Engelstein, "Lesbian Vignettes."

55. Engelstein, *The Keys to Happiness*, 159–60.

56. Bekhterev was founder and director of St. Petersburg's Psychoneurological Institute (1908), and by the war was an acknowledged leader in studies of the physiology of the brain as well as of hypnosis and psychotherapy; A. S. Nikiforov, *Bekhterev* (Moscow: Molodaia gvardiia, 1986), 234–44.

57. Bekhterev testified for the defense in the 1913 trial in Kiev of Mendel Beilis, a Jew accused of ritual murder of a Christian child. A jury acquitted Beilis: Engelstein, *The Keys to Happiness*, 326n.

58. Bekhterev, "Lechenie vnusheniem prevratnykh polovykh vlechenii i onanizma," 9.

59. Bekhterev, "Lechenie vnusheniem prevratnykh polovykh vlechenii i onanizma," 9.

60. J.-M. Charcot and V. Magnan, "Inversion du sens genital," *Archives de neurologie* 3 (1882): 53–60, 296–322; on hypnosis in 1890s, Tikhon I. Iudin, *Ocherki istorii otechestvennoi psikhiatrii* (Moscow: Medgiz, 1951), 125; V. M. Bekhterev, *Gipnoz, vnushenie i psikhoterapiia* (St. Petersburg, 1911).

61. Bekhterev's reflexology resembled physiologist I. P. Pavlov's ideas about reflexes on a superficial level. Early disputes between Bekhterev and Pavlov over the former's failure to duplicate the latter's results in animal physiology experiments led Pavlov to accuse Bekhterev's staff of poor work; the result was "one of the bitterest feuds in Russian scientific history," Joseph Wortis, *Soviet Psychiatry* (Baltimore: Williams & Wilkins, 1950), 36.

62. Bekhterev, "O polovykh izvrashcheniiakh, kak patologicheskikh sochetatel'-nykh refleksakh," 5.

63. Bekhterev promoted this message to both general audiences and professional educators: Bekhterev, "O polovom ozdorovlenii," *Vestnik znaniia* (1910): 9: 924–37, 10: 1–19; idem, "Ob izvrashchenii i uklonenii polovogo vlecheniia," in *Polovoi vopros v svete nauchnogo znaniia*, ed. V. F. Zelenin (Moscow: Gosizdat, 1926); idem, "O polovom izvrashchenii, kak osoboi ustanovke polovykh refleksov."

64. In 1900, exile for simple sodomy was amended to a term of imprisonment of four to five years, and the religious penance for Orthodox offenders was dropped, Nabokoff, "Die Homosexualität in Russischen Strafgesetzbuch," 1161. In England, "buggery" (anal intercourse) was punishable by death until 1861, then ten years to life until 1967. In Germany, paragraph 175 of the criminal code between 1871 and 1935 punished "unnatural vice" with a five-year prison term. See V. D. Nabokov, "Plotskie

prestupleniia po proektu ugolovnogo ulozheniia" *Vestnik prava* 9–10 (1902), reprinted in V. D. Nabokov, *Sbornik statei po ugolovnomu pravu* (St. Petersburg, 1904), 112–13; and Jeffrey Weeks, *Coming Out*, 14.

65. James Scott describes euphemism as a political tool that presents a facade of unanimity and respectability in regimes intolerant of public insubordination; James C. Scott, *Domination and the Arts of Resistance: Hidden Transcripts* (New Haven: Yale University Press, 1990), 44–57.

66. On Wilde, see Weeks, *Coming Out*, 21–22 and passim; on Eulenberg, James D. Steakley, "Iconography of a Scandal: Political Cartoons and the Eulenburg Affair in Wilhelmine Germany," in Duberman et al., *Hidden from History;* on Austria-Hungary's Redl, Istvan Deak, *Beyond Nationalism: A Social and Political History of the Habsburg Officer Corps, 1848–1918* (New York: Oxford University Press, 1990), 144–45.

67. Poznansky, *Tchaikovsky's Last Days*, 2–3. Engelstein notes the absence of symbolic politicization of homosexuality and proposes Prince Meshcherskii as a "Russian Eulenberg" had one been needed, Engelstein, *The Keys to Happiness*, 58.

68. "At the beginning of the 1870s, one of Petersburg's highest administrative figures was found guilty of pederasty and was swiftly removed from his post and exiled abroad without a court hearing or publicity." Tarnovskii, *Izvrashchenie polovogo chuvstva*, 72.

69. Later, a newspaper allegation of improper sexual relations at the Moscow Conservatory weighed heavily on the composer, who taught there, despite the fact that his name was not mentioned; Poznansky, *Tchaikovsky's Last Days*, 10, 18.

70. W. E. Mosse, "Imperial Favorite: V. P. Meshchersky and the *Grazhdanin*," *Slavonic and East European Review* 59 (1981): 529–47.

71. Mosse, "Imperial Favorite," 533–34; Poznansky, *Tchaikovsky's Last Days*, 4. On his accession, Nicholas II expressed some initial distaste, but he soon resumed subsidies to *Grazhdanin* and corresponded privately with Meshcherskii, who by this time was well connected with the government and military, Mosse, "Imperial Favorite," 542–47. The scale of the second scandal is evident from the denunciation of the capital's "tetki" dating from the late 1880s or early 1890s, reproduced in Bersen'ev and Markov, "Politsiia i gei," 105–16.

72. Diarists show these facts were notorious in elite society; see Simon Karlinsky, "Russia's Gay Literature and Culture," in Duberman et al., *Hidden From History*, 351; Nina Berberova, *Chaikovskii* (St. Petersburg: Limbus, 1997 [first published 1937]), 18–19; Poznansky, *Tchaikovsky's Last Days*, 5. Note also diary entries of Grand Duke Konstantin Romanov in Maylunas and Mironenko, *A Lifelong Passion: Nicholas and Alexandra*.

73. Nabokov, "Plotskie prestupleniia," 124.

74. Piatnitskii, *Polovye izvrashcheniia*, 13. Piatnitskii's survey, using data from successive *Svody statisticheskikh svedenii po delam ugolovnym*, which counted consensual sodomy (art. 995), aggravated sodomy (art. 996), and bestiality (art. 997, eliminated in 1903) as one category. He argued plausibly that bestiality convictions were so insignificant that the numbers could be taken to indicate both types of sodomy convictions alone (Moscow court records appear to support this claim). Of these, consensual sodomy accounted for about 20 percent of convictions; he based this conjecture on the proportion of cases of single individuals (78 percent) versus cases in which more than one person was convicted (22 percent), Piatniskii, *Polovye izvrashcheniia*, 11, 31.

75. Piatniskii, *Polovye izvrashcheniia*, 14. The ratio of sodomy convictions to all convictions for each occupational category was the following: state servitors (0.68:3.22 percent), free professions (5.23:1.04 percent), craftsmen (11.59:5.91 percent), and ser-

vants (2.45:1.26 percent). Those in agriculture were underrepresented (31.59:47.77 percent), while factory workers were as likely to be convicted of sodomy as of all other crimes (34.32:34.66 percent). City dwellers, accounting for some 12.8 percent of the population and responsible for 27 percent of all crime in this period, took 45 percent of all sodomy convictions, showing that enforcement was also more prevalent in towns.

76. Piatniskii, *Polovye izvrashcheniia*, 16.

77. Piatnitskii, *Polovye izvrashcheniia*, 88; Fuks, *Gomoseksualizm*, 75.

78. Piatnitskii, *Polovye izvrashcheniia*, 11; Fuks, *Gomoseksualizm*, 75–76.

79. Piatnitskii, *Polovye izvrashcheniia*, 11. This source says 1,066 men (and 4 women) were indicted for sodomy (arts. 995 and 996) from 1874 to 1904; of these, 440 men and no women were convicted. An 1895 census of 7,068 male inmates at the Sakhalin prison colony showed only 6 had been convicted and exiled to this island for "sodomy," *Sakhalinskii kalendar' i materialy k izucheniiu ostrova Sakhalina* (1895), 110. I am grateful to Sergei Ivashkin for this source.

80. Piatnitskii, *Polovye izvrashcheniia*, 33, cites an article claiming no prosecutions under article 995 were pursued in St. Petersburg between 1890 and 1903 ("Preniia v SPb Iurid. Obshchestve po dokladu Nabokova" *Pravo* [1903], 122). Cf. Fuks, *Gomoseksualizm*, 83. Holdings for the Moscow circuit court in TsGIAgM (f. 142) support a similar conclusion for the situation in Moscow, with the last example of a trial for consensual sodomy held in 1888 (f. 142, op. 2, d. 142). Subsequent sodomy trials heard up to 1917 in this court were for male "rape" prosecuted under article 996.

81. Merzheevskii, *Sudebnaia ginekologiia*, 241.

82. GARF, f. 564, op. 1, d. 260, ll. 37–37 ob. (Koni dossier).

83. TsGIAgM, f. 142, op. 2, d. 142.

84. Fuks, *Gomoseksualizm*, 83.

85. Piatnitskii, *Polovye izvrashcheniia*, 31–32.

86. Merzheevskii, *Sudebnaia ginekologiia*, 219–20, 245–48; Tarnovskii, *Izvrashchenie polovogo chuvstva*, 91–93. A Tashkent physician took this notion to its logical conclusion, when he argued against Tarnovskii that pederasts had greater control over this muscle than the "normal man," A. Shvarts, "K voprosu o priznakakh privychnoi passivnoi pederastii (Iz nabliudenii v aziatskoi chasti g. Tashkenta)," *Vestnik obshchestvennoi gigieny, sudebnoi i prakticheskoi meditsiny* 6 (1906): 816–18.

87. A 1907 case document noted the presence of a scar on the penis of the alleged offender, "which in the opinion of Dr. Zybin, could have resulted about ten days ago during forcible sodomy." TsGIAgM, f. 142, op. 1, d. 2532 ("Delo po obvineniiu Kolesnikova N. P., . . . v iznasilovanii krest'ianina Kuznetsova A. E."), l. 4. A doctor testifying in the 1913 case of a brutal rape of a six-year-old boy by a forty-four-year-old laborer combined his observations of the victim's bruises with the boy's testimony and his own conjecture to conclude that the trauma was the result of rape, TsGIAgM, f. 142, op. 3, d. 186 ("Delo po obvineniiu Bukhvalova S. F., . . . v iznasilovanii maloletnego Fedotova, A. A."), ll. 49–49 ob. A 1915 examination explained blood blisters on the foreskin of a prisoner accused of raping a seventeen-year-old cellmate, as the probable result of "great stress to the foreskin, for example, during the introduction of the penis into the anus of another person." TsGIAgM, f. 142, op. 12, d. 99, l. 14 ("Delo po obvineniiu Savel'eva D. N. i Bezrukova V. V. v iznasilovanii arestanta Belousova S. G.").

88. Data for 1905–13 from annual editions of the Ministry of Justice's *Svody statisticheskikh svedenii po delam ugolovnym* (St. Petersburg: Senatskaia tipografiia, 1905–13).

89. Neuberger, *Hooliganism*, 164.

90. From 1874 to 1904, 1,066 persons had been indicted, about 34 indictments yearly; from 1905 to 1913, there were 911 indictments, or 101 annually. The number of convictions rose from 440 between 1874 and 1904 (i.e., about 14 each year), to 504

convictions from 1905 to 1913, an average of 56 annually. This average gives a false impression, for there was a late surge in convictions, with annual rates much higher than the average: in 1905, there were 10 convictions for sodomy; in 1906, 7; in 1907, 25; in 1908, 30; in 1909, 69; in 1910, 68; in 1911, 73; in 1912, 96, and in 1913, 126.

91. Breakdowns of solo convictions versus those with accomplices were not published in 1909 and 1913. Total convictions less those years equaled 309, of which 242 were solo convictions.

92. One-third of all indictments from 1905 to 1913 were raised in the Tiflis district. Only 8 convictions were recorded in St. Petersburg and Moscow, out of the 504 registered between 1905 and 1913.

93. Slavic and European nationalities (Russians and other Slavs, plus Greeks, Jews, Poles, Baltic peoples, Germans) constituted between 50 and 71 percent of all convicted "sodomites," 1905–07; in the same period, Caucasian nationalities (Armenians, Georgians, Tatars, and "members of mountain tribes of the Caucasus") made up between 14–30 percent of convictions. By 1911 to 1913, the roles had reversed, with Russians and Europeans accounting for 16–27 percent of convicted "sodomites," and Caucasians constituting 67–78 percent. The number of Central Asians ("Sarts," "Turkmen and other nationalities of Central Asia") was insignificant.

94. Grigorii Iokhved, "Pederastiia, zhizn' i zakon," *Prakticheskii vrach* 33 (1904): 871–73, quotation, 871.

95. Shvarts, "K voprosu o priznakakh privychnoi passivnoi pederastii."

96. E. V. Erikson, "O polovom razvrate i neestestvennykh polovykh snosheniiakh v korennom naselenii Kavkaza," *Vestnik obshchestvennoi gigieny, sudebnoi i prakticheskoi meditsiny* 12 (1906): 1868–93.

97. Erikson, "O polovom razvrate i neestestvennykh polovykh snosheniiakh v korennom naselenii Kavkaza," 1886–88; the reputation of the region's hotels and bathhouses reached Austria, see Stern, *Geschichte der Öffentlichen Sittlichkeit in Russland*, 570.

98. Erikson, "O polovom razvrate," 1886.

99. On the empire's internal Orient, see Brower and Lazzerini, *Russia's Orient.*

100. Iokhved, "Pederastiia, zhizn' i zakon," 873.

101. Piatnitskii, *Polovye izvrashcheniia;* Fuks, *Gomoseksualizm;* V. P. Serbskii, *Rukovodstvo k izucheniiu dushevnykh boleznei* (Moscow, 1906), 64, 67–68; idem, *Psikhiatriia* (Moscow, 1912), 71, 74, 476–77.

CHAPTER FOUR

1. Ushakovskii, *Liudi srednego pola,* 7. Using "queer" to translate *strannyi* is slightly provocative here; the Russian word, like the English, means "strange, funny, odd," but lacks "queer's" extended meaning of "homosexual." No Russian word performs the work that "queer" does in English; to achieve the homophobic force intended by users of "queer" during most of the twentieth century in the English-speaking world, Russian relies on derivatives of pederast (*pedik*) and homosexual (*gomik*). (The word *urod* was applied to deformities such as birth defects.)

2. *Wings* (Kryl'ia) was first published in 1906 in *Vesy,* a prominent literary journal, then issued separately in St. Petersburg in 1907 and republished repeatedly until 1923. See Karlinsky, "Death and Resurrection of Mikhail Kuzmin," 92–96; idem, "Russia's Gay Literature and Culture: The Impact of the October Revolution," 354–55. For an English translation, Mikhail Kuzmin, *Wings: Prose and Poetry* (Ann Arbor: Ardis, 1972).

3. N. Gumilev, *Sobranie sochinenii* (Washington, 1968), 4: 307, cited in Karlinsky, "Death and Resurrection of Mikhail Kuzmin," 93n.

4. Contemporary European fictions about male same-sex love almost invariably ended in degradation and death or were wreathed in apologetic moralizing; see, e.g., Oscar Wilde, *The Portrait of Dorian Gray* (1890), in which opium addiction necessarily stands in for homosexuality; Abel Acácio de Almeida Botelho, *O Barão de Lavos* (Lisbon, 1891); André Gide, *L'Immoraliste* (1902); Robert Musil, *Die Verwirrungen des Zöglings Törless* [Young Törless], (1906); Thomas Mann, *Der Tod in Venedig* [Death in Venice], (1912). Gide's apology for homosexuality, *Corydon* (written between 1907 and 1920), circulated privately during its long gestation, and Gide repeatedly hesitated to publish it; see Martha Hanna, "Natalism, Homosexuality, and the Controversy over *Corydon*," in Merrick and Ragan, *Homosexuality in Modern France* (New York: Oxford University Press, 1996). On Botelho's little-known novel of Lisbon homosexual life, see David Higgs, "Lisbon," in *Queer Sites: Gay Male Urban Histories*, ed. D. Higgs (London: Routledge, 1999).

5. *Tridtsat' tri uroda*, (St. Petersburg, 1907). Translated by Samuel Cioran as Lydia Zinovieva-Annibal, "Thirty-three Freaks," *Russian Literature Triquarterly* 9 (1974): 94–116.

6. Burgin, "Laid Out in Lavender," 183.

7. Gippius's review of Zinov'eva-Annibal's *Tridtsat' tri uroda* in *Vesy* 7 (1907): 61, cited in Burgin, "Laid Out in Lavender," 184.

8. Burgin, *Sophia Parnok*, 137–38.

9. The best general introduction to sex in late-tsarist literature is Engelstein, *The Keys to Happiness*, 359–420. For an introduction to works of the era celebrating homosexuality, see Karlinsky, "Russia's Gay Literature and Culture," 354–56; on salon culture and gender dissidents, Holmgren, "Stepping Out/Going Under," 233–34; for samples in translation from the works of Kuzmin, Viacheslav Ivanov, Nikolai Kliuev, and other male contributors to this milieu, see Moss, *Out of the Blue: Russia's Hidden Gay Literature*, 69–159.

10. Ushakovskii, *Liudi srednego pola*, 7.

11. Originally published as "Le roman d'un inverti," ed. Dr. Laupts, *Archives d'anthropologie criminelle* 9 (1894): 212–15, 367–73, 729–37; 10 (1895): 131–38, 228–41, 320–25. On this text, see Vernon A. Rosario, "Inversion's Histories/History's Inversions: Novelizing Fin-de-Siècle Homosexuality," in *Science and Homosexualities*, ed. V. Rosario (New York: Routledge, 1997).

12. P. A. Näcke, "Ein Besuch bei den Homosexuellen in Berlin," *Archiv für Kriminalanthropologie und Kriminalistik* 15 (1904). On Näcke's polemic with French medical experts over the character of same-sex love in France and Germany, see Vernon A. Rosario, "Pointy Penises, Fashion Crimes, and Hysterical Mollies: The Pederasts' Inversions," in Merrick and Ragan, *Homosexualities in Modern France*, 165.

13. P. Brouardel, "Les attentats à la pudeur," *Annales d'hygiène publique* (August 1907); and possibly A. von Schrenk-Notzing, "Beiträge zur forensischen Beurtheilung von Sittlichkeitsvergehen mit besonderer Berücksichtigung der Pathogenese psychosexueller Anomalien," *Archiv für Kriminalanthropologie und Kriminalistik* 1 (1898–99): 5–25, 137–82.

14. Marc-André Raffalovich, "L'affaire Oscar Wilde," *Archives d'anthropologie criminelle* 10 (1895): 445–77. Russian émigré and London dandy, Raffalovich had been an intimate of Wilde's until they quarreled in the early 1890s; he had no medical training but wrote extensively in this journal on "*unisexualisme*," or homosexuality. See Rosario, "Inversion's Histories/History's Inversions," 97–98.

15. Ushakovskii, *Liudi srednego pola*, 213.

16. Ushakovskii, *Liudi srednego pola*, 211–26. Like some other apologists for homosexual love, this author also sought to minimize the role played by "pederasty" (i.e.,

anal intercourse) in "the loving relations between men who incapable of loving women," 226.

17. Magnus Hirschfeld, *Tret'ii pol Berlina. Dokumenty bol'shogo stolichnogo goroda*, trans. V. N. Pirogov (St. Petersburg, 1908), first published as *Berlins Drittes Geschlecht* (Berlin and Leipzig, 1904). It appears that Hirschfeld's exhaustive work on same-sex love, *Die Homosexualität des Mannes und des Weibes* (Berlin: Louis Marcus, 1914), was never translated into Russian, although a copy in German is held in the Russian State Library (Moscow). The journal of the Scientific-Humanitarian Committee, published by Hirschfeld (*Jahrbuch für sexuelle Zwischenstufen*), for 1899–1918, is held at the Russian National Library, St. Petersburg. A handful of offprints from this journal are held by the State Central Scientific Medical Library, Moscow.

18. Gavelok Elli [Havelock Ellis], *Polovoe izvrashchenie. Etiudy polovoi psikhologii*, trans. I. D. Florinskii (St. Petersburg: N. S. Askarkhanov, n.d.). This was a translation of the 1909 second English edition. Florinskii translated other works on "sexual psychopathy."

19. Eduard Karpenter [Edward Carpenter], *Promezhutochnyi pol* (Petrograd: M. V. Pirozhkov, 1916). This edition had two portraits of the author and a lengthy appendix of citations on same-sex love from Ellis, Albert Moll, and Krafft-Ebing.

20. Krafft-Ebing's *Psychopathia Sexualis* was translated into Russian in 1887 and 1909; Iwan Bloch's *Das Sexualleben userer Zeit in seinen Beziehungen zur modernen Kultur* (1907) appeared in Russian translations in 1910 and 1911; Albert Moll's *Untersuchung über die Libido sexualis* (1897) was translated in 1910. For several more sexological studies and their Russian publication details, see Engelstein, *The Keys to Happiness*, 132n.

21. A. Koffin'on, *Izvrashchennyi mir (O polovom voprose)* (Moscow: E. Konovalova i Ko. 1908). Fauconney wrote numerous vivid tracts, under pseudonyms Caufeynon and Coffignon, on sexual perversions, recycling other doctors' material; see Sautman, "Invisible Women," in Merrick and Ragan, *Homosexuality in Modern France*, 186.

22. Koffin'on, *Izvrashchennyi mir*, 37, 42.

23. In their complaint, the press committee wrote, "Perhaps it is necessary for criminologists and psychopathologists to know about the secrets of sadism (*sadomiia*) and masochism, of pederasty, to be informed about how vice is spread in Paris, but it is impossible to regard the distribution of this book among a wide public as anything but extremely harmful in view of its pornographic character." The indictment condemned the description of perversion "without being a scientific work." TsGIAgM, f. 142, op. 1, d. 2619, ll. 2–2ob, 33. Konovalova pleaded guilty and received a fifty-ruble fine and a ten-day prison sentence. The entire print run was ordered destroyed, but no evidence in the case file confirms this took place (a copy of the book is held in St. Petersburg's Russian National Library).

24. A. Borisov, *Izvrashchennaia polovaia zhizn'. Boleznennye izmeneniia polovoi sfery* (St. Petersburg, 1907); A. Bekov, *Izvrashchennaia polovaia zhizn'. Zhestokosti polovogo chuvstva* (St. Petersburg: Kommer. skoropechat., 1908); P. I. Kovalevskii, *Psikhologiia pola. Polovoe bezsilie i drugie polovye izvrashcheniia i ikh lechenie* (St. Petersburg, 1905, 1909); *Uzhasy razvrata (Polovoe bezumie)* (Lodz: Mysl', 1911). On the appetite for such tracts and their circulation beyond the medical fraternity, see Evgenii Bershtein, " 'Psychopathia sexualis' v Rossii nachala veka: Politika i zhanr," in Levitt and Toporkov, *Eros i pornografiia v russkoi kul'ture / Eros and Pornography in Russian Culture*.

25. V. M. Bekhterev, "O polovykh izvrashcheniiakh, kak patologicheskikh sochetatel'nykh refleksakh," 1–26, quotation, 9. This incident apparently occurred in approximately 1899.

26. Belousov, "Sluchai gomoseksuala-muzhskoi prostitutki," 315. Krafft-Ebing first

used "nature's stepchildren" to describe practitioners of same-sex love in *Psychopathia sexualis* (2d ed.), vi.

27. Her psychiatrist appeared to have heard these arguments from his patient, to judge by the firmness with which he insisted on refuting them; N. I. Skliar, "O proiskhozhdenii i sushchnosti gomoseksualizma," 1919–23. For a similar case, see Sudomir, "K kazuistike i sushchnosti gomoseksual'nosti," 375.

28. Protopopov, "Sovremennoe sostoianie voprosa o sushchnosti i proiskhozhdenii gomoseksualizma," 52.

29. Engelstein, *The Keys to Happiness*, 391.

30. Novopolin, *Pornograficheskii element v russkoi literature;* on Novopolin's politics, see Engelstein, *The Keys to Happiness*, 378n.

31. Novopolin, *Pornograficheskii element v russkoi literature*, 163–65.

32. Novopolin, *Pornograficheskii element v russkoi literature*, 155, 164.

33. Novopolin, *Pornograficheskii element v russkoi literature*, 157, 169.

34. Novopolin, *Pornograficheskii element v russkoi literature*, 169.

35. Ruadze, *K sudu!* Ruadze justified his book in pious opening and closing remarks that he admitted were at odds with the amusing tone of the rest of the text. He referred to the Eulenburg scandal in Germany, where a "sect" practicing "homosexual vice" had penetrated "ruling circles." St. Petersburg's inhabitants could hardly imagine how developed the vice had become in "our magnificent capital on the Neva," where Ruadze linked it to hooliganism, unemployment, and the influence of "same-sex pornography" inaugurated with Kuzmin's *Wings*. The danger facing Russia was not vice in high places, but the corruption of male youth. Ruadze, *K sudu!*, 3–5, 113–17.

36. Matiushenskii, *Polovoi rynok i polovye otnosheniia;* chapters entitled "Unnatural Vice" and "A Pornographic Club" alerted readers to same-sex prostitution and propaganda for homosexuality in lurid settings. My thanks to Stephen Smith for this reference.

37. Rozanov, *Liudi lunnogo sveta;* citations here from a reprint [Moscow: Druzhba narodov, 1990]); for an introduction to Rozanov and his influential works, see Engelstein, *The Keys to Happiness*, chapter eight, "Sex and the Anti-Semite: Vasilii Rozanov's Patriarchal Eroticism."

38. The "pud" and "funt" were traditional Russian measures of weight; Rozanov, *Liudi lunnogo sveta*, 166. For a perceptive analysis of Krafft-Ebing's interactions with his middle-class "pervert" subjects and readers, see Harry Oosterhuis, "Richard von Krafft-Ebing's "Step-Children of Nature": Psychiatry and the Making of Homosexual Identity," in Rosario, *Science and Homosexualities.*

39. Rozanov, *Liudi lunnogo sveta*, 203.

40. Engelstein, *The Keys to Happiness*, 303–4.

41. N. S. Timasheff, "The Impact of the Penal Law of Imperial Russia on Soviet Penal Law," *American Slavic and East European Review* 12, no. 4 (1953): 441–62.

42. Engelstein, *The Keys to Happiness*, 57–71; Koni referred to the "supposed scientific defenders and apologists of Professor Aletrino's type" who propagandized for "the unnatural vice." See Koni, *Na zhiznennom puti*, 153. Aletrino, a physician, defended sodomy decriminalization in 1901 at the Fifth International Congress of Criminal Anthropology in Amsterdam. On the *skoptsy*, see Laura Engelstein, *Castration and the Heavenly Kingdom: A Russian Folktale* (Ithaca: Cornell University Press, 1999).

43. On Hirschfeld, see Manfred Herzer, *Magnus Hirschfeld: Leben und Werk eines jüdischen, schwulen und sozialisticshen Sexologen* (Frankfurt: Campus, 1992).

44. Engelstein, *The Keys to Happiness*, 67–70. Engelstein notes the influence on Nabokov of P. von Feuerbach's 1813 Bavarian criminal reform (deleting sodomy); Nabokov's brief mention of the lack of a sodomy ban in the "Romance" nations led

by France suggests he was also aware of, if less impressed by, the secularization of criminal codes during the French revolution and Napoleonic conquest, Nabokov, "Plotskie prestupleniia," 112.

45. Engelstein, *The Keys to Happiness*, 62.

46. Piatnitskii, *Polovye izvrashcheniia i ugolovnoe pravo;* Fuks, *Gomoseksualizm kak prestuplenie.*

47. Gert Hekma, Harry Oosterhuis, and James Steakley, "Leftist Sexual Politics and Homosexuality: A Historical Overview," in Hekma et al., *Gay Men and the Sexual History of the Political Left*, 20, 23.

48. See, e.g., Goldman, *Women, the State, and Revolution;* Stites, *The Women's Liberation Movement in Russia.*

49. On biopower, Foucault, *The History of Sexuality: An Introduction, Vol. 1*, 135–59.

50. Alexandra Kollontai, "Sexual Relations and the Class Struggle," in *Selected Writings of Alexandra Kollontai*, trans. Alix Holt (London: Allison & Busby, 1977), 241.

51. Goldman, *Women, the State, and Revolution*, 55–57.

52. By the time of Bebel's death in 1913, this "unofficial Bible of the European Marxist movement" (Stites, *The Women's Liberation Movement in Russia*, 234) had been issued in numerous editions and translations, circulating well beyond women's sections of the left. On sexuality in Bebel, see Goldman, *Women, the State, and Revolution*, 36–37.

53. See, e.g., A. Bebel', *Zhenshchina i sotsializm*, 34th ed. (1902), trans. V. A. Posse, (St. Petersburg: Vestnik Znaniia, 1909), pt. 1, 142.

54. Hekma et al., "Leftist Sexual Politics and Homosexuality," 14–15, 21.

55. Hekma et al., "Leftist Sexual Politics and Homosexuality," 36 n45.

56. Goldman, *Women, the State and Revolution*, 35.

57. The WLSR included in its platform a call for the decriminalization of homosexual relations. On Soviet involvement in the WLSR, see chapter 5.

58. In her most developed prerevolutionary statement on sexuality, she noted, "History has never seen such a variety of personal relationships" including "marriage in *threes* and even the complicated marriage of *four people*—not to talk of the *various forms* of commercial prostitution" (my emphasis). This was an extremely rare hint from Kollontai at possibilities beyond heterosexuality; Kollontai, "Sexual Relations and the Class Struggle," 241.

59. Hekma et al., "Leftist Sexual Politics and Homosexuality," 17–19, 22; Healey, "Evgeniia/Evgenii," 93–94.

60. Hekma et al., "Leftist Sexual Politics and Homosexuality," 22; for a Russian example, contrast the views of psychiatrist and later Bolshevik supporter Bekhterev, "O polovom ozdorovlenii," 9: 924–37, 10: 1–19, in which he argued against open debate about homosexuality on sexual hygiene grounds, and idem, "O polovom izvrashchenii, kak osoboi ustanovke polovykh refleksov," in which he asserted a private gathering of homosexuals was harmless to the public.

61. Stites, *The Women's Liberation Movement in Russia*, 376–79; Goldman, *Women, the State and Revolution*, 1–58.

62. The phrase was one Armand proposed using in a pamphlet, see V. I. Lenin, *Polnoe sobranie sochinenii*, 5th ed. (Moscow: Politicheskaia literatura, 1960), Letter to I. F. Armand, 17 January 1915) 49: 51–52, and Letter to Armand, 21 January 1915) 49: 54–57. These letters were only published in 1939 (in the theoretical journal *Bol'shevik*), apparently to signal that changes to family policy in the 1930s had Leninist origins.

63. Here he contradicted Kollontai, who had argued that it was "unforgivable" to put off thinking about revolutionary sexuality; refuting its relegation as a superstruc-

tural problem of the new order, she insisted that sexuality was already evolving as the struggle for socialism took place. Kollontai, "Sexual Relations and the Class Struggle," 237–39, 249.

64. Written immediately after Lenin's death in January 1924 and published in Klara Tsetkin, *O Lenine. Vospominaniia i vstrechi* (Moscow: Moskovskii rabochii, 1925); for an English translation of the chapter on marriage, sex and family, see Clara Zetkin, *Lenin on the Woman Question* (New York: International Publishers, 1934).

65. Indeed, in 1904–5, Lenin himself expressed such sentiments, albeit always with the proviso that prostitutes be "educated" to the norms of social democracy; see Lenin, *Polnoe sobranie sochinenii*, 11: 223. This reference appeared in an article of September 1905, reflecting the exuberance of the revolutionary era: "not long ago a worker asked me in a letter why not agitate among prostitutes (*prostitutki*)." For a 1904 reference to prostitution as social oppression, see a scheme for lectures on social democracy, *Polnoe sobranie sochinenii*, 9: 392–93.

66. Zetkin, *Lenin on the Woman Question*, 7; my emphasis.

67. Many Western queer theorists and activists support a movement of endlessly diverse sexual alterity, and (contradicting Lenin) view transgressive gender and sexuality as politically transformative. With Lenin they share the view that pleading for acceptance from conventional ("straight," "bourgeois") morality, as homophile and gay politics allegedly did and do, merely capitulates to heteronormativity. See, e.g., Butler, *Gender Trouble*; Jagose, *Queer Theory*; Morton, *The Material Queer: A LesBiGay Cultural Studies Reader*; Califa, *Sex Changes*.

68. The one relatively senior Bolshevik known to have been homosexual, Commissar of Foreign Affairs Grigorii Chicherin (in office 1918–30), apparently conformed unswervingly to this ethic.

69. Zetkin, *Lenin on the Woman Question*, 11; my emphasis.

70. Zetkin, *Lenin on the Woman Question*, 10.

71. V. D. Nabokov, *The Provisional Government* ed. Andrew Field (Brisbane: University of Queensland Press, 1970), 95–96; Timasheff, "The Impact of the Penal Law of Imperial Russia," 443–44. A. Shreider, in early 1918 the first Deputy Commissar of Justice, noted that the Provisional Government's law commission had generated a new draft code, but the statute had not been fundamentally revised, GARF, f. A353, op. 2, d. 164, l. 36. No proposed draft appears in Robert Browder and Alexander F. Kerensky, eds., *The Russian Provisional Government 1917: Documents* (Stanford: Stanford University Press, 1961).

72. Based on a review of GARF, f. A353 ("Narodnyi kommissariat iustitsii RSFSR, 1917–1946 gg.") opisi 1–12 and 16s, and in particular, on the protocols of the Justice Commissariat's collegium for the period.

73. Karlinsky, "Russia's Gay Literature and Culture," 357; idem, "Introduction: Russia's Gay Literature and History," 24.

74. Healey, "The Russian Revolution and the Decriminalisation of Homosexuality," 26–54, esp. 34.

75. Engelstein, "Soviet Policy toward Male Homosexuality," 165.

76. GARF, f. A353, op. 2, d. 164 (Proekt "Ugolovnogo Ulozheniia" i ob"iasnitel'naia zapiska k nemu. 1918 g.), l. 29; on LSR control of this commissariat, see G. V. Shvekov, *Pervyi sovetskii ugolovnyi kodeks* (Moscow: Vysshaia shkola, 1970), 105.

77. GARF, f. A353, op. 2, d. 164, ll. 36–37.

78. GARF, f. A353, op. 2, d. 164, ll. 30–33.

79. The text of this article reads:

215. [One is] guilty of sodomy:
If sodomy is committed:

1. with a minor from fourteen to sixteen years, without his [*ego*] consent or although with his consent, but through abuse of his innocence,

2. knowingly with someone incapable of understanding the character and significance of that which is being committed on him or of governing his acts for reason of pathological disorder of mental activity, or unconscious condition, or mental retardation, as a result of bodily defect or illness,

3. with someone incapable of expressing his refusal to the perpetrator, without his consent to sodomy, then the guilty person [male gender] is punished: by deprivation of freedom for a term not less than three years.

If sodomy is committed:

1. with a child under fourteen years,

2. with a person under the power [*pod vlast'iu*] or guardianship of the guilty person,

3. with a person coerced into it by means of force on the individual or threats of murder, with grievous bodily harm to the threatened person or a member of his family, if such a threat could cause the threatened person to fear it would be implemented,

4. with a person placed in an unconscious condition for that [purpose] by the perpetrator himself or with his participation, then the guilty person is punished: by deprivation of freedom for a term not greater than eight years.

GARF, f. A353, op. 2, d. 164, ll. 115–16; except for the legalizing of adult consensual sodomy, the article is virtually identical to legislation in the 1903 code, N. S. Tagantsev and P. N. Iakobi, eds., *Ugolovnoe ulozhenie 22 marta 1903 g.* (Riga: Leta, 1922), 1064–67.

80. Nabokov, "Plotskie prestupleniia," 108–9.

81. Nabokov, "Plotskie prestupleniia," 110. Tsarist jurists were aware of male prostitution in Russian cities, Tagantsev and Iakobi, *Ugolovnoe ulozhenie,* 1065–66.

82. GARF, f. A353, op. 2, d. 164, ll. 37–39.

83. GARF, f. A353, op. 2, d. 3, l. 3; Shvekov, *Pervyi sovetskii ugolovnyi kodeks,* 114–16.

84. Shvekov, *Pervyi sovetskii ugolovnyi kodeks,* 126.

85. Shvekov, *Pervyi sovetskii ugolovnyi kodeks,* 119–25; Peter H. Solomon, Jr., *Soviet Criminal Justice under Stalin* (Cambridge: Cambridge University Press, 1996), 24–25.

86. GARF, f. A353, op. 3, d. 745 ("Dokumenty o kontrrevoliutsionnoi agitatsii monakhov Novoirusalimskogo monastyria i po obvineniiu episkopa Palladiia v rastlenii mal'chika, 1919 g.").

87. John S. Curtiss, *The Russian Church and the Soviet State 1917–1940* (Gloucester, Mass.: Peter Smith, 1965), 93; Dimitry Pospielovsky, *The Russian Church under the Soviet Regime 1917–1982* (Crestwood, N.Y.: St. Vladimir's Seminary Press, 1984), 1: 39.

88. GARF, f. A353, op. 3, d. 745: Eighth Department dispatched secret police operative to seek witnesses against Palladii in Belev and Saratov 16 September 1919 (l. 24, albeit the protocols of these were not obtained until 20 and 24 October); interrogated Palladii's "victim" Volkov, on 25 September (l. 28 ff.) and consigned him to the Institute for Defective Child for forensic tests (26 or 27 September, l. 29 ob.); obtained full testimony from Palladii and several Zvenigorod and Moscow witnesses by 13 October (ll. 30–31, 32 ff.).

89. The collegium appointed Krasikov himself to serve as "public accuser" in the case, GARF, f. A353, op. 3, d. 745, l. 13; Palladii noted the frequent presence of jurist N. A. Cherlunchakevich during his interrogations, and the intercessions he made on his behalf, ll. 55, 58 ob., 61 ob.; after the trial, on 4 November, the collegium rejected a request for an immediate appeal of the verdict from Palladii, GARF, f. A353, op. 3, d. 4, l. 80.

90. N. P., "Monakhi pred sudom v roli razvratitlei maloletnikh i nesovershennoletnikh," *Ezhenedel'nik sovetskoi iustitsii* 42 (1922): 13–15; S. N., "Monastyri—pritony razvrata—pri svete sovetskogo suda (Protsess arkhimandrita Sergiia, nastoiatelia Sretenskogo monastyria v Moskve)," *Ezhenedel'nik sovetskoi iustitsii* 19–20 (1922): 19; M. Sheinman, *Religioznost' i prestupnost'* (Moscow: Bezbozhnik, 1927), 55–56.

91. Healey, " 'Their Culture.' "

92. The Eighth Department used the paraphernalia of science in its antireligious propaganda work, calling on doctors to examine exhumed relics and make pronouncements before cine-cameras about their inauthenticity. In the Palladii case, psychiatrists at the Institute of the Defective Child found nothing wrong with Volkov, and their report was suppressed. Prosecutor Krasikov offered an improvisatory scientific analysis of Palladii's "unnatural" sexual tastes: GARF, f. A353, op. 3, d. 745, l. 45.

93. GARF, f. A353, op. 3, d. 4, l. 94; op. 4, d. 301, ll. 4–4 ob.; Shvekov, *Pervyi sovetskii ugolovnyi kodeks*, 126; on Kozlovskii's volte-face, see Solomon, *Soviet Criminal Justice under Stalin*, 24–25.

94. The following discussion is based on documentation in GARF, f. A353, op. 4, d. 301 (Dokumenty po podgotovke Ugolovnogo kodeksa RSFSR, 1920 g.). The various chapter heading schemes found in this file are undated; I have imposed a chronological order upon them, based on my interpretation of textual changes toward Kozlovskii's full draft of his Chapter V "Crimes against the Life, Health and Dignity of the Individual" (ll. 10–12 ob.).

95. GARF, f. A353, op. 4, d. 301, l. 9.

96. GARF, f. A353, op. 4, d. 301, ll. 6–6 ob. "Property" in this chapter heading was an obvious error, which the collegium corrected to read "dignity" (*dostoinstvo*). The final variant was thus arrived at, cf. ll. 5–5 ob.

97. GARF, f. A353, op. 4, d. 301, l. 11 ob. The text of this article read: "SODOMY. Sodomy is punishable when it is committed: 1. with the mentally ill, 2. with a person incapable of expressing resistance to the guilty person, 3. with a child under fourteen years, 4. with a person coerced to it by means of force or threats of murder or grievous bodily harm to the threatened person [i.e., the victim] or his family. The punishment is increased if such action is committed with the rendering in an unconscious condition for that [purpose] of the corresponding individual by the perpetrator himself or with his participation." This draft code did not specify punishments for the offenses it enumerated.

98. "As the experience of history teaches us, all significant legislative works were developed and took effect not at the moment of intense revolutionary struggle, but rather in the epoch when the *results* of revolutionary upheavals had become apparent, when revolutionary battles took on a clear and conclusive character. Thus the great codifications incorporating in legal norms the battles of the French Revolution (*code penal, code civil, code de commerce, code d'instruction criminelle, code d'instruction civil* [sic]) appeared in the first decade of the nineteenth century, when the achievements of the third estate seemed clear and irreversible, when civil peace reigned in France, and the new ideas together with Napoleon's army completed a triumphant march across the continent of Europe." GARF, f. A353, op. 4, d. 301, ll. 25–25 ob.

99. Michael Sibalis, "The Regulation of Male Homosexuality in Revolutionary and Napoleonic France, 1789–1815," in Merrick and Ragan, *Homosexuality in Modern France*, 82–83, 89–92.

100. GARF, f. A353, op. 4, d. 301, l. 26 ob.

101. GARF, f. A353, op. 4, d. 301, l. 27 ob.

102. GARF, f. A353, op. 4, d. 1, l. 131.

103. Shvekov, *Pervyi sovetskii ugolovnyi kodeks,* 130, 132; GARF, f. A353, op. 4, d. 1, l. 63; this commission's papers do not appear in RSFSR Justice Commissariat archival holdings. Savrasov, the commissariat's representative to the Cheka (secret police) since June 1920, had participated in revising the chapter on crimes against the person over the previous two years.

104. Shvekov, *Pervyi sovetskii ugolovnyi kodeks,* 136–37; GARF, f. A353, op. 4, d. 1, l. 117. No draft of the institute's code appears in GARF holdings, and only the general part was published.

105. GARF, f. A353, op. 4, d. 1, l. 131; Nikolai Krylenko, "Ob izmeneniiakh i dopolneniiakh kodeksov RSFSR," *Sovetskaia iustitsiia* 15, no. 7 (1936): 1–5.

106. Shvekov, *Pervyi sovetskii ugolovnyi kodeks,* 146, 152–59.

107. On the "minimalism" pursued by Soviet lawmakers, see Engelstein, "Soviet Policy Toward Male Homosexuality," 165.

108. The tsarist terminology included *liubostrastnye deistviia* (nonpenetrative sexual assault), *liubodeianie* (heterosexual rape), *muzhelozhstvo* (sodomy), and *krovosmeshenie* (incest). GARF, f. A353, op. 4, d. 301, ll. 11 ob.-12; cf. *Ugolovnyi kodeks RSFSR (1922). Sobranie uzakonenii i rasporiazhenii rabochego i krest'ianskogo pravitel'stva* (1922), no. 15, item 153; see Special section, Chapter V(4) "Crimes in the field of sexual relations," articles 166–71. Later revised as *Ugolovnyi kodeks RSFSR (1926). Sobranie zakonov i rasporiazhenii raboche-krest'ianskogo pravitel'stva SSSR* (1926), no. 80, item 600; Special section, Chapter VI, (no subtitle), articles 150–155.

109. E.g., *liubodeianie* was treated in three different articles, with "sexual intercourse with persons not having reached sexual maturity" punished under article 166 of the 1922 RSFSR Criminal Code; aggravated forms of *liubodeianie* became "sexual intercourse . . . accompanied by defloration or with the satisfaction of sexual lust in perverted [*izvrashchennye*] forms" (article 167), while the article 169 dealt with ordinary "rape." *Liubostrastnye deistviia* became "corruption of children or minors accomplished by depraved (*razvratnye*) acts in relation to them" (article 168).

110. According to articles 166 and 167 of the 1922 code, and article 151 in the 1926 code.

111. The 1926 criminal code rationalized the organization of certain articles (by combining articles 166 and 167 of the 1922 code on sexual offenses against young persons in the new article 151; prostitution crimes were similarly treated). It elevated a 1923 amendment to article 169, outlawing sexual harassment of women, to a discrete article 154, and set maximum sentences where previously minimums were listed. The new redaction was meant to retain a firm penal policy on sex crimes while permitting judges more latitude to consider circumstances (class background, age, education) in sentencing: D. Kurskii and P. Stuchka, "Instruktivnye pis'ma. Direktivnoe pis'mo NKIu i verkhsuda RSFSR po primeneniiu Ugol. Kod. redaktsii 1926 g.," *Sudebnaia praktika RSFSR* 1 (1927): 8–11.

112. In the 1922 code, only article 171 (procuring women for prostitution) was gender-specific; in the 1926 edition, articles 154 (sexual harassment) and 155 (procuring) used language specifying female victims. Article 153 of the 1926 code (against rape) acquired a subsection, on rapes by groups of perpetrators, whose victims were specified as female, yet the main definition of rape continued to be gender neutral.

113. Punishable with a minimum five years under the 1922 code; the penalty was altered to a maximum of eight years in 1926.

114. A. A. Zhizhilenko, *Polovye prestupleniia (st. st. 166–171 Ugolovnogo Kodeksa)* (Moscow: Pravo i zhizn', 1924), 15; cf. B. Zmiev, *Ugolovnoe pravo. Chast' osobennaia. Vypusk I Prestupleniia protiv lichnosti i imushchestvennye* (Kazan': Izd. NKIust. Avtomnoi Tatarskoi SSR, 1923), 26; P. I. Liublinskii, *Prestupleniia v oblasti polovykh otno-*

shenii (Moscow-Leningrad: Iz-vo L. D. Frenkel', 1925), 122; E. P. Frenkel', *Polovye prestupleniia* (Odessa: Svetoch, 1927), 11.

115. Poznyshev, *Ocherk osnovnykh nachal nauki ugolovnogo prava*, 61.

116. Liublinskii, *Prestupleniia v oblasti polovykh otnoshenii*, 122–23; see also Zmiev, *Ugolovnoe pravo. Chast' osobennaia*, 26.

117. Zmiev, *Ugolovnoe pravo. Chast' osobennaia*, 26; Frenkel', *Polovye prestupleniia*, 11.

118. Jurists who thought homosexual rape was understood by the article: Zhizhilenko, *Polovye prestupleniia (st. st. 166–171 Ugolovnogo Kodeksa)*, 19; Liublinskii, *Prestupleniia v oblasti polovykh otnoshenii*, 122; Frenkel', *Polovye prestupleniia*, 14. Those who reserved rape for heterosexual acts: Zmiev, *Ugolovnoe pravo. Chast' osobennaia*, 27; Poznyshev, *Ocherk osnovnykh nachal nauki ugolovnogo prava*, 58; D. A. Karnitskii and Iu. Trivus, *Voprosy ugolovno-sudebnoi i sledstvennoi praktiki* (Moscow: Iuridicheskoe iz-vo NKIu RSFSR, 1927), 61–62; D. A. Karnitskii, G. K. Roginskii, and M. S. Strogovich, *Ugolovnyi kodeks RSFSR. Postateinyi kommentarii* (Moscow: Iuridicheskoe iz-vo NKIu RSFSR, 1928), 265–71. Tsarist court documents routinely used the word "rape" (*iznasilovanie*) to refer to sodomitical assaults between males prosecuted under the old regime's article 996.

119. Soviet authorities could prosecute someone for an act analogous to one in the criminal code; they justified this drastic departure from liberal legal principles by arguing that the isolated and young socialist state could not anticipate all the possible acts of its enemies, Solomon, *Soviet Criminal Justice under Stalin*, 31–32. The implications of gender-neutral language were clear to deputy OGPU chief G. Iagoda in 1933 when he drafted the decree to recriminalize sodomy. It explicitly reaffirmed the viability of existing sexual offenses, including "criminal responsibility . . . for the rape of persons of both sexes," "Iz istorii Ugolovnogo kodeksa: 'Primerno NAKAZAT' etikh Merzavtsev,'" 165, citing APRF, f. 3, op. 57, d. 37, ll. 25–26. The enactment of the new sodomy law with its second clause prohibiting coercive acts was thus a significant redundancy, making explicit what had previously been implicit to but a few observers.

120. F. Pfäfflin, ed., *Mitteilungen des Wissenschaftlich-humanitären Komitees, 1926–1933* (Hamburg: Faksimile-Nachdr., 1985), 147.

121. In 1805, to settle a case turning on sodomy's status in criminal law, Napoleon wrote "We are not in a country where the law should concern itself with these offenses. Nature has seen to it that they are not frequent. The scandal of legal proceedings would only tend to multiply them. It would be better to give the proceedings another direction." Police were told to impose administrative penalties; Sibalis, "The Regulation of Male Homosexuality," in Merrick and Ragan, *Homosexuality in Modern France*, 89–92. In 1921, the British House of Commons voted to extend the Labouchère Amendment (the law against gross indecency between men used against Oscar Wilde) to acts between women; the Lords rejected extension, arguing that giving publicity to the offense would increase it, Weeks, *Coming Out*, 106–7.

122. Only in Italy did a similarly progressive outcome occur. Unification imposed the French-influenced law of the north on the entire Kingdom by 1900. In Germany, Prussia's ban on male same-sex acts was forced on principalities that had decriminalized sodomy under French influence. In Austria-Hungary, male and female same-sex relations were prohibited, and successor states inherited the ban. See Flora Leroy-Forgeot, *Histoire juridique de l'homosexualité en Europe* (Paris: Presses Universitaires de France, 1997), 66–67; Greenberg, *The Construction of Homosexuality*, 352.

CHAPTER FIVE

1. Protopopov, "Sovremennoe sostoianie voprosa o sushchnosti i proiskhozhdenii gomoseksualizma," 49.

2. Susan Gross Solomon, "Social Hygiene and Soviet Public Health, 1921–1930," in Solomon and Hutchinson, *Health and Society in Revolutionary Russia;* idem, "The Expert and the State in Russian Public Health."

3. Neil B. Weissman, "Origins of Soviet Health Administration," in Solomon and Hutchinson, *Health and Society in Revolutionary Russia.*

4. G. R., "Protsessy gomoseksualistov," 16–17. The author may have been Grigorii Ryndziunskii, who in 1922 wrote in this journal on comparatively humble *bytovye* (everyday) subjects: family law and inheritance, bills of exchange, and municipal land use.

5. The key articles are the following: for the raid on the Petrograd club, Protopopov, "Sovremennoe sostoianie voprosa o sushchnosti i proiskhozhdenii gomoseksualizma"; V. M. Bekhterev, "Polovye ukloneniia i izvrashcheniia v svete refleksologii," 644–746, esp. 720–21, 740; idem, "O polovom izvrashchenii, kak osoboi ustanovke polovykh refleksov," 167–71. My thanks to Frances Bernstein for providing me with a copy of this exceptional source on the raid. For Evgeniia's marriage to a woman, see Edel'shtein, "K klinike transvestitizma," 273–82.

6. "In his expert testimony, Academician Bekhterev explained that although the deviation of these abnormal people could not be criminally punished [*ne mogut byt' ugolovno-nakazuemymi*], nevertheless, the public display of their desires, the involvement of other unstable persons in the circle of perverted interests, in a word, the declaration to a wide public of homosexual tastes and acts is harmful from the public point of view and must not be permitted, and the establishment of clubs or dens for such purposes should be criminally punishable"; G. R., "Protsessy gomoseksualistov," 16.

7. Diverse historians have generally regarded "Protsessy gomoseksualistov" as evidence of early Bolshevik disapproval of homosexual emancipation and (in the totalitarian interpretation) of all same-sex erotic relationships. See, e.g., Timasheff, "The Impact of the Penal Law of Imperial Russia on Soviet Penal Law," : 441–62, esp. 458; Karlinsky, "Introduction: Russia's Gay Literature and History," in *Out of the Blue,* 24; Healey, "The Russian Revolution and the Decriminalisation of Homosexuality," 26–54, esp. 34. A recent reading still assigns great importance to the article as indicative of Bolshevik views: Engelstein, "Soviet Policy Toward Male Homosexuality," 168.

8. This presumption lies behind Karlinsky's description of the cases as "show trials staged right after the appearance of the 1922 [criminal] code, "Introduction: Russia's Gay Literature and History," 24. There is no indication whether the trial of the Petrograd men was open or closed; no trial of the women had yet taken place, G. R., "Protsessy gomoseksualistov," 16–17. On responses to directives from the center by local justice operatives at this time, see Solomon, *Soviet Criminal Justice under Stalin,* 54–60.

9. ". . . it would seem that acts of this type . . . should be punishable, even if [*khotia by*] by application of article 176 [i.e., against hooliganism] of the Criminal Code." G. R., "Protsessy gomoseksualistov," 17.

10. Commentaries ignoring advice of "Trials of Homosexuals": Poznyshev, *Ocherk osnovnykh nachal nauki ugolovnogo prava; Ugolovnyi kodeks. S predisloviem D. I. Kurskogo* (Moscow: Izd. moskovskogo gubernskogo suda, 1924); Frenkel', *Polovye prestupleniia;* Karnitskii and Trivus, *Voprosy ugolovno-sudebnoi i sledstvennoi praktiki;* D. A. Karnitskii et al., *Ugolovnyi kodeks RSFSR. Postateinyi kommentarii.* Commentaries advising use of hooliganism statute against public consensual sodomy: Zmiev, *Ugolovnoe pravo. Chast' osobennaia;* Zhizhilenko, *Polovye prestupleniia;* Liublinskii, *Prestupleniia v oblasti polovykh otnoshenii.*

11. Frenkel', *Polovye prestupleniia,* 12.

12. Liublinskii, *Prestupleniia v oblasti polovykh otnoshenii* 124–27; medical reasons for decriminalization were also given by Zmiev, *Ugolovnoe pravo. Chast' osobennaia,* 27.

13. Liublinskii, *Prestupleniia v oblasti polovykh otnoshenii*, 117–20; Frenkel', *Polo-vye prestupleniia*, 11–12; S. V. Poznyshev, *Ocherk osnovnykh nachal nauki ugolovnogo prava. II. Osobennaia chast'*, 60; A. A. Zhizhilenko, "Polovye prestupleniia. Iuridicheskie ocherk," in *Polovye prestupleniia*, eds. A. A. Zhizhilenko and L. G. Orshanskii (Leningrad-Moscow: Iz-vo Rabochii sud, 1927), 10.

14. Edel'shtein, "K klinike transvestitizma." Both the Evgeniia in "Protsessy gomo-seksualistov" and Edel'shtein's Evgeniia Fedorovna M. presented themselves in public as men, altering their identity papers using the masculine form of their name, Evgenii; both had managed to marry their female partner at a ZAGS office in 1922. In "Pro-tsessy," Evgeniia was said to be an insistent defender of her right to the privacy of her "intimate life" (*intimnaia zhizn'*), and a clever legal strategist, having "complicated [the case] with various collateral circumstances and complaints, raised by the accused as a result of her clear mental imbalance." The woman described by Edel'shtein robustly defended the rights of what she called the "intermediate sex" in a long text she was said to have written for the doctor. This "History of my illness" with its lucid homosexual emancipationist arguments was reproduced by Edel'shtein as evidence of Evgeniia's compulsive fantasizing.

15. Edel'shtein, "K klinike transvestitizma," 274: "It should be noted that the Justice Commissariat recognized the marriage as legal, as having been concluded by mutual consent." Edel'shtein textually represented this observation as a fact from Ev-geniia's anamnesis, isolating it in the case history from his claims about her "'com-pulsive fantasizing.'" His treatment of this extraordinary detail suggests he had inde-pendent confirmation of it. In the Justice Commissariat's account, the possibility of just such an outcome was not ruled out. The unnamed provincial investigator's tactics were inadequate, and the case against Evgeniia/Evgenii was threatened with failure, "Protsessy gomoseksualistov," 16.

16. Archival holdings of the collegium of the RSFSR Justice Commissariat for the 1920s (at GARF) make no mention of the decision to recognize Evgeniia Fedorovna M.'s marriage, presumably a lower court ruling, in a provincial jurisdiction unnamed in any source.

17. Historians have viewed the timing of this trial, coming after the enactment of the new code, as crucial: Timasheff, "The Impact of the Penal Law of Imperial Russia," 458; Karlinsky, "Introduction: Russia's Gay Literature and History," 24; Healey, "Rus-sian Revolution and the Decriminalisation of Homosexuality," 34. Engelstein, "Soviet Policy toward Male Homosexuality" accepts the trials occurred *after* the 1922 code was enacted, but notes "G. R.'s" 1922 article failed to influence the 1926 criminal code revision, 166–68.

18. Bekhterev, "Polovye ukloneniia i izvrashcheniia v svete refleksologii" 720–21, 740; idem, "O polovom izvrashchenii, kak osoboi ustanovke polovykh refleksov" 167–71; for interviews with ten men arrested in the same raid described by Bekhterev, see Protopopov, "Sovremennoe sostoianie voprosa o sushchnosti i proiskhozhdenii gomo-seksualizma."

19. He said the case arose "a short time ago," and he reported that Bekhterev testified that "these abnormal people's deviation *cannot be criminally prosecuted*," suggesting the new code was in effect at the time of the trial; G. R., "Protsessy gomoseksualistov," 16.

20. Bekhterev, "Polovye ukloneniia i izvrashcheniia v svete refleksologii," 720. Some sources say 95 persons were arrested.

21. He presented a paper describing these men to the Petrograd Institute for the Study of the Brain on this date, Bekhterev, "Polovye ukloneniia i izvrashcheniia."

22. Bekhterev, "O polovom izvrashchenii, kak osoboi ustanovke polovykh reflek-sov," 166–71.

23. Bekhterev, "O polovom izvrashchenii," 169.

24. Bekhterev, "O polovom izvrashchenii," 171.

25. Waters, "Victim or villain: Prostitution in post-revolutionary Russia," 161, 167–68. In these debates and institutions, "prostitution" was virtually always assumed to be heterosexual, exclusively involving women and girls selling sex to men. On male prostitution in Russia, see Dan Healey, "Masculine Purity and 'Gentlemen's Mischief': Sexual Exchange and Prostitution between Russian Men, 1861–1941" *Slavic Review* 60, no. 2 (2001): 233–65.

26. Lebina and Shkarovskii, *Prostitutsiia v Peterburge*, 142–43; Waters, "Victim or Villain," 167; Wood, *The Baba and the Comrade*, 113–16.

27. On the new discipline of social hygiene, see Solomon, "Social Hygiene and Soviet Public Health, 1921–1930"; the field included sexology in its broad remit, but its interest in homosexuality remained very slight.

28. Semashko's remarks were reported in *Jahrbuch für sexuelle Zwischenstufen* 23 (1923): 211–12. On the film, see *Goodbye to Berlin?: 100 Jahre Schwulenbewegung* (Berlin: Verlag rosa Winkel, 1997), 82–84.

29. Solomon, "Social Hygiene and Soviet Public Health, 1921–1930," 179.

30. Solomon, "Social Hygiene and Soviet Public Health, 1921–1930," 183.

31. Grigorii Batkis, *Die Sexualrevolution in Russland* (Berlin: Syndikalist, 1925), 22. Claims that this pamphlet represented official Bolshevik views or, conversely, that it was released to mislead foreign sex reformers and leftists, are based on assumptions that the early Bolsheviks had a consistent policy on homosexuality. The pamphlet is cited as evidence that official policy backed emancipation, most forcefully expressed in Lauritsen and Thorstad, *The Early Homosexual Rights Movement (1864–1934)*, 62–63, and opposed by Karlinsky, "Russia's Gay Literature and Culture," 556n; also Wayne R. Dynes, *Homosexuality: A Research Guide* (New York, 1987), 141. The question of the distribution of Batkis's pamphlet within Russia remains open; a copy in German (translated "from a Russian manuscript") is held by the Russian National Library, St. Petersburg.

32. Her membership on the committee is noted in: World League for Sexual Reform, *Proceedings of the 2nd Congress (Copenhagen, 1928)* (Copenhagen, 1929), 9–10; idem, *Proceedings of the 3rd Congress (London, 1929)* (London, 1930). See also a letter addressed to Kollontai, from the WLSR chairman, Dr. J. H. Leunbach of Copenhagen, dated 4 August 1928, in which she is named on the committee along with Batkis and Kiev professor Nikolai Pasche-Oserski, RGASPI, f. 134, op. 1, d. 448, ll. 1–3.

33. A note to herself in her Party archive file suggests Kollontai may have had mixed feelings about her association with the sex question by 1923. She was pleased to be nominated to the British Society for Sex Psychology, but doubted whether the Soviet press would treat the appointment with anything but derision: "The English society for the study of sex psychology /British Soc. for Sex Psychology/ *has elected me an honorary member, on a level with* Havelock Ellis and others. I wondered: will it be published in our newspapers? After all, not many Russian women are nominated to scientific associations, even less so in 'proud' Britain . . . But then I realized, there's no need. Sex-psychology? What's that? Expert on sexual questions? 'Spets' in charge of 'sex matters'? Cynicism, vulgarizations. . ."; RGASPI, f. 134, op. 4, d. 17, l. 9.

34. She did, however, participate in the 1926 debate over family law reform; see Goldman, *Women, the State, and Revolution*, chapter 6.

35. Demands for a return to "control" in sexual life were heard in the debates over the new Soviet marriage code (1926–27) and in the moral and political panic following the Chubarov Alley gang rape scandal (1926) in Leningrad. On these events and on calls from below for control see Farnsworth, "Bolshevik Alternatives and the Soviet

Family," in Atkinson et al., *Women in Russia;* Wendy Z. Goldman, "Working-Class Women and the 'Withering Away' of the Family: Popular Responses to Family Policy," in *Russia in the Era of NEP,* eds. Sheila Fitzpatrick, Alexander Rabinowitch, and Richard Stites (Bloomington: Indiana University Press, 1991); Naiman, "The Case of Chubarov Alley," 1–30; Fitzpatrick, "Sex and Revolution," 252–78.

36. Alexander Lipschütz, *The Internal Secretions of the Sex Glands: The Problem of the "Puberty Gland"* (Cambridge, England: W. Heffer, 1924), 369. The experiment was reported in E. Steinach and R. Lichtenstern, "Umstimmung der Homosexualität durch Austausch der Purbertätsdrüsen," *Münch. mediz. Wochenschr.* 6 (1918).

37. Magnus Hirschfeld, *Künstliche Verjüngung. Künstliche Geschlechtsumwandlung. Die Entdeckungen Prof. Steinachs und ihre Bedeutung* (Berlin: Johndorff, 1920); on Hirschfeld's interaction with Steinach, see Sengoopta, "Glandular Politics," 445–73.

38. N. K. Kol'tsov, ed., *Omolozhenie,* 2 vols. (Moscow-Petrograd: Gosizdat, 1923); A. V. Nemilov et al., eds., *Omolozhenie v Rossii* (Leningrad: Meditsina, 1924). The cultural fascination with sex-gland science in Soviet Russia was captured in Mikhail Bulgakov's story "Sobach'e serdtse" (The Heart of a Dog, written in 1925; first Soviet publication, 1987), see M. O. Chudakova, "Posleslovie" in M. Bulgakov, *Sochineniia: Roman, povesti, rasskazy* (Minsk: Universitetskoe, 1988), 412–14; note also Mikhail Zolotonosov, "Masturbanizatsiia: 'Erogennye zony' sovetskoi kul'tury 1920–1930-kh godov," 97; Naiman, *Sex in Public,* 144–47.

39. Bekhterev described his note-taking with Mishutskii in "Polovye ukloneniia i izvrashcheniia v svete refleksologii," 720; he reconstructed his impressions of the interviews with legal documents on not less than seven men in "O polovom izvrashchenii, kak osoboi ustanovke polovykh refleksov," 167–70.

40. Protopopov, "Sovremennoe sostoianie voprosa o sushchnosti i proiskhozhdenii gomoseksualizma." This article appeared not in a Bekhterev-sponsored journal, but in the Commissariat of Enlightenment periodical *Nauchnaia meditsina,* in which Protopopov had already published two works in the previous three years.

41. Ia. I. Kirov, "K voprosu o geterotransplantsii pri gomoseksualizme," *Vrachebnoe delo* 20 (1928): 1587–90. "Heterotransplantation" refers not to sexual orientation, but the source of the tissue grafts used, that is external to the patient herself. On Protopopov's career, see Tikhon I. Iudin, *Ocherki istorii otechestvennoi psikhiatrii,* 426.

42. For descriptions of these implants used in rejuvenation therapy on women, see A. V. Nemilov, "Fiziologicheskie osnovy 'omolozheniia,'" in Nemilov et al., *Omolozhenie v Rossii,* 27–28.

43. Gannushkin's work in the psychiatric clinic of First Moscow State University, his supervision of young psychiatrists until his death (from natural causes) in 1933, and his contributions to the neuropsychiatric section of the Health Commissariat's Expert Medical Council, left a legacy focused on the problems of "minor psychiatry," the study of borderline states and personality adjustments. He preferred an exogenous etiology for homosexuality but acknowledged dissenting views respectfully. See P. M. Zinov'ev, "Osnovnye etapy nauchnoi raboty P. B. Gannushkina," *Sovetskaia nevropatologiia, psikhiatriia i psikhogigiena* 2, no. 5 (1933): 3–6; Iudin, *Ocherki istorii otechestvennoi psikhiatrii,* 406–7; A. O. Edel'shtein, "P. B. Gannushkin kak uchitel'," *Sovetskaia nevropatologiia, psikhiatriia i psikhogigiena* 2, no. 5 (1933): 7–9. On homosexuality: P. B. Gannushkin, *Klinika psikhopatii: Ikh statika, dinamika, sistematika* (Moscow: Sever, 1933), 116–17.

44. M. Ia. Sereiskii, *Problemy endokrinologii v psikhiatrii* (Moscow, 1925); M. O. Gurevich and M. Ia. Sereiskii, *Uchebnik psikhiatrii. S predisloviem P. B. Gannushkina* (Moscow-Leningrad: Gos. izdatel'stvo, 1928). Gurevich had led the team from the Institute of the Defective Child, which in 1919 had examined fourteen-year-old

monastic novice Ivan Volkov, the "victim" in the trial for "pederasty" of Bishop Palladii.

45. V. Rozhanovskii, "Sudebno-meditsinskaia ekspertiza v dorevoliutsionnoi Rossii i v SSSR," 75; Iudin, *Ocherki istorii otechestvennoi psikhiatrii*, 372, 406.

46. Krasnushkin and Kholzakova, "Dva sluchaia zhenshchin ubiits-gomoseksualistok," 105–6. In 1919, Dr. Kholzakova had, like M. O. Gurevich, participated in the team that examined the boy Volkov in the trial of Bishop Palladii. Her career is difficult to reconstruct; she published one study of schizophrenia in the 1930s with an adult male case history briefly mentioning an episode of "sodomy": N. G. Kholzakova, "Chastichnaia utrata (stoikoe snizhenie) trudo-sposobnosti pri shizofrenii," in *Problemy pogranichnoi psikhiatrii (Klinika i trudosposobnost'),* ed. T. A. Geier (Moscow-Leningrad: Gos. iz-vo biologicheskoi i medtsinskoi literatury, 1935).

47. In the mid-1920s, Hirschfeld's influence on Krasnushkin's work was at its height. Sexual intermediacy and same-sex desire are discussed in similarly Hirschfeldian terms in E. K. Krasnushkin, "Sudebno-psikhatricheskie ocherki. Posobie dlia iuristov i penitentsiarnykh rabotnikov [1925]," in *E. K. Krasnushkin: Izbrannye trudy,* ed. V. M. Banshchikov (Moscow: Medgiz, 1960), 114–15.

48. Krasnushkin and Kholzakova, "Dva sluchaia zhenshchin ubiits-gomoseksualistok," 105–6.

49. E. K. Krasnushkin, "K psikhologii i psikhopatologii polovykh pravonarushenii," in *Pravonarusheniia v oblasti seksual'nykh otnoshenii,* eds. E. K. Krasnushkin, G. M. Segal, and Ts. M. Fainberg (Moscow: Moszdravotdel, 1927), 14, 18.

50. N. P. Brukhanskii, *Materialy po seksual'noi psikhopatologii,* 6–8. Brukhanskii testified in one of the two cases observed in the V. P. Serbskii Forensic Psychiatry Institute and described by Krasnushkin and Kholzakova, the 1924 murder of Ol'ga Shch. by Valentina P.

51. N. P. Brukhanskii, *Sudebnaia psikhiatriia* (Moscow: M. i S. Sabashnikovy, 1928), 77.

52. Solovtsova and Orlov, "Gomoseksualizm i reaktsiia d-ra Manoilova," 547.

53. Solovtsova and Orlov, "Gomoseksualizm i reaktsiia d-ra Manoilova," 545–46. Solovtsova's contribution to this article consisted of a separate report on blood tests conducted on twenty subjects displaying "sexual anomalies" (from intersexual states to psychosexual variations, primarily homosexuality). She said nothing about the social origins or histories of these subjects. For another study of this type, see R. I. Livshits, "Reaktsiia d-ra Manoilova kak pokazatel' narusheniia sekretornoi funktsii polovykh zhelez pri seksual'nykh prestupleniiakh," *Leningradskii meditsinskii zhurnal* 2 (1925): 11–14.

54. Herzer, *Magnus Hirschfeld,* 44–45.

55. None mention Hirschfeld's visit in their publications, nor does it appear in any archival documents of the Health Commissariat.

56. Malmstad and Bogomolov, *Mikhail Kuzmin: A Life in Art,* 348. Kuzmin in his diary wrote that Hirschfeld was "dying to make [his] acquaintance," but the feeling was hardly reciprocated as the poet maintained a studied indifference to all explanations for homosexuality. Kuzmin's works had been warmly reviewed in several German newspapers before 1914, as Hirschfeld's scientific yearbook had noted: *Jahrbuch für Sexuelle Zwischenstufen* (1914): 69–70.

57. The Psychoneurological Institute was renamed "Psychoreflexological Institute" in 1919; Iudin, *Ocherki istorii otechestvennoi psikhiatrii,* 125, 128, 405; Nikiforov, *Bekhterev,* 234–44.

58. Bekhterev, "Polovye ukloneniia i izvrashcheniia v svete refleksologii," an article of 102 pages.

59. In that year, 100,000 copies of a 183-page medical textbook on women's sexual pathology for psychiatrists and gynecologists appeared: A. M. Sviadoshch, *Zhenskaia seksopatologiia* (Moscow: Meditsina, 1974).

60. Bekhterev, "Polovye ukloneniia i izvrashcheniia v svete refleksologii," 671, 745–46.

61. Bekhterev, "Polovye ukloneniia," 656–61.

62. A Bekhterev student, V. P. Osipov (1872–1947), assumed control of the Leningrad Institute for the Study of the Brain from 1929 until his death in 1947; Wortis, *Soviet Psychiatry*, 190. Osipov was more open than his teacher to endocrinological explanations of homosexuality (in the early 1920s), and he also valued Freud more highly than did Bekhterev. See V. P. Osipov, *Kurs obshchego ucheniia o dushevnykh bolezniakh*; idem, *Rukovodstvo po psikhiatrii* (Moscow-Leningrad: Gosizdat, 1931).

63. The journal was published from 1910 to 1914. "Homosexuality" featured in a discussion of Freud's biographical account of Leonardo da Vinci: V. S., "Freid o Leonardo-da-Vinchi," *Psikhoterapiia* 4 (1911): 195–203.

64. Martin Miller, *Freud and the Bolsheviks: Psychoanalysis in Imperial Russia and the Soviet Union* (New Haven: Yale University Press, 1998), 88–92.

65. Aleksandr Etkind, *Eros nevozmozhnogo: Istoriia psikhoanaliza v Rossii* (St. Petersburg: Meduza, 1993).

66. In Russia, a distinction was made between "major psychiatry" (*bol'shaia psikhiatriia*), dealing with aspects of insanity (later schizophrenia and other disorders requiring long-term institutionalization of the patient), and "minor psychiatry." Analogous disciplinary divisions were present in German, French, and American practice, see Henry Werlinder, *Psychopathy: A History of the Concepts: Analysis of the Origin and Development of a Family of Concepts in Psychopathology* (Uppsala: University of Uppsala, 1978), chapters 4, 5; Elizabeth Lunbeck, *The Psychiatric Persuasion: Knowledge, Gender, and Power in Modern America* (Princeton: Princeton University Press, 1994), 46–47.

67. Etkind, *Eros nevozmozhnogo*, 137–39. Bekhterev was more categorical than Gannushkin in his opposition to Freud, no doubt because of his institution-building in reflexology.

68. Krasnushkin and Rozenshtein attended "little Friday" seminars on psychoanalysis before 1914, see Magnus Ljunggren, "The Psychoanalytic Breakthrough in Russia on the Eve of the First World War," in *Russian Literature and Psychoanalysis*, ed. Daniel Rancour-Laff2rière (Amsterdam: 1989), 184. On Rozenshtein, W. Reich, "Psikhoanaliz kak estestvenno nauchnaia distsiplina," *Vestnik kommunisticheskoi akademii* 35–36 (1929): 345–350. Reich's peculiar assessment of the actual influence and appeal of psychoanalytic therapies in Soviet Russia was challenged there and in Europe, see Miller, *Freud and the Bolsheviks*, 91–92.

69. L. M. Rozenshtein, "Psikhiatricheskaia Germaniia," in *Sovetskaia meditsina v bor'be za zdorovye nervy: Sbornik statei i materialov*, eds. A. I. Miskinov, L. M. Rozenshtein, and L. A. Prozorov (Ul'ianovsk: Izd. Ul'ianovskogo kombinata PPP, 1926), 192. Kronfeld emigrated to the USSR in 1936, later working on "soft" (*miagkaia*) schizophrenia with Mark Sereiskii; Ingo-Wolf Kittel, "Zur historischen Rolle des Psychiaters und Psychotherapeuten Arthur Kronfeld in der frühen Sexualwissenschaft," *Sozialwissenschaftliche Sexualforschung* 2 (1989): 33–44.

70. The institute's reports of activity for 1928–29 ranked "questions of sexual life" as fifth among six mental hygiene issues in clinical services to workers, while plans for training Pioneer leaders included sessions on child sexuality and sex education; GARF, f. A406, op. 12, d. 2734, ll. 8–9.

71. Ella Winter, *Red Virtue: Human Relationships in the New Russia* (London: Victor Gollancz, 1933), 169. Winter apparently visited Russia just before publication of this book in 1933.

72. Shtess, "Sluchai zhenskogo gomoseksualizma," 1–19. A psychiatrist in Kiev displayed a thorough grounding in psychoanalytic concepts but concluded that there was no satisfactory "single psychological understanding of the essence of homosexuality," A. K. Sudomir, "K kazuistike i sushchnosti gomoseksual'nosti." I. S. Sumbaev, a lecturer (*dotsent*) at the Irkutsk psychiatric clinic of the Eastern Siberian Medical Institute, did not explicitly mention psychoanalysis, but spoke of "the language of the unconscious" and the " 'deep layers' of the mind," and employed free-association techniques, I. S. Sumbaev, "K psikhoterapii gomoseksualizma," *Sovetskaia psikhonevrologiia* 3 (1936): 59–68, (quotations, 59, 67). This article on "psychotherapy for [male] homosexuality" betrayed no awareness that sodomy had been recriminalized some two years before its publication.

73. This case is described in detail in Healey, "Evgeniia/Evgenii," 83–106. On Freud and hypnosis, see Etkind, *Eros nevozmozhnogo*, 143; Freud on homosexuality, see, e.g., Jeffrey Weeks, *Sexuality and Its Discontents. Meanings, Myths, and Modern Sexualities* (London: Routledge, 1985), 149–56.

74. At least ten primary psychiatric cases, featuring numerous additional individuals, appeared in Soviet medical journals and monographs: Osipov, *Kurs obshchego ucheniia*, two case histories, 355–56, 365; Shtess, "Sluchai zhenskogo gomoseksualizma" (one case history, with numerous partners); Skliar, "O proiskhozhdenii i sushchnosti gomoseksualizma" (one case history); Krasnushkin and Kholzakova "Dva sluchaia zhenshchin ubiits-gomoseksualistok" (two case histories of two pairs of women; one couple described in Brukhanskii, below); Edel'shtein, "K klinike transvestitizma" (one case history); Brukhanskii, *Materialy po seksual'noi psikhopatologii*, two case histories involving two pairs of women, 53–65; Riasentsev, "Dva sluchaia i praktiki," 152–56 (reviews of a case later discussed by Brukhanskii above); Kirov, "K voprosu o geterotransplantatsii pri gomoseksualizme" (one case); E. K. Krasnushkin, *Prestupniki psikhopaty*, one case history, 11–12. A biologist described a woman imprisoned in Leningrad for "same-sex attraction" and embezzlement in R. I. Livshits, "Reaktsiia d-ra Manoilova," 13. There are cases of individual "female homosexuals" in sexological surveys and pedagogic literature of the period as well.

75. Osipov, *Kurs obshchego ucheniia*, 365.

76. Skliar, "O proiskhozhdenii i sushchnosti gomoseksualizma," 1919.

77. Brukhanskii, *Materialy po seksual'noi psikhopatologii*, 59–60.

78. Krasnushkin and Kholzakova, "Dva sluchaia zhenshchin ubiits-gomoseksualistok," 107, 112, 115; Edel'shtein, "K klinike transvestitizma," 273–74.

79. Of the ten principal subjects of the studies enumerated in note 72 above, five were women who "passed" as men.

80. These were Evgeniia Fedorovna M. (described by Edel'shtein); a woman identified only as "P. A." (described by Skliar); and a female soldier (described by Osipov). The other passing women were a letter carrier (Fedosiia P., described by Brukhanskii) and the NEP-market trader known as "Aleksandr Pavlovich" (described by Shtess).

81. Izrail G. Gel'man, *Polovaia zhizn' sovremennoi molodezhi*, 119.

82. See, e.g., Shtess's NEP-market trader; and the 26-year-old woman imprisoned for embezzlement (*rastrata*) described as wearing a man's clothes and carrying "herself in a masculine manner," Livshits, "Reaktsiia d-ra Manoilova." For positive descriptions of the omnicompetent "active" female homosexual from a criminologist, see Orshanskii, "Polovye prestupleniia."

83. Kenneth M. Pinnow, "Making Suicide Soviet: Medicine, Moral Statistics, and the Politics of Social Science in Bolshevik Russia, 1920–1930" (Ph.D. diss., Columbia University, 1998), 178–95. Similar views were expressed about women's masturbation, A. B. Zalkind, *Polovoe vospitanie* (Moscow: Rabotnik prosveshcheniia, 1928), 47; and women's criminality in general, Brukhanskii, *Sudebnaia psikhiatriia*, 13.

84. Semashko, "Nuzhna li 'zhenstvennost'"?," 205–6.

85. Tarnovskii, *Izvrashchenie polovogo chuvstva*, 8–27.

86. Engelstein, *The Keys to Happiness*, 132, 164.

87. Bekhterev, "Lechenie vnusheniem prevratnykh polovykh vlechenii i onanizma"; idem, "O polovykh izvrashcheniiakh, kak patologicheskikh sochetatel'nykh refleksakh," 1–26. Similar silence on effeminacy prevails in two other case histories in S. Liass, "Izvrashchenie polovogo vlecheniia," *Obozrenie psikhiatrii, nevrologii i eksperimental'noi psikhologii* 6 (1898): 415–16. A rare explicit description of the "youth who tries to be feminine" appears in P. I. Kovalevskii, *Sudebnaia psikhiatriia* (St. Petersburg: M. Akinfiev & I. Leont'ev, 1902), 125.

88. Osipov, *Kurs obshchego ucheniia*, 354–55.

89. Belousov, "Sluchai gomoseksuala-muzhskoi prostitutki," 309–17.

90. G. R. "Protsessy gomoseksualistov"; Bekhterev, "O polovom izvrashchenii, kak osoboi ustanovke polovykh refleksov," 171; Belousov, "Sluchai gomoseksuala—muzhskoi-prostitutki." During the civil war in the town of Kamenets-Podol'sk, a provocatively effeminate homosexual man known as "Karolina Ivanovna" was arrested by the Cheka (on suspicion of disloyalty) even after turning in five former lovers who had supported Petliura's short-lived Ukrainian national regime. "Karolina" was transferred by Kursk city police to a psychiatric hospital: "The policeman accompanying the patient was incapable of explaining anything" about the case, and a psychiatrist kept him under observation for three weeks before concluding (following Krafft-Ebing) that no change in this "profoundly degenerate" case was possible. See S. P. Vysotskii, "Sluchai prevratnogo polovogo chuvstva," *Vestnik Kurskogo gubernskogo otdela zdravookhraneniia* 6–7 (1921): 9–11.

91. Brukhanskii, *Materialy po seksual'noi psikhopatologii*, 66–69; A. K. Lents, *Kriminal'nye psikhopaty (Sotsiopaty)* (Leningrad: Rabochii sud, 1927), 45–46.

92. A Dane in St. Petersburg in 1869 said, of a pederast-extortionist, "I understood . . . that he was prepared to offer himself for sodomy (*sebia predlozhit' dlia muzhelozhstva*); it was understood from his manner of addressing me, which had the appearance of feminine courtesy (*zhenskaia liubeznost'*)," Merzheevskii, *Sudebnaia ginekologiia*, 254. Associating effeminacy with sodomy may have been a European perception; elsewhere in Merzheevskii little effeminacy was reported, but sex roles were clearly divided into active (male) and passive (female) categories, e.g., a male bathhouse attendant was reported saying "[the male client] lies with me like with a woman, or orders me to do with him as with a woman, only in the anus," 238.

93. Bekhterev, "O polovom izvrashchenii, kak osoboi ustanovke polovykh refleksov," 170.

94. Protopopov, "Sovremennoe sostoianie voprosa o gomoseksualizme," 50. On anal intercourse among homosexuals, Osipov wrote: "Just as in normal intercourse one side plays the active and the other the passive role, so we find the same among pederasts, with the difference that in natural conditions the active role belongs to men, and the passive to women; while here both roles are filled by men," *Kurs obshchego ucheniia*, 353.

95. See entry under "*upotrebliat*ˣ" in D. A. Drummond and G. Perkins, *Dictionary of Russian Obscenities* (Oakland: Scythian, 1987), 77. A 1941 criminal investigation and

trial recorded defendants using the verb *ispol'zovat'* in this sense: case file of Andreevskii and two others (1941), ll. 29, 108 ob.

96. " 'Sodomy' and 'unnatural' intercourse inverted 'proper' relationships, by putting a woman in the dominant 'male' position, or another man in the passive 'female' position." Eve Levin, "Sexual Vocabulary in Medieval Russia" in Costlow et al., *Sexuality and the Body in Russian Culture*, 45.

97. In one case, of a patient who fellated bathhouse attendants, an attendant "supposedly used him in the mouth"; Bekhterev, "Lechenie vnusheniem prevratnykh polovykh vlechenii i onanizma," 8.

98. For example, "I gave in to him, and we committed a sexual act. First, I took the role of a woman, then he did," case file of Andreevskii and two others (1941), l. 16; "We became close and then committed acts of sodomy . . . First he used me, and then I, him," ll. 57–58; see also in this complete case record ll. 29, 57 ob., 100, 108 ob.; "Pavlov, for whom the active role was physically impossible [because of a war wound], was the object of Shelgunov, but nevertheless his active strivings he expressed in his emotional ties with Shelgunov, who on this level played the role of a woman (*igral rol' zhenshchiny*)"; sentence of Bezborodov and eleven others (1935), ll. 241–42.

99. Tarnvoskii, *Izvrashchenie polovogo chuvstva*, 63–64; Protopopov, "Sovremennoe sostoianie voprosa o sushchnosti i proiskhozhdenii gomoseksualizma," 56; Osipov, *Kurs obshchego ucheniia*, 354–55; Lents, *Kriminal'nye psikhopaty (Sotsiopaty)*, 45.

100. Later examples of the desexualized male homosexual appeared in a case history discussed by Brukhanskii, *Materialy po seksual'noi psikhopatologii*, 66–69, and as a "latent homosexual" (*latentnyi gomoseksualist;* a rare early use of the term in Russian) in Sumbaev, "K psikhoterapii gomoseksualizma." In both cases the psychiatrist appeared to be urging sympathy for the patient who had restrained perverse impulses or was capable of rehabilitation.

101. See, e.g., Shtess, "Sluchai zhenskogo gomoseksualizma," 9 (patient's affair with Al'ga, who leaves to get married); Edel'shtein, "K klinike transvestitizma," 274 (S.'s affair with male coworker); Krasnushkin and Kholzakova, "Dva sluchaia zhenshchin ubiits gomoseksualistok," 117 (Ol'ga's decision to get married drives Valentina P. to murder her).

102. Krasnushkin and Kholzakova, "Dva sluchaia zhenshchin ubiits-gomoseksualistok" (two masculinized female homosexuals murdered their partners); Shtess, "Sluchai zhenskogo gomoseksualizma," 9 (patient beats partner to point of hospitalization); Kirov, "K voprosu o geterotransplantatsii pri gomoseksualizme," 1588 (patient "scornful" of "*baby*" [women] she pursued).

103. Krasnushkin and Kholzakova, "Dva sluchaia zhenshchin ubiits-gomoseksualistok," 116.

104. These fits were said to be caused by epilepsy or degenerative neuropathies, Tarnovskii, *Izvrashchenie polovogo chuvstva*, 27–31.

105. Bekhterev, "Polovye ukloneniia i izvrashcheniia v svete refleksologii," 731–34, 739.

106. V. M. Bekhterev, "Lechenie vnusheniem prevratnykh polovykh vlechenii i onanizma," 1–11; for doubts in effeminacy-linked cases, see idem, "Ob izvrashchenii i uklonenii polovogo vlecheniia," in *Polovoi vopros v svete nauchnogo znaniia*, ed. V. F. Zelenin (Moscow: Gosizdat, 1926). Protopopov described one manly sailor who said he preferred "men who are masculine in appearance and do not try to make women of themselves." Protopopov believed his "pederasty" was acquired in the single-sex marine environment and believed such men would resume heterosexual relations if exposed to women, "Sovremennoe sostoianie voprosa o sushchnosti i proiskhozhdenii gomoseksualizma," 51, 56.

107. Lents, *Kriminal'nye psikhopaty. (Sotsiopaty)*, 21, 45–46.

108. Approximately forty-seven case histories of male homosexuals appeared in Soviet Russia's psychiatric publications (central journals, edited collections, and monographs) in the 1920s, if one includes seventeen out of the ninety-five men arrested in the 1921 Petrograd "pederasts' club" raid (Bekhterev, "O polovom izvrashchenii, kak osoboi ustanovke polovykh refleksov," seven cases; and Protopopov "Sovremennoe sostoianie voprosa o sushchnosti i proiskhozhdenii gomoseksualizma," ten cases). Psychiatric cases of male homosexuality after 1923 appeared generally in *forensic* publications and described criminals, usually youths whose sexuality was discussed in contexts of *bezprizornost'* (homelessness) or institutional care.

109. Only one Soviet psychiatrist, Bekhterev, apparently accumulated enough anecdotal data—much of it dating before 1917—to assert convincing claims of authority on sexual deviance.

110. Osipov, *Kurs obshchego ucheniia*, 356.

111. Bekhterev, "Ob izvrashchenii i uklonenii polovogo vlecheniia"; Krasnushkin and Kholzakova, "Dva sluchaia zhenshchin ubiits-gomoseksualistok"; Levko Kvint and Robert Geshvandtner, "Pro germafroditizm i gomoseksualizm," *Ukrainskii medichnyi arkhiv* 2–3 (1927): 1–19; Brukhanskii, *Materialy po seksual'noi psikhopatologii*; Sudomir, "K kazuistike i sushchnosti gomoseksual'nosti"; Solovtsova and Orlov, "Gomoseksualizm i reaktsiia d-ra Manoilova."

112. For Hirschfeld's research, see James Steakley, *"Per scientiam ad justitiam:* Magnus Hirschfeld and the Sexual Politics of Innate Homosexuality," in Rosario, ed., *Science and Homosexualities;* the U.S. Committee produced a report: George W. Henry, *Sex Variants: A Study of Homosexual Patterns* (New York: Hoeber, 1941); on the committee's activity, see Jennifer Terry, *An American Obsession: Science, Medicine, and Homosexuality in Modern Society* (Chicago: University of Chicago Press, 1999), chapter 6.

113. On social hygiene's use of questionnaires to study sexological issues and prostitution, see Solomon, "The Expert and the State in Russian Public Health," 202. On suicide studies conducted by forensic physicians and moral statisticians, Pinnow, "Making Suicide Soviet."

114. Pinnow makes this argument for forensic medicine in "Making Suicide Soviet," chapter 2, "Cutting and Counting the Suicide: The Individual and the Social Body in Soviet Forensic Medical Practice." Medical education in the 1920s promoted the ideal of the "physician-sociologist," see Solomon, "The Expert and the State in Russian Public Health."

115. "We [only] had on hand a rather elderly male rhesus, of whose testicles the seminal function was impossible to guarantee." M. M. Zavadovskii, "Issledovanie semennika gomoseksualista," *Trudy po dimanike razvitiia (Prodolzhenie "Trudov laboratorii eksperim. biologii Mosk. Zooparka")* 6 (1931): 66.

116. Kirov, "K voprosu o geterotransplantatsii pri gomoseksualizme," 1589. Two surgeons in Tashkent noted that it was rarely possible "to obtain the transplant tissue from a man" (meaning, human testicular tissue) yet they insisted that "therapy for homosexuality" was technically within the reach of surgery. Only a few "technical failures" in the procedure still needed to be addressed, see M. A. Zakharchenko and N. S. Pereshivkin, "Po povodu khirurgicheskogo lecheniia gomoseksualizma u muzhchin," *Novaia khirurgiia* 11 (1930): 24–29.

117. Thus both Western and Soviet human sex-hormone study concentrated on existing maternity clinics as sites for gathering hormones from women. On Dutch research, see Oudshoorn, *Beyond the Natural Body.* Soviet work with hormones, derived

from the urine of pregnant women, culminated in the promotion of a urine-based drug, "gravidan," developed by A. A. Zamkov, from 1933 to 1937 the director of a "Scientific Research Institute of Urogravidanotherapy" in Moscow. Thousands received injections of gravidan, including author Maksim Gor'kii, party luminary Clara Zetkin, and Politburo member Valerian Kuibyshev; see Zolotonosov, "Masturbanizatsiia," 97; Naiman, *Sex in Public*, 290–91.

118. Hirschfeld had referred (presumably unhappy) homosexual patients to Richard Mühsam for testicular graft therapy, with mixed success; by 1926 Mühsam had given up the procedure as only temporarily effective. Hirschfeld admitted reluctantly in the late 1920s that gland transplant therapy had been " 'greatly overvalued' " earlier in the decade; Sengoopta, "Glandular Politics," 465n, 468–69.

CHAPTER SIX

1. The history of Soviet antireligious campaigns is underdeveloped. Confessional viewpoints are cataloged in D. V. Pospielovsky, *A History of Soviet Atheism in Theory and Practice, and the Believer*, 3 vols. (London: Macmillan, 1987–88). An early secular interpretation from published sources is Curtiss, *The Russian Church and the Soviet State, 1917–1940*. For an institutional history, using new archival materials from Moscow and Iaroslavl', Daniel Peris, *Storming the Heavens: The Soviet League of the Militant Godless* (Ithaca: Cornell University Press, 1998). An excellent discussion of resistance to these campaigns is William B. Husband, "Soviet Atheism and Russian Orthodox Strategies of Resistance, 1917–1932," *Journal of Modern History* 70, no. 1 (1998): 74–107.

2. Sex as a theme in the movement's agitation deserves further study. The first issue of its journal relayed stories of monastic storehouses groaning with grain and wine, and tied to the sexual appetites of monks and abbesses. One archimandrite hoarded "several dozen extremely uncensored postcards" along with luxurious food; others, "corrupt children" and "organize orgies" in monasteries. Exhumations of infant skeletons accompanied the closure of convents. "Pod flagom religii; Za monastyrskoi stenoi," *Revoluutsiia i tserkov'* 1 (1919): 22–26. In the 1920s, the movement's central organ, *Bezbozhnik*, confined discussions of sexuality to a hygiene-related stream of stories (focusing on reproduction, especially the novel discoveries about the sex glands). After the civil war, stories about sexual disorders among the religious were relegated to a back-page column for courtroom reportage. Local antireligious press, more populist in tone, (for example, Moscow's *Bezbozhnik u stanka*) combined innuendo with prudery. The Justice Commissariat's weekly review also carried reports of religious crime in the early 1920s. For a general view of sex crime as a "professional crime" of monks and clerics, see M. Sheinman, *Religioznost' i prestupnost'*, 50–58.

3. N. P., "Monakhi pred sudom v roli razvratitlei maloletnikh i nesovershennoletnikh," 14.

4. S. N., "Monastyri—pritony razvrata—pri svete sovetskogo suda (Protsess arkhimandrita Sergiia, nastoiatelia Sretenskogo monastyria v Moskve)," 19. In this case, staged as a show trial in a workers' club in Moscow in late May 1922 (on the eve of the new criminal code), Archimandrite Sergii was officially only charged with "minor assaults," "because Kurtasova [his victim] is an adult woman" who entered voluntarily into a sexual liaison with him. Despite this weakness of the prosecution's case, the trial lasted two days and exposed the "monstrous refinements" of Sergii's sexual tastes with women. For the preponderance of heterosexual cases, Sheinman, *Religioznost' i prestupnost'*, 52–55.

5. Sheila Fitzpatrick, "Ascribing Class: The Construction of Social Identity in Soviet Russia," *Journal of Modern History* 65 (1993): 745–70. On the Stalin constitution, see

J. Arch Getty, "State and Society under Stalin: Constitutions and Elections in the 1930s," *Slavic Review* 50, no. 1 (1991): 18−35.

6. N. P., "Monakhi pred sudom v roli razvratitelei," 14.

7. N. P., "Monakhi pred sudom v roli razvratitelei.

8. Such a defense was possibly advanced by a Leningrad deacon in a 1927 show trial, who apparently claimed he himself was "a victim" (of what was not stated): Al. Kh-ov, "Delo 'sviatoi troitsy' (Pokazatel'nyi protsess v Okhtenskom Dome Proseshcheniia v Leningrade)," *Bezbozhnik*, 4 September 1927, 3. No information on de-ense claims in same-sex clerical sex cases appeared in K. Petrova, "Protsess d'iakona Tkachenko (Gor. Vladikavkaz)," *Bezbozhnik*, 16 October 1927, 5; "Sviatye razvratniki," *Bezbozhnik*, 12 November 1928, 6; F. U-v, "Ikh 'kul'tura,'" *Bezbozhnik*, 20 December 1930, 8.

9. He declared the chief defendant "mentally healthy." "There is only senile per-versity [*starcheskaia izvrashchennost'*], a high degree of depravity [*raspushchennost'*]": Kh-ov, "Delo 'sviatoi troitsy.'" These phrases separated the defendant from the sexual psychopath who might be forgiven his transgressions as signs of an illness. The defen-dant was thus left with his moral judgment and criminal responsibility intact. Orshan-skii read widely in Western sexology and had written about these issues for a domestic audience; see L. G. Orshanskii, "Polovye prestupleniia," in Zhizhilenko and Orshanskii, eds., *Polovye prestupleniia.*

10. Ordinary "open" trials took place in courtrooms, spatially and symbolically humble places; "show" trials were often mounted in places of popular entertainment, such as workers' clubs, theaters, and "houses of enlightenment." For examples of justice brought to places of entertainment to promote Bolshevik values, see Stephen Kotkin, *Magnetic Mountain: Stalinism as a Civilization* (Berkeley: University of California Press, 1995), 256−58.

11. Petrova, "Protsess d'iakona Tkachenko."

12. Petrova, "Protsess d'iakona Tkachenko."

13. Kh-ov, "Delo 'sviatoi troitsy.'" Sexual interference had reportedly taken place with boys between six and twelve years of age, and with one girl ten years of age.

14. A 1930 show trial of a cleric for the defloration of a sixteen-year-old girl netted a similar five-year sentence, but with five years' banishment from Moscow province after release; see Rybtsov, "Po zaslugam," *Bezbozhnik*, 6 January 1930, 8.

15. Petrova, "Protsess d'iakona Tkachenko." In this case, it was found that Tka-chenko's syphilis had long since passed the infectious stage, but it was claimed he had endangered parishioners during religious services (via shared communion vessels). He was given a four-month sentence with "compulsory therapy," presumably for syph-ilis.

16. The Soviet release of a popular Hungarian two-part film entitled *Sodom i Go-morra* (Sodom and Gomorrah) may have inspired Iaroslavskii and others to enter this discussion; see an advertisement for the picture, which opened in Petrograd in late April 1923, in *Krasnaia gazeta*, 22 April 1923, 7.

17. E. Iaroslavskii, "Sodomitskie greshniki i sodomitskie pravedniki," in E. Iaros-lavskii, *Protiv religii i tserkvi* (Moscow: Bezbozhnik, 1932−33), 5: 114−18. The essay was first published in *Bezbozhnik*, 22 April 1923. Daniel Peris contrasts Iaroslavskii's "culturalist" approach to antireligious campaigning with the impatient styles of his rivals; Iaroslavskii expected secularization to be a long educational process and that to succeed the movement for atheism would need leaders with wide historical, cultural, and scientific knowledge. See Peris, *Storming the Heavens*, 50−51.

18. RGASPI, f. 89, op. 4, d. 6, ll. 119-21 (Iaroslavskii's notes of his contacts with

Masliankovskii). Iaroslavskii's original article did in fact refer with sarcasm to the sexual significance of *poznat'*, and it placed Lot's offer to the Sodomites of his virgin daughters as a substitute for the angel-visitors within the context of "the customs of hospitality."

19. E. Iaroslavskii, "V zashchitu biblii protiv sodomlian," *Bezbozhnik*, 9 May 1923, 3, When reprinted in 1930, the last four sentences of this passage and two similar passages were not reproduced: Iaroslavskii, *Protiv religii i tserkvi*, 5: 370–71.

20. "Sodom i Gomorra," *Bezbozhnik u stanka* 8 (1923): 10–11. Accompanying cartoons portrayed Lot and the angels as corpulent and cowardly; the Sodomites and their "disgusting" sexual tastes were not represented in these illustrations. On the aggressively "interventionist" campaigning style at *Bezbozhnik u stanka*, see Peris, *Storming the Heavens*, 50–51.

21. The first criminal code of Soviet Azerbaidzhan was approved in December 1922 and came into force on 1 February 1923; it prohibited "sodomy" (*muzhelozhstvo*) unlike the SFSR code; see M. S. Khalafov et al., eds., *Istoriia gosudarstva i prava Azerbaidzhanskoi SSR (1920–1934 gg.)* (Baku: Iz-vo ELM, 1973), 373. Evidence that "an article on sodomy" existed in Soviet Georgia by 1928, Iu. Kratter, "Rukovodstvo sudebnoi meditsiny. Dlia vrachei i studentov. Ch. IV. Sudebnaia seksologiia. Avtorizovannyi perev. so 2-go nemetsk. izd. pod red. i s dopolneniiami Ia. Leibovicha (Prodolzhenie)," *Sudebno-meditsinskaia ekspertiza* 10 (1928): 58.

22. Not all republican codes formally set apart "Crimes in the field of sexual relations" under a specific subheading, as the RSFSR code of 1922 did.

23. The most sensitive study of the *bacha* (plural *bachi*) is I. Baldauf, *Die Knabenliebe in Mittelasien: Bačabozlik* (Berlin: Das Arabische Buch, 1988). The *bachi* tradition was the local variant of a more general Asian Islamic pattern of love between men and youths, Murray and Roscoe, *Islamic Homosexualities*, 14–54, 204–221. For tsarist medical views, Tarnovskii, *Izvrashchenie polovogo chuvstva*, 50–51; Shvarts, "K voprosu o priznakakh privychnoi passivnoi pederastii (Iz nabliudenii v aziatskoi chasti g. Tashkenta)," 816–18. For European reports, see Hirschfeld, *Die Homosexualität des Mannes und des Weibes*, 600. For a sanitized description of *bachi* as simply dancers, Elizabeth Bacon, *Central Asians under Russian Rule: A Study in Culture Change* (Ithaca: Cornell University Press, 1966), 88. The story of the *bachi* is ripe for investigation from a culturally sensitive queer theoretical perspective.

24. N. D. Durmanov, *Ugolovnoe pravo. Osobennaia chast'. Prestupleniia, sostavliaiushchie perezhitki rodogo byta* (Moscow: Iuridicheskoe izd. NKIu SSSR, 1938), 68.

25. A similar chapter of customary crimes was appended to the RSFSR criminal code in 1928. It was directed at non-European minorities within the Russian republic's borders, (primarily in Kazakhstan, until 1936 an autonomous republic within the RSFSR), but it was silent about sodomy or same-sex offenses. For a pioneering study of gender and "survivals of primitive custom," which ignores the *bachi* and antisodomy legislation, see Gregory J. Massell, *The Surrogate Proletariat: Moslem Women and Revolutionary Strategies in Soviet Central Asia, 1919–1929* (Princeton: Princeton University Press, 1974). On the effects of gender campaigns inside the Uzbek party, see Douglas Northrop, "Languages of Loyalty: Gender, Politics, and Party Supervision in Uzbekistan, 1927–41," *Russian Review* 59, no. 2 (2000): 179–200.

26. The 1926 edition of the RSFSR article stated the following: "Compulsion of a woman to enter into a sexual liaison by a person in relation to whom the woman is materially or professionally dependent, [is punished by] deprivation of freedom for up to five years." *Ugolovnyi kodeks RSFSR (1926). Sobranie zakonov i rasporiazhenii raboche-krest'ianskogo pravitel'stva SSSR* (1926), no. 80, item 600, article 154. The Uz-

bek text read as follows: "Compulsion of a man to sodomy [*besakalbazstvo*] by a person in relation to whom the victim is materially or professionally dependent, or is in the guardianship of, entails deprivation of freedom for up to five years." Article 278 of "Ugolovnyi kodeks Uzbekhskoi SSR" in D. S. Karev, *Ugolovnoe zakonodatel'stvo SSSR i soiuznykh respublik. Sbornik* (Moscow: Iuridicheskaia literatura, 1957), 217. The same code prohibited the sexual harassment of women in article 215.

27. Karev, *Ugolovnoe zakonodatel'stvo SSSR i soiuznykh respublik,* article 283. Article 217 of the 1926 Uzbek code prohibited the same offense against women. Cf. articles 171 and 155 of the 1922 and 1926 RSFSR criminal codes respectively, against procurement of women for prostitution.

28. The Turkmen criminal code forbade anal intercourse ("unnatural sexual intercourse in the form of sodomy") with children or minors (article 157 of the Turkmen SSR criminal code), maintenance of *bachi* or dens for their exploitation (article 163), and the conclusion of contracts between parents and procurers (article 164); "Ugolovnyi kodeks Turkmenskoi SSR," Karev, *Ugolovnoe zakonodatel'stvo SSSR,* 431. The practice may also have been silently pursued in Islamic regions of the RSFSR; statistical tables of criminal convictions prepared in the 1930s–40s listed *bachebazstvo* (keeping *bachi*) as a discrete crime under the heading "survivals of primitive custom," despite the absence of this offense in the RSFSR criminal code. No figures were ever entered against this category, GARF, f. A353, op. 16, d. 19, ll. 24–29 ob., d. 23, ll. 31–34 ob., d. 27, ll. 41–42 ob., d. 31, ll. 99–104 ob., d. 38, ll. 123–126 ob.

29. Liublinskii, *Prestupleniia v oblasti polovykh otnoshenii,* 132–33.

30. Frenkel', *Polovye prestupleniia,* 3, 6, 12.

31. Zhizhilenko merely acknowledged the existence of such differences in a footnote in his "Polovye prestupleniia. Iuridicheskie ocherki," 10.

32. Pfäfflin, *Mitteilungen des Wissenschaftlich-humanitären Komitees, 1926–1933,* 147.

33. Sheila Fitzpatrick, "Cultural Revolution as Class War," in *The Cultural Front: Power and Culture in Revolutionary Russia* (Ithaca: Cornell University Press, 1992), 138–39.

34. See Sheila Fitzpatrick, ed., *Cultural Revolution in Russia, 1928–31* (Bloomington: Indiana University Press, 1978); Katerina Clark, *Petersburg: Crucible of Cultural Revolution* (Cambridge, Mass.: Harvard University Press, 1995).

35. Krasnushkin and Kholzakova, "Dva sluchaia zhenshchin ubiits-gomoseksualistok," 105–20. The cases, and the Russians' problematic use of Hirschfeld's term "transvestite" as denoting *all* sexual intermediaries including homosexuals, are discussed in chapter 5.

36. A. O. Edel'shtein, "K klinike transvestitizma," 273–82, and V. A. Belousov, "Sluchai gomoseksuala-muzhskoi prostitutki," 309–17. Belousov's criticism of Krasnushkin was entirely implicit in his diagnosis; he acknowledged Krasnushkin's "valuable instructions" on this case.

37. Belousov, "Sluchai gomoseksuala-muzhskoi prostitutki," 316. Belousov, in contrast to Edel'shtein, vaguely favored a constitutional predisposition for homosexuality, citing Kraepelin, but he devoted almost all his attention to the social factors generating P.'s "psychopathy." Like Edel'shtein, Belousov eschewed any mention of homosexuality's supposed links with aesthetic talent, or of historical figures said to be homosexual, or of popular prejudice against homosexuals, all featured in the Krasnushkin and Kholzakova 1926 article.

38. For an equally pessimistic view of the social value of the "homosexual," arguing vehemently against the existence of a "special type of normal person with only a partic-

ular, abnormal sexual inclination" (the Hirschfeld apology for homosexuals), see Skliar, "O proiskhozhdenii i sushchnosti gomoseksualizma," 1919–23. This Astrakhan' psychiatrist also posited a psychopathic etiology for same-sex love.

39. Belousov, "Sluchai gomoseksuala-muzhskoi prostitutki," 317 (original emphasis). Belousov viewed thirty-two-year-old P.'s thefts as an "attribute of the particular phase of his career," as an older and less desirable male prostitute; the psychiatrist likened this to thefts committed by "female heterosexual prostitutes" in the same age bracket.

40. E. K. Krasnushkin, "K psikhologii i psikhopatologii polovykh pravonarushenii," in Krasnushkin et al., *Pravonarusheniia v oblasti seksual'nykh otnoshenii,* 17–18; idem, *Prestupniki psikhopaty* (Moscow: Izd-vo pervogo Moskovskogo gos. universiteta, 1929), 10–12, 23–25.

41. The request, for both surgical intervention and the right to change his civilly registered sex, had been relayed to Moscow from the Tatar republic's own Commissariat of Justice (the Tatar ASSR was an autonomous republic within the RSFSR). In Moscow, RSFSR Commissar of Justice N. M. Ianson, and the collegium of his commissariat, had asked the Health Commissariat to comment on the issues raised by the citizen's request. (Justice Commissariat archives do not record these transactions.) The earliest documented European case of surgical intervention to transform a man into a woman was undertaken in 1930–31, resulting in the death of the patient, Danish artist Einar Wegener; see Hausman, *Changing Sex: Transsexualism, Technology and the Idea of Gender,* 15–19. Sex-reassignment techniques considered successful were not devised until the late 1940s and early 1950s in the United States and Europe; Soviet doctors reportedly began conducting similar procedures in the 1960s: David Tuller, *Cracks in the Iron Closet: Travels in Gay and Lesbian Russia* (Boston & London: Faber & Faber, 1996), 158. For late–Soviet era case histories of transsexualism, see G. S. Vasil'chenko, *Chastnaia seksopatologiia* (Moscow: Meditsina, 1983), 2: 53–66.

42. Leibovich's intervention: GARF, f. A482, op. 25, d. 575, l. 1. (*Zasedaniia Nevropsikhiatricheskoi komissii U. M. S., 2/I-1929 g. Protokol no. 1*). For regulations permitting the change of sex shown in identity documents of hermaphrodites after medical examination, see "Ob ispolnenii zapisei v registratsionnykh knigakh rozhdeniia pola imeni i familii germafroditov" (a circular of the NKVD RSFSR, no. 146 of 22 April 1926), in Ia. Leibovich, *Sudebnaia ginekologiia: Rukovodstvo dlia vrachei i iuristov* (Khar'kov: Iurdicheskoe iz-vo Narkomiusta USSR, 1928), 126–27.

43. It is not clear who replaced the term "hermaphrodite" with "transvestite," but the presidium instructed Expert Medical Council secretary L. Ia. Brusilovskii (a psychiatrist) to write a report for Commissar Semashko, justifying a "mixed commission of doctors and jurists" to do more work on "transvestites"; GARF, f. A482, op. 25, d. 479, l. 18 ob. (*Zasedaniia prezidiuma U.M.S., 29/I-1929 g.*).

44. Jay Prosser, "Transsexuals and the Transsexologists: Inversion and the Emergence of Transsexual Subjectivity," in Bland and Doan, *Sexology in Culture: Labelling Bodies and Desires.*

45. GARF, f. A482, op. 25, d. 478, l. 85; Edel'shtein, "K klinike transvestitizma."

46. GARF, f. A482, op. 25, d. 478, l. 85 ob. The stenographic record does not indicate which passages Brusilovskii read, but Evgeniia's "History" used several terms—excluding "transvestite"—to refer to herself: intermediate sex, pseudo-hermaphrodite, homosexual.

47. Kol'tsov perhaps treated his patient with the drug "Spermokrin" marketed by the Health Commissariat's Institute for Experimental Endocrinology; for an advertisement, see GARF, f. A406, op. 12, d. 2223, l. 215 (and see fig. 13). He was well acquainted with the Steinach rejuvenation techniques and publicized them in his journal *Priroda;*

see Bernstein, "What Everyone Should Know about Sex," 67–71. The biologist in 1916 founded the Moscow Institute of Experimental Biology, remaining its director until 1938; Mark B. Adams, "Science, Ideology and Structure: The Kol'tsov Institute, 1900–1970," in *The Social Context of Soviet Science*, ed. Linda L. Lubrano and Susan Gross Solomon (Boulder, Col.: Westview Press, 1980).

48. GARF, f. A482, op. 25, d. 478, ll. 85 ob.-86.

49. The status of "homosexuals" in the Red Army during the early Soviet regime was not explicitly codified. Until a 1925 Law on Obligatory Military Service regularized recruitment policies, little thought was probably given to screening sexual deviants out of the military. Provisions under the 1927 "Decree on Military Crimes" regulated the moral behavior of servicemen, calling for "the observance of the rules of military honor and politeness, and also of the personal dignity of the serviceman." It is not difficult to imagine such language being applied to sex acts between men, or between women, uncovered in the military. On recruitment, see von Hagen, *Soldiers in the Proletarian Dictatorship*, 206–10; on military crimes decree ("Polozhenie o voinskikh prestupleniiakh TsIK i SNK SSSR 27 iiulia 1927g."), V. M. Chkhivadze, *Sovetskoe voenno-ugolovnoe pravo* (Moscow, 1948), 357–59.

50. GARF, f. A482, op. 25, d. 478, l. 86.

51. GARF, f. A482, op. 25, d. 478, l. 86 ob.

52. On epidemiological metaphors used to describe disciplinary and political problems in the Red Army, Pinnow, "Making Suicide Soviet," chapters 4 and 5. A Leningrad military psychiatrist used "mental infection" (*psikhicheskaia zaraza*) to describe the demoralizing effect psychopathic personalities had on the army: N. A. Iurman, *Instruktivnye materialy po profilaktike dushevnykh boleznei v krasnoi armii* (Leningrad: Izd. Voenno-sanitarnogo upravlenie LVO, 1930), 17. The only mention of sexual perversion in this manual was embedded in a sample questionnaire for doctors examining men accused of *military crimes:* "Data on behavior . . . 5. Sexual deviations (masturbation, sexual perversions)," 32. A contrasting view was offered by a Smolensk psychiatrist, who thought "sociopsychopathic" youths could be cured by army service; V. I. Pliashkevich, "Psikhiatricheskaia ekspertiza voennoobiazannykh," in *Trudy psikhiatricheskoi kliniki (Gedeonovka). Vyp. 1*, ed. R. I. Belkin (Smolensk: Smolenskii gos. universitet, 1930), 175–76. Both authors gave first priority to violent crime, alcoholism, and suicide generated by mental defects. On concern over alcohol abuse, suicide and discipline in the military, see von Hagen, *Soldiers in the Proletarian Dictatorship*, 193–95, 305–8.

53. GARF, f. A482, op. 25, d. 478, l. 86.

54. GARF, f. A482, op. 25, d. 478, ll. 85 ob., 86.

55. GARF, f. A482, op. 25, d. 478, l. 86.

56. The procedure laid down in 1926 for altering a citizen's registered sex was in the domain of forensic gynecologists (such as Leibovich, whose dispute with psychiatrists over the framework for this discussion has been mentioned above). It was intended solely to accommodate hermaphrodites identified by these experts. It apparently fell into disuse, perhaps during the 1940s; another decree authorizing such bureaucratic sex changes for hermaphrodites was issued in 1974. On the fascinating tangles of red tape this generated in late-Soviet life, see I. V. Golobueva, *Germafroditizm (Klinika, diagnostika, lechenie)* (Moscow: Meditsina, 1980).

57. GARF, f. A482, op. 25, d. 478, ll. 86–86 ob. No other traces of this case have yet come to light in Moszdrav or Commissariat of Health archives.

58. Sex transformation in animals, based on the manipulation of gland functions, was the object of scholarly research and popular fascination in the Soviet 1920s. See

Bernstein, "What Everyone Should Know about Sex," 64–130. The "creation of certain organs or the removal of superfluous ones (creating an artificial vagina, removing a hypertrophied [*sic*] clitoris)" would in fact be undertaken, supposedly with success, on Soviet hermaphrodites as early as 1932; see E. E. Rozenblium, M. G. Serdiukov, and V. M. Smol'ianinov, *Sudebno-meditsinskaia akushersko-ginekologicheskaia ekspertiza* (Moscow: Sovetskoe zakonodatel'stvo, 1935), 208–10. For an even earlier report of a failed operation to produce an "artificial vagina" (in unclear circumstances), N. N. Malinovskii, "Redkoe pozdnee oslozhnenie posle operatsii obrazovaniia iskusstvennogo vlagalishcha," *Kazanskii meditsinskii zhurnal* 8 (1928): 763–66. On the origins of Western medical paternalism that counseled (and continues to promote) these interventions, see Alice Domurat Dreger, *Hermaphrodites and the Medical Invention of Sex* (Cambridge, Mass.: Harvard University Press, 1998).

59. GARF, f. A482, op.25, d. 478, ll. 86 ob.-87.

60. GARF, f. A482, op.25, d. 478, l. 80 ob.

61. Mark Sereiskii, "Gomoseksualizm," *Bol'shaia meditsinskaia entsiklopediia*, 1st ed. (Moscow, 1929): 7: 668–672; idem, "Gomoseksualizm," *Bol'shaia sovetskaia entsiklopediia*, 1st ed. (Moscow: Sovetskaia entsiklopediia, 1930): 17: 593–96. "G" is the fourth letter of the Russian alphabet, and the first Soviet volumes of these encyclopedias had only been published. Of course, the deliberate decision to include articles on homosexuality was not coincidental, but reflected the utopianism of the era. Production of subsequent volumes for the rest of the alphabet spanned the 1930s, and articles headed under letters later in the alphabet reflected changing political views. Thus a 1940 article headed "Sexual Life," under letter "P" (*Polovaia zhizn'*), would be highly critical of libertarianism, while an article under "Sexual Anomalies" (*Polovye anomalii*), promised at the end of A. Abrikosov, "Germafroditizm," in *Bol'shaia sovetskaia entsiklopediia* (Moscow: Sovetskaia entsiklopediia, 1929), 16: 439–41, failed to appear eleven years later, readers consulting that heading were redirected to see the article on "Sexual Life"—but instead of anomalies, "perversions" were discussed. See D. Gorfin, "Polovaia zhizn'," in *Bol'shaia sovetskaia entsiklopediia*, 1st ed. (Moscow: OGIZ RSFSR, 1940), 46: 163–69.

62. I cannot agree with Simon Karlinsky, who interprets Sereiskii's articles as "morbidizing" and, therefore, unremittingly harmful to "gays," see his "Russia's Gay Literature and Culture," 358. Karlinsky's readings, correct in linguistic detail, ignore Sereiskii's continual return in these articles to the authority of Magnus Hirschfeld, the era's leading homosexual emancipationist who claimed scientific credentials, and the sexologist rated highest for his expertise by the Expert Medical Council in its "transvestites" discussion. Hirschfeld's biomedical model of homosexuality was fundamental to his strategy of pursuing justice for homosexuals through science. Acknowledging controversy between "conditional" and "constitutional" theories for the etiology of homosexuality, Sereiskii puts Hirschfeld first among the constitutionalists, before Steinach or Kretschmer, and highlights Hirschfeld's language of sexual variation, a key aspect of his antipathologizing arguments for a congenital model. ["Hirschfeld . . . considers H[omosexuality] an inborn anomaly, a biol[logical] variation ('sexual, intermediary stage'), based on the teachings of Steinach" (*Bol'shaia meditsinskaia entsiklopediia*, 7: 668)]. Sereiskii's apparent attempts to cure homosexuality with partial testicular transplants (7:671) should be set next to Hirschfeld's own referrals of homosexuals for the same treatment to German specialists (Sengoopta, "Glandular Politics," 465.). Sereiskii opens the medical encyclopedia article on homosexuality by flatly rejecting as outdated the psychopathological model (citing Krafft-Ebing, but certainly here taking aim at Edel'shtein and Belousov). He then comments on the highly orga-

nized social life of homosexuals observable in Germany: "in Berlin alone there are about 120 clubs for homosexuals and a special newspaper 'Die Freundschaft,' with approximately 20,000 subscribers despite the high cost, is published" (668). He does not label these phenomena pathological, degenerate, or evidence of mental illness. Finally, Sereiskii's sharp criticism of foreign laws punishing homosexuality as "absurd" and "harmful to the homosexual's mind" can only be interpreted as sympathetic and humane. For a sensitive partial translation (by Laura Engelstein) of the version of these articles published in the *Great Soviet Encyclopedia,* see Mark Blasius and Shane Phelan, eds., *We Are Everywhere: A Historical Sourcebook of Gay and Lesbian Politics* (New York: Routledge, 1997), 214–15.

63. See "Gomoseksualizm," *Bol'shaia sovetskaia entsiklopediia,* 17: 596. Preobrazhenskii was an authority on ancient Greek and Roman civilizations, and his selection to write this supplementary sketch suggested editorial sympathy with and awareness of European homosexual discourses of anthropology used to illustrate noble traditions of same-sex love in non-European cultures. Bleys, *The Geography of Perversion,* 207–65.

64. Solomon, "Social Hygiene and Soviet Public Health," 189.

65. Iudin, *Ocherki istorii otechestvennoi psikhiatrii,* 386–87; Joravsky, *Russian Psychology,* 339–41.

66. GARF, f. A482, op. 24, d. 742, l. 1.

67. Iudin, *Ocherki istorii otechestvennoi psikhiatrii.* 386–87; Rozenshtein's 1929 report for the Moscow Institute for Neuropsychiatric Prophylaxis criticized its research for reflecting "individual interests of the Institute's staff" and haphazard choices made in its clinic, rather than Institute priorities, see GARF, f. A482, op. 10, d. 1748, l. 53. Criticism of "individualism" in research: P. Emdin, "Sovetskaia nevropatologiia," in *13 let nauchnoi meditsiny na severnom Kavkaze,* ed. I. L. Ben'kovich (Rostov-na-Donu: Severnyi Kavkaz, 1934), 130; M. Ia. Sereiskii, E. M. Zalkind, and E. V. Maslov, "Uspekhi nauchnoi psikhiatrii," in *13 let nauchnoi meditsiny na severnom Kavkaze,* 162.

68. See, e.g., I. A. Beilin, M. B. Maizel', and M. I. Khurgich, "Rannee polovoe sozrevanie s akromikriei, anomaliei 5-go pal'tsa i rannim klimakteriem," *Sovetskaia nevrologiia, psikhiatriia i psikhogigiena* 3, no. 8 (1934): 141–46; N. I. Skliar, "Sluchai polovogo metatropizma v rannem detskom vozraste," *Sovetskaia nevropatologiia, psikhiatriia i psikhogigiena* 2, no. 8 (1934): 124–27; N. G. Kholzakova, "Chastichnaia utrata (stoikoe snizhenie) trudo-sposobnosti pri shizofrenii," in *Problemy pogranichnoi psikhiatrii (Klinika i trudosposobnost'),* ed. T. A. Geier (Moscow-Leningrad: Gos. iz-vo biologicheskoi i meditsinskoi literatury, 1935).

69. Solomon, "Social Hygiene and Soviet Public Health," 189–90; Bernstein, "What Everyone Should Know about Sex," 387–97; Mark B. Adams, "Eugenics in Russia," in Adams, *The Wellborn Science: Eugenics in Germany, France, Brazil and Russia.*

70. E.g., Kollontai in 1921 lambasted criminal anthropology for blaming the prostitute's biology for her plight, rather than considering her social position; Alexandra Kollontai, "Prostitution and Ways of Fighting it," in *Selected Writings of Alexandra Kollontai,* 264; Semashko and colleagues indulged in this criticism freely during the 1920s, Bernstein, "What Everyone Should Know about Sex," 388. On the campaigns for worker promotion and against "bourgeois specialists," see Fitzpatrick, "Cultural Revolution as Class War."

71. Just as the dialectical march of history could not be reversed, there could be no return to a previous stage of biological development; A. Nemilov, "Lozh' i pravda v voprose ob omolozhenii," *Priroda* 8 (1932): 710–38, cited in Naiman, *Sex in Public,* 296–97.

72. The consequences for Sereiskii as author of these pieces were doubtless uncomfortable, although he continued to practice and publish during the 1930s. In 1934, after the recriminalization of sodomy, a British Communist and homosexual working for the English-language *Moscow Daily News* wrote (in a letter to Stalin) that his managing editor advised him "that I should not ascribe much significance to the article on homosexuality in the Great Soviet Encyclopedia, because—as he put it—the author himself is a homosexual, and the article was published at a time when a whole range of deviations (*uklony*) had not yet been discovered." Garri Uait [Harry Whyte], "Mozhet li gomoseksualist sostoiat' chlenom kommunisticheskoi partii?" *Istochnik* 5–6 (1993): 185–91, quotation, 189. This letter is discussed in chapter 7.

73. Zavadovskii, "Issledovanie semennika gomoseksualista," 66.

74. Zavadovskii, "Issledovanie semennika gomoseksualista," 66, 69–70. The article was accompanied by lavish illustrations of the tissue sections and photographs of the unclothed soldier, from the front and behind.

75. On the failure of confidence in the Steinach techniques among German and Austrian biologists by 1925, see Sengoopta, "Glandular Politics." In 1925, an Astrakhan' psychiatrist, a supporter of the psychopathy model, had reviewed European attempts to duplicate Steinach's claims in a little-noticed article, Skliar, "O proiskhozhdenii i sushchnosti gomoseksualizma." A pair of surgeons in Tashkent reported their 1924 failure to cure a male homosexual using transplants of human testicular tissue, Zakharchenko and Pereshivkin, "Po povodu khirurgicheskogo lecheniia gomoseksualizma u muzhchin" (1930). Their optimism that one day the technical difficulties in the procedure could be overcome was an expression of cultural revolution utopianism; they contended that surgery could soon lead "the way to a cure for homosexuality," leaving psychiatry's failures behind. Zavadovskii did not refer to their work in his 1931 article.

76. Osipov, *Rukovodstvo po psikhiatrii*, 573, 575; P. B. Gannushkin, *Klinika psikho putil*, 117. Gannushkin was the subject of political pressures on two fronts. An 1926 article on "early acquired invalidism," one of his few published works, inspired a bitter debate into the late 1920s over the mental hygiene of Party activists; while the Moscow Society of Neuropathologists and Psychiatrists, which he led, was forced in November 1929 to recognize Party leadership by admitting three hundred new members and renouncing its "elitist" autonomy; see Joravsky, *Russian Psychology*, 336–39.

77. Osipov, *Rukovodstvo po psikhiatrii*, 574–75. Osipov cited a foreigner, Kraepelin, on male femininity, in a passage about male homosexual occupations: "Among persons who do heavy physical labor (workers in heavy industry, stevedores, day laborers) sexual psychopaths are rarely encountered; they more often occupy professions less physically demanding, somewhat corresponding to female ones—decorators, upholsterers, restaurateurs, women's dress designers, actors (Kraepelin), bathhouse attendants . . ." Osipov proposed that proletarian Russia would be comparatively free of "sexual psychopaths" by virtue of the inherent health of the physical laborer, with the single exception (familiar to Petersburgers) of the bathhouse prostitute. It was a striking reversal of his 1923 conjecture that between eight and nine million sexually perverted persons, of whom two to three million were homosexuals, probably lived in Russia; Osipov, *Kurs obshchego ucheniia o dushevnykh bolezniakh*, 356. The citing of foreigners to license discussion of Soviet sexual cultures also occurred in venereology in the late 1920s; see Susan G. Solomon, "The Soviet-German Syphilis Expedition to Buriat Mongolia, 1928," *Slavic Review* 52, no. 2 (1993): 204–32.

78. While from 1923 to 1941 the proportion of persons examined at Moscow's V. P. Serbskii Forensic Psychiatric Institute judged to be "psychopaths" fluctuated between 17–21 percent, the number pronounced not criminally responsible (*nevmeniaemyi*) fell:

Year	Percentage of Psychopaths among all Examined Individuals	Percentage of Psychopaths Judged nevmeniaemyi
1922	9.8	46.5
1923	19.8	28.9
1924	22.3	35.7
1925	18.0	19.2
1926	20.2	25.0
1927	19.8	17.6
1928	17.0	22.6
1929	16.6	13.0
1930	12.8	6.4
1931	19.6	7.9
1932	17.8	10.0
1933	14.1	9.9
1934	16.7	8.2
1935	20.4	3.0
1936	23.6	3.7
1937	20.6	3.4
1938	17.3	4.4
1939	20.7	4.3
1940	21.1	4.3
1941	21.6	6.2

Source: Ts. M. Feinberg, *Sudebno-psikhiatricheskaia ekspertiza i opyt raboty instituta sudebnoi psikhiatrii im. prof. Serbskogo za XXV let* (Moscow: Tsent. n.-i. institut sudebnoi psikhiatrii im. prof. Serbskogo MZ SSSR, 1947), 15.

79. See, e.g., S. Ia. Bulatov, "Vozrozhdenie Lombrozo v sovetskoi kriminologii," *Revoliutsiia prava* 1 (Jan.–Feb. 1929): 42–61; I. Sapir, "Freidizm, sotsiologiia, psikhologiia," *Pod znamenem marksizma* no. 7–8 (July–Aug. 1929): 207–36; G. I. Volkov, "Krizis sotsiologicheskoi shkoly i freidizm v ugolovnom prave," *Revoliutsiia prava* 6 (Nov.–Dec. 1929): 106–25; A. Gelovani, "Protiv burzhuaznykh izvrashchenii kriminologii. (Ob izuchenii prestupnosti v sovetskoi Gruzii)," *Sovetskoe gosudarstvo* no. 4 (Apr. 1932): 121–34.

80. Krasnushkin attacked, see Bulatov, "Vozrozhdenie Lombrozo v sovetskoi kriminologii"; on Brukhanskii, see I. Il'inskii, "Obshchestvennost' i bolezni byta [Po povodu knigi N. P. Brukhanskogo: "Materialy po seksual'noi psikhopatologii"]." and T. Segalov, "Po povodu stat'i I. Il'inskogo," *Molodaia gvardiia* no. 5 (1928): 175–93. Krasnushkin practiced psychiatry in Moscow province during the 1930s and later served as chief Soviet forensic psychiatrist to the Nuremburg trials. Brukhanskii took up a post in the faculty of psychiatry at Smolensk University. His career was ignored in Iudin's 1951 history of the psychiatric profession, *Ocherki po istorii otechestvennoi psikhiatrii.*

81. Feinberg, *Sudebno-psikhiatricheskaia ekspertiza,* 5–10; A. M. Khaletskii, "Poniatie umen'shennoi vmeniaemosti v sudebno-psikhiatricheskoi otsenke psikhopatii," in Ts. M. Feinberg, ed., *Psikhopatii i ikh sudebno-psikhiatricheskoe znachenie* (Moscow: Sovetskoe zakonodatel'stvo, 1934), 99–102; V. A. Vnukov, "Sudebno-psikhiatricheskaia ekspertiza psikhopatii," in Feinberg, *Psikhopatii i ikh sudebno-psikhiatricheskoe znachenie,* 15–16. On the high turnover of the Serbskii Institute's staff during the cultural revolution, see Joravsky, *Russian Psychology,* 416.

82. See "Sotsial'nye problemy raspredeleniia. Trud i kul'tura" in *Piatiletnii plan narodnokhoziaistvennogo stroitel'stva SSSR* (Moscow, 1929), 2: 242, cited in G. A. Bor-

diugov, "Sotsial'nyi parazitizm ili sotsial'nye anomalii? (Iz istorii bor'by s alkogolizmom, nishchestvom, prostitutsiei i brodiazhestvom v 20e–30e gody," *Istoriia SSSR* 1
(1989): 60–73. In the categories of "social anomaly," homeless adults, dealt with by
these plans, should be distinguished from orphaned and homeless children, who were
wards either of the Commissariats of Education, Health, or Internal Affairs, see Alan
M. Ball, *And Now My Soul Is Hardened: Abandoned Children in Soviet Russia, 1918–
1930* (Berkeley and London: University of California Press, 1994).

83. Lebina and Shkarovskii, *Prostitutsiia v Peterburge*, 152.

84. The decrees were "O merakh po bor'be s prostitutsiei" (issued 29 July 1929 by
RSFSR Council of People's Commissars) and "O merakh po likvidatsii nishchenstva i
besprizornosti vzroslykh"; Bordiugov, "Sotsial'nyi parazitizm ili sotsial'nye anomalii?"
66. The Health Commissariat retained only those therapeutic-labor prophylactoria
within its venereal treatment clinics. In their study of female prostitution in Peters-
burg-Leningrad, Lebina and Shkarovskii argue for this reading of institutional conflict
over the first Five Year Plan's projects for the *sotsanomaliki*, and they offer local archival evidence of the division of views at municipal level to support their conclusions;
see their *Prostitutsiia v Peterburge*, 153–55. My discussion of the "social anomalies"
is greatly indebted to their research. For a view of the process as untroubled by conflict
between Health and Welfare Commissariats, see Bordiugov, "Sotsial'nyi parazitizm ili
sotsial'nye anomalii?" 66–67.

85. Lebina and Shkarovskii, *Prostitutsiia v Peterburge*, 155–58. The quotation, cited
by Lebina and Shkarovskii, appeared in P. Verzhbilovskii, "Nado postroit' rabotu po
bor'be s sotsanomaliiami," *Sotsial'noe obespechenie* 9 (1933): 6.

86. The 27 December 1932 decree "On the Establishment of a Unified Passport
System in the USSR and on the Obligatory Registration of Passports" gave as one of
its objects, "the removal . . . from populated centers of persons not associated with
production and work in enterprises or schools . . . and also in order to cleanse (*v tseliakh
ochistki*) these population centers of concealed kulaks, criminal, and other antisocial
elements." Cited in Kuzmin, *Dnevnik 1934 goda*, 234 n65. On the use of the passport
system to purge undesirables, Fitzpatrick, "Ascribing Class," 761. Official publications
celebrated the "sharp decline in the percentage of nonworking elements (bourgeoisie,
clergy, declassed elements) in the urban population" as a result of the first Five Year
Plan. "Nonworking" social groups constituted 5.1 percent of city dwellers in 1926, but
had dropped to 1 percent by 1931, while the proportion of proletarians had jumped
from 68.5 percent to 88 percent, *Summary of the Fulfillment of the First Five Year Plan
for the Development of the National Economy of the USSR* (Moscow: State Planning
Commission, 1933), 189.

87. David Shearer, "Crime and Social Disorder in Stalin's Russia: A Reassessment
of the Great Retreat and the Origins of Mass Repression," *Cahiers du Monde russe* 39,
no. 1–2 (1998): 119–49, esp. 134–37. Lebina and Shkarvoskii argue that the state's
decree of 1929 on prostitution (transferring control from medical to welfare officials)
virtually legalized the intimidation of single women in dormitories, flophouses, railway
stations, and restaurants. Police "secret agents" specialized in identifying prostitutes,
with the Ligovka district chief (a woman), going undercover to pursue them: *Prostitutsiia v Peterburge*, 174. Note also the Politburo's decision to step up measures against
"criminal and déclassé elements in the city of Moscow" taken 23 December 1933,
RGASPI, f. 17, op. 3, d. 937, item 45/26. See as well on these points Paul Hagenloh,
" 'Socially Harmful Elements' and the Great Terror," in *Stalinism: New Directions*, ed.
Sheila Fitzpatrick (London: Routledge, 1999).

88. A memoir source claims "a number of homosexuals" were caught in the wave
of arrests that took away historian S. F. Platonov and Leningrad academic colleagues;

Philip Jason [pseud.], "Progress to Barbarism," *Mattachine Review* 3, no. 8 (1957): 20. Poet Mikhail Kuzmin's flat was searched by security police in 1931; prior to this his lover, Iurii Iurkun, had been repeatedly called to the GPU to persuade him to inform on Kuzmin, see S. V. Shumikhin, "Dnevnik Mikhaila Kuzmina: Arkhivnaia predystoriia," in *Mikhail Kuzmin i russkaia kul'tura XX veka: Tezisy i materialy konferentsii 15–17 maia 1990g.*, ed. G. A. Morev (Leningrad: Sovet po istorii mirovoi kul'tury AN SSSR, 1990), 144.

89. Smolensk archive, WKP 261, ll. 60–61, quotation l. 60 ob.

90. The OGPU summary says nothing further about Natal'ia/Vasilii, and so her motives for adopting a man's persona can only be guessed. Lynne Viola plausibly interprets the gesture as a carnivalesque inversion, consistent with the vigorous culture of peasant resistance: Lynne Viola, *Peasant Rebels under Stalin: Collectivization and the Culture of Peasant Resistance* (Oxford: Oxford University Press, 1996), 194. This would be consistent too with the apparently public nature of her self-transformation, which contrasts with the concealment of the crossing of gender usually practiced by Russia's "passing women."

91. She was thus perhaps a distant relative of the masculine woman, "resembling a man in [her] appearance, movements, voice," or the "hermaphrodite-woman," described by peasant informers to lexicographer Vladimir Dal' in the first half of the nineteenth century. None of the words to label her were insulting in the way that equivalents for the feminine man were; see chapter 2.

CHAPTER SEVEN

1. On collectivization and peasant response, see Viola, *Peasant Rebels under Stalin.* On the famine, Robert Conquest, *The Harvest of Sorrow: Soviet Collectivization and the Terror-Famine* (Oxford: Oxford University Press, 1986).

2. On the Plan's industrial achievements and problems, see R. W. Davies, M. Harrison, and S. G. Wheatcroft, eds., *The Economic Transformation of the Soviet Union, 1913–1945* (Cambridge: Cambridge University Press, 1994); on rural-urban migration, Sheila Fitzpatrick, "The Great Departure: Rural-Urban Migration in the Soviet Union, 1929–33," in *Social Dimensions of Soviet Industrialization.* eds. William G. Rosenberg and Lewis H. Siegelbaum (Bloomington: Indiana University Press, 1993); on Magnitogorsk, Kotkin, *Magnetic Mountain;* statistics on Moscow housing, David L. Hoffmann, *Peasant Metropolis: Social Identities in Moscow, 1929–1941* (Ithaca: Cornell University Press, 1994), 139.

3. Moshe Lewin, *The Making of the Soviet System: Essays in the Social History of Interwar Russia* (London: Meutheun and Co., 1985), 221–22.

4. J. Arch Getty, *Origins of the Great Purges: The Soviet Communist Party Reconsidered 1933–1938* (Cambridge: Cambridge University Press, 1985).

5. Until the Nazi-Communist propaganda war, homophobic political discourse (which I define as evoked by hostility toward the modern, Western European self-proclamation of the "homosexual") had been confined to national politics particularly in Britain, Germany, France, and the United States. After the exploitation of the issue by right and left on the international stage in the 1930s, homophobic propaganda became an evolving (but still inadequately researched) fixture of relations between states, especially during the cold war, leading to purges of homosexuals in government and society in the United States and Britain; see John D'Emilio, *Making Trouble: Essays on Gay History, Politics, and the University* (New York: Routledge, 1992); Weeks, *Coming Out.*

6. On the homosexual movement's political goals and activities, see Steakley, *The Homosexual Emancipation Movement in Germany.*

7. Manfred Herzer, "Communists, Social Democrats, and the Homosexual Move-

ment in the Weimar Republic," in Hekma et al., *Gay Men and the Sexual History of the Political Left*, 206.

8. Herzer, "Communists, Social Democrats, and the Homosexual Movement in the Weimar Republic," 204–6, 212–13. Both Communists and Social Democrats had inherited Bebel's policy supporting the abolition of paragraph 175. Kurt Hiller, a Hirschfeld associate in the Scientific-Humanitarian Committee and not linked to any party, in 1930 noted the KPD's unblemished parliamentary record on homosexual emancipation.

9. The book was *Braunbuch über Reichstagbrand und Hitler-Terror* (Basel: Universum-Bücherei, 1933), cited in Harry Oosterhuis, "The "Jews" of the Antifascist Left: Homosexuality and Socialist Resistance to Nazism," in Hekma et al., *Gay Men and the Sexual History of the Political Left*, 232–33.

10. Friends of van der Lubbe published a defense (*Roodboek Van der Lubbe en de Rijksdagbrand* [Amsterdam: Internationaal Uitgeversbedrijf, 1933]), which tarred Nazis with homophobic rhetoric; later, the Nazis' own defense of their elimination of Röhm would cloak itself in the same language of moral purity (*Weissbuch über die Erschiessungen des 30. Juni* [Paris: Editions du Carrefour, 1934]); see Oosterhuis, "The 'Jews' of the Antifascist Left," 233, 253n. Herzer argues (against Oosterhuis) that the European left's exploitation of homophobic themes was alien to its "subcultures," which were, nevertheless, subordinate to an all-powerful, heterosexist bourgeoisie: Herzer, "Communists, Social Democrats, and the Homosexual Movement," 218. This interpretation overlooks the role of the USSR, and the Comintern, in dogmatizing and promoting the discourse (whether invented by the left or not).

11. Among the critics of *Männerbund* were Wilhelm Reich, Erich Fromm, and the International Association of Socialist Physicians; Oosterhuis, "The 'Jews' of the Antifascist Left," 237–45; idem, "Medicine, Male Bonding and Homosexuality in Nazi Germany," *Journal of Contemporary History* 2 (1997): 187–205.

12. Students of a physical education college ransacked the institute, then SA men carried off much of the library; these books joined the pyre of "un-German" publications burned in Opernplatz on 10 May. On the earliest moves by Nazis to destroy the homosexual subculture, see Günter Grau, ed., *Hidden Holocaust?: Gay and Lesbian Persecution in Germany 1933–45* (London: Cassell, 1995), 26–61; Richard Plant, *The Pink Triangle* (New York: Henry Holt, 1986), 50–52. On the principles of "national community" and the "battle for the birthrate" applied in Nazi views of the homosexual, see Detlev J. K. Peukert, *Inside Nazi Germany: Conformity, Opposition and Racism in Everyday Life* (London: Penguin, 1989), 219.

13. See the discussion of the archives of the Ministry of Internal Affairs (ordinary police), of the Federal Security Service (custodian of the archives of its predecessors the OGPU/NKVD and KGB), and of the President of the Russian Federation, in the introduction.

14. "Iz istorii Ugolovnogo kodeksa: 'Primerno NAKAZAT' etikh Merzavtsev,'" 164–65.

15. "Iz istorii Ugolovnogo kodeksa: 'Primerno NAKAZAT' etikh Merzavtsev.'" The letter bears the notations "Correct! L. Kaganovich" and "Of course. It is necessary. Molotov."

16. "Iz istorii Ugolovnogo kodeksa: 'Primerno NAKAZAT' etikh Merzavtsev,'" citing APRF, f. 3, op. 57, d. 37, ll. 25–26.

17. "Iz istorii Ugolovnogo kodeksa: 'Primerno NAKAZAT' etikh Merzavtsev,'" citing l. 24 of the APRF documents; the same text may be found in RGASPI, f. 17, op. 3, d. 936, l. 18. The decree was published 17 December 1933 [1934] *1 Sobranie zakonov i rasporiazhenii raboche-krestianskogo pravitel'stva soiuza sovetskikh sotsialisticheskikh respublik* (Moscow: 1934), item 5.

18. GARF, f. 1235, op. 141, d. 1591, l. 1. This version included the use of force (*s nasiliem*) as an aggravated form of sodomy not found in Iagoda's draft adopted the previous day in the Politburo.

19. 7 March 1934, *15 Sobranie zakonov i rasporiazhenii raboche-krestianskogo pravitel'stva soiuza sovetskikh sotsialisticheskikh respublik* (Moscow: 1934), item 110. Moscow city court documents and RSFSR Supreme Court determinations refer to the "law of 7 March 1934"; individuals who committed sodomy after this date were judged criminals, e.g., Sentence of Bezborodov and eleven others (1935), ll. 238–45.

20. The RSFSR criminal code amendment read:

> 154-a. Sexual intercourse of a man with a man (sodomy)—deprivation of liberty for a term of three to five years.
>
> Sodomy committed with the use of force or with the use of the dependent situation of the victim—deprivation of liberty for a term of three to eight years.

The offense of consensual sodomy was usually referred to in judicial documents as "154a-I"; aggravated sodomy, as "154a-II."

21. See " 'Primerno NAKAZAT' etikh Merzavtsev,' " 165, citing Iagoda's 13 December proposal to Stalin from APRF, f. 3, op. 57, d. 37, ll. 25–26, and GARF, f. 1235, op. 141, d. 1591, l. 1 (VTsIK RSFSR, sekretnaia chast'). My thanks to David Shearer for this reference.

22. As late as 28 February 1934, the Iagoda draft mentioning prostitution and public sex was approved by RSFSR VTsIK and Sovnarkom; on this date it was distributed to the RSFSR Commissariat of Justice and the Supreme Courts of the Soviet Union and RSFSR. The simplified final version dropping these elements may have been suggested in one of these arenas. GARF, f. 1235, op. 141, d. 1591, ll. 5–6

23. All other sex offenses in the RSFSR criminal code had sentencing maximums, which generally encouraged judges to take the class character and other circumstances of a case into account when pronouncing a penalty; nevertheless, since the 1926 Chubarov Alley group rape case, judges had instructions to retain "sufficiently firm" sentencing values in sex crime cases, see D. Kurskii and P. Stuchka, "Instruktivnye pis'ma. Direktivnoe pis'mo NKIu i verkhsuda RSFSR po primeneniiu Ugol. Kod. redaktsii 1926 g.," *Sudebnaia praktika RSFSR* 1 (1927): 8–11. The USSR TsIK Presidium decree in Iagoda's draft and in the final published form carried no explicit language to explain the reason for the antisodomy law, but the decree's preamble in its insistence that "voluntary relations, regardless of whether one of the participants has not reached sexual maturity," would be a crime, also suggests that legislators expected courts would be reluctant to view this with the harshness deemed appropriate; GARF, f. 1235, op. 141, d. 1591, l. 1.

24. Bemused jurists drew attention to the variation by juxtaposing the text of the all-union decree with the hastily incorporated article 161-I, suggesting by implication that the former's sentencing values and language took precedence, "Ugolovnyi kodeks Ukrainskoi SSR" in D. S. Karev, *Ugolovnoe zakonodatel'stvo SSSR i soiuznykh respublik. Sbornik* (Moscow: Iuridicheskaia literatura, 1957), 114.

25. "Ugolovnyi kodeks Tadzhikskoi SSR" in Karev, *Ugolovnoe zakonodatel'stvo SSSR i soiuznykh respublik*, 345 (article 223).

26. Karev, *Ugolovnoe zakonodatel'stvo SSSR i soiuznykh respublik*, 159 (Belorussian SSR), 384 (Armenian SSR), 254 (Georgian SSR). The Armenian and Georgian codes both had sections dealing with customary crimes, which theoretically could have borne the antisodomy statute; in Georgia the preexisting sodomy prohibition was already situated in a discrete section headed "Crimes in the field of sexual relations," in other words, in a section reflecting "modern" sexual ethics.

27. Karev, *Ugolovnoe zakonodatel'stvo SSSR i soiuznykh respublik*, 345 (Tadzhik

SSR), 217 (Uzbek SSR). In Uzbekistan as in Georgia, the preexisting placement of the statute did not change.

28. Karev, *Ugolovnoe zakonodatel'stvo SSSR i soiuznykh respublik*, 433 (Turkmen SSR), 299 (Azerbaidzhan SSR).

29. Solomon, *Soviet Criminal Justice under Stalin*, chapters 3 and 4.

30. These subcultures were linked to the declining bourgeoisie and survivals of their old ways of life in A. Gertsenzon, "Klassovaia bor'ba i perezhitki starogo byta," *Sovetskaia iustitsiia* 2 (1934): 16–17. The signal for such linkages was given a year earlier in speeches from Stalin and V. Molotov about declassed remnants of the bourgeoisie and their concealed struggle against the victories of socialism, see I. Stalin, *Itogi pervoi piatiletki (Doklad na ob'edinennom plenume TsK i TsKK VKP(b) 7 ianvaria 1933 g.)* (Moscow: Partizdat TsK VKP(b), 1937), 62–63; V. Molotov, "Tasks of the First Year of the Second Five-Year Plan" [a speech from the same plenum] in *From the First to the Second Five Year Plan* (Moscow-Leningrad: Cooperative Publishing Society of Foreign Workers in the USSR, 1933), 118–26.

31. Given that police awareness of female prostitution and criminal subcultures was acute, it appears probable that both ordinary and security police were well aware of the existence and character of the male homosexual subculture. On discussions of the policing of women's prostitution in the late 1920s in publications of the Commissariat of Internal Affairs, see G. A. Bordiugov, "Sotsial'nyi parazitizm ili sotsial'nye anomalii?"; Lebina and Shkarovskii, *Prostitutsiia v Peterburge;* Elizabeth Waters, "Victim or Villain: Prostitution in Post-revolutionary Russia".

32. Some years earlier, Professor S. Mokrinskii, a jurist with experience of codification in the central Asian republics, had made these arguments about the criminal codes of the RSFSR and Ukraine, S. P. Mokrinskii and V. Natanson, *Prestupleniia protiv lichnosti. Kommentarii k VI glave* (Khar'kov: Narkomiusta USSR, 1928), 117.

33. Uait, " 'Mozhet li gomoseksualist sostoiat' chlenom kommunisticheskoi partii?' " 185–91. (The subtitle of this publication—"Humor from the special collection"—is indicative of the confused political interpretations of the 1993 sodomy decriminalization decree emanating even from the Presidential Administration. These circumstances are addressed in the epilogue.) This article does not indicate when in May Whyte's letter was written; I have inferred that it predated Maksim Gor'kii's article "Proletarian Humanism," which is discussed below. Whyte's letter is attributed to APRF, f. 3, op. 57, d. 37, ll. 29–45, i.e., from the same file as the Iagoda-Stalin correspondence on the sodomy law of 1933–34, published in the same issue of *Istochnik*, 164–65. Whyte told Stalin that he had been named a "head of the editorial staff" (*zaveduiushchii redaktsiei*) and a top shock-worker, but his name does not appear on the masthead of the *Moscow Daily News*. The paper published one book review by Whyte in 1933: H. O. Whyte, "Koltsov—The Journalistic Artist," *Moscow Daily News*, 3 April 1933, 2.

34. Uait, " 'Mozhet li gomoseksualist sostoiat' chlenom kommunisticheskoi partii?' " 185, 188–91. Whyte also cited Kaganovich's speeches to the congress on population growth in the USSR to deny there was any harm to this aspect of national prosperity; and he pointed to the prestige of open homosexual André Gide as "ardent friend of the USSR." Whyte's interpretation of Marxism and awareness of its historical views of homosexuality was not exceptional, as demonstrated in Hekma et al., *Gay Men and the Sexual History of the Political Left.*

35. " 'Mozhet li gomoseksualist sostoiat' chlenom kommunisticheskoi partii?" 191.

36. Maksim Gor'kii, "Proletarskii gumanizm" *Pravda*, 23 May 1934, 3; *Izvestiia*, 23 May 1934, 2. The same article was published that year in German as "Gegen der Faschismus: Proletarischer Humanismus," *Rundschau über Politik, Wirtschaft und Arbeiterbewegung* 34 (1934): 1298, cited in Oosterhuis, "The 'Jews' of the Antifascist Left," 236.

37. In Russian, "*unichtozh'te gomoseksualistov—fashizm ischeznet.*" Gor'kii's slogan (casually advocating the destruction of a group of human beings) has an unmistakably genocidal resonance. Regrettably, this effect has been overlooked as the slogan is often translated as "Destroy homosexuality and fascism will disappear." See, e.g., Reich, "The Struggle for a 'New Life' in the Soviet Union," 255; Engelstein, "Soviet Policy toward Male Homosexuality," 170; Masha Gessen, *The Rights of Lesbians and Gay Men in the Russian Federation* (San Francisco: International Gay and Lesbian Human Rights Commission, 1994), 8; Laurie Essig, *Queer in Russia: A Story of Sex, Self and the Other* (Durham: Duke University Press, 1999), 5; Malmstad and Bogomolov, *Mikhail Kuzmin: A Life in Art*, 350.

38. With access to APRF, f. 3, op. 57, d. 37, this hypothesis might be substantiated. There is a gap of two pages in this file between those published in *Istochnik* comprising the Iagoda-Stalin correspondence on the new sodomy legislation, ll. 24–26, and Whyte's letter, ll. 29–45. On Gor'kii's house arrest under Iagoda and decline into "a broken man and an obedient instrument of the authorities" from May 1934, see Vitalii Shentalinskii, *Raby svobody: V literaturnykh arkhivakh KGB* (Moscow: Parus, 1995), 362. Similar articles linking Fascism and homosexuality were reportedly written by the journalist M. E. Kol'tsov; Reich, "The Struggle for a 'New Life' in the Soviet Union," 255.

39. Shumikhin, "Dnevnik Mikhaila Kuzmina: Arkhivnaia predystoriia," in Morev, *Mikhail Kuzmin i russkaia kul'tura XX veka.*

40. Shumikhin, "Dnevnik Mikhaila Kuzmina: Arkhivnaia predystoriia," 140–41.

41. He praised the acquisition of the Kuzmin archive in B. Bonch-Bruevich, "Novye vklady v nashe literaturnoe nasledstvo," *Za kommunisticheskoe prosveshchenie* 3 June 1934: 2, cited in the commentary to Kuzmin, *Dnevnik 1934 goda*, 210 n77.

42. RGASPI, f. 17, op. 120, d. 111, l. 2. Shumikhin, "Dnevnik Mikhaila Kuzmina," in Morev, *Mikhail Kuzmin i russkaia kul'tura XX veka*, 143–45.

43. Iurkun's fate is chronicled from the secret police dossier of poet B. Livshits, whose arrest led to Iurkun's. See Eduard Shneiderman, "Benedikt Livshits: Arest, sledstvie, rasstrel," *Zvezda* 1 (1996): 82–126. See also Shumikhin, "Dnevnik Mikhaila Kuzmina," in Morev, *Mikhail Kuzmin i russkaia kul'tura XX veka.*

44. On 29 April 1934, Stalin vetoed the publication of a study of Mozart—the fruits of a lifelong hobby of former Commissar of Foreign Affairs Chicherin; T. E. O'Connor, *Diplomacy and Revolution: G. V. Chicherin and Soviet Foreign Affairs, 1918–1930* (Ames, Iowa: 1988), 167.

45. I. M. Gronskii, "O krest'ianskikh pisateliakh (Vystuplenie v TsGALI 30 sentiabria 1959 g.). Publikatsiia M. Nike," in *Minuvshee: Istoricheskii al'manakh* 8 (1992): 148–51. I am grateful to Natal'ia Lebina for bringing this item to my attention. Gronskii, who spent sixteen years in confinement after arrest in 1937, participated during the Khrushchev "thaw" in the commission to liquidate the consequences of the Stalin cult. He spoke about the Kliuev episode during a long address on "peasant writers" to literary specialists in 1959, evidently justifying his actions against Kliuev by emphasizing his strangeness as a homosexual to an audience that had lived with the Stalinist antisodomy ban for a quarter century.

46. Shentalinskii, *Raby svobody*, 265–74. In both the Russian and English versions of his book, Shentalinskii censors his account of Gronskii's story, removing all references to Kliuev's homosexuality to construct a purer anti-Communist victim; see Dan Healey, "Ghosts Come out of KGB Closet [review of Vitaly Shentalinsky, *The KGB's Literary Archive* (London: Harvill, 1995)]," *Moscow Tribune*, 27 April 1996, 40. We cannot know what references to the poet's sexuality Shentalinskii has omitted from his account of the NKVD documents (to which he had exclusive access).

47. I disagree with the pseudonymous chronicler of homosexual St. Petersburg,

who characteristically shrugs that further inquiry into this question "is not worth the effort"; Rotikov, *Drugoi Peterburg*, 180. The state of our knowledge on the point is a textbook example of homophobic evasion in literary studies, a desire to sustain the myth of Russia's sexual innocence.

48. "Mozhet li gomoseksualist sostoiat' chlenom kommunisticheskoi partii?" 186, 188–89. The fate of Whyte, and his lover, remains unknown.

49. The decree of 7 April 1935, extending harsher sanctions for juvenile crime, furnishes an excellent example. The decree itself, edited by Stalin, caught procuracy and court officials by surprise, but they quickly issued circulars and rulings to clarify its application. A similar flurry of communications followed the recriminalization of abortion on 27 June 1936. Solomon, *Soviet Criminal Justice under Stalin*, 200–21. The following GARF holdings were unsuccessfully trawled for directives regarding the anti-sodomy law: f. 8131, op. 27, 28s (Prokuratura SSSR, 1933–49 gg.); f. 9474, op. 16s (Verkhovnyi Sud SSSR, 1924–70 gg.); f. A353, op. 10 (NKIust RSFSR, prikazy, tsirku-liary . . . 1925–36 gg. [contains in addition to circulars, relevant protocols of Justice Commissariat collegium for 1933–34, without mention of the new law]); f. A353, op. 16s (Tsirkuliary NKIu RSFSR, 1923–50 gg.). Of course, archives of the Interior Ministry (for the regular police) or of the former KGB (for political police) may hold this type of document.

50. Secrecy of Justice Commissariat and procuracy directives and instructions expanded in the early 1930s; Solomon, *Soviet Criminal Justice under Stalin*, 419–20.

51. Sentence of Bezborodov and eleven others (1935), l. 243.

52. Sentence of Bezborodov and eleven others, l. 245.

53. Feinberg, *Psikhopatii i ikh sudebno-psikhiatricheskoe znachenie*, 168, terse definition of "*gomoseksualizm*"; V. A. Vnukov and Ts. M. Feinberg, *Sudebnaia psikhiatriia. Uchebnik dlia iuridicheskikh vuzov* (Moscow: OGIZ, 1936), 246–47, ignores homosexuality.

54. E. A. Popov, "O klassifikatsii polovykh izvrashchenii," in *Problemy psikhiatrii i psikhopatologii*, ed. S. N. Davidenkov (Moscow: Biomedgiz, 1935), 527–28. Popov had been a student of Protopopov at the Khar'kov Psychiatric Institute during the late 1920s, at one point publishing a study of sex perversion challenging his teacher's endocrinological theories: E. A. Popov, "K voprosu o geneze nekotorykh form mazokhizma (passivnogo flagelliantizma)," *Vrachebnoe delo* 7 (1928): 527–31. His article on "sexual perversions" in the second edition of the *Great Medical Encyclopedia* extolled the nurturist hypothesis: idem, "Polovye izvrashcheniia," 25: 942–52. The major currents in Soviet psychiatry on sexual perversion were thus embodied in three successive academic generations (Bekhterev, Protopopov, and Popov).

55. In 1931, an audit by the Workers' and Peasants' Inspectorate expressed "complete dissatisfaction with forensic medical affairs" and directed the Health Commissariat to implement sweeping changes in the education of specialists and the outlay of resources to the discipline. A new central institute was established. Ia. Leibovich, Chief Medical Expert during the 1920s, was replaced during the cultural revolution by V. M. Smol'ianinov. Most significantly, the Health Commissariat was able to see off an attempt by the Commissariat of Internal Affairs to take over responsibility for forensic medicine; see GARF, f. A482, op. 24, d. 301, ll. 1–4ob.

56. GARF, f. A-482, op. 25, d. 879, ll. 22–29 (*Pravila ambulatornogo sudebno-meditsinskogo akusher.-ginekologicheskogo issledovaniia*).

57. GARF, f. A-482, op. 25, d. 879, l. 24. The use of the word "pederasty" in this document may be linguistic evidence of influence by police or Party on the authors of this paragraph.

58. Forensic medicine, supervised by the Commissariat of Health, was given a crucial role in furnishing expertise in sex crime trials after the revolution. Medical exami-

nations were required in cases of rape, defloration, and the sexual abuse of persons not having attained "sexual maturity." A lack of funding and trained experts hampered the realization of this role during the 1920s, and there were lively disputes about the definition of "sexual maturity"; see Predsedatel' UKK Verkhsuda RSFSR Chelyshev, "Doklad UKK o praktike po delam o polovykh prestupleniiakh za vtoruiu polovinu 1926 goda," *Sudebnaia praktika RSFSR* 6 (1927): 4–8; "Rasshirennyi nauchnyi s'ezd sudebnykh vrachei i predstavitelei iustitsii v g. Ivanove-Vosnesenske 23–25 dekabria 1927 g.," *Sudebno-meditsinskaia ekspertiza* 9 (1928): 135–64.

59. Rozenblium et al., *Sudebno-meditsinskaia akushersko-ginekologicheskaia eksper-tiza,* 45.

60. Rozenblium et al., *Sudebno-meditsinskaia akushersko-ginekologicheskaia eksper-tiza,* 46.

61. Popov had asserted in the book's introduction that "in our conditions" sodomy was rare; Rozenblium et al., *Sudebno-meditsinskaia akushersko-ginekologicheskaia ek-spertiza,* 9.

62. Rozenblium et al., *Sudebno-meditsinskaia akushersko-ginekologicheskaia eksper-tiza,* 47.

63. A late-Stalin-era textbook confidently discussed sodomy between males, as a sexual crime routinely identified by forensic doctors, rehearsing the acknowledged stig-mata of "pederasty" with an exemplary "Document of Forensic Medical Expertise" in a case of consensual sodomy; no reference to psychiatric etiologies, or political dogma, was made. M. I. Avdeev, *Sudebnaia meditsina,* 3d ed. (Moscow: Gosiurizdat, 1951), 375–76.

64. Nikolai Krylenko, "Ob izmeneniiakh i dopolneniiakh kodeksov RSFSR," 1–5.

65. "Declassed elements" were said to be perpetrators of a range of "*bytovye* [daily life] crimes" (group rape, brawling, and hooliganism), Gertsenzon, "Klassovaia bor'ba i perezhitki starogo byta." Members of "criminal circles," unemployed declassed per-sons, and "professional beggars" were to be tried by special NKVD troikas according to an order signed by Iagoda and USSR Procurator Vyshinskii (9 May 1935), GARF, f. 8131, op. 28s, d. 6, ll. 62–64. Professional beggars had been treated as "social anoma-lies" during the first Five Year Plan. Gang rapes by men of individual women were the focus of special concern by the mid-1930s in studies produced by the Institute of Criminal Policy reviewing "general criminality . . . of class enemies, the declassed and criminal elements" in 1934 and 1935, GARF, f. 9474, op. 16s, d. 80, ll. 39–46, 82; GARF, f. 8131, op. 27, d. 48, ll. 229–30. See also Shearer, "Crime and Social Disorder in Stalin's Russia," 119–49.

66. Krylenko, "Ob izmeneniiakh i dopolneniiakh," 1, 3. Needless to say, he did not mention his involvement in the approval of the section of the 1922 RSFSR criminal code that had decriminalized sodomy.

67. Krylenko, "Ob izmeneniiakh i dopolneniiakh," 3–4 (my emphasis). Krylenko's tough-man persona extended beyond his aggressive courtroom behavior and his milita-ristic shaved head; he was an energetic promoter of mountaineering and hunting as well: Donald D. Barry, "Nikolai Vasil'evich Krylenko: A Re-evaluation," *Review of Socialist Law* 2 (1989): 131–47.

68. Claudia Schoppmann, "National Socialist Policies towards Female Homosexual-ity," in *Gender Relations in German History: Power, Agency and Experience from the Sixteenth to the Twentieth Century,* eds. Lynn Abrams and Elizabeth Harvey (London: UCL Press, 1996); for documentary extracts, see Grau, *Hidden Holocaust?* 71–84.

69. Leon Trotsky, *The Revolution Betrayed* (Garden City, N.Y.: Doubleday, Doran, 1937); Timasheff, *The Great Retreat;* for a detailed and nuanced reworking of these views, see Stites, *The Women's Liberation Movement in Russia.*

70. Lapidus, *Women in Soviet Society;* Janet Evans, "The Communist Party of the Soviet Union and the Woman's Question: The Case of the 1936 Decree 'In Defense of Mother and Child,'" *Journal of Contemporary History* 16 (1981): 757–75; Goldman, *Women, the State, and Revolution.*

71. Evans, "The Communist Party of the Soviet Union and the Woman's Question," 771.

72. The drop was ascribed to upward social mobility, working women's increased desire to limit family size, and to the drop (produced by the population losses of war and revolution) in the number of women who would come to childbearing age in the late 1930s; see Goldman, *Women, the State, and Revolution,* 292–93. For a version of the 1934 study, see S. G. Strumilin, "K probleme rozhdaemosti v rabochei srede," in *Izbrannye proizvedeniia v piati tomakh* (Moscow: Akademiia nauk SSSR, 1963–68). (Thanks to David Hoffman for bringing this to my attention.) On the 1920 abortion discussions, Solomon, "The Demographic Argument in Soviet Debates over the Legalization of Abortion in the 1920s," 59–82.

73. Goldman, *Women, the State, and Revolution,* 291, 331–33; on abortion see also Donald Filtzer, *Soviet Workers and Stalinist Industrialization: The Formation of Modern Soviet Production Relations* (London: Pluto Press, 1986), 131–33; on a possible increase in rural women's resort to abortion in the early 1930s, see Solomon, "The Demographic Argument in Soviet Debates over the Legalization of Abortion in the 1920s," 74; on the secret withdrawal of contraceptives, Solomon, *Soviet Criminal Justice under Stalin,* 212. In December 1935, male doctors in the Health Commissariat discussed whether the pain of having a baby was genuine ("What is pain?" one asked), and agreed that research into the "pain reduction of normal childbirth" for Soviet women should be undertaken. GARF, f. A482, op. 25, d. 896, ll. 69–125ob. At the same time, the commissariat's researchers were studying the effects of pregnancy on women in aviation and recommending that women at Aeroflot be diverted from positions of responsibility, see GARF, f. A482, op. 25, d. 896, l. 35 and GARF, f. A482, op. 25, d. 897, ll. 6ob.–7.

74. Lapidus, *Women in Soviet Society,* 112, citing Rudolf Schlesinger, comp., *Changing Attitudes in Soviet Russia—The Family in the USSR* (London: Routledge, 1949), 252. Lenin's 1915 correspondence with Armand appeared in *Bol'shevik* 13 (1939): 59. The *Great Soviet Encyclopedia* declared that "Stalin's concern for the mother, for the child, for our youth, for its upbringing, has created all the conditions for the development of a strong, joyful generation." D. Gorfin, "Polovaia zhizn'," in *Bol'shaia sovetskaia entsiklopediia,* 1st ed. (Moscow: OGIZ RSFSR, 1940), 46: 168–69.

75. Evans, "The Communist Party of the Soviet Union and the Woman's Question," 761–64. On reactions to the alimony measures, see Sarah Davies, *Popular Opinion in Stalin's Russia: Terror, Propaganda and Dissent, 1934–1941* (Cambridge: Cambridge University Press, 1997), 66.

76. On the *obshchestvenitsy,* see Fitzpatrick, *The Cultural Front,* 231–35; Rebecca B. Neary, "Mothering Socialist Society: The Wife-Activists' Movement and the Soviet Culture of Daily Life, 1934–41," *Russian Review* 58 (1999): 396–412.

77. Neary, "Mothering Socialist Society," 410.

78. Schoppmann, "National Socialist policies towards female homosexuality."

79. On the class distribution of the new family values promoted by *obshchestvennitsy,* see Fitzpatrick, *The Cultural Front,* 234–35. Neary argues that *obshchestvennitsy* also recruited from ordinary workers' ranks, but her evidence (of the changing designations given the movement) could also suggest embarrassed leaders sought euphemisms for the exclusivity of their movement. The material privileges embodied by wife-activism (dependency on a breadwinner, access to "culture" and the trappings of femininity) probably limited the participation of worker-wives.

80. GARF, f. A482, op. 25, d. 879, ll. 23–23 ob. The word used for "masculinization" is based on Russian roots (and therefore would be more readily understood by less cosmopolitan practitioners).

81. Rozenblium et al., *Sudebno-meditsinskaia akushersko-ginekologicheskaia eksper-tiza*, 45–47.

82. Louis Martineau, *Leçons sur les déformations vulvaires et anales produites par la masturbation, le saphisme, la défloration, et la sodomie* (Paris, 1883). On Martineau's influence on tsarist discussions of forensic gynecology, see Engelstein, *The Keys to Happiness*, 131–32, 153.

83. Fitzpatrick, *The Cultural Front*, 237.

84. See, e.g., *obshchestvennitsa* Galina Shtange's diary entry describing a formal visit of wife-activists to the Lenin Locomotive Works in 1936; Garros et al., *Intimacy and Terror: Soviet Diaries of the 1930s*, 175–77.

85. Goldman, *Women, the State, and Revolution*, 342.

86. On the patina of culture (*kul'turnost'*) avidly pursued by the newly promoted elite of the 1930s as "a scarce and essential commodity" and "the means and manners of a lifestyle appropriate to the new masters of the Soviet state," see Fitzpatrick, *The Cultural Front*, 218.

CHAPTER EIGHT

1. On these issues, see the appendix. Vladimir Kozlovskii interviewed ex-prisoners in Moscow in the 1970s, and they told him that in the mid-1930s "several thousands of homosexuals" arrived in the labor camps, "adding another rivulet to the Gulag flood waters." See Kozlovskii, *Argo russkoi gomoseksual'noi subkul'tury*, 155.

2. See, e.g., Merle Fainsod, *Smolensk under Soviet Rule* (Cambridge, Mass.: Harvard University Press, 1958), 192; Jerry F. Hough and Merle Fainsod, *How the Soviet Union is Governed* (Cambridge: Harvard University Press, 1979), 170–78.

3. Solomon, *Soviet Criminal Justice under Stalin*, 458.

4. Solomon, *Soviet Criminal Justice under Stalin*, 193, 458–59. Solomon notes that Harold Berman earlier pointed out the simultaneous coexistence of law and extralegal force, see Harold J. Berman, *Justice in the USSR: An Interpretation of Soviet Law* (Cambridge, Mass: Harvard University Press, 1963), 7–9.

5. For example, Boris I. Nicolaevsky *Power and the Soviet Elite: "Letter of an Old Bolshevik" and Other Essays* (London: Pall Mall, 1966), 31. The "Letter of an Old Bolshevik" describes a "so-called *homosexual conspiracy*" led by an "assistant of the German military attaché . . . under cover of a homosexual 'organization'" running a network of agents in Moscow, Leningrad, Khar'kov, and Kiev. Soviet authorities were thus "compelled to intervene" at the end of 1933. Wilhelm Reich, in "The Struggle for a 'New Life' in the Soviet Union," published in 1936 (reprinted in his *The Sexual Revolution* [New York: Pocket Books, 1969]), linked "politically motivated" arrests of homosexuals in January 1934, in Moscow, Leningrad, Khar'kov, and Odessa to espionage fears and the propaganda war using homosexuality as a charge against Fascism. Although Sidney and Beatrice Webb regarded the new law as "this drastic action," they attributed it to conspiracy centers led by "certain foreigners who were summarily expelled from Soviet territory," *Soviet Communism—A New Civilisation*, 2d ed. (London: V. Gollancz, 1937), 1060n.

6. This application of article 155, while it explicitly gendered victims as "women," recalled that suggested by the Justice Commissariat's "G. R." in 1922 (discussed in chapter 4). See Jason, "Progress to Barbarism," 18–21.

7. "Iz istorii Ugolovnogo kodeksa: 'Primerno NAKAZAT' etikh Merzavtsev,'": 164–65. The anonymous publisher of these APRF documents writes that 130 persons had been arrested by the time of Iagoda's letter of 15 September 1933.

8. Borodin reportedly told Whyte that "he personally has a negative attitude toward homosexuality but along with this he said that I was a sufficiently good Communist who could be trusted, and that I may lead whatever private life I liked"; Uait, " 'Mozhet li gomoseksualist sostoiat' chlenom kommunisticheskoi partii?' " 186, 188.

9. The file cited in *Istochnik* (APRF, f. 3, op. 57, d. 37), which is evidently devoted to the implementation of the antisodomy statute, contains at least forty-five pages while only nineteen were employed in the 1993 publication. Editors would have wanted to avoid any discomfort to Ukrainian authorities, which the admission of raids on homosexuals in Kiev, Khar'kov, or Odessa (places mentioned by memoirists) might generate. Awkward questions over the retention in the Ukrainian SSR antisodomy statute of the Iagoda-inspired language against male prostitution and public homosexuality could also arise.

10. Sentence of Bezborodov and eleven others (1935), see l. 244 for dates of arrests.

11. Case file of Andreevskii and two others (1941), ll. 14–14 ob.; "victims," possibly colluding with police once uncovered, were apparently the source of denunciations initiating two other trials, Sentence of Siniakov (1937) ll. 128–31, and Sentence of Leont'ev and Baikin (1939) ll. 187–88. Sexual denunciations, which Sheila Fitzpatrick suggests were comparatively rare in Soviet practice, logically may have gone to procurators and police rather than to newspapers or high public figures (whose archives are her chief sources), especially given the element of shame they entailed. See Sheila Fitzpatrick, "Signals from Below: Soviet Letters of Denunciation of the 1930s," in *Accusatory Practices: Denunciation in Modern European History, 1789–1989*, eds. Sheila Fitzpatrick and Robert Gellately (Chicago: University of Chicago Press, 1997), 106–7. It is, nevertheless, undeniable that denunciations of homosexual behavior were rare. Note that criminal investigations of rape in the 1920s and early 1930s could only be initiated by denunciations or complaints from victims, see Predsedatel' UKK Verkhsuda RSFSR Cholylhov, "Doklad UKK o praktike po delam o polovykh prestupleniiakh za vtoruiu polovinu 1926 goda," *Sudebnaia praktika RSFSR* 6 (1927): 5; S. P. Mokrinskii and V. Natanson, *Prestupleniia protiv lichnosti. Kommentarii k VI glave* (Khar'kov: Narkomiusta USSR, 1928), 113; V. Gromov, *Tekhnika rassledovaniia otdel'nykh vidov prestuplenii* (Moscow: Sovetskoe zakonodatel'stvo, 1931), 47.

12. Sentence of Belov and six others (1937), ll. 169–72. The testimony of witnesses was the primary evidence used against this group.

13. Sentence of Tereshkov and nine others (1938), l. 42.

14. It seems likely that in one case of two men, both arrested on 5 September 1935, described as meeting and having sex in public toilets and on boulevards, that police surveillance of "meeting places" led to their arrest, Sentence of Anisimov and Brodskii (1935). A second case involving a pair of men, arrested later that month, were described only tersely but appeared to have come to police attention through earlier raids or investigations of persons already under arrest.

15. Sentence of Bezborodov and eleven others (1935), l. 241.

16. Diaries: Sentence of Siniakov (1937), Sentence of Stepanova (1940); quotations from search dockets: Case file of Andreevskii and two others (1941), ll. 11, 53.

17. The USSR TsIK Presidium antisodomy decree of 17 December 1933 had explicitly insisted that "voluntary relations, regardless of whether one of the participants has not reached sexual maturity" would be a crime: GARF, f. 1235, op. 141, d. 1591, l. 1. The decree of 7 April 1935, "On the Struggle against Juvenile Crime" lowered the threshold of criminal responsibility for a short list of serious crimes to age twelve. The list did not include sexual offenses, but decreed that adults who led minors to prostitution were to be sentenced to a minimum five years' imprisonment. Decree text: Karev, *Ugolovnoe zakonodatel'stvo SSSR i soiuznykh respublik*, 23. On the decree, see Solomon, *Soviet Criminal Justice under Stalin*, 197–203.

18. Sentence of Tereshkov and nine others (1938), l. 44. Although Svechnikov was proven to have done no more than touch Kirill's genitals, the charges against him were qualified as voluntary sodomy with the application of article 19 of the RSFSR Criminal Code (preparation for crimes to be prosecuted as though a crime had occurred). Svechnikov was sentenced to three years' imprisonment, but in circumstances described below, on appeal the sentence was suspended in September 1938.

19. Sentence of Siniakov (1937), ll. 128–31.

20. One sea cadet was sixteen; all the rest whose ages were given were eighteen and over, and thus adults according to criminal code and marriage code definitions.

21. Sentence of Bezborodov and eleven others (1935), ll. 241–42.

22. Sergeev admitted "he engaged in pederasty with men unknown to him in summer 1937 in the basement of a building located not far from the toilet at Nikitskie Gates, he had sexual intercourse, playing the role of passive pederast (*passivnyi pederast*), with two men whom the investigatory organs have been unable to identify," Sentence of Tereshkov and nine others (1938), l. 42.

23. It is difficult to establish from Moscow's surviving trial records how differences between consensual and aggravated sodomy affected the resort to expertise. Individual Moscow city trials with forensic expertise from this era: TsMAM, f. 901, op. 1, d. 1352 (1950; consensual sodomy; forensic psychiatric expertise only); TsMAM, f. 1921, op. 1, d. 69 (1955; consensual sodomy; forensic medical expertise only); TsMAM, f. 901, op. 1, d. 1534 (1949; forcible sodomy; forensic medical expertise); TsMAM, f. 1919, op. 1, d. 136 (1952; sodomy with minors; forensic medical expertise only); TsMAM, f. 1919, op. 1, d. 238 (1955, forcible sodomy later reduced to consensual; forensic medical expertise); TsMAM, f. 901, op. 1, d. 394 (1955, forcible sodomy; forensic medical and psychiatric expertise). On the development of this expertise after Stalin, see the epilogue.

24. In March 1939, the physical education instructor Leont'ev (who had engaged in sexual acts with boys and youths) pleaded for a forensic psychiatric evaluation, in an appeal for a reduction of his five-year sentence; it was refused: Sentence of Leont'ev and Baikin (1939), l. 188.

25. Sentence of Siniakov (1937), l. 130.

26. This was the classic Bolshevik euphemism for disorderly sexual or personal conduct that was not commensurate with Party membership. "*Bytovoe*" in this context signified "lifestyle" or "personal life," indicating that side of existence (*byt*) regarded as trivial, personal, and politically insignificant (except when marked by excesses such as Siniakov's). The euphemism was frequently used in political rhetoric to mask a personal life devoted to alcoholism or heterosexual promiscuity.

27. Show trials of the1930s evolved from the practice of what Solomon describes as NEP-era "demonstration trials" (although the term, *pokazatel'nye protsessy,* was identical to that given the famous trials of Old Bolsheviks in 1936–38); Solomon, *Soviet Criminal Justice under Stalin,* 44–46, 238–39. On the use in the 1930s of circuses and theaters to house trials, and their function as popular entertainment in one region, see Kotkin, *Magnetic Mountain,* 188–89.

28. Two trials conducted openly differed in no discernible way from the others, see Sentence of Anisimov and Brodskii (1935), ll. 297–99 and Sentence of Leont'ev and Baikin (1939), ll. 187–88.

29. Ben De Jong, " 'An Intolerable Kind of Moral Degeneration': Homosexuality in the Soviet Union," *Review of Socialist Law* 4 (1982): 341–57, see 346. De Jong based this claim on trials of prominent dissident artists, so his observation could not be said to apply to cases of routine judicial practice. TsMAM post-1945 archives hold two closed sodomy trials (1949, 1950) and two open ones (both 1955); again, the sample is too small to justify generalizations.

30. Sentence of Bezborodov and eleven others (1935), l. 241.

31. Personal communication, Viktor Gulshinskii of the Russian Library of Lesbians and Gays (GenderDok), 4 November 1995. In July or August 1937 near this toilet, the gregarious Tereshkov met someone he had had sex with the summer before in the same spot, Sentence of Tereshkova and nine others (1938), l. 43.

32. Case file of Andreevskii and two others (1941), l. 83. "Sodomy" (*muzhelozhstvo*) in Soviet-era police and court documents might mean any manual, oral, or anal sexual contact between males.

33. Levin met Fedorov, one of the named defendants in this case file, in the Trubnaia toilet in May 1940, and they slept together twice; it was evidently this contact that led to Levin's arrest. Levin claimed he only slept with men when he drank "as a result of the fact that I am ill with schizophrenia." He was transferred to the Butyrskaia Prison's medical unit to be examined by a forensic psychiatric specialist; the police investigator directed Levin's case be separated from the rest of the Andreevskii case file, and further information about him does not appear in the Moscow city court archives. Case file of Andreevskii and two others (1941), ll. 83–85.

34. Case file of Andreevskii and two others (1941), ll. 57, 106 ob.

35. Sentence of Anisimov and Brodskii (1935), l. 297.

36. On reconstruction, see Evan Mawdsley, *Blue Guide: Moscow and Leningrad,* (London: A. & C. Black, 1991), 120–22; Timothy Colton, *Moscow: Governing the Socialist Metropolis* (Cambridge, Mass.: Harvard University Press), 326–28. Much of the terrain in front of the Bol'shoi Theater and near the adjoining metro station has acquired subcultural designations, but history of this folklore is obscure. See, e.g., entries under "Direktor pleshki" (an ironic reference to the Marx monument overlooking the square), "Goluboi zal," "Gomodrom," "Shliapki" (a reference to an erstwhile milliner's shop nearby) and "Shtrikh," in Kozlovskii, *Argo russkoi gomoseksual'noi subkul'tury,* 45, 73. As a gathering spot for homosexual men, the square in front of the Bol'shoi survived into the 1990s. See David Tuller, *Cracks in the Iron Closet: Travels in Gay and Lesbian Russia* (Boston: Faber and Faber: 1996), 22, 98, Laurie Essig, *Queer in Russia: A Story of Sex, Self and the Other* (Durham: Duke University Press), 88–89. In 1997, the city administration with private sponsor Daimler-Benz remodeled the square's street furniture and removed foliage to expose it to easier surveillance, ending its subcultural career.

37. Sentence of Siniakov (1937), ll. 128–29. The sailors' surnames have been replaced with letters to preserve anonymity.

38. "Soso" was Georgian diminutive for Iosif, the forename this performer shared with Stalin.

39. Sentencing documents mention that pairs of men had "sexual intercourse" or "intimate relations" repeatedly over sustained periods of time without describing the emotional context: Sentence of Tereshkov and nine others (1938), l. 44; Sentence of Leont'ev and Baikin (1939), ll. 187–88. Records of interrogations in Case file of Andreevskii and two others (1941) show that police asked pointed questions about the nature of friendships, contacts, and associations.

40. Sentence of Bezborodov and eleven others (1935), l. 241.

41. Sentence of Bezborodov and eleven others (1935), l. 245. Of the other four accused, one was acquitted for lack of evidence, one given a suspended one-year sentence (on medical grounds), and two received three-year sentences. One of these last persons was acquitted on appeal (see below).

42. Sentence of Tereshkov and nine others (1938), ll. 46–47.

43. Sentence of Anisimov and Brodskii (1935): Brodskii had "extorted" nine thousand rubles from Anisimov and was initially sentenced to five years (under article 154a-

I only); the sentence was lowered on appeal to three years. Sentence of Belov and six others (1937): Belov, a "ringleader" figure in this case, got four years under article 154a-I and ten years for counterrevolutionary activity with no reduction on appeal, l. 172. Case file of Andreevskii and two others (1941): Andreevskii, also a "ringleader" figure, was first given six years under article 154a-II (aggravated sodomy, maximum penalty, eight years), then appealed and received requalification as simple sodomy with a reduction in sentence to five years, ll. 123, 129.

44. Article 151 (six convictions) forbade sexual intercourse with a person not having achieved sexual maturity; article 152 (thirteen convictions) prohibited "corruption of minors" by "depraved [i.e., nonpenetrative] acts"; article 153 (fifty-seven convictions) dealt with rape by individuals (part I) and groups (part II). Cases under articles 154 (sexual harassment) and 155 (procuring for prostitution, etc.) were negligible. The convictions were culled from sentencing documents of the Moscow city court, TsMAM, f. 819, op. 2, dd. 9–42.

45. Naiman, "The Case of Chubarov Alley," 1–30.

46. Gertsenzon, "Klassovaia bor'ba i perezhitki starogo byta"; GARF, f. 9474, op. 16s, d. 80, ll. 39–46, 82; GARF, f. 8131, op. 27, d. 48, ll. 229–30.

47. ". . . the political significance [of the case] gave the court the basis to apply article 59/3 of the criminal code," TsMAM, f. 819, op. 2, d. 12, ll. 171–173. Eight defendants were tried by a woman judge heading a *spetskollegiia* of the Moscow city court on 20–21 May 1935; medical evidence was used along with the testimony of the group to secure these convictions. On these special chambers (of the regular judicial system) for politicized offenses, see Solomon, *Soviet Criminal Justice under Stalin,* 231.

48. Sentence of Belov and six others (1–2 April 1937; appeals denied on 1 June 1937). The case was heard by the Moscow city court *spetskollegiia,* beginning as one against anti-Soviet agitation using articles 58 and 59 of the RSFSR criminal code; only later were four defendants also charged under article 154a-I. Even here, the sentences that three of the four defendants received specifically for the sodomy charges were *not* the five-year maximum: two men were given three years, the other, four (ll. 169–172).

49. Compare, e.g., group rape cases in TsMAM, f. 819, op. 2, d. 18, l. 89 (1936: sentences between eight and three years), f. 819, op. 2, d. 32, ll. 233–236ob. (1939: sentences between eight years to acquittal, no change on appeal), f. 819, op. 2, d. 38, ll. 59–62 (1940: sentences between eight to one year, no change on appeal); versus sodomy trials of Tereshkov et al. (1938: one maximum sentence given with no change on appeal, the rest substantially below maximum), of Belov et al. (1937: sentences below maximum for article 154a-I despite aggravating counterrevolutionary agitation charges), of Andreevskii et al. (1941: RSFSR Supreme Court requalified Moscow city court's below-maximum six-year penalty under article 154a-II to a maximum five years under 154a-I, still a relative softening—and this just days after the start of the war).

50. Twenty-five per cent of those convicted under article 154a (sodomy) got reductions on appeal; cf. 17.5 percent of convicts under both sections of article 153 (rape), 33 percent of convicts under article 151 (sex with "sexually immature" persons, defloration), and 31 percent of convicts under article 152 (depraved acts with children/minors).

51. Quote is from RSFSR Supreme Court's determination, which released three defendants by suspending the remainder of their three-year sentences in Sentence of Tereshkov and nine others (1938), l. 47. Two others in this case were released on similar grounds, l. 46. All had advocates arguing for them. "Family situation" could have referred to having dependent parents or relatives, since all of these men were unmarried. Note also reduction of sentence (from five to three years) for Brodskii, said by his advocate to have been "lured into the crime" by his partner, in Sentence of Anisimov and Brodskii (1935), l. 299.

52. Few were launched, but compare Leont'ev's claim that he was "a mentally abnormal personality" and therefore deserved a milder sentence (Sentence of Leont'ev and Baikin, 1939, l. 188) with a 1950 plea for leniency from a man convicted of consensual sodomy; his appeal (which might have been more plausible given his history of mental health troubles) was also refused, on the same grounds: TsMAM, f. 901, op. 1, d. 1352, ll. 56a, ll. 87–89.

53. Case file of Andreevskii and two others (1941), ll. 123–123ob., 129. Another successful defense based on rhetorical dispute seems to have been available soon after the antisodomy law was decreed. A man given a three-year sentence by the Moscow city court in 1935 for his role in the case against Bezborodov et al. was later acquitted by the RSFSR Supreme Court, having argued that no homosexual acts after 1928 had been attributed to him by the lower court. No advocates were recorded as present and the Supreme Court's decision was based on a "report" from the presiding judge; Sentence of Bezborodov and eleven others (1935), l. 245.

54. Ringleaders' unsuccessful appeals: Sentence of Bezborodov and eleven others (1935), Bezborodov himself was denied any reduction; Sentence of Tereshkov and nine others (1938), Tereshkov denied leniency. Corrupters of youth: Sentence of Siniakov (1937), under article 154a-II, most of Siniakov's "victims" were soldiers and sailors; he was denied leniency; Sentence of Leont'ev and Baikin (1939), Leont'ev, a physical education teacher sexually involved with his students, denied leniency. Counterrevolutionary crimes: Sentence of Belov and six others (1937), Belov, Shuvalov, and Shapovalov denied leniency for sodomy offenses in overall sentencing, probably because of charges under arts. 58 and 59.

55. The juxtaposition of "depraved acts" and "sodomy" probably indicates that a distinction between nonpenetrative acts, often referred to as "depraved" in legal discourse, and penetrative ones, was intended. Sentence of Leont'ev and Baikin (1939), ll. 187–190. In this case the Supreme Court's irritation with sophisticated defense strategies was probably redoubled by Leont'ev's advocate's plea for mercy on psychiatric grounds, mentioned above. Both appeals were considered in the same sitting by the same personnel.

56. The figures consisted of the following: fifteen bachelors; three married; six family men (*semeinye*); four divorced; one widower; and seven civil status unstated in the documents. All six described as *semeinye* were defendants in a single trial, Sentence of Bezborodov and eleven others, (1935), and court records described none in this case as "married," suggesting the categorizations were interchangeable.

57. One "family man" was immediately acquitted, and the second was released upon appeal (successfully argued by an advocate); in both cases their acquittals were based on the procurator's failure to demonstrate that they had engaged in sodomy after 7 March 1934 and had close ties to "the group of pederasts" on trial. Of the remaining four "family men," three (including ringleader Bezborodov) got five years' imprisonment (the maximum) and one, three years. Their appeals were unsuccessful.

58. Sentence of Krasin and Popov (1935).

59. Sentence of Tereshkov and nine others (1938), l. 45.

60. Case file of Andreevskii and two others (1941), ll. 57–57 ob., 62, 79–82.

61. Case file of Andreevskii and two others (1941), l. 101 ob.

62. Case file of Andreevskii and two others (1941), ll. 103–103 ob. The outcome of this pregnancy was not registered in the trial documents. Markovskii had a child by his first marriage, and his second wife mentioned this in her unprompted first statement to the court. This child lived with its mother in Moscow.

63. Case file of Andreevskii and two others (1941), l. 68.

64. Case file of Andreevskii and two others (1941), ll. 99 ob.

65. Case file of Andreevskii and two others (1941), l. 110.

66. Case file of Andreevskii and two others (1941), l. 109. Her statement contradicted her husband's claim, earlier in the trial, that they had "lived together" in the hotel (l. 104). "To live together, cohabit" (*sozhit'*) is often a euphemism for "to have sexual relations." Markovksii's advocate's questions (not recorded in the trial transcript) prompted her to state, "I always had him [Markovskii] in my sight. Fedorov also was with us. Relations between Markovskii and Fedorov were the same as those between the others and Fedorov" (l. 109 ob.).

67. Case file of Andreevskii and two others (1941), l. 123–123 ob. Further protestations of normal sexuality were heard from Levin, the fourth man in this case whose file was diverted as a result of his claim of mental illness. Levin said: "About my sex life I may say that as a youth I masturbated but when I married I quit masturbating. I lived with my wife from 1929 to 1939, although with long interruptions. I find women attractive even now, but when I drink, men begin to attract me. . . . When I am sober, acts of sodomy seem unpleasant to me" (ll. 83–83 ob.).

68. Riasentsev, "Dva sluchaia iz praktiki," 152–56; see also Brukhanskii, *Materialy po seksual'noi psikhopatologii*, 62–65. These slightly differing accounts make uncertain which criminal code article was used against Fedosiia. Brukhanskii said she was charged under article 168 (1922 redaction); Riasentsev did not give the article. If, as Riasentsev said, acquittal turned on Nina's "sexual maturity" (*polovaia zrelost'*) before her affair with Fedosiia, the court used the language of article 167, which punished "sexual intercourse with persons not having attained sexual maturity, when accompanied by defloration or the satisfaction of sexual passion in perverted forms." Article 168 forbade "depraved acts" (*razvratnye deistviia*), regarded as the nonpenetrative sexual abuse of children or minors.

69. Riasentsev, "Dva sluchaia iz praktiki," 153.

70. Brukhanskii, *Materialy po seksual'noi psikhopatologii*, 65.

71. Riasentsev, "Dva sluchaia iz praktiki," 154. Note that in Brukhanskii, *Materialy po seksual'noi psikhopatologii*, 62–65, the psychiatrist did not mention the acquittal nor its gynecological basis, but terminated his account abruptly with his psychiatric diagnosis of her homosexuality.

72. Riasentsev, "Dva sluchaia iz praktiki," 154.

73. She was said to have worked "for hire since 1922 as a researcher in cinematography [*assistent po kinematografii*] and researcher of history [*assistent istorii*]"; she had been a member of the Party since 1922 as well: Sentence of Stepanova (1940), l. 17.

74. Sentence of Stepanova (1940), ll. 17–18. Only sentencing and appeal documents were located for this case and do not indicate who raised the original complaint, nor whose diary fell into police hands. The diary became pages nine to thirty of the full case file, which was evidently destroyed.

75. Sentence of Stepanova (1940), l. 17. A Russian émigré to the United States, commenting on her encounters with "homosexuals" in 1930s artistic and Party circles, pointed to the existence of women who had affairs with women, hiding behind the veil that concealed privileged living standards enjoyed by officialdom, Harvard University Project on the Soviet Social System—Schedule "A" Interviews (1950–1953), interview no. 386, 58–59. My thanks to Amy Randall for this reference.

76. Poliakova, "Poeziia Sofii Parnok," 36. On the domestic sphere and women's role as bearers of witness to repression (although usually of husbands), see Beth Holmgren, *Women's Works in Stalin's Time: On Lidiia Chukovskaia and Nadezhda Mandelstam.* (Bloomington: Indiana University Press, 1993), 9–10.

77. No reference to the criteria used is found in the sentencing documents for this case. The 1934 guidelines stipulated that a "combination" of the ability to bear a child,

the intellectual development required to rear it, and the readiness for an independent social existence, constituted sexual maturity "from the point of view of forensic medical practice"; see GARF, f. A482, op. 25, d. 879, ll. 24, 27–27 ob; Rozenblium et al., *Sudebno-meditsinskaia akushersko-ginekologicheskaia ekspertiza*, 20–21.

78. As in cases of sodomy between adults and minors, this sentence document emphasized the inducements used by the adult to corrupt the object of the crime. Stepanova "finally suborned Anna Zhukova to her influence by buying her sweets and with the promise of giving her an education worthy of the era [*sic!*]"; she was thus "lured to the city of Moscow," Sentence of Stepanova (1940), l. 17.

79. In a punitive ruling not observed in the men's sodomy cases, Stepanova was also ordered to pay the costs of the forensic expertise, the defense counsel, and the summoning of witnesses.

80. The most senior well-known homosexual Bolshevik, Grigorii Chicherin, commissar of Foreign affairs (1918–1930), died of natural causes in 1936. His fall from favor with Stalin could have been exacerbated by his homosexuality (he was discreet and repressed), but undoubtedly it was primarily the result of Stalin's mistrust of intellectual Old Bolsheviks, the shifting diplomatic climate of the late 1920s, and the commissar's chronic illness; see O'Connor, *Diplomacy and Revolution*, 153–67.

81. All were in service or consumer sectors of the economy. There were three cooks, one tram driver, one electrician, one shop assistant, and one theater usher.

82. Ten were white-collar/clerical (*sluzhashchie*); there were eight artists (actors, musicians); four educators (school teachers, one lecturer); four professional/managerial (two senior engineers; a doctor; a film-studio executive). Of these, four were from "former classes": Siniakov (1937) and Baikin (1939) were ex-nobles; two others from the Belov case (1937) linking counterrevolutionary activity to sodomy, were described as from former merchant and tsarist bureaucrat's families.

83. Two were men in their mid-fifties, and no current occupation was recorded for them; they were tried in the 1935 Bezborodov case. A third was tried in 1937 in the Belov case, for counterrevolutionary activity and sodomy. He was just thirty-two, was still an active priest, and had been born into the nobility; he had already been exiled to the Far North once by the OGPU "for counterrevolutionary activity," from 1930 to 1933. The sodomy charges against him were ultimately dropped, but he still received ten years for anti-Soviet propaganda.

CHAPTER NINE

1. In 1939, over half of the 2.962 million convicts under NKVD control were in labor colonies (sentences under three years) or camps. Just under one million persons were held in "labor settlements," where large-scale industry or resource extraction was undertaken. For a summary of the types of places of confinement and their populations in 1937 and 1939, see S. G. Wheatcroft and R. W. Davies, "Population," in *The Economic Transformation of the Soviet Union, 1913–1945*, ed. R. W. Davies, Mark Harrison, and S. G. Wheatcroft (Cambridge: Cambridge University Press, 1994), 70. On the Gulag, see Alexander Solzhenitsyn, *The Gulag Archipelago*, 3 vols. (London: Collins/Fontana, 1973–78). For a view of life inside the labor settlements, see Thomas Lahusen, *How Life Writes the Book: Real Socialism and Socialist Realism in Stalin's Russia* (Ithaca: Cornell University Press, 1997).

2. A further 2.75 million were "special settlers," remnants of deported small nationalities exiled to distant northern and eastern locations; John Keep, *Last of the Empires: A History of the Soviet Union, 1945–1991* (Oxford: Oxford University Press, 1996), 13.

3. Researchers, e.g., would want to interview survivors of the period, but the prospect of finding willing subjects for an oral history of homosexual experience is not as

simple, say, as locating interviewees prepared to talk about their lives as Soviet women. I have in mind the excellent collection of interviews in Barbara Alpern Engel and Anastasia Posadskaya-Vanderbeck, eds., *A Revolution of Their Own: Voices of Women in Soviet History* (Boulder: Westview Press, 1998). When one considers the obstacles encountered and overcome by these collaborators, the challenges of gathering material from sexual and gender dissidents seem immense. Nevertheless, there have been some impressive attempts to gather this kind of data, which are mentioned in this section.

4. Kozlovskii, *Argo russkoi gomoseksual'noi subkul'tury*, 94.

5. The view that this sexual culture is "more or less stable and universal" in Russia's penal history is suggested in Kon, *The Sexual Revolution in Russia*, 221; the suggestion that Stalinist camps contributed to the proliferation of homosexuality in Soviet society is found in Mikhail Stern, *Sex in the USSR* (New York: Times, 1980), 217, 267, 278.

6. N. Bek, "V zakrytom zavedenii. (Otryvki). Rozhdestvo v tiur'me" *Ural*, 31 December 1902, 2. I am grateful to Aleksei Kilin for sharing this article with me.

7. Bek, "V zakrytom zavedenii."

8. Bek, "V zakrytom zavedenii." In 1915, a Moscow court heard the case of the rape while in custody of seventeen-year-old S. G. Belousov by fellow prisoners Savel'ev and Bezrukov; another prisoner offered Belousov forty kopeks for sex after the first assault, TsGIAg.M, f. 142, op. 12, d. 99, ll. 17–18, 20–21 ob.

9. Tan, "Tiuremnye mysli," *Vestnik Evropy* (November 1911), 130, cited in M. N. Gernet, *V tiur'me. Ocherki tiuremnoi psikhologii* (Moscow: Izd. Pravo i zhizn', 1925), 79–80.

10. Gernet, *V tiur'me*, 77.

11. Nowhere did Lass define what he meant by "active" or "passive" forms of pederasty; D. I. Lass, "Polovaia zhizn' zakliuchennykh," in *Izuchenie prestupnosti i prenitentsiarnaia praktika* (Odessa: Izd. Odesskogo tsentral'nogo DOPRA, 1927), 19.

12. See Lass, *Polovaia zhizn' zakliuchennykh*, 4, 32–33; Gernet, *V tiur'me*, 77–80.

13. L. Mel'shin [P. Iakubovich] *V mire otverzhennykh. Zapiski byvshego katorzhnika* (St. Petersburg, 1899), 2: 200–1, 234–35, cited in Kozlovskii, *Argo russkoi gomoseksual'noi subkul'tury*, 87–89.

14. Gernet, *V tiur'me*, 77. Meanwhile, Lass, using formal interviews and a standard questionnaire to probe the details of his prisoners' sex lives, was unable "to obtain frank answers about this question [pederasty]." The anthropology of prison "pederasty" was something he observed, but would not describe without the legitimation provided by questionnaire data. Lass, *Polovaia zhizn' zakliuchennykh*, 18.

15. Ozeretskii, "Polovye pravonarusheniia nesovershennoletnikh," in Krasnushkin et al., *Pravonarusheniia v oblasti seksual'nykh otnoshenii*, 149–50; Ball, *And Now My Soul Is Hardened*, 125.

16. V. Markman, *Na kraiu geografii* (Jerusalem, 1979), 81–83, cited in Kozlovskii, *Argo russkoi gomoseksual'noi subkul'tury*, 104.

17. Eduard Kuznetsov, *Mordovskii marafon* (Jerusalem, 1979). An entire chapter from this memoir describes how "in big camps [in the 1930s] passive 'queers' [*gomiki*] lived in separate barracks, run by . . . a brothel madame," that is, a male prisoner acting as a procurer; cited in Kozvlovskii, *Argo russkoi gomoseksual'noi subkul'tury*, 200–10. For descriptions of similar operations inside a labor camp of the 1970s, see Stern, *Sex in the USSR*, 264–65.

18. Vladimir Bondarenko, "Golubye v seroi stae," *Kristofer* 1 (1992): 32–33.

19. V. Aleksandrov, "Arestantskaia respublika," *Russkaia mysl'* 9 (1904): 68–84; and V. Trakhtenberg, *Blatnaia muzyka* (St. Petersburg, 1908), cited in Kozlovskii, *Argo russkoi gomoseksual'noi subkul'tury*, 89–90.

20. To refer to an inmate using the feminine-gendered past tense verb, or labels

such as *suka* (bitch) or *baba* (peasant woman) were mortal insults, reserved for putting that person into the realm of "passive pederasts"; Aleksandrov, "Arestantskaia respublika"; P. Fabrichnyi, "Iazyk katorgi," *Katorga i ssylka* 6 (1923), both cited in Kozlovskii, *Argo russkoi gomoseksual'noi subkul'tury*, 91.

21. For post-1953 accounts, A. Amal'rik, *Zapiski dissidenta.* (Ann Arbor: Ardis, 1982), 187–88; Markman, *Na kraiu geografii*, 81–83; and an interview recorded in 1973 by Kozlovskii; all cited in Kozlovskii, *Argo russkoi gomoseksual'noi subkul'tury*, 94–95, 105, and passim.

22. Stern, *Sex in the USSR*, 258–66; Kozlovskii, *Argo russkoi gomoseksual'noi subkul'tury*, 94–110; Kon, *The Sexual Revolution in Russia*, 218–22, 257; Bondarenko, "Golubye v seroi stae," partially translated in Moss, ed. *Out of the Blue;* Masha Gessen, "We Have No Sex: Soviet Gays and AIDS in the Era of Glasnost," *Outlook* 3, no. 1 (1990): 42–54; idem, *The Rights of Lesbians and Gay Men in the Russian Federation* (San Francisco: International Gay and Lesbian Human Rights Commission, 1994); Iaroslav Mogutin and Sonia Franeta, "Gomoseksualizm v sovetskikh tiur'makh i lageriakh," *Novoe vremia* 35–36 (1993): 44–47 (no. 35), 50–54 (no. 36).

23. E. K. Krasnushkin, "Chto takoe prestupnik?" *Prestupnik i prestupnost'. Sbornik I* (1926): 6.

24. Jacques Rossi, *The Gulag Handbook: An Encyclopedic Dictionary of Soviet Penitentiary Institutions and Terms Related to the Forced Labor Camps*, trans. W. A. Burhaus (New York: Paragon, 1989), 231–32. On 13 July 1941, convicted sodomite Andreevskii was dispatched from Moscow's Butyrskaia prison to the NKVD's "Viatlag" at Ia-Fosforitnaia, while his codefendant Federov served his sentence in Butyrskaia prison: Case file of Andreevskii and two others (1941), ll. 128, 130.

25. Solzhenitsyn, *The Gulag Archipelago*, 1: 499–512.

26. For a description of late-Soviet prison camp men's hierarchies from the perspective of a professor of archaeology who spent three years imprisoned for sodomy in the 1980s, see Lev Samoilov, "Puteshestvie v perevernutyi mir," *Neva* 4 (1989): 150–64.

27. For French women prisoners' culture, see Sautman, "Invisible Women," in Merrick and Ragan, *Homosexuality in Modern France*, 195–94.

28. Gernet, *V tiur'me*, 80–81.

29. Lass, *Polovaia zhizn' zakliuchennykh*, 19.

30. Lass, *Polovaia zhizn' zakliuchennykh*, 11, 15, 19. Social hygienists and educators deplored the sharing of beds with varying degrees of frankness about the possibly sexually perverse outcomes; see, e.g., V. Z. Land, "Opyt izucheniia effektivnosti sanitarno-prosvetitel'noi raboty na predpriiatii," *Vrachebnoe delo* 22 (1929): 1437–40; idem, "Opyt planirovaniia sanitarno-prosvetitel'noi raboty iz predpriiatii," *Vrachebnoe delo* 17 (1930): 1237–40; Moskalevich-Karetnikova, "Seksual'nye pravonarusheniia nad maloletnimi kak so storony samikh nesovershennoletnikh, tak i vzroslykh sub'ektov po dannym Leningradskogo Komones'a za period vremeni s 1926 po 1927 god i Gubsuda za 1927 g.," *Voprosy izucheniia i vospitaniia lichnosti* 3–4 (1929): 59–64.

31. Gernet, *V tiur'me*, 80.

32. This could mean that Gernet misunderstood the term he reported, or that it underwent a reversal of meanings during the 1920s and 1930s; see Kozlovskii, *Argo russkoi gomoseksual'noi subkul'tury*, 126. For a recent psychiatric text that notes the use of the term among present-day female prisoners to denote "active" partners or "husbands," V. N. Volkov, S. I. Kalinichenko, and A. V. Pishchelko, *Seksual'nye izvrashcheniia u osuzhdennykh-zhenshchin* (Domodedovo: MIPK rabotnikov OVD, 1992), 55.

33. See, e.g., the psychiatric portrait of a so-called "Marquise of Ligovka" (a seedy district of Leningrad) in A. K. Lents, *Kriminal'nye psikhopaty (Sotsiopaty)* (Leningrad: Rabochii sud, 1927), 48–50; and the description of a female homosexual in prison

described in R. I. Livshits, "Reaktsiia d-ra Manoilova kak pokazatel' narusheniia sekretornoi funktsii polovykh zhelez pri seksual'nykh prestupleniiakh," *Leningradskii meditsinskii zhurnal* 2 (1925): 11–14.

34. For a study of female homosexuality derived mainly from prisoner-subjects, see Derevinskaia, "Materialy k klinike, patogenezu, terapii zhenskogo gomoseksualizma"; see also Volkov et al., *Seksual'nye izvrashcheniia u osuzhdennykh-zhenshchin.*

35. Elinor Lipper, *Eleven Years in Soviet Prison Camps* (London: Hollis & Carter, 1951), 158.

36. E. Olitskaia, *Moi vospominaniia* (Frankfurt, 1971), 2: 243–44, cited in Kozlovskii, *Argo russkoi gomoseksual'noi subkul'tury,* 111.

37. M. Ulanovskaia, "Konets sroka—1976 goda," *Vremia i my* 10 (1976): 153–55, cited in Kozlovskii, *Argo russkoi gomoseksual'noi subkul'tury,* 114–16. All references in this paragraph to Ulanovskaia's text are from this passage in Kozlovskii, *Kobel,* pronounced with a final ë sound, used to denote a female "who fulfills the sexual function of a man" in prison slang from the 1940s onward, appears to be a corruption from *kobel'* (male dog), see Kozlovskii, *Argo russkoi gomoseksual'noi subkul'tury,* 126.

38. Ulanovskaia cited a *chastushka* she heard sung by one criminal lesbian inmate: *Oi, spasibo Stalinu / Sdelal s menia baryniu / I korova ia, i byk, / Ia i baba, i muzhik* (Oy, thank you, Stalin / You made a gentleman of me / A cow I am, and a bull / I'm a woman and a man). Kozlovskii, *Argo russkoi gomoseksual'noi subkul'tury,* 115.

39. Evgeniia Ginzburg, *Krutoi marshrut* (Milan, 1979), 113, cited in Kozlovskii, *Argo gomoseksual'noi subkul'tury,* 113; Solzhenitsyn, *The Gulag Archipelago,* 2: 234–35; Vasily Grossman, *Forever Flowing* (London: Collins Harvill, 1988), 116–17.

40. Olga Zhuk, "The Lesbian Subculture: The Historical Roots of Lesbianism in the Former USSR," in *Women in Russia: A New Era in Russian Feminism,* ed. Anastasia Posadskaya (London: Verso, 1994); idem, *Russkie amazonki: Istoriia lesbiiskoi subkul'tury v Rossii XX vek* (Moscow: Glagol, 1998).

41. Zhuk, "The Lesbian Subculture," 150; see also Bondarenko, "Golubye v seroi stae."

42. Volkov et al., *Seksual'nye izvrashcheniia u osuzhdennykh-zhenshchin,* 56.

43. Early estimates of the number of returnees ran as high as seven to eight million, Roy A. Medvedev and Zhores A. Medvedev, *Khrushchev: The Years in Power* (Oxford: Oxford University Press, 1977), 20. For archive-based recent figures, see G. M. Ivanova, *GULAG v sisteme totalitarnogo gosudarstva* (Moscow: Moskovskii obshchestvennyi nauchnyi fond, 1997), 77; Keep, *Last of the Empires,* 13, 77.

44. For the abortion decree, issued by the Presidium of the USSR Supreme Soviet on 23 November 1955, see Karev, *Ugolovnoe zakonodatel'stvo SSSR i soiuznykh respublik,* 35. On other measures mentioned, see Berman, *Justice in the USSR,* 72–76.

45. Minimum penalties had been included in 1934 to impress upon judges the seriousness with which the crime was to be treated. In the 1960 RSFSR Criminal Code the antisodomy statute was renumbered from article 154a to article 121. Its text now read: "Sexual intercourse of a man with a man (sodomy)—is punished by deprivation of liberty for a period of up to five years. Sodomy committed with the use of physical force, threats, or with a minor, or by exploiting the dependent position of the victim—is punished by deprivation of liberty for a period of up to eight years."

46. In Germany in 1945, male homosexuals in Nazi concentration camps and prisons were not always liberated. U.S. and British jurists could rule they were criminals and order them to serve out their sentences. No compensation was offered them, and in West Germany the Nazi legislation against male homosexual relations enacted in 1935 was not repealed until 1969. The Communist regime in East Germany retained the Fascist version of the antihomosexual paragraph until 1967; Plant, *The Pink Triangle,* 181.

47. A survivor of the 1980s penal camp regime claimed that prisoners' culture in the men's camps was extremely resilient and, in fact, powerful enough to impose significant limits to any control claimed by the authorities; Samoilov, "Puteshestvie v perevernutyi mir," 154–57.

48. Women composed 24 percent of camp inmates in 1945, and 38 percent of labor colonies' inhabitants; after this date, their proportion of the total Gulag population fell; Keep, *Last of the Empires,* 13.

49. Evidence for this reasoning remains to be discovered, but one of Khrushchev's famous outbursts may illustrate the tone of his thoughts on the subject. In December 1962 in Moscow he attended an exhibition (officially sanctioned) of non–Socialist Realist art of the "thaw." Exasperated with incomprehension, the leader of the Communist Party exploded with rage, calling the artists *"pederasy"* (an illiterate variant of "pederasts" found in the slang of the camps). See Kozlovskii, *Argo russkoi gomoseksual'noi subkul'tury,* 161. During this conversation between men, Khrushchev was evidently groping for the most damning term of abuse he could imagine. The coarse language that had shaped Party thinking on the original antisodomy statute in 1933–34 lived on in the imagination of the leader who might otherwise (if the logic of de-Stalinization had been observed) have dismantled this law. More circumstantial evidence of this anxiety could be in the studies of homosexuals undertaken by isolated researchers during this era, discussed below.

50. On chemical swabs and digital rectal examinations for evidentiary purposes, I. G. Bliumin, "K voprosu sudebnomeditsinskoi ekspertizy muzhchin pri polovykh prestupleniiakh," in *Voprosy travmatologii, toksikologii, skoropostizhnoi smerti i deontologii v ekspertnoi praktike. Vypusk 3* (Moscow: Meditsina, 1966). On the advantages of "sphincterometry" and "sphincterograms" (*sfinkterometriia, sfinkterogramy*) (using an apparatus to measure muscle tone via hydraulic displacement), over the crude guesswork of the digital examination, see I. G. Bliumin and L. S. Gel'tenbein, "Ob odnom diagnostiheskom priznake pri ekspertize polovykh sostoianii muzhchin," in the same volume.

51. I. G. Bliumin, "O nekotorykh funktsional'nykh priznakakh gomoseksualizma," in *Voprosy seksopatologii (Materialy nauchno-prakticheskoi konferentsii),* ed. D. D. Fedotov (Moscow: Moskovskogo n.-i. institut psikhiatrii MZ RSFSR, 1969), 32–33.

52. Shvarts, "K voprosu o priznakakh privychnoi passivnoi pederastii (Iz nabliudenii v aziatskoi chasti g. Tashkenta)," 816–18 (see chapter 3).

53. Kon, *Seksual'naia kul'tura v Rossii,* 179.

54. Sexological seminars and publications began to appear in the mid-1960s; Kon, *Seksual'naia kul'tura v Rossii,* 179–81.

55. E. M. Derevinskaia, "Materialy k klinike, patogenezu, terapii zhenskogo gomoseksualizma."

56. Kon, *Seksual'naia kul'tura v Rossii,* 181. A. M. Sviadoshch, *Zhenskaia seksopatologiia* (Moscow: Meditsina, 1974), was issued in a print run of 100,000 and circulated well beyond the medical profession.

57. There were a few exceptions, studies of experiments in psychotherapy-and-drug cures for male homosexuality with only handfuls of patients, perhaps diverted deliberately from the penal system; see N. V. Ivanov, *Voprosy psikhoterapii funktsional'nykh seksual'nykh rasstroistv* (Moscow: Meditsina, 1966), 134–39; Ia. G. Goland, "K voprosu o psikhoterapii gomoseksualizma," in *Voprosy psikhoterapii v obshchei meditsine i psikhonevrologii,* ed. A. L. Groisman (Khar'kov, 1968); idem., "O stupenchatom postroenii psikhoterapii pri muzhskom gomoseksualizme," in *Problemy sovremennoi seksopatologii (sbornik trudov),* ed. A. A. Portnov (Moscow: Moskovskii nauchno-issledovatel'skii institut psikhiatrii, 1972); Bliumin's studies (discussed above) served

police requirements and displayed no ambition to claim the "homosexual" for psychiatry, by, e.g., suggesting therapeutic rather than penal solutions to the "problem."

58. Derevinskaia, "Materialy k klinike, patogenezu, terapii zhenskogo gomoseksualizma," 50; for three histories of this type, see 140–48. Derevinskaia acknowledged the assistance of two doctors at the MVD labor camp, see 253.

59. By nationality there were sixty-nine Russians, seventeen Ukrainians, five Armenians, two Latvians, one each of Lithuanian, Jewish, and "gypsy" origin. Eighty-eight women had something less than an incomplete secondary education, and of these, over half had four years of schooling or less. Of the fifty-three women with work experience, forty could be considered workers (e.g., cobblers, lathe operators, drivers, seamstresses, cleaners, kitchen staff); twelve, white-collar employees (bookkeepers, salespersons, secretaries). There was one milkmaid, the sole peasant in the group. Derevinskaia, "Materialy k klinike, patogenezu, terapii zhenskogo gomoseksualizma," 47–52.

60. Derevinskaia consulted 175 foreign sexological works on homosexuality and the psychology and physiology of sexuality, including Krafft-Ebing in a 1908 translation, Alfred Kinsey's studies of male and female sexual behavior, Freud's study of a case of female homosexuality, and Steinach and Lichtenstern's 1918 report of their testicular transplant on a male homosexual. There were several lesser U.S. studies from the 1930s and 1940s in her bibliography. Among Russian authorities (110 titles), she cited Bekhterev, Osipov, Sereiskii, and E. A. Popov.

61. Derevinskaia, "Materialy k klinike, patogenezu, terapii zhenskogo gomoseksualizma," 73–76, 104, 116–20.

62. This might, however, include what Derevinskaia believed to be unorthodox sexual demands put to male partners once "passive" women had reverted to heterosexual relations: "Thus G. L. and F. R. explained that they succeeded in convincing their husbands to invoke sexual arousal in them by the means that their female partners had used. Their desire for women disappeared." Derevinskaia, "Materialy k klinike, patogenezu, terapii zhenskogo gomoseksualizma," 140.

63. Aminazine was used during the 1960s–1970s as a "punitive" tool in Soviet psychiatric institutions, where its sedative properties were valued for muting troublesome "patients." Dosages were reportedly exceeded routinely and could lead to impaired liver function and death; see Alexander Podrabinek, *Punitive Medicine* (Ann Arbor: Karoma, 1980), 88–89.

64. Derevinskaia, "Materialy k klinike, patogenezu, terapii zhenskogo gomoseksualizma," 204–5, 236–37.

65. Sviadoshch, *Zhenskaia seksopatologiia,* 165–67.

66. Kon, *Seksual'naia kul'tura v Rossii,* 182.

67. Kon, *Seksual'naia kul'tura v Rossii.*

68. On late-Soviet medical ethics, see Richard De George, "Biomedical Ethics," in *Science and the Soviet Social Order,* ed. Loren R. Graham (Cambridge, Mass.: Harvard University Press, 1990).

69. Gessen, *The Rights of Lesbians and Gay Men in the Russian Federation,* 17–18. See also Catherine Durand and Catherine Gonnard, "Pas de pérestroïka pour Olga," *Lesbia Magazine* 88 (November 1990): 14–15; C. D., "L'amour traité en hôpital psychiatrique," *Gai Pied Hebdo* 457 (14 February 1991): 56.

70. Gessen, *The Rights of Lesbians and Gay Men,* 18.

71. See, e.g., a letter written in the early 1990s from a lesbian in Vologda, who when sent by her mother to a "sexopathologist," underwent urine analysis; "the doctor said, if I am a man according to the test, he could send me to be 'redone' (*na peredelku*) in Moscow!" Ol'ga Krauze, "Vashi pis'ma," *Gay, Slaviane!* 2 (1994): 90.

72. On the social evolution of late-Soviet life, see Moshe Lewin, *The Gorbachev*

Phenomenon: A Historical Interpretation (London: Hutchinson Radius, 1988); Robert
G. Kaiser, *Why Gorbachev Happened: His Triumphs, His Failure, and His Fall* (New
York: Simon & Schuster, 1992); David Lane, *Soviet Society under Perestroika* (London:
Routledge, 1992). On post-1991 Russia, see Richard Sakwa, *Russian Politics and Society,*
2d ed. (London: Routledge, 1996).

73. On the evolution of the subculture in these years in the capital, see Dan Healey,
"Moscow," in *Queer Sites: Gay Urban Histories since 1600,* ed. David Higgs (London:
Routledge, 1999), 51-57.

74. Julie Dorf, "On the Theme: Talking with the Editor of the Soviet Union's First
Lesbian and Gay Newspaper," *Outlook* 1 (1990): 55-59.

75. The literature on the emergence of lesbian and gay voices and demands for
the human rights of "sexual minorities" in Soviet and post-Soviet Russia is growing.
See Gessen, *The Rights of Lesbians and Gay Men;* Olga Zhuk, "The Lesbian Subculture:
The Historical Roots of Lesbianism in the Former USSR," in *Women in Russia: A New
Era in Russian Feminism,* ed. Anastasia Posadskaya (London: Verso, 1994); Igor S. Kon
and James Riordan, eds., *Sex and Russian Society* (London: Pluto, 1993); Kon, *The
Sexual Revolution in Russia;* idem, *Seksual'naia kul'tura v Rossii;* Riordan, "Sexual Mi-
norities," in Marsh, *Women in Russia and Ukraine;* Tuller, *Cracks in the Iron Closet;*
Daniel Schluter, "Fraternity without Community: Social Institutions in the Soviet Gay
World" (Ph.D. diss., Columbia University, 1998); Essig, *Queer in Russia.*

76. On the rise of the gay liberation movement, its American origins, and its global-
ization, see: Dennis Altman, *The Homosexualization of America, the Americanization
of the Homosexual* (New York: St. Martin's Press, 1982); Barry Adam, *The Rise of a
Gay and Lesbian Movement* (Boston: Twayne, 1987); D'Emilio, *Making Trouble;* Barry
D. Adam, Jan Willem Duyvendak, and André Krouwel, eds., *The Global Emergence
of Gay and Lesbian Politics: National Imprints of a Worldwide Movement* (Philadelphia:
Temple University Press, 1999).

77. This scrutiny was fueled by the expansion of gay publications and the cultivation of a lesbian and gay readership. By 1980, several gay newspapers and magazines
in Western nations had run detailed accounts of mostly male gay life in the USSR
and had followed stories about individuals charged under the antisodomy law. See,
e.g., Tom Reeves, "Red and Gay: Oppression East and West," *Fag Rag* 6 (fall 1973):
3-6; George Schuvaloff, "Gay Life in Russia," *Christopher Street* (September 1976);
Simon Karlinsky, "The Case of Gennady Trifonov," *Christopher Street* (January 1979);
"G," "The Secret Life of Moscow," *Christopher Street,* (June 1980): 15-21.

78. For translations of Trifonov's open letter and "Letter from Prison," see Moss,
Out of the Blue, 226-32; on Trifonov's case, see also Simon Karlinsky, "Russia's Gay
Literature and Culture." For Pezzana's activities in Moscow and his protest, see Karl-
Heinz Steinle, "Gay Liberation von 1969 bis heute: DDR und UdSSR," in *Goodbye
to Berlin?: 100 Jahre Schwulenbewegung,* eds. Monika Hingst et al. (Berlin:Verlag rosa
Winkel, 1997), 301.

79. Sakharov, e.g., refused to assist Pezzana because he feared being labeled a homosexual himself according to Steinle, "DDR und UdSSR." The first feminist unofficial
(samizdat) journal, issued in Leningrad in 1979, evoked angry denunciation from "both
sides," dissidents and official press alike; see Mamonova, *Russian Women's Studies,* 138-
42.

80. The "Gay Laboratory's" activities deserve to be better documented; this description relies on Kon, *Seksual'naia kul'tura v Rossii,* 367, and Sergej Shcherbakov, "On
the Relationship between the Leningrad Gay Community and Legal Authorities in
the 1970s and 1980s," in *Sexual Minorities and Society: The Changing Attitudes toward
Homosexuality in 20th Century Europe,* ed. Udo Parikas and Teet Veispak (Tallinn:

350 NOTES TO PAGES 248-49

Institute of History, 1991). A transcription of a cassette tape, made by group member and received in January 1984 by the International Gay Association, is held in the archive of the Schwulesmuseum in Berlin. This statement opens by summarizing what foreign gays know about Russia (". . .the police, KGB, dissidents, Sergei Paradjanov, prisoners and public toilets. C'est la vie en Russie, charmant cocktail à la russe."). The speaker identifies himself as a twenty-seven-year-old member of the Communist Party and an inhabitant of Leningrad. He continues: "I do not think [our country's] antigay policy is good. I think it acts as a destructive force in our society. It makes people hostile toward our political and social system. Homophobia undermines the international prestige of the Soviet Union and compromises the ideals of socialism and communism. It makes it difficult to counterattack anti-Soviet forces in the West who say the Soviet Union is an inhuman country and that Russians are barbaric and underdeveloped. As a Soviet patriot, I will never tolerate cynical and demagogic propaganda aimed against the millions of gays and lesbians, citizens of the USSR . . ." He observes that the chief abusers of Soviet gays and lesbians are not the "ignorant masses of heterosexual men and women," but the "corrupt bureaucrats and their servants who have nothing to do with socialism and communism." He argues that these forces no longer have the upper hand, since mass terror has been eschewed by the post-Stalin political system and because the country is no longer as isolated as it was in Stalin's time. Optimistically, he concludes that with the assistance of foreign gay organizations, "we can have a quite different cocktail à la russe. This new cocktail consists of courage, passion, solidarity, and knowledge . . . The time for gay liberation in the USSR has come."

81. M. Shagorodskii and P. Osipov, *Kurs sovetskogo ugolovnogo prava. Chast' 3* (Leningrad: Izd-vo LGU, 1973), 645–48. This commentary on criminal law was unusual in this respect; for a description of it and its juridical context, see De Jong, "'An Intolerable Kind of Moral Degeneration,'" 341–57.

82. Kon, *Seksual'naia kul'tura v Rossii,* 359. Ignatov had in 1974 successfully defended his doctoral thesis (on sex crimes), which called for the decriminalization of sodomy, against the objections of Party functionaries; see Gessen, *The Rights of Lesbians and Gay Men,* 10.

83. G. S. Vasil'chenko, *Obshchaia seksopatologiia. Rukovodstvo dlia vrachei* (Moscow: Meditsina, 1977); idem, *Chastnaia seksopatologiia. Rukovodstvo dlia vrachei,* 2 vols. (Moscow: Meditsina, 1983); I. S. Kon, *Vvedenie k seksologiiu* (Moscow: Meditsina, 1988); Kon's book had been published in translation in the two Germanies in 1985.

84. See, e.g., Vasil'chenko, *Chastnaia seksopatologiia,* 2: 109–14. This section was written by Moscow psychiatrist Ia. G. Goland, a specialist in psychotherapeutic treatments for homosexuality; note, e.g., his "K voprosu o psikhoterapii gomoseksualizma," in *Voprosy psikhoterapii v obshchei meditsine i psikhonevrologii,* ed. A. L. Groisman (Khar'kov, 1968); idem, "O stupenchatom postroenii psikhoterapii pri muzhskom gomoseksualizme," in *Problemy sovremennoi seksopatologii (sbornik trudov),* ed. A. A. Portnov (Moscow: Moskovskii nauchno-issledovatel'skii institut psikhiatrii, 1972). This literature does not acknowledge the use of electroshock therapy to "cure" homosexuals, which was, however, reputedly employed during the late 1950s and 1960s at the Institute of Higher Nervous Functions, Moscow.

85. A. Ignatov, "K razrabotke novogo ugolovnogo zakonodatel'stva: Ob otvetstvennosti za polovye prestupleniia," *Sovetskaia iustitsiia* 3 (1988): 28–29.

86. Kon, *Seksual'naia kul'tura v Rossii,* 360–61.

87. Gessen, *The Rights of Lesbians and Gay Men,* 24–25.

88. On these developments, see, e.g., Kon, *The Sexual Revolution in Russia;* Tuller, *Cracks in the Iron Closet;* Riordan, "Sexual Minorities." For the proceedings of the Estonian conference, Parikas and Veispak, eds., *Sexual Minorities and Society.*

89. Schluter, "Fraternity with Community"; Essig, *Queer in Russia.*

90. Gessen, *The Rights of Lesbians and Gay Men,* 24. For the decree, see "Zakon Rossiiskoi federatsii o vnesenii izmenenii i dopolnenii v Ugolovyi kodeks RSFSR, Ugolovno-protsessual'nyi kodeks RSFSR i Ispravitel'no-trudovoi kodeks RSFSR," *Rossiiskaia gazeta,* 27 May 1993, 6.

91. "Iz istorii Ugolovnogo kodeksa: 'Primerno NAKAZAT' etikh Merzavtsev,' " 164–65. The failure of gay/lesbian campaigning groups to achieve genuine political influence, and the presidency's ambivalence about sodomy decriminalization, were evident in the presentation of the Whyte-Stalin letter (from the same archival file), which accompanied the Iagoda-Stalin revelations. The Whyte letter was subtitled "Humor from the Special Collections" and was treated as a bizarre find; see Garri Uait [Harry Whyte], "Mozhet li gomoseksualist sostoiat' chlenom kommunisticheskoi partii?" *Istochnik* 5–6 (1993): 185–91. Both *Sovershenno sekretno* (1996) and *Trud* (2000) republished this material, supplying their own commentaries and photomontages to entertain readers. (*Trud* added a sidebar offering another archival curiosity, a 1935 Kremlin memo on letter-opening hygiene, circulated after someone posted Stalin an envelope full of excrement.) Bad taste aside, these releases of otherwise inaccessible archival documents were a frequent political maneuver of the Yeltsin Presidency; R. W. Davies, *Soviet History in the Yeltsin Era* (London: Macmillan, 1997), 111–14.

92. Gessen, *The Rights of Lesbians and Gay Men,* 12 (statistics), 28–33 (lack of amnesty).

93. I. V. Smirnov, ed., *Ugolovnyi kodeks Rossiiskoi federatsii priniat Gosudarstvennoi Dumoi 24 maia 1996 goda* (St. Petersburg: Al'fa, 1996), 64–65, article 132. For reaction, see Gessen, *The Rights of Lesbians and Gay Men,* 25–27; Kon, *Seksual'naia kul'tura v Rossii,* 373–75.

94. The post-Soviet Russian criminal code's language on sexual crime is characterized by a proliferation of conditions and aggravated circumstances described explicitly, when compared with terse Soviet statutes. Penalties for heterosexual "rape" (article 131) and "Sodomy, lesbianism or other acts of a sexual character with the use of force or the threat of its use" (article 132) attract sentences ranging from three to fifteen years. Aggravating circumstances in each case are identical. The code also punishes "Compulsion to acts of a sexual character" (article 133) and "Sexual intercourse or other acts of a sexual character with a person who has not attained 16 years of age" (article 134), nominating "sodomy" and "lesbianism" explicitly alongside "sexual intercourse," a term reserved for heterosexual acts presumably of a penetrative nature. It also punishes "Depraved (*Razvratnye*) acts" with children under fourteen years (article 135), retaining this Soviet legal term for nonpenetrative sexual activity; see Smirnov, ed. *Ugolovnyi kodeks Rossiiskoi federatsii,* 63–66.

CONCLUSION

1. Quoted in Karlinsky, " 'Vvezen iz-za granitsy . . .'?"

2. Kotkin, *Magnetic Mountain.*

3. Terry Martin, "Modernization or Neo-traditionalism? Ascribed Nationality and Soviet Primordialism," in *Stalinism: New Directions,* ed. Sheila Fitzpatrick (London: Routledge, 1999).

4. Kotkin, *Magnetic Mountain,* 355–66.

5. Martin, "Modernization or Neo-traditionalism?" 355, 361.

6. Sedgwick, *Epistemology of the Closet,* 85.

7. Novopolin, *Pornograficheskii element v russkoi literature,* 169.

8. The Elista HIV scandal of 1988 dramatized this mapping of perversion. The infection of twenty-seven hospitalized infants in Elista, Kalmyk ASSR, through the

use of unsterilized syringes in a maternity ward was traced to a Soviet merchant seaman who had had a blood transfusion in the Congo in 1981. He later infected his wife and her newborn child. An article about the first Soviet AIDS patient, "a gay engineer who caught the virus in Africa," also emphasized this "geography of perversion." AIDS was also portrayed in the Soviet press as a disease of depraved foreigners and those Soviet citizens sufficiently antisocial to consort with them. On Elista and AIDS in late-Soviet journalism, see Dan Healey, "Can Glasnost Cope with Aids?" *The Pink Paper*, 18 March 1989, 2; on the first Soviet person with AIDS, Riordan, "Sexual Minorities," in Marsh, *Women in Russia and Ukraine*, 161.

9. Martin, "Modernization or Neo-traditionalism?" 360–61. For an example of the sanitization of folklore in practice, see the delicate mention of a tsarist-era denial of same-sex love as an element of Russian *pobratimstvo* (religious and lay unions between unrelated men) in M. M. Gromyko, *Traditsionnye formy povedeniia i formy obshcheniia russkikh krest'ian XIX v.* (Moscow: Nauka, 1986), 86. On the sanitization of anthropologists' descriptions of these traditional Christian unions, see John Boswell, *Same-Sex Unions in Premodern Europe* (New York: Villard Books, 1994), 267–79. For comment on the distinctions between *pobratimstvo* and male same-sex love in Russian history, see Healey, "Moscow," 41–42.

10. Bleys, *The Geography of Perversion*, 267.

APPENDIX

1. "We will probably never know how many suffered, perhaps up to a quarter of a million": see Neil McKenna, "Men of the Lunar Light," *Him* 32 (1990): 49. Most attempts to set a figure have relied upon an approximate number of convictions during the 1960s of 1,000 per year, see De Jong, " 'An Intolerable Kind of Moral Degeneration,' " 341–57; Kon, *Lunnyi svet na zare*, 311; Sergei Shcherbakov, "Sotsial'nye posledstviia prebyvaniia golubykh v nevole," *Gay, Slaviane!* 1 (1993): 71.

2. See, e.g., Iurii Trifonov, "Sovetskie gomoseksualisty," *Gay, Slaviane!* 1 (1993): 15 (editors' notes); "Pervyi v Rossii obshchestvennyi tsentr geev i lesbiianok," *Tsentr Treugol'nik: Informatsionnyi biulleten'* 1 (1996): 1. The equation of Soviet and Nazi oppression of male homosexuals serves totalitarian school interpretations of Russian history. A serious historical comparison of the two regimes' approaches is needed; no one denies that both created living hells for homosexual men. On compulsory castration, hormonal "experiments" and other aspects of the Nazi treatment of imprisoned homosexuals, see Wolfgang Röll, "Homosexual Inmates in the Buchenwald Concentration Camp," *Journal of Homosexuality* 31, no. 4 (1996): 1–28; Günter Grau, ed., *Hidden Holocaust?: Gay and Lesbian Persecution in Germany, 1933–45* (London: Cassell, 1995).

3. Kozlovskii, *Argo russkoi gomoseksual'noi subkul'tury*, 155.

4. The table listing criminal convictions for this year, located in the archive of the RSFSR Ministry of Justice, breaks them down by location. The single largest cluster it shows are 20 sodomy convictions handed down in the last quarter of 1950 in Tula province, a manufacturing center just south of Moscow: GARF f. A353, op. 16s, d. 121, l. 21 ob. Tula city police may have been unusually successful in uncovering a network of friends and contacts; yet this suggests that big city police forces paid relatively little attention to homosexuals at this time.

5. Daniel Schluter, "Fraternity without Community: Social Institutions in the Soviet Gay World" (PhD, Columbia University, 1998), 179. My own conversations with Moscow homosexuals in 1995–1996 confirmed this assertion.

BIBLIOGRAPHY

ARCHIVAL SOURCES

1. Court Cases (1935–41)

To preserve the anonymity of individuals tried from 1935 to 1941 for sodomy and other sex crimes in Moscow city court (*Moskovskii gorodskoi sud*) criminal cases used in this study, I assign pseudonyms to named defendants. All documents are held in TsMAM. Full references for each short title are as follows, in chronological order:

Sentence of Bezborodov and eleven others (1935): TsMAM, f. 819, op. 2, d. 11, ll. 238–245

Sentence of Krasin and Popov (1935): TsMAM, f. 819, op. 2, d. 10, ll. 283–285

Sentence of Anisimov and Brodskii (1935): TsMAM, f. 819, op. 2, d. 10, ll. 297–299

Sentence of Siniakov (1937): TsMAM, f. 819, op. 2, d. 25, ll. 128–131

Sentence of Belov and six others (1937): TsMAM, f. 819, op. 2, d. 24, ll. 169–172

Sentence of Tereshkov and nine others (1938): TsMAM, f. 819, op. 2, d. 30, ll. 41–47

Sentence of Leont'ev and Baikin (1939): TsMAM, f. 819, op. 2, d. 33, ll. 187–188

Sentence of Stepanova (1940): TsMAM, f. 819, op. 2, d. 38, ll. 17–18

Case file of Andreevskii and two others (1941): TsMAM, f. 819, op. 2, d. 51

2. Other Court Cases

Other sodomy and relevant sex crime cases were located in the following archival holdings:

TsGIAgM, f. 203 (Moskovskaia dukhovnaia konsistoriia)

TsGIAgM, f. 142 (Moskovskii okruzhnyi sud)

TsMAM, f. 901 (Moskovskii narodnyi sud, Leningradskii raion, 1942–1960 gg.)

TsMAM, f. 1921 (Moskovskii narodnyi sud, Sokol'nicheskii raion, 1946–1960 gg.)

TsMAM, f. 1919 (Moskovskii narodnyi sud, Zheleznodorozhnyi raion, 1945–1957 gg.)

GARF, f. 564, op. 1 (Dokumental'nye materialy, sobrannye A. F. Koni, dlia svoikh rabot)

3. Other Archival Materials

GARF, f. A353 (Narodnyi komissariat iustitsii RSFSR)

GARF, f. A482 (Narodnyi komissariat zrdavookhraneniia RSFSR)

GARF, f. A406 (Narodnyi komissariat raboche-krest'ianskoi inspektsii RSFSR)

GARF, f. R8131 (Prokuratura SSSR 1924–49 gg.)
GARF, f. R9492 (Verkhovnyi sud SSSR, Ministerstvo iustitsii SSSR)
GARF, f. R9474 (Verkhovnyi sud SSSR 1924–70 gg.)
GARF, f. R1235 (VTsIK Sovetov rabochikh, krest'ianskikh, i krasnoarmeiskikh deputa-
    tov, 1917–38 gg.)
RGASPI, f. 17 (Tsentral'nyi komitet KPSS)
RGASPI, f. 134 (A. M. Kollontai)
RGASPI, f. 159 (G. V. Chicherin)
RGALI, f. 232 (M. A. Kuzmin)
RGALI, f. 612 (Gosudarstvennyi literaturnyi muzei)

PUBLISHED SOURCES

1. Periodicals

Newspapers, Periodicals, Scientific Journals (1861–1941)

Arkhiv psikhiatrii neirologii i sudebnoi psikhopatologii
Arkhiv sudebnoi meditsiny i obshchestvennoi gigieny (later *Vestnik obshchestvennoi gi-
    gieny, sudebnoi i prakticheskoi meditsiny*)
Bezbozhnik
Ezhnedel'nik sovetskoi iustitsii
Izvestiia
Jahrbuch für sexuelle Zwischenstufen (Leipzig)
Kazanskii meditsinskii zhurnal
Klinicheskii arkhiv genial'nosti i odarennosti
Molodaia gvardiia
Nauchnaia meditsina
Obozrenie psikhiatrii, nevrologii i refleksologii
Pod znamenem marksizma
Pravda
Pravo i zhizn'
Prestupnik i prestupnost'
Revoliutsiia i tserkov'
Revoliutsiia prava
Saratovskii vestnik zdravookhraneniia
Sotsial'naia gigiena
Sovetskaia iustitsiia
Sovetskoe pravo
Sud idet
Sudebno-meditsinskaia ekspertiza
Voprosy izucheniia i vospitaniia lichnosti
Vrach
Vrachebnaia gazeta (later *Sovetskaia vrachebnaia gazeta*)
Vrachebnoe delo
Sovetskoe gosudarstvo i revoliutsionnoe pravo
Zhurnal nevropatologii i psikhiatrii im. S. S. Korsakova (later *Sovetskaia nevropatologiia,
    psikhiatriia i psikhogigiena; Nevropatologiia i psikhiatriia*)

2. Primary Sources

Avdeev, M. I. *Sudebnaia meditsina.* 3d ed. Moscow: Gosiurizdat, 1951.
Banshchikov, V. M. "Zasluzhennyi deiatel' nauki professor E. K. Krasnushkin (Zhizn'
    i nauchnaia deiatel'nost'). 1885–1951 gg." In E. K. Krasnushkin, *Izbrannye trudy.*
    Ed. V. M. Banshchikov. Moscow: Medgiz, 1960.

Batkis, Grigorii. "Sex Problems in Soviet Russia at the Time of Socialistic Reconstruction." In *World League for Sexual Reform: Proceedings of 4th Congress in Vienna.* Vienna, 1932.

Bekhterev, V. M. "Lechenie vnusheniem prevratnykh polovykh vlechenii i onanizma." *Obozrenie psikhiatrii* 8 (1898): 1–11.

———. "O polovom ozdorovlenii." *Vestnik znaniia* (1910): 9: 924–37, 10: 1–19.

———. *Gipnoz, vnushenie i psikhoterapiia.* St. Petersburg, 1911.

———. "O polovykh izvrashcheniiakh, kak patologicheskikh sochetatel'nykh refleksakh." *Obozrenie psikhiatrii* 7–9 (1915): 1–26.

———. "Polovye ukloneniia i izvrashcheniia v svete refleksologii." *Voprosy izucheniia i vospitaniia lichnosti* 4–5 (1922): 644–746.

———. "Ob izvrashchenii i uklonenii polovogo vlecheniia." In *Polovoi vopros v svete nauchnogo znaniia.* Ed. V. F. Zelenin. Moscow: Gosizdat, 1926.

———. "Polovaia deiatel'nost' s tochki zreniia refleksologii." In *Polovoi vopros v svete nauchnogo znaniia.* Ed. V. F. Zelenin. Moscow: Gosizdat, 1926.

———. "O polovom izvrashchenii, kak osoboi ustanovke polovykh refleksov." In *Polovoi vopros v shkole i v zhizni.* Ed. I. S. Simonov. Leningrad: Brokgauz-Efron, 1927.

Belousov, V. A. "Sluchai gomoseksuala-muzhskoi prostitutki." *Prestupnik i prestupnost'. Sbornik* 2 (1927): 309–17.

Bentovin, B. I. *Torguiushchie telom. Ocherki sovremennoi prostitutsii.* St. Petersburg: Leonid Krumbiugel', 1909.

Bliumin, I. G. "K voprosu sudebnomeditsinskoi ekspertizy muzhchin pri polovykh prestupleniiakh." In *Voprosy travmatologii, toksikologii, skoropostizhnoi smerti i deontologii v ekspertnoi praktike. Vypusk 3.* Moscow: Meditsina, 1966.

———. "O nekotorykh funktsional'nykh priznakakh gomoseksualizma." In *Voprosy seksopatologu (Materialy nauchno-prakticheskoi konferentsii).* Ed. D. D. Fedotov. Moscow: Moskovskogo n.-i. institut psikhiatrii MZ RSFSR, 1969.

Bliumin, I. G., and L. S. Gel'fenbein. "Ob odnom diagnosticheskom priznake pri ekspertize polovykh sostoianii muzhchin." In *Voprosy travmatologii, toksikologii, skoropostizhnoi smerti i deontologii v ekspertnoi praktike. Vypusk 3.* Moscow: Meditsina, 1966.

Bloch, Iwan. *Das Sexualleben unserer Zeit in seinen Beziehungen zur modernen Kultur.* Berlin: Louis Marcus, 1908.

Borisov, A. *Izvrashchennaia polovaia zhizn'. Boleznennye izmeneniia polovoi sfery.* St. Petersburg, 1907.

Brailovskii, V. "Kogda nuzhen psikhiatr v ugolovnom protsesse." *Pravo i zhizn'* 7 (1927): 109–13.

Bron, T. M. "Problema izucheniia byta." *Gigiena i epidemiologiia* 2 (1927): 25–33.

Brukhanskii, N. P. "K voprosu o skotolozhestve." *Zhurnal nevropatologii i psikhiatrii im. S. S. Korsakova* 2 (1926): 59–71.

———. *Materialy po seksual'noi psikhopatologii.* Moscow: M. i S. Sabashnikovy, 1927.

———. *Sudebnaia psikhiatriia.* Moscow: M. i S. Sabashnikovy, 1928.

———. "Krizis ucheniia o psikhopatiiakh." In *Trudy psikhiatricheskoi kliniki (Gedeonovka).* Ed. R. I. Belkin. Smolensk: Smolenskii gos. universitet, 1930.

Bulatov, S. Ia. "Vozrozhdenie Lombrozo v sovetskoi kriminologii." *Revoliutsiia prava* 1 (Jan.–Feb. 1929): 42–61.

Buneev, A. N. *Sudebnaia psikhiatriia.* Moscow: Gos. iz-vo iuridicheskoi lit., 1954.

Buneev, A. N., Ts. M. Feinberg, and A. M. Khaletskii. *Sudebnaia psikhiatriia.* 3d ed. Moscow: Gos. iz-vo. iuridicheskoi literatury, 1949.

Chaikovskii, P. I. *Dnevniki, 1873–1891.* Moscow-Petrograd: Gos. iz-vo Muzykal'nyi sektor, 1923.

Cherlunkachevich, N. A. "Ob ugolovnom kodekse." *Ezhenedel'nik sovetskoi iustitsii* 5 (1922): 9.

Cheron, George. "The Diary of Mixail Kuzmin, 1905–1906." *Wiener Slawistischer Almanach* 17 (1986): 391–436.

Chizh, V. F. *K ucheniiu ob "izvrashchenii polovogo chuvstva" (Die conträre Sexualempfindung)*. *Soobshcheno obshchestvu Peterburgskikh morskikh vrachei v zasedanii 1-go fevralia 1882 goda*. [St. Petersburg], 1882.

Chlenov, M. A. *Polovaia perepis' moskovskogo studenchestva i ee obshchestvennoe znachenie*. Moscow, 1909.

Ciliga, Anton. *The Russian Enigma*. London: Ink Links, 1979.

Derevianko, I. M. *Gomoseksualizm. Prichiny i lechenie*. Stavropol': Stavropol'skoe kn. iz-vo, 1990.

Derevinskaia, Elizaveta M. "Materialy k klinike, patogenezu, terapii zhenskogo gomoseksualizma" [Materials on the clinical presentation, pathogenesis, and therapy of female homosexuality]. Kandidatskaia dissertatsiia meditsinskikh nauk, Karagandinskii gosudarstvennyi meditsinskii institut, 1965.

Drokov, S. V. "Protokoly doprosov organizatora Petrogradskogo zhenskogo batal'ona smerti." *Otechestvennye arkhivy* 1 (1994): 50–66.

Durova, Nadezhda. *The Cavalry Maiden: Journals of a Russian Officer in the Napoleonic Wars*. Transl. M. Zirin. Bloomington: Indiana University Press, 1988.

Durmanov, N. D. *Ugolovnoe pravo. Osobennaia chast'. Prestupleniia, sostavliaiushchie perezhitki rodogo byta*. Moscow: Iuridicheskoe izd. NKIu SSSR, 1938.

Edel'shtein, A. O. "K klinike transvestitizma." *Prestupnik i prestupnost': Sbornik* 2 (1927): 273–82.

Ellis, Havelock. *Studies in the Psychology of Sex*. 3d ed. 7 vols. Philadelphia: F. A. Davis, 1925.

Eratov, L. "Nakazuema li prostitutsiia?" *Ezhenedel'nik sovetskoi iustitsii* 4 (1922): 4–6.

Erikson, E. V. "O polovom razvrate i neestestvennykh polovykh snosheniiakh v korennom naselenii Kavkaza." *Vestnik obshchestvennoi gigieny, sudebnoi i prakticheskoi meditsiny* 12 (1906): 1868–93.

Fedotov, D. D., ed. *Voprosy seksopatologii (Materialy nauchno-prakticheskoi konferentsii)*. Moscow: Minzdrav RSFSR, Moskovskii nauchno-issledovatel'skii institut psikhitrii, 1969.

Feinberg, Ts. M., ed. *Psikhopatii i ikh sudebno-psikhiatricheskoe znachenie*. Moscow: Sovetskoe zakonodatel'stvo, 1934.

———. *Sudebno-psikhiatricheskaia ekspertiza i opyt raboty instituta sudebnoi psikhiatrii im. prof. Serbskogo za 25 let*. Moscow: Tsent. n.-i. institut sudebnoi psikhiatrii im. prof. Serbskogo MZ SSSR, 1947.

Frenkel', E. P. *Polovye prestupleniia*. Odessa: Svetoch, 1927.

Fuks, I. B. *Gomoseksualizm kak prestuplenie. Iruidich. i ugol.-politich. ocherk*. St. Petersburg: Obshchestvennaia Pol'za, 1914.

G. R. "Protsessy gomoseksualistov." *Ezhenedel'nik sovetskoi iustitsii* 33 (1922): 16–17.

Gakkebush, V. M., and I. A. Zalkind. *Kurs sudebnoi psikhopatologii*. Khar'kov: Iurid. iz-vo Narkomiusta UkrSSR, 1928.

Gannushkin, P. B. *Klinika psikhopatii: Ikh statika, dinamika, sistematika*. Moscow: Kooperativnoe Izdatel'stvo Sever, 1933.

Gel'man, I. G. "Anketnyi list dlia sobraniia svedenii po polovomu voprosu." *Sotsial'naia gigiena* 2 (1923) : 111.

———. *Polovaia zhizn' sovremennoi molodezhi. Opyt sotsial'no-biologicheskogo obsledovaniia*. Moscow and Petrograd: Gosizdat, 1923.

Gernet, Mikhail N. *Moral'naia statistika.* Moscow: Izdanie TsSU, 1922.

———. *V tiur'me. Ocherki tiuremnoi psikhologii.* Moscow: Pravo i zhizn', 1925.

———, ed. *Prestupnyi mir Moskvy.* Moscow: Pravo i zhizn', 1924.

Gertsenzon, A. "Klassovaia bor'ba i perezhitki starogo byta." *Sovetskaia iustitsiia* 2 (1934): 16–17.

Gide, André. *Retour de l'URSS.* Paris: Gallimard, 1936.

Gofmann, Eduard. *Uchebnik sudebnoi meditsiny.* Trans. I. M. Gvozdev et al. Kazan': Tip. imperatorskogo universiteta, 1878.

Golomb, Ia. D. *Polovaia zhizn' normal'naia i nenormal'naia.* Odessa: Chernomorskii mediko-sanitarnii otdel, 1926.

———. *Polovoe vozderzhanie (za i protiv).* Odessa: Svetoch, 1927.

Goland, Ia. G. "K voprosu o psikhoterapii gomoseksualizma." In *Voprosy psikhoterapii v obshchei meditsine i psikhonevrologii.* Ed. A. L. Groisman. Khar'kov, 1968.

Golenko, V. F. "Pederastiia na sude." *Arkhiv psikhiatrii, neirologii i sudebnoi psikhopatologii* 9, no. 3 (1887): 42–56.

Golosovker, S. Ia. *O polovom byte muzhchiny.* Kazan': Izd. Kazanskogo meditsinskogo zhurnala, 1927.

Gor'kii, Maksim. "Proletarskii gumanizm." *Izvestiia,* 23 May 1934, 2.

———. "Proletarskii gumanizm." *Pravda,* 23 May 1934, 3.

Gronskii, I. M. "O krest'ianskikh pisateliakh (Vystuplenie v TsGALI 30 sentiabria 1959 g.). Publikatsiia M. Nike." *Minuvshee: Istoricheskii al'manakh* 8 (1992): 148–51.

Gurvich, B. R. "Prostitutsiia, kak sotsial'no-psikhopatologicheskoe iavlenie (Predvaritel'noe soobshchenie)." In *Sovetskaia meditsina v bor'be za zdorov'e nervy: Sbornik statei i materialov.* Ed. A. I. Miskinov, L. M. Rozenshtein, and L. A. Prozorov. Ul'ianovsk: Izd. Ul'ianovskogo kombinata PPP, 1926.

Gurevich, Z. A., and F. I. Grosser. *Problemy polovoi zhizni.* Khar'kov: Gos. Iz-vo Ukrainy, 1930.

Halle, Fannina W. *Women in Soviet Russia.* London: Routledge, 1934.

Hirschfeld, Magnus. *Das Ergebnis der statistischen Untersuchungen uber den Prozentasatz der Homosexuellen.* Leipzig: Max Spohr, 1904.

———. *Tret'ii pol Berlina.* Trans. V. N. Pirogov. St. Petersburg, 1908.

———. *Die Transvestiten.* Leipzig, 1910.

———. *Die Homosexualität des Mannes und des Weibes.* Berlin: Louis Marcus, 1914.

———. *Künstliche Verjüngung. Künstliche Geschlechtsumwandlung. Die Entdeckungen Prof. Steinachs und ihre Bedeutung.* Berlin: Johndorff, 1920.

Iaroslavskii, E. "V zashchitu biblii protiv sodomlian," *Bezbozhnik,* no. 20 (9 May 1923), 3.

———. "Sodomitskie greshniki i sodomitskie pravedniki," in E. Iaroslavskii, *Protiv religii i tserkvi* (Moscow: Bezbozhnik, 1932–33), 5: 114–18. First published in *Bezbozhnik,* 22 April 1923.

———. *Bibliia dlia veriushchykh i neveriushchykh, chast' 2: Kniga bytiia.* Moscow: 1936.

Iaroslavskii, E., ed. *Polovoi vopros.* Moscow: Iz-vo GIZh, 1925.

Il'inskii, I. "Obshchestvennost' i bolezni byta [Po povodu knigi N P Brukhanskogo: "Materialy po seksual'noi psikhopatologii"]." *Molodaia gvardiia* 5 (1928): 175–93.

Iokhved, Grigorii. "Pederastiia, zhizn' i zakon." *Prakticheskii vrach* 33 (1904): 871–73.

Ishlondskii, N. E. *Liubov', Obshchestvo i Kul'tura: Problema pola v bio-sotsiologicheskom osveshchenii.* Berlin: Iz-vo Sovremennaia Mysl', 1924.

Iudin, T. I. *Polovoe vlechenie i nenormal'nosti polovogo povedeniia.* Moscow: Narkomzdrav RSFSR, 1928.

Iurman, N. A. *Instruktivnye materialy po profilaktike dushevnykh boleznei v krasnoi armii.* Leningrad: Izd. Voenno-sanitarnogo upravlenie LVO, 1930.

Ivanov, N. V. *Voprosy psikhoterapii funktsional'nykh seksual'nykh rasstroistv.* Moscow: Meditsina, 1966.

Jason, Philip [pseud.]. "Progress to Barbarism." *Mattachine Review* 3, 8 (1957): 18–21.

Karev, D. S. *Ugolovnoe zakonodatel'stvo SSSR i soiuznykh respublik. Sbornik.* Moscow: Iuridicheskaia literatura, 1957.

Karnitskii, D. A., and Iu. Trivus. *Voprosy ugolovno-sudebnoi i sledstvennoi praktiki.* Moscow: Iuridicheskoe iz-vo NKIu RSFSR, 1927.

Karnitskii, D. A., G. K. Roginskii, and M. S. Strogovich. *Ugolovnyi kodeks RSFSR. Postateinyi kommentarii.* Moscow: Iuridicheskoe iz-vo NKIu RSFSR, 1928.

————. *Ugolovnyi kodeks RSFSR: Posobie dlia slushatelei vuzov.* Moscow: 1935.

Kechek, K. S. "Sudebno-meditsinskii i bytovoi analiz ekspertiz zhivykh lits za 1916 [1926] god po gg. Rostovu n/D. i Nakhichevani n/D." *Sudebno-meditsinskaia ekspertiza* 8 (1928): 100–5.

Khaletskii, A. M. "K probleme psikhopatii." *Zhurnal nevropatologii i psikhiatrii im. S. S. Korsakova* 12 (1952): 61–66.

Kirov, Ia. I. "K voprosu o geterotransplantatsii pri gomoseksualizme." *Vrachebnoe delo* 20 (1928): 1587–90.

Koffin'on, A. *Izvrashchennyi mir.* Moscow, 1908.

Kollontai, Alexandra. "Sexual Relations and the Class Struggle." In *Selected Writings of Alexandra Kollontai.* Trans. Alix Holt. London: Allison & Busby, 1977.

Kol'tsov, N. K., ed. *Omolozhenie.* Vols. 1–2. Moscow-Petrograd: Gosizdat, 1923.

Koni, A. F. *Na zhiznennom puti. Iz zapisok sudebnogo deiatelia. Zhiteiskie vstrechi.* Vol. 1. St. Petersburg, 1912.

Kosarev, V. K. "K voprosu o sudebno-psikhiatricheskom znachenii gomoseksualizma." In *Aktual'nye voprosy seksopatologii.* Ed. D. D. Fedotov. Moscow: Moskovskii n.i. institut psikhiatrii MZ RSFSR, 1967.

Kovalev, K. N. *Polovoe razmnozhenie v obshchebiologicheskom i biosotsial'nom osveshchenii.* Moscow: Izdatel'stvo Kul'turno-Prosvetitel'nogo Obshchestva Prometei, 1930.

Kovalevskii, P. I. "Prof. V. M. Tarnovskii. Izvrashchenie polovogo chuvstva 1885 g. [review]." *Arkhiv psikhiatrii neirologii i sudebnoi psikhopatologii* 5–6, no. 3 (1885): 262–64.

————. *Psikhologiia pola. Polovoe bezsilie i drugie polovye izvrashcheniia i ikh lechenie.* St. Petersburg, 1909.

Kraepelin, E. *Vvedenie v psikhiatricheskuiu kliniku.* 3d ed. Moscow: Narkomzdrav, 1923.

Krafft-Ebing, Richard von. *Psychopathia Sexualis.* 12 ed. Transl. F. Klaf. New York: Stein & Day, 1965.

Krasnushkin, E. K. *Sudebno-psikhiatricheskie ocherki.* Moscow: M. i S. Sabashnikovy, 1926.

————. *Prestupniki psikhopaty.* Moscow: Izd-vo pervogo Moskovskogo gos. universiteta, 1929.

————. *Izbrannye trudy.* Ed. V. M. Banshchikov. Moscow: Medgiz, 1960.

Krasnushkin, E. K., and N. G. Kholzakova. "Dva sluchaia zhenshchin ubiits-gomoseksualistok." *Prestupnik i prestupnost'. Sbornik 1* (1926): 105–20.

Krasnushkin, E. K., G. M. Segal, and Ts. M. Fainberg, eds. *Pravonarusheniia v oblasti seksual'nykh otnoshenii.* Moscow: Izdanie Mozdravotdela, 1927.

Kratter, Iu. [Julius Kratter]. "Rukovodstvo sudebnoi meditsiny. Dlia vrachei i studentov. Ch. 4. Sudebnaia seksologiia. Avtorizovannyi perev. so 2-go nemetsk. izd. pod red. i s dopolneniiami Ia. Leibovicha (Prodolzhenie)." *Sudebno-meditsinskaia ekspertiza* 9–10 (1928): 1–38, 67–114.

—. *Lehrbuch der gerichtlichen Medizin.* Stuttgart: Ferdinand Enke, 1921.

Krylenko, Nikolai. "Ob izmeneniiakh i dopolneniiakh kodeksov RSFSR." *Sovetskaia iustitsiia* 15, no. 7 (1936): 1–5.

Kul'teleev, T. M. *Ugolovnoe obychnoe pravo kazakhov (S momenta prisoedinenii Kazakhstana k Rossii do ustanovleniia sovetskoi vlasti).* Alma-Ata: Akad. nauk Kazakhskoi SSSR, 1955.

Kuzmin, M. A. *Dnevnik, 1905–1907.* Eds. N. A. Bogomolov and S. V. Shumikhin. St. Petersburg: Iz-vo Ivana Limbakha, 2000.

—. *Dnevnik 1934 goda.* Ed. G. A. Morev. St. Petersburg, Iz-vo Ivana Limkakha, 1998.

—. "Kryl'ia." In *Podzemnye ruch'i. Izbrannaia proza.* St. Petersburg: Severo-Zapad, 1994.

—. "Mikhail Kuzmin. Dnevnik 1921 goda." Eds. N. A. Bogomolov and S. V. Shumikhin. *Minuvshee. Istoricheskii al'manakh* 12–13 (1993): 423–94, 457–524.

Kvint, Levko, and Robert Geshvandtner. "Pro germafroditizm i gomoseksualizm." *Ukrainskii medichnyi arkhiv* 2–3 (1927): 1–19.

Lass, D. I. *Polovaia zhizn' zakliuchennykh.* Odessa, 1927.

Lebedev, D. A. *Sviatye razvratniki.* Moscow: Gosizdat, 1927.

Leibovich, Ia. "Tri goda sudebnoi meditsiny." *Ezhenedel'nik sovetskoi iustitsii* 7 (1922): 7–8.

—. "Piat' let sudebnoi meditsiny." *Ezhnedel'nik sovetskoi iustitsii* 34 (1923): 775–77.

—. "Sudebno-meditsinskaia ekspertiza pri NEP'e." *Ezhenedel'nik sovetskoi iustitsii* 2 (1923): 36–38.

—. "Godovoi otchet po sudeb.-meditsinskoi ekspertize v RSFSR za 1925 g." *Sudebno-meditsinskaia ekspertiza* 5 (1927): 96–128.

—. *Sudebnaia ginekologiia: Rukovodstvo dlia vrachei i iuristov.* Khar'kov: Iurdicheskoe iz-vo Narkomiusta USSR, 1928.

Lents, A. K. *Kriminal'nye psikhopaty (Sotsiopaty).* Leningrad: Rabochii sud, 1927.

Liass, S. "Izvrashchenie polovogo vlecheniia." *Obozrenie psikhiatrii, nevrologii i eksperimental'noi psikhologii* 6 (1898): 415–16.

Liberman, L. L. *Vrozhdennye narusheniia polovogo razvitiia. Genetika, "patogenez," klinika.* Leningrad: Meditsina, 1966.

Liublinskii, P. I. *Prestupleniia v oblasti polovykh otnoshenii.* Moscow-Leningrad: Iz-vo L. D. Frenkel', 1925.

Livshits, R.I. "Reaktsiia d-ra Manoilova kak pokazatel' narusheniia sekretornoi funktsii polovykh zhelez pri seksual'nykh prestuplenniiakh." *Leningradskii meditsinkii zhurnal* 2 (1925): 11–14.

Matiushenskii, A. I. *Polovoi rynok i polovye otnosheniia.* St. Petersburg, 1908.

Merzheevskii, V. *Sudebnaia ginekologiia. Rukovodstvo dlia vrachei i iuristov.* St. Petersburg, 1878.

Meyendorff, Alexander. "My Cousin, Foreign Commissar Chicherin." *Russian Review* (April 1971): 173–78.

Morev, G. A., ed. *Mikhail Kuzmin i russkaia kul'tura XX veka: Tezisy i materialy konferentsii 15–17 maia 1990 g.* Leningrad: Sovet po istorii mirovoi kul'tury AN SSSR, 1990.

Nabokoff [Nabokov], Vladimir D. "Die Homosexualität in Russischen Strafgesetz-buch." *Jahrbuch für sexuelle Zwischenstufen* 3 (1903): 1159–71.

———. "Plotskie prestupleniia po proektu ugolovnogo ulozheniia." *Vestnik prava* 9–10 (1902). Reprinted in *Sbornik statei po ugolovnomu pravu*. Ed. V. D. Nabokov. St. Petersburg, 1904.

Nekliudov, N. A. *Osobennaia chast' Russkogo ugolovnogo prava. Vyp. 1. Posiagatel'stva na lichnost'.* St. Petersburg, 1888.

Nemilov, A. V., et al., eds. *Omolozhenie v Rossii.* Leningrad: Meditsina, 1924.

Neugebauer, Franz L. *Hermaphroditismus beim Menschen.* Leipzig: Dr. W. Klinkhardt, 1908.

Newsholme, Sir Arthur. *Red Medicine: Socialized Health in Soviet Russia.* London: Heinemann, 1934.

Novopolin, G. S. *Pornograficheskii element v russkoi literature.* St. Petersburg, 1909.

Obolonskii, N. A. "Izvrashchenie polovogo chuvstva." *Russkii arkhiv patologii, klinicheskoi meditsiny i bakteriologii* (1898): 1–20.

———. "Izvrashchenie polovogo chuvstva." *Universitetskie izvestiia (Kiev)* (1898): 1–11.

Osipov, V. P. *Kurs obshchego ucheniia o dushevnykh bolezniakh.* Berlin: RSFSR Gosizdat, 1923.

———. *Rukovodstvo po psikhiatrii.* Moscow-Leningrad: Gosizdat, 1931.

Pasche-Oserski, Nikolai. "Sexualgesetzgebung in der Sowjet-Union." In *World League for Sexual Reform: Proceedings of 2nd Congress.* Copenhagen, 1928.

Piatnitskii, B. I. *Polovye izvrashcheniia i ugolovnoe pravo.* Mogilev, 1910.

Popov, Ardalion. *Sud nakazanii za prestupleniia protiv very i nravstvennosti po russkomu pravu.* Kazan': Imperatorskii universitet, 1904.

Popov, E. A. "K voprosu o geneze nekotorykh form mazokhizma (passivnogo flagelliantizma." *Vrachebnoe delo* 7 (1928): 527–31.

———. "O klassifikatsii polovykh izvrashchenii." In *Problemy psikhiatrii i psikhopatologii.* Ed. S. N. Davidenkov. Moscow: Biomedgiz, 1935.

———. "Polovye izvrashcheniia." In *Bol'shaia meditsinskaia entsiklopediia.* 2d ed. Vol. 25. Moscow: 1962.

Portnov, A. A., ed. *Problemy sovremennoi seksopatologii (sb. trudov).* Moscow: Moskovskii n.-i. institut psikhiatrii MZ RSFSR, 1972.

Porudominskii, I. M. *Polovye rasstroistva u muzhchin. Etiologiia, klinika i lechenie.* Moscow: Medgiz, 1960.

Poznyshev, S. V. *Ocherk osnovnykh nachal nauki ugolovnogo prava. II. Osobennaia chast'.* Moscow: Iuridicheskoe iz-vo NKIust, 1923.

Protopopov, V. P. "Sovremennoe sostoianie voprosa o sushchnosti i proiskhozhdenii gomoseksualizma." *Nauchnaia meditsina* 10 (1922): 49–62.

"Rasshirennyi nauchnyi s'ezd sudebnykh vrachei i predstavitelei iustitsii v g. Ivanove-Vosnesenske 23–25 dekabria 1927 g." *Sudebno-meditsinskaia ekspertiza* 9 (1928): 135–64.

Reich, Wilhelm. "Dialekticheskii materializm i psikhoanaliz." *Pod znamenem marksizma* 7–8 (July–Aug. 1929): 180–206.

———. "Psikhoanaliz kak estestvenno-nauchnaia distsiplina." *Vestnik Kommunisticheskoi Akademii* 35–36 (1929): 345–50.

———. "Psychoanalysis in the Soviet Union." In *Sex-Pol: Essays, 1929–1934.* Ed. Lee Baxandall. New York: Random House, 1966.

———. *The Sexual Revolution.* New York: Pocket Books, 1969.

Riasentsev, V. A. "Dva sluchaia iz praktiki. 1. Gomoseksualizm?" *Sudebno-meditsinskaia ekspertiza* 2 (1925): 152–56.

Rozanov, Vasilii. *Liudi lunnogo sveta: Metafizika khristianstva.* St. Petersburg: A. S. Suvorin-Novoe Vremia, 1913. Reprint, Moscow: Druzhba narodov, 1990.

Rozenbakh, P. Ia. "K kazuistike polovogo izvrashcheniia." *Obozrenie psikhiatrii, nevrologii i eksperimental'noi psikhologii* 9 (1897): 652–56.

Rozenblium, E. E., M. G. Serdiukov, and V. M. Smol'ianinov. *Sudebno-meditsinskaia akushersko-ginekologicheskaia ekspertiza.* Moscow: Sovetskoe zakonodatel'stvo, 1935.

Rozhanovskii, V. "Sudebno-meditsinskaia ekspertiza v dorevoliutsionnoi Rossii i v SSSR." *Sudebno-meditsinskaia ekspertiza* 6 (1927): 1–105.

Ruadze, V. P. *K sudu! Gomoseksual'nyi Peterburg.* St. Petersburg, 1908.

Rybakov, F. E. "O prevratnykh polovykh oshchushcheniiakh." *Vrach* (1898): 22: 640–43, 23: 664–67.

———. *Granitsy psikhicheskogo zdorov'ia i pomeshatel'stva.* Moscow, 1906.

Sapir, I. D. "Freidizm i marksizm." *Pod znamenem marksizma* 11 (1926): 59–87.

———. "Freidizm, sotsiologiia, psikhologiia." *Pod znamenem marksizma* 7–8 (1929): 207–36.

Semashko, N. A. "Nuzhna li 'zhenstvennost'? (v poriadke obsuzhdeniia)." *Molodaia gvardiia* 6 (1924): 205–6.

Serbskii, V. P. *Rukovodstvo k izucheniiu dushevnykh boleznei.* Moscow, 1906.

———. *Psikhiatriia.* Moscow, 1912.

Sereiskii, M. Ia. "Gomoseksualizm." *Bol'shaia meditsinskaia entsiklopediia.* 1st ed. Vol. 7. Moscow: Sovetskaia entsiklopediia, 1929.

———. "Gomoseksualizm." *Bol'shaia sovetskaia entsiklopediia* 1st ed. Vol. 17. Moscow, 1930.

———. "K psikhopatologii fetishizma." In *Trudy psikhonevrologicheskoi kliniki.* Ed. M. Ia. Sereiskii. Novocherkassk: Severo-Kavkazskii gosudarstvennyi meditsinskii institut, 1934.

Shchedrakov, V. I. "K voprosu o polovykh pravonarusheniiakh." *Izvestiia Severo-Kavkazskogo gosudarvstvennogo universiteta* 1, no. 14 (1930): 219–35.

Shcherbak, A. E. "K voprosu ob anomaliiakh polovogo chuvstva i vlecheniia." *Zhurnal nevropatologii i psikhiatrii im. S. S. Korsakova* 2–3 (1907): 282–98.

Sheinman, M. *Religioznost' i prestupnost'.* Moscow: Bezbozhnik, 1927.

Shtess, A. P. "Sluchai zhenskogo gomoseksualizma pri nalichii situs viscerum inversus, ego psikhoanaliz i gipnoterapiia." *Saratovskii vestnik zdravookhraneniia* 3–4 (1925): 1–19.

Shvarts, A. "K voprosu o priznakakh privychnoi passivnoi pederastii (Iz nabliudenii v aziatskoi chasti g. Tashkenta)." *Vestnik obshchestvennoi gigieny, sudebnoi i prakticheskoi meditsiny* 6 (1906): 816–18.

Skliar, N. I. "O proiskhozhdenii i sushchnosti gomoseksualizma." *Vrachebnoe delo* 24–26 (1925): 1919–23.

———. "O gruppirovke psikhopatii." In *Problemy nevrologii i psikhiatrii.* Ed. T. I. Iudin. Kiev: Gos. meditsinskoe izdatel'stvo USSR, 1939.

Sigerist, Henry Ernest. *Socialized Medicine in the Soviet Union.* London: V. Gollancz, 1937.

"Sodom i Gomorra." *Bezbozhnik u stanka* 8 (1923): 10–11.

Solovtsova, A. S., and N. F. Orlov. "Gomoseksualizm i reaktsiia d-ra Manoilova." *Klinicheskaia meditsina* 5, no. 9 (1927): 541–47.

Sudomir, A. K. "K kazuistike i sushchnosti gomoseksual'nost." *Sovremennaia psikhonevrologiia* 5, no. 11 (1927): 371–77.

Sukhanov, S. A. "K kazuistike seksual'nykh izvrashchenii." *Nevrologicheskii vestnik* 8, no. 2 (1900): 164–68.

Sumbaev, I. S. "K psikhoterapii gomoseksualizma." *Sovetskaia psikhonevrologiia* 5 (1936): 59–68.

Tagantsev, N. S., and P. N. Iakobi, eds. *Ugolovnoe ulozhenie 22 marta 1903 g.* Riga: Leta, 1922.

Tarnovskaia, P. N. *Zhenshchiny-ubiitsy. Antropologicheskoe issledovanie.* St. Petersburg, 1902.

Tarnovskii, I. M. *Izvrashchenie polovogo chuvstva u zhenshchin.* St. Petersburg, 1895.

Tarnovskii, V. M. *Izvrashchenie polovogo chuvstva. Sudebno-psikhiatricheskii ocherk.* St. Petersburg, 1885.

——. *Polovaia zrelost', eia techenie, otklonieniia i bolezni.* St. Petersburg, 1886.

Uait, Garri [Harry Whyte]. "Mozhet li gomoseksualist sostoiat' chlenom kommunisticheskoi partii?" *Istochnik* 5–6 (1993): 185–91.

Ucbevatov, A. "Iz byta prostitutsii nashikh dnei." *Pravo i zhizn'* 1 (1928): 50–60.

Ugolovnyi kodeks Uzbekskoi Sovetskoi Sotsialisticheskoi Respubliki. Po sostoianiiu na 1 noiabria 1954 goda. Tashkent: Gos. izdanie Uzb. SSR, 1954.

Ushakovskii, P. V. [pseud.] *Liudi srednego pola.* St. Petersburg, 1908.

Uspenskii, A. N. "K kazuistike anomalii polovogo chuvstva." *Obozrenie psikhiatrii, nevrologii i eksperimental'noi psikhologii* 12 (1898): 927–28.

Vasilevskii, L. M. *Polovye izvrashcheniia.* Moscow: Novaia Moskva, 1924.

——. *Golgofa rebenka. Bezprizornost' i deti ulitsy.* Leningrad-Moscow: Kniga, 1924.

Vasilevskii, L. M., and L. A. Vasilevskaia. *Prostitutsiia i novaia Rossiia.* Tver: Oktiabr', 1923.

Vnukov, V. A. *Problema izucheniia lichnosti prestupnika v svete marksistskoi kriminologii.* Khar'kov: Iuridicheskoe iz-vo NKIu USSR, 1930.

Vnukov, V. A., and Ts. M. Feinberg, *Sudebnaia psikhiatriia. Uchebnik dlia iuridicheskikh vuzov.* Moscow: OGIZ, 1936.

Volkov, V. N., S. I. Kalinichenko, and A. V. Pishchelko. *Seksual'nye izvrashcheniia u osuzhdennykh-zhenshchin.* Domodedovo: MIPK rabotnikov OVD, 1992.

Vysotskii, S. P. "Sluchai prevratnogo polovogo chuvstva." *Vestnik Kurskogo gubernskogo otdela zdravookhraneniia* 6–7 (1921): 9–11.

Winter, Ella. *Red Virtue: Human Relationships in the New Russia.* London: V. Gollancz, 1933.

Zakharchenko, M. A., and N. S. Pereshivkin. "Po povodu khirurgicheskogo lecheniia gomoseksualizma u muzhchin." *Novaia khirurgiia* 11 (1930): 24–29.

Zalkind, A. B. *Ocherki kul'tury revoliutsionnogo vremeni.* Moscow: Rabotnik prosveshcheniia, 1924.

——. *Revoliutsiia i molodezh'.* Moscow: Kommunistich. in-ta im. Sverdlova, 1924.

——. *Polovoi fetishizm. K peresmotru polovogo voprosa.* Moscow: Vserossiiskii proletkul't, 1925.

——. *Polovoi vopros v usloviiakh sovetskoi obshchestvennosti.* Leningrad: Gos. izd. Leningr. otd. im. tov. N. Bukharina, 1926.

Zavadovskii, M. M. "Issledovanie semennika gomoseksualista." *Trudy po dinamike razvitiia (Prodolzhenie "Trudov laboratorii eksperim. biologii Mosk. Zooparka")* 6 (1931): 65–70.

Zetkin, Klara. *Lenin on the Woman Question.* New York: International Publishers, 1934.

——. *Reminiscences of Lenin.* New York: International Publishers, 1934.

"Zakrytie raboty s"ezda. 26 dekabria 1936 g." In *Trudy vtorogo s"ezda psikhiatrov i nevropatologov. 25–29 dekabria 1936 g. vyp. 2.* Moscow, 1936.

Zhizhilenko, A. A. *Polovye prestupleniia (st. st. 166–171 Ugolovnogo Kodeksa).* Moscow: Pravo i zhizn', 1924.

Zhizhilenko, A. A., and L. G. Orshanskii, eds. *Polovye prestupleniia.* Leningrad-Moscow: Iz-vo Rabochii sud, 1927.

Zmiev, B. *Ugolovnoe pravo. Chast' osobennaia. Vypusk 1. Prestupleniia protiv lichnosti i imushchestvennye.* Kazan': Izd. NKIust. Avtomnoi Tatarskoi SSR, 1923.

Zuk, Dr. "O protivozakonnom udovletvorenii polovogo pobuzhdeniia i o sudebno-meditsinskoi zadache pri prestupleniiakh etoi kategorii." *Arkhiv sudebnoi meditsiny i obshchestvennoi gigieny* 2, sec. 5 (1870): 8–13.

3. Secondary Literature

Abraham, Richard. "Mariia L. Bochkareva and the Russian Amazons of 1917." In *Women and Society in Russia and the Soviet Union.* Ed. Linda Edmondson. Cambridge: Cambridge University Press, 1992.

Adam, Barry D. *The Rise of a Gay and Lesbian Movement.* Boston: Twayne, 1987.

Adams, Mark B., ed. *The Wellborn Science: Eugenics in Germany, France, Brazil, and Russia.* New York: Oxford University Press, 1990.

Anikeev, M. " 'Liudi byli zagnany v tualety, i ot etogo ikh kul'tura—tualetnaia'." *Uranus* 1 (1995): 46–47.

Atkinson, Dorothy, Alexander Dallin, and Gail Warshofsky Lapidus, eds. *Women in Russia.* Stanford: Stanford University Press, 1977.

Attwood, Lynne. *The New Soviet Man and Woman: Sex-role Socialization in the USSR.* Basingstoke: Macmillan, 1990.

Baldauf, I. *Die Knabenliebe in Mittelasien: Bačabozlik.* Berlin: Das Arabische Buch, 1988.

Ball, Alan M. *And Now My Soul Is Hardened: Abandoned Children in Soviet Russia, 1918–1930.* Berkeley: University of California Press, 1994.

Berlin Museum. *Eldorado: Homosexuelle Frauen und Männer in Berlin, 1850–1950. Geschichte, Alltag und Kultur.* Berlin: Frölich & Kaufmann, 1984.

Berman, H. J. *Soviet Criminal Law and Procedure: The RSFSR Codes.* Cambridge, Mass.. Harvard University Press, 1966.

Bernstein, Frances L. "Envisioning Health in Revolutionary Russia: The Politics of Gender in Sexual-Enlightenment Posters of the 1920s." *Russian Review* 57 (1998): 191–217.

———. "What Everyone Should Know about Sex: Gender, Sexual Enlightenment, and the Politics of Health in Revolutionary Russia, 1918–1931." Ph.D. diss., Columbia University, 1998.

Bernstein, Laurie. *Sonia's Daughters: Prostitutes and Their Regulation in Imperial Russia.* Berkeley and Los Angeles: University of California Press, 1995.

Berrios, German E. *The History of Mental Symptoms: Descriptive Psychopathology since the Nineteenth Century.* Cambridge: Cambridge University Press, 1996.

Bersen'ev, V. V., and A. R. Markov. "Politsiia i gei: Epizod iz epokhi Aleksandra III." *Risk* 3 (1998): 105–16.

Bérubé, Allan. *Coming Out under Fire: The History of Gay Men and Lesbians in World War Two.* New York: Plume, 1990.

Bleys, Rudi C. *The Geography of Perversion: Male-to-Male Behaviour outside the West and the Ethnographic Imagination, 1750–1918.* New York: New York University Press, 1995.

Bobroff, Anne. "Russian Working Women: Sexuality in Bonding Patterns and the Politics of Daily Life." In *Powers of Desire: The Politics of Sexuality.* Ed. Ann Snitow, Christine Stansell, and Sharon Thompson. New York: Monthly Review Press, 1983.

Bogomolov, N. A. *Mikhail Kuzmin: Stat'i i materialy.* Moscow: Novoe literaturnoe obozrenie, 1995.

Bogomolov, N. A., and John E. Malmstad. *Mikhail Kuzmin: Iskusstvo, zhizn', epokha.* Moscow: Novoe literaturnoe obozrenie, 1996.

Bonnell, Victoria E., ed. *The Russian Worker: Life and Labor under the Tsarist Regime.* Berkeley: University of California Press, 1983.

Bordiugov, G. A. "Sotsial'nyi parazitizm ili sotsial'nye anomalii? (Iz istorii bor'by s alkogolizmom, nishchestvom, prostitutsiei i brodiazhestvom v 20e–30e gody.)" *Istoriia SSSR* 1 (1989): 60–73.

Boswell, John. *Same-Sex Unions in Premodern Europe.* New York: Villard Books, 1994.

Bradley, Joseph. *Muzhik and Muscovite: Urbanization in Late Imperial Russia.* Berkeley: University of California Press, 1985.

Bravmann, Scott. *Queer Fictions of the Past: History, Culture, and Difference.* Cambridge: Cambridge University Press, 1997.

Bray, Alan. *Homosexuality in Renaissance England.* London: Gay Men's Press, 1982.

Brooks, Jeffrey. *When Russia Learned to Read: Literacy and Popular Literature, 1861–1917.* Princeton: Princeton University Press, 1985.

Brower, Daniel R. *The Russian City between Tradition and Modernity, 1850–1900.* Berkeley: University of California Press, 1990.

Brower, Daniel R., and Edward Lazzerini, eds. *Russia's Orient: Imperial Borderlands and Peoples, 1700–1917.* Bloomington: Indiana University Press, 1997.

Brown, Julie V. "The Professionalization of Russian Psychiatry, 1857–1911." Ph.D. diss., University of Pennsylvania, 1981.

———. "Heroes and Non-heroes: Recurring Themes in the Historiography of Russian-Soviet Psychiatry." In *Discovering the History of Psychiatry.* Ed. Mark S. Micale and Roy Porter. New York: Oxford University Press, 1994.

Burds, Jeffrey. "The Diary of Moscow Merchant Pavel Vasil'evicha Medvedeva, 1854–1864." Department of History, Northwestern University, Boston, Mass. Photocopy.

Burgin, Diana Lewis. "Sophia Parnok and the Writing of a Lesbian Poet's Life." *Slavic Review* 51, no. 2 (1992): 214–31.

———. "Laid Out in Lavender: Perceptions of Lesbian Love in Russian Literature and Criticism of the Silver Age, 1893–1917." In *Sexuality and the Body in Russian Culture.* Eds. Jane T. Costlow, Stephanie Sandler, and Judith Vowles. Stanford: Stanford University Press, 1993.

———. *Sophia Parnok: The Life and Work of Russia's Sappho.* New York: New York University Press, 1994.

Butler, Judith P. *Gender Trouble: Feminism and the Subversion of Identity.* New York: Routledge, 1990.

Carr, E. H. *The History of the Russian Revolution.* 14 vols. London: Macmillan, 1950–77.

Chalidze, Valerii. *Ugolovnaia Rossiia.* New York: Khronika, 1977.

Chauncey, George. "From Sexual Inversion to Homosexuality: Medicine and the Changing Conceptualization of Female Deviance." *Salmagundi* 58–59 (1982–83): 114–46.

———. *Gay New York: Gender, Urban Culture, and the Making of the Gay Male World, 1890–1940.* New York: Basic Books, 1994.

Chirkov, Petr M. *Reshenie zhenskogo voprosa v SSSR (1917–1937 gg.).* Moscow: Mysl', 1978.

Clements, Barbara E. *Bolshevik Feminist: The Life of Aleksandra Kollontai.* Bloomington: Indiana University Press, 1979.

———. *Bolshevik Women.* Cambridge: Cambridge University Press, 1997.

Clements, Barbara Evans, Barbara Alpern Engel, and Christine D Worobec, eds. *Russia's Women: Accommodation, Resistance, Transformation.* Berkeley and Los Angeles: University of California Press, 1991.

Cocks, Geoffrey. *Psychotherapy in the Third Reich: The Göring Institute.* New York: Oxford University Press, 1985.

Cohen, Stephen. *Rethinking the Soviet Experience.* New York: Oxford University Press, 1985.

Connell, R. W. *Masculinities.* Cambridge, U.K.: Polity Press, 1995.

Costlow, Jane T., Stephanie Sandler, and Judith Vowles, eds. *Sexuality and the Body in Russian Culture.* Stanford: Stanford University Press, 1993.

Crisp, Olga, and Linda Edmondson, eds. *Civil Rights in Imperial Russia.* Oxford: Clarendon Press, 1989.

Crompton, Louis. "The Myth of Lesbian Impunity: Capital Laws from 1270–1791." *Journal of Homosexuality* 6, 1–2 (1980–81): 11–25.

Curtiss, John S. *The Russian Church and the Soviet State, 1917–1940.* Gloucester, Mass.: Peter Smith, 1965.

D'Emilio, John. *Making Trouble: Essays on Gay History, Politics, and the University.* New York: Routledge, 1992.

David, Hugh. *On Queer Street: A Social History of British Homosexuality, 1895–1995.* London: HarperCollins, 1997.

Davies, R. W. *Soviet History in the Yeltsin Era.* Basingstoke: Macmillan, 1997.

Davies, Sarah. *Popular Opinion in Stalin's Russia: Terror, Propaganda, and Dissent, 1934–1941.* Cambridge: Cambridge University Press, 1997.

De Jong, Ben. "'An Intolerable Kind of Moral Degeneration': Homosexuality in the Soviet Union." *Review of Socialist Law* 4 (1982): 341–57.

Dekker, Rudolf M., and Lotte C. van de Pol. *The Tradition of Female Transvestism in Early Modern Europe.* New York: St. Martin's Press, 1997.

Dollimore, Jonathan. *Sexual Dissidence: Augustine to Wilde, Freud to Foucault.* Oxford: Oxford University Press, 1991.

Donoghue, Emma. *Passions between Women: British Lesbian Culture, 1668–1801.* London: HarperCollins, 1993.

Dose, Ralf. "The World League for Sexual Reform: Some Possible Approaches." In *Sexual Cultures in Europe. National Histories.* Eds. Franz X. Eder, Lesley Hall, and Gert Hekma. Manchester: Manchester University Press, 1999.

Dreger, Alice Domurat. *Hermaphrodites and the Medical Invention of Sex.* Cambridge, Mass.: Harvard University Press, 1998.

Duberman, Martin B., Martha Vicinus, and George Chauncey, Jr., eds. *Hidden From History: Reclaiming the Gay and Lesbian Past.* New York: New American Library, 1989.

Dunham, Vera. *In Stalin's Time: Middleclass Values in Soviet Fiction.* Cambridge: Cambridge University Press, 1976.

Edmondson, Linda. *Feminism in Russia, 1900–17.* London: Heinemann Educational, 1984.

Eklof, Ben, and Steven Frank, eds. *The World of the Russian Peasant: Post-Emancipation Culture and Society.* Boston: Unwin Hyman, 1990.

Engel, Barbara A. *Between the Fields and the City: Women, Work, and Family in Russia, 1861–1914.* Cambridge: Cambridge University Press, 1994.

Engelstein, Laura. "Lesbian Vignettes: A Russian Triptych from the 1890s." *Signs* 15, no. 4 (1990): 813–31.

———. *The Keys to Happiness: Sex and the Search for Modernity in Fin-de-Siècle Russia.* Ithaca: Cornell University Press, 1992.

———. "There Is Sex in Russia—and Always Was: Some Recent Contributions to Russian Erotica." *Slavic Review* 51, no. 4 (1992): 786–90.

———. "Combined Underdevelopment: Discipline and the Law in Imperial and Soviet Russia." *American Historial Review* 98, no. 2 (1993): 338–53.

————. "Soviet Policy toward Male Homosexuality: Its Origins and Historical Roots." In *Gay Men and the Sexual History of the Political Left*. Eds. Gert Hekma, Harry Oosterhuis, and James D. Steakley. New York: Harrington Park Press, 1995.

————. *Castration and the Heavenly Kingdom: A Russian Folktale*. Ithaca: Cornell University Press, 1999.

Essig, Laurie. *Queer in Russia: A Story of Sex, Self, and the Other* (Durham, N.C.: Duke University Press, 1999).

Etkind, Aleksandr. *Eros nevozmozhnogo: Istoriia psikhoanaliza v Rossii*. St. Petersburg: Meduza, 1993.

Evans, J. "The Communist Party of the Soviet Union and the Woman's Question: The Case of the 1936 Decree 'In Defense of Mother and Child.' " *Journal of Contemporary History* 16 (1981): 757–75.

Faderman, Lillian. "The Morbidification of Love between Women by 19th-Century Sexologists." *Journal of Homosexuality* 4, no. 1 (1978): 73–90.

————. *Odd Girls and Twilight Lovers: A History of Lesbian Life in Twentieth-Century America*. New York: Columbia University Press, 1991.

————. *Surpassing the Love of Men: Romantic Friendship and Love between Women from the Renaissance to the Present*. New York: Morrow, 1981.

Farnsworth, Beatrice, and Lynne Viola, eds. *Russian Peasant Women*. New York: Oxford University Press, 1992.

Fausto-Sterling, Anne. "The Five Sexes: Why Male and Female Are Not Enough." *Sciences* (March–April 1993): 20–24.

————. *Myths of Gender: Biological Theories of Women and Men*. New York: Basic Books, 1985.

Field, Mark G. *Doctor and Patient in Soviet Russia*. Cambridge: Harvard University Press, 1957.

————. *Soviet Socialized Medicine: An Introduction*. New York: Free Press, 1967.

Fitzpatrick, Sheila. "Sex and Revolution: An Examination of Literary and Statistical Data on the Mores of Soviet Students in the 1920s." *Journal of Modern History* 50 (1978): 252–78.

————. *The Russian Revolution, 1917–1932*. Oxford: Oxford University Press, 1982.

————. *The Cultural Front*. Ithaca: Cornell University Press, 1992.

————. "Signals from Below: Soviet Letters of Denunciation of the 1930s." In *Accusatory Practices: Denunciation in Modern European History, 1789–1989*. Eds. Sheila Fitzpatrick and Robert Gellately. Chicago: University of Chicago Press, 1997.

————, ed. *Stalinism: New Directions*. London: Routledge, 1999.

Fitzpatrick, Sheila, Alexander Rabinowitch, and Richard Stites, eds. *Russia in the Era of NEP: Explorations in Soviet Society and Culture*. Bloomington: Indiana University Press, 1991.

Foucault, Michel. *The History of Sexuality: An Introduction Vol. 1*. Transl. Robert Hurley. London: Penguin, 1990.

Frank, Stephen P., and Mark D. Steinberg, eds. *Cultures in Flux: Lower-class Values, Practices, and Resistance in Late Imperial Russia*. Princeton: Princeton University Press, 1994.

Freeze, Gregory. "Bringing Order to the Russian Family: Marriage and Divorce in Imperial Russia, 1760–1860." *Journal of Modern History* 62, no. 4 (1990): 709–46.

Frieden, Nancy M. *Russian Physicians in an Era of Reform and Revolution, 1856–1905*. Princeton: Princeton University Press, 1981.

Garros, Veronique, Natalia Korenevskaya, and Thomas Lahusen, eds. *Intimacy and Terror: Soviet Diaries of the 1930s*. New York: New Press, 1995.

Gessen, Masha. "We Have No Sex: Soviet Gays and AIDS in the Era of Glasnost." *Outlook* 3, no. 1 (1990): 42–54.

———. *The Rights of Lesbians and Gay Men in the Russian Federation.* San Francisco: International Gay and Lesbian Human Rights Commission, 1994.

Getty, J. Arch. *Origins of the Great Purges: The Soviet Communist Party Reconsidered, 1933–1938.* Cambridge: Cambridge University Press, 1985.

———. "State and Society under Stalin: Constitutions and Elections in the 1930s." *Slavic Review* 50, no. 1 (1991): 18–35.

Getty, J. Arch, and Roberta Manning, eds. *Stalinist Terror: New Perspectives.* Cambridge: Cambridge University Press, 1993.

Goldman, Wendy Z. *Women, the State, and Revolution: Soviet Family Policy and Social Life.* Cambridge: Cambridge University Press, 1993.

Golod, S. I. *XX vek i tendentsii seksual'nykh otnoshenii v Rossii.* St. Petersburg, Aleteiia, 1996.

Goodbye to Berlin? 100 Jahre Schwulenbewegung. Ed. Monika Hingst et al. Berlin: rosa Winkel, 1997.

Goscilo, Helena, and Beth Holmgren, eds. *Russia—Women—Culture.* Bloomington: Indiana University Press, 1996.

Graham, Loren R. *Science in Russia and the Soviet Union.* Cambridge: Cambridge University Press, 1993.

Grau, Günter, ed. *Hidden Holocaust?: Gay and Lesbian Persecution in Germany, 1933–45.* London: Cassell, 1995.

Greenberg, David F. *The Construction of Homosexuality.* Chicago: University of Chicago Press, 1988.

Gromyko, M. M. *Traditsionnye formy povedeniia i formy obshcheniia russkikh krest'ian XIX v.* Moscow: Nauka, 1986.

Gulshinskii, Viktor. "Istochniki po russkoi gei-istorii: Opyt predstavleniia" [Sources in Russian gay history: Preliminary suggestions]. GenderDok, Biblioteka lesbiianok i geev, Moscow, 1995. Photocopy.

Hahn, Pierre. *Nos ancêtres, les pervers: La vie des homosexuels sous le Second Empire.* Paris: Olivier Orban, 1979.

Hansen, Bert. "American Physicians' 'Discovery' of Homosexuals, 1880–1900: A New Diagnosis in a Changing Society." In *Framing Disease: Studies in Cultural History.* Eds. C. E. Rosenberg and J. Golden. New Brunswick, N.J.: Rutgers University Press, 1992.

Hausman, Bernice. *Changing Sex: Transsexualism, Technology, and the Idea of Gender.* Durham, N.C.: Duke University Press, 1995.

Hazard, John. *Communists and Their Law.* Chicago: University of Chicago Press, 1968.

———. "Soviet Law: The Bridge Years, 1917–1920." In *Russian Law: Historical and Political Perspectives.* Ed. William E. Butler. Leyden: A. W. Sijthoff, 1977.

Healey, Daniel. "The Russian Revolution and the Decriminalisation of Homosexuality." *Revolutionary Russia* 6, no. 1 (1993): 26–54.

———. "Evgeniia/Evgenii: Queer Case Histories in the First Years of Soviet Power." *Gender and History* 1 (1997): 83–106.

———. "Moscow." in *Queer Sites: Gay Urban Histories since 1600.* Ed. David Higgs. London: Routledge, 1999.

———. "'Their Culture': Clerical Same-sex Offenses in the Discourse of Bolshevik Militant Atheism." Department of History, University of Wales Swansea, 1998. Photocopy.

———. "'Man or Woman?': Hermaphroditism as a Medical Problem in Tsarist and

Soviet Russia." Paper presented to European Social Science History Conference, Amsterdam, 13 April 2000.

———. "Masculine Purity and 'Gentlemen's Mischief': Sexual Exchange and Prostitution between Russian Men, 1861–1941." *Slavic Review* 60, no. 2 (2001): 233–65.

———. "Unruly Identities: Soviet Psychiatry Confronts the 'Female Homosexual' of the 1920s." In *Gender in Russian History and Culture, 1800–1990.* Ed. Linda Edmondson. London: Palgrave, 2001.

Hekma, Gert, Harry Oosterhuis, and James Steakley, eds. *Gay Men and the Sexual History of the Political Left.* New York: Harrington Park Press, 1995.

Herdt, Gilbert, ed. *Third Sex, Third Gender: Beyond Sexual Dimorphism in Culture and History.* New York: Zone Books, 1993.

Herzer, Manfred. *Magnus Hirschfeld: Leben und Werk eines jüdischen, schwulen und sozialistischen Sexologen.* Frankfurt am Main: Campus, 1992.

Hoffmann, David L. *Peasant Metropolis: Social Identities in Moscow, 1929–1941.* Ithaca: Cornell University Press, 1994.

Hohmann, J. S. "Zum rechtlichen und sozialen Problem der Homosexualität." In *Sexualforschung und -politik in der Sowjetunion seit 1917: Eine Bestandsaufnahme in Kommentaren und historischen Texten.* Ed. J. S. Hohmann. Frankfurt am Main: P. Lang, 1990.

Holmgren, Beth. "Stepping Out/Going Under: Women in Russia's Twentieth-Century Salons." In *Russia—Women—Culture.* Eds. Helena Goscilo and Beth Holmgren. Bloomington: Indiana University Press, 1996.

Hutchinson, John F. *Politics and Public Health in Revolutionary Russia, 1890–1918.* Baltimore: Johns Hopkins University Press, 1990.

Iudin, T. I. *Ocherki istorii otechestvennoi psikhiatrii.* Moscow: Medgiz, 1951.

Jackson, Peter A. "Thai Research on Male Homosexuality and Transgenderism and the Cultural Limits of Foucaultian Analysis." *Journal of the History of Sexuality* 1 (1997): 52–85.

Jagose, Annamarie. *Queer Theory: An Introduction.* New York: New York University Press, 1996.

Johnson, Robert. *Peasant and Proletarian: The Working Class of Moscow in the Late Nineteenth Century.* New Brunswick, N.J.: Rutgers University Press, 1979.

Joravsky, David. *Russian Psychology: A Critical History.* Oxford: Basil Blackwell, 1989.

Juviler, Peter H. *Revolutionary Law and Order.* New York: Free Press, 1976.

Gleason, A., P. Kenez, and R. Stites, eds. *Bolshevik Culture: Experiment and Order in the Russian Revolution.* Bloomington: Indiana University Press, 1985.

Kannabikh, I. V. *Istoriia psikhiatrii.* 1928. Reprint, Moscow: TsTR MGP VOS, 1994.

Karlinsky, Simon. "Russia's Gay Literature and History." *Gay Sunshine* 29–30 (1976): 1–7.

———. "Przhevalsky: The Russian Livingstone." *University Publishing* 5 (1978).

———. "Death and Resurrection of Mikhail Kuzmin." *Slavic Review* 38, no. 1 (1979): 92–96.

———. "Gay Life before the Soviets: Revisionism Revised." *Advocate* 339 (1 April 1982): 31–34.

———. "Russia's Gay Literature and Culture: The Impact of the October Revolution." In *Hidden from History: Reclaiming the Gay and Lesbian Past.* Eds. Martin Duberman, Martha Vicinus, and George Chauncey, Jr. New York: New American Library, 1989.

———." 'Vvezen iz-za granitsy. . .'? Gomoseksualizm v russkoi kul'ture i literature." In *Erotika v russkoi literature. Ot Barkova do nashikh dnei. Literaturnoe obozrenie.*

Spetsial'nyi vypusk. Ed. I. D. Prokhorova, S. Iu. Mazur, and G. V. Zykova. Moscow: Literaturnoe obozrenie, 1992.

———. "Introduction: Russia's Gay Literature and History." In *Out of the Blue: Russia's Hidden Gay Literature.* Ed. Kevin Moss. San Francisco: Gay Sunshine Press, 1996.

Kashchenko, Evgenii A. "Institutsionalizatsiia seksual'noi kul'tury voennosluzhashchikh v Rossiiskoi armii" [The institutionalization of the sexual culture of military personnel in the Russian army]. Avtoreferat dissertatsii na soiskanie uchenoi stepeni doktora sotsiologicheskikh nauk. Moscow: Rossiiskii institut kul'turologii, 1997.

Katz, Jonathan Ned. *Gay American History.* New York: Thomas Crowell, 1976.

———. *The Invention of Heterosexuality.* New York: Dutton, 1995.

Kelly, Catriona, and David Shepherd, eds. *Constructing Russian Culture in the Age of Revolution, 1881–1940.* Oxford: Oxford University Press, 1998.

Kittel, Ingo-Wolf. "Zur historischen Rolle des Psychiaters und Psychotherapeuten Arthur Kronfeld in der frühen Sexualwissenschaft." *Sozialwissenschaftliche Sexualforschung* 2 (1989): 33–44.

Kon, Igor' S. *The Sexual Revolution in Russia.* New York: Free Press, 1995.

———. "Istoricheskie sud'by russkogo Erosa." In *Seks i erotika v russkoi traditsionnoi kul'ture.* Ed. A. I. Toporkov. Moscow: Ladomir, 1996.

———. *Lunnyi svet na zare: Liki i maski odnopoloi liubvi.* Moscow: Olimp, 1998.

———. *Seksual'naia kul'tura v Rossii: Klubnichka na berezke.* Moscow: O.G.I., 1997.

Kotkin, Stephen. *Magnetic Mountain: Stalinism as a Civilization.* Berkeley and Los Angeles: University of California Press, 1995.

Kozlovskii, Vladimir. *Argo russkoi gomoseksual'noi subkul'tury: Materialy k izucheniiu.* Benson, Vt.: Chalidze Publications, 1986.

Kuhn, Thomas S. *The Structure of Scientific Revolutions.* Chicago: University of Chicago Press, 1962.

Lapidus, Gail W. *Women in Soviet Society: Equality, Development, and Social Change.* Berkeley: University of California Press, 1978.

Lauritsen, John, and David Thorstad. *The Early Homosexual Rights Movement (1864–1934).* New York: Times Change, 1974.

Lebina, N. B., and M. B. Shkarovskii. *Prostitutsiia v Peterburge.* Moscow: Progress-Akademiia, 1994.

Legendre, Paul. *V poiskakh sebia: Polozhenie geev i lesbiianok v sovremennoi Rossii.* Moscow: Charities Aid Foundation, 1997.

Leont'eva, T. G. "Byt, nravy i povedenie seminaristov v nachale XX v." In *Revoliutsiia i chelovek: Byt, nravy, povedenie, moral'.* Ed. P. V. Volobuev et al. Moscow, 1997.

Leroy-Forgeot, Flora. *Histoire juridique de l'homosexualité en Europe.* Paris: Presses Universitaires de France, 1997.

Lesbian History Group. *Not a Passing Phase: Reclaiming Lesbians in History, 1840–1985.* London: Women's Press, 1989.

Levin, Eve. *Sex and Society in the World of the Orthodox Slavs, 900–1700.* Ithaca: Cornell University Press, 1989.

Levitt, M., and A. Toporkov, eds. *Eros i pornografiia v russkoi kul'ture / Eros and Pornography in Russian Culture.* Moscow: Ladomir, 1999.

Lewin, Moshe. *The Making of the Soviet System: Essays in the Social History of Interwar Russia.* London: Metheun and Co., 1985.

Lumsden, Ian. *Machos, Maricones, and Gays: Cuba and Homosexuality.* Philadelphia: Temple University Press, 1996.

Lunbeck, Elizabeth. *The Psychiatric Persuasion: Knowledge, Gender, and Power in Modern America.* Princeton: Princeton University Press, 1994.

Malmstad, John E. "Mixail Kuzmin: A Chronicle of His Life and Times." In M. A. Kuzmin, *Sobranie stikhov/Gesammelte Gedichte*. Ed. John E. Malmstad. Munich: W. Fink, 1977.

Malmstad, John E., and Nikolay A. Bogomolov, *Mikhail Kuzmin: A Life in Art*. Cambridge: Harvard University Press, 1999.

Mamonova, Tatyana. *Russian Women's Studies: Essays on Sexism in Soviet Culture*. New York: Pergamon, 1985.

Marsh, Rosalind, ed. *Women in Russia and Ukraine*. Cambridge: Cambridge University Press, 1996.

Massell, Gregory J. *The Surrogate Proletariat: Moslem Women and Revolutionary Strategies in Soviet Central Asia, 1919–1929*. Princeton: Princeton University Press, 1974.

Maynard, Steven. " 'Horrible Temptations': Sex, Men and Working-Class Male Youth in Urban Ontario, 1890–1935." *Canadian Historical Review* 78, no. 2 (1997): 191–235.

McIntosh, Mary. "The Homosexual Role." *Social Problems* 16 (1968): 182–92.

Merrick, Jeffrey, and Bryant T. Ragan, Jr., eds. *Homosexuality in Modern France*. New York: Oxford University Press, 1996.

Miller, Martin. *Freud and the Bolsheviks: Psychoanalysis in Imperial Russia and the Soviet Union*. New Haven: Yale University Press, 1998.

Mogutin, Iaroslav, and Sonia Franeta. "Gomoseksualizm v sovetskikh tiur'makh i lageriakh." *Novoe vremia* (1993): 35: 44–47, 36: 50–54.

Morton, Donald, ed. *The Material Queer: A LesBiGay Cultural Studies Reader*. Boulder: Westview Press, 1996.

Moss, Kevin, ed. *Out of the Blue: Russia's Hidden Gay Literature*. San Francisco: Gay Sunshine Press, 1996.

Mosse, George. *Nationalism and Sexuality: Respectability and Abnormal Sexuality in Modern Europe*. New York: H. Fertig, 1985.

———. *The Image of Man: The Creation of Modern Masculinity*. New York: Oxford University Press, 1996.

Mosse, W. E. "Imperial Favorite: V. P. Meshchersky and the *Grazhdanin*." *Slavonic and East European Review* 59 (1981): 529–47.

Murray, Stephen O., ed. *Oceanic Homosexualities*. New York: Garland, 1992.

Murray, Stephen O., and Will Roscoe, eds. *Islamic Homosexualities: Culture, History, and Literature*. New York: New York University Press, 1997.

Naiman, Eric. "The Case of Chubarov Alley: Collective Rape, Utopian Desire and the Mentality of NEP." *Russian History/Histoire Russe* 17, no. 1 (1990): 1–30.

———. *Sex in Public: The Incarnation of Early Soviet Ideology*. Princeton: Princeton University Press, 1997.

Neary, Rebecca B. "Mothering Socialist Society: The Wife-Activists' Movement and the Soviet Culture of Daily Life, 1934–41." *Russian Review* 58 (1999): 396–412.

Neuberger, Joan. *Hooliganism: Crime, Culture, and Power in St. Petersburg, 1900–1914*. Berkeley: University of California Press: 1993.

Nikiforov, A. S. *Bekhterev*. Moscow: Molodaia gvardiia, 1986.

Norton, Rictor. *The Myth of the Modern Homosexual: Queer History and the Search for Cultural Unity*. London: Cassell, 1997.

Nye, Robert A. "Sex Difference and Male Homosexuality in French Medical Discourse, 1830–1930." *Bulletin of the History of Medicine* 63 (1989): 32–51.

Oosterhuis, Harry. "Medicine, Male Bonding and Homosexuality in Nazi Germany." *Journal of Comtemporary History* 2 (1997): 187–205.

Oudshoorn, Nelly. *Beyond the Natural Body: An Archeology of Sex Hormones*. London: Routledge, 1994.

Parikas, Udo, and Teet Veispak, eds. *Sexual Minorities and Society: The Changing Atti-*

tudes toward Homosexuality in the 20th Century Europe. Talinn: Institute of History, 1991.

Petrovsky, Arthur. *Psychology in the Soviet Union: A Historical Outline*. Moscow: Progress, 1990.

Pinnow, Kenneth. "Making Suicide Soviet: Medicine, Moral Statistics, and the Politics of Social Science in Bolshevik Russia, 1920–1930." Ph.D. diss., Columbia University, 1998.

Plant, Richard. *The Pink Triangle: The Nazi War against Homsexuals*. New York: H. Holt, 1986.

Poliakova, S. "Poeziia Sofii Parnok." In *Sofiia Parnok: Sobranie stikhotvorenii*. Ed. S Poliakova. Ann Arbor, Mich.: Ardis, 1979.

Poznansky, Alexander. *Tchaikovsky: The Quest for the Inner Man*. New York: Schirmer Books, 1991.

————. *Tchaikovsky's Last Days: A Documentary Study*. Oxford: Clarendon Press, 1996.

Prosser, Jay. "Transsexuals and the Transsexologists: Inversion and the Emergence of Transsexual Subjectivity." In *Sexology in Culture: Labelling Bodies and Desires*. Eds. Lucy Bland and Laura Doan. Cambridge: Polity Press, 1998.

Reeves, Tom. "Red and Gay: Oppression East and West." *Fag Rag* 6 (fall 1973): 3–6.

Rey, Michael. "Parisian Homosexuals Create a Lifestyle, 1700–1750: The Police Ar chives." In *'Tis Nature's Fault: Unauthorized Sexual Behavior during the Enlightenment*. Ed. Robert P. Maccubbin. New York: Cambridge University Press, 1985.

Riordan, James. "Sexual Minorities: The Status of Gays and Lesbians in Russian-Soviet-Russian Society." In *Women in Russia and Ukraine*. Ed. Rosalind Marsh. Cambridge: Cambridge University Press, 1996.

Rocke, Michael. *Forbidden Friendships: Homosexuality and Male Culture in Renaissance Florence*. New York: Oxford University Press, 1996.

Roper, Michael, and John Tosh, eds. *Manful Assertions. Masculinities in Britain since 1800*. London: Routledge, 1991.

Rosario, Vernon A., ed. *Science and Homosexualities*. New York: Routledge, 1997.

Rotikov, Konstantin K. "Epizod iz zhizni 'golubogo' Peterburga." *Nevskii arkhiv: Istoriko-kraevedcheskii sbornik* 3 (1997): 449–66.

————. *Drugoi Peterburg*. St. Petersburg: Liga Plius, 1998.

Rowse, Alfred Leslie. *Homosexuals in History: A Study of Ambivalence in Society, Literature, and the Arts*. London: Weidenfeld and Nicolson, 1977.

Sautman, Francesca C. "Invisible Women: Lesbian Working-class Culture in France, 1880–1930." In *Homosexuality in Modern France*. Eds. Jeffrey Merrick and Bryant T. Ragan, Jr. New York: Oxford University Press, 1996.

Schluter, Daniel. "Fraternity without Community: Social Institutions in the Soviet Gay World." Ph.D, diss., Columbia University, 1998.

Schoppmann, Claudia. "National Socialist Policies towards Female Homosexuality." In *Gender Relations in German History: Power, Agency and Experience from the Sixteenth to the Twentieth Century*. Eds. Lynn Abrams and Elizabeth Harvey. London: UCL Press, 1996.

Scott, James C. *Domination and the Arts of Resistance: Hidden Transcripts*. New Haven: Yale University Press, 1990.

Scott, Joan W. "Gender: A Useful Category of Historical Analysis." *American Historical Review* 91 (1986): 1053–75.

Sedgwick, Eve K. *Epistemology of the Closet*. Berkeley and Los Angeles: University of California Press, 1990.

Seel, Pierre. *Liberation Was for Others: Memoirs of a Gay Survivor of the Nazi Holocaust*. Transl. J. Jeugroschel. New York: Basic Books, 1995.

Sengoopta, Chandak. "Glandular Politics: Experimental Biology, Clinical Medicine, and Homosexual Emancipation in Fin-de-Siècle Central Europe." *Isis* 89 (1998): 445–73.

Shearer, David. "Crime and Social Disorder in Stalin's Russia: A Reassessment of the Great Retreat and the Origins of Mass Repression." *Cahiers du monde russe* 39, no. 1–2 (1998): 119–49.

Shentalinskii, Vitalii. *Raby svobody: V literaturnykh arkhivakh KGB.* Moscow: Parus, 1995.

Shereshevskii, A. M. "Nekotorye voprosy istorii psikhiatricheskoi ekspertizy v Rossii (po materialam Meditsinskogo Soveta)" [Some questions in the history of psychiatric expertise in Russia (from materials of the Medical Council)]. Avtoreferat dissertatsii na soiskanie uchenoi stepeni kandidata meditsinskikh nauk. Leningrad: Voenno-meditsinskaia ordena Lenina Akademiia im. S. M. Kirova, 1966.

Shlapentokh, Vladimir. *Love, Marriage, and Friendship in the Soviet Union: Ideals and Practices.* New York: Praeger, 1984.

Shtern, Mikhail. *Sex in the USSR.* New York: Times, 1980.

Shvekov, G. V. *Pervyi sovetskii ugolovnyi kodeks.* Moscow: Vysshaia shkola, 1970.

Solomon, Peter H., Jr. *Soviet Criminal Justice under Stalin.* Cambridge: Cambridge University Press, 1996.

Solomon, Susan Gross. "David and Goliath in Soviet Public Health: The Rivalry of Social Hygienists and Psychiatrists for Authority over the *Bytovoi* Alcoholic." *Soviet Studies* 41, no. 2 (1989): 254–75.

———. "Social Hygiene and Soviet Public Health, 1921–1930." In *Health and Society in Revolutionary Russia.* Eds. S. G. Solomon and J. Hutchinson. Bloomington: Indiana University Press, 1990.

———. "The Demographic Argument in Soviet Debates over the Legalization of Abortion in the 1920s." *Cahiers du Monde Russe et Soviétique* 33, no. 1 (1992): 59–82.

———. "The Soviet-German Syphilis Expedition to Buriat Mongolia, 1928." *Slavic Review* 52, no. 2 (1993): 204–32.

———. "The Expert and the State in Russian Public Health: Continuities and Changes across the Revolutionary Divide." In *The History of Public Health and the Modern State,* ed. Dorothy Porter. Amsterdam: Editions Rodopi B. V., 1994.

Solomon, Susan Gross, and John Hutchinson, eds. *Health and Society in Revolutionary Russia.* Bloomington: Indiana University Press, 1990.

Solzhenitsyn, Alexander. *The Gulag Archipelago.* 3 vols. London: Collins/Fontana, 1974–78.

Steakley, James. *The Homosexual Emancipation Movement in Germany.* New York: Arno, 1975.

Stein, Edward, ed. *Forms of Desire: Sexual Orientation and the Social Constructionist Controversy.* New York: Routledge, 1990.

Stites, Richard. *The Women's Liberation Movement in Russia: Feminism, Nihilism, and Bolshevism, 1860–1930.* Princeton N.J.: Princeton University Press, 1978.

———. *Revolutionary Dreams: Utopian Vision and Experimental Life in the Russian Revolution.* New York: Oxford University Press, 1989.

Szasz, Thomas. *The Manufacture of Madness: A Comparative Study of the Inquisition and the Mental Health Movement.* London: Paladin, 1973.

Terry, Jennifer. "Lesbians under the Medical Gaze: Scientists Search for Remarkable Differences." *Journal of Sex Research* 27, no. 3 (1990): 317–39.

———. *An American Obsession: Science, Medicine, and Homosexuality in Modern Society.* Chicago: University of Chicago Press, 1999.

Timasheff, N. S. *The Great Retreat.* New York: E. P. Dutton, 1946.
———. "The Impact of the Penal Law of Imperial Russia on Soviet Penal Law." *American Slavic and East European Review* 12, no. 4 (1953): 441–62.
Tuller, David. *Cracks in the Iron Closet: Travels in Gay and Lesbian Russia.* Boston and London: Faber & Faber, 1996.
Viola, Lynne. "Bab'i Bunty and Peasant Women's Protest during Collectivization." *Russian Review* 45 (1986): 23–42.
———. "The Peasant Nightmare: Visions of Apocalypse in the Soviet Countryside." *Journal of Modern History* 62, no. 4 (1990): 747–70.
———. *Peasant Rebels under Stalin: Collectivization and the Culture of Peasant Resistance.* New York: Oxford University Press, 1996.
von Hagen, Mark. "The New Soviet Man in the Red Army: Regulating Sex and the Body during the Civil War and NEP." Department of History, Columbia University, New York. 1987. Photocopy.
———. *Soldiers in the Proletarian Dictatorship: The Red Army and the Soviet Socialist State, 1917–1930.* Ithaca: Cornell University Press, 1990.
Ward, Chris. *Stalin's Russia.* London & New York: Edward Arnold, 1993.
Waters, Elizabeth. "The Female Form in Soviet Political Iconography, 1917–32." In *Russia's Women: Accommodation, Resistance, Transformation.* Eds. Barbara Evans Clements, Barbara Alpern Engel, and Christine D. Worobec. Berkeley and Los Angeles: University of California Press, 1991.
———. "Victim or Villain: Prostitution in Post-revolutionary Russia." In *Women and Society in Russian and the Soviet Union.* Ed. Linda Edmondson. Cambridge: Cambridge University Press, 1992.
Weeks, Jeffrey. *Sexuality and Its Discontents: Meanings, Myths and Modern Sexualities.* London: Routledge & Kegan Paul, 1985.
———. *Coming Out. Homosexual Politics in Britain from the Nineteenth Century to the Present.* London: Quartet Books, 1990.
———. *Against Nature: Essays on History, Sexuality and Identity.* London: Rivers Oram Press, 1991.
Weindling, Paul. "German-Soviet Medical Cooperation and the Institute for Racial Research, 1927–c.1935." *German History* 10, no. 2 (1992): 177–206.
Werlinder, Henry. *Psychopathy: A History of the Concepts: Analysis of the Origin and Development of a Family of Concepts in Psychopathology.* Uppsala: University of Uppsala, 1978.
Wheelwright, Julie. *Amazons and Military Maids: Women Who Dressed as Men in the Pursuit of Life, Liberty and Happiness.* London: Pandora, 1989.
Wood, Elizabeth A. *The Baba and the Comrade: Gender and Politics in Revolutionary Russia.* Bloomington: Indiana University Press, 1997.
Worobec, Christine. *Peasant Russia: Family and Community in the Post-Emancipation Period.* Princeton, N.J.: Princeton University Press, 1991.
Wortis, Joseph. *Soviet Psychiatry.* Baltimore: Williams & Wilkins, 1950.
Zhuk, Ol'ga. "Lesbiiskaia subkul'tura. Istoricheskie korni lesbiianstva v byvshem SSSR (postanovka voprosa)." *Gay, Slaviane!* 1 (1993): 16–20.
———. *Russkie amazonki: Istoriia lesbiiskoi subkul'tury v Rossii, XX vek.* Moscow: Glagol, 1998.
Zolotonosov, Mikhail. "Masturbanizatsiia: 'Erogennye zony' sovetskoi kul'tury 1920–1930-kh godov." In *Erotika v russkoi literature: Ot Barkova do nashikh dnei (Literaturnoe Obozrenie. Spetsial'nyi vypusk).* Eds. I. D. Prokhorova, S. Iu. Mazur, and G. V. Zykova. Moscow: Literaturnoe obozrenie, 1992.